One Woman's War: *Da* (Mother)

The author holding a weapon given to her in March 1980

One Woman's War

Da (Mother)

The Memoirs of

Seyyedeh Zahra Hoseyni

Translated from the Persian with an Introduction by

Paul Sprachman

Since 1980
Mazda Publishers
Costa Mesa, California 2014

Publication of this book was made possible by a grant from
The A. K. Jabbari Trust

Mazda Publishers, Inc.
Academic publishers since 1980
P.O. Box 2603, Costa Mesa, California 92628 U.S.A.
www.mazdapub.com
A. K. Jabbari, Publisher

Library of Congress Cataloging-in-Publication

Husayni, Zahra, 1963 or 1964-
[Da. English]
One Woman's War: Da (mother): the Memoirs of Seyyedeh Zahra Hoseyni / translated from the Persian with an introduction by Paul Sprachman.
pages cm
Includes bibliographical references.
ISBN 978-1-56859-273-2 (alkaline paper)
1. Husayni, Zahra, 1963 or 1964- 2. Iran-Iraq War, 1980-1988—Personal narratives, Iranian. 3. Kurds—Iran—Biography. 4. Women, Kurdish—Iran—Biography. 5. Khurramshahr (Iran)—Biography. I. Title. II. Title: One Woman's War: Da. III. Title: One Woman's War. IV. Title: Da (mother).
CT1888.H874A3 2014
305.40955—dc23
2014013468

Cover inset:
Photograph by Abbas Kowsari, *Shade of Earth,Raihan Noor,* Iran-Iraq border, 2007, 105 x 70 cm, in Abbas Daneshvari, *Amazingly Original: Contemporaray Iranian Art at Crossroads*, Mazda Publishers:2014.

Translator's Dedication

To Susan.
Special thanks to editor, Kerry Kern, who not only read the book at least two times, but exhibited great curiosity about the topic, and by asking for clarifications of places, names, and phrases helped make the memoir more accessible. And thanks to Dawn Patterson who was generous with her time and made sure the manuscript was in good shape for the publisher.

CONTENTS

Translator's Introduction

I. *Da* as Cultural Phenomenon

One Woman's War: Da (Mother) the Memoirs of Seyyedeh Zahra Hoseyni is many things.[i] Part autobiography, part oral history of the Iran-Iraq War (1980–88), the work is the story of Zahra Hoseyni, a female descendant of the Prophet Mohammad (thereby termed a *seyyedeh*), whose Kurdish family found refuge in Iran after being expelled from their native Iraq. There are three parts to the book. The first speaks of the author's early life—her childhood in Iraq, her family's emigration to Iran, and their struggles adapting to life in Khorramshahr, a port city on the Persian Gulf. The second and largest part deals with Zahra Hoseyni's experiences during the first three weeks of the Iran-Iraq War (September 22–October 13, 1980), including her activities as a collector of body parts and washer of corpses, her role as a nurse to wounded civilians and soldiers, and her activities as a combatant in the defense of Khorramshahr. The final part of the book is devoted to Zahra Hoseyni's recovery from shrapnel wounds received on the battlefield and to her married life, spent in two homes: one in a suburban area of southwestern Iran within commuting distance of the front and the second in an urban apartment house in central Tehran.

Da is the product of more than a thousand hours of Zahra Hoseyni's interviews with Seyyedeh A'zam Hoseyni (a woman with the same family name but no relation to the narrator). The book was part of a larger project to record the oral histories of Iranian women who took part in the Iran-Iraq War. Administering the project was the Center for the Study and Research on Resistance Literature, a division of the Artistic Center of the Islamic Development Organization. In 2000 the Center compiled a list of women who had active roles in the War, and A'zam Hoseyni contacted many of them personally for interviews.[ii]

Having outsold or gone through more reprints than all other Iran-Iraq War memoirs by a factor of a hundred, the Zahra Hoseyni-A'zam Hoseyni collaboration has been and continues to be a cultural phenomenon in the Islamic Republic. The nature of its extraordinary sales, however, has been the subject of debate. Official figures are suspect because of the many copies bought and distributed free of charge by government organizations. Zahir Tavakkoli, a journalist and poet, speaks of the "deceptive" (*kazeb*) purchasing of the book in his article "The Sorrowful Tale of the Book *Da* and the Injustice Visited upon it."[iii] He reports that among his acquaintances none had actually had to buy *Da*; they received the book as a gift, and one of them even reported having eight free copies at home. In Tavakkoli's view the "pointless" (*gotreh-i*) gifting of the book by officials does a significant work like *Da* a disservice. He is not alone in thinking the book could have stood on its own merits; indeed, there is ample evidence that broad swaths of the Persian reading public have spent relatively large sums for the 800-page volume, which up to now has only been published in hardcover.[iv] Needless to say, this is startling in the case of a work that critics of state-supported publications generally dismiss as "commissioned" (*sefareshi*) writing.[v]

What might be termed the institutionalization of *Da* began less than a year after it first appeared in September 2008. Early in the spring of 2009, Seyyed Mohammad Reza Mirtajeddini, a Principalist[vi] member of Iran's legislature from Tabriz and Vice-President for Parliamentary Affairs under President Ahmadinezhad, proposed ways to publicize and disseminate *Da* at a meeting honoring its creators and publisher.[vii] With the New Year imminent, he suggested the book be presented to deputies so they could read it over the two-week holiday recess. Mirtajeddini further proposed the memoir be awarded to deserving students in schools, universities, and cultural centers.[viii]

Da was a hit with more than just hard-line politicians like Mirtajeddini. The reformist Mohammad Ali Abtahi, a former Vice President of Iran and close associate of Mohammad Khatami (President 1997–2005), recalls that his wife brought the book home, but he was too busy with the 2008 presidential elections to read it.[ix] Abtahi eventually found ample opportunity to do so after going to prison in June 2009. *Da* was among the reading materials brought by a visitor to one of Abtahi's suite mates in Tehran's Evin Prison. Zahra Hoseyni's account of how, as a seventeen-year-old, she resisted the Iraqis and was prepared to sacrifice her life to defend the ideals of the Islamic Revolution made her a transcendent figure for Abtahi. He was so moved by the scenes of raw emotion and privation in the memoir that he would often burst into tears while reading it. Abtahi's reaction is typical. Many readers see *Da* as an epic of grief and suffering that evokes the formative event in Shiism: the martyrdom in 680 of Imam Hoseyn, his family, and a small band of followers at Karbala. To the documentary filmmaker Mohammad Mehdi Khaleqi, Zahra Hoseyni's accounts of the martyrdom of her father and brother are so remarkable that they take the place of the most moving (*sangintarin*) eulogies (*rowzeh`ha*) commemorating the suffering at Karbala.[x] In this reading, the Zahra Hoseyni–A'zam Hoseyni collaboration functions like the traditional dirges or passion pageants (*ta'ziyeh*) performed during the month of Moharram. *Da*, in effect, brings the archetypal Shii narrative of martyrdom from the seventh century into the twentieth and thereby contemporizes the slaughter at Karbala in the context of the Iran-Iraq War.

The phenomenon that has been described as "*Da*-reading fever" continues to this day in Iran.[xi] One website attributes the book's popularity among the country's politicians and members of its entertainment community to the Supreme Leader's praise. Ayatollah Khameneh'i said the book was "capable of being advanced on a global level."[xii] In one of its recent incarnations as cultural icon, the book was spotted on the desk of the newly elected President of Iran, Hassan Rouhani. With its telltale red-and-white cover, *Da* became part of the office "décor" at a session with the press on the 100th day of the new administration.[xiii] This inspired a website headline writer to ask: "Is Rouhani Reading *Da*?" The news conference happened to fall in Basij Week, an annual event commemorating the selflessness of young, mobilized paramilitaries (*Basiji*s) who fought and were maimed and/or killed in the Iran-Iraq War. The headline writer's speculation about whether Rouhani was actually reading the book was, of course, rhetorical; however, the author of the article suggests the book was purposely placed on the President's desk as a fitting reminder of *Basiji* sacrifices.

Not unexpectedly, given the book's phenomenal popularity, *Da* generated serious interest outside of politics. Academics were particularly quick to realize its potential and to make use of it in their research. Scholarly studies began to emerge less than three years after the book came out. In a paper published in 2011, three social science researchers combed through Zahra Hoseyni's war experiences to see if they conformed to international models of crisis management.[xiv] The paper begins with a comprehensive survey of the literature in the field and then proceeds to a detailed analysis and sequencing of the chaotic events of the first weeks of the War, as narrated in *Da*. The general conclusion of their research is that Zahra Hoseyni's experiences fall neatly into crisis management categories found in the current literature on the subject. One example of the researchers' findings is that Zahra Hoseyni's account of what happened at the Jennatabad corpse-washing and shrouding facility exemplified the 3- and 5-stage crisis frameworks as defined by Mitroff and Pearson, two pioneers in the field.[xv] Interestingly, although the paper adheres to the standard format of international academic research and makes liberal use of refereed source materials, two aspects of the final report undermine its formal claims to scholarly rigor and objectivity. First, reflecting the popular misreading of the memoir mentioned above, the paper consistently identifies *Da* as a "novel" (*roman*) and not as a memoir or oral history. Second, one can see the influence of Islamic Republican speech on the research in the way it uses—as does *Da* itself—the pejorative term *Monafeqin* ("Hypocrites") for the anti-Islamic Republican group known as the *Mojahedin-e Khalq* (the MEK or People's Mojahedin, which until 2012 had been on the U.S. government's list of terrorist organizations).[xvi]

In addition to the crisis management study, two dissertations reflect how academia has embraced *Da*. Payam-e Nur (Message of Light) University reports awarding a Ph.D. to Esma'il Ashhab in 2011 for his dissertation, "A Study of the Story Elements in the Book *Da*."[xvii] The other Ph.D., far broader in scope, is Mohammad Abbas Nezhad's "A Meta-Analysis of Writings, Criticism,

Interviews, Research, and Dissertations on the Book *Da*" (February 2012), which reports that since *Da*'s publication there have been eleven dissertations and more than seventy seminars and roundtable discussions on the work.[xviii]

Da also quickly entered the worlds of animation and the cinema. In an attempt to bring the book to the large audience of nonreaders in Iran, the publisher, Howzeh-ye Honari (Artistic Center), allowed the production of a 120-episode animated feature that began airing on television in June 2011.[xix] Fifty-five of Iran's leading theater, cinema, and television artists lent their voices free of charge to the program. In this way the animated *Da* is comparable—and perhaps an indigenous response—to *Persepolis*, Marjane Satrapi's successful graphic novel and animation with characters voiced by such stars as Catherine Deneuve and Gena Rowlands. Of course, as the director of the television *Da*, Sina Ata'ian, readily admits, although the film contains moving imagery (*tasvir-e motaharrek*), it does not rise to the level of a truly animated feature like *Persepolis*.[xx] *Da*'s translation to motion picture has not been as smooth as its path to motion drawing. One of the first to express interest in making a film of the work was Tahmineh Milani, director of some of the highest grossing films in Iran. Milani has been accused of being "anti-revolutionary" for her outspoken criticism of the psychological and social pressures on Iranian women and her treatment of sensitive topics such as what happened in the country in the years immediately after the 1979 Revolution. Zahra Hoseyni strongly objected to having Milani direct the film of her memoir because she believed Milani to be a *zed-e arzeshi* director, one whose values deviate from those of the Islamic Republic.[xxi] Accordingly, Howzeh-ye Honari gave the task of making a film of *Da* to Homayun Asadian, whose values are more consonant with those expressed in the book.

The brief controversy about the choice of director is indicative of how *Da* is something more than an ordinary memoir. Like mega cultural phenomena in other places, *Da* turned into a battleground for opposing views on basic moral and ethical questions. On one side was the narrator of the book, with her unshakeable fidelity to proper veiling (*khosh hejabi*). Throughout *Da* there is a constant pull between the necessity to remain covered and the demands war makes on veiled women. In Chapter 9, for example, Zahra Hoseyni recalls being tossed around in the back of a van carrying food for the troops. As the vehicle swerves to avoid bomb craters in the road, she is forced to keep one hand on her immodestly flapping chador while steadying pots of rice and stew with the other. In Chapter 20, her commitment to gathering corpses puts the need to maintain propriety at all costs to a severe test. Zahra Hoseyni describes how she and two male companions trudge through a marshland near the front to retrieve a body left out in the sun for a number of days. Because her companions refuse to touch the rotting corpse unless it is covered with something, Zahra Hoseyni has no choice but to remove her chador and use it as a shroud. The very act of de-veiling—however necessary—violates a principle of adult femininity, which became second nature the moment she got her first chador (also described in the book).

Despite being near contemporaries and both having lost a brother in the War, the social, economic, and cultural divide between the narrator of *Da* and its putative director could not be deeper. According to the Persian Facebook entry,[xxii] Milani was born in Tabriz in northwestern Iran in September 1960 to a family that placed a high value on women's education. Her mother is the eldest daughter of Mirza Ali Khan Hashemzadeh, a respected member of the Azerbaijani gentry. Milani's father is a retired internist from a town near Tabriz, where Milani attended a French-language missionary school. Twice weekly her mother took her to the Metropol Cinema, where she saw many western movies—often more than once. Milani's mother continued to expose her daughter to films after her husband was transferred to Qazvin. Milani's background would have placed her in the upper strata of Iranian society. As a native Persian user, educated in a European language, exposed to Western art and music as a child, and brought up in a secular household indifferent to veiling, she was poised to prosper in the rapidly Westernizing Iran under Shah Mohammad Reza Pahlavi (ruled 1941–79).

Zahra Hoseyni, by contrast, comes from an impoverished refugee family from Iraq with two home languages (Kurdish and Arabic), which put her on the lowest rung of the Persian-dominant society of Iran. Her father, Hoseyn Hoseyni, was a low-wage laborer, a political dissident in both Iraq and Iran, and a devoted follower of anti-monarchist Shii spiritual authorities, some of whom were living in exile in Iraq. Opposed to the mandatory coeducation in public schools under the Shah, he refused to allow Zahra to continue her education. But the advent of war changed Hoseyn Hoseyni's ideas about the role of women. In his eyes the need to repel the Iraqi invasion was more important than keeping his daughter out of society. This change of heart enabled Zahra to continue her schooling, albeit using a curriculum necessitated by conflict: dealing with the dead, nursing the wounded, and operating weapons. As it was for many of the young people in southwestern Iran who suddenly became combatants in a conflict they had not started, the War became a kind of post-secondary education for Zahra. The indiscriminate shelling of the city also made it necessary for those from two distinct speech communities (Arabic and Persian) to communicate. Thus, Zahra's fluency in Arabic changed from being a marker of social inferiority to a needed skill, one that gave her entrée to circles in male society that ordinarily would have been closed to her.

The wide social and cultural gap between Zahra Hoseyni and Tahmineh Milani is also reflected in their choice of a spouse. Habib Maz'ali, Zahra's husband, is an Iranian Arabic speaker and a commander who spent the War serving in the southern battlefields. *Da* often describes him coming home with his uniform soaked in the blood of one of his men whom he has driven to the hospital. Zahra also mentions her husband's frequent dreams of martyrdom. Mohammad Nikbin (b. 1953), Milani's husband, spent his youth studying in the United States: the University of Colorado at Boulder (1971-79?) and the University of Minneapolis Twin Cities (1977-79), from which he graduated with a masters degree in architecture. Nikbin returned to Iran after the Revolution and established Atabin, an architecture firm with around thirty employees (including Tahmineh Milani as a consulting architect) that frequently worked with an American design, planning, and management concern.[xxiii] Unlike Habib Maz'ali, whose sights Zahra Hoseyni tells us were often set on the enemy and eternity, Nikbin, according to a 2007 profile in the journal *Entrepreneurs*, looked forward to a time when management principles he had learned in Minnesota would apply to the business of building in Iran.

II. Reading *Da* in Iran

The *Da*-occasioned divide between Tahmineh Milani and Zahra Hoseyni, however brief, typifies a larger and more lasting fissure in Iranian society today. At the time of this writing more than a quarter century has passed since the end of the War. Many members of the under thirty generation have no direct memory of it, nor are they eager to hear or read about it. Moreover, some young people view the public commemoration of the War and state-sponsored fiction and nonfiction works on it as regime propaganda. These they dismiss as a means of inculcating and reinvigorating such basic revolutionary values as allegiance to the supreme leader, self-sacrifice, modesty, belief in the miraculous nature of the holy Imams, etc. Research in Sacred Defense [i.e., Iran-Iraq War] Studies indicates a large number of young people doubt the official version of why it was fought. One narrative espoused by the post-War generation has it that Iraq attacked Iran in response to the latter country's efforts to export its revolution and not—as officials maintain—because the War was "imposed" (*tahmili*) on Iran by the superpowers and their surrogates.[xxiv] In this narrative, Iranian soldiers become the aggressors and the Iraqis the victims of their aggression, which goes against doctrine in Sacred Defense writing. But the positive reaction to the book and the popularity of the animated version suggest that not everyone has been as skeptical of the appeal of the Zahra Hoseyni–A'zam Hoseyni collaboration as some members of the post-War generation and that there is something about *Da* that—state-generated sales not withstanding—makes it a best seller.

Many Iranian writers have tried to explain why *Da* has proven to be such a hit. Dr. Ali Reza Kamari[xxv] argues that the multidisciplinary field of cultural studies is better suited to explain the book's popularity than exclusively aesthetic or sociological approaches.[xxvi] The broader view allows Kamari to identify two types of discourse (*gofteman*) in the book: manifest and latent. On the surface the book seems to uphold the official view of the war; namely, that it was an entirely male enterprise, a holy struggle fought by Persian boys and men in the defense of the Islamic Revolution and Shii values. At the same time, however, in *Da* are the less evident discourses of ethnicity (*qowmiat*) and gender (*jensiat*), which seem to complicate the official narrative. Kamari believes *Da* to be exceptional among War memoirs because details only a woman would notice come to the fore in the book, while the concerns of fighting men recede in the background. As an example he cites how Zahra Hoseyni often notices what the female victims of the Iraqi assault were wearing when they died. Kamari thinks *Da,* with its latent discourses, became popular because it came at a time of national reassessment, when Iranians were seeking alternatives to the official views of the Iran-Iraq War.

An analogous explanation of *Da*'s popularity came in an article published in spring 2013. It studies *Da*'s latent feminist discourse features by applying the methods of Critical Discourse Analysis developed by Norman Fairclough.[xxvii] One of the findings of the authors, Mohammad Reza Javadi-Yaganeh and Seyyed Mohammad Ali Sohofi, is that by having a woman narrate what men ordinarily do, *Da* represents a new type of text in war literature. In their opinion, *Da* is among the few texts that challenge conventional thinking on the conflict in general and the clichés about women in war specifically. It is this iconoclastic approach that explains *Da*'s exceptional popularity. The authors see Zahra Hoseyni fundamentally as a seventeen-year-old "struggling to free herself from the clutches of women's roles." The most salient features of the book are the many ways Zahra Hoseyni acts as a man. For example, after her father's death, she assumes the role of head of the family, and other women comment on her masculine demeanor; she usurps the ordinarily male job of gravedigger and buries her father and brother with her own hands for which—as said above—she becomes widely known; and she goes to the front and engages in the archetypal male endeavor—soldiering. She also speaks publicly about the treachery of former Iranian President Banisadr and is denounced by men for jeopardizing revolutionary solidarity with her unfeminine outspokenness.

As noted above, *Da* not only looks backward almost three decades to the start of the War, it also evokes the most consequential event in Shii history: the seventh-century slaughter of innocents at Karbala. In popular accounts of the battle, one woman stands out more than any other figure both as a victim of the tragedy and a resister of the tyranny and aggression that caused it: Zeynab, the daughter of the first Imam Ali and sister to the martyred third Imam Hoseyn. As the interviewer of Kamari points out, reader response polling indicates that many identify Zahra Hoseyni with Zeynab. Certain biographical details abet the identification. Both women had to endure the killing of a father and their beloved brother at the hands of a hated enemy. In her grief Zahra Hoseyni occasionally seems to be patterned on Zeynab—or, at least, on the Zeynab portrayed in elegies (*nowheh*, *marsiyeh*) Shiis recite during Moharram, the month of mourning. An Urdu poem by Mir Babar Ali Anis (1802–74) has Zeynab ask, "Would that you could bury me too, beside my brother."[xxviii] Zahra Hoseyni similarly mourns her her brother Ali and, at times, even envies him his martyrdom. The incident—mentioned above—of Zahra Hoseyni removing her chador and using it as a shroud will also strike a chord with those steeped in Shii devotional literature. It is reported that after her capture Zeynab was subjected to the indignity of having her veil removed. As she looks down at her brother's headless body, the poet Anis has her say:

> How will I lift up your corpse?
> My head lacks any veil, which I might spread out for you.[xxix]

Zahra Hoseyni also has a blood tie with Zeynab. As a *seyyedeh*, she traces her ancestry back to the Prophet Mohammad, Zeynab's grandfather. In *Da* we often see how members of the Hoseyni family, despite their relatively low status in Iranian society as Iraqi Kurdish refugees, are privileged among their neighbors and others because they are *seyyed*s. The tie that binds *seyyed*s over the ages, however, is more than one of blood. *Seyyed*s, as a whole, form a collective of uncommon pain and suffering. Late in *Da* Zahra Hoseyni recalls how her grandfather explains what it means to be descended from the Prophet Mohammad. He tells her *seyyed*s come into the world to suffer, which is what distinguishes them among all other believers. Suffering tests their faith and their "strength" (as the present work renders the Persian *sabr*) in the face of unbearable hardship and injustice. Such suffering also can be redemptive; the greater the torment *seyyed*s endure in this world, the greater their reward in the next. As the scholar of Shii beliefs Mahmoud Ayoub points out, the suffering of *seyyed*s on earth can turn into immeasurable bliss in the afterlife.[xxx] The extreme difference between the terrestrial existence of *seyyed*s and what they will see in heaven is illustrated in the saga of Fatemeh (also Fatimah, 605 or 615–633, the daughter of the Prophet, wife of the murdered first Imam Ali, and mother of the arch-martyr, Imam Hoseyn). Shii eschatology tells us:

> Fatimah's humiliation will be amply rewarded. The poverty and privation, which she endured in life, will be matched with unimaginable glory. All creatures, men, angels, and *jinn*, will be dazzled by her radiant light as she stands before God to pass judgment on her persecutors and grant intercession to those who love *ahl al-bayt* [the Prophet's family]. The mistress of the House of Sorrows will be the mistress of the Day of Judgment.[xxxi]

The function of the uncommon grief and suffering *seyyed*s must endure is very clear from this; they make the most abject creature on earth one of the most powerful beings in heaven.

Not all opinion on *Da* in Iran has been as positive about the book as the cultural studies and *Da*-as-dirge readings outlined above. An unattributed critical analysis of the book was published on the site Iranpardis in October 2010.[xxxii] The review responds to the misreading of *Da* as a novel by employing the very criteria used for judging fiction. It finds the book wanting on several counts. The anonymous critic objects to Zahra Hoseyni's frequent reminiscences because they interrupt the flow of the narrative. The review also considers other novelistic elements, including *Da*'s character development (of both well-known figures and those rescued from obscurity by the memoir), dialogue (paltry), diction (uneven), theme (well realized), and naturalistic depictions of war (strongest Sacred Defense feature). The review's harshest criticism is reserved for the narrator. It points out that during the first third of the book Zahra

Hoseyni is a marginal figure, a young child in Basra and a schoolgirl coming of age in Iran. With the outbreak of war, however, she suddenly achieves Zelig-like proportions, often appearing at the center of major events in the first three weeks of the Iraqi invasion. According to the reviewer, the largest section of the memoir is an occasional exercise in egotism that exaggerates the narrator's actual contributions.

One example of *Da*'s self-centered narration comes in Chapter 10, in which Zahra Hoseyni recalls coming upon the corpses of two acquaintances in the hospital morgue. She sees Shahnaz Hajjishah, a girl from her school whom she got to know after the outbreak of the War, and Shahnaz Mohammadi. With the help of an older woman, Zahra tries to lift the corpse of Hajjishah onto a stretcher, but the woman drops the feet, leaving Zahra holding an arm separated from the body by the fall. *Da* devotes many heartfelt words to the traumatic effect this has on the narrator. She finds the thought of being responsible for the post-mortem dismemberment of a friend particularly horrifying. Before the publication of *Da*, its publisher had also produced works containing oral histories that mention the martyrdom of Shahnaz Hajjishah. One of these, *In the Alleys of Khorramshahr,* compiles a number of reminiscences of the War's first weeks.[xxxiii] In the book (p. 138), Shahnaz Hajjishah's sister Shahla recalls hearing the news of her death, but even though Shahla is speaking of the death and burial of an older sibling, she does so succinctly and does not place her own thoughts and emotions at the center of the narrative. The same can be said of Bahjat Salehpur's memory of seeing the corpses of the "two Shahnazes," who had been among her closest friends:

> The scenes were horrifying. I had never even imagined much less actually seen such things. They had laid out the bodies of the martyrs on the ground so they faced Mecca. I couldn't make out who they were, but felt I had to do something. We put three of the bodies and six or so of the wounded in the back of the truck on a load of apples meant for the troops and sent them on to the hospital. Although I would never have dared look at a corpse in the past, my best friends were now dying in

> my arms: Shahnaz Hajjishah, who passed away the moment the doctor asked her name, and Shahnaz Mohammadi, who lived on fifteen minutes longer.[xxxiv]

Another criticism of *Da* also takes the book to task for its excessive foregrounding of the narrator's emotions and feelings. Gholamreza Azari Khakestari, a scholar of oral history, has studied a number of Iran-Iraq War memoirs published by Howzeh-ye Honari. He finds that although these works are important first steps along the path to understanding what happened during the War, they are too concerned with the narrators' psychological states to be considered reliable primary sources. In his review of *Da*, Azari Khakestari uses the book to illustrate the failings of memoirs as oral history.[xxxv] The narrative style of the book, he writes, is often so unlike a historical document, so similar to popular literature, in fact, that it overshadows the events of the War the work describes. This, in turn, causes the reader to doubt its truthfulness. In this view, what has captivated many consumers of *Da*, i.e. its thriller-like readability, disqualifies it from being history. Another failing of the book Azari Khakestari often mentions is that long periods of time pass between when events described in the book take place and the time of their telling. In the beginning of *Da*, we read a five- or six-year-old child's memories of her life in Basra. Zahra Hoseyni was at an age when she could not fully comprehend the facts of her family life—the imprisonment of her father, her uncle's position as the head of a school in Basra, emigration to Iran, etc. The written record of those facts is the product of an adult mind and therefore influenced by what she had heard at family gatherings after the events had taken place. The same criticism applies to what Zahra Hoseyni remembers of the first weeks of the war in Khorramshahr. According to Azari Khakestari, the passage of time may have to some degree degraded or distorted those memories. If, rather than being dictated by one person and turned into Persian prose by another almost two decades after the events it describes, *Da* had been based on a diary (*ruz-nevesht*), readers would be in a better position to judge its reliability as oral history.

Azari Khakestari's critique also contrasts *Da* with the oral histories of other women active in the Iran-Iraq War. He specifically cites Maryam Amjadi's *The Boots of Maryam* as a kind of anti-*Da*.[xxxvi] The comparison is apt; Maryam Amjadi and Zahra Hoseyni (as *Da* readily attests) share many things. Both were seventeen when the Iraqis invaded; both nursed the wounded; both took up arms and fought shoulder to shoulder with men; and both lost their fathers in the War. Azari Khakestari contrasts how the two narrators remember the same events and finds a simplicity of expression in Amjadi's book that makes it seem an account of exactly what she said. On the other hand, Zahra Hoseyni's reminiscences with their "endless descriptive passages" (*towsifat-e bi-hadd*) seem novelistic to readers.

III. The Translation

As has been often said, translations by nature are a series of compromises that betray original texts. It is only a slight exaggeration to say that those able to contrast the original to the present translation will find treachery in every chapter. Some of the ways the English version of *Da* differs from the Persian, or pales by comparison to it, are described below.

Footnotes: *Da*'s publisher anticipated criticism of the work's failings as oral history by annotating the text with a number of footnotes, some of which are taken verbatim from historical sources. One of these is an explanation of the "Arab insurrection" (*gha'eleh-ye 'arab*) in Chapter 3 (pages 60–63 in the original).[xxxvii] This footnote does not appear in the translation. It was felt that a personal memoir was not an appropriate place to raise the issue of Arab separatism in southwestern Iran, a complex and controversial topic that comes up frequently in the modern history of the country. In addition, the excessively detailed account of the uprising that took place at the beginning of the Revolution breaks the flow of Zahra Hoseyni's story. Apart from this footnote, almost all other notes in the original have been translated as is, incorporated in the text, or consigned to the glossary that follows the translation.

To Die or Be Martyred: *Halaliat*: Having translated three fiction works on the Iran-Iraq War,[xxxviii] I have often thought about how to render *shahid* ("martyr") or *be-shahadat rasidan* ("to be martyred"). As they do in all Sacred Defense writing, casualties in *Da*—both civilian and military—do not "die"; they are "martyred" or "achieve martyrdom." To use such terms exclusively in the translation would make the memoir read like church history or hagiography. An amalgamated approach seemed to be in order. Thus, casualties in this translation more often than not "die," but when people close to the narrator (father, brother) pass away, they are "martyred." This is to reflect the deeply emotional impact of the death rather than to assert that the deceased is heaven-bound, which—it is believed—only God can determine. The extended passages on impending death or martyrdom in *Da* also entail the notion of *halaliat*, literally "the state of being *halal* or "free of sin." The term is used when survivors ask the departed to be absolved of committing any slight, wrongdoing, or transgression. It involves a deeply felt amalgam of guilt and shame for not having behaved well toward someone. Translations can only approximate such a tangle of feelings and memories. Chapter 9, for example, has the translated Zahra begging her martyred father's "forgiveness," which faintly renders the emotional force and intent of the Persian. "Absolution" was a possibility, but it seemed too freighted with non-Muslim associations to be at home in the memoir of a devout Shii. An analogous use of *halal* comes in Chapter 12 when Zahra, sensing her brother's martyrdom is at hand, asks her mother to "make [her] peace with Ali." The original is *shirat`ru halalash kon*, literally "make the milk you fed him as a child *halal*." The English compromise is cold and clinical.

***Mojahedin* or "Hypocrites":** Translating *Monafeqin* ("Hypocrites"), a staple of Sacred Defense usage, also presented a problem. As mentioned above, the narrator consistently uses this pejorative term, which is taken from the Quran, to refer to the Islamo-Marxist group *Mojahedin-e Khalq*. It is part of a purposeful demonization of the organization, which carried out a number of attacks on Iran's top leadership and sided with the Iraqis during the War. On one hand, to translate *Monafeqin* as "People's Mojahedin of Iran" would be to neutralize both regimist and popular hostility toward the group. On the other, using "Hypocrites" would make the translation resemble official texts. In this case the translation has erred on the side of antipathy.

***Gharib*:** *Gharib*, literally "strange" or "stranger," is another term with a long history that defies easy translation. In Chapter 9

Zahra recites a dirge in Arabic about the martyrdom of the innocents at Karbala, in which *gharib* is translated as "forlorn." Zahra's mother uses it when standing at the gravesite of her dead husband and says to him, "We're burying you like some stranger." Though all but one of her children are with her, the absence of her father and brothers at the funeral is almost as painful as the death of her spouse. In this way Hoseyn Hoseyni goes to a grave that will soon be overrun by the Iraqis as one "estranged" or "dispossessed." He is not only bereft of life but abandoned—like the martyrs of Karbala—by all but those nearest to him. As in the case of other terms with deep roots in Arabic and Persian literature, the English equivalents used here cannot fully convey the intent and emotional impact of *gharib*.

***Dagh-del*: "seared of heart":** After the start of the War, public expressions of deep sorrow and grief normally reserved for Moharram pageants or for recitation of Karbala elegies became common in Khorramshahr. *Da* often pairs the qualifier *dagh* ("scalding hot") with *del* ("heart, gut") to convey these feelings. *Dagh* can be paired with *kabab* to mean kebab "straight from the grill." A "bazaar" can also be *dagh* when there is a "hot market." The terms *dagh* and *del* are often used to mark the ineffable feelings that come with the loss of a loved one. The usage is a common trope in the rich tradition of elegiac literature in Persian. In Chapter 4 a dirge describes the Prophet Mohammad's heart as being "seared," which once again does not do justice to the sentiment in the original. "Heartburn," of course, was rejected for its gastric associations, and "heart-scalded" seemed a misleading neologism.

***Mazlumiat va ma'sumiat*: "victimhood and innocence":** In Chapter 7 Zahra describes her father's eyes as "brimming" with *mazlumiat* and *ma'sumiat*. The English paraphrase "the look of an innocent victim" doesn't quite capture the religio-cultural import of the phrase. Hoseyn Hoseyni has made his peace with the world. Realizing he is about to die, he formally hands responsibility for the family over to his eldest daughter. As one on the verge of martyrdom, he is innocent in two senses: "incapabable of harm" or "put upon" (*mazlum*) and "untainted by sin" (*ma'sum*). In this way he is like the holy Imams, who are considered sinless, but victimized by the forces of tyranny.

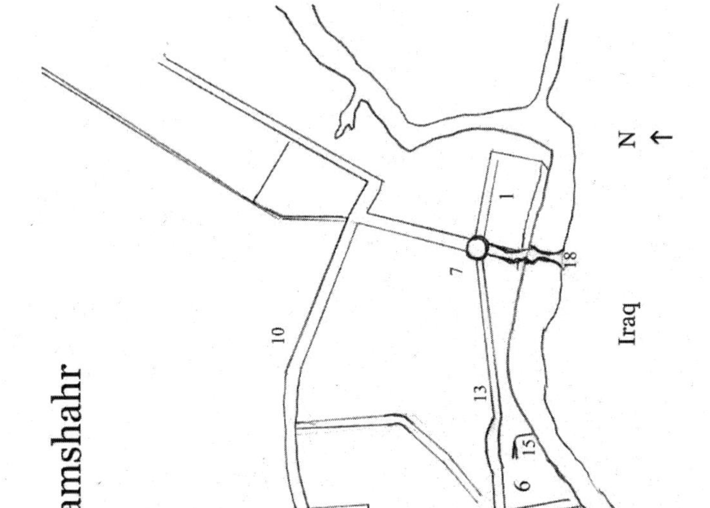
Khorramshahr
1
2
3
4
5
6
7
8
9
10
11
12
13
14
15
16
17
18
19
20
21
Iraq
N

Map Legend

The map of Khorramshahr, which is not drawn to scale, represents the city as it was during the initial stages of the War. It is based on the one found in *Khorramshahr dar Jang-e Tulani* ("Khorramshahr in the Long War"), Mehdi Ansari, Mohammad Dorudian, and Hadi Nakha'i. Tehran: *Markaz-e Motala'at va Tahqiqat-e Jang*, 2006, pp. [176a-b].

Legend

1. Mosaddeq Hospital
2. Persian Gulf Avenue
3. Dieselabad
4. Shatt al-Arab (Arvandrud)
5. Ferdowsi Avenue
6. Congregational Mosque
7. Farmandari Circle
8. Stadium
9. Road to Shalamcheh
10. Ring Road
11. Jennatabad
12. Darvazeh Traffic Circle
13. Forty Meter Road
14. Hafez Avenue
15. Safa Market/Bazaar
16. Road to Ahvaz
17. [Road] Police
18. Bridge
19. Moqbel Circle
20. Port and Customs Area
21. Sentab Gate

---

[i] The Persian title of the work is: *Da* [Kurdish for "mother"]*: the Memoirs of Seyyedeh Zahra Hoseyni as told to and set down by Seyyedeh A'zam Hoseyni*, but it is commonly known as *Da*.
[ii] http://www.farsnews.com/php?nn=8801250450. On the genesis of the book, how it has been read and translated into nonprint formats, see Laetitia Nanquette, "An Iranian Woman's War Memoir on the Iran-Iraq War: The Production and Reception of *Da*" (*Iranian Studies* 46: 6; published online July 11, 2013).
[iii] The story is "*Dastan-e ghamangiz-e ketab-e da va setami keh bar an raft*." It is dated August 7, 2013, and filed at: http://alef.ir/prte7n8zzjh8ozi.b9bj.html.
[iv] Over the course of its more than 150 reported printings (see "*Ketab-e* Da *bish az 150 bar chap shodeh ast*" http://www.farsnews.com/php?nn=13910822001451), the book has ranged between the equivalent of ten and fifteen dollars.
[v] One blogger at Zambur (http://zambur.blogfa.com/post-174.aspx) reports hearing that many intellectuals, who have no truck with the Sacred Defense and are even antiwar, have extolled (*tamjid kardeh-and*) *Da*.
[vi] Principalist or *Osuli* politicians adhere strictly to articles of faith of the Islamic Revolution of 1979, among which is the belief that a Shii Jurist (*faqih*) is the rightful and supreme leader of the Islamic Republic. The first such *faqih* was Ayatollah Khomeini; the second is his successor Ayatollah Ali Khamene'i.
[vii] See http://dsrc.ir/Contents/ContentFrame.aspx?ID=1720&PF=true.
[viii] In his remarks Mirtajeddini termed the work a *roman-e haqiqi* or a "real novel," which may remind English readers of Truman Capote's characterization of *In Cold Blood* as a "non-fiction novel." Because *One Woman's War* at times reads like a thriller, it has often been mistaken for fiction. Needless to say, Zahra Hoseyni stands by the truth of everything she relates in the book.
[ix] See http://www.webneveshteha.com/weblog/?m=06&y=1389, a blog dated September 22, 2010.
[x] See his review of *Da* posted at http://zambur.bogfa.com/post-174.aspx.
[xi] Iman Motahhari Manesh uses the phrase "*tab-e da-khvani*" in the article "The Book with the Most Adventures in 2009" (*por majartarin ketab-e sal-e 1388*) at http://asha.ir/archives/2432.
[xii] See http://asha.ir/archives/2432. Ayatollah Khameneh'i calls the book "*qabel-e tarh dar sath-e jahani*" at: http://www.asriran.com/fa/news/113741.
[xiii] *Aya rowhani ketab-e da mikhvanad* at http://www.spidezh.ir/tab-266/2%.

[xiv] "A Study of Models of Crisis Management in the Novel *Da,*" by professor Hamid Taboli of Payam-e Nur University and two graduate researchers Samaneh Karimi Afshar and Elham Ashrafzadeh at Islamic Azad University, was published in the journal *Perseverance Literature* (*Adabiayt-e Paydari*) of the Faculty of Letters and Social Sciences of Shahid Bahonar University and is available at: http://www.noormags.com/view/fa/articlepage/957050.

[xv] In Ian I. Mitroff and Christine M. Pearson, *Crisis Management: A Diagnostic Guide for Improving Your Organization's Crisis-Preparedness* (San Francisco, CA: Jossey-Bass, 1993).

[xvi] On these terms, see the glossary at the end of the translation.

[xvii] *Bar'rasi-e anaser-e dastan dar ketab-e da*, http://dsrc.ir/View/dissertation.aspx?id=147.

[xviii] "*Da* Transported the Literature of Perseverance of Iran beyond Boundaries" (Da *adabiyat-e paydari-e Iranra be-an su-ye marzha sader kard*), a Javan newspaper article dated November 6, 2013, published at http://www.javanonline.ir/fa/news/617094.

[xix] See the article in *Hamshahri* at: http://hamshahrionline.ir/print/137042. The series is available at: http://www.youtube.com/watch?v=jacTR-EenyXM.

[xx] See http://alijazayeri.blogfa.com/post-231aspx.

[xxi] See the article in *Serat News* dated July 1, 2012 at: http://www.seratnews.ir/fa/news/69611.

[xxii] See https://m.facebook.com/profile.php?v=info&expand=1&id=221980407833833.

[xxiii] From an interview with Nikbin published in *Majalleh-ye Karafarinan* ("Entrepreneurs") dated December 20, 2007. Nikbin left Iran in 2008 and works in Los Angeles.

[xxiv] The speculation was voiced at a seminar on the animated *Da* with Arts Center officials hosted by the *Pazhuheshgah-e 'Olum va Ma'aref-e Defa'-e Moqaddas* (The Research Center for Sacred Defense Science and Learning) at: http://dsrc.ir/Contents/ContentsFrame.aspx?ID=6808&PF=true.

[xxv] Ali Reza Kamari is a scholar of Sacred Defense literature. One of his works is a collection of writings of Fahimeh Baba'iyanpur (Tehran: Howzeh-ye Honari, 1990), a woman active in the resistance to the Iraqi invasion of Khorramshahr.

[xxvi] Kamari's views appear in an interview with Zahir Tavakkoli republished in *Farhang Shenasi* at: http://www.farhangshenasi.ir/persian/node/771.

[xxvii] "*Revayat-e zananeh az jang: tahlil-e enteqadi-ye ketab-e khaterat-e* Da," Mohammad Reza Javadi- Yaganeh, Seyyed Mohammad Ali Sohofi; *Naqd-e Adabi* 6: 21(Spring 2013): 85–110.
[xxviii] David Pinault, "Zaynab bint 'Ali and the Place of the Women of the Household of the First Imams in Shi'ite Devotional Literature," in *Women in the Medieval Islamic World: Power, Patronage*, *and Piety,* ed. Gavin R.G. Hambly (NY: St. Martin's, 1998, p. 84).
[xxix] Pinault, p. 86.
[xxx] Mahmoud Ayoub, *Redemptive Suffering in Islam: A Study of the Devotional Aspects of 'Ashura in Twelver Shiism* (The Hague, Paris; NY: Mouton, 1978, p. 24).
[xxxi] Ayoub, p. 213.
[xxxii] See http://www.iranpardis.com/showthread.php?t=62373.
[xxxiii] *Dar Kucheh`ha-ye Khorramshahr*, ed. Maryam Shanaki (Tehran: Howzeh-ye Honari, 1991).
[xxxiv] *Dar Kucheh`ha-ye Khorramshahr*, p. 170.
[xxxv] "*Negahi beh ketab-e* Da" ("A Look at *Da* as Oral History") at http://ohwm.ir/show.php?id=740.
[xxxvi] Maryam Amjadi and Fariba Taleshpur, *Putin`ha-ye Maryam* (Tehran: Sureh-ye Mehr, 2002).
[xxxvii] The footnote is taken from *Khorramshahr dar Jang-e Tulani* ("Khorramshahr in the Long War"), Mehdi Ansari, Mohammad Dorudian, and Hadi Nakha'i. Tehran: Markaz-e Motala'at va Tahqiqat-e Jang, 2006, pp. 54-57.
[xxxviii] All three were published by Mazda: *Journey to Heading 270 Degrees* (2006) by Ahmad Dehqan; *Chess with the Doomsday Machine* (2008) and A *City Under Siege: Tales of the Iran-Iraq War* (2010) by Habib Ahmadzadeh.

Author's Introduction

When I was around fourteen, I read the book *Zanan-e Qahreman* ("Women Heroes"). Apart from the lives of the women of early Islam, what interested me was the figure of Djamila Boupacha, though it was hard to accept that a young woman would, with all her being, enter into a one-sided struggle against the occupiers of her country. To preserve the honor and independence of her people, she bore all the barbarous tortures of the French but never gave in to the disgrace of occupation.

Several years later, after the Baathists had savagely attacked Iran, slaughtering the people of my hometown, it seemed that living a life of comfort no longer had any meaning. I realized then that comfort amounted to a type of humiliation that was nothing short of self-annihilation. I had never imagined during those days of fire and gore that I would be burying with my own hands the innocent children of the town, as well as my own relatives, covering them with earth pink with their own blood. This was when, under normal circumstances, I couldn't stand to be away from these relations, even if only for a few days.

But these were the realities I faced, and even now after several years, they are still fresh in my mind. During those years, though individuals from a variety of places have repeatedly come to interview me, insisting I speak about my experiences, I have always refused, feeling if what I had done during the war pleased God in some way, I didn't have to shout it from the rooftops. But there came a time when the situation changed, and those who had served their country, preserving the sacred Islamic Republican system, were being accused of warmongering. At that point I decided to defend the Holy Defense itself, and there was no other way to do this but to record my memories of what had happened during the war.

One day in late April or early May 2001, someone from the women's unit of the Office of Resistance Literature and Art at the Arts Council (hereafter the Office) contacted me, requesting an interview. Because I was not sufficiently familiar with the organization and its staff, I refused. I did so because I wanted to make sure the interviewers were trustworthy people with only the purest of motives. So I began reading the books published by the Office and this—praise God—put my mind at rest, and I could tell them what I remembered. After some preliminary meetings and discussions, it was decided Ms Seyyedeh Azam Hoseyni would interview me. Because of my physical condition, the interviews had to be conducted in my home, which forced Ms Hoseyni to travel back and forth regularly.

Because my aim in these interviews was to show how we were the injured parties in the war, how we had right on our side, I was content to answer the questions in general terms, keeping many painful memories and feelings to myself. This phase of the interviews lasted about thirty hours and yielded three hundred pages of written text. The text, which was not altered in any way, met with the approval of specialists at the Office, but all of them thought many of the topics were not told in sufficient detail and needed clarification. Regardless, it was not easy for me to agree to more interviews, because recalling the details of what had happened would have been distasteful to me and emotionally trying. Thus, my memories were compiled without more interviews. After a period, Ms Hoseyni and I got to know each other better, having traveled together to Iraq with a group of other people to conduct a two-week picture and book exhibit.

This trip and our later association led me to a more precise understanding of interviewing and the process of recording my memories. This was why, when I had the chance to go over the text of my recollections again, and by the time I read the questions raised for clarification, the relationship between Ms Hoseyni and me had become so close that I was now able to open myself up to her. During the second round of interviews, which also took place in my home, Ms Hoseyni followed up, went over, analyzed, and finalized each issue and incident in a gentle and understanding way; but this forced me to recall painful scenes, which even after the passage of a number of years had remained vivid in my mind.

Recalling these things often increased the psychological strain on me, raising my blood pressure and giving me severe headaches. Nevertheless, I persevered until it got to the point where my very soul rebelled against the process. The conflict that raged between my mind and spirit manifested in physical illnesses that interrupted the interviews a number of times. The need for quiet during the interviews also kept my children in their room for hours, depriving them of their horseplay and favorite TV programs. My husband and son would return home later and later each day so they would not disturb the interviews, and the work could reach a conclusion. During this period, my oldest daughter, in addition to providing hospitality, assumed all the household chores.

As the work continued, Ms Hoseyni and I cemented our relationship, becoming so close that when I had to recall something particularly painful, I no longer felt embarrassed to have tears flowing down my cheeks in her presence. But on several occasions my physical and mental condition and other daily concerns made me regret agreeing to the interviews, and I sought various excuses to end them. At each such time Ms Hoseyni patiently, without using any pressure and with a proper understanding of the situation, encouraged me to go on. Her tolerance, in fact, convinced me in the end to keep up my end of the conversations.

Those also were the days when I was working part-time at the Martyrs Museum and attending classes three days a week. At one point, the pressure of work caused a piece of shrapnel lodged near my spinal cord to act up, forcing me to remain bedridden at home. On the strict orders of a physician, I had to avoid any kind of stress or excitement that might affect my nerves. This stopped the interviews for a number of months. After I had returned to relative good health, the conversations restarted both at my home and at the Office.

Conversations at the Office were not without headaches. The small size of the interview room, people coming and going, telephones ringing, and the racket coming from the courtyard and the basement often interrupted my train of thought. I also had to wrap myself in a blanket to keep out the cold, which seeped in the room through cracks in the door and the window. Because sitting hours on end in a chair made my back ache, I had to get up periodically and walk around or stretch out on the floor for a few minutes. During this phase of the interviews, I would spend six or seven hours expanding on what I remembered. Ms Hoseyni then jotted down what I said word for word so I could answer her questions about the incidents in as much detail as possible.

The process went on like this from September 2005 to June 2006. My recollections, which covered the period from the beginning of the war to my coming to Tehran, amounted to more than 1,000 hours....

Here I feel it necessary to express my sincere thanks to Mr. Mehdi Farahani for his expert and sympathetic advice. Likewise I am grateful to Mr. Ali Reza Kamari and Mr. Morteza Sarhangi, both of whom read the manuscript of this book and favored me with their informed opinions and guidance.

I have called the book *Da* ("mother") to pay homage to the sacrifices of all the mothers of the martyrs, especially my own long-suffering and patient mother who devoted all her love and the very essence of her existence to the Lord. If it hadn't been for these adoring and grief-stricken mothers, the soldiers would never have made their way to the battlefields. The protection and support provided by these women heroes allowed their proud sons to remain steadfast in the face of an eight-year enemy assault and to sacrifice their souls for the sake of today's freedom and tranquility. Finally, I hope Khorramshahr shall one day regain its splendor and become the Lord's country, which it had been in the past.

1

Early Life in Iraq

We had no word of father for several months. His political activities kept him away from home so often we had gotten used to his absences. But this time was different; he had been gone for a very long time. Mother told us father had gotten involved in politics, meeting secretly with people after he had stopped working in grandfather's mill and had started in the gunny-sack bazaar.

The owner of the place where father worked was a merchant of Iranian origin whom they called "Hajji." He was aware of father's political activities, and it seemed he himself and his other workers were also involved.

In father's absence, Hajji looked after our family and would pass on messages about his welfare to us. From time to time when father was home, a message would come saying things were dangerous and he had to leave.

When our neighbors asked about father, which they often did, mother would tell them he had gone to a village near Basra and, because it was far away, he would be coming home late.

Those years we were living in the port city of Basra in southern Iraq. Our home was in the Rabat neighborhood, which was quite green because it was near the Tigris. Here immigrants lived in mud houses with sloping roofs made of reeds and straw matting. Those days most of the homes in Basra were made that way. They had large inner courtyards surrounded on all sides by living quarters. The better Basran homes were made of baked brick and were located in the

Ashshar Quarter and its bazaar, which was considered the center of town.

One of father's male cousins had a home in the Ashshar Quarter. I always looked forward to the times we visited there, because unlike our part of the city it had electricity. The light in our house was from kerosene lamps. Mother polished the chimneys of the lamps, which were called "tulips" in those days, and as soon as it got dark she would light the wicks. She placed several of these around the house. Because there was no electricity, we would normally go to bed early. At night the Ashshar Quarter with its square lined on all sides with shops was as bright as day. The ample lighting on the doors of the shops invited customers to enter and look at the goods inside. When I had mother's permission, I would spend hours gaping at the bright electric lights, which made passersby's eyes sparkle, and at the food. The bazaar in our neighborhood had no such luster. People from the villages would just sell their produce from baskets or carts.

Father and mother had come to Basra from the Kurdish village of Zarinabad near Dehloran. This was before their marriage, which took place at the end of the 1950s. My four siblings and I were born in the city: Ali in 1961, and afterwards with one year between us Mohsen, myself, and Leila. The last child, born three years after Leila, was Mansur.

Having grown up in Basra, we were all fluent in Arabic, but at home or when with fellow Kurdish immigrants we spoke Kurdish. We dressed the way the Arabs of the region dressed: in long-sleeved over-shirts known as dishdashas. Mother, whom we called in Kurdish "Da," had been living in Basra since she was an adolescent and had long since grown used to the customs of the area. She spoke Arabic so fluently that people scarcely believed she was a Kurd. She even dressed the way the Arab women did, with a silk shawl wound around her head like a headdress and a long cloak like a chador.

Most of the men in our neighborhood worked like father, in the gunnysack bazaar or on the docks. All of them had a relatively low standard of living. For extra income we rented out two rooms near the entrance to our home, and we lived in a large room at the end of the courtyard.

Mother prepared meals on a pressure stove outside of the room under an overhang made of reed mats and wooden supports. She made a variety of local dishes like hilsa fish, okra goulash, and chopped fish soup. Sometimes she would make a rice casserole with "meat" balls made of mashed bulgur and yogurt fried in animal fat, which relatives had brought as a souvenir.

In the summer we mostly ate outside under the overhang I mentioned. All the children except Mansur, who was nursing, slept on a large wooden platform covered by mosquito netting.

Renting out the two rooms covered most of our expenses. Mother helped out by buying gunny sacking and weaving it into loofahs, which she sold in the bazaar. Father, of course, would provide money for her when he was at home.

When he did come home after long absences, the house became totally different. He would hug and kiss us, laugh and kid around; in short, he would do everything to show his love for us. At night we would all gather round and listen to him tell about the mischief he got into when he was a boy. It was interesting because father, not knowing Arabic very well, spoke in Kurdish. So when he was home, the household language was Kurdish. Father told us he had lost both of his parents when he was two years old, so he was raised by his mother's brother. Because he was the last of his line, everyone, especially his uncle, made sure he was well looked after. "Uncle, who was a hunter," he recalled, "would regularly take me on hunting trips in the mountains. He loved to smoke a pipe and I had the job of preparing it for him. Soon I got fed up with this and began to search for a way to get out of it. Then one time I packed the bowl with some gunpowder and covered it with tobacco. I handed it to uncle, who was sitting with his friends. He lit the pipe and when the flame reached the powder, the thing exploded singeing his mustache and beard. The gathering broke into wild laughter. Afraid of what uncle would do to me, I ran away and hid in a tree. On one hand uncle was furious, but on the other he feared that I'd be torn to pieces by a wild animal. He ran after me shouting, 'Come back. I'm not going to do anything to you!' My trick worked and, from that day on, uncle packed his pipe himself."

As a four- or five-year-old child myself, I couldn't get enough of the stories about the mischief father got into when he was my age.

Father also told us the story of how he came from Iran to Basra and how he and mother got married. Seyyed Hoseyn Hoseyni (my father) and Seyyedeh Shah-Pasand Hoseyni (my mother) were related and came from the same village. Father, who was three years younger than mother, was born in 1936. At eighteen he left the village to work with his elder brother in Basra. There he caught the eye of my grandfather, Seyyed Najaf, a generous family man. Grandpa was working at a government mill at the time, and because he understood what it meant to be a stranger in a strange land, he took father under his wing, arranging work for him at the mill. Later, having seen for himself what a good worker father was and how devout he was, grandfather arranged the marriage between his daughter and my father. Father rented a home near grandfather, and it was there that they began their married life. They were very well suited; I never heard mother complain about father's long absences.

One time I remember mother, her back to the door, was sweeping under the beds. We children were playing in the corner of the room. All of a sudden father entered and we all were about to rush into his arms, when he waved his hands, signaling to us not to say anything. Unaware of what was happening, mother continued to sweep. Father crept up behind her and put his hands over her eyes.

Mother was staggered "Who's that?" she gasped. "Good God in heaven!" The joy of seeing father combined with mother's panic made us all burst out laughing. With father at home everybody woke up when he called out to us at the crack of dawn. He was in the habit of exercising after prayer. He would work out with a metal exercise bar and do push-ups, all the while reciting verses of heroic poetry, and every time Imam Ali's name was mentioned in the poetry, he'd send up prayers to him. After exercising he would turn on a small, two-band radio. The radio was only operated when father was home; other times we didn't have permission to use or even go near it. It was father's property, and honoring him meant that we didn't touch his things. Later he bought a larger radio with the dimensions of a large, cardboard box. After you turned it on, it took a long time to warm up. Father explained, "The tubes have to be on for a while before it'll work." I listened to the radio while he and mother saw to the other children. He was very considerate toward her and the rest of the family, realizing, given the short time we had together, he had to try to provide what we needed so he could again leave with a clear conscience. I never actually saw him leave, as he waited for us to go to sleep before he exited the house. But after his departures, the hardships for mother would begin again: the children's tears and the excuses, father's friends coming around asking questions and the made-up answers, and, worst of all, the raids of the state security agents. Whenever we heard the pounding on the door, we knew they were after us again, and we would all run to mother, who was white-faced with fright. Her fear affected us and we started trembling like willows in the wind. She had instructed us ahead of time to keep our mouths shut and stay in our room. We took her seriously, even though we didn't understand what was happening. Seeing our peace and security in danger was enough to keep us from doing something stupid, which would make matters worse. After peppering mother with questions and terrifying us, and having gotten nothing for their troubles, the agents would storm out the door. We were certain, however, that they would be back.

After they had gone, mother would lean against the wall, and, in a voice choked with tears, say, "There is nothing to this Hasan al-Bakr; Saddam Hussein is the one pulling all the strings." Then she would curse Saddam calling him "the spawn of Shemr's bastard son." Regaining her calm, she would point to the framed picture of Seyyed Mohsen Hakim hanging on the wall and say, "Why expect the person who cut off the water supply to Hakim's family, showing no mercy to the great scholar, to take pity on the likes of us?"[1]

---

[1] Ayatollah Seyyed Mohsen Tabataba'i Hakim (1888-1970) did his seminary studies under professors of the day like Ayatollahs Akhond Khorasani, Zia al-Din Eraqi, Mirza Hasan Na'ini, and Mohammad Khvansari. At the age of twenty-four, he became licensed to give juridical opinions. He participated in the Iraqi independence movement against British military forces. His term as a source of emulation began in 1946 with the death of Ayatollah Seyyed Abu al-Hasan Esfahani. Ayatollah Hakim opposed the monarchy of Feisal, the communist government of Abd al-Karim Qasem, the Baathist rule of Hasan al-Bakr, and the anti-Islamic activities of the Imperial Iranian government. After the death of Ayatollah Bo-

Mother's words frightened me even more than the security agents. Though I was too young to know about such things, I had no trouble spotting them. The few times that I opened the front door for them, I was too scared to talk. They had thick mustaches and generally wore brownish suits. I clearly remember once one of them sat down on his haunches, made a sweet face at me, and said, "If you tell me where your daddy is, I'll buy you some baklava."

Scared beyond my wits, and with mother's warning echoing in my head, I said, "I don't want any baklava." Baathists agents were everywhere. No matter what or where, whenever something happened, they would descend on our neighborhood and arrest a few people. Most of the people there were Kurdish refugees, whom the agents suspected of every crime. People like father who participated in politics came under even more suspicion.

Father's comings and goings and his activities continued. One day a man with a wife and a daughter rented a room from us. He didn't seem like an ordinary person, staying at home for a few days and then vanishing for a time, but always keeping us under surveillance. He would often take us children aside and question us about father. He even tried to get our other border, Naneh Papi (a Kurdish woman whose son was Papi) to talk. The poor woman would always tell him that she didn't know anything. Mother was very afraid of this man and, playing on his name "Ali," would curse, "May Ali break his back. The man's an enemy of the Shiis, a spy for the security agency. He calls himself 'Ali' to fool people." She warned us not to tell him anything. As it turned out her fears were not misplaced. It was around

---

rujerdi in 1961, Shah Mohammad Reza Pahlavi conferred the title of Source of Emulation on Ayatollah Hakim. This was a move on the part of the Shah to shift the center of emulation from Iran and thereby weaken the religious authority of the Qom religious establishment. But Ayatollah Hakim's support of the Islamic resistance under the leadership of Ayatollah Khomeini thwarted the Shah's move. Ayatollah Hakim published a number of pronouncements on such issues as the Iranian security forces' attack on the Feyziyeh Seminary, the 15th of Khordad killings, and the issuing of death sentences for members of the Islamic Nations Party. Ayatollah Hakim's scholarly works include a fourteen-volume "Encyclopedia of Jurisprudence."

this time father's long absence began. Security agents would come and go, asking about him. After a while, they came for uncle and took him away.

Because uncle's home and ours had a common wall, security agents arrested him thinking that they could get information about father from him. Uncle told them that he had nothing to do with his brother's activities, which they doubted given that his house was right next door. But they soon realized that uncle was not involved in father's politics and released him.

Father's absence dragged on for months until one day we finally got word that the Baathists had imprisoned him in Khanaqin for being an Iranian spy. Not long after that our Arabic-speaking boarder moved out.

2

Moving to Iran

Mother did everything she could to get permission to visit father in prison. She made daily trips to various government offices, only to return fed up and tired, telling grandfather and mother's Aunt Mimi where she had been and to whom she had spoken. Ali and I would be all ears when they talked, and, after mother had spoken to grandfather and Mimi, we nagged and nagged her about seeing father. Doubtful herself that anything could be done, she would pat our heads and say, "God willing, we'll see."

Mother's constant visits to government offices and her prayers finally worked. On a spring day in 1968 she left the younger children with grandfather and auntie and brought Ali and me to visit father.

In those days people normally traveled on foot or in horse carriages, but because the prison was very far away, we had to go by taxi. This was the first time for me in a car, which as I recall was an old blue Chevrolet. I also remember going a long way. Ignoring mother's nervous state, Ali and I never stopped fidgeting and clowning in the car, raising and lowering the windows and staring at the passing scenery. But the excitement of being in a car for the first time didn't stop us from pestering mother about when we would see father. She only shook her head, saying nothing.

After several hours we reached Khanaqin. The car stopped in front of a multistoried building with a wide stairway. Two armed guards in military uniforms stood beside its large brown door, but inside the building everyone was in civilian clothes. One of the men brought us up the central stairway. It was dimly lit inside; I had never seen such a place and had a bad feeling about it. We stood at the end of the second-floor hallway in front of a window with steel bars. The window was too high up for me to look through it. Mother picked me up, and I grabbed the bars. In the semidarkness I saw a room with several cells, each with a prisoner inside. They opened the door of the cell where father was crouching. He had trouble crawling out of the cell and, as though his whole body was stiff, he couldn't straighten his back and knees. I wasn't more than five years old at the time, and the scene terrified me. The excitement of seeing father again disappeared. Viewing him in that state, I was terrified, and the closer he came the more afraid I became. His features had changed a lot; there was no life in his face, which had become boney, making his cheeks jut out. His hair was matted. There was no sign of the spark that was always in his eyes; instead they were red and lifeless. It seemed he had lost a lot of weight. But in spite of it all, he maintained his usual dignity and aplomb.

As soon as mother saw the condition he was in, she began to sob, making Ali and me burst into tears. Though father was an emotional person, he tried to hide his feelings, but the tears came rolling down his cheeks when he saw mother crying. He reached out through the bars to hold and caress me. Then he put me down and hugged Ali and kissed him. Poor mother had to keep holding me in her arms the whole time we were there; Ali was able to climb onto the bars and pull himself up.

I felt father was upset because Ali and I were there. He asked mother, "Why did you bring the kids?" It was as if he didn't want us to see him that way. Then he said, "Try to leave the country. Take the kids and go back to our homeland."

It was not a good visit. I wanted to leave as soon as possible and wouldn't stop crying. Father patted my head to calm me; he tousled my hair and said in Kurdish, "Don't cry, little mother."

After our visit, I couldn't stop wondering why father was in that place. Why did he have to go to prison? I finally came to the conclusion that he was innocent, and it was only because he was faithful to Imam Ali that they put him there. I had heard from mother some people were against those friendly toward Imam Ali. I wished I were strong enough to break the bars and free father from his cell myself.

In the days and nights following the visit, I imagined the prisoners in those cells marching past me. My mind was so preoccupied with these thoughts that every window, every metal bar I saw would remind me of the prison. But despite it all, we were happy to see him; the visit lessened the pain somewhat.

Following father's instructions, mother visited the Iranian consulate in Basra and petitioned to return to Iran. Because we had never taken Iraqi citizenship, we didn't have identity cards. Father had even gotten our birth certificates from the Iranian consulate. This was why our exit would not be that difficult. We just had to wait a few months until they issued permission. The problem was elsewhere; leaving grandfather and his family was going to be very painful for us. What would we do without them? We were part of their family. Grandfather's protection and support for us knew no limits, and his love for father was very strong.

The children adored grandfather. We would spend all day and night at his home, which was only a few alleys away from ours. We'd go there at the break of dawn and have breakfast with him. He'd give us whatever small change he had in his pocket. Even when father was home and didn't permit us to go to grandfather's, my grandmother, Bibi Ezzat, would come around with a breakfast tray and money and cajole father into accepting it.

After breakfast we would normally go to Uncle Salim and Aunt Salima's house in Shakha and bring mother's geese and ducks with us. Shakha was a very pretty spot watered by a branch of the Tigris, which explained its lush palm groves. The other girls and I would roll up our pants and play in the river, while the boys fished. Sometimes Uncle Salim and Ali would climb the palms and pick their dry, yellow dates and give them to us. We had such a good time there we forgot all about the time. When the sun was overhead, we'd return to grandfather's house, leaving the geese and ducks to fend for themselves, but knowing they'd return on their own by sundown.

As soon as we got to grandfather's house, we'd make a beeline for the rope swing that he had hung from the awning poles. The blazing afternoon sun scorched our heads and bare feet, but we didn't mind. We'd just run over to the clay water-cooling jar and have some cold water when it got too hot. We'd also always have one eye on the front door, waiting for grandfather to come home. In the summer he'd always return with a watermelon tucked under his arm. He'd wash it and stick it into an ice chest. After it had cooled, he'd cut it open, give each of us a piece, and say, "Now, go home."

Grandmother spoiled us as much as grandfather, treating us the same way she treated her own children. She was so loving and generous that until her dying day we didn't realize she was our mother's stepmother and that Uncles Nad Ali and Salim were grandfather's stepchildren. Grandfather married Bibi several years after the death of his first wife, the mother of my mother, and Uncle Haqq Ali had died. Bibi was also a Seyyed. People said that the inhabitants of Zarinabad, all said to be descendants of Ebrahim, son of Imam Mohammad Baqer, only married with Seyyeds.

After grandfather's marriage to Bibi there was a drought, and he had to abandon farming in the village to join his family in Basra.

Bibi gladly took on the role of mother to his children and was especially fond of my mother. Because of this kindness we also became attached to her. Unfortunately, as fate would have it, something terrible happened to take her from us. Early one Ramadan morning, Bibi lit the brazier to prepare the predawn meal, but as she poured kerosene on the coals, she caught fire and was badly burned. Hearing her screams, grandfather came running to help her, but he was unable to douse the flames, burning his arms in the process. That morning they sent word of what happened, and we came immediately. We could still see traces of the fire in the compound beside the small pool to which the burning Bibi had fled.

Mother looked after Bibi during her dying days at the hospital. Bibi was very thirsty, but the doctors wouldn't let her drink, and, after enduring a few days of pain, she died. Grandfather had her buried in Najaf. Bibi's death took a heavy toll on mother.

After the incident, Aunt Mimi took over managing the house. Mimi had come to grandfather's home a few years before and had been helping Bibi with the housework. Mimi told us she had married at nine, and some years after her marriage God gave her a son, who was apparently very smart but died of measles at the age of eight. Two years later her husband died, leaving her all alone in the world. Mimi was a young woman at the time and for that reason went to live with her only brother. She never got over the death of her son. Whenever we did something that upset her, she would sit in the corner, going on and on about her son and crying. We children all adored Mimi. She went out of her way to take care of us, treating us like a mother would. In addition to us, she also helped raise our cousins on both sides of the family. I preferred to be with her most of the time, because when I was home I was so busy playing I wouldn't hear mother calling me in Kurdish to take care of Mansur. When I didn't answer, she would get mad and say in Kurdish, "Little brat, where were you?"

Mimi, on the other hand, didn't care what we did. We would jump up and down on the beds, and play with Aunt Salima using dolls we made from straw, a metal tin, and scraps of cloth. When Uncle Nad Ali became fed up with all the noise, he would break up our game or untie the rope swing. Then we would be quiet for a time, waiting until uncle's anger died down or until he went out so we could start playing again.

Mimi would sleep outside in the compound every night under a mosquito net on a separate bed grandfather had for her. When we slept out there with her, we—especially Mohsen and I—would fight. To get us to fall asleep, Mimi would get between us, hold our heads, and tell us many stories and recite poetry.

Though he couldn't read or write, grandfather would tell us stories from the *Shahnameh* and recite the poetry of Rumi and Hafez. He was the elder of the clan. He had a family tree that bore the seals and signatures of Ayatollah Mohsen Hakim, Sheikh Morteza Ansari, Ayatollah Golpayegani, Ayatollah Marashi Najafi, and many other clergymen. He was very protective of this document, and a few times he took it out of the metal casing he had made himself, very carefully exhibiting it to us with the utmost of respect and countless prayers.

Grandfather was quite a sight when he stood in the middle of the compound and, dressed in his robe and black turban, gave the call to prayer. His glowing face imparted a peculiar sense of serenity, and even at the end of his life, when he was very frail, he continued to declaim his prayers to the congregation. Anything they gave him by way of alms or charity, he would bring to us.

I'll never forget the first time I prayed. I came to grandfather, and he sensed I wanted to pray, which made him very happy. He hugged and kissed me and said, "I'll teach you myself." I stood up, and grandfather told me to repeat what he said. Whenever I made a mistake, he patiently corrected me. When it was over, he gave me some money. Afterwards, he never failed to encourage me when I prayed.

There was a kind of prayer and pageant hall called a Hoseyniyeh near grandfather's house. During Ramadan, I would go there with the neighborhood kids just before dawn and stand by the door waiting for the call to prayer. The moment the sound came from high up on the mosque's minaret, we scattered into the alleys, each of us racing home and shouting, "The call, the call!" Because the sound of the muezzin did not reach every part of the neighborhood, and because most homes had no radio, this told everyone it was time for the predawn meal.

Sometimes mother would go to the market, taking Ali and me with her. The path took us over the wooden bridge on the irrigation canal known as the Shatt al-Khandaq. Located on the canal was grandfather's mill or, as we called it, the "flour machine," which along with one or two other mills supplied the needs of the whole town. Before kerosene and electric generators were installed, water from the canal powered the millstone. When we got to the mill, mother would normally leave the path and look for grandfather to see how he was. We couldn't wait, rushing ahead of her to find grandfather. He would call me "*dalakam*" in Kurdish, which means "my little mother," which delighted me because it showed how much affection he had for me.

We knew grandfather wore a skullcap in the mill instead of his black turban. He also wrapped his green shawl firmly around his waist and tucked the ends of his dishdasha in it so he could work more freely. I felt sorry for him every time I saw him in that blazing Basran sun, wiping the sweat from his sunburned face with a bandana he kept in the pocket of his dishdasha. The last thing I wanted to see was grandfather lifting heavy gunnysacks packed with flour. But these thoughts didn't last.

As soon as Ali and I reached the flour machine, we'd get into mischief. Inside the mill it was generally dark; it was only around noon that the sunlight would stream through the skylight. While mother was asking after grandfather, we would scamper over the flour sacks and the apparatus, getting into everybody's hair. Grandfather kept an eye on us even as he spoke with mother and occasionally said, "Don't climb on the flour; it's a gift from God. It's wrong, get down from there at once!"

But we didn't listen and just went on doing what we were doing. One time when playing with Ali, I jumped down from one of the sacks, but my foot slipped, and I landed in a pile of flour. All at once everything went white, and I couldn't see. I couldn't breathe, either. Flour went in my mouth and up my nose, and I was choking. I used all my strength to scream, "Help!"

Mother and grandfather heard me fall into the flour and quickly pulled me out. Grandfather said irritably, "How many times did I tell you not to go in there?" But when he saw how scared I was, he just blew the flour from my face and dusted off my clothes, asking, "Little mother, why can't you just sit still? You don't want to turn into a little devil, do you?"

Such childhood memories and countless others like them made it impossible for me to understand why we had to leave grandfather behind. In the meantime, mother was busy auctioning off the contents of our home, which were her dowry. Each day a few neighbors would come in and buy household items for less than they were worth. Everything was for sale at a low price: mother and father's metal bed with the pleated white spread I loved; the blue, Japanese and Chinese ceramic cups painted with birds and trees full of blossoms; the double-door wooden wardrobe with the full-length mirror in the middle; the dish closet; Mansur's cradle. Leila and I were on the verge of tears, seeing mother putting our possessions in the for-sale pile. Whenever she put her hands on something else I begged her not to sell it, but she would only say, "It can't be helped, Zahra." When I insisted, she explained, "We can't take all this to Iran." But when she took my cloak, the dam burst, and tears started rolling down my face. She consoled me by saying, "Where we're going they're Persian; they don't wear this type of thing."

But it didn't do any good; I loved that cloak. It was silk with gold threads and piping. When I wore it and went around carrying a basket woven from date palms, I felt all grown up. That was why I cried my eyes out when mother tried to sell it. Mother saved only those things we absolutely needed. We were also forced to sell the house, and we moved into a room next to grandfather's house that he had rented for us. The landlady, an old woman living alone, was a poor creature who lived off the rent and what she earned selling odds and ends near her front door. We didn't stay there long.

When they sent word from the Iranian Consulate that we could go, the long goodbyes began. Grandfather's home took on an air of mourning. Family, friends, and neighbors came in groups to wish us farewell. We could only cry; we were very upset. It hurt most of all to say goodbye to grandfather and Mimi.

While this was going on, Uncle Hoseyni, mother's brother who lived in Khorramshahr, got word to us that father was there. The news of father's release made us very happy, especially at the moment we were leaving Iraq. All the same, the pain of leaving grandfather was still unbearable.

The day of our departure, we all went to customs in Basra: grandfather, Mimi, Uncle Salim, Uncle Nad Ali, and Aunt Salima. Everybody was crying, especially Mimi and mother; until that day I had never seen grandfather cry. When we got on the launch he tried to cheer us up saying, "You go, and we'll gather and come right after you."

Uncle Nad Ali, no more than eighteen then, accompanied us to the water border with Iran. We cried the whole time we were in the launch. Uncle played the clown to cheer us up, but it did no good. In the end, he was crying too.

The look on grandfather's and Mimi's faces when they said goodbye stayed with me; the thought that we were leaving them behind was torture. But Ali was different; somehow he was able to keep himself amused. He was his curious, naughty self. Ali pestered the captain so much that the poor man allowed him to steer the launch for a considerable way.

There was another family originally from Elam in the launch. They also tried to console us by saying, "God is great; someday, if He wills it, you'll be reunited," which was no comfort. In my own childish way I thought, "Easy for you to say. You're all together—you even have your daughter-in-law and your grandchild with you. You didn't have to leave anybody behind in Basra."

The Consulate arranged for an Iranian boat to meet us at the border. They transferred us from the Iraqi launch to the boat. Staying behind in the launch, Uncle Nad Ali went to pieces. As the Iranian boat moved away, the launch remained where it was, which was probably what he wanted. I could see him crying; but soon he became a dot disappearing over the horizon.

3

In Iran Before the War

We got to Iranian customs at evening prayer time. Uncle Hoseyni came to look after us. It took a little time to go through customs and immigration. Father was waiting outside the customs area. It had been months since we last saw him. At first we shied away from him, but soon we went toward him. He hugged and kissed each of us, as tears rolled down his cheeks. Then we went to Uncle Hoseyni's house. On the way father exchanged the small Iraqi coins grandfather had given us for Iranian coins, saying, "These are not worth anything here."

Uncle had arranged a gathering to welcome us to his home, which was completely different from the houses in Basra. Instead of a dirt yard, the courtyard was covered in tiles. Most of the guests spoke Persian, and, knowing only Arabic and Kurdish, we couldn't understand what they were saying. Persian seemed very strange to my ears.

That night I remember having a water fight in the yard. Uncle's wife came, saying something in Persian and stopping our game. The only word of hers I understood was *khees* ("wet"), which in Arabic is "to stink." What kind of water was this—I asked myself—that makes your hands smell bad?

When it was time for dinner, uncle's wife spread a cloth on the roof because it was hot, and there wasn't enough room in the house. It was weird going up a tiled stairway to reach the roof, because in Basra we only had wooden ladders.

That night I realized that after he was expelled from Iraq, father had had to walk all the way to Khorramshahr. As a result his feet were cut and calloused. For several days uncle kept his feet in marsh water to let the salt disinfect them. It was a long time before he could walk properly. Later he told me the real reason for what happened to his feet: Iraqi security agents had beaten him.

The rooms uncle lived in were rented, and he was the sole support of his family, which included his mother-in-law them. For this reason, father immediately tried to find a separate place for us. Eventually he found a room on an alley called Shahabad (later renamed Taleqani).

Father also tried to find work for a time, although imprisonment and torture had left him in a bad way mentally and physically. Mother was very attentive to his needs and saw to it we did not annoy him by making a racket or getting into mischief. When he returned from work, he would immediately go and lie down, and I would massage his arms and legs, doing everything I could to ease the fatigue of the day. Father would bless me under his breath and call on God to repay the kindness.

Father's spiritual crisis soon passed, but there was something else troubling him. Often he would go out in the morning to look for work but would return with nothing to show for it. Because of his political activities, he couldn't be hired in government offices. The need to feed his children and pay the rent took a heavy toll on him. Some even suspected father of loafing. When this became clear to me, my heart went out to him. I wanted to tell people they had it all wrong, but there was nothing I could do but call on God for help. When he couldn't find work that matched his capabilities, father had no choice but to rent a handcart and become a porter in the market. He also did a little plumbing, construction, and welding on the side.

After some months father gathered Ali and Mohsen and went to Elam to see relatives and get an identity card. As fate would have it, while he was there, the military base in Elam was blown up, killing the commander. SAVAK arrested father as a possible suspect in the bombing. We had no idea this had happened. Some time passed and still we had no word of them, which was worrying. On the one hand, when we got in touch with our relatives in Elam, they told us that father and the children had left. On the other, they hadn't returned to

Khorramshahr. Having no news was irksome; we didn't know what to do. Without grandfather and Mimi to help us, life became very difficult. The time of the evening prayer was especially hard on us. When the call came, I would pull mother's cloak over us, and we would sob, wondering what our relatives in Iraq were doing. Mother would sit in a corner and cry so much the neighbors came around to console us. Sometimes they would yell at her, "You're the mother of these children. What do you think you are doing? Instead of calming these innocents, you just sit in the corner and weep along with them?" Then they tried to comfort us. But it was no good; wailing became our nightly routine. Uncle Hoseyni would drop by, behaving very much like a grandfather. We adored him, and whenever one of us took an oath in his name, there was no doubting the truth of what the person said. Uncle was well off. While in Iraq, he worked as a translator for the Consulate and assistant principal of the school for Iranian residents of Basra. In Khorramshahr he was employed at a vegetable oil firm. He never visited us without gifts, and sometimes helped—so to speak—mother with the household expenses.

At that time Khorramshahr exported a great deal of dates. The storehouse managers would bring freshly plucked dates to people's homes for cleaning and collect them the next day; then they would wash the dates in the factories, where they stuffed them with walnuts, coated them with sesame seeds, or sweetened them with date syrup. They exported them to Arab countries and Europe. Mother would get crates of dates and put them on a tray so we could help her with them. To keep our minds on the work, she would recite poetry to us. We would open the dates and remove the stones; then we would toss them into the crate. We'd get one tuman (ten rials) for each thirty-kilo box; later this was raised to thirteen rials.

This was our job during the summer and winter months. In winter the dates became rigid, making them hard to cut with a knife. To make the job easier, mother would put the tray over a brazier; this would soften the dates and warm the room. This was how we earned a living while father was in prison in Elam. We had a neighbor by the name of Abdol Hoseyn Harbi, a very good man who looked after us. He was very respectful of Seyyeds. His wife would bring us fruit and other things from time to time, but mother wouldn't accept them, saying with characteristic pride, "We don't need anything."

Mother was a very private person. Never one to empty her heart to others, she preferred to bear the weight of life on her own shoulders without complaining. Often when she dusted the framed pictures we had, I saw her crying. I always tried in one way or another to share these private moments with her, but I was powerless.

After three or four months, father returned with the boys. They were very pale and skinny. Ali was eight at the time, and Mohsen was seven. The filthy conditions in prison gave Mohsen a case of diarrhea, which because of the lack of medical attention worsened, becoming bleeding bowels. Despite father's repeated pleas, the prison officials refused to bring in a doctor, saying, "There's nothing wrong with him, and even if he dies, we're better off—one less terrorist pup." They tried to get father to confess to bombing the military base, but he would ask them, "If I had wanted to blow it up, would I have brought these kids along?" The interrogators wouldn't listen, and it took quite a while before even they had to admit that he had nothing to do with the bombing.

After his release, father rented a two-room apartment with its own entrance on Shahabad. The room made of baked brick was where we entertained guests, and the room made of adobe we used as a kitchen and sitting room. The house lacked running water but had electricity. The main entrance to the house led to a small courtyard, from a kind of foyer that opened onto a larger yard, where our rooms were. In the small courtyard was a stairway to the roof, where we slept during the hot summer months. Father always warned us to be careful on the roof because there was no railing. The nearly three years we lived in that house gave us a chance to get used to life in Khorramshahr, and we hoped that grandfather and the rest of our family would join us there.

In the spring of 1969, when I was six years old, Uncle Nad Ali came to stay with us from Basra. The Iranians required that he immediately do his military service; but whenever he had leave, he came to stay with us to make it easier on Uncle Hoseyni's wife. When he saw the sorry state of our finances, he chose to stay with uncle, not wanting to be a burden. Two years later, before the Baath regime expelled all Iranians living in Iraq, grandfather and other relatives came.[1] This was the luckiest day of my life, I felt, because now we were all together.

Grandfather rented a home near ours, and the rounds of visits began again. Every day after school Ali, Mohsen, and I would make a beeline for grandfather's place. The old man would give us money, as he had in the old days. One time we came but didn't find him there; nevertheless, we ate lunch. Mimi, who knew about the allowances, gave us our money and said, "You should go home; your mother's waiting for you." She sent Aunt Salima out to help us cross the road; then Salima went home.

We stood in a corner watching her leave, then we continued on our way, making a detour at the greens market. We knew that grandfather went to the mosque for the noon prayer, after which he would go to the Chasbi Bridge[2] and sit and talk with his friends. We went there and saw grandfather, who hugged and kissed us and introduced us to his friends. He also gave us our usual allowances, but we didn't tell him that we had already gotten money from Mimi. We went merrily back home. When Mimi later found out what had happened, there was a row.

In 1971 our landlord, who lived in Shadegan, told father to vacate the house. Father quickly got busy finding another house, and, while he and mother were doing this, they left the younger children at home in my care. They locked us in the compound to keep us from going into the alley by ourselves.

On that day our next-door neighbors were having a circumcision ceremony. Mohsen went up on the roof to watch. I was busy playing with Mansur in the room when I heard Leila shrieking, "Zahra come

---

[1] At the time the president of Iraq was Ahmad Hasan al-Bakr, but in reality Saddam Hussein, his deputy, was in charge. Saddam declared that the Arvand River (or, as it known in Arabic, the Shatt al-Arab) belonged to Iraq, and he used this dispute with Iran as a pretext for expelling all Iranians living in the country.

[2] Now known as "Allah Circle." The water channel is dry today, and there is no trace of the old bridge because of new roads. The water branched off from the Karun River east of the city.

quickly, Mohsen's dead!" I thought that she was kidding, but when she swore on Uncle Hoseyni's life, I didn't know what I was going to do with the baby but I raced into the courtyard just the same. Mohsen lay unconscious by the stairway, his eyes swollen and black, bulging from their sockets, but there was no sign of blood.

Seeing Mohsen like that, I started shrieking and clawing at my face. Leila was also very scared. We started to cry and strike ourselves. At that point, someone knocked on the front door; it was Mrs. Nowruzi's daughter who lived across the street. From behind the door she said, "My mother wants to know what's making you screech like that."

"Mohsen's dead," I said. "He fell off the roof."

"So why don't you open the door?" she asked.

"Father and mother have gone out and locked the door," I said.

With that, our neighbor, Naneh Jasem, a strong women with a powerful physique, came and gave the door such a kick that it opened. When she saw Mohsen, she said, "He's unconscious; we'd better get him to the hospital. Where are your parents?"

"They've gone out to look for a place to rent," I explained. "But now they're probably at the home of one of our family members."

She said, "You should go and tell them to come yourself."

The whole way there I was trying to figure out how to tell mother what had happened without terrifying her. She was pregnant with another child, after all. When I arrived, everybody was surprised to see me.

"Why are you here?" mother asked.

"Aunt Hajar has come from Elam," I lied; I had never seen Aunt Hajar in my life.

Father said, "How was it possible for her to come all this way?"

"I don't know," I said, "But she's here. She introduced herself to me."

It was the best story I could make up at the time, but the bruises on my face told another one. There was no point in lying, and they continued to question me so much that I was forced to admit, "Mohsen fell and he's in a bad way. I was so scared I started clawing at my face, but it's nothing. He'll be fine. Naneh Jasem's with him now."

Mother fainted when she heard this.

By the time we got back home, they had already taken Mohsen to the hospital. We had yet to arrive when we saw Mimi coming toward us, crying and beating her chest. As the one who raised Mohsen, she was very attached to him, considering him her own son. She couldn't stand seeing something bad happen to him, giving up another boy.

I don't know how they found out what had happened, but soon friends and acquaintances crowded into our house. All of them were weeping, thinking the situation was hopeless.

While Mohsen lay unconscious in a hospital bed, our house was in mourning. Neighbors brought us food as though there were a funeral. They insisted we eat but it was no use; no one was in the mood.

The children were just as affected as the rest of the people. There was an unknowable bond between us, making the love and affection we had quite special. I was worst of all. One night when I was spreading the bedding, my eyes fell on the place where Moshen would have been between Ali and Mansur. The lump in my throat burst, and I started to wail. Father tried his best to calm me. No matter how many times he told me that he had seen Mohsen that day, and that he was fine, I continued to cry. The poor man even went to the store to buy me something to eat, but it didn't do any good. I don't know why I felt sure that we had lost Mohsen.

I cried so much I started hiccupping uncontrollably. To reassure me father had to bring me to the hospital that night, but they wouldn't let me see Mohsen. Father left me in the care of the attendant, a kind old man who sat me down beside him and tried to comfort me.

After a bit, father returned saying that Mohsen was okay. I believed him and calmed down.

Mohsen's coma lasted three or four days. When he came to, he had lost his memory. He didn't recognize anyone. He was released from the hospital after ten days, but he was never the same. The doctors said that he needed time to recover.

It was as if he'd suddenly become stupid. His mind didn't seem to work properly. For example, when we gave him money to buy bread he'd return empty-handed or he would get lost. Even when he spent the money, he didn't know what he spent it on or what we had sent him out to do. The poor thing was in the third grade at the time. Before the accident he was a very good student, but afterwards his schoolwork took a nosedive, and he became indifferent to studying. Father tried mightily to encourage him, but it did no good. He dropped out of the school in junior high. He remained in this state for a long period.

Moshen's accident delayed moving to a new house. It was in the old house that Hasan, mother's sixth child was born. Around that time grandfather and Mimi made a pilgrimage to the shrine of Imam Reza in Mashhad. The accident had also caused Uncle Hoseyni's wife and his mother to bring mother to the Khombeh Hospital.[3] Father had yet to find a good job, and our financial situation was bleak. For this reason, Uncle Hoseyni's mother-in-law paid mother's hospital bill, which amounted to fifty tumans. Later father paid her back. I nursed mother after they brought her home, which was truly difficult for an eight-year-old girl.

In the midst of all this, our landlord gave us an ultimatum to pack up our things and move. The new house was in reality two parts, a front portion and a back one joined by a long, narrow hallway. The people living in the back had to go through the front, passing through the part where the landlord and we lived. There were many things about the new place that were annoying. Our old landlords were good people, but the new one was a real horror. While we were his tenants, he would turn off the water in the morning and leave. At first we all thought that there was a shortage, but in the evening when he returned it would come back on and we figured it out. The poor man's wife was not like him. She would grumble at him, "What you're doing is not right. These people have young children." But he wouldn't listen and said, "Wrong! They're one big family that uses a lot of water, which costs a lot."

The neighbors also objected, saying that they also paid a share of the water bill, but he would just go on turning off the water in the morning. Mother complained bitterly about the way he tormented us.

By contrast, one of the neighbors was very good and humane, but we didn't see him that often. He was a driver who went to towns on the desert highways. He would bring back fruits grown in those towns

---

[3] Also known as "Mosaddeq," located near the Farmandari circle.

and share them with the neighbors. He was single. Father would always say, "May God reward him; he's a decent man." We children knew he was home when we heard the sounds of a stringed instrument he played called a *sehtar*. We loved to gather outside his window and listen to the music.

The miseries of adult life never stop children from getting into mischief. Our lives seemed to travel on a different track. The days would come and go, and we remained in our own little world. The fall of that year I entered first grade, but not more than two months into the term something happened to me. One of our neighbors had a pile of used lumber that he had brought from the port and stored next to his compound. The neighborhood kids would climb up the pile and jump down. Once when we were playing, the pile suddenly collapsed. I fell, and a large nail sticking out of one of the pieces of lumber went deep into my calf, so far that one of the kids had to hold my leg while the other yanked on the wood to extract the nail. They finally managed to get it out, but my leg was badly hurt. I couldn't move, so the kids went to get mother.

Although I was terrified, the whole time I tried to find a way to explain it to mother. When she arrived she didn't say anything. She was so scared she probably forgot to have it out with me. She quickly put her arms around me and brought me home. Then she burned some cloth and fastened the ashes tightly over the wound to stop the bleeding.

Several days later, my leg was severely swollen and so stubbornly crooked I couldn't walk and had to drag myself along the ground. It hurt so much I wouldn't let anyone touch it. Finally, she put me over her shoulder and brought me to a local dispensary. The doctor said, "Her leg is very infected; if it goes untreated, she'll be paralyzed."

That was the worst day of my life. The doctor along with one of the nurses held me up and forced me to walk. It was really hard; when my foot touched the floor, the pain was unbearable. I shrieked with each step as blood and pus emerged from the wound. After a while they put me on a bed. I thought it was over, but a doctor came with a pair of tweezers. He inserted them into the wound and cleaned it out. After he was finished, he looked at the wound. It was like a balloon with the air let out. He told mother, "You've got to bring her here every day so we can change the dressing."

Each time she was about to take me to the clinic I started howling, "I won't go. They torture me there." But despite all the grief I gave her, she'd hoist me on her shoulder and go to the clinic on foot. With each step my foot throbbed more. Going to the clinic and coming home nearly killed me. I missed a month of school because of the accident. The principal assumed the family had forbidden me from going to school, because girls generally had a hard time getting an education. So they sent somebody around to ask about me, and the next morning mother went to the school explaining, "She's not well. Her leg is in such a bad state she can't go to school."

But they didn't believe her and said, "She's got to come in person."

The next day the poor thing hoisted me on her shoulders and carried me to school, where they looked at my leg. They said, "For the time being there's no problem, but the minute she's able to go to school, she has to appear in class."

It took a month and a half for me to be able to get up and walk by leaning on walls. I didn't have carfare, so I had to limp along this way to get to school. Although it was very difficult, the desire to continue my education gave me the strength to continue and make up what I had missed. Of course, Mrs. Foruzandeh, my teacher, helped a lot. Her understanding and my efforts combined to make me first in my class by the end of spring.

With school over we moved and got away from our nasty landlord. Then began a period of going from one house to another every so often in the Shahabad neighborhood. Each place had its advantages and disadvantages; we had no choice but to take the good with the bad. One place had a good landlord who looked out for us, while another had a nasty one who would do things to annoy us. One landlord would do everything in his power to make us comfortable, while another wasted no opportunity to harass us. For example, one house we rented had a big yard (around 300 meters) with rooms along two of its sides. On one side were the landlord's rooms and the one room that we rented; in the other rooms were three other men each with their own families.

In the summer each family would spread carpet before their entryways and eat dinner. The hospitality families showed to one another was very interesting; when anyone cooked something, everybody in the other households got a taste. The place was very serene and genial. Every night after dinner the landlord would bring out the television and put it in the middle of the compound where all could sit around and watch it.

People stayed in their rooms in winter. The same room served as our guest and sitting room, bedroom, and our study. The only entertainment was the nightly story on the radio. My favorites were the tale of Sohrab and Rostam from the *Shahnameh* and other epic stories.

Mother continued to help with the expenses by cleaning dates. All of us children—even Ali and Mohsen—helped, but after a few hours, we started to drift away one by one and go to sleep.

Father worked as a porter in the market until one day he found a job with the city as a sweeper. He would get up at 5:00 a.m. every day, pray, then go off to work. Ali and I would leave the house at 7:00 and sometimes we'd see father sweeping the streets on our way to school. We ran to him and kissed his hand. He would pat our heads and say, "Go, you'll be late for school." My school was called Salur and Ali's was The 25th of Shahrivar; both were located on Persian Gulf Avenue.

That year father bought a chador for me. It was made of cheap fabric with a floral pattern of roses and green leaves on a dark background. It was supposed to be only for the house, but I liked to wear it outside so I could feel all grown up. Father would warn me, "You can't keep it clean; one day you'll fall in the mud and get it filthy."

I couldn't openly oppose him, given who he was, but there were times I'd slip the chador to Ali, who would leave for school before me. When we got to the end of the alley, I'd take it from him and put it on. By the time I got to school, I was covered up to my waist in mud and dust, which was natural after all because, except for the main roads, all the streets in town were unpaved and whenever it rained they turned to mud. So every day I had to wash the chador and my shoes and socks in the small pool the school had for ablutions. I hung the wet chador over the second-floor railing to dry.

For a time there was a minibus to take one of the neighbors' girls and me to school. It was cheaper than a cab, which cost five rials per person. The bus was three rials, but the driver counted us as one fare and we took turns paying two rials per trip, while the other person paid one.

For most of my school years I served as class monitor, a job I liked and did well. In those days there were free student lunches consisting of milk, cake or an egg sandwich, and, sometimes, fruit. For a time they also gave us Danish cheese, which wasn't to the children's liking because it would dry out once the packaging was opened. That was why we used to call the dried pieces of cheese "rocks" and would toss them at one another. On sandwich days, the teacher and I would make the sandwiches and put them in special red or blue baskets, which I would bring into the classroom. The school authorities insisted we eat lunch on the premises, but most of the students brought food home because they didn't want to eat alone. Ali, Mohsen, and I felt the same way, so we brought our food home and ate with mother and the rest of the kids. We even kept some food for father, but when it was offered, his eyes would fill with tears and he'd say, "Eat it yourselves; I don't want it. They give me a lot of this kind of thing at work." But we knew that father would never eat anything without us.

In the summer of 1974 Mr. Behruzi, one of the engineers at the municipality, asked father if he would like us to live at his house. He was looking for a dependable person to look after his house during the summer when he was in Tehran. He was a charitable man and had asked his friends to recommend a needy family man for the job.

With the addition of Sa'id and Zeynab the family was complete. Father raised us never to be a bother to the neighbors or to make noise. Mr. Behruzi was very taken with us, and for that reason instead of three months we stayed in his house for a whole year.

Engineer Behruzi's place was a spacious and attractive villa located in the area of Railroad Square. It had two doors; we entered and exited through the courtyard door, which opened on the alley, while Behruzi's family used the main door, which had access to the avenue.

Power Authority employees and city engineers lived in the neighborhood. The houses were separated by dead-ends where people parked cars. The doors to the yards, which were rectangular gardens filled with trees, opened onto these alleys. The large gardens were divided into smaller plots by pathways paved with stones. There were also ablution pools with blue walls. At the far end of our yard was an area where Mrs. Behruzi kept chickens, and beside it was a pen for the watchdog.

In another corner of the yard there were two rooms separated by a narrow hallway. Mrs. Behruzi used the room on the left as a place to store extra tools. The room on the right, which was the bigger of the two, she gave to us. At the end of the hallway was a cement bench that came out from the wall. We put a gas canister under the bench and a three-burner range over it. Father also made some wooden shelves that he nailed to the wall for our kitchen utensils. The room was furnished with a small wooden wardrobe and what people called an "under-the-bed" cupboard for dishes. We covered the floor with loose-weave carpets called *zilu*s and spread rectangular cushions all around the room so people could lean against them when sitting on the floor. On the walls were the usual framed pictures of the great clergymen like Ayatollahs Borujerdi and Hakim, whom father held in the most amazing esteem. The holiest objects in our home were: first, the Quran, and, second, those photographs on the wall, which he taught us to respect.

After a few months, we felt at home and at peace at the Behruzi's. There were no niggling landlords, no noisy neighbors. The engineer and his wife were good people who respected our privacy. We had the run of the compound as if it belonged to us. For the children it was great; the yard was my favorite place. Uncle Hoseyni's children liked it as much as we did and loved to visit us; but uncle, aware of our finances, wouldn't let them stay too long. Father, however, insisted on looking after them. It was at the Behruzi's that we finally felt like a family again, and our corner of the compound became an open house. The children spent their time playing on the swings father put up. Among the trees in the garden was one lotus that was very special to Mrs. Behruzi. She once told us about the time she woke up in the middle of the night and saw a light coming from the tree, and, though an educated woman, she believed it was a sign there was a good person living in the tree. Acting on that belief, she dug a narrow trench around it and every Thursday night would fill it with water and put lighted candles all around, making a very pretty sight. Whenever she went on vacation, she would give me the candles, and I would light them for her.

It was also in this home that for the first time I completed the Ramadan fast. In previous years I would try to keep the fast, but I always cheated. That year Mrs. Behruzi asked mother if she could give me the breaking of the fast meal at night. Although she would normally send food around for us, she insisted that I come to her home so she could host me personally, but father said, "First break the fast here with water and dates and then go there."

The moment they broadcast the special benedictions over the loudspeakers, Mrs. Behruzi would reply, "Say a prayer for me and my children. Your Seyyed prayers are bound to be answered." All of Mrs. Behruzi's children were educated and held important positions, except for Shahram, who was a bit slow; although he was eighteen, he acted like a child. The first time I saw him it alarmed me a bit, but he was the kind of boy who wouldn't hurt a fly. Whenever anyone came to his house, he would immediately offer the guests food, forcing them to accept it. If they didn't, he'd complain to his mother.

Mrs. Behruzi was a solitary old woman unable to carry out all her household chores by herself. I tried to help her whenever I could, but at the Now Ruz holidays, when her children visited, things got hectic. Her daughter, Parivash, who lived in Abadan, was overjoyed to see me helping Mrs. Behruzi. She kissed me saying, "Good for you! I'm really grateful that you're looking after mother." Then she gave me a twenty-tuman bill as a kind of New Year's gift. I was delighted because in those days twenty tumans was real money.

The year we spent at the Behruzi's was wonderful, but the peace and quiet we enjoyed there was not to last. Mr. Behruzi was transferred to Tehran, and we had to return to Shahabad.[4] Father found a room for us in a house on Mina Avenue near Jennatabad.[5] Though on the surface the landlord seemed decent, inwardly he was anything but,

---

[4] Several years later, mother, while getting off a bus in Tehran, saw Mrs. Behruzi, who told her that her husband had died. Mother said that Mrs. Behruzi had aged greatly, and she couldn't get her address during the rush of getting out of the bus.

[5] Jennatabad (Heaven's Abode) was the old name for the cemetery in Khorramshahr. Now it is called *Golzar-e Shohada* (Martyr's Meadow).

engaging in vile things like drinking alcohol. Father often tried to warn him about this, but it did no good. In the end his behavior caused us to move to another place.

Unfortunately, the new landlord was no better than the old one. He stole building materials from job sites in the neighborhood and brought them home. When father discovered this, he confronted him saying, "Why are you doing that? It's not right to take other people's property like that." But again it did no good; in fact, matters got worse. One day the landlord out of spite went up to the roof with a pickax and dug a hole in the mud, sending earth and debris down on our belongings. Had it not been for the neighbors, it seems, he would have brought the whole house down on our heads. They had tremendous respect for Seyyeds and were very angry with the landlord. That night they all came by and advised father to swear out a complaint against the landlord. At first father refused, but they finally persuaded him to do it. The next day the police came and took the landlord away, but father changed his mind and withdrew the complaint.

Ali, who had witnessed all this strife as a child, was the first of us to go to work. In the dead of summer or in winter when it got cooler, he would sell gum to people at the gas station (famous as Dieselabad) on the Ahvaz-Khorramshahr road. He would also sell corn on the cob roasted over a fire. One day I insisted he take me with him so I could see how he did it. I wouldn't take no for an answer. Then he became quite the little man, saying that a place where drivers and garage boys hung out was no place for a girl. I kept begging him to take me. He finally gave in to my nagging. Having seen how he and the other children did it, I thought I'd try my hand. I worked on mother so much that she finally agreed to let me go with Ali. When father found out about it, he became very upset, and there was an argument. "Why are you sending them off to work?" he asked. He was not in favor of Ali working in the first place, and so when I started … well. Given our finances, mother had no choice but to let us sell food without telling father. I eagerly grabbed the pot of cooked chickpeas she made and stormed out of the house. Ali also wasn't happy about having his sister work, but because of mother he didn't say anything. Every day at the crack of dawn we took our places by the road among the twenty or so half-pints and bigger children. We placed the pots of food in front of us and waited for customers. God was good to all the children, providing everyone with a living, but Ali and I sold out before the others because mother scrubbed our pots so they sparkled and was compulsive in the way she prepared the food. The drivers would come around and ask us to lift the lids on our pots. They went down the line examining all the offerings, but would end up buying from Ali and me. Ali tried to see to it that I sold out before he did so I could go home. Whenever a driver bought from me, Ali would come forward to stand by me protectively and say, "We're together."

Though we needed the income from selling food ourselves, Ali would sometimes stop me from making a sale when he saw there was a child more in need of money than we were. He would tell the kid to go ahead of him with the gum and chocolates. It made me happy to see Ali letting the poor kids take his place. Though he was only in second or third grade, I accepted everything he did without question.

Aware of our finances, Uncle Hoseyni asked my parents if he could raise Ali himself, thinking it would make it easier for the boy's intelligence and talents to develop. He could study and advance without having to worry about supporting the family by selling gum. Ali eventually went to live with uncle, but only a few days later he returned. He looked around and asked me, "What did you have for lunch?" "Nothing," I said. "Why?" he asked. "Well, because there was nothing in the house," I said. Father, who hadn't been in favor of Ali's going but finally gave in, asked him in a gentle way why he was back. Ali said nothing. Mother insisted that Ali should not give up this opportunity. Uncle came around and kept trying to persuade him, but Ali did not agree. Several days later I asked him about it. He looked at me and said, "I want to be in my own home. I want to eat whatever we eat together—everybody equal."

Ali apparently gave up many things by returning. Uncle wanted to enroll him in the National School, which was considered a private school. For the few days Ali was at uncle's house, uncle drove him and his own children to and from school. Uncle's house was furnished with many things a child would find entertaining. He had a television all to himself, while in our entire neighborhood there was only one set. This was probably a reason to stay, but Ali came back and resumed working. Ali's capacity for sympathy kept us fast friends. When the boys rolled out of school making a terrible racket, he raced ahead of them and waited in front of my school to keep me from being stampeded by the crowd. On the way back we took out our lunches and showed them to each other. There were times when we didn't have the heart to eat and brought the food home. We often spoke about of what we wanted from life. One thing was a house of our own, which would rid us from having landlords.

One of the homes we rented belonged to a wife-beater. After pummeling his wife with his fists, this landlord would smoke a cigarette and go out drinking with his buddies, who were worse than he was. The whole time we were there, father and Ali stayed up nights keeping watch over us. The resulting stress forced us to think about a place of our own.

The nights we slept on the roof Ali and I would point to the stars and say to Leila and Mohsen, "That one's mine. Mine is brighter." Ali would say, "I wish everybody's heart shined like those stars. If only all people were united. If only the rich gave a thought to the poor and distributed their riches among them; that way there'd be no poor people."

This made me think. I suggested we go to a certain rich man and ask him to portion out his money. Ali said, "That's impossible. These people are rich exactly because they love money and are not prepared to spend it on others." So I asked how we could make them understand that there were poor people. We went on talking this way until we fell asleep.

Once one of my shoes was badly torn. I needed shoes for school and didn't have another pair. Ali said, "Don't worry; you can use mine." That year we went to school in shifts: Ali in the morning, me in the afternoon. As soon as his shift was over, he raced home, took off his sneakers, and gave them to me. The shoes were too tight for him and too loose for me and they skidded. When I had them on, my foot would slide forward and my toe would emerge from a hole in the canvas. When I passed through the neighborhoods where the rich kids lived, I was very careful not to let the toe show, because the spoiled brats were just waiting for an excuse to make fun of anyone less privileged than they were. My feet began to hurt as I walked through the neighborhood. When I told Ali the shoes were a little big for me, he stuffed them with cotton, but it wasn't much help, especially in the warm weather when my feet started sweating and the cotton became tight little balls that fell out of the shoes, which only made the misery begin all over again. This went on until Ali used the money he earned to buy a pair of shoes of his own, and father also used some of his money to buy me a pair.

Around the beginning of 1977, the municipality started building housing for its workers in an area known as the Old Cemetery. Father was hired to work on the project, doing things like being a watchman, handing out building materials, and overseeing the laborers. After a lifetime of going from place to place, mother couldn't believe the good news. It was a joy to think that in a few months we'd have a place of our own. But the hell our landlord put us through with his pickax finally became too much for father. He moved us to another house, which was more like a shelter with four walls and not much else. He tried to make up for it by using plastic sheeting as "windows." The good news was: we were now free from the agonies of renting from vile landlords.

The Old Cemetery slowly turned into a suburb. In the first year of construction we often saw that when workers dug new ground, they would uncover the bones of the dead. The only grave that remained undisturbed was that of the twelve-year-old daughter of a Seyyed known as Hashemiyeh. The people believed she was a saint; they prayed to her and their prayers were answered. Each time one of the city bulldozers came near the grave, something would make it stall. In the end the excavaters kept away from the spot, and people vowed—if their prayers were answered—to make a shrine for her. There was also a family sepulcher on the site belonging to a chief of one of the Arab clans of Khorramshahr. Later they turned the place into a mosque. It was said that the graveyard originated during World War II when it had been part of the city precincts. When British forces entered the city, people took cover there to resist them and bury their dead. I also heard about two boys, who, while looking for scrap copper, found a grenade there. When they pounced on it, the grenade went off, killing both of them.

Occasionally, when his workload became too much for him, father was sidelined for a time. At those times, when the workers found a skeleton, they would bring it to a piece of land that was to become a garden spot. Father would say, "It is sinful what they're doing with the bones; you can't just bury them any old place." Sometimes when we were playing we would come across a skeleton and call out to father. He would dig a hole for it and tell us to lift it gently and bring it to the hole. When we weren't careful with a skeleton, he remind us that it wasn't a club we were wielding; these are, he'd say, the body parts of a human being who may have died a while ago, but still deserved respect. We would also say what one normally said over the dead: "In the name of God," and we'd send up prayers for the departed. Working together we'd try to extract the skeletons whole, but some without even touching them would turn to powder. Sometimes all that was left was the skull. This was probably why, later on, I had no fear of the dead or skeletons.

Everybody valued father for the care and attention he brought to his work. He used a little pad to issue receipts to the drivers, but because he only had a reading knowledge of the Quran and couldn't write, I had to fill it in for him. I'd leave the number of the truck and the date of delivery blank. When he took delivery of the materials from the drivers, they would fill out two pages of the pad, and he'd stamp them and get signatures. One page he'd give to the driver, the other he'd keep. The drivers became such good friends with father they'd send him presents from their hometowns, and when he wasn't at work, they'd even come by the house for a visit.

Whenever father had to go somewhere else to work, he'd let Ali take his place, knowing that his son was disciplined enough to carry out any task he gave him. And the older he got, the more difficult were the jobs he took on. Working beside father, Ali gradually learned construction, plumbing, and welding. His eyes became bloodshot from the welding, and the pain would keep him awake all night. But, by the time he was eighteen, he was a master welder and mason. In those days most buildings were one-story; anything higher was a rarity. Ali did the welding for the two-story Mehr hospital and the three-story Behbehanian Clinic near the bazaar. On our trips to the market, mother and I often saw him working on the scaffolding. We couldn't miss him because of the bright bandana he ordinarily wore on his head. The heat and the blinding light of the welding torch hurt his eyes. By sundown they would be all red and swollen, and he would moan constantly. He relieved the pain by putting raw potato slices over his eyes. The next morning, though, he'd be back at work again. Ali wasn't the only one who worked like a dog; Mohsen also did. Before he fell off the roof he was a clever student, but after the fall he said studying no longer interested him. Father forced him to continue, but after he failed several subjects in high school, he quit and went to manual labor, at which he was as successful as Ali. Mohsen liked construction work, while Ali loved to weld. The two of them showed so much work ethic and interest in what they did they were treated like professionals.

Although Ali earned money at a great personal cost to himself, he turned his whole salary over to father. I often saw father's eyes tear up when he took the money from him. Father would kiss him and say, "Honey, take this money and spend it on yourself. I know that you are working to lighten the burden on me and I'm grateful, but it's yours, spend it on yourself." But Ali refused, saying that he wasn't working for himself but for the family. In addition to working, Ali also went to karate and military exercise classes. He was a black belt and sometimes he would teach me some moves at home. He was also always practicing his penmanship and, without a teacher, was able to write like a master calligrapher. Most boys in Khorramshahr could swim, thanks to having the Shatt al-Arab nearby, but Ali's swimming skills reached the professional level because he worked out at the Red Crescent (formally Lion and Sun) Youth Club pool. Whatever it was—reciting the Quran, sports, calligraphy—Ali was always getting awards, which made mother so happy she declared he had a knack for everything.

The complex of houses for city workers was finally finished a year later. We moved our belongings into a place at the end of the complex that had been allotted to us. There was a vast salt marsh in a sunken area behind the homes. Whenever it rained the marsh turned into an artificial lake. They made the homes in the British style, without courtyards and high walls; the only thing separating one home from the next was a chain-linked fence usually hedged with evergreens. Many of the residents, including father, were sensitive about the lack of privacy. The first day we were there, father brought one of his builder friends along so he, working with Ali and Mohsen, could build walls around the compound and keep the prying eyes of neighbors from looking in. They also tiled the yard and put up a porch.

Ali mortared the walls, while Mohsen and father did the welding. Leila and I also helped; I prepared the mortar and we poured it into a carrier, which Leila brought to father. We changed places from time to time so we wouldn't get tired. At 10:00 a.m. that day father lit the primus stove and made omelets for us. He'd froth up the eggs and then pour them into a greased skillet and add onions. When they were done, he'd plate them with a grilled tomato. Eating the eggs with onions and drinking glasses of tea in the compound hit the spot.

With everyone helping, the house was soon finished. What a relief it was to have our own home, where we would no longer have to put up with depraved landlords, where we could enjoy comfort and security. It was during that year that the first rumblings of the revolution began to reach our ears. Ali was the first to get involved in the movement. He put his studies aside. Ordinarily father would have insisted on Ali and Mohsen stay in school; but because of his own background in politics, he not only fully backed Ali's decision, he also joined the movement. They would sit at home at night and discuss what was going on. I was very curious and tried to understand what they were saying, but I couldn't make heads or tails of it. Late at night they would go out and distribute leaflets and audiotapes made by Imam Khomeini that Ali brought home. The situation caused Ali's political awareness to blossom. It also affected him physically. Owing to his influence I also matured and became interested in reading the books he read. Father was always watching out for us during this period. One time Ali brought home a poster of Che Guevera, who symbolized the struggle against imperialism for some. When father saw the poster hanging on the wall, he got upset and took it down, stashing it in Ali's closet. Father was always very wise and careful about images; despite all the love he had for the Twelve Holy Imams, he had no use for the pictures that were painted of them. He explained that a number of miscreant Jews had made these imaginary portraits to lead people astray from the true faith.

When the underground revolutionary movements became more public, taking the shape of street demonstrations, Ali bought a camera and a small tape recorder, which he used to document the people's protests. Father did not leave Ali's side and brought Mohsen along with him. Father arranged with his friends to provide water to the demonstrators in the streets. They bought large chunks of ice, put them in water barrels, and lugged them around in a pickup truck. Father wouldn't let Leila and me participate in the demonstrations. He reminded us we were girls, and he didn't want us to fall into the clutches of SAVAK.

It had been two years since I left school. Although I did well, the mixing of boys and girls in one building caused father to take me out of school despite my tantrums and tears. Before I left, I had a teacher by the name of Mrs. Najjar, a woman who wore the veil. In that period, because she was religious, no matter what school she went to, after a certain amount of time they would fire her. Mrs. Najjar's sister had been a classmate of mine who brought various books for me from their home. Among them was a series of books I found interesting with the title "Why the Youth?" whose author I believe was Ahmad Beheshti. When she saw my interest in reading, she supplied me with more books. Reading them opened my mind. In addition, the more I saw of Ali and father's activities, the more I wanted to take part in the demonstrations. Leila was no less excited about taking part than I was, and sometimes we would get to the demonstrations secretly, although it might have been when they were almost over. Nevertheless, this seemed to satisfy us. We would stand around so long as we were certain father would not return during that time, but all the while my heart was in my mouth, afraid that I wouldn't get home in time.

Those were strange days; it was as if all the people were in the streets. The army positioned tanks in most of the main arteries, especially Forty Meter Road, Ferdowsi, the avenues around the Congregational Mosque—places they knew there would be trouble. The soldiers thought they could make the people disperse that way. The leaders of these demonstrations were the young people of the city and the clergy, people like Hajj Aqa Mohammadi and Hajj Aqa Nuri, who made things happen. The people started to attack and set fire to the liquor stores, most of which were along the Shatt waterway. They also pulled down the statue of the Shah at the Farmandari Circle. SAVAK arrested many of these young people, and we expected that

Ali would fall into one of their traps any minute. He would always say a person had to be on his toes, stay sharp to escape with his life.

During the demonstrations I got acquainted with women who were active in a Quran school. Through them I began to take part in Quran interpretations classes that were held at the Hashtrudi High School. My ties to the school gradually developed. The person responsible for the school was a woman called Khadijeh Abedi, the wife of Mehdi Albooghabeesh, whom I knew for his revolutionary activities. Along with a number of others, he planned and led the street demonstrations. The school also ran programs for conducting the Komeyl and Nodbeh prayers. The lecture series by professors invited from Qom was especially popular.

During one of the days when the demonstrations were especially wild, we got word that father fell on his way back from the mosque and was in bad shape. We rushed to see him. He told us that he was returning from prayer when he came face to face with a demonstration. Police were firing on the crowd and using tear gas. By chance one of the gas canisters landed at his feet, and he found himself caught in the stampede. He fell and was trampled, and as a result had trouble breathing. Finally some people came to his aid and carried him from the scene. God was merciful that day.

In the end, the people's struggle bore fruit. One evening I was returning from a demonstration when I stopped to look at the headlines at a newspaper stand. One read:

Imam Returns Tomorrow

I couldn't contain the joy and excitement. Victory, it seemed, was certain. In those days news of Imam Khomeini's return was everywhere. Father surprised us by buying a television. He had a special respect for the audiotapes of the late Ahmad Kafi and the Quran of Abd al-Baset, which he would play for us. But we were always nagging him to get a television, so he played one of the Kafi's tapes in which he says, "O you who have a television in your homes, beware. Those who broadcast the programs on television want to make depravity an everyday thing." At the moment in history when Imam Khomeini entered Iran, father put the television on the table. All of us sat around, and when we saw the Imam reach the airport over the opposition of remnants of the Pahlavi regime, we sent up prayers, clapped our hands, and jumped with joy. During the celebration, I looked at father and saw tears rolling down his cheeks; it was clear he was also overjoyed. This reminded me of the days when he would send me into the avenue to find out for him whether such-and-such person, whose address he had given me, was around. He made it a point to tell me to come and go naturally. No matter how many times I tried to find out who these people were, he'd say, "Don't ask." Later I found out they were local security or SAVAK agents monitoring father.

The era of our moving from house to house and all the misery of that nomadic life had come to an end. Father was no longer under suspicion. Gone was the nightmare of having SAVAK—like the Iraqi secret service before it—after him. I often wondered what he had done to deserve that much surveillance. I tried to look more closely into his affairs, but he kept to himself, not wanting others to know too much about them. In this respect he was very different from other men in the family. But even under those harsh conditions, whenever members of mother's family visited Khorramshahr and stayed with us, he was a generous host. But I could tell that no one understood father; he remained a stranger to the family. On the other hand, I knew that despite the mystery surrounding his activities, he was on good terms with a series of people that he kept from us. Often he would greet certain people in the street unemotionally and go on his way. From their looks or the ways they interacted I could tell that they knew one another well, but behaved impersonally in public.

Ali was rarely at home after the victory of the revolution. He joined the Civilian Construction Corps to help in farming and the development of villages in deprived regions. Many nights he went on public safety patrols and didn't return until morning. Not many months had passed after the revolution when word spread in the town that some of the heads of the Arab clans wanted independence from Iran. These were the same people who collaborated with SAVAK before the revolution and now were mounting terrorist plots, using arms and explosives they received from Iraq to make people sorry they had participated in the revolution. Every day there was a bombing somewhere in the city, slaughtering many innocent people. There were several targets, vulnerable places where crowds gathered: the Congregational Mosque, the Seyf Market, the sports stadium, etc. One time in the Congregational Mosque there was a speech and ceremonies attended by lots of people. A grenade was thrown into the crowd, wounding and killing many. Taking advantage of the support they received, the opposition groups expanded their activities. They would identify young people who had been active in the revolution and throw bombs and grenades into their homes. This brought chaos to the city, but their real objective was to separate the southern province of Khuzestan from the rest of Iran and merge it with Iraq. They drew maps using Arabic names for Persian places—for example, "Mohammerah" for Khorramshahr, "Naseriyah" for Ahvaz, and "Abbadan" for Abadan.

Though they were short on weapons and equipment, the revolutionary forces put up fierce resistance to the Arab separatists. Ali told us to gather as many blankets and as much gasoline as we could. Leila, father, Mohsen, and I went around to the neighbors and to relatives asking for clean blankets and soap and sent them to Ali and his friends. Finally the battle between the two sides came to a head in a three-day pitched battle. The Arab separatists surrounded the military-cultural building that was the headquarters of the revolutionary forces and, after an armed struggle, took a number of people prisoner. Things got so bad that reinforcements from Tehran and Khorramabad entered the city and took the pro-Iraqi school located in a building on the avenue that ran along the Shatt. After the taking of the first and most important source of the insurrection, documents were found that made the nature of the separatist movement and its ties to Iraq clear for all to see. A number of the conspirators were captured while others fled to Iraq.

With this, the Arab insurrection appeared to be put down, but it did not disappear and its agents continued to operate. There were nightly attacks on people and threatening leaflets were thrown into the houses of youth active in the revolution. To contain the problem city officials told the young people to keep a low profile and, if possible, leave Khorramshahr for a time. Ali was among those told to go. The only place we had relatives was Elam, where as a nine-year-old

Ali had spent three or four months of his life in jail. He went to Elam and continued with his activities there. He wrote us regularly, commenting that the people there lived in extreme poverty. They even had to get their drinking water from the river. There wasn't one pharmacy or clinic in the town to treat those victims of separatist attacks. He asked us to buy medicines for the villagers and send them to him. Ali became a one-man construction corps around Elam; he even helped out in farm work.

The winter of 1979-1980 was a time of bad flooding in Khorramshahr and the surrounding areas. Many of the villages were under water, causing untold damage. Ali returned to Khorramshahr to help the flood victims. Sepah and Construction Corps members gave the victims food and shelter. They also pulled their belongings out from under the rubble, and, when the flooding stopped, helped to rebuild the villages. Ali returned after some time, bringing several large sacks of clothing with him. He explained that the boys from Aqajari were newcomers in town, but they were very helpful in the aid work. He brought the stuff home to be washed so we could help them out. I was aware of the groups of young people from Aqajari that had come to Khorramshahr for training. After completing their training, they wanted to create a Construction Corps of their own in their town. I always would count the hours for Ali to come, because the work he was doing was so inspiring I would put body and soul into anything he wanted me to do. He brought so many clothes in the first batch that there wasn't enough room on the roof to spread them out. Any time we found that the clothing needed repair we would stitch them with a sewing machine we borrowed from the neighbors and then iron them. One time I said to Ali, "It's embarrassing for me to go to the neighbors and borrow their machine. If you want us to do the job, we'll have to have one of our own." The next day around noon Ali came to the house with a machine he bought in Abadan.

Although he was working for the Construction Corps, Ali had long before applied to join the Pasdars. In the late fall of 1979 word came that he had been accepted. The day he appeared in his Pasdar uniform was a treat for us. The looks father gave him told me how proud he was of Ali. I also took pride in the fact that I had such a brother, especially since the Pasdar uniform for me was a kind of holy garb. Seeing him in it I felt it was something that not just anybody could wear. The thought became stronger as time passed. I realized the work the people in the Pasdars did was not for their own personal satisfaction, for the salary or the benefits; rather, it was to please God. Even when Jahan Ara, the commander of the Pasdar, approved giving them wages, they had other things in mind. Ali gave away his first paycheck to the poor. In subsequent months he gave money to Leila, mother, and me and pooled the rest with his friends to buy necessities for the people, delivering things at night to the doorsteps of those they had identified as needy. Later on he was delegated with several others to go to Shadgan to set up a Construction Corps.

This was a beautiful period in our lives. Everyone worked together without expecting anything in return. One of the gifts of the revolution was an atmosphere of peace and security. Father gave Leila and me permission to take part in the demonstrations and marches. I also took responsibility for the housework, trying my best not to leave any task undone.

It was almost the spring of 1980 and for the first time father let Leila, Mohsen, and me go to the Now Ruz celebrations with Uncle Hoseyni's family. Very early one morning we boarded a truck and, with family friends of uncle's, went to the shrine of Ali, one of the sons of Imam Hoseyn at Shalamcheh. Around the shrine there was a small grove of tall date palms as well as pomegranate and lotus trees. We hadn't been there long when we saw Ali patrolling the area. He had just returned to Khorramshahr from four or five months in Shadgan, where he had been stationed with other Pasdars to control the border. Ali saw us and walked over. After the usual greetings, he said to uncle that we shouldn't stay in the area too long in case the Iraqis started shooting in our direction. We found it hard to believe that they would attack just like that. I remembered that in 1970 there had been a minor skirmish between the two countries. Our home was in Dieselabad in those days, near the Ring Road, and I had seen military vehicles travelling toward the Iraqi border. Some of the trucks carrying soldiers would stop, take a break, and then go on to their posts on the border. For the Iraqis the excuse was the border dispute in the waterway between the two countries (they called it the Shatt al-Arab; we the Arvand River). This resulted in the expulsion of Iranians from Iraq. We had no inkling of what the Iraqis had in store for us now, but it didn't take long for the first incident to take place.

On June 1, 1980, two Pasdars from Khorramshahr named Abbas Ferhan Asadi and Musa Bakhtur were killed by Iraqi forces in the border region. The incident confirmed what the Pasdars had been saying; namely, that all the Iraqi border activity and provocations had but one purpose—starting a war with Iran. But their reports had little effect.

On the day the two Pasdars were buried, Leila and I went to Jennatabad, where we saw father and Mohsen. A large crowd gathered, among them many Pasdars. From the looks on their faces it was easy to see how affected they were by the death of their two comrades. They beat their chests and cried. The situation in the town critical and threats of Arab separatist bombing, so several Pasdars were stationed on the roof of the mortuary.

After the two were buried—if memory serves—I recall that Hajj Aqa Nuri, the Congregational preacher of Khorramshahr, delivered a speech and the Pasdar comrades of the two fallen men sang a dirge, parts of which I still remember:

We are Pasdars of Khomeini, ready to sacrifice our souls.
Never shall we retreat till the last measure of our souls.
O Khomeini, O Brother,
Command us, so we can wash for martyrdom.
From our veins blood will flow,
And from our blood, tulips will grow.
The ground will be a garden thick with tulips and roses.

This scene was not something you saw everyday. It was unnerving, heart wrenching; but at the same time the pact the Pasdars made with their martyr comrades was both stirring and majestic.

That night when Ali came home, he was very disturbed. Abbas and Musa were two of his closest friends. He spoke of them warmly to us many times. He told us that after the funeral, he and some of the Pasdars went to Abbas's home, where everyone but Abbas's mother was sobbing. She was calm and, when she saw how upset they were, she tried to console them, saying "Abbas traveled the path he chose for himself, a path that is not open to everyone. You should be happy for him. Why cry?"

The next day I saw to Ali's pack, as I normally did. There were some bloodstained clothes and a pair of boots in it. I pulled the clothes out, washed them, and hung them to dry on the clothesline. A couple of hours later, Ali returned. As soon as he saw the clothes on the line, he let out a deep sigh and said testily, "Why did you touch those clothes? They belonged to Abbas and I wanted them to stay the way they were—with the blood from his passing and all, to remember him." Then he gathered the clothes along with the boots and put them in the wardrobe. Now I felt sorry about washing those clothes. I went to the wardrobe and, when saw them again, I felt sick.

The death of Musa and Abbas affected Ali deeply. He had changed in a way that I had never seen before. The old Ali, who had infected us with his verve and enthusiasm, was now very unemotional. It seemed he was thinking about leaving home. Several days passed, and I thought Ali would snap out of it. That day I had gone to grandfather's house for a couple of hours. When I returned I saw Ali beside the window that looked out on the courtyard; he was dressed in black and was holding a framed picture. It was a photo of himself, which I had never seen. Mother was sitting in the yard. I said hello to both of them and asked, "What's this about, Ali? Why did you frame a picture of yourself?"

"I want it for that day," he said calmly and turned to mother with a smile. But I could tell from the expression on her face how much these words upset her. I knew Ali was her favorite; she was always singing his praises and saying how devoted she was to him. The rest of us accepted that he was the best, for the way he was always helping and, despite all his own problems, how he would try to shoulder others' burdens. I desperately wanted to know whether he was thinking about martyrdom, so I asked, "Which day, Ali?"

"The day that I'll make all of you proud," he said.

"The day of martyrdom, you mean?" I asked.

Mother's angry look stopped me from saying more. Ali said, "I had this picture taken so that after I'm martyred you'll hang it up on one of those columns with the mirrors and lights, and people will see that my heart and soul were in the path I chose."

He stopped for a moment and began again, "I don't want you to cry when I'm martyred. You've got to be like Abbas's mother. Come to it with patience and quiet defiance. You be the ones to comfort others."

I didn't know what to say to him. But with mother on the verge of hysterics, I tried to relieve the tension by joking around.

From the time Ali joined the army, handling a weapon was very painful for him. Two of his fingers on both hands were fused from birth, and when he cocked the weapon they would get caught. His fingers were always bandaged and sometimes the bleeding was very bad, making washing for prayers torture. At times the cuts were very deep, requiring stitches. He played down the pain, telling us not to worry, but it upset mother, who would complain to him, "Why do you have to bring this misery on yourself?"

Father wanted more than anything to save enough money for an operation, but in those days he didn't make more than 1,300 tumans, and the surgery would have cost around 20,000. Not only were his fingers joined; two toes on both feet were also fused. His skin would swell up when he took his socks off. It was difficult for me to see this, and I would rush to him with lotion but he wouldn't let me apply it.

Eventually Commander Jahan Ara asked Ali to think about doing something about this. The army arranged for him to go to Tehran for an operation. The day he left was the darkest one of my life. On the one hand, he was leaving for a good cause; on the other, his absence, even if for short time, would be hard to take. Ali wasn't only my brother; he was my friend and confidant. I told him things that I couldn't even tell mother. When I told him what I wished for, he would try to make my wishes come true. When he couldn't do anything he would raise the issue with father in such a way that he couldn't tell it was my wish. Leila also loved Ali very much. The day father bought him a wardrobe, Leila and I insisted that he put it in our room so that Ali would visit us more. Although after he joined the army, he didn't come home more than twice a week, we still would straighten it out and dust it every day. We consoled ourselves when he was away by just looking at his possessions.

The day before he was scheduled to fly to Tehran, he came home very late. I packed everything I thought he would need in a suitcase:

clothes, camera, tape recorder, prayer mat. When he came home, I showed the suitcase to him. He thanked me. That night I couldn't sleep and in the morning when he was about to leave, I hugged him and, all choked up, I told him how devoted I was to him and kissed him. He said, "Stop. That's enough. Why are you going on like this?" But I couldn't help it; I stroked his beard and kissed his hands. This made him angry. I held up the Quran so he could pass under it and all the way to end of the alley I kept clasping his hands. Father then pulled me away, and he and mother took Ali to the airport. Mother was also on her way to Tehran for an appointment for an eye operation.

When I got back I felt that the light had gone out of our house. I was very worried; they said Ali's operation would be complicated. A team of surgeons was going to operate on his brain, nerves, arteries, and bones. They were going to straighten out the bones in his foot and graft skin from his legs on to his hands. Imagining what he had to go through made the pain of his being away several times worse. I went to the shelf where the picture was, the one he wanted for his martyrdom memorial, and I kissed it several times.

We had expected Ali to return after two weeks, but it was a month before he came home. They had only operated on his right hand. He said that mother didn't have the patience to stay. He spent that night at home and was off the next day, and I felt worse than when he had left the first time. I had a bad a feeling about it, as if something had been wrenched from my being. I even wished Ali had not come home if it was only going to be temporary. Why did he have to come only to leave so soon? Something deep inside me said that this was the last time I would see Ali.

I called the hospital regularly to ask about him. He would always ask me about what was happening in town. I could tell how much it bothered him to hear about the death of his friend Seyyed Jafar Musavi and the skirmishes on the border. He tried to hide the emotion in his voice from me. I stopped telling him the bad news, but he was in contact with his friends in Khorramshahr. During those last days of summer, the situation for our border forces got worse and worse, and there were more incidents, which would be hard to keep from him.

As the fighting on the border intensified, people from those areas started to leave their villages and come to the city. Most were farmers who tended the date palms and sold their produce by the side of the road. Some also sold things like milk, cream, and yogurt at the market in town. The skirmishes wiped out all the livestock and herds of these ranchers and farmers. A number of these poor folk found shelter in the building that was burned during the Arab separatist crisis.

Sleeping on the roof gave us a chance to see the fire fights between our forces and the Iraqis. Father explained that we didn't let any Iraqi firing go unanswered, so as not to give them a pretext, but we could see them getting more brazen by the day. Their assaults got to the point where their naval vessels entered our waters. They also invaded on land and shelled our positions, leaving our forces with no choice but to engage with them.

4

The Invasion

On September 22, 1980, we expected the next day to be like any other, with the kids going to school: Sa'id to first grade, Hasan to second, and Mansur to the first year of middle school. Father had given us money a few days before to buy school supplies for them. I took the boys myself to the Darvazeh traffic circle and bought—as much as our budget would allow—what they needed. They were excited about what we had bought, especially Sa'id. Because they had to be up early the next day, I made them go to sleep before their usual bedtime that night.

On the morning of September 23 I said my prayers, laid out breakfast, and woke the kids. I had my heart set on bringing Sa'id and Hasan to school myself. The excitement made me feel it was my own first day of school. I remembered how happy I was to go to school. I held Sa'id by the hand, looking this way and that as we crossed the street, but it wasn't a normal day; the streets seemed deserted. When we got to the school, the doors were locked. I was about to knock when I saw one of the neighbors and asked about the doors.

"Don't you know that the Iraqis bombarded the city last night?" she asked.

"When?" I said in surprise.

"In the middle of the night."

It was unbelievable to me that they would attack just like that. I couldn't figure out why I hadn't heard anything.

I didn't waste a minute getting the kids back to the house. Then I went to the avenue to learn more about what happened from anyone who went by. As I frantically tried to find someone, I noticed Ahlam Ansari, a classmate of mine from elementary school. Her face was all red and she was crying. I went over and, though we hadn't seen each other for ages, I got right to the point, "Ahlam, what happened? Why are you crying?"

"My uncle was killed," she said.

"Killed? How?"

"Weren't you in town last night? Don't you know they bombarded the city?" she asked.

I said, "Sure I was, but I don't understand. What happened?"

Unable to control her sobs, Ahlam said, "Uncle was visiting when they hit our house. He was killed in his sleep."

Terribly upset by what she said, I asked, "Where are you going now?"

"Jennatabad. They took him there."

Although I didn't want to leave Ahlam alone at that point, I thought I would be of more help at the hospital. I said goodbye and started out for the Mosaddeq Hospital, but there were no taxis. I walked down Forty Meter Road, the main street of the city [now Ayatollah Khamene'i Avenue]. The number of cars and ambulances racing to the hospital increased the closer I got to the Farmandari traffic circle. By contrast, there were very few pedestrians on the street. The few people I saw seemed to be in shock. Having passed Farmandari, I saw a large crowd gathered behind the hospital, which was strange. I could make out weeping and wailing as I got closer to the crowd; people were screeching, beating their chests in mourning, and shouting out the names of their loved ones. There were bloodstains on some; others were covered in grime. Many of the women were sitting on the ground, beating themselves. I tried to maneuver my way through them but, as I got to the entryway, the attendants thrust open the doors and a mass of people spilled out into the courtyard, all scurrying in different directions. The only thing I could hear was the screaming. Inside the hospital all hell had broken loose; patients were lying everywhere. I went toward the emergency room on the right side of the building past the information desk. I knew where to go because I had brought my brothers and sisters there before. A guard stood in front of the door warning people who insisted on entering, "It's too crowded in there. Where do you think you're going? You'll never come out if you go in."

I waited outside the door for the guard to step aside and rushed in when he wasn't looking. But he saw me and, crying out, ran a few steps toward me. I ignored him and disappeared in the crowd. I had never seen the emergency room in such chaos. There were blood trails on the floor leading from the entrance to the interior; people drenched in blood lay all over the floor. There were footprints in the blood. When I had been there before, the floor was so spotless it reflected the moonlight, and the only thing I could smell was alcohol. Now I smelled the stench of dirt, blood, and gunpowder in the air. Nurses were running this way and that, holding bags of serum and dragging trolleys filled with medical supplies. Ordinarily their uniforms were stylish and neat, but the volume of work gave them another look. There was no trace of makeup on their faces, and their white uniforms and shoes were spattered with the blood of the wounded. The pins holding their caps together had come undone and their hair had fallen over their faces and shoulders. Those nurses in headscarves were no better off than their coworkers. The doctors were working at a frantic pace. The rooms overflowed with the injured. The wounded people lying in the corridors were being treated with serum bags nailed to the walls. Some were on stretchers, while others were on blankets. Most were staring lifelessly into space, apparently because of losing so much blood. Some were moaning in pain. Only one person at the end of the room was actually saying something intelligible: "Help! I'm dying."

I ran to the back of the room. The man's wounds did not seem worse than those of the others. He was shouting out of fear, it seemed. Patients near him said, "Quiet! Let them help those who are in worse shape. Wait your turn."

I didn't know what to do. I was terrified seeing all those wounded people, but I wanted with all my heart to do something to help the nurses who were swamped and exhausted. Maybe I could see to some of the wounded who had been there longer. But I didn't have any training in first aid or other skills called for in the situation. It felt so frustrating being of no use to anyone.

I left the building and stood in the yard, which was still a madhouse. A number of people were waiting outside the morgue to collect the bodies of their relatives. These people were in worse shape than the people waiting for their wounded family members. Their wails cut my heart to the quick, and seeing the children sobbing was torture for me. Then I went to the wards in the hope of doing something. They were even more chaotic than the emergency room; most of the wounded were just spread out on the floors without anything underneath them. Relatives were standing over them holding the serum bags. There was no sign of the quiet that normally reigned in these places, giving patients a sense of security. It was all heartrending cries and moans. Not knowing what else to do, I stood over the wounded and asked, "If there's anything I can do for you, tell me. Is there anything you need?"

Most were parched from losing blood and asked for water. Some said that they were in pain and wanted me to fetch a doctor. The poor doctors didn't know whom to go to first. When I saw them attending to people in even worse shape, I regretted having spoken to them about the others. Having noticed me there, the nurses started screaming, "What the hell is this about? Why are you making such a fuss?"

As I stood in the corridor not knowing where to go, the sound of a woman moaning caught my attention. I looked at her; she was very thin and her face didn't seem to match her voice, which was that of a young woman. But she was so scared and bloody just looking at her made me sick to my stomach. I tried to control my feelings, and at the same time I felt sorry for her. She was in an awful state. Blood-soaked bandages ran vertically and horizontally around her head and her feet were in splints. I took her hands. She opened her eyes and looked at me. I asked her if she needed anything, if I could help her in any way. She squeezed my hands feebly and gasped, "Go and bring a doctor. It hurts. My head is splitting open, my eyes are falling out."

"They didn't give you a sedative?" I asked.

"It didn't do any good."

The way she squeezed my hand told me how much pain she was in. I told her to go to sleep so she wouldn't feel the pain, and I would get a doctor.

She closed her eyes and feebly mouthed the words, "The pain won't let me sleep."

I got up and turned around to see a nurse emerging from one of the rooms with several serum bags in her hand. I ran to her. All the color was drained from her face; she was dead tired and it was clear she hadn't slept in ages. "Pardon me," I said, "that woman there is in a lot of pain. Can't something be done for her?"

"What can I do?" she said. After a pause, she said, "It's been non-stop hell for all of us since last night. We're in agony too; it feels like were going to die. We're short-staffed, and she's not the only one. She'll have to put up with it."

I watched as she quickly receded in the distance. She seemed to be around twenty-eight or so. Her hair had come undone, which made her seem more frazzled. Her clothes were reddish-purple, not from iodine but from blood; her hose, which were torn, were hiked up her calves. It felt bad to see how tired she was and how grubby she looked. My thoughts were interrupted by the sound of child. A few feet beyond the woman who wanted me to get a doctor was a four-year-old girl with her mother sitting by her side. Each time her child shrieked, the mother raised her head from the blanket she was lying on and hugged her, trying to comfort her; but the mother was also crying. The child's legs were in splints wrapped in bandages. Her swollen fingers were covered in bloody gauze. I went over and looked at her. She was a beautiful girl with delicate features. Her hair, which lay on her shoulders, was an attractive brown but matted. She was in a yellow dress with a blue and green flower print that had turned purple from the blood. I stood there watching her and noticed that whenever she raised her head and saw her legs, she screamed in horror. I told her mother, who had obviously rushed to the hospital without changing out of her house dress, to cover her child's legs with something.

The woman was in tears and said, "I don't have anything. You see how I'm dressed."

I said, "No problem," and covered the little girl with a corner of the blanket.

The woman seemed to be paying attention to me, but her crying and moans made me speak more directly. "If you go on this way, you'll make it worse for the child. You've got to get yourself under control first and then try to calm the child."

"You have a point, but I'm dying inside. There's nothing I can do for her."

I sat down and caressed the child's face. I wanted with all my heart to do something to soothe her but couldn't. Just then I heard a man say, "Where do I give blood?" This gave me a start, as I realized: At last, here's something I can do. I quickly ran toward the man and followed him into the room where they took blood. It was full of metal cabinets with glass doors. There were also nurses cutting lengths of adhesive and sticking them on the side of a trolley. Before the man could speak, I said, "I want to give blood; where should I go?"

The nurse looked up and asked, "How old are you?"

"Not quite seventeen."

"Impossible. You can't give blood."

"What's wrong with me?" I asked.

"You're under eighteen and you're on the thin side. We only take blood from people over eighteen, who also have the right weight."

I was so frustrated. Here was one thing that I thought I could do, but even that was impossible. Now what was I supposed to do?

I thought I would go home and take a page out of father's book, because he had been a great help to the boys at the mosque when there was the problem with the Arab separatists. He told Leila and me to go around to the neighbors to collect sheets, petrol, and soap. I had made up my mind by the time I left the ward. As I was leaving, I saw a nurse poke her head out of one of the rooms and said to a man, "Go tell the morgue attendant to come by. Another one's gone and needs to be taken to the freezer."

This made me think of the martyrs. I ran into the courtyard. There was a lot of noise coming from the morgue. Men and women were standing in front of it beating themselves and calling out the names of their loved ones. There was a man standing in front of the door, stopping the mourners from rushing inside. He kept repeating, "Why are you crowding around here? We're going to eventually transfer all of them to Jennatabad. You have to go there if you want to take possession of your dead."

I said to myself: Go to Jennatabad and see what's happening there and maybe you can do something to help. There were two ways to go there, and, after leaving the hospital, I stopped to decide which way was best. One was the Ring Road that went through the wasteland outside the city; the other was the main Forty Meter Road. I decided to go on the main road, but the vehicles that passed were all full of people, so there was no chance of catching a ride. I was walking past a furniture store when a white Peykan appeared. I waved my hand and it stopped; there were only two women passengers inside. The driver asked, "Where to?"

"Straight ahead. I want to go to Jennatabad."

"We're going up to the entrance of Congregation Mosque," he said.

"So I'll get off at the corner of Mosque Avenue," I said.

I got out at the corner and when I tried to pay the driver, he wouldn't accept the money, saying, "Pray for me." I thanked him and headed for Jennatabad. The cemetery was near our house; I had been there many times so I wasn't that afraid of the dark atmosphere there or of corpses. I remembered one time I was with mother and Zeynab going home from uncle's house, and we were standing on the Ring Road, waiting and waiting but there were no taxis. It was getting dark and Zeynab was tired and crabby. We had no choice but to walk. As we passed Jennatabad I said to mother, "Let's cut through the cemetery."

She said, "It's not good to walk there at sundown, especially in the middle of the week."

"What's the problem?" I asked. "The people resting here were just like us." Then I walked toward the cemetery, forcing mother to follow. I remembered what the kids in the neighborhood had said about being afraid of the place, but I wasn't scared. As we walked among the graves, I noticed that my shoelace was untied. I knelt down to retie it and noticed a coffin a few feet away from us. I was curious to look inside, but mother said, "You've got no business looking at coffins. Let's get out of here."

"Wait a second; I'm coming," I said. I raised the lid a crack and looked inside. There was a body wrapped in a shroud. Mother, who was now really frightened, didn't wait for me and hurried off. I said a quick prayer for the dead and ran after her. We got to the place where they washed the bodies, just as a pickup was entering the cemetery. I wondered whether they were transferring corpses to another place.

It wasn't long before I reached the cemetery. All hell had broken loose. Waves of people were there, moaning and wailing to the heavens. I had never seen Jennatabad like that before. They had laid out row after row of corpses on white sheets and packed them with chunks of ice. Blood from the dead mixed with the water from the melting ice, and small pinkish streams flowed out from under the corpses. A few people were standing over each corpse reciting dirges and pounding on their heads and clawing at their faces. The fury of their mourning made a person tremble; the way the women grieved was especially heartbreaking. Some of them had gouged their cheeks so deeply their blood had begun to flow. Some also tore at their hair so ferociously that tufts of it were in their fists. There were others who had fainted, while those around them tried to revive them by slapping their faces, forcing water into their mouths, and massaging their shoulders. Even some of the men, unable to be taken in the catastrophe, fainted. Some pounded their heads against the wall or threw themselves on the corpses. There were also people who had heaped mud and dirt on their heads and shoulders. Most of the Arab women mourners formed a circle to mourn as though it were Moharram. One of them sung the lines of a dirge, while the others responded and beat their heads and chests. I sobbed as I walked through the crowd and heard the dirge leader sing in Arabic:

> *O woe! O woe! Everyone say, Woe!*
> The women answered: *O woe! O woe!*
> The leader said: *O woe unto us! Ours are the martyrs!*
> The women answered: *O woe! O woe!*
> The leader said: *Woe unto us for Mohammad's heart is seared!*

Whenever they said the name of one of the martyrs, the crowd would shriek. Then they would immediately start with rapid-fire face-slapping and choral responses: "Hooo Haaa…." Some couldn't take it any longer and lost consciousness. Those were strange scenes, and even though I had seen mourning processions during the course of the revolution, which celebrated martyrdoms from the Arab separatist trouble and the Hypocrites' bombings, this time the number of killed was greater. This time the dead were innocents buried and bloodied in their sleep. The sun was merciless, and the smells of earth, blood, and gunpowder filled the air. All these things made me sick to my stomach; I felt so terrible I couldn't stand. It was as if I'd lost every ounce of strength in my body. I was dizzy and everything went blank. My knees weak, I was forced to lean on a nearby pillar. But that was no use, and I slid to the ground. The scenes were just like the descriptions of Karbala. I scolded myself: What's wrong? Why are you so weak? This was how I tried to regain control of my body. I got up and walked toward the place where they washed women's corpses. Men and women were massed behind the door, sitting on the ground waiting to take possession of their dead. As soon as the door opened they charged inside, wanting to be there when they washed the bodies and wrapped them in shrouds. But the door would close immediately after a body emerged. One person had a list of people in his hand and would send out bodies in order of the names on the list. After pushing myself forward only to retreat several times, I finally managed to cut a path through the crowd. I knocked on the door but they didn't open it. I waited until they sent out another body and, using the force of the crowd, hurled myself inside. I waited in the middle of a room for someone to ask testily what I thought I was doing there. My heart was racing as I looked around, stunned and confused. There were two rooms connected to each other and only one entrance. The room I was in was about 120 square meters. The walls and floor were made of cement painted with a leaden color that caused the atmosphere in the room to be even more dismal. In front of me was a window with a green wooden frame. Sunlight from the window combined with the faint glow of electric lamps to light the room. Everything in the place was cold and soulless, which made it seem even more morbid to me. But what really broke my heart was seeing the bodies of women lined up from the walls to the center of the room. As soon as I saw them, I instinctively stepped back; the bodies were all aligned with the heads facing me and the feet pointing toward the wooden door separating the two rooms. Some eyes and mouths were open; others were full of blood. The faces and stringy hair of the dead were blood-soaked. All the corpses were those of young women. Their arms and legs hung limp from the rest of their bodies. Some didn't have arms and legs at all, and one that made my heart break had her arms torn off leaving two jagged gashes at the elbows. I recalled that whenever mother was distressed, beseeching God for something, she swore by the two severed hands of the revered Abbas.

Seeing the bodies made me weak again; then I felt nauseous. I wanted nothing more than to have someone splash water in my face and say, "Get up. This is just a nightmare," but the screeches and wailing coming from outside the body-washing room and the combined smells of blood, camphor, and wet earth told me otherwise. The bitter truth was that there was no escaping the scene, and I was sorry I had entered the room. I asked myself: What the hell were you thinking coming here? Why didn't you get off at the mosque where there was probably a lot for you to do?

On the right-hand side of the room there was a cement bench and in front of it a metal cabinet. Beside the bench was a thickset old woman, soaked in sweat. She was in such a bad state that she didn't notice I had entered. She seemed to be taking a breather. I stood there not know what to do, when a thin, relatively short woman entered from the back room. She was in dark, loose-fitting clothing and had a red cotton cloth on her head. Her face was olive bordering on yellow. As she passed me, I got a strong whiff of tobacco, and I realized her lips were so bluish because she was a heavy smoker. As she went to the cabinet, she glanced at me. I was petrified, thinking that there would be an argument. In a raspy voice she asked, "Are you here to help or are you looking for your dead?" At a loss I only said, "I've come to help."

I didn't know what my face told her I was feeling, but she asked me, "You're not afraid?"

I sensed that there were still signs in my expression of the weakness I felt. I said, "I'll try not to be."

"Come and help us, then."

"Okay," I said.

She pulled lengths of muslin from a drawer and said, "Take these and help that woman cut it into shrouds."

I took the fabric and walked toward the old woman and, as I did, I glanced at her; there was no color in her face. Her blouse was so damp it clung to her body. Strands of her gray hair had crept out from under her head cloth and were splayed over her forehead. Her thin, braided forelocks, red with henna, also protruded from the cloth.

I gathered my chador and squatted on the floor in front of her. To break the silence I said, "Looks like you've been working hard?" She nodded and took the fabric from my hands and measured it out with her thumb. Then she had me hold one end while she cut the other with a pair of scissors.

As she was cutting the fabric, I heard sounds coming from the other room. I was curious to see what was going on. I could hear a woman say in a caring voice, "Bring the hose over here and hold it right. Why are you doing it that way? Now this poor creature's going to fall. Point the hose that way…."

When she mentioned falling, I felt a pain in my heart. I moved around trying to see what was happening in the room. The door was ajar and I could see a woman laid out on a bench with water flowing over her limp hair. Gloved hands were pouring pails of water over the body. The scene was familiar to me; about a year ago Nahid, the sister of Uncle Nad Ali's wife, had died not from the burns when the brazier she was fanning exploded—they were minor—but from kidney failure. Nahid's long locks were spread out over the body-washing stone, waving and dancing as the water flowed through them. The scene stayed with me for a long time; there was something troubling about it. Now I was seeing the same thing.

After the fabric was cut into shrouds, the old woman said, "Put them in the cabinet." I did this and walked toward the back room. My heart was in turmoil. After going through all that to get inside in the first place, snaking through the crowd and, above all, doing so without my parents' permission, I needed to accomplish something so that, if I had to leave, it would give me a reason to return. There was another thing also; I wanted to experience everything I could. I stepped into the other room even though I found it difficult to look at the corpses laid out that way. Seeing the floor swamped in a pink mixture of blood and water, I hoisted my chador. The first thing that caught my eye was the small cement pool in the middle of the room that was ringed with a narrow drainage channel filled with blood. I immediately thought of the slaughterhouse that was near our home when we lived on Mina Avenue. Sometimes mother and I along with the wives of the neighbors would go there to buy sheep heads and trotters for a stew. I had also been curious to see what went on in that place. There was a steady stream of blood from the carcasses hanging from the ceiling. My sympathies were with the sheep.

Two sides of the room were lined with cement benches protruding from the wall. The bodies were laid out on the benches. The panes in the translucent windows were etched with floral patterns and covered with muslin so nothing could been seen from the outside. Light from a naked bulb suspended from the ceiling shone on the water. Several aged women were helping the body washers. A few others operated the spigot, undressed the corpses, or filled buckets with camphor water from the pool and, in the final stages of preparing the bodies for burial, poured it over them with a red plastic cup. As soon as one corpse had been washed, they lifted another from the corner and placed it on a bench. The wounds on some of the dead were so bloody they looked like slaughtered sheep. When they poured water over the wounds, a trickle of blood would become a flood. The sight pained my soul and turned my stomach. As if that weren't enough, the creaking of a rusty bucket handle got on my nerves. The leaden bucket was the last straw; I nearly threw throw up at the sight of it.

As I stood there looking around, one seemingly competent woman, who may have been in charge, turned around. I recognized her immediately: Zeynab Rudbari, a city employee at Jennatabad. She was wearing a dark blue coat and pants and a black head cloth. Her boots and gloves were also black, and there was a dark shawl wrapped around her waist. Her house was one alley over from ours, and I would occasionally see her in the neighborhood or at the market where we'd say hello to each other. During Moharram when as part of our vows we would make food for the neighbors, I would bring dishes to her home. Now she was so busy with what she was doing she didn't even have time to acknowledge my greeting.

I stood there without knowing what to do. The bodies lying on the floor made me stop and think; I was of two minds. On one hand, I wished I hadn't come there at all. On the other, I thought it had been a good idea. I was debating with myself when I saw a woman put her bucket down and rub her back. She swayed back and forth, hoping to relieve the weariness she felt. Zeynab, so busy with her work she didn't notice the woman had put her bucket down, called for water. I lunged to pick up the bucket, and then dipped it in the fount, which was now half full. After pouring the water, I put the bucket on the bench. Zeynab looked at me and said, "Thanks."

"I've come to help. Tell me what you want me to do," I said.

One of the women standing near Zeynab asked, "You're not afraid?"

"No. At first I would have been, but now it seems normal to me."

She nodded her head and said, "God bless you for that."

That was how it started. I operated the spigot, turning the water on and off for the body washers. They began to order me around, telling me to fetch camphor or cotton from the cabinet or pour water or hold the hose, and I wasted no time doing whatever they asked.

The women, all old and established people, were evidently thankful someone had come to help them—especially since they were so exhausted. The thing that worried me as I got involved in the work was how mother would view it. I was afraid she'd come and start a fight about me working there, and how I would have to answer to father about it. But the worst thing was to have father come and fetch me himself. I always had my ears cocked for a familiar voice from outside so I could get ready to fight. But I only heard the droning and crying of the people outside the body washers'. The sounds got louder whenever they put a body out or whenever people took possession of their dead. I could hear people mourning in many tongues: Arabic, Turkish, Luri, Bakhtiyari, Shirazi Persian, Esfahani Persian….

The women stopped working when the noon call to prayer sounded. "Come; let's pray and take a break," they said.

As they were finishing up with one of the dead, I lifted the hose and washed down my arms and legs. No matter how hard I tried not to get blood on my clothing, the hem of my chador and my pants got stained when I lifted the bodies. I washed my face and head cloth and cleaned my shoes.

I stepped gingerly from the building with the body washers, careful not to get my shoes bloody again. We waded through the crowd, which parted before us, and I said to Zeynab, "I'm going to go straight home. My mother hasn't had word from me since morning. She must be worried. If father lets me, I'll come back."

Zeynab thanked me and we said goodbye. Working there for a few hours had made me very tired—that was to be expected, but what I really couldn't believe were the scenes that I had just witnessed. In the space of a few hours, I had received several shocks. Never in the world had I imagined that those innocent white sheets, so familiar to me from home, would be used as shrouds. To that point I had thought of shrouds as something holy, since that was how a person was dressed before making the final journey. Now even the thought of plain sheets as shrouds gave me an empty, chilling feeling.

The closer I got to home, the more thoughts of the body washers receded in my mind, only to be replaced by another worry. I didn't know what to say to father, how to convince him that what I did was right. Although I loved him very much, I was also afraid of him. When he got mad, the way he looked sent shivers through me. He was never angry without a reason, of course. He wasn't happy that his children spent time playing in the alley. I had left the house without telling anybody where I was going; now whatever I got I deserved. I also knew that in my absence mother was forced to do chores that ordinarily I would have done. On account of this I was sure she had told on me to father. At the door I knocked and made a loud greeting and sent up prayers. I heard Hasan and Sa'id playing inside the compound. As soon as they heard me knocking, they ran to open the door.

When the door opened, mother poked her head out of the kitchen door, which opened on the yard. She looked me up and down; then she glanced at the window of the sitting room. I followed her gaze and saw father through the window, deep in thought with his chin resting on his hands. He seemed very upset.

My throat was dry with fear and I swallowed hard before saying hello.

Whenever he was angry at me, father had the habit of not answering my "Peace be upon you" or of saying something like "No peace upon you"; but this time he took his hands from his chin and answered normally.

He wasn't gruff, thank God—more absentminded. Clearly he didn't know how long I had been away from home. Stepping into the yard I went by mother who barked in Kurdish, "You little brat, where the hell were you? Your father's going to kill you!"

Before I could answer, father seemed to notice only then that I was there. He asked, "Where were you?"

To justify my absence, I quickly listed the reasons why I was away. "I was in Jennatabad; there were millions of bodies there; I was helping out."

"Jennatabad! What were you doing there?" he asked.

"I was helping out at the body washers'; it was wall-to-wall corpses."

"What do you mean you helped out?"

"I was helping to wash the bodies and cutting the shrouds," I said.

His face softened. He looked at me more carefully and asked, "You weren't afraid?"

"Sure, very, at first. I was also sick to my stomach." I was about to say that I fainted, but swallowed my words and said, "I tried to keep myself under control and work."

He said, "That's right, child. Good for you! Nowadays we all have to pitch in."

Relieved now, I asked, "So you're okay with me going to help out?"

"Yes, it's alright with me so long as you know for certain you're needed there."

"Even if I get home late because the workload?" I asked.

"Try to be back before sunset, but even if it's later than that, there won't be a problem," he said.

I almost jumped for joy, never imaganing the conversation with father would go so well. I went to the window, took his hands from behind the window bars, and kissed them. He chuckled and said, "What do you think you're doing, child?" As I continued to kiss his hands, he said more affectionately, "Don't, sweet child." I couldn't contain myself; I wanted to kiss his face. I rushed into the house and, when I got to the entrance to the hall, mother, her voice raised, asked, "Where to? Where to?"

I understood what she really meant and said, "I'm going to wash."

"First, get out of that chador." I took off my head cloth and chador and put them in a corner of the yard. "Take off those socks, too," she said testily.

Then I heard father's voice saying, "Leave her alone. She's tired. Stop pestering her."

I added, "Wait a second, mother; I'm going to the bathroom." She said, "You can't come in with your legs like that." I went to the spigot in the yard. I got out of my socks and washed my legs. Then I entered the sitting room barefoot. Father was still standing behind the window deep in thought. I said, "I thank you, father. I was really afraid that I'd come home and have it out with you."

He turned around and said, "Why would I argue with you? You didn't do anything wrong."

I said, "No, but I was worried about going off without permission and staying so long."

"No, you did the right thing, what was necessary. May God reward you. If God's okay with it, I'm okay."

This made me want to jump into his arms, but, blocking me with his arms, he said, "No so fast. Wait a second."

I realized I had been handling corpses and hadn't done the proper ablutions. I clasped my hands around his neck and kissed his face. Then, as I kept kissing him, I looked him straight in the eye, something his sense of decorum would never allow. More out of joy than uncertainty, I asked him again, "So you're saying I can go, right?"

He kissed my face and unlocked my hands from around his neck. He looked at me and said, "Yes, today everyone must help. The differences between men and women don't matter anymore. Everybody must lend a hand in the defense. We can't let a foreigner invade our country and take our land, dignity, and self-respect. Both men and women must stop this from happening." He paused and then said, "I was at Jennatabad myself, and saw what was going on there. They sent us to dig graves; the gravediggers they had couldn't cope with all the bodies, after all."

I asked, "So you were there?"

"Yes, but I couldn't stand it. I couldn't take being in Jennatabad only to dig graves—I need to go to the front and fight the enemy. I can do more than just dig." Then he said, "So tell me what it was like at the body washers'?"

I explained the conditions there: the large number of poor souls I saw, people slaughtered like that, how tired the body washers were. Leila listened to what I was saying as she went in and out. Father's expression showed how deeply he was affected by what I said; I had the feeling that he was now deeper in thought than when I first came into the compound. Suddenly he left the room without a word.

Father's giving his permission was a relief to my physically. What he said also lifted my spirits, and I decided that moment to go back to Jennatabad.

As I was leaving the hall, Leila said she wanted to go, too.

"Go where?" I asked, "And do what?"

"The same place as you. Why are you going?"

"I'm helping."

"Fine, I'll help, too."

"That won't be necessary; you'll be of no use there. You'll just get in the way," I said.

"How do you know?" she asked.

"The things I saw there made me go to pieces; there's no telling what they'd do to you," I said.

She didn't say anything. I went to the spigot and washed for prayer on the veranda. I felt much better after praying; the pressures on my heart were gone. I picked up my socks and put them on, and although I had washed them thoroughly, they still smelled of camphor. At that point five-year-old Zeynab walked over to me. She hadn't seen me since morning, and I knew she wanted a hug. I said to her, "Don't come near me, sweetie. My clothes are filthy." She made a face and looked at me in disbelief with those almond-shaped eyes gleaming like two stars,.

"I'm going," I said. "Tonight when I come back, I'll change my clothes and then I'll give you a big hug. So, tell me now, what have you been doing all morning?"

Hearing my voice in the yard, mother emerged from the kitchen and, using that tone of hers when she wanted to show her disapproval, said, "Okay, now; have a nice trip?"

"I am going back to Jennatabad," I said.

"How come?" she asked in Kurdish.

"Dad gave me permission—you saw."

"And what am I supposed to do? You've been gone since morning, leaving me all alone here."

I knew it wasn't just havging to do the housework that made her cranky; the children listened to me more than they did to her. With me gone things got out of hand, and she confirmed it by saying, "The children are driving me crazy."

"Well, there's always Leila," I said.

"Yeah, there's always Leila," she repeated crossly.

She was upset but as I put on my chador she asked, "What about lunch? Hold on; let me make a lunch for you."

"I don't want it. I have no appetite, can't keep anything down."

I left the house and headed for Jennatabad. I was lost in thought. I was overjoyed by father's reaction, but it still puzzled me. I began to think about the things he was going through. He wasn't a person to sit by in quiet acceptance, but it seemed to me that he had given up things he was most attached to.

With these thoughts on my mind, I returned to Jennatabad to find the situation was no better than it had been that morning. I was more at ease, though; the pangs were gone. I felt more at home at the body washers', but as I worked I still cried and tried to keep myself from seeing many things. Suddenly, among the bodies that they had sent in

I noticed a familiar face. I was trembling. She was one of our former neighbors, and the bodies of her two children were beside her. I got all choked up and suddenly everything went dark. When they were washing her and preparing the shroud, I heard her husband wailing outside the door, making sounds that would melt the hardest of hearts. I wondered what was going through his mind. He was a young man with a light complexion who had fallen head over heels for this dark-skinned girl. She wasn't pretty or well built—almost a mirror opposite of her husband—but they loved each other passionately and, over the objections of both families, got married. In spite of the fact that the marriage produced two grandchildren, the boy's family remained bitter about it. In the end they forced their son to separate from his wife, but he couldn't stand being away from her and, after a few weeks, returned. This hadn't happened that long ago, and I figured he was probably in agony over the hurt he had caused his wife. When they were handing over the three bodies, I went out of the building with them. The husband threw himself on the corpses and howled with all his being. Then he let them go and began to beat himself and heap dirt on his head, shouting, "God!"

I was moved beyond tears by that scene. I wanted nothing more than to calm him, saying that I understood his pain, but modesty prevented it. I could no longer look at him and quickly went inside. Again I felt dizzy and faint, and was plagued by questions that had no answers. Why? Why did this have to happen? What crime did these people commit?

The sound of Zeynab's voice interrupted my thoughts. "Go to the cabinet and fetch more camphor," she said angrily. Her tone surprised me. From that morning until now the woman never raised her voice to anyone despite the heavy workload. Why she would do so now was puzzling. She was probably dead on her feet, I thought. So I didn't take it to heart, and did what she said, passing by the dead bodies on my way to the cabinet. All of a sudden it was as if there was an electric shock running through me; I jumped back. Once again I saw another familiar face: Effat. We lived on the same block a few years back. Now she was lying on the floor of the body washers' with her one-year-old son in her arms. I heard that she had had a second child recently. She'd been married about eight years, but hadn't conceived. She and her family tried everything: vows, special prayers, and pilgrimages—so that God would favor her with a child, and one year ago it happened. The birth transformed their lives, restoring the thrill to their marriage. Her son was just a toddler when she got pregnant again. Sitting by her body, I saw that her head had been wounded by shrapnel but her body was still intact. Shrapnel had severed the throats of her child and shredded the baby's sides, however. They had brought the pregnant woman and her toddler to the body washers' as a family: a mother with her two children in her arms. The lump in my throat grew as I looked around at all the dead women, asking myself why they had to end up like that. I knew her; she waited seven or so years to have the children by her side. I couldn't take any more and told the workers a little about Effat's life, and they reacted by regularly saying how sorry they were and cursing Saddam. This was too much to bear. When they told me to bring Effat to the slab, I told them I couldn't.

"Tired, so soon?" they asked.

All choked up, I said, "No, it's not that. I knew this one personally. It's hard for me to touch her."

I stormed out of the building. The crowd seemed to have thinned. The remaining people had cried themselves into semi-consciousness over the graves of loved ones in various parts of the cemetery. I was afraid I would see Effat's husband among them. What would I say to him? After years of hoping for a child, to have his wishes come true finally, only to lose everything in one night. I was disgusted with myself, with life, with everything—disgusted with myself for surviving and being a witness to such sights. I walked a bit around the cemetery and saw how many graves had been dug, and the day was not even over. I walked toward the exit, searching the avenue for a change of scenery. I hadn't reached the gate when I saw an old woman, tall and thin, in mourning. Her age was clear from the wrinkles on her face; nevertheless, she seemed to be in good shape. Her temples, the skin around her eyes, under her lower lip, and on her chin was full of bluish tattoos. She was wearing a dark silk shirt with a floral print. On her head was a large silk head cloth tied Arab style, but her forelocks protruded from her head cloth and lay on her shoulders the way Kurds wore them.[1] Strangest of all were the tufts of hair that she had yanked from her skull and wrapped around her fingers. She was moaning softly and reciting a dirge in Kurdish. As she walked she brought her fists over her head, turned them slightly, and than brought them down hard against her bony chest with an audible thud. I heard her saying in Kurdish, "O my darling, I am the living dead because of the infidel." Then she cursed Saddam, hoping for the day when his heart like hers would be ablaze at the sight of a dead child. "What can I say," she continued, "it was God's wisdom to spare me and take my child."

I looked up to the sky and begged God to come to the aid of these people. All the terrorist bombings, the Arab separatist troubles—how long would we have to endure such miseries? Then I comforted myself with what I had heard people saying all that day: Today or tomorrow the army will drive them back. Planes will come and bomb their positions. Once the army gets here, the Iraqis won't dare stay any longer. The Arab troubles will be over very soon and....

Reassured, I returned to the body washers'. Zeynab was busy washing Effat, while Maryam, the heavy smoker, was washing her child. However much I tried to remain indifferent to Effat, I couldn't. Her lips, once red and full, were now bluish and her eyes, which had been bright, were now closed forever. I couldn't stand to watch them unbraid her long hair and ran into the next room, crushed by the sight. It was hard to breathe, and I felt a terrible pain in my throat—as if it had closed. There was an awful weight on my chest, and the last thing I wanted was for somebody to ask me about it. I waited for them to finish with Effat. Out of curiosity I went outside as they handed over the body and, as bad luck would have it, saw her mother and sister. It was astonishing. I knew that they had come from Azna for Effat's pregnancy. Now they wanted to bring her back to the town. Although they didn't know me that well, I didn't want them to see me there, so I hid behind Zeynab. The mother was speaking in their dialect to Ef-

---

[1] With people of various ethnic backgrounds living together in Khuzestan, cultural practices were bound to blend.

fat as though she were still alive. The poor thing had no tears in her eyes, which surprised me until I saw that she wasn't herself. She would beat her head and chest so hard you'd think she wanted to do away with herself. Effat's sister, who was crying, tried to stop her mother from beating herself. I thought I would tell her to cry to make her feel better and did, but she lashed out at me, "Why should I cry? I came here for the public bath of Effat's pregnancy!" Then she said to her daughter, "Go burn some incense for your sister. Why are you crying?" When she laid her head on Effat's belly, I got the impression that she was trying to see whether the baby was alive or not. This tore my insides to pieces. Now, I thought, she'd remember the time when she had Effat in her belly.

It was almost dark when they left. There was no one around to take possession of the nameless bodies that had been prepared for burial. These had been wrapped in canvas and put aside in the hope someone would claim them. Each time they opened the canvas to reveal the faces of the dead, I almost blacked out. As it was late, the person who recorded the particulars of the dead said to Zeynab, "Come and wait for the clergy and people in charge so that we can bury these also." She nodded and went along with them. It bothered me that they were going to bury the poor souls anonymously, without their loved ones knowing where. In addition to these, there were a number of bodies still inside the body washers'. They had names, but there was no telling what had happened to their relatives.

Zeynab returned to find the old and round woman who washed bodies smoking a water pipe and Maryam a cigarette. The rest of her staff was busy with other things. She called me and said, "Come and grab her head." She meant the body of a young girl. I had resisted doing such things. Until this point, I would only lift corpses if they were on stretchers, but now I had to lay my hands on one of them. I looked at the body; she was about my age—the only difference between was my being thin and olive-complexioned, while she was light-skinned and curvy. She was wearing a dark brown blouse and crème colored corduroy pants that suited her quite well. She was obviously very stylish; the color of her head cloth, which was hanging off her head, went with the ensemble. Exhausted from all the work,

Zeynab had little patience for my shilly-shallying and asked brusquely, "What's gotten into you, girl?"

I wanted to say that I couldn't do it, but I was unable. The woman's full-bodied, coifed hair had been singed and her clothes, although chic, were bloody and shredded from all the shrapnel. I bring get myself to lift her, but Zeynab was already bent over the body saying, "Hurry up; it's late."

I had no choice if I wanted to keep working. So I hiked up my chador and, imagining the girl looking at me, said, "Let me take her by the feet."

"What difference does it make?" asked Zeynab.

"No difference. It's just that I'm more comfortable at this end," I said and stood at the girl's feet.

"Up to you, girl," said Zeynab.

Holding the corpse by the legs, it felt for a moment like a bullet shot through my spine and my hair stood on end. All the strength I had drained from my body and I became limp. My heart started racing and seemed as if it was going to burst from my chest. It felt like I had been running for hours; my throat was burning and I couldn't catch my breath. Seeing me like this, Zeynab said, "Get a good grip and say 'Ya Ali,'—that's what we say when we're doing heavy lifting."

I said, "Ya Ali!" and grabbed the girl around her knees and hoisted her up under my arm.

After the last of the unclaimed bodies was washed, the washers went to the one who kept the list and said, "Don't admit any more. We're dead on our feet and we've got homes to go to. We'll take care of the rest tomorrow."

We began to swab the rooms. It was dark inside, and because of the Iraqi planes, we couldn't turn on the lights. Despite the darkness, I was sure that the walls were bloody from the bodies leaning against them. The corpses were charred from the explosions and left traces of smoke on the walls. Still, I couldn't touch them with my hands. Zeynab and Maryam were wearing gloves as they washed the walls, saying if we don't clean off the blood and gore, tomorrow it'll reek in here. I hosed down the floor of the building. Then we washed our hands and feet and left. I was the last helper left in the place. There wasn't a soul outside our building, but there were still a few people standing outside the men's body washers', beating themselves and wailing. One of the women seemed familiar to me. I stepped forward. It was Mrs. Nuri, my elementary school teacher. She was in very bad shape. Her cries were heartbreaking. She was such a happy person. I never saw her without a smile on her face. She always had a good word and joked with her colleagues, but now she was trying to yank off her chador to give full vent to her wailing. I said hello and offered my condolences. She answered me in tears and repeated several times, "God forbid you lose your brother; it's unbearable." Her sisters, especially the younger ones, were even more grief-stricken. When they delivered the body, a roar went through Jennatabad. They brought his corpse along with an unidentified body that Zeynab and Maryam had prepared to the mosque, where the prayer for the dead was recited. Then they went to the cemetery. Since Mrs. Nuri was an acquaintance I greatly respected, I joined in the procession. Zeynab and one or two others buried the unknown corpse. Mrs. Nuri's sisters threw themselves on the grave of their brother. Their mother had fainted, and the father was crying and saying in Kurdish, "Brother, Qeytas. Brother Qeytas."

I knew that Qeytas was their oldest son who had been studying in America. When Mrs. Nuri's father said his name, it made me think that he had returned and was killed. The person who wrote the names of the dead on the placards they put by the graves asked, "The deceased's name?"

I asked Mr. Nuri directly, "Father, what was his name? Qeytas, was it?"

All of a sudden, as if he had been set on fire, the father screamed at me, "Don't say Qeytas. Never, ever, mention that name or I'll kill myself. My Qeytas is dead to us!" I was staggered and began to tremble. "Sorry," I said, "I was mistaken."

Later I asked the family, "The deceased, which son was he?"

"Bizhan," they said, "the last son."

They wrote "Bizhan" on the placard. At first the mother and sisters wouldn't let them put the body into the grave, but they finally relented. His face looked out from the shroud as they lowered him, and his sister, who did not seem much older than the boy, began to screech, “Bury me instead of Bizhan!” This was first time I saw the kind of hole they dug for the graves. It seemed very narrow and dark. The men were getting fed up with the antics of Bizhan’s sisters. I looked into the pretty face of one of them, now contorted with grief. I felt sorry for her and tried to comfort the girl, who was around my age, but she continued to screech and then passed out. Her chador fell off and it was worrying to see her in that state. However much I repeated, “God wouldn’t like this; try to control yourself; your dead brother will be upset; ask God for the patience to bear this,” she wouldn’t listen—she wasn’t even paying attention. After the hole was filled in, they sat around the grave in a circle and mourned with men and women from the family.

After Zeynab and Maryam returned from the burial of the nameless corpse, they said a prayer over Bizhan’s grave and offered their condolences to the Nuri family. Then Zeynab, seeing me struggling with Bizhan’s sister, whispered in my ear, “Don’t you want to go home? They will probably be staying here until midnight. You don’t want to stay that long, do you?”

“I know these people,” I said. “I want to help this girl come to grips with it. You go ahead, I’ll be along soon.”

Zeynab said, “We’ll go then.”

I heard Bizhan’s sister saying to him, “I’m staying with you. I’m not going anywhere. I want to say the prayer that will help you get through the horrors of the grave.” I said to her, “The body washers do that for the dead,” but she wouldn’t listen. In the end the family pried the sisters away from the grave. I helped the young one get up myself and accompanied her to the car. When they all were inside, I returned to Jennatabad.

They were giving the call for the sundown prayer. I walked over to the door for the men’s body washers’, which was right next to where Zeynab worked. Having told Bizhan’s sister that the body washers would say a prayer for the horrors of the grave, I wanted to be sure that was correct. I asked an older man, whom I had seen several times since morning about it. He said, “We don’t have time to say it for each and every one, but when we can, especially if someone makes a point of it, we will say that prayer over their dead. Let's face it; nobody's going to ask these poor souls anything, so what do they need a prayer for the horrors of the grave for?"

I thanked him and was about to leave when I saw Ali Reza, the husband of the dark-skinned woman. I was surprised; he stayed there from morning until now. My heart when out to him; he seemed to have lost all his senses. He would take a few steps and fall to the ground. He would get up, and then walk aimlessly among the graves. He moved without making a sound, as if in a stupor.

I didn't have much time. I went to Zeynab and Maryam's room to say goodbye. They were changing out of their work clothes and talking. Maryam was saying, "Today I didn't even have time to smoke a cigarette they way I would like." That made me laugh, because she sat down to smoke whenever she had the chance. Zeynab answered, "Yeah, I've got a headache; I think it's because I didn't have any tea." Then they spoke about the day's work and how tired they were, both agreeing that they were too tired to stand up. These two carried most of the load that day. The older body washer didn't last; after all with that bulk there was no way she could stay on her feet. She'd take frequent breaks and sit in the corner smoking the water pipe. She went home early with her husband, also a very round person who worked at the men's body washers'.

When Zeynab and Maryam started to talk about their work, I didn't feel right about listening in. I passed by their door and said, "I'm leaving now."

Both of them thanked me. Then Zeynab came to the door and asked, "Are you coming tomorrow?"

"I don't know. Let's see what tomorrow brings."

I said goodbye and headed home. I felt that Zeynab and I, despite the difference in our ages (she was more than twice mine), had formed a bond. We became close and whenever she called out to me she would use the endearing "mother" or "daughter." This showed how kind and sympathetic she was. Maryam was also a fine person, but not in Zeynab's league.

As I walked home, I went over the events of the day. I couldn't stop thinking about these things: Bizhan and his sisters; the body of Effat, the wife of Khoda Rahm; that dark-skinned woman whose husband's name—Ali Reza—was the only thing I knew about her.

I couldn't figure out why the afternoon had been more troubling to me than the morning. It was dark when I got home and it felt like my heart was chock-full of all the troubles of the world. In the morning I was just afraid of what was going on, but in the afternoon fear gave way to something gloomier—depression. I saw several women from the neighborhood in the alley: Mrs. Goruhi, Eskandar the local grocer's wife, etc. I said hello and tried to pass them without a word, but Mrs. Goruhi asked, "How's it going? What's new?"

I had no idea how she knew I was at Jennatabad. "It was a mad house," I said "Very upsetting." Then I added, "By the way, Effat the wife of Khoda Rahm was killed. They also brought her child in."

Mrs. Goruhi immediately bit her hand, showing how much the news upset her. The other women asked her who Effat was. She was about to explain when I begged to be excused; I didn't have the strength to listen.

When I got home, Mansur opened the door for me. I went into the yard. Mother was standing in front of the porch. She seemed exhausted. She answered my greeting sarcastically, "So, you're home. How strange!"

She was obviously exasperated. I answered playfully, "Did you want me to come back?"

She glared at me and disappeared into the kitchen. I sat by the small pool to wash my socks. "What's going on, mother?" I asked.

"What do mean what's going on? You're the one who left me high and dry."

"Where's dad?" I asked.

"After you left, he came straight home. Then he went out again, saying, 'Don't wait up for me; they've sounded the general alarm.'"

When she saw me by the spigot, she said, "Get up. Get up and go to the bathroom."

"I will," I said.

I was dead tired, but I knew that if I didn't listen to her, I'd never hear the end of it. I got up and dragged myself to the bathroom and stood under the shower in my clothes. I looked at my hands, amazed that they had been touching corpses. Although the water was so cold it made me shiver, it was soothing just the same. It lifted my spirits, but I didn't even have the strength to wash. Waiting impatiently for me behind the door, Leila took the clothes. I heard mother say to her, "Don't put these on the clothesline; put them on the fence."

Then I said to myself: Imagine what mother would say if she had seen the situation at the body washers'. As I did the ablution for touching the dead, I thought about the corpses that I had washed that day. The only difference between them and me, it seemed, was that I was washing myself. As I left the bathroom the only thing I wanted to do was collapse on my bed, but I had housework to do so mother would not have an excuse to scold me.

Leila dogged my steps as I went this way and that, bombarding me with questions. She wanted to know what it was like at Jennatabad. I was worn out and didn't feel like talking. We brought out dinner and spread the food cloth on the floor. The children sat around the cloth, behaving badly as they ate. I gave them a look. Although my stomach was rumbling, I didn't touch the food; I had absolutely no appetite. The sight of meat turned my stomach. Mother kept asking, "Why don't you eat? You've been on your feet all day."

I wanted to tell her about the storm raging in my heart, but I made do with a simple, "I'm not hungry." I broke off a lump of bread and went into the yard. I forced it down to make the knot in my stomach go away. I also had a few cups of tea to quench my thirst and pep me up a bit. Then I went to clear the dinner things and spread the bedding. The everyday things like eating and sleeping no longer had any meaning, I thought, in the face of death; life could be lived on a much more basic level. When I was washing the dishes with Leila, she said, "I'm coming with you tomorrow."

"No way," I said. "If you go, mother will be left here all by herself and she'll complain to father. He won't let either of us go then." Then I told her some of the things that I had seen at Jennatabad that day. Mother came in and out of the room, hearing parts of what I said, and cursed Saddam. She said, "This one will never leave us in peace. All our suffering is from him; in Iraq, in Iran—it makes no difference."

When we were finished washing up, I said my prayers and went to bed. I was really tired, but Zeynab wouldn't let me sleep. From the minute I entered the house, she had latched on to me and wouldn't let go, and no matter how many times I told her to go away and sleep, she wouldn't listen. She came into the room and said in her baby voice, "I want to sleep by you." I didn't have the heart to say no. She lay down beside me and I stroked her hair. With her beside me, so innocent and fragile, I didn't want to think any more about Jennatabad, but she asked me, "Where were you?"

"Jennatabad."

"What did you do there?" she asked.

I was at a loss. I paused and said, "There was some work. Now I'm really tired." Then to distract her I asked, "Tell me what you did today?"

"Nothing. I was bored being in the house all day. Mother wouldn't let me go out. She's says it's dangerous. Father was gone also."

"Mother's right. You shouldn't go out. Father wherever he is will be back."

Then I said to myself: It doesn't matter whether she stays in the house or goes out. It's dangerous everywhere. Zeynab forced me to tell her a story. Telling her I was tired and wanted to sleep did no good. Finally I made something up and she left, but Leila, who was next to me, started her questions. She was worse than Zeynab, not satisfied with anything I said, but when she finally relented I was so exhausted I couldn't sleep. When I closed my eyes, the nightmares would start. I saw myself in a grave, and there was someone pulling me down deeper. I tried to resist but I couldn't break free. As I struggled, from not that far away all sorts of strange faces began to threaten me. I tried to climb out of the grave and escape, but my feet were held tight. There was no escape. As those faces got closer, I woke up covered in sweat with my heart beating so hard it was about to burst from my chest. I sent up prayers and thanked the Lord that I had awakened in time; otherwise I would have been done for. I went to sleep again and in my dreams there were all sorts of jumbled scenes that were upsetting. I woke myself up several times that night with my labored breathing. Once I jumped out of bed, hearing mother say to father, "Why don't you talk to that girl? Why don't you stop her from going to Jennatabad." I was very upset thinking it was all over now, but I heard father say, "This is not the time for such talk. We all have to look out for one another. Suppose I don't let her go; then the neighbor will do the same thing. Who would stop the enemy then? They're going to invade any day now, occupy the whole country, and rob us of our dignity. You don't know what depravity these Baathists are capable of. They have no respect for anything: not for a person's good name or religion or faith. Some are worse than wild beasts." I was reassured by what he said.

The last time I woke up that morning there was the call to prayer. Getting out of bed to pray, I asked mother, "About what time did father come in?"

"Late at night."

"Where is he now?" I asked.

"He left when the call to prayer sounded."

I wanted nothing more than to return to bed and sleep until noon, but I had to get cracking if I wanted to go to Jennatabad. Leila also jumped out of bed and the two of us started working like fiends. We prepared breakfast and spread the cloth. I woke the children and Leila folded the bedding. I fed the children some breakfast and poured a glass of tea for myself and ran. I put on some clothes. When mother saw Leila and I were about to leave, she said, "Where to?"

"Jennatabad," we said in unison.

"Both of you? One of you at least should stay and help."

I said, "I can't stay. I told them yesterday I would be back. I promised."

Leila pleaded, "I want to go and help, too."

"We'll try to come back early to help you," I repeated.

Mother was silent. We didn't wait for her to say anything and raced from the door. As we walked toward Jennatabad, I was worried about Leila joining me. She was an emotional girl and was afraid she couldn't take what she saw there. How would it affect her psychologically? If she couldn't do the job, I'd never hear the end of it. I couldn't understand it; the more I described the horrifying scenes at Jennatabad, the more she insisted on coming. There was one explanation: since we were only one year apart and always worked together, she preferred to be with me. Not to do a job helpful to people was the last thing she wanted. This made me feel better about her coming. I said to her, "The moment we arrive, you'll have to get busy, right? Don't dawdle or say I can't do something. Whatever they ask you to do you'll have to do."

The poor thing wanted so badly to come with me she agreed to do whatever they asked.

We reach Jennatabad very quickly. It was the beginning of the day, and the place wasn't crowded. We stood outside the building as the body washers changed into their work clothes. When Zeynab emerged wearing her boots and gloves, I said hello. She smiled and said, "You brought reinforcements?"

"This is Leila, my sister," I said.

"Two young people! God bless you both for coming to help," Zeynab said. She turned to Leila and continued, "Your sister was a big help to us yesterday. She was exhausted." Then we walked toward the body washers'. Before we reached the entrance I saw a number of dead piled up behind the door. Zeynab said, "They brought them from the hospital."

I kept my eye on Leila. As soon as she saw the corpses her eyes went round, and she stared at them nervously, almost in shock. It was as if she realized for the first time what had actually happened—or maybe despite all her questions, she had to see the reality before she could believe it. She now understood the depth of the tragedy. She stood there staring with the same startled expression. Then she looked at me as if to say: You didn't tell me it was going to be like this.

In order to ground her and make the situation seem routine, I said, "Let's visit the grave of Mrs. Nuri's brother." I had told her about him and Bizhan the night before. Mrs. Nuri was Leila's favorite teacher at the Salvar School.

At the gravesite, Leila recited from the Quran and cried. The lump in her throat she had tried to stifle by the entrance to the body washers' burst. Then we got up and returned to the building. Leila, surprised by the number of graves dug in twenty-four hours, said, "Gosh, Zahra, just two days ago this was all wasteland! How did it get filled so fast?"

She was right. Early in 1980 the city announced that Jennatabad was closed, telling people that they would have to bring their dead to a new graveyard near the shrine of Ali, son of Hoseyn, on the road to Shalamcheh. After this announcement, visits to Jennatabad went down a lot. Exceptions to the prohibition were made in the case of martyrs; three of them—Musa Bakhtur, Abbas Ferhan, and Seyyed Jafar Musavi, who were all killed in skirmishes—were buried at Jennatabad. But in the space of two days with so many people killed, the cemetery was packed with new graves.

Although we hadn't been away half an hour, we found the entrance to the body washers' now swarming with people. Unlike the day before, they hadn't bolted the door and we had no trouble entering the building. Leila looked around with a mixture of curiosity and astonishment at the bodies being washed. She seemed transfixed by what she saw and her expression spoke volumes about what she felt. She looked at me as if to say: What am I supposed to do with this? But this didn't last long, and she quickly got down to work. Maybe she remembered what I had told her about not hesitating; nevertheless, she kept her distance from the bodies as I did the day before. She fetched water, cut shrouds, and helped shift the bodies on stretchers. It seemed that she was able to get used to the unfamiliar environment at the body washers' more easily and sooner than I did. My descriptions of the place had probably set the scene for her. My presence was also, no doubt, reassuring. I found that having her there bolstered my confidence that I could do a good job. I knew I had to work even more seriously than I had the day before. Necessity also helped me in this process.

My thoughts were interrupted by the sound of Zeynab, who was calling for me. She said, "Hold the edges of that wound and see if you can make the bleeding stop." When I saw she was referring to a large gash on a woman's side, I panicked and said, "I can't do that. Tell me to do anything else, but I don't have it in me to do that. I'm sorry."

Zeynab folded several pieces of cotton and put them on the wound. She said, “You’ve got to get used to this. You’ll probably have to see worse things. Now put pressure here; maybe it’ll staunch the bleeding.”

I stepped forward with my body all pins and needles in anticipation of touching the cotton. For a moment I felt as if I was trapped in molasses with my brain locked. My stomach turned over and I stood motionless with my hand on the folded cotton. The paralysis, I thought, would last forever. The bloodier the cloth became, the queasier I got. Afraid they’d throw me out of the room in front of Leila, I didn’t dare show any emotion, but deep in my heart I was asking myself: Why did you come here? With everything else that needed to be done, why here? Why here?

I turned around so that the others wouldn’t see how I was feeling, but as luck would have it I saw the bodies of several girls that they had just brought into the building. They had the looks, and I imagined they also had sweet voices. I was angry at myself for thinking these children were delicate, innocent blossoms that would be buried beneath the ground.

Once Zeynab finished her job, she called me over to help tear the clothing off the corpses. This was very difficult. Out of modesty, I didn’t look at the naked bodies. It took all my strength not to react. All my life I was used to seeing people clothed; now I had to cut the clothes off the corpses stacked on the floor. The prayers of the body washers mixed with the moans and cries coming from outside the building.

In the end, it was huge workload that forced me to take the bull by the horns. I went over to one of the corpses. I don’t know what it was that finally made me roll up my sleeves—the sense of shame of seeing the bodies of the children or the fatigue of the body washers or the injustices visited upon the dead. One of the women and I lifted the corpse of a dark-skinned Arab woman about fifty from the floor and put her on the washing bench. I cut off her clothes and got ready to wash the body.

I hesitated before reaching for the soap and the bath mitt. I wasn’t wearing gloves, so I had to handle something that had been in contact with the corpses. This was a tremendous spiritual challenge for me, but I said to myself: You'd better do this now, otherwise there's very little value to your being here. I glanced over at Leila. The well-fed, pampered girl, who always had had her own way in life, now bowed to circumstances and carried out whatever they asked without a peep. Feeling nauseous, I began to wash the body. I thanked God that the bulky old woman was helping me, because I was incapable of washing the head and the hair of the dead. In the middle of it all the water ran out. But that wasn't the worst of it; blood wouldn't stop oozing through the frizzy grey hair of the Arab woman, a problem when there was no water.

They finally managed to rig a hose from a tanker to the body washers' and work continued. The sound of the Arab woman's daughter crying "Mama!" came nonstop from behind the door. They wouldn't let her in, because in the past when some of the family members were present at the washing, they would beg the women washers to be gentle with their relatives.

After finishing the washing, I got a shroud and wrapped the body in it, wondering what I had done to deserve this. How did I come to be doing this? How did I get so hard-hearted that I was now washing corpses? Putting these feelings aside, I got the next corpse and the next and the next.

There were certain things I just wouldn't touch. The fetuses aborted by wave after wave of bombings, for example, had horrible expressions on their tiny faces that scared me out of my wits. I also drew the line at infants and small children; just carrying them ate away at my very being. When it came time to wash little boys and girls, I would merely help the others. There was one six-month-old they had brought from the hospital that broke my heart. They had opened his throat and there was a bandage around his chest. Despite his dark skin he was very cute, quite loveable for his long eyelashes and the curls on his head. When they told me to lift him, I said I couldn't. Putting my hands on his calves, I felt that they were rough; it was clear that he had started crawling. The sound of low-flying jets breaking the sound barrier gave me a start. Everybody stopped working and said a benediction under their breaths. My eyes were still on the infant; he made me think of our own Zeynab, Sa'id, and Hasan. I missed them terribly and worried about what would happen to them. I asked God to watch over them and protect our family. Then there was the sound of explosions and everybody prayed that they hadn't hit the bridge. Because the bridge was our only way out of the city, the Iraqis tried to destroy it. While all this was going on, a woman standing in front of the door shouted, "You're not finished with that child, yet? The father is waiting here to take possession."

Hearing the word "father," I decided I would try to find my father after the attack was over. He had told us that they wanted him to dig graves, so he was undoubtedly in Jennatabad. I waited all morning for a chance to go see him, but it never came. I missed father. Mother wasn't happy about our working in Jennatabad, but I had no worries on that score, because I knew that father backed the decision. Still, I wanted to talk to him to make double sure that mother wouldn't get him to change his mind. I managed to break free from the body washers' around noon. I made my way through the graves to the new section, and my heart skipped a beat when I saw father there. It had been almost a day. He was digging with others with picks and shovels. The closer I got the better I could make out his torso rising above a grave. He was wearing a white shirt with blue stripes and dark pants. I knew that he put his body into the work, but his spirit longed to be at the front. I wanted to run to him but I knew that he wouldn't be pleased if I did this in front of his coworkers. I quickened my pace and, when I got close, said hello. He had his back to me. He looked around and stepped back, saying, "Hi, darling. Are you okay? Where have you been?"

"At the body washers'," I said.

He put his shovel down and climbed out of the grave. I locked my hands around his neck and kissed him. He returned my kisses. I massaged his hands, which were raw and red from digging. I kissed them several times. Father kept saying, "Don't do that. It's bad manners with people looking." Then he asked, "What do you do there?"

"There's a lot to do. Many people have been killed."

"You're not scared?" he asked.

"I was at first but not any more. Even so, every once in a while something comes over me and I don't feel too well."

"These people are like us; we're all human. There's nothing to be afraid of. They used to be alive and now they're even more alive. The only difference is that they have gone on to eternity, while we're still stuck in the temporary world."

"What's troubling you father?" I asked. "Why are you so upset?"

"Why shouldn't I be upset? They're mowing down our youth, massacring our women and children, and instead of fighting they've got us digging graves. I for one am going to the front. They can do to me whatever they want; let them throw me out, those pen-pushers sitting behind their desks ordering us to dig graves."

To calm him I said, "What difference does it make? Work is work—whether you serve in a cemetery or on the battlefield."

"No," he said, "there is a difference, a big difference between someone like me who knows how to use a weapon and one who doesn't. I can do a better job. It's my responsibility to go and fight the Baathist infidels."

I didn't know what to say to this. He knew about all kinds of weapons, light and otherwise. He was the one who taught us how to use a G3 assault rifle and the Colt that Ali had brought back from his time in the army. Even when blindfolded he could dismantle them and put them back together in no time. It seemed that he'd been preparing for this kind of warfare all his life. He would often tell us to work like "partisans."

Some mornings after his usual exercises, he would tie knots in a rope and attach one end to the roof and throw the other end into the yard. He would scamper up the rope to the roof by toeing the knots. Then he would untie the knots and, locking his feet around the rope, slide down to the yard. He would also use a metal porch support to climb up to the roof, then let go and do a drop-and-roll back onto the ground. I was amazed at how multi-talented he was, and, when he saw me watching him admiringly, he said, "Come on, child. You try, too."

"No, I'm afraid," I said.

"I'll spot you."

I declined. I often insisted he tell me where he had learned these things, but no matter how many times I asked, he wouldn't say anything.

No wonder he wasn't satisfied with digging graves. Given the crisis we were facing, how could such a spirited man remain calm?

I gave up trying to sooth him and said, "Dad, with your permission, I'll go now. There's a lot of work."

"Go, darling, goodbye."

I said, "Dad, there's so much work here, I've got to come every day. Sometimes it'll go on for a long time and I'll stay with the others until it's finished. Any objections?"

"No. Now is the time to work. Everybody's got to work. Just try not to be too late so the streets aren't completely deserted by the time you get home."

I said, "Mom's all by herself during the day, and Leila is with me. She might get mad about being alone."

"Try to work out something so your mother won't get that upset being all alone," he said.

That was a relief. I kissed his hands again and said goodbye.

Back inside I noticed they were out of cotton and camphor. Zeynab said, "Go to the office and get some; see a man by the name of Parvizpur."

I left the building. The Jennatabad administrative office was one of three adjoining rooms not far from the body washers'. I knocked on the door and entered the office, where a tall, thin man around thirty-six was sitting behind a desk. He had a fair complexion and was wearing horn-rimmed glasses. There was a large registry in front of him. I had seen him several times before out of the office when he was wearing sunglasses. He was working with another man around his age recording the particulars of the dead given to them by two other men, who were grieving. I stood there waiting for them to finish. As people came in and out of the office, I learned that Parvizpur was the one behind the desk; his colleague was called Salarvand. With his jacket and vest Parvizpur seemed more the teacher type rather than someone in charge of a graveyard.

After the room had cleared, I greeted him and said, "They sent me from the body washers'; Mrs. Rudbari needs more cotton and camphor."

Parvizpur got up from his desk, went to a metal cabinet, and got what I asked for. From that time on, they always sent me to the office for supplies. He knew my father and, after learning I was the daughter of a Seyyed, showed me a lot of respect. Though normally a serious and humorless man, Parvizpur handled my requests with immediate attention. The second or third time I came to the office he asked me to help him with recording the particulars of the females unclaimed by their relatives. Someone waited outside the door while we described these poor souls to him. He took a registry out of the desk drawer and handed it to me, saying, "Write down the particulars of the women without names here and give them to me so I can record the statistics in the main registry." In the body washers' I drew columns in the book and recorded physical descriptions of the dead lying in a corner waiting to be washed: their skin and hair color, approximate ages, whether they were Arab or Persian, height and body types, and occasionally other particulars. I also told the people cutting the clothes from the bodies to pin sample swatches in the book. I thought this might make it easier for their next of kin to identify them. If they found valuables on the body, I would put them in bags and record them in the relevant registry page. The bags were kept in a cabinet. A representative of the courts would come and we would prepare minutes. Then we would hand over the valuables to him.

Sometimes when I was outside the body washers', I noticed that a municipal pickup would come with gravestones and black metal placards, and workers would place them at various spots in the cemetery. Workers would write the names of the dead on the placards with a calligraphy brush and plant them in the ground at the head of the graves. Often, when I couldn't find a city worker, I would write the names myself. When there were no placards, I would write the names on broken pieces of cement that couldn't be used as gravestones. Ordinarily we would run out of placards and stones and the pens by sunset. At that point I had to use a piece of wood for a pen and pieces of cardboard that I stuck in the ground by the grave.

At times I'd get bitter, but remembering father's words made the mood go away. He gave me the energy and courage I needed to help with the corpses. One afternoon Maryam and two other women were lifting the body of a woman off the ground. She was around forty and, although she was wearing a head cloth, her hair was showing. She didn't seem Arab on the surface; her pants were dark with cream-colored designs and she was wearing a black shirt. I folded her arms over her chest. When I raised her head a little, she seemed to sit up, and I noticed that her body was still soft and supple. By contrast the bodies that had been lying around for hours felt stiff like pieces of wood when we hoisted them. Maryam and the two women grabbed the woman by the waist and legs, and, when we tried to lift her and put her on the slab, a horrifying noise echoed through the room, giving everyone a jolt.

The planes had come again, making the windowpanes rattle. The old wooden door of the building vibrated so much it seemed that someone was trying to break in. Maryam and the two women who were bent over the body remained frozen in place, staring at me questioningly. The roar of the airplanes came again and suddenly there was pandemonium in the room. The clothes cutters and the shroud makers all stopped what they were doing. I put the corpse back on the ground and joined Zeynab, who was looking out the window. We both tried to follow the course of the planes in the sky, but no matter how much we crooked our necks, the trees and the cemetery wall got in the way. People outside the building were in an uproar. Women ran from it seeking shelter outside. I went to the door and saw that the crowd had scattered. It was a sight; women and children running around screeching. A person was shouting, "Enemy planes! Take cover!" Another person said, "Don't be afraid; those are our Phantoms. They're bombarding the Iraqis." After a while the sounds died down and, feeling things had returned to normal, we got back to work. I don't know how long it was, but once again there was a sound again, loud enough to split open the sky and shake the building to its foundation. Because the planes hadn't dropped bombs the first time, people were less afraid. The person who had tried to assure the others asked, "Didn't I say that they were ours?"

The other man contradicted him, "No those are Iraqi planes, only they have come to reconnoiter, not to bomb." As soon as he said this there was a terrible explosion and more yelling from the already terror-stricken crowd. Another person tried to calm the crowd by saying that the bombs landed by the bridge and the municipal building; but people, ignoring him, continued to scream. The planes left but the crowd remained as terrified as ever. It was quite a while before they settled down.

By evening I couldn't stay in the building any longer. All of us were exhausted. The body washers grumbled that no one had come to relieve them. "How long," they asked, "must we tear away at these corpses? It's driving us out of our minds."

At other times their bickering would turn ugly, and I looked for any excuse to escape. I didn't want the others to know how little strength I had left. They counted on me; everybody around us said to Leila and me, "I swear, you two have stuck it out really well considering how young you are."

When I heard a man say from behind the door, "Someone come and help me bury this woman; she's been here since morning and nobody's come by," I saw my chance. I said to Zeynab and Maryam, who were busy with the shrouds, "Come let's help bury this body he's talking about. It wouldn't be right for a man to do it."

Maryam, never without a cigarette, didn't have the strength to lift anything. On the other hand, Zeynab, who couldn't wait to get out of the room with its suffocating odor of camphor and blood, nodded and said, "I'm coming as soon as I finish with this." Then we went outside.

The three bodies or so, which we had sent out since morning, lay next to the building. A man had pulled aside the canvas bags to reveal their faces so their loved ones could identify them. The similarity of their faces, and that fact that they had all been found together, made me think they were members of one family. They brought some stretchers and, with the help of some others there, we piled them on the stretchers and brought them to the small mosque at Jennatabad. Hajj Aqa Nuri and another cleric they called Hajj Aqa Sedaqat said the prayer for the dead over them. The large number of corpses forced them to chant the prayer over seven or eight bodies at a time. After the prayers, we carried the corpses to the gravesites. One of the men issued a loud "There-is-no-God-but-Allah," and the rest gave the response. We got to the graves and put the dead on the ground. Zeynab climbed down into one of holes. The women lifted a body by the shroud, which was bloody, to pass it to Zeynab. When I noticed she didn't have the strength to take the body by herself, I got into the grave myself so the men wouldn't touch the corpse. For a moment thoughts of the torments of burial, which I had heard from the time I was a child, flashed through my mind. I thought: There's nothing to fear—it all seems ordinary enough. A person's actions are more important than what happens in the grave. The men untied the straps on the stretcher, and three women passed the body down to Zeynab and me. The weight of the body put so much strain on my back it took my breath away. I didn't waste any time resting the corpse on the bottom of the hole, but there was not enough room for us to position it the way Zeynab wanted: on the right side. So I quickly got out of the grave to make room. Zeynab uncovered the face. The old man in charge of saying prayers for the dead came over and recited two verses from the Quran. The poor man was nearly out of breath there were so many dead. With some of the men helping, I went and dragged over some stones to serve as grave markers. I gave the heavy stones to Zeynab and together we covered the grave.

Despite all our efforts, there were still ten or twelve bodies of women to be buried at sundown, but we were so tired that as soon as one of the body washers declared the workday over, we all agreed to see to them the next day. Everyone it seemed was just waiting for her to call it quits. Leila, who had been working all day without complaining, gave me a look that said she welcomed the end with all her heart.

After they had delivered the last of the unnamed dead, Zeynab told me to burn the clothes we had stripped from the bodies. A large pile of clothing had grown in a corner since noon. I got a wheelbarrow from the garden and shoveled the clothing into it. It wasn't my favorite thing to burn the clothes, so I wheeled them to a barren spot near the prewar graves and dug a half-meter hole in the soft sand there. You couldn't call them clothes really; they had been torn apart by shrapnel and cut from the bodies by us. The pile was not as large as it could have been because the rags were damp. After putting them in the hole I patted them down with the shovel. I put quicklime that I had found in a bag by the building over them and covered the pile with dirt so the wild dogs wouldn't dig them up.

Leila was waiting for me when I returned. We said goodbye to the others and searched and searched for father but couldn't find him. He had told me the day I kissed his hands that he would no longer be coming to Jennatabad; however, I had seen him there working a few times. He probably had gotten fed up and left.

As we were leaving the cemetery, we saw several of his coworkers. They had also knocked off for the day and were about to leave. I said hello and asked about father.

One of them said, "The Seyyed stopped working around noon and left."

Another said, "He was very upset. By noon his patience had run out, it seems."

"Where did he go?" I asked.

"Don't know; maybe to the mayor's."

"So he hasn't been around since noon?" I repeated.

"No."

I walked back to where Leila was standing. I was very worried about father, but I couldn't share my fears with her.

She was in a bad way, almost sullen. I could tell she was tired and hungry. But, more than that, the sight of all those mangled bodies, I was sure, had an emotional effect on a sixteen-year-old girl. It wasn't just seeing the wounds and broken bones; she also had to come to grips with the nakedness, which had to violate her sense of modesty. That had been the most stressful thing for me. Nevertheless, just having her there gave me the strength to handle the emotional strain. As we walked by the houses and lanes of our neighborhood, I tried to get her to talk by saying, "Maybe it'll be our turn tomorrow."

As if not hearing what I said, Leila asked, "So tomorrow it'll be just like that or is it over?" As we got near the house, there was absolute quiet. The people had heeded what the authorities kept saying on the radio about observing the blackout, about sandbagging their windows and covering them with gunnysacks. It was as if there was a pall over the whole quarter; there wasn't a sound to be heard or a light to be seen. Absent also were the people who normally stood around talking in front of their homes. The one or two people we came upon disappeared quickly. We were surprised to find our door open when we got home; normally it was locked. We saw mother in the compound and said hello. She replied cheerfully, "What's happening out there?"

Leila said, "Nothing, just one dead body after another—so many corpses we couldn't bury them all."

"Any news of father?" I asked.

"He stopped by, grabbed some Quran and preaching tapes and left."

"Is he coming back tonight?" I asked.

"I don't know. He didn't say."

"Is there water?" asked Leila. "I want to take a shower."

"There's none in the pipes, but I managed to save some."

I started to laugh. Afraid we would come home sinfully filthy, mother had collected water in some big pots and put a kettle on the kerosene stove so that there would be hot water when we returned. We went to the bathroom. Since there wasn't enough water to wash clothing, she gave us a large towel to put our clothes in. She looked at the things we had taken off with disgust and wrinkled her nose; they smelled of camphor. Then she piled them in a corner of the yard. She said, "Aren't you afraid, girl, they'll take you for a corpse—dressed the way you are?"

"No," I said.

From the moment we entered the compound, I was waiting for mother to restart the why-do-you-have-to-work-at-the-morgue argument, but she remained calm, in a good mood. I thought: father probably had had a word with her.

When we emerged from the bathroom, dinner was ready. We spread the cloth on the floor. Sa'id, Hasan, and Zeynab danced around us. Hasan said he was happy there was no school, but Sa'id, who liked to go, was disappointed and asked me, "When can we go back?"

Not knowing what to say, I took his hand and sat him down on the floor by the cloth.

Dead tired I said my prayers and, without so much as a bite of food, went straight to bed. Leila had gone to the bedroom before me and was stretched out in the dark. Mother asked us to come to dinner several times, but I kept saying I had no appetite. She said nothing after that, even when it came time to clear the dishes and do the washing up. The door to the bedroom was open a crack, and we could hear Hasan, Mansur, and Sa'id playing and teasing one another. I asked Leila, "Did you ever think that one day we would be involved in this kind of work? Can you believe we've become body washers?"

In a dull voice she said, "Zahra, I think that I'm sleeping and this is all a nightmare. You really feel the same, don't you?"

"Yesterday and last night, I did. I felt I wasn't anchored to the ground, floating in space; but today I felt better. I'm more used to it now."

The children's laughter interrupted our conversation. How could people, I wondered, commit such atrocities? Was it just for a stupid patch of ground they were slaughtering others? They didn't care how many they had to sacrifice to reach their goal. I turned to Leila and asked, "You think that they'll bomb our house, too? Can you imagine what would happen if they brought us the bodies of those kids when we're at Jennatabad? I'd go mad."

Leila's eyes, which were closed, suddenly opened wide, and she stared at me in horror. "Why should we think the worst?" I said immediately. "Forget it. God is great." I didn't say more, but those terrible thoughts wouldn't go away, making me toss and turn. My whole body ached. My spine felt like it was about to snap. Because of the severe pains in my back and the fatigue, my legs began to shake. It took a long time for me to get to sleep. The nightmares of last night returned: everywhere I went the dead appeared before me; I tried to not to sink beneath the pool of blood by treading with my hands and feet. "Help, help me!" I shouted. There was no escape. Then the faces of the corpses I had washed kept materializing before me; they were spinning and spinning so fast it made me dizzy.

5

More and More Dead

The third day was extremely busy. The number of dead increased, especially in the residential areas that took direct hits. Most of the dead were women and children, which meant the female body washers would be under even more pressure to finish their work. By contrast, the number of people volunteering to help decreased. Some of the volunteers stayed for a couple of hours and left saying they would return but never did. Of course not everyone was cut out for this kind of work. Even though the municipal tanker trucks came regularly to replenish the water supply, there were shortages. If there had been fewer corpses, we could have made do with the water in the pool, but the supply did not meet the expanded need. This was especially true when the body washers gave the corpses a careful scrubbing. The second time we ran out of water, we called the city for more, but Salarvand said, "The Shatt is under such heavy fire it's impossible to draw water from it."

By noon the situation was desperate. Ambulances kept bringing bodies from the hospitals. Relatives of the dead wrapped their loved ones in blankets or sheets and wailed behind the building. A number of volunteers, who had been riding around the city in pickups, brought in the corpses they had found. They were full of information about what was going on in the city: what neighborhoods were experiencing the heaviest shelling, how far the Iraqi forces had advanced, and where they were at the time. When we asked them how the Iraqi attack progressed so easily despite the heavy resistance, they complained about shortages in manpower and weapons. The sounds of explosions kept coming from places nearby and far away, confirming what the men had been saying. We tried to work even harder. Salarvand furiously wrote numbers on pieces of paper and pinned them to the clothes of the dead, and, after they were brought inside the building, we recorded their particulars in the register. Jennatabad was also running out of graves. The increase in volume of the dead was not only a problem for the women body washers; because of the fighting more men had been killed and there was also a shortage of workers among the men. I couldn't guess how they were managing. Zeynab and Maryam looked exhausted. They had become weak and irritable from lack of sleep. Zeynab said, "Last night the dogs wouldn't even let us sleep. We hardly shut our eyes, afraid they'd go after the corpses or after us. They smelled blood; there was nothing we could do!"

Ordinarily very even-tempered, Zeynab was now short with me when she was kept waiting for something. Her tone of voice changed and she'd bark, "Move, girl! What are you doing?" Or when I hesitated for a moment, shocked by something I saw, she would say sharply, "Don't just stand there; do something!"

She didn't understand that I could no longer cope with the scene in front of me. All I wanted to do was to curl up in a corner, close my eyes, and not think about anything. When this mood came over me, I didn't want anybody to talk to me. I craved silence so I could grapple with my thoughts.

We emerged from the building at one point when there were no Iraqi planes to bury the bodies we had washed that morning. I was aware there were people milling about outside, who might help us and then leave. Leila, Zeynab, and I brought some stretchers, and people took them from us. Saying "heave-ho" and offering prayers, we managed to hoist the bodies, but we had to put the stretchers down a few times before finally reaching the graves. They were so heavy I couldn't straighten my back, and I felt dizzy for a time as things went dark before my eyes.

Two of the people who were big helps to us were an Arabic-speaking boy of about twenty with fine frizzy hair and a thin mustache and an older man named Jaber Jabbarzadeh. The boy, whose name I don't remember, was a straightforward person and a real worker. He did his job without saying a word. He was quick to help support the stretchers or coffins when they brought them. He also carried the gravestones. Once the bodies were in the graves he covered them with dirt, but he would never touch a corpse. He showed up regularly at Jennatabad as long as there was work. Occasionally he would chant when accompanying the dead to the grave. Though he couldn't pronounce some of the words, he chanted enthusiastically. He would substitute "f" for "p" so his cry of "war, war, until victory (*piruzi*)" sounded like "war, war, until fictory."

We went back and forth a number of times until we buried all the corpses. Seeing a gravedigger had stopped using his pick, exhausted by the work, I said to him, "Give it to me."

"This is not a plaything. You can't dig graves," he said.

I got mad and said, "Why not? Is that what you men think? We're weak just because we're women?"

I took the pick from him and started to dig. It wasn't easy. I began to sweat as I drove it into the ground. The man seemed sorry he gave me his pick. He insisted I give it back, but to spite him I finished digging the grave. Later my hands began to hurt and swell up.

It was very warm and the sun was ruthless. It seemed to get stronger with the constant wailing of the bereaved and the dust. I stood over the grave that I had dug and then bent down to see if the hole was the right size. I said to myself: Now that dying is so easy perhaps I'll be in one of these holes one day. Amid the din made by the mourners I made out someone saying, "Water, water."

It was a young boy who had put some ice in a bucket and was serving people cold water. I was about to ask him for some when I saw an old man standing in a grave and telling some people who wanted to bury one of the dead, "No, no. You can't bury him that way." I didn't know what he meant. I continued to look in that direction and saw the old man climb from the grave. He said to one of the men, "Hold this; it's gotten stiff" and he pointed to the bent leg of the corpse. Then he jumped up and landed with all his weight on the corpse, breaking the leg. We could hear it snap like a twig. The dead person's family and the men nearby all went into fits of wailing and moaning. There were also cries of "There's no God but God." I was shaking from head to foot. I couldn't believe what I had just seen. I looked down at my own bent knees and felt pain shoot through them.

One of the women—I don't know how she was related to the deceased—after witnessing this scene began to shriek and beat her chest. Then she scooped up some dirt and poured it over her head and shoulders. She pulled her hair and clawed her cheeks. Then she threw herself to the ground and, like a child, tumbled over, twitching her legs. The poor creature was writhing in agony, unable to stop. Some of the women dragged her aside, poured water over her head, and massaged her shoulders. She didn't come to. I found this scene very disturbing. With the intense heat my nerves were completely frazzled. I asked the boy with the water for a glass. He submerged the glass in the bucket and handed it to me, saying, "Drink and say, 'Praise be to Hoseyn!'"

The water was very cold. I drank it down and gave back the glass. I returned to the body washers' with the scene of the leg breaking and the sound of that crack etched in my memory. I didn't feel well; my chest was on fire. I was on the verge of spitting up the water I had drunk.

I went for more supplies, but Parvizpur said there was nothing left and I'd have to go and get them myself. He got up from his desk and closed the registry, which meant he was leaving. I asked him for a ride home if it wasn't too much trouble. I wanted to see what was happening there, to see if father had come back. I was worried. Parvizpur said, "No problem."

We got into his van and left. It wasn't far. After we turned into our lane, Parvizpur asked me, "Are you going back to Jennatabad?" "Yes," I said. "Why do you ask?" "I'll wait. You do what you have to and I'll take you back." I thanked him and as I got out of the van, I noticed that the neighbors had gathered. Knowing where I had been, my relatives greeted me and said, "It's been a long day for you."

Parvizpur, who knew Uncle Gholami, got out of the van, said hello, and shook hands with him. Then uncle turned to me and said, "You've done us all proud, my sweet. Bravo, my brave niece!" If he only knew the truth. I felt I was about to die from exhaustion or I couldn't bear the horrors another minute; but I didn't say a word.

The women crowded around me and asked, "Seyyed's daughter, what's going on in Jennatabad?"

"Nothing," I said, "it's all wailing and moaning, wall-to-wall calamity and anguish, as the dead keep coming in droves."

Uncle's wife said, "I couldn't hold up for a minute there. I think I'd have a heart attack just setting foot in the place. God, it's great that someone your age is able to cope!"

Naneh Reza also said, "Yeah, you've done us all proud."

What they said came as a surprise to me; I didn't think my working at Jennatabad was all that important to them or that they even knew about it. Not wanting to keep Parvizpur waiting, I excused myself and entered the house. "Any word from father?" was the first thing I asked mother.

Irritated she said, "Nothing. What word!"

Although agitated myself, I told her not to worry.

Then I went quickly to the wardrobe, took off my earrings and gold necklace and put them on a shelf. These were the first pieces of gold jewelry that father had bought for me as a New Year's present. The necklace was my favorite and from the moment he put it around my neck until now I hadn't taken it off. But during the past three days, when I bent down to lift or wash a corpse, it would slip down, which was annoying. Besides, with death all around material things seemed to have lost the meaning they once had for me. How could gold be important when people were losing body and soul? I'd yet to close the door of the wardrobe when I heard mother asking, "Why did you take those things off?"

"They're of no use to me now."

"What that's supposed to mean?" she asked.

I didn't answer. I opened my watchband, but then, thinking I would need my watch, put it on again. I said to her, "Mom, I'm going to spend the night at Jennatabad. Don't worry about me."

"Why? Your father'll be worried?"

I said, "Why should he be? I won't be alone; everybody's there. Besides, father saw what's going on there with his own eyes."

"You know best," she said. "But you'll have to answer to him."

"Okay," I said and left the house. We got into Parvizpur's van and headed for the city social services office. When we pulled up in front of it, Parvizpur said, "You come also." I entered the building with him. He told one of the men to fill our order for bolts of shroud fabric. Then he said, "Wait here until I get back." After ten or fifteen minutes the same man returned carrying the fabric we needed. He put it in a gunnysack and handed it to me. A moment later Parvizpur came back. He lifted the sack and put it in the back of the van, which was already loaded with several big rolls of cotton, a couple of large registries, and a sack labeled "camphor." I realized that during the time he was away, he had gathered all those supplies. We got in the van and went to Jennatabad.

By 4:00 p.m., everybody was so zonked we didn't have the strength to stand; the workload was so heavy there wasn't time for lunch. I felt weak working on an empty stomach, and my hands shook; but it was absolutely impossible for me to think of food at that point. I would get dizzy and everything would go black when I bent down to pick up a corpse. In any case I had no appetite, and even if I had there wasn't any proper food. The body washers scrounged up some biscuits from the rusty armoire and offer them to me, but I refused to eat.

When they insisted, I would pick one up and bring it to my lips, but before I could get it in my mouth, the stench of blood and camphor assaulting my nose made me gag. Then scenes of bodies not only crushed by the force of the explosions but also twisted and mangled, and the sight of people with their eyes gouged out and their throats torn open would appear before my eyes. This was enough to make me fed up with life, robbing me of any desire for food. A few times during the day the old men body washers would come by asking for tea. Maryam would take off her black gloves, the ones that turned my stomach, to fill the kettle and put it on the stove. She poured the boiling water into a teapot, added some tea, and gave it to the men, who were sitting outside the building having a smoke. She also poured some tea for herself into an old jam jar. Although I was dying for a cup, I didn't have the strength to get some. But Maryam insisted I have some tea as a pep-me-up. I tried to refuse, saying that I couldn't drink on an empty stomach. Two days of war had passed and, instead of decreasing, the number of bodies and the frequency of the explosions had increased. This was especially true at Jennatabad, which was near a military base, where there had been heavy shelling. Sitting there with the others, I thought: We cannot go on like this. We're dead on our feet. We have to have replacements, otherwise how are these old men and women going to cope with the growing volume of bodies?

On another front I was curious to know how things were going at the Congregational Mosque. I had heard reports that the mosque was the distribution point for the weapons given to recruits sent to front. But more important than that was to get some idea of how long the war was going to last. Echoing in my mind was what Zeynab had told me about the dogs, their nightly attacks, and her not being able to sleep a wink, having to throw stones at the beasts. I turned to the others and said that I was going to the mosque.

"What for?" asked Zeynab.

"We've got to tell them what's going on here so they can figure something out for us. There's no telling when this thing is going to be over, and we still have no word about replacements. You see what it's like here, don't you? Look at yourself. You're all worn out. We've got to tell them to send in fresh people before one of us dies from exhaustion and we have to bury her."

She said, "Who's going to help with all of this going on? Who's going to listen to you? Nobody's in charge there; who're you going to tell? This is something a man should do, go there and demand new people."

"So how long do we have to wait for the men to act?" I said, "What's wrong with us? We have tongues, don't we? We'll go and say what we have to. Eventually we'll find someone who'll look into what's happening here. The longer it goes on like this, the worse it'll be."

Zeynab didn't say anything. I left the building and, as I was leaving the cemetery, I saw several of father's coworkers. They had knocked off for the day and were about to go. I walked over to them and asked about father. They didn't know anything.

As I was about to leave, one of them said, "I saw the Seyyed this morning. He was with several soldiers from the 106th heading toward the police station. I asked him, 'Seyyed, is everything okay? Where are you off to?' He told me he was going to the front. 'What about your work?' I asked. He said that his work today was to fight the enemy. 'Haven't you heard,' I asked, 'the city declared that anyone who isn't at work will be expelled?' But the Seyyed said, 'The hell with work! With the enemy here, driving us from our homes, the city is going to expel me? My duty is to fight.'"

I was glad to hear father finally had gotten involved in the defense. It bothered me that no one from our family to that point had become a defender. I was sure that had Ali been here, he would have been at the front by now. I secretly wished they would allow me to go.

As I left the cemetery, I noticed a large number of soldiers stretched out, lying by the wall. They seemed thin and worn out. A Chieftain tank was parked a few meters away. Given the circumstances, it made me mad to see these soldiers, some of whom were smoking, just lounging on the ground with nothing to do. I walked over to them and said belligerently, "You should be ashamed of yourselves lolling about here while the enemy is in the city slaughtering people! Don't you see that they want to take the city?"

One of them said, "Fine, but what can we do? There's nobody in command."

Even more put out I barked, "What do mean: What can we do? You're already dead; we should bury you alive! Get up and do something! There may be no one in command, but you still have your pride. At least get on your feet and help us bury the dead."

"Okay, but what do you expect us to do without orders?"

"Why do you have to wait for someone to give you orders?" I said. "Let your conscience do that!"

What I said had some impact; a few of the soldiers rose to their feet and went to the cemetery. Others grumbled, "What are we supposed to do when nobody's in charge?"

As I made my way to the mosque I saw other soldiers in the streets milling about. The city looked totally different; it was now a war zone. Smoke from the fire at the oil refinery in Abadan blackened the sky. Almost every house showed signs of being hit by shrapnel. Some of the houses were reduced to rubble, and most of the shops were closed. The few people I saw looked anxious and upset; some had tears in their eyes. The bloom was off the greenery and flowers on the avenues and the decorative palms lining them. Everything was shrouded in dust and grime. Cooped up in the body washers' these past few days, I had only heard about how the city had changed. How quickly, I thought, did war revealed its ugly and brooding face. People were losing their homes to the war. I consoled myself with the thought that it wouldn't last. As soon as reinforcements arrived, the enemy would be expelled and people would join hands to make the city better than before. I badly wanted to see every part for myself.

From the Ordibehesht Circle I went to the Gate Circle so that I would end up at the entrance to the mosque from Fakhri Razi Avenue. Gate Circle was the center of the city, so to speak, and I was anxious to see what had happened there. It was my favorite part of town, with sidewalks that were lined with Good-for-Nothing Palms with their layered branches and tapered leaves.[1] In the middle of the circle was a relatively large pool ringed by hedges, rose bushes, verbena, and grass. The trees and greenery made the place very beautiful and, when it was very warm, the spray from the fountain in the pool was refreshing. The traffic circle was where several roads and lanes leading to the markets converged. It was, in short, the hub of the city. But now there was no sign of the pre-war hustle and bustle. The stores were all closed and the fountain was dry. The trees and flowers were covered in soot. I looked in the direction of Hafez Avenue and saw the cinema and market complex had taken a direct hit. Singed limbs from the decapitated palms and clumps of earth lay in the middle of the road. The closer I got to the mosque, the more pedestrians and vehicles I saw. All types of people were outside the building: from military personnel to militia and paramilitary youth in trucks. I didn't know whom I should see in the mosque. I noticed the Fakhri Razi-side door was open, and there were a number of people inside standing around a desk and talking in loud voices. There was a young man with frizzy hair and dark skin sitting behind it, talking on a telephone. Every once in a while, he told the people around him to quiet down.

The conversations around the desk continued. Some men were demanding weapons so they could go to the front. Some had weapons on their shoulders and were asking for transport. Several wanted a vehicle so they could ferry wounded back from the front; they said that boys with simple wounds were bleeding to death for lack of

---

[1] Good-for-Nothing was the local name for a kind of umbrella palm that produced inedible fruit.

treatment. One man demanded officials see to devastated parts of the city quickly to prevent water from being cut off.

I walked past these people and entered the central courtyard, looking for someone who would listen to our problems. To my left were some people making Molotov cocktails. Arrayed around them were many types of soap: Yas, Johnson, even the green Borujerdi stuff that must have come from people's homes. Scattered about there were also containers of various sizes and manufacture. Two people were filing down the hard soap and several others were filling the containers with gasoline using a funnel. Near the prayer room were sacks and cartons filled with goods, and next to them stood a tall girl with olive skin. I liked the way she looked, standing there calmly and quietly. She was wearing a blue-purple headscarf held tightly around her face and a navy coat. There were many other women and some children scattered about the courtyard and in the prayer room. Some were squatting in the corners. All the women looked anxious and afraid, as they waited for something bad to happen. A sense of horror was palpable among the adults, but the children were playing as if they didn't have a care in the world. There was a cleric without the traditional robe listening to some old men who apparently had come from the market. As he listened to what they were saying, he appeared to be deep in thought. Mash Mammad, the keeper of the mosque, was forever going up and down the steps to his room, bringing things that they wanted and carrying out chores for them. His face was lined with fatigue from running around so much.

I returned to the desk next to the entrance to the mosque and stood among the people making demands. The young man behind the desk tried to respond politely. After the crowd had thinned out, I approached him and said, "Excuse me. Who am I supposed to talk with here?"

"Talk about what?" he asked.

"About the dead," I said.

"I don't know. Go in the mosque and ask. Eventually you'll find somebody who'll tell you."

"What's going on here?" I said irritably. "Who should I talk to? Give me a name. Or am I just supposed to stand in the middle of the courtyard and shout until someone comes?"

My outburst made him laugh and he asked, "Okay, what's your problem?"

"The dead are lying on the ground in Jennatabad," I said. "We're all alone there. There's no water and we're short of shrouds. Wild dogs are attacking the corpses."

He said, "Now calm down and get control of yourself. I'll call the boys to arrange for them to send people to Jennatabad. Okay?"

I turned without saying another word and went back to Jennatabad. As soon as Zeynab saw me looking riled up, she asked, "What happened?"

"I went there and explained. They said they'd send somebody to help and keep guard."

"I hope to God that's so," she said. Then, when I was about to go back into the building, she added, "Come on, pet, let's bury these poor souls. There's no more water in the tank anyway. Our hands are tied."

We took hold of a stretcher and walked to the graves. As we passed the men's building several people came to help us with the stretchers. Jennatabad was almost deserted; no more than a dozen mourners were there. We got to an empty grave and put the stretcher down. We were about to hoist the body to maneuver it into in the grave, when suddenly we heard the terrifying roar of planes breaking the sound barrier. We desperately scanned the sky overhead and saw two MIGs. Before we knew it they had launched the first series of missiles.

The horrible explosions sounded so close that I thought they had hit Jennatabad. There was total pandemonium. A thick cloud of dust rose into the air. Everybody dove for cover, as shrapnel struck the ground all around us. As soon as I heard the explosion, I let go of the body and dove head first into the grave. As I did, I shouted to Zeynab, "Get down!" As I lay prone in the grave I expected the next round to land by my head, but nothing happened. I looked up to see how Zeynab was, all the while begging the revered Abbas to protect me. Zeynab was huddled on the ground using the corpse for cover. Several of the men, who had also found shelter in the graves, raised their voices in prayers of thanks.

Then the sounds of explosions started to come from the direction of the base, and all of a sudden planes were raking Jennatabad with machine guns. Bullets ploughed the ground about fifty meters from us. I hid my head again. The bullets made a peculiar sound when they burrowed into the earth. I was concerned about Zeynab. Though I found myself plastered to the ground for a few terrifying moments, there was something about the experience I found fascinating. Whatever it was, it only lasted a few seconds. After things had quieted, another thought occurred to me: If I had been hit by one of the shells, the grave where I found cover would have been my eternal resting place. I stayed in it for several minutes to see what it would be like, going over the steps in the burial process in my mind: putting the body on the proper side, face down, laying the gravestone by the head; then darkness and solitude. I was suddenly struck with horror as I reviewed my good and bad deeds and watched scenes of my life pass by. I prayed to God to take me from this world after all my sins had been forgiven—in a state of grace if that what it was—so I wouldn't be terrified when death finally did come.

Zeynab's voice brought me back to life, "Why are you doing down there, girl?"

"I wanted to sample a taste of death," I said. "Shovel some dirt on me so I can see what it's like to be a corpse."

"On your feet. This is no time for jokes."

"So that's it! This one belongs to you and you're evicting me?" I joked.

She laughed and said, "No, the owner is this poor soul. I'm just her representative and only heir." Then she extended her hand and pulled me out of the grave. Fearing that the MIGs would return, we hurriedly buried the body. Then we walked to the place where the shells had landed and noticed that some had hit a few of the graves, while others had ploughed into the ground around them. People had already collected some of the shells and were looking at them in shock and awe. They were big—at least five centimeters. One man joked, "One of these is enough to bring down an elephant. These bastards have come to kill us."

From there we went to the Sabaean cemetery.[2] It was located in an empty lot between Jennatabad and the homes built for educators. There were fifty or sixty cement graves, each a considerable distance from the other. The first round of rockets landed in this cemetery, obliterating the graves there. We didn't stay long.

Toward evening Jennatabad emptied completely. All of us worked so hard we could hardly stand. I couldn't straighten my back. There were still corpses to be buried. The body washers said that it wouldn't be good to bury them in the dense night air.

When I saw that they were stopping for the day, I told Leila to go home.

"You're not coming?" she asked.

"No."

"So why do I have to go, if you're not?"

"I have to stay."

"Fine, I'll stay, too."

"No," I said. I didn't feel she should remain there and go through the hardships of the graveyard at night. During the day, I could see how hard working there was on her, how much pressure she was under from all the running around. The other thing was that mother would be angry with both of us away from home all night.

She got up reluctantly and said goodbye to the women. I accompanied her to Daneshsara Avenue. When we were about to part, I told her to tell mother not to worry about me. I'd be with Zeynab and Maryam.

She nodded and left. I felt terrible sending her away like that. I stood there for a while and, after she had disappeared from view, returned.

As soon as I came back to the cemetery, the evening call to prayer sounded on a radio belonging to one of the old men. I washed for prayer and went into the women body washers' lounge. The room was bare but for faded carpeting on the floor, a metal cabinet for

---

[2] The Sabians are followers of the Prophet Yahya [John the Baptist] and place particular importance on the stars. Because of their religious practices, they generally live near rivers.

clothes, and a couple of blankets. As I looked around, I wondered how we were going to cope with all the work?

It didn't take long for me to regret staying the night. Why, I asked myself, should I stay here? It would have been better to go home and rest. At least I would have gotten a good night's sleep and return energized. Mother also could have slept with peace of mind. But then I consoled myself with the thought that there was a reason for staying. This wasn't such a bad place. If I had gone home, I wouldn't have slept a wink; my mind would have been here. It was definitely God's will that I stay.

I found some consolation in these thoughts, but the scenes of what happened that day began to flash before my eyes. Of all the horrors at the body washers', the things that terrified me the most were the aborted fetuses. They came in weird sizes and shapes, some with their features contorted, as if they had been put in a clothes press. It was said that the shock and terror produced by the explosions and the falling debris caused women to abort. I didn't get around to seeing the dead fetuses until late afternoon, and by that time there were many little bodies wrapped in shrouds and stacked in a corner. In order to clear them away I had to touch them. Though I was run ragged going back and forth between the cemetery and the body washing room, I picked up two of the small corpses. They had become very heavy. The cold from the little things penetrated my body, giving me the shakes. Just the memory that one of them still had its pacifier in its tiny mouth and that the other had dried milk on its lips, made me want to die. But my curiosity wouldn't permit me to do what others would ordinarily have done: leave the corpses unexamined. I looked at their outer clothing and swaddling cloths. From these things I could tell what kind of families they came from, whether they were from the class we called "the oppressed" or whether their parents had some means.

Again I wondered why we, Leila and I of all people, had to face such scenes. It was strange because previously we would faint at the sight of blood and we had no tolerance for seeing even the smallest cut. When father was working as a welder or a builder, his legs would be all cuts and bruises. He'd come home and sit on the porch, asking for us to bring salve and gauze. Even these small wounds so upsetting to us we couldn't look at them. How did things change? It made me dizzy to think about it. I asked God to end this misery as soon as possible and grant me the strength to go on.

While prostrate in prayer, I cried my eyes out. I got up and tried to process my thoughts. I rubbed my eyes to make the tiredness go away, but the faces of the dead still haunted me. Then I heard Zeynab's voice, "Where are you, girl? Get up and join us out here. Stop moping in the dark."

I pulled myself together and went out to sit by the others. In front of them was an old tray with some boiled potatoes on it. Someone brought bread and onions. After an "in-the-name-of-God," they began eating. As she peeled the potatoes, Maryam said, "I wish we had made a stew with the onions."

One old man said, "Dream on, sister."

Another said, "It'd be impossible. Where would we get the cooking grease? Besides there's no stove."

Everyone sat around in the darkness, balling up the bread and onions. When they saw I wasn't joining in, they insisted I eat, but I said I wasn't hungry and thanked them.

That wasn't true. I was famished but couldn't eat. I didn't feel comfortable with these people who had been around cemeteries, washing bodies all their lives. When Zeynab saw that the potatoes were almost gone, she offered to get some skins for me.

I said, "No thanks," but I knew that eventually she would make me eat. So, to stop her from force-feeding me the skins, I picked up a small potato, and peeled and salted it. I shoved it in my mouth and swallowed it without chewing, but it seemed to force open up my throat as it went down and I finally felt like eating. I tore off some bread and ate the rest of the potato with it. I was thinking about what she said, about the wild dogs and whether we would have to confront them. The sound of dogs barking came from far away, conjuring up what we might have to face that night. Again they insisted I eat more, but I wouldn't. They wolfed down the potatoes and bit into the bread they had packed with onion. Then they made tea and offered some to me, but I refused.

As they had their tea, they spoke about their families and some of the strange things they had seen during the past days. It occurred to me that more than any other people, they were able to understand one another because of the type of work they did. It was like they were members of one family.

I listened to them as they hopped from one subject to another. Zeynab said, "I'm not worried—my daughter is with my husband, who took her away from the shelling. If he hadn't, I would have never been able to work here. Whenever I heard a sound, I'd think that it was our house that was bombed."

I knew her daughter. Her name was Maryam, and she was in the habit of pacing on their roof when she had to study for school. I used to see her around regularly and we would greet each other from a distance.

Maryam, the body washer, spoke about her son-in-law, whom she called Yedi. He was a member of the Special Forces, who gave her news about the front. She pointed to her cigarette and said, "God bless him, he also brings me these. I told him to pack up his wife and kids and leave. Yedi insisted that I come, too, but I refused."

Unable to listen to more of this, I got up and began to walk around. Moments later I was joined by Zeynab. It was around 11:00 p.m. and Zeynab kept yawning as we strolled. She was clearly very tired, but kept speaking about her daughter, whom she missed very much.

When we reached the pile of unburied dead, I was sick. My heart went out to them lying there helpless. I wanted to do something, but Zeynab wouldn't let me pursue these thoughts. She asked, "Are you with me?"

"Yeah," I said, but my thoughts were soon back to the dead. When they were born? How happy were their parents when they brought them home? What were their expectations? What did they do to fulfill them? I also had my share of desires; I wanted to restart my education. Ever since the time Ali told me about the deprivation and lack of medical services in the villages, I had redoubled my efforts so I could do something about the poverty.

As the night wore on, the howling of the dogs grew louder. When they got close, I picked up a rock and threw it in their direction. The situation was getting serious. We started to hear the sound of the dogs gnashing their teeth coming from the trees, which meant they were getting ready to attack. I shuddered as I imagined them snapping at my heels. Zeynab started hollering and beating the ground with a stick to frighten them, which didn't make any sense to me because there were so many of them. We could see their eyes flashing in the pitch-black night. We picked up as many stones as we could carry in our chadors, waiting for them to attack. As I left the wooded part of the cemetery, I thought I could feel them behind me. I turned around in horror and saw a pack of sharp-toothed dogs foaming at the mouth, and it scared the life out of me. My legs began to shake and I tried to stay glued to Zeynab. We started to throw stones. Bending down to pick up more stones and then standing upright reminded me of the agony in my back and shoulders from lifting corpses.

The high-pitched whines of the dogs told us some of the stones hit their mark. The pack began to thin out and soon they left. Dead tired, we went back to the changing rooms. I stopped for a moment to look at the dozen or so unidentified bodies we had put in front of the mosque.

I thought: Where are your families now? Are they searching for you?

Zeynab said, "This is exactly why I didn't go home."

We didn't stay there long. I hoped the helpers the young man at the mosque had promised would show up soon. When we got back to the room there was no sign of them, though. Maryam and her colleague were still busy talking. The old man was stretched out listening to BBC radio. The other man was sleeping nearby. Zeynab stopped to chat and I went inside. I stretched out in the enclosure formed by the walls and the metal cabinet and pulled my chador over me. A few minutes later Zeynab asked, "You're not sleeping outside, pet?"

"No," I said and soon Zeynab followed by Maryam entered and lay down on the carpeting. "Why are you sleeping like that?" they asked. "Come here and make yourself comfortable."

"I'm more comfortable this way," I said. The truth was that I didn't want to sleep on that filthy carpeting. Not only was it old and threadbare, it probably hadn't been washed in years. In contrast to the crisp air outside, the atmosphere in the room was heavy and dank. Despite this I closed the wooden door before going to sleep.

"Why did you do that?" asked Maryam. "We'll suffocate."

"For our own peace of mind," I said.

"Who's going to see us in the dark?" she asked.

They made me get up and open the door a crack. I tried to sleep but before I could close my eyes, horrifying noises echoed in my head and I jumped to my feet in a fright. I looked around and realized where I was. I sent up prayers and started to drift into sleep, but a few minutes later I was awake again. Zeynab and Maryam were sound asleep, as if their day hadn't been as dreadful as mine. There was also the old woman sleeping outside and snoring as if she was sawing wood. This, combined with the low gurgle of Maryam, put my nerves on edge. If the nightmares weren't enough to keep me awake, these sounds certainly were.

One time I woke up thinking I couldn't breathe; the thick, clammy air was suffocating. It felt like the walls were crushing me. I got up and went outside, passing the old woman who was sleeping in front of the entrance. I inhaled several times and felt better. Afraid of startling the old woman if she woke and saw me standing there, I went for a walk in the graveyard. It was very dark, and the stars twinkling in the sky did nothing to relieve the gloom. I couldn't see more than five meters ahead. I chanted a few prayers, which calmed me down. I thought: Suppose the Iraqis, or the Hypocrites or some other were to appear. How would I defend myself? There was also the sound of the wild dogs, which seemed to get closer by the minute. I returned to the room and closed the door. It squeaked, waking Zeynab. "Why did you get up?" she asked.

"I woke up suddenly and couldn't get back to sleep."

"Come lie down. You'll go back to sleep."

"I can't. I just can't sleep. I can hear the dogs getting closer. If they attack what are we going to do about the bodies?"

"Do you want to go for a walk?" she asked.

"You can't sleep either?" I asked.

"No."

She got up. Maryam turned over in her sleep and growled, "Go to sleep. Why are you making all that racket?"

Zeynab whispered, "Go back to sleep. This has nothing to do with you." With that she got to her feet. We left the room and began to patrol. It was clear from the sounds that the dogs would soon appear. I looked desperately for something to use to keep them off me, but found nothing. Luckily the sounds seemed to recede in the distance and Zeynab said, "Let's go back."

As we passed the bodies, I said in Arabic, "Peace be upon you, martyrs."

Zeynab, imitating my "classical" Arabic accent responded, "And upon you be peace."

"I was greeting the martyrs," I explained.

"What if one of them answered; what would you do?"

"Nothing," I said, "I'd probably run."

We laughed and went back to the room. Zeynab lay down and said, "Come, you stretch out here and before its morning we'll catch a few winks."

"No, I'll stay where I am." Zeynab was nice and all, but there was no way I was going to lay down on that ratty carpeting where they washed the dead. It didn't take long for Zeynab to fall fast asleep, but I remained awake wrestling with my thoughts. The sounds of explosions, some nearby, some from far away, made the concerns cascade in my mind. To escape them I thought I'd go out again. This time Zeynab didn't see me going.

The graveyard was large but had no gate. It was surrounded by old walls that could be climbed easily. There was an asphalt road extending the length of the body washers' building. Trees had been planted on both sides of the road. The wind whistled through the branches and the leaves, making the place seem menacing in the darkness. Often I used to sleep on the roof of our house to escape the heat, and every time before I went to sleep, I would look up into the sky and stare at the moon and the stars. The silver sheen of the stars stood out against the navy blue sky. Nights in our town were so filled with stars that sometimes I feared the sky would buckle under their weight, sending them crashing to the ground. A poem that Mimi used to recite in her compound came to my mind: "O beautiful moon, did you not see father on the road? With his rifle on his shoulder he went hunting."

I could have used the light of the moon and those stars then, but the clouds deprived me of the sight. I walked toward the unburied bodies. When we were talking earlier that night, Maryam mentioned the wild dogs weren't the only beasts that might feed on the dead. Now that I was here, I wasn't going to let my insomnia go to waste. I didn't want to wake up the next day to find the corpses half-eaten. But my heart was filled with a strange dread. I was afraid that one of the bodies laid out here would suddenly rise. What would I do then? I had heard stories of how some of the dead would show signs of life after being in the morgue for a few hours—in a coma they had been taken to the morgue by mistake. For this reason, it had been ordered that the hospital issue a death certificate before bodies were brought to Jennatabad. It was creepy being out there, alone in the darkness with just those gruesome thoughts.

I listened intently to the sounds around me. As soon as I heard something, I would stop, all ears, trying to figure out what it was. Dogs barked and explosions went off in the distance. The unfamiliar sounds of the wind whistling in the trees gave me a start. I managed with some difficulty to break off a dry branch from a tree to defend myself. I trimmed the leaves and, holding it like a club, felt more secure as I patrolled around the corpses. Although I knew that the bodies had been there for a while, it seemed as if they had been killed not more than an hour ago; there wasn't the slightest hint of an odor.

I looked up at the sky. The moon now appeared. As I walked I had the sense it was moving with me. Then it disappeared behind a cloud and everything was pitch-black again.

At one point as I walked around the dead, it felt like I had stepped on something soft. The hairs on the back of my neck stood up. I didn't dare move or reach down to touch my foot. The sense I had stepped in something slimy got stronger by the minute. I froze but beads of sweat formed on my forehead just the same. I reached down gingerly and felt my foot. When I realized what had happened, a chill when up and down my spine. I was ankle deep in the bowels of a corpse. It was hard to pull my foot out. Unwieldly and lifeless, it seemed like it didn't belong to me. I limped along until I reached a stretch of dirt. I took off my shoe and lay on the ground, which didn't do any good. I took off my sock, but I still couldn't move my foot. I took a handful of dirt and rubbed it on my shoe and foot. Then I went to the entrance of the building and picked up the ewer we used in the toilet. Leaning on a tree, I washed my shoe and sock with dirt and water. I rubbed my shoe and the curb to get rid of the slime. Then I slowly rinsed it with water. The earth beneath my foot became mud, making things even more difficult, but I finally managed to get everything clean. There wasn't that much water but I had to make do with what I had. Then I went back into the room. I was shivering in the cold. My heart was racing so fast it seemed it would burst from my chest. I tried to sleep the bad feeling away, but it was no use; the palpitations wouldn't stop. I couldn't wait for it to be morning to drive the darkness away, and for people to come to free me from the torments of my conscience.

6

Search for Help

I finally fell asleep in the wee hours, only to be awakened by the old man body washer calling us to prayer. It was hard to get up; every bone in my body ached. After prayers, I wished I had been home sleeping; there was no escape here. Zeynab and Maryam were talking. Seeing me crumpled into a ball in the corner trying to snooze, Zeynab said, “My God! You didn’t sleep a wink all night, did you, girl?”

“Not true. I napped,” I said.

“Sleeping sitting up is no way to rest. We were fast asleep, but we still got up woozy, and we want to go back to bed. But you!” Then she turned away and said, “I wish to God they’d say the war’s over, and the Iraqi’s have gone. That way there’d be no more bodies, and we’d know where we stand.” She got up and brought the kerosene lamp outside. I could hear one of the men saying, “The kerosene’s out in this one, and the wick’s burned through. With your permission, I’ll use it without the wick. How are we going to find a wick anyway, the bazaars being what they are? Then there’ll be no tea for anyone.”

The sun was up by the time they had the tea brewing. Zeynab and I spent the intervening time walking in the yard between the building and the mosque, which had no minaret or dome and was used for prayers for the dead. The weather was great, but every breath I took came with a whiff of gunpowder. The shelling, which had gone on all night, continued. It would stop for a half hour and then resume. By now I was used to the explosions. I said, “Night or day, it makes no difference to them.”

Zeynab asked, “What’s gotten into them?”

The walk did wonders for the kinks in my muscles, but my stomach was sticking to my ribs and I felt weak. I sat by a container of water they used for cooking and washed my hands and face. I drank some water and gargled, but I was suddenly sick with a bitter taste in my mouth. I couldn't get up. It felt like my teeth had sunk back into my gums. The muscles in my neck were knotted. To top it off, there was no feeling in my hands.

I got on my feet feeling dazed, as if the ground had collapsed under me and I was falling into an abyss. It was a struggle to walk back to the room.

Breakfast was a few potatoes and pieces of bread left over from the night before. Maryam added some petit beurre biscuits. It was a chore even to get down a few biscuits. I ate them only to stop feeling nauseous, but they actually tasted good and made me feel better.

The male body washers looked at the potatoes and bread and said, "We can't work on empty stomachs. If this is all there is, we won't even be able to stand up."

It occurred to me that I should go to the Congregational Mosque and tell them to do something about the food. If things went on like this, we'd never last. But then I thought: With all the people I saw there, they still hadn't sent anyone to help us. Why should they do anything about rations for the body washers? While it was true that the body washers who stayed out here were probably getting overtime, it was hardly enough considering what they were doing. Besides they were risking their lives. They could have quit and left.

It made me mad to think I had been fooled into thinking that reinforcements would come any minute. I made up my mind to go back after breakfast, and, if that young man tried to feed me a bill of goods again, I'd have it out with him. "I'm going," I announced.

"Where to?" asked Zeynab.

"The mosque."

"To do what?"

"To see what they can do for us," I said.

"Weren't you there yesterday? Have they done anything yet?" she asked.

"They probably forgot. Today I'm going to make sure they'll remember us." I started walking and by the time I got to the mosque my blood was boiling. I was on Ordibehesht when I saw a battered van coming. The driver stopped and said his route took him past the mosque and, if I was also going that way, he'd give me a lift.

I felt so worn out that it made no difference to me the man was a stranger. I thanked him and hopped in the back. Along the way every time he saw a pedestrian the driver would stop and ask if they needed a ride. Two men sat in the front and a woman with a four-year-old sat in the back. Two other men were added, but they got off at the Imam Sadeq mosque; the rest of us were going to the Congregational Mosque.

Despite the chaos I managed to find the same young man. People called him "Ebrahimi." He was in constant motion, talking to this person and that, and whenever the telephone rang he would run to answer it. No matter how busy he was, he was always cordial responding to people's demands. When he returned to the desk and before the phone could ring again, I saw my chance and said, "Hello."

"And hello to you," he said.

"Pardon me but the forces you sent to help us haven't arrived yet. I'm here to find out what happened."

He laughed and said, "Wait a second while I take this call."

I paid no attention to his conversation and looked into the courtyard, which was a mob scene. A number of people were arranging equipment and relief supplies. They put women and the children in the prayer room; the constant moaning and howls were getting on people's nerves. I returned to the desk where the young man was sitting. He put down the receiver and asked, "Well, what can I do for you?"

I sensed that he had forgotten all about me. I said, "Don't you remember? I came here yesterday asking for you to arrange for more people to come to Jennatabad?"

He paused and said, "Jennatabad. Yes. Yes."

"So, where are the fresh forces you promised?"

"Where am I supposed to find them?" he asked.

"Seems like you forgot that I had come yesterday," I said. "You didn't know who I was. You call yourself a serious person! Why did you promise to do something when you knew you couldn't? If you had just told me that yesterday, I would have gone and asked somebody else."

"I'm telling you now; it's not going to happen," he said irritably. "Go ask somebody else."

Angrily I said, "Now, I don't care how but either you dig up some people or you give me some weapons!"

"Really? Did I give you a guarantee or something?" he said.

"Search me," I said, "I didn't guarantee that I'd stay in Jennatabad. I just know it's my duty. By sitting behind that desk, you also should feel a sense of responsibility. So now you've got to do your duty."

"What do you want me to do?"

"Try to do something about the situation at Jennatabad. We need more people. It's not the handful of body washers' fault that they have more work than they know what to do with. During the last several days, they've been working from morning till night without even being able to go home, and nobody feels their pain. We don't have any weapons to defend ourselves against the wild dogs that come around. Now no matter how much I complain about the situation there's nobody here to help me. What happens when the dogs come and attack one of the corpses or takes it away? Then what?"

After I said this, I noticed that a number of people had gathered around. "She's right," they said. "It's a crazy situation. You've got to do something for them. It can't go on...."

The young man was trapped, "I don't doubt what the sister says—but what can I do about it? It's not my job."

"I didn't say it was your job," I said, "but there's a telephone on your desk. Get in touch with someone who can help and describe the situation in Jennatabad to them. Tell them that I'll be back every day to pester you. If you put it that way, they'll be forced to think of something."

"Okay. I'll do it. If all it takes is a telephone call, I'll do it," he said.

"I'm staying here until you do, now," I warned him. "I don't want it to be like yesterday. If you ignore me again, I'll be back to scream my head off until somebody does something."

He laughed and said, "So what else is new? Why should you be any different from the others who come here to shout at me?"

This made me feel sorry for him. After a pause, I said, "God bless you." Then I said goodbye and headed for Jennatabad. I felt miserable; I had high hopes of returning with more people and weapons. I knew that when they saw me coming back empty-handed, Zeynab and the others would say, "Told you so."

Sounds of explosions came from all directions as I walked back to the cemetery. When I got to Ordibehesht Circle, I saw several dogs coming from the slaughterhouse. They began to whimper and run toward me. The noises they made were a mixture of fear and pleading. I realized that they weren't going to attack; they were just looking for shelter amidst all the shelling. They were also, I guessed, hungry; when there was no food for people, who would feed stray dogs?

Still whimpering, they followed me down Ordibehesht Avenue. They seemed to be begging me to take them wherever I was going. Dogs were not unfamiliar to me; I seemed to know what they were thinking. I turned and said, "Why are you following me? Where am I supposed to take you? To Jennatabad? If I did that, the others would just make fun of me, saying, 'Are these the reinforcements you were talking about? We have enough problems with dogs. Get rid of them!'"

I did everything I could to shoo them away several times, but it did no good. They insisted on following me. I wagged my chador at them and pretended to kick them whenever they got close. It was so frustrating I had to laugh. What would someone think if they saw me lunging and feinting like that? I finally gave up and let them follow me. It reminded me of at time the winter before, when we were returning from grandfather's house, passing an empty lot where they were supposed to plant grass. I saw some puppies, not more than a few days old, and kids from the area were throwing rocks at them and kicking them. The poor things were whining and snuggling together trying to escape their tormentors. It was heartbreaking; I wanted to do something, but I knew that father would never let me keep puppies in the house. Besides, we were still at Behruzi's home, and father was by no means on good terms with the engineer's dog. He believed that God's angels would not set foot in a home with a dog, and he'd never change his mind about this. In back of our house was an empty lot, which troublemakers might use to get in through the roof. Father was always warning us to keep on the lookout when we were on the roof. We were always telling him that a dog would solve the problem. The dog, we argued, would bark at any intruder; but he wouldn't budge.

I told Ali about the puppies after I got back home, and at first he was also opposed to the idea of keeping them, but when I described how the neighborhood kids were torturing them, he went out to see for himself. He came back and told me he wanted to keep them too. He told Mansur and me to go and get one. He promised to mollify father. I was so happy that I nearly fainted. Mansur, Leila, and I raced to where the puppies were. There were only two left but the one I wanted, which was white with a few black markings around its eyes, was gone. I asked Mansur and Leila which one they wanted, but just at that moment several boys said, "These are ours."

I said, "These puppies have been here since morning with no one claiming them. Now they're yours? We've come to take them away."

They softened and asked, "Auntie, do you think we could have just one of them?"

"Okay," I said, "take the one you want."

They took one of the yellow puppies and I asked them, "What are you going to do with it?"

"We'll take it home and raise it," they said.

"Don't hit it," I warned. "Be nice to it or you'll feel God's anger."

"No, auntie," they promised, "we won't hurt it."

Mansur wrapped the other puppy in a cloth and picked it up. Then we walked home with big smiles on our faces, but it was just our bad luck that father was standing by the front door. When he saw us, he asked, "Where were you?"

"Just down the way, dad," we said uneasily.

"What were you doing there?" he asked.

We started hemming and hawing. All of a sudden Mansur brought the puppy out from behind his back and said, "Ali said we should go and get this."

Father looked first at Mansur and then at Leila and me and said, "What did you think you were doing, bringing this home?"

We were almost too scared to breathe. "It's not my fault," Mansur said and, pointing at Leila and me, added, "they made me."

Father looked at us again and said, "Bring it here now; let's take a look at this thing."

Mansur raised his hands and the little thing struggled to get out of the cloth. Suddenly father said angrily, "Why did you do that to the defenseless creature?" He looked at the puppy for a moment and continued, "Don't let it run around in the yard; it'll make a mess." I felt a little better after he said that. I got the sense that Ali had already spoken to father and had received his permission—dad was just joking.

Mansur, now happy, said, "What should we do with it?"

"Put it in a box," father said, "so it won't run wild in the yard."

We kept the puppy in a big kerosene tin for several days. Afterwards father and Mohsen made a doghouse on the roof for it. They also made a rope leash so it could only go so far. Father would sometimes untie the leash to let the dog run free on the roof. I brought it its food. The boys found playing with the puppy on the roof so much fun they no longer hung out in the alley. The puppy with its golden coat got bigger, more attractive, and even more energetic by the day. He felt at home and whenever he saw one of us, he would become insufferably adorable and try to rub up against our feet and lick us. We didn't get all that close to him, and with these ground rules we got to know what made the dog Hasan and Mansur named "Jimmy" tick. This is why I felt the dogs following me were just looking for protection.

When I got to Amir Kabir Avenue, the sounds of explosions got worse. They were hitting the areas around Chasbi and Persian Gulf Avenues. When the dogs realized that I was not going to be of any help to them, they scattered to the four winds looking for shelter.

I went straight to the body washers' and noticed Leila had gotten to Jennatabad before me. They had also brought in a number of corpses. Everyone was busy working, and I tried not to be noticed so they wouldn't ask questions. I entered the building feeling tired and depressed. I hoped to God that they wouldn't ask about reinforcements so they could say, "Told you it wasn't going to do any good."

As soon as I said hello they could tell from my expression that I'd come back empty-handed. Maryam asked, "What's new?"

"Nothing," I said. "No change; they made the same promise as yesterday."

Zeynab said, "Lord knows it's a mistake to have any hope from other people. We'll just do what we have to do here and let God take care of the rest."

Seeing I was very glum, she said, "There's no reason for you to get upset about it. You don't have to go there and plead with them. They're the ones who should think of something. After all, it's not as if we're working just for ourselves. Any volunteer is welcome, but even if they don't come, well God be with them also."

Both Maryam and one of the old women agreed with her, but several minutes later when Parvizpur came by, they said, "You'd best be looking for new people; we're dead on our feet."

He said, "I swear we're on it, doing everything we can, but things are such a mess; it's every man for himself. Some of the men have gone to get their families away from the shelling. Others have gone to the front. The rest have to provide backup for them. There's no one left to come here." I was in such a state that I didn't even ask Leila what happened at home the night before. Could it be that mother had said nothing about my absence? Leila also saw I wasn't in the mood to talk. Zeynab and Maryam were talking, but I remained in my shell, wondering what was stopping them from getting this place in order. They must have thought it was the municipality's responsibility. Fighting was the duty of the military. Why should anybody else get involved? Taking care of the wounded was the medics' sole job. So, they probably figured, since everyone had their own work to do, why should they help Jennatabad?

The volume of dead bodies was so great I worked nonstop, which gradually helped my mood. I was still stewing on the inside and tormented spiritually, though. Again there were only a handful of volunteers and, again, our supplies were running out. The last body we washed that morning belonged to a woman fifty plus years old who appeared to be very well preserved. Her hair was in two long braids and her blouse suited her quite well. It was made of a fine fabric with a bright blue background and turquoise colored roses; her pants were navy with tiny gold and crème flowers. It took four of us to hoist her on the bench. There were no wounds on her body. When we were finished the old woman body washer brought a shroud and said, "She's the last one."

The shroud was too small; we had to jam the woman into it. With the sound of the noon call we all broke for prayer. We were standing by the water truck, when I saw Salarvand had brought a lunch consisting of bread, cheese, and watermelon, which he had gotten from the mosque. Walking behind Salarvand was Parvizpur, who announced, "The hospital called. They want to deliver a load of corpses because there's no more room in the morgue."

An hour later a pickup arrived with about fifteen bodies stacked one upon the other, a terrifying sight. They had tried to separate the women from the men, but the bodies had shifted during transport. All were covered in mud and grime and some of the bodies had deep wounds, which meant they had been pulled out from under rubble. Every body cavity and orifice was filled with dirt, even the eyes and mouths. Noticing how shocked I was by what I saw and hearing me sigh, the driver explained, "There were even more, but they sent them to Abadan."

I noticed the corpse of a schoolgirl on top of the pile. She had an elongated body and wore a simple blouse and had a dark scarf around her neck. I reached out and, with the help of the pickup driver, hoisted the girl onto my shoulder. Her ample, radiant hair hung down from her head. It felt like the bones in parts of her body were broken; it was very elastic. I felt sick, and my body shook as I carried her. I managed to put her in a corner and returned to the truck. With Zeynab's help I carried another body inside, but suddenly I had had it. I stayed inside. When Zeynab entered she said to Leila, "Help me carry these so we can empty the place."

She meant the two or three bodies that had remained in one corner. I had the feeling she realized the state I was in and purposely turned to Leila for help. I didn't have the heart to abandon her, so I helped them bring the stretchers and together we loaded the bodies onto them. Leila and I took one stretcher, while some men helped Zeynab. We had to put the stretcher down several times before we reached the graves. My back was breaking, but Leila, who was more muscular, was better able to cope. We were waiting for the old man to say the prayers, when a number of men and women appeared, wanting to take a look at the bodies. They didn't find any of their kin among them, so we covered the faces of the corpses and put them in the graves.

As we returned from the cemetery, I noticed a green jeep with two passengers entering the compound. It pulled up in front of us and the driver, a slim boy, asked, "What should we do with this body?"

"Give us a second," said Zeynab, "and we'll bring a stretcher to take her into the body washers'."

While we waited, I looked in the back of the jeep and saw the body of woman with a black chador over her face. I asked the passenger, who, unlike the driver, was chubby with sparse hair covering his forehead, "Is she a relative?"

"No," he said. "We don't know her."

"Where did you find her?" I asked.

"We were driving up Naqdi Avenue looking for cars that needed a tow. They had hit the area, and we saw the woman lying in a doorway. We asked all around if anybody knew her but didn't get a straight answer. So we brought her here."

From their dark overalls, I guessed they were garage workers. Zeynab came with the stretcher, and we put the corpse on it. The chador fell off revealing that it was the body of young woman. The two men helped us bring the stretcher to the building. We learned their names; the larger one, who showed signs of shaving regularly, was Reza, while the driver, who had a full head of hair, a silky beard and large, piercing eyes, was Khosrow. They took great care in lifting and putting down the stretcher, a sign they were responsible, principled young men. We could appeal to them to help us. More importantly: they had a jeep.

I decided to take the plunge and asked, "With that vehicle of yours it would be a good deed to go around town and pick up dead and wounded."

"Where would we collect them?" asked Khosrow.

"Anywhere that's been hit is where you'll find them."

They looked at each other. "Aren't you going around the city to tow cars anyway? Fine, you can look for bodies as you make your rounds."

They said, "Okay. Let's see how it goes. There are bad problems with gas and spare parts; but we'll do our best."

While I was very happy to have these two helpers, they weren't enough. I went back the Congregational Mosque five or six times asking for more people. I still couldn't get over the shock of stepping on that corpse; it had gotten worse and poisoned my overall attitude. I was less patient with people who promised they were going to help us at Jennatabad. The only way to rid myself of this plague was to go and shout my head off. They'd have to answer me then.

I thought they had forgotten about us, and I had to do whatever it took to get them to take the dead at Jennatabad seriously. Though I was exhausted and my arms and legs ached—even my finger joints were swollen from the strain of lifting the bodies—I still went to the mosque but achieved nothing. My irritability was so bad that I was even ashamed. I realized I kept repeating myself, but I was at a loss. The mosque, I noticed, was now command headquarters, a place where decisions were made, where the food and security needs of terror-stricken people were met. It was the one place to find people with answers: military commanders, mosque board members, city leaders. I didn't know them well, so I spoke to anyone I could find. They would tell me to see so-and-so, to talk to this or that Hajj Aqa. As far as I can remember I spoke to Hajj Aqa Mohammadi and Hajj Aqa Nuri (the Congregational preacher of Khorramshahr), as well as to a Mr. Soleymani and a Mahmud Farrokhi….On occasion I would raise my voice without knowing it. I recall describing the situation at Jennatabad to Hajj Aqa Nuri, who was holding a weapon at the time. I told him we were out of water and shrouds.

"Well," he said, "the situation is desperate. You can bury the bodies without washing them with water and without shrouds. Khorramshahr is a war zone now, and the dead have the status of martyrs on the field of battle. There is no need for washing, and they can be buried in their own clothes. People who touch the corpses are absolved from performing the ablution for the dead."

"There is a way to get water," I replied. "They have trucked it in with a tanker in the past. The only problem is that we don't have enough personnel. You've got to figure out how we can get new people."

"And where am I going to find them?" he asked.

"Well," I said, "if you can't provide us with personnel, at least let me have the weapon you're holding."

He refused, but I wouldn't budge trying to get the weapon any way I could. He got irritated. I got equally angry and said, "God be praised! You have neither forces nor weapons. There's no way I'll allow anything to happen to our dead; I'll protect them with sticks and stones if I have to. Tomorrow it may be your turn to die. Do you really want the dogs to tear your corpse to pieces?"

The same tall girl with dark features that I saw the previous day stepped forward and said, "What's the matter with you? Why are you making such a fuss?"

All at once I was on the verge of tears, but I described the situation at Jennatabad to her. Thinking that I had found a sympathetic face, I poured my heart out to her, as my body went into spasms I was weeping so much.

"Which high school were you in?" she asked sympathetically.

"I didn't go to high school," I said.

"So what made you go to Jennatabad?" she asked.

"They needed me there," I said. Then I asked, "What's your name?"

"Maryam Amjadi. What's yours?"

"Zahra. Seyyedeh Zahra Hoseyni, but on my ID they wrote by mistake Zohreh."

Speaking with Maryam made me feel better. Several other girls gathered around us while we were talking. It appeared that they were a group of well-bred young woman, all of whom became friends while working in the mosque. They were on a first-name basis. Maryam introduced me to them. Sabah Vatankhah was a slender girl with a dark complexion, tall with a unibrow and almond-shaped eyes. She wore a cloak with a floral check print and dark brown and white stripes. Her oversized crème-colored headscarf was fastened tightly under her chin.

Zohreh Farhadi like Sabah was tall and thin; but, unlike the others, very quiet and composed. When she did speak, I thought, she showed considerable strength and personality. She didn't say much not because she was self-effacing but self-reliant. I also met Ra'na Najjar, Elaheh Hejab, Ashraf Farhadi, and Afsaneh Qazizadeh.

They had heard my conversation with Nuri and tried to console me, "Don't get upset; everything will turn out okay. What good does it do to torture yourself? You just keep on doing what you're doing, and good things will happen. Just think how those martyrs you're helping will intercede for you in heaven! Look at us; we're content just to work here. We wish we could be as brave as you."

"What do you do here?" I asked.

"We wait for them to bring in the wounded, and we act as nurses."

Snooping around, I had noticed they had turned the right side of the mosque into a small clinic with a bed, a hospital screen, a small table, a drug cabinet, and a trolley.

"Now, since you don't seem to be busy, why don't we all go to Jennatabad?" I suggested. "There's no end of work there and you could help out."

They were silent for a moment and stared at me. Sabah said, "The truth is I'm afraid. Not exactly afraid, but I think I'd be sick to my stomach if I worked there. That's probably what the other girls are thinking also."

"Why do you say you can't?" I asked. "How do you know unless you try? It was hard for me at first, but I did it and stayed. Why not go and see if you could stick it out?"

Sabah was again very direct, "Why are you trying to strong arm us? We're frightened. Understand?"

"Are you afraid of me now?" I asked.

"No, why should we be?"

"So, if I were to die right now, then you'd be afraid?"

"Yeah."

"That makes no sense," I said. "Alive I can hurt you, but after I'm gone what harm could I do?"

She smiled and said, "But you'd look different; you'd be stone cold and I couldn't go near you."

This annoyed me and I said, "You claim that you've come here to work. So let's go; work is work—it makes no difference if it's here or there. No more excuses."

"But that's so beyond what we can do," said the other girls.

The severe spiritual strain I was under left no room for the normal niceties. I didn't care whether I offended them or not. All I could see were the martyrs lying in piles. That was the reason I was so blunt. I didn't have it in me to return to Jennatabad empty-handed again. Even so, after all the running around and speaking to this person and that, the only people I could convince were a bunch of schoolgirls. I persuaded most of them to come to Jennatabad. Only Maryam Amjadi refused, saying she couldn't abandon the mosque.

She went up the stairs to the second floor of the mosque and stood there. From what I understood, she was in charge of a small arms and ammunition cache, distributing guns and bullets to those who had permits for them. So I set out with Sabah, Zohreh, Afsaneh, and Ashraf Farhadi, a cousin of Zohreh. But it was only Afsaneh who, after all my badgering, agreed to come and help voluntarily.

I asked her, "Aren't you scared?"

She said, "No, we were there to work and we've got to do anything we can."

What she said pleased me, because here was at least one girl who was going to help with all her heart. But when we got to Jennatabad, Ashraf and Zohreh found they just couldn't manage it. Sabah also said to me, "I'm afraid. I guess I'm not as cold-blooded as you."

She went inside the body washers' building to see what had to be done. When Afsaneh entered with me and saw the conditions there, she blanched. Registering her reaction, I said, "Okay, if you're scared, you don't have to touch them."

"No, I will," she said as if under an obligation. Then she rolled up her sleeves and together we dry-washed one of the bodies. After we had finished, she said, "I can't stay. This is no place for me."

I didn't say anything. I couldn't force her to stay. We left the building together, and as we did I saw Zohreh sweeping the room and Sabah arranging some of the supplies. Then all the girls said their prayers. Zohreh turned her sweet and sympathetic face to me and said, "Sister Hoseyni, you were right to raise hell at the mosque. Nobody's really going to come to your rescue. No matter how much you run after this person or that, you'll only be running in circles."

7

MIGs and Dogs

It was late afternoon on the September 26, 1980. I was standing outside the body washers' building with the other girls. Leila had also taken a break and come outside. I introduced her to Sabah, Zohreh, Ashraf, and Afsaneh, telling them that we were sisters. As we exchanged pleasantries, I heard father's voice calling me. I can't describe how happy that made me; not having seen him for two days, I missed him terribly. Noticing my reaction, Leila and the other girls turned and saw him. Leila and I ran toward father. He took me in his arms first, then Leila. He said hello to the other girls, then stood quietly. He seemed very tired. There was a strange sadness in his expression. After Leila and the other girls left, he wasted no time getting to the point, "Zahra, I have a favor to ask you."

I had a bad feeling in the pit of my stomach. "What kind of favor?" I asked uneasily.

He looked down saying nothing. I examined his features. His face was drained of color, which told me he hadn't been sleeping lately. The spark was gone from his eyes, those eyes that always had the look of an innocent victim. This was exactly his expression in the Iraqi state security prison, when he gave mother formal responsibility for the family and asked Ali and me to be good and not to cause her any grief.

I sensed he was searching for the right words. My eyes were fixed on his mouth and I couldn't breathe. I struggled to anticipate what he would to say. Finally he raised his head and looked directly into my eyes. I couldn't bear him staring at me like that and turned away. Then he broke the silence and in a gentle voice said, "Ali is not around and Mohsen, as you know, is not the most capable child. Until Ali comes back from Tehran, I am entrusting the care of the children and your mother to you. I'm going and I might not be back. Anything could happen. I could be killed, taken prisoner, wounded. So I'm going into this with my eyes open. Of course there is always God, but responsibility for the family after me, is yours."

It was impossible for me to take this in, but I saw how calm he was, how determined. He had cut his ties with all that was dear to him; he was ready even to leave us—me!—behind and go. I tried with all my might to keep the intense feelings we had for each other under control. I had to answer him in such a way that would convince him he hadn't made a mistake relying on me. I couldn't dash his hopes, but I had to tell him that we still needed him. It was too soon to leave a seventeen-year-old alone in charge of a family. In our private moments, didn't he tell me that I—apart from mother and grandfather—meant the world to him? How then could he so easily cut his ties with us?

I couldn't breathe; it felt like there was a weight on my chest. The air had suddenly become too thick to take into my lungs. I wanted to relieve myself of all the stress I felt and rail at him: What kind of pledge do you want from me? It's too early for you to saddle me with such a heavy responsibility. Don't ask this of me, at least. But in the end the answer I gave him was personally reassuring and, at the same time, one that would end the conversation sooner than it needed to. "What kind of talk is this? God willing, you'll go and come back without a scratch. We're going to cut those Baathists to ribbons. We can't lose."

In a voice choked with emotion, father said, "We'll always be victorious, my daughter, barring treachery. And with the treachery that's going on there's no turning back. During the past several days I was with the highway patrol, I met soldiers and other military people. They're all running around without any orders. Banisadr won't let the regular military get involved. The traitors have gotten us into this mess."

He emphasized the idea of betrayal by banging his fist on a nearby road sign. I didn't know what to say. A teary film covered my eyes, and a fierce battle was raging in my soul. I didn't want my tears to weaken his resolve, but on the other hand, I wanted to shout with all my being that this wouldn't be the last time I was going to see him.

After a pause, he said, "I've got to go." We walked toward the gate and he took my right hand in his and knitted our fingers. I wanted to keep him there forever but couldn't. As we got closer to the gate he squeezed my hand harder, and I felt I would always be the closest to him. He unhooked his fingers and held me around the waist, which allowed me to rest my head on his chest. I breathed in his smell, making sure it would remain with me always. I also committed all the signs of his love for me to memory: his embrace, the kindness in his voice, the gentle pressure of his hand on mine. I wanted again to say: Don't leave me alone. Why do you want to go at the very time when I need you most? Why are you leaving me with this unbearable burden? My whole being was full of words, recriminations, but not a single sound emerged from my mouth. As we reached the gate, my heart started pounding, and my gut was in an uproar. I wanted to be by his side forever.

Leila saw that he was about to leave and came running. I left his embrace and he took her in his arms. I thought: Poor Leila doesn't suspect how precious these moments are.

I heard him tell her, "Now mind what your sister says. Take care of yourself and try to stay together at all times." Leila stared at father stunned. Her face was strained with the effort to keep her emotions in check, but she couldn't stop the tears. Father hugged her again and with his usual kidding about her chubbiness, said, "Don't cry, my little Chieftain. We will all have to watch out for one another."

Leila calmed down. Father hugged me again. Then he walked away quickly, and, without a backward glance, left the cemetery. I was certain he was now divorced from the real world and everything in it. We stood there watching him go, the father that we adored. Leila asked, "Zahra, why was father speaking that way? What did he mean?"

Choked up, I said, "It was like his last will and testament. We will probably never see him again. He's going to his martyrdom."

Her tears started flowing again. Father's leaving set off waves of emotion in me. I couldn't stand still. All the girls had left, though I had hoped one or two would have stayed.

The sun faded and Jennatabad emptied out, leaving no more than seven or eight of us standing by a graveside. We wanted to bury a boy of ten or twelve. Some earth had spilled into the grave and one of the men was digging it out. The old man who said the prayers, too tired to stand, sat on the loose earth. He was short, around sixty, with a light complexion. He came each morning to Jennatabad, preferring not to spend the night there. He would always take off his shoes and hang up his street clothes and change into a pair of loose-fitting pajamas. He wore a white skull cap and went around the cemetery barefoot. He rolled up the pajama pants so they wouldn't get in the way when he worked. I felt very sorry for him. With his skull cap he reminded me of grandfather. Before all this happened I would regularly visit grandfather's house but it had been several days that I had no word from him.

When the grave was ready, the old man went inside and they passed the body down. As they were uncovering the boy's face and reading the prayer, I went to get two gravestones. The old man said to me, "Give me that stone, my daughter. Be careful, don't throw it" (after he had gotten to know me, he always called me "daughter").

But before he could finish, we heard the sound of jets coming from the south. We all looked in that direction but didn't see anything. Suddenly someone shouted, "There coming from that direction, that direction—behind you!"

The two MIGs were flying faster than sound, so we saw them first and then heard a terrifying roar later. I felt so much pressure on my eardrums, I though they were about to burst from whatever held them in place. The sound went through my heart, causing it to quake, and I didn't know why I couldn't breathe. It was like a violent wind had blown all the air away from my face. The MIGs went by so quickly I couldn't tell anything about their size; the only thing that was apparent was that they were extremely low to the ground. The jets started coming at the beginning of the war, but yesterday, the third day, the bombing intensified. Aware that there was no antiaircraft, the pilots started flying low to the ground. I had heard from military people who were scattered about that the AWACs came to reconnoiter, and the MIG 21s and 23s were Russian fighter planes. They dropped their bombs on the base and in the wasteland between the base and the houses on Abbasabad Lane. The ground shook under my feet. The air was filled with the sounds of the blasts and plumes of dust. We could even hear the sound of glass shattering on Abbasabad Lane. The ugly roar reminded me of what happened during the solar eclipse that happened when I was in school one day. Everything went dark and there was a terrible storm with lashing rain and thunder and lightning that split the sky with a piercing blare. All the children were terrified and most were crying. The MIGs brought back that kind of fear. We all lay flat on the ground with our hands covering our ears, waiting for what would happen next. When I got up to see, someone yelled, "Down, girl! Why are you getting up?"

Out of curiosity I couldn't help following the flight of the MIGs as I sat there. After dropping their bombs, they returned to where we were, this time hitting the area near the Police Station. There was a thick cloud of black smoke rising over part of the city. Clearly they had hit some of the garages in Dieselabad. The sounds of explosions also came from Farmandari Circle, which certainly meant that they were going after the bridge. Everything was happening very fast, but, as I sat there, it seemed to take ages. The MIGs circled in the sky several times and then headed for Shalamcheh. I was worried that if they bombed Jennatabad, they would destroy the graves, making it impossible to sort out the remains afterwards. When I was certain they had gone, we got up and went on with our work. One of the men cursed, "Goddamn the lot of you, you heathen Baathists! May you and your whole generation be wiped off the earth! You've murdered everyone dear to me, and now you've no mercy for their graves! What the hell have we done that you don't even let our dead rest in peace?" Another said consolingly, "If our Phantoms had been flying, they wouldn't have had the nerve to do what they did."

The men continued burying the dead. As there were no female corpses, I went to fetch the wheelbarrow beside the building. I managed to put several gravestones in it and wheel them away. The terrain in Jennatabad was uneven, which made handling the wheelbarrow difficult. It would hit a hole and lurch to one side, causing me to cry out. I had to bend over and put so much into wheeling it over the bumpy ground I couldn't straighten my back when I reached the graves. The gravestones were cement slabs about 40 x 65 centimeters.

The men said, "Don't bother with the stones. They're too heavy; you can't lift them."

"Yes I can," I said defiantly.

As I struggled with the wheelbarrow, I saw a young man rapidly photographing the empty graves and the bodies beside them. He seemed out of place in those grim surroundings, too clean-cut and stylish. He was wearing jeans and a tee shirt, and his hair was combed over his shoulders. He was in constant motion, bending down, standing upright, and, at times, kneeling as he fiddled with his camera. He even went into the graves. One of the men asked, "What are you doing?"

"I'm taking pictures of the dead," he said.

"What for?" asked the man.

"No reason. I'm a photographer and I've come to take photos of the martyrs at Jennatabad."[1]

"What do you want the pictures for?" I asked joining the conversation.

"For an exhibition," he said. "For posterity, so history won't be forgotten. When future generations see them, they will know what happened here. There are pictures, for example, from World War II that tell people what it was like during that time."

I felt what he was saying did not go with how he looked. Suddenly it occurred to me: Maybe he could take pictures of the unidentified bodies. I placed the wheelbarrow by the grave and then approached him. He was thoroughly involved in taking pictures. I said, "Listen. We have a number of bodies here that haven't been claimed by family members. We are burying them as 'unknowns.' It might be a good idea for you to photograph them so that later on we could show the pictures to people looking for their loved ones."

"Okay, but even if you show them the pictures, they still won't know where their dead are buried."

---

[1] According to Parvizpur, his name was Mojtahedi.

I said, "We thought of that. We have recorded their particulars and noted the locations of the graves. But it would be much better if we had pictures. Come with me and we'll tell Parvizpur about it?"

He nodded and we headed for the office. When Parvizpur saw the photographer, he asked him, "Did you take your pictures?"

"Yes."

"Would it be a good idea for him to take pictures of our unknowns, Mr. Parvizpur?" I asked.

"That's just what I was speaking to Salarvand and the others about," he said.

"We can record their particulars and paste their pictures in the register next to them," I suggested.

"Can I see this register?" asked the young man.

"Sure, come in," said Parvizpur.

We entered the room and Parvizpur took out from the drawer the little, twenty-page notebook with the plastic green cover and showed it to him. The young man paged through the notebook, which was almost one-third full, and said, "This is fine, but it would have been better if it were bigger so we could record the particulars of the dead and paste in their pictures."

As soon as the photographer got to work, Parvizpur divided a larger register into categories written across the top of the page: gender, age, distinguishing marks. We also were to make educated guesses about the ethnicity of the deceased from the type of clothing they wore, their features, the neighborhoods where they were found. We put a swatch of clothing next to the names, along with a photograph of the unclaimed body. They put the register in the room. For every unknown female, Leila or I would record their vitals. The photographer, who waited outside the door of the body washer room, would take the picture. Sometimes the dead were so disfigured it was impossible to tell the gender.

The photographer was to provide prints two days after taking the photographs.

After he left, I returned to my work washing bodies. By sundown I had run out of steam. Without telling anybody, I left and headed for home, wanting to know if father was still there. The streets were deserted; it seemed everybody had fled the city. Just as mother opened the door, the Iraqi batteries started up again, shelling mercilessly.

Though I hadn't seen mother since noon the day before, as soon as she opened the door, I asked without so much as a hello, "Mom, you're still here?"

Seeing me, her face lit up and she said, "Where have you been? I can't tell you what I've been through waiting here for you to come home." Then she looked around and asked, "Where's Leila?"

I said, "Don't worry. Leila is still at Jennatabad." Then I asked, "So why didn't you leave? Why are you still here?"

"Where am I supposed to go?" she grumbled. "This is home."

"Mom, it's not good for you to stay here. Go to the Congregational Mosque. Everybody's gathered there. It's not just the bombs and the tanks; the neighborhood has emptied out, and there are Fifth Column elements and Hypocrites around, and they are more dangerous than the Iraqis. Why inflict this on the children? What have they done to deserve it?"

She gave me such a murderous look I didn't dare argue further with her. I asked, "Any news of grandfather and them?"

She said, "Uncle Hoseyni came in the morning saying he had told grandfather and Mimi to get ready. He's going to come for them and take everybody to Khorramabad, to his wife's family's home. Uncle Nad Ali is also taking his family to Sar Bandar."

I took the opportunity to continue the conversation about leaving. "So what did you say to him? I wish you had gone with Uncle Hoseyni with the children."

She said, "He kept insisting that I go, but how could I? I told him that Ali was not around. Suppose he comes all the way from Tehran and sees the house empty? He'll run around frantically trying to find us. My older girls are also never here and their father has gone off to war."

"Father came home?" I asked.

"He came in the afternoon to say goodbye. He took his prayer cloth and left." Her voice cracked when she spoke about father. She went on, "Your father didn't tell you to tell me to go. We have to know what's going to happen to us. With all of these kids, where am I supposed to go?"

I pointed to Mansur, Hasan, Sa'id, and Zeynab, who had gathered around us as we were speaking, and said, "I'm begging you, Mom, for our sakes, go to the mosque. Don't make us worry so much. I'm not saying you have to go to Khorramabad; just go somewhere safer."

She said, "Nowhere is safe. The way it's going now, you can't tell what's going to happen. It makes no difference whether we go or stay. My heart tells me something bad is going to happen, Zahra."

I comforted her and said to the children, "Don't upset mother. Don't leave the house either. The block's totally empty." Sullen and withdrawn, they didn't say anything in response. I turned and looked in the corner of the yard where the sheep and a goat, which were bought for Moharram, had been. It was empty. I asked mother, "Why aren't the sheep there?"

"Your father brought them to the mosque. He also said they'd be around later for rice and cooking oil to prepare food for the troops."

For two years now we had been holding recitals of the mourning for Imam Hoseyn during the beginning of Moharram. On the ninth and the tenth we would host the sheep sacrifice. Father believed that the animals had to be fed pure grain before they were slaughtered to produce the best meat in honor of the Imam. Anything, he said, dedicated in the name of the Holy Imams had to be of the utmost purity. He would buy the sheep several months before Moharram and fatten them or he would have them brought from Elam. He bought our home based on this vow; every year before the advent of Moharram he would drape it in black to prepare for the recitals, which were very well attended. So many people piled into our living room that there was scarcely enough space to turn around. The recitalist was Alawiyeh, who had studied in the Religious Studies Center in Qom. After her recital we served cinnamon tea or cake or halva.

I spoke and spoke to mother until I finally convinced her to go. Once I was certain she wouldn't remain there, I left. As I walked away, I reviewed her features in my mind; she had gotten very thin and pale. The woman who always seemed steadfast and calm was now showing signs of anxiety and fear.

I found myself in front of the Congregational Mosque. As soon as Ebrahimi saw me, he said, "God help us, look who's here: the cyclone has come to clean out the cobwebs around here!"

"If you saw the situation there," I objected, "you wouldn't say such things. The only reason why I'm running around like this is to get some results."

He said, "Why don't you see Jahan Ara himself and explain what's going on? He's the commander. If there's a way, he won't disappoint you."

"Where do I find him?" I asked.

"Don't know really. At the war room, the mayor's, the mosque, at the front—he's everywhere."

"What an answer! I can't spend my whole life chasing him."

From the way he averted his eyes, it was clear he had reached the end of his rope. Then he pointed and said, "Go ask those brothers over there," indicating several Revolutionary Guards standing in the courtyard of the mosque, apparently waiting around for someone or something. The whole time I was there, they had been coming and going in and out of the courtyard and talking to people.

As if he had just found the key to getting rid of me, Ebrahimi now called out to them saying, "I beg you, guys, please come over here and see what the sister wants."

They walked over to us and, after exchanging greetings, asked, "What happened? What's the matter?"

I said, "I don't know whether you can help or not, but I don't think you know how things have been at Jennatabad during these last few days. The dead are stacked up like firewood, and there's no one to help shroud and bury them. It's way beyond what the old body washers can do, and no matter how many times I come here begging them to help us, it doesn't do any good. It's true that Jennatabad is a cemetery, but that doesn't make it any less of a military issue. The war is the reason why things are the way they are there. It is precisely why the dead are piling up. It wouldn't be right to leave them in that state."

The young guards looked at one another; clearly what I said had had an effect. One of them said, "Yeah, I saw what it's like there. It's really bad."

"We've got to tell brother Jahan Ara," said another.

"Can I be sure you'll tell him?" I asked. I wondered how I could be so calm given the lump in my throat and my anger. One of them said, "Give us a chance and maybe we can find Mammad. You can update him."

Then they all went over to Ebrahimi's desk. One of them took the receiver and dialed the phone. For a moment fear gripped me. This was more than embarrassing. I had heard many things about Jahan Ara from Ali and others. To them he had a special presence and dignity. I prayed he wouldn't act gruff because he was forced to keep up a military bearing or that he wouldn't be in a foul mood because of the difficult conditions. The last thing I wanted was to have him bark at me, "What am I supposed to do about it?"

As I struggled to keep my emotions in check, the young soldier was calling everywhere he could, trying to reach Commander Jahan Ara. After several failed attempts and being told to hold, he said, "Thank God. I found him."

When Jahan Ara came on the line, the young guard explained a little about the situation at Jennatabad. Then he said, "There's a sister here who needs to speak with you herself."

I nervously took the receiver, praying to God I would be able to explain things so well he would react with good grace. Unable to mask the fear in my voice, I sheepishly said hello and continued, "My name is Hoseyni, sister of Seyyed Ali Hoseyni."

He returned my greeting and said amiably, "We miss Ali a lot; he's a real man. It would be a big help to have him here now—both as a tactician and a man of action. He could do many things. He's a strong and brave boy. I pray that he gets well soon and can be with us again." Then he asked, "What's going on at Jennatabad? What problems have come up?"

Assured by what Ali had told me about Jahan Ara, I felt confident telling him the truth. "There are very few of us working in Jennatabad. We can't bury all the bodies. At night the dogs attack them and we have to throw stones to keep them at bay. Even though Jennatabad is not secure, we feel it's our responsibility to stay there through the night protecting the dead. We have no weapons or any other thing to keep the dogs away. There aren't even any guards to protect us."

"How many people total?" he asked.

"Five women and two men," I said.

"You mean that's all you have? Without any guards, without weapons?" he said in disbelief.

"Yes," I said.

His tone changed and obviously put out he said, "God willing you'll be rewarded by the martyrs and the Prince of Martyrs. I will definitely follow up on this. Something's got to be done about the water and the shrouds, too."

I thanked him and said, "You are my only hope."

"I'll follow up on it, and you've accomplished your first goal, which was telling me about it."

I said goodbye and put down the receiver. The young guards asked, "What happened? You got your answer, we hope?"

"Yeah, he's going look into it, and the situation there will be put right."

Ebrahimi, who was listening the whole time, put his hands together in mock prayer and said laughingly, "Thank God! Praise the Lord! Jennatabad's going to be right as rain."

I couldn't help laughing; the poor guy was really fed up with me. I said to the guards, "If it's not too much trouble, could you give me brother Jahan Ara's number? He said himself that I should monitor what's being done."

They wrote the number on a piece of paper and handed it to me, and I felt relieved. I left the mosque, but before I stepped into the street I saw a young woman shrieking. Several older men in charge of affairs at the mosque were insisting that she return. It was late, and she had no business being outside. She was clearly a refugee and they wanted to keep her safe in the mosque, but she seemed a little simple-minded and refused to go inside. The men were at a loss as to how to communicate with her; they tried Persian mixed with a sprinkling of Arabic words, but they apparently did not know the language. The girl, no doubt in a bad way, began to swear.

I stared at her in amazement; she was a very odd creature of around thirty in horrible physical shape. Her emaciated face was filled with large, festering pockmarks. Her eyes, barely open, made me think at first she was blind.

As I stared at her, I heard Ebrahimi saying, "Sister Hoseyni, before you go, would you get her to come in?"

"Who is she?" I asked.

"Some poor thing with a screw loose. She's been giving us hell since morning. She doesn't understand what we say to her. She just screeches, not listening to a word we're saying. She walks around aimlessly and then returns to the mosque. I can't make up my mind whether she's really crazy or pretending to be. Farsi is not one of her strengths."

I nodded and walked over to the young woman, thinking that by talking to her I could calm her. As soon as I said, "Come, let's go to the mosque," she clawed my face.

I pulled back saying, "Why did you do that? I'm talking to you."

When she began to curse in Arabic, I shouted, "Shut your filthy mouth!"

This frightened her and she said in Arabic, "That wasn't meant for you."

"Who was it for?" I asked.

"For them," she said pointing at the men.

"They're not around. They're over there," I said.

"It wasn't meant for you," she repeated.

I heard the men calling her Genoa, so I said, "Genoa, why are you behaving like that? Why do you want to leave the mosque?"

"They're bothering me," she said.

"No, they're good people. The street's not safe; that's why they want you in the mosque. They'll get you with a fifty-five caliber machine gun if you're not careful!"

"My house is on the border," she said in Arabic. "I want to go home."

"The Iraqis are there now. They've crossed the border," I said.

"I'm not afraid of the Iraqis; they'll leave me alone."

I said, "So they're harmless like first cousins on your father's side, then? Believe me, if they see you, they'll shoot."

In that strange voice she said, "No, Saddam is one of us. He won't kill Arabs."

I nearly had a fit. Saddam's propaganda, I said to myself, had even reached this sick woman. Baathist radio was continually encouraging people—especially the Arabs—to leave the city or to flee in the direction of their army, enticing them with offers of hospitality. They claimed that the Arabs of Iran were on their side; they were brothers. It was only the Khomeini regime that they were fighting.

I didn't say anything as I mulled over what she said. She stared at me, then suddenly as if remembering something, asked, "Who's your father?"

I laughed saying, "If I tell you his name, will you know him?"

Ignoring me, she asked, "Aren't you the daughter of Hajj Khalaf?"

"I'm the daughter of Hajj Salbookh," I said mockingly. I had heard the name mentioned in satire. It meant rough terrain full of gravel and sand, but we kids would always call each other Salbookh as a joke.

"I don't know any Hajj Salbookh, girl," she said mystified.

I laughed and gave her a hug. With my skin prickling from being close to her, I said, "Come let's go into the mosque."

Even under her loose-fitting shirt I felt the boils on Genoa's skin, how uneven it was, and nearly threw up. What puzzled me was why, in addition to her scary looks, was she so grubby and foul smelling? When was the last time she bathed? Had water even touched her skin? Her bare feet were cracked and calloused, and her matted hair, which looked like sackcloth, had escaped from her head cloth. The most disgusting thing was that lice had the run of her forehead. I got more nauseous when I noticed them.

She was disgusting but I felt obligated to bring her into the mosque. It was worth wading through her mire if only to get her to talk. Genoa liked the show of affection and hugged me tighter. I didn't pull back even though I couldn't stand the odors coming from her. She said in Arabic, "I love you so much, my dearest."

"Enough." I said "Promise me you'll stay in the mosque. Why do you want to leave anyway?"

"I'm hungry," she said simply.

"There's food and water here. You don't need to go outside," I said.

"Who should I tell that I want food?" she asked.

"It doesn't matter. They'll feed you whoever you tell. They'll give you biscuits."

Then she suddenly went off on a tangent and said, "I want cake."

This made me laugh "Where are they going to find cake in all of this? What's wrong with you? Did you think there's a wedding going on here? We're under fire now. There's a war on, understand? What do you mean *cake*?"

She shrugged like a little girl and said, "What am I supposed to do? I want cake."

She was driving me mad, and I was at the point of leaving her on her own, when someone brought a package of petite beurre biscuits and offered them to her. As soon as she opened them, she began to noodle around on the ground. I said, "See! They've got everything here. Don't go out. There are other women here, and they don't wander around outside. Just tell them whatever you want."

Absorbed in eating, she didn't register what I said.

I left the mosque and headed for Jennatabad with my mind on the conversation with Jahan Ara and Genoa's antics. I hadn't reached the avenue when I heard someone behind me calling, "Sister, sister."

I stopped and turned around. Two boys thin as rails were coming toward me. One of the boys, taller and darker than the other, had an M1 rifle slung over his shoulder. They had been at the mosque when I was speaking to Ebrahimi. When I had raised my voice, I noticed they had come nearer to hear what we were arguing about. They said hello and one of them asked, "Do you need people at Jennatabad?"

"Yeah," I said.

"We're ready to help," they said.

I looked at them and wondered: How could these two runts help move heavy bodies around? They seemed so young. How could they be expected not to run away when they saw the corpses? Many older and heftier men couldn't stand the sight and left without so much as a backward glance. Then I had second thoughts and scolded myself: Not so fast, girl! Don't pretend you didn't faint the first time you were in Jennatabad. What makes you think that you're any better than these two? How do you know they're not strong? At least they're males and have more tolerance for that type of thing than females. Finally I said to them, "The work there is very tough. You've got to wash the bodies and then shroud them. You've also got to carry the bodies to the graves. If you think you've got the stomach for it, more power to you."

The boy with the M1 said, "But you were saying that you need armed people for guard duty."

"Yeah, that's right."

"Fine, so we'll be guards, and, if we're able, we'll help with the other things, too."

"That'll be a big help, thanks. Can you come now?" I asked.

"Yeah," they said.

In order to put Ebrahimi's mind at rest, I said to them, "So let's go back to the mosque. I'll tell them you're going to Jennatabad."

We went back to find Ebrahimi again. As usual he was busy talking to many people, answering the phone, and just smiling when people like me started brow-beating and yelling at him. Once in a while he would lose his temper, but this didn't last long and he became calm again. What a patient man, I said to myself.

I managed to make my voice heard over the uproar. I said I thought I should tell him about the two boys. But, I added, that this didn't mean that he should give up on sending more people to Jennatabad.

He said, "Don't worry; I'll do my best to make sure they look into it."

As we were walking back to Jennatabad, the boys asked me questions about the conditions there. I gave them a complete rundown. They got very upset when I told them that the bodies were piling up with nobody to wash them. They said, "If we had known, we would have come earlier. We've been sitting around in the mosque the past days with little to do. We were getting bored—wish we'd known about Jennatabad."

Then they asked, "You're sister Hoseyni, aren't you?"

"Yeah, so?" I asked in surprise.

"We've heard your name a lot."

I didn't ask how my name had come up, but I guessed that because of all my visits to the mosque and the shouting, I had become the talk of the town. Seeing that they knew my name, I decided to ask theirs. The shorter one said, "I'm Abdollah Moavi; my brother, Hasan, is in the army."

The other one said, "My name is Hoseyn Eidi."

He looked familiar. I wondered where I had seen Hoseyn Eidi before.

Finally I said, "Your face is familiar, but I can't remember where I've seen you."

He got all bashful and said, "Our house is on Mina Avenue across from the bakery."

Then I remembered. He was one of the kids in the neighborhood who was now all grown up.

"Are you the same Hoseyn that the kids used to call 'black frizz-head'?" I asked.

He laughed and said, "Yeah, that's me."

The closer we got to Jennatabad, the more anxious I became. I hoped the workers there wouldn't have the same doubts as I about the two kids' ability to stick it out and say, "So this is what you meant by fresh forces, huh?" Thank God that didn't happen. Everybody greeted the two boys warmly, which made me happy. I said, "You want to help? Go to the place where they wash the men."

The poor things. They wanted to be guards, but they went to the body washers' without a peep. Zeynab and I along with two of the men grabbed a stretcher with a corpse. The body was very heavy, and carrying it strained my back. I had to rest after we returned from the grave. Then I saw a girl coming toward me, a girl that I had seen at the mosque that afternoon; she had been sitting on some boxes stacked by a wall. She said, "Come here, sister."

Puzzled, I asked, "Are you talking to me?"

"Yeah," she said. "You don't know me, but I've heard a lot about you. They talk about what a fine job you've done at Jennatabad, how you're really brave staying here. I'd be scared to bury the dead like you do."

"Yeah," I said.

She told me her name at that point: Nahid. Then she came nearer and asked, "Wouldn't you rather sleep in the mosque?"

"No, I stay here at night," I said.

"Here?" she said in disbelief.

"Yeah, and this is not my first night," I said.

Her tone changed all of a sudden. It surprised me to see the kind girl she had been suddenly turn so bossy and quarrelsome. She said, "It's not proper for a young girl to sleep here!"

"It's got nothing to do with age; I'm not alone here. The others also stay."

"You mustn't," she insisted. "I'm going to bring it up with the committee."

That made me very angry. "What? You're going to do what? What the hell does it have to do with you? You like to play boss, honey, don't you? Go and take it up with the committee, for all I care!"

"You'll answer to me eventually. I'll show you," she threatened.

Now I was steaming mad. "You're threatening me now? Go and do whatever the hell you want."

Zeynab, who had overheard our run-in, said to her, "What are you doing here? Get out and mind your own business!"

The girl was around twenty something and relatively chubby and short. She walked away in a huff only to come back less than half an hour later.

It had gotten dark and I was going to wash for prayer when Zeynab said, "Zahra, come here. That girl is back, and she's got an official with her."

The man was thin and short and his white shirt was not tucked into his pants. He seemed to be one of those thick-headed types, indifferent to logic. When they got close, he asked, "Who's Sister Hoseyni?"

"That's me. You want something?"

In a voice full of disapproval, he asked, "I want you to explain why you're spending the night here. Who gave you permission?"

I said, "This is not my first time. My father has given his approval. Besides, what's the problem with my staying here in your opinion?"

"Problem, I'm saying for your sake it's a problem, because it's not safe here. You're a young girl, after all. Taking care of this place at night is a man's job."

I said, "I know about this place, and incidentally, it's because there's no security here that I'm staying. The bodies of the fallen would be all alone otherwise. Nobody's given a thought to protecting them. Why don't you show me the men who're coming here? Come to think of it why don't you spend the night here, and I'll go home?"

"I can't do that; I have tons of work already. Besides, what do the dead need with protection anyway?"

"If you'd kindly come with me," I said with mock deference, "I'll show you."

We walked to the body washers' building. I showed him the rows of corpses lying by the path and said, "These need protecting. At night when the dogs get aggressive, you'll see what goes on here. Last night we couldn't let our guard down for a minute, and this morning you can see how the dogs had rutted around in the cemetery. There's more: the Hypocrites. When they went to Taleqani Hospital to claim 'their' bodies, they wouldn't deliver them, saying they needed a letter. It became clear they were stealing bodies to hike up their own martyr count for propaganda purposes. So whether the dogs attack or the Hypocrites, what can you expect a handful of old men and women to do to defend the place?"

"In any case, it would be better if you didn't stay here," he said.

"I agree," I said, "just provide us with some armed men, and you'll have a clear conscience."

He said, "I'll go and see what I can do."

That was the end of the conversation, and they left with their heads hanging. I was really upset finding the whole thing offensive. How dare they come here and get on their high horse with me in the middle of all this!

After a few hours it was completely dark. Everybody stopped working. Dinner that night was bread and canned fish; I had no appetite for either. Ignoring the food, I got up and sat with Leila and Zeynab by the small garden near the mosque. Hoseyn and Abdollah were sitting a few feet away. They would occasionally get up, walk to the door, and come back.

The sound of dogs barking could be heard over the din of the explosions. The sound got louder and closer as the night wore on. The sounds had been coming from the wasteland behind the Sabaean cemetery, but soon we could here them from all around us. We all pricked up our ears, anxious to see what would happen next. Zeynab said, "The dogs had so much blood they're rabid."

I recalled how they were on the previous night: ready to attack with foam dripping from their mouths. All at once the sounds started coming from the part of the cemetery where the wall was broken. Zeynab, Leila, and I immediately ran to that side. Hoseyn and Abdollah got there right after us. Hoseyn said, "You shouldn't go farther, they'll flank us. I'll shoot them."

"That's sinful. Why do we have to kill these dumb animals?"

"If I don't kill them they'll tear us apart."

I said, "Shoot in the air; that'll probably scare them off."

I hadn't finished speaking when the forms of dogs appeared, and the sound was now coming from the garden area. They were running toward us. We were all crouched on the ground gathering stones, which we threw at the dogs. This only made them bolder, and they came at us more quickly, and at the same time increased the space between them. Some went to the left, others to the right. Two or three also attacked from the center. In an instant they had formed a semicircle around us, ready to pounce. They gnashed their teeth, and there was fury in their eyes. When they were four meters away, they stopped and began to bark. Their sharp teeth were glistening in the semi-darkness. The savagery in their looks scared me out of my wits; it seemed they could devour us just with their eyes. Obviously we were all terrified, but I was even more worried about Leila. We warned one another not to approach them, because the dogs were definitely rabid.

When a couple of the dogs stepped closer, the others followed and Zeynab began to shriek like a baby, which I found both ridiculous and irksome. Here was a woman who had remained firm in the face of all that went on at the cemetery, who supported me, now breaking down. It was totally unexpected. "Don't shriek," I said. "It'll only encourage them."

She kept on screaming, though. "They can't get any more vicious than this! They're going to tear us to pieces any minute now!"

Hoseyn cocked his rifle, but I said, "Don't shoot; it's not right."

Zeynab and Leila said in unison, "Let him fire. Shoot, Hoseyn!"

Abdollah, angered by what I said, yelled, "What do you mean: Don't shoot? You want them to eat you alive to be sure they're rabid?"

"The dogs are innocent," said Hoseyn. "We're the guilty ones here. They're going to eat us now," and he fired several shots in the air. The sound of the gun wound its way around the cemetery, and the dogs stopped moving. At the same time I threw a rock at a large dog, which seemed more dangerous than the rest. Since it wasn't entirely dark, I could aim and hit it on the snout. The dog growled and retreated; the rest followed suit and ran away, looking back at us as they did. Hoseyn and Abdollah ran after them. Fear of the dogs had taken so much out of the rest of us we fell to the ground and lay there for a few minutes waiting to catch our breaths. I sat with my back against a tree and stretched out my legs. I looked up to see clouds moving across the sky. They covered the moon and it got pitch dark. As they scudded along, it seemed as though the moon was moving along behind them.

Able to breathe again, we returned to the building. Maryam and the others, still afraid, looked around nervously. One of the old men had a shovel and greeted us by saying, "I was going to come and help but they wouldn't let me. They said I might fall if I tried to run."

Maryam said, "We were very afraid for you. I thought they'd tear you to shreds."

I took out the piece of paper with Jahan Ara's number from my headscarf and went to make a call. I told them who I was calling as I dialed.

It took a while for him to come to the phone. I told him about the dogs, saying that we had won one battle, but they might be back at any moment, and we couldn't beat them back a second time.

He said, "Don't worry. God will reward you for the way you've put yourselves on the line." His message was: we must continue to resist. I thanked him and joined the others.

A couple of hours later we were eating a supper of bread and watermelon, when the phone rang. One of the old men answered. Then he said to me, "It's for you, sister."

I was surprised, but then I realized that it was probably the mosque calling. Jahan Ara was on the line, asking whether the people they had sent had arrived yet.

"No," I said.

"We've collected some shroud material and sent it along. They should be arriving soon, but the corpses have to stay piled up, because we don't have people to spare. We've decided to move the bodies from Jennatabad to nearby cities—to Abadan and Mahshahr. A truck will come in the morning to pick them up."

A short time after he hung up, two young men on a motorcycle arrived. They said, "Brother Jahan Ara sent us." They brought several bolts of denim with them. The body washers put in a call to Parvizpur asking him to come and help with the shrouding. We lit some pressure lamps, but only enough to give off a dim light; the bodies were male and we didn't want them fully exposed. The women only cut the fabric for the shrouds outside the building. The men carried the bodies inside, cut their clothes off, and dry-washed them. Then they wrapped them in the shrouds. One of the young men who had arrived on motorcycle recorded the particulars of each corpse on the shrouds. I glanced at the bodies in the darkness, and I was so torn by the sight that I felt justified in going again to the Congregational Mosque or anywhere to raise hell on their behalf. Some of the ones I saw had died in battle; they had given the last measure of their lives as soldier-martyrs. It was a disgrace for their bodies to be neglected like this. The only one I recognized among them was Esma'il Sa'bari, the son of our neighbor and the most precious one in the world to his mother. I can't say how much my heart went out to her when I saw him lying there. There was no sign of motherly affection for his corpse, which had been out in the sun for three days, so long we feared it would swell up and explode. I thought: If Esma'il's mother saw the state her son was in, she'd burn the place down.

Before the job of shrouding the dead had been completed, I went to Parvizpur's office to call the mosque. Even at that hour of the night, Ebrahimi picked up the phone. I said, "Brother Jahan Ara promised to send a truck in the morning to pick up the dead and transfer them to another city. We're in the process of getting the bodies ready. I'm asking you to see to it that the truck actually comes."

He promised to have the truck reach us at the crack of dawn. I said goodbye and walked back to the building to find the shrouding was over, and Parvizpur and the young men were leaving. After they left, I went into the other room.

I was so tired that, unlike the previous night, I curled up next to Leila and was fast asleep quickly. In the middle of the night, I woke up in a strange state of overexhaustion. I desperately missed home and wanted father to come and bring Leila and me home, where I could then sleep for a couple of days straight—sleep so much it would wipe from my mind all the things I had seen at Jennatabad. Then suddenly I could hear father saying: You're responsible for your mother and the kids until Ali returns. Then the word "treachery" rang in my ears ... "treachery." I could see the look on father's face when he had pounded the sign; his face seemed to spin as it came and went in my imagination. I raised my arms to put them around his neck, but he wasn't there. The scene returned several times that night as the air grew heavier.

I turned over and looked at Leila; I could only fee heartache for her. I didn't know what the hell was wrong with me. I wanted to hug and kiss her and cry, but I was afraid she'd wake up. I was in a really bad way, wanting to scream, to cry out for father, so loud that he'd hear me wherever he was and come to me. Then I felt something weighing down on my lungs, and I couldn't breathe. The only way to remove the weight, I thought, was to go outside and shout. At that point I sensed Zeynab was also awake.

"Mama, are you awake?" I asked, calling her that because she wanted us to.

"Yes, my darling. You haven't slept?" she asked.

"It's not that; I just woke up."

"You got some sleep, thank God," she said.

"You want to go outside and take a walk?" I asked.

"What for?" she asked.

"I don't know—maybe to see if someone has come. To look in on the boys."

"Okay," she said.

We got up and quietly left the room. We stood for a moment on the porch so that we wouldn't make Hoseyn and Abdollah jumpy. When we saw Abdollah pacing in front of the body washer building, we approached him and said hello. Zeynab asked him, "You haven't slept, son?"

He said, “We’re taking turns sleeping so we wouldn’t be tired at the same time. Since Hoseyn was tired, I took the first watch.”

His eyes looked so tired we knew he didn’t even have the energy for a stroll. I asked, “Anything to report?”

“No, nothing,” he said.

We walked over to the bodies with him and walked around the area. Then we went back to the building and Zeynab said to Abdollah, “You want us to stay with you, baby, so you won’t fall asleep?”

Seemingly taken by surprise, Abdollah said in his peculiar accent in which “r” almost became “q,” “No, I won’t fall asleep. When my shift is over, I’ll wake up Hoseyn.”

We went back into the building.

8

Transporting Bodies

At the crack of dawn on the fifth day I waited impatiently for the truck to come, poking my head out of the gate every so often, looking down the avenue for any sign of it. The sun had just risen when two vans—one a Nissan, the other a Peykan—pulled into Jennatabad and stopped in front of the body washers' building. The two young men who had delivered the shrouds the night before along with a number of guards stepped out of the vans. The two young men led them straight for the bodies. Because their felt markers had run out of ink the night before, they brought new ones to finish writing the names of the dead on the shrouds. Then all of us grabbed stretchers to carry the dead to the vans. Some of the bodies were very heavy, and it took three people to lift one stretcher. The guards stacked the bodies in the back of the vans. It was gratifying to see that all the running around I had done had paid off; it made me work even harder now. Everybody was relieved that there weren't as many corpses on the ground as we had thought.

Zeynab said, "Girl, I hope good things will happen for you because of this."

While we were carrying the bodies, I overheard the drivers say that the Nissan would go to Mahshahr, while the Peykan, which didn't have a motor to speak of, would have to go to nearby Abadan. They loaded twelve bodies into the Peykan, and Zeynab and a couple of guards went with it. Since Abadan was closer, and therefore was a safer journey, I told Leila to go with them.

I said to Zeynab, "Take care of yourself and Leila."

"Don't worry. I'll keep a closer watch on her than you do. Let me say she's become quite the young lady." After the Peykan left, we filled the Nissan with eighteen bodies. I said goodbye to Maryam and the others and sat down on the space between the end of the van and the bodies. Hoseyn and Abdollah rode shotgun on opposite sides of the tailgate. One of the guards said, "Miss, you should sit in front."

"No, I'm more comfortable right here," I said. The guard sat in front and we were off. When we got to the Congregational Mosque the Nissan stopped and the guard got out, reporting to Ebrahimi that we were transporting eighteen bodies to Mahshahr and that the other van was carrying twelve to Abadan.

As soon as he heard this Ebrahimi jumped to his feet and made his way through the crowd around his desk. He stopped short when he saw me, saying hello. I greeted him, and Ebrahimi with a look of distress on his face surveyed the bodies. He seemed stunned and, waving his arms at the pile, he yelled, "What is all this? Where did all these come from?"

"Now you know why I kept coming back and making such a fuss; these are the bodies I was talking about," I explained.

"Yes, now I see why you put yourself through all that hell! What do you want to do with them now?" he asked.

"Since there's no water or people here, and with all the bombing, we thought we'd bury them somewhere else."

He said nothing and merely stared at us with a look of disbelief. Finally he said, "Well, I sure gotta hand it to…."

"Who do you have to hand it to?" I asked.

"I don't know. To you, to them? I don't know who," he said.

At that point the guard who had been in the truck came with another guard carrying a G3 battle rifle. Abdollah climbed onto the roof of the van and sat down. The guard with the G3 took his place in the back.

When the van got going I said goodbye to Ebrahimi. He answered me calmly, "God be with you."

Because the road along the Shatt was in range of Iraqi artillery, the driver turned around and took the Forty-Meter Road. Ebrahimi watched us as we raced toward the Khorramshahr Bridge. Once over the bridge we got stuck in the traffic waiting to fill up at the gas station.

It was ridiculous sight. People were fed up, shouting and blowing their horns. There was so much noise you couldn't hear yourself think. Abdollah was shouting at the top of his lungs for the cars to get out of the way so we could pass.

The driver was honking madly, but it did no good. All at once Abdollah began firing into the air, causing people to turn and look at us in terror. There had been an air raid that morning, and fear was still etched on their faces. I said to him, "These people are terrified enough. Don't shoot anymore, brother."

We weren't that far from the bridge but still stuck in traffic, when a guard with a G3 appeared and shouted angrily, "Why were you firing? What's the point of trying to scare people already frightened to death?"

"We wanted to clear a path through the traffic," said Hoseyn and Abdollah in unison.

"Everybody wants to do that!" shouted the guard. "Everybody wants to be on their way."

"We've got dead back here," explained the boys.

"Okay, so you do, but you've got to wait your turn just like everybody else!"

I knew the guard slightly. His name was Majed, and he had a bright and very attractive face. His family were Kurds from Elam who had been driven from Iraq. Father sometimes said hello to Majed's father. But the way he was acting upset me. I got up and said heatedly, "Why are you shouting? We've got to get these bodies where they're supposed to go quickly."

He said, "Wait a little."

"That's not possible," I said. "They've been out in the sun three days now and they'll rot. Come and see what they're like."

He stepped forward and when he saw blood flowing out from the crimson shrouds, he blanched and started apologizing. Then he ran around trying to clear a path through the cars for us. When the van started to move he hopped on the side of the cab, waiting for the next bottleneck to form. Then he would try his best to move the cars out of the way. Other drivers tried to help, but some of the cars had run out of gas and had to be pushed to the side. The avenue, despite its width, was completely snarled in traffic. In order to maintain order around the station, Majed was forced to fire into the air himself. We all were shouting at the other cars to get out of the way, which attracted people's attention. Some of them approached the van and, seeing the bodies, started weeping. Several old women began to chant dirges and wail. Others were stunned by what they saw and asked, "Is that how we're going to end up? With this war going on, we're all going to perish." Some of the people even began to help Majed clear the way for us.

All the shouting was wearing me down little by little. The sun was directly overhead hammering us, and the sweat was pouring down my face. Now that the bodies were out of the shade, I knew they would decompose in the heat. Despite all the effort to free us from the traffic, we still hadn't reached the gas station. But just as we got there, jets appeared in the sky, spoiling the relief of reaching the station. That instant the crowd began to sound weird. Drivers stumbled from their vehicles, leaving them parked in the middle of the avenue with their doors open. Women and children were shrieking in terror, running in every direction. Everyone was frantically searching for cover. People cried out, "Lord!" and "O Hoseyn!" I could see women clutching one child to their breasts, while holding another by the hand, running for their lives.

It was a strange sight. Masses of people got caught up in the stampede, some of them falling to the ground and getting trampled. Assured there was nothing to stop their attack, the jets flew low to the ground, so low their menacing shadows fell on the people. Faced with certain death, people looked up at the sky and raced in every direction.

I was no less afraid than the others, but my fear was of a different kind. From the bottom of my heart I prayed to God not to let these damned things stop the dead in the van from reaching their final resting places. I prayed that He would bring the jets down before they could drop their bombs on us.

It didn't take but a few seconds for the jets to veer off toward Taleqani Hospital and drop their bombs between the hospital and a rural area southeast of the city. There were several explosions that sent smoke and dust into the air, followed immediately by the sound of breaking glass. The quaking of the earth was so terrible it felt like a whole had opened up and we were being swallowed by it. There was so much dust in the air I couldn't open my eyes to see whether the hospital had been flattened. But I could hear the jets coming back for a second round, firing their missiles at the bridge; fortunately they went astray and exploded in the Shatt, raising the water level nearly twenty meters. The sound this time was muffled, and the earth didn't quake as much as before. From our vantage point on the van we had a better view of what had happened than most and could see there was an unexploded rocket on the banks of the Shatt.

The planes had gone, but I was still trembling, afraid that they wouldn't take pity on the poor souls in the back of the truck. People remained motionless for a time, fearing the jets would be back. Some had taken shelter in unfinished houses. Some were lying in the sewer ditches lining the road or in the irrigation channels in the date grove across the way. Some hadn't gotten far and were lying in the avenue, their hands clawing at the pavement. Even more ridiculous were two men who had jumped into empty barrels beside the road. Everyone thought that the jets would return, so Majed and the other guards shouted, "Everybody, get your cars out of the road. The planes have dropped their load and won't be returning." But no one believed them. After things had quieted down somewhat, I heard people saying, "Let's go to the next gas station. Let's go to Abadan; it makes no sense to stay here."

I also saw several women crying, refusing to budge from where they were. In all the commotion an argument between a woman and her husband happened to catch my attention. They were walking by the road with their four-year-old daughter, trying to hail a passing car. The man, who had dark skin, frizzy hair, and a thick mustache, was holding a sack in one hand and his daughter in the other. The woman, who, unlike her husband was squat and relatively plump, had a bundle in her hand. They were both around thirty. Occasionally the man walked ahead of the woman, dragging the child behind him. The woman followed saying, "Where are we going? Our home is here. Why should we leave? For the love of God, let's go back!"

In a southern accent the man answered, "Stay here and do what? We'll be killed!"

The woman started to cry. She took the girl by the hand and pulled her. The man said, "Look, woman! Everybody's leaving."

"So, this is everybody in the city?" the woman asked tearfully.

"If we stay, we'll die!" the man shouted.

The woman said, "We're just like everybody else. We'll stay and whatever happens, happens. We'll die just like everybody else."

The little girl remained suspended between the parents, each pulling her in a different direction. Whenever her mother raised her voice and teared up, the child also cried. My heart went out to the woman; she had the right to dig in her heels. Her husband wouldn't budge. No match for him, she finally went along but in tears. After the Nissan driver filled up, the attendant refused to take his money, and we were quickly on our way. Despite its heavy load of bodies and the five or six of us non-dead, the van moved at a rapid pace. Along the route we saw the signs of fifty-caliber bursts. There were also the occasional mortars that landed in the road or in fields, sending shrapnel in all directions. Ignoring everything, the driver kept his foot on the gas and raced along. As we passed Taleqani Hospital we saw throngs of people waiting outside, a token of the bedlam inside the building. On the outskirts of Abadan, the crowds were very unruly. Many people had sought refuge at the Seyyed Abbas Shrine, hoping the blessed saint would protect them from the shelling.

When we got to the area around the bridge over the Bahman Shir River, I could see crowds forming around any vehicle that went by. When they saw only four of us in the back of the Nissan, they thought there was room for more and they stormed the vehicle. We told them that there was no room, but they accused us of holding out. Hoseyn said, "Come and see what's in the back, and if you find space, hop on." When they got closer and saw the dead, they sheepishly retreated. Some sent up prayers and recited verses from the Quran.

Once over the bridge we got on the Abadan-Mahshahr Road. The crowds got thicker, and, naturally, the van had to slow down. The driver kept honking to open a path through the throngs. My heart went out to these refugees from the fighting; all of them looked pale and exhausted. Many were barefoot and could barely drag along the bundles and boxes they had with them. Some gave into the fatigue and were stretched out on the sloping ground beside the road. We kept encountering people begging for a ride, and Hoseyn and Abdollah became fed up with trading words with them. Abdollah started to be brutal, "I'm telling you there's no room. Okay, come and sit on my head. You want me to get down so you can ride?"

The most pitiful ones were those that got to the van and, seeing our cargo, turned away in disgust. In despair they abandoned the vehicle and kept on walking.

Then, in all the chaos, the planes returned, flying so low and fast that people lost the will to go on. Stricken with fear and exhausted, they ran from the road and scattered in the desert. The jets flew so low their shadows fell on the van. Some people yelled, "Fire at them; you have weapons. SHOOT! SHOOT!" When Hoseyn did take aim and fired, other people shouted, "Don't shoot. They'll bomb this place and massacre all of us!"

The crowds thinned out and the driver took advantage of the open road to speed up. It was getting toward noon, and the heat from the the metal bars I was leaning against began to scorch my back. Drenched in sweat, I fanned myself with my chador but it offered no relief. I couldn't take much more heat; my lips were parched and my throat was on fire. I craved a glass of cold water. I had been dying of thirst since we were at the gas station where I had shouted at the guard. Now I had no strength to go on. The state of the bodies was also more troubling than ever. Blood and other liquids began to slosh about in the back of the van; my palm was red with blood.

I ignored the crowds and the noise and turned my attention to the dead—particularly to Esma'il Sa'bri, whom they called Eidi at home. His mother loved him passionately. His stepfather hadn't been in good health and was bedridden for a time. As a child I was especially friendly with his sister Raqiyeh, and that way I got to know about their circumstances. Both Esma'il and Ebrahim had to work to help out with their mother's expenses. The mother also did her damnedest to see to it her children didn't suffer. After their father had died, the weight of supporting the family fell on the boys' shoulders. And this was how Esma'il was rewarded for his efforts!

There was also an Iraqi among the dead our boys had delivered. The body washers told us that he was in the process of surrendering when he was hit from behind. We had buried a number of Iraqis before, and all I recorded in the register was a number and the fact that they were Iraqi.

I could see the Iraqi's face clearly. A bullet had entered the back of his head and exited from his forehead, making his face a bloody mess. He seemed to be around twenty-seven or eight. His skin was very dark, and he was on the hefty side. On his shroud they had written: Iraqi soldier. I wondered: What will they tell his family? Though he had been killed by his own forces, they would probably offer the bold-faced lie he had been taken prisoner or was missing. Now we were bringing his corpse to Mahshahr, while his loved ones waited in vain for him to return. I could also imagine them telling his family their son was a traitor and then harassing the poor souls.

I put these thoughts behind me and noticed numbers of people walking toward Mahshahr. This would be my first time there. Not knowing much about the city, I imagined it wasn't different from Abadan, because like Abadan it had a petrochemical complex and, of course, foreign forces had been stationed there. But when we got there, I saw it was mostly dry wasteland. It seemed as if the sun was fiercer here—everywhere I looked was baked salt marsh. The city still had a traditional layout, and the dryness seemed to cast a pall over everything. People were in constant motion in the alleyways and on the main streets and avenues.

The van left the main road and entered a side street, sending up clouds of dust. I had to cover my face with my chador. The crowds hunting for vehicles grew thicker as we proceeded. When they saw our cargo, they sent up prayers for the dead. Now what concerned me was where to deliver the bodies. To the military, the mayoralty, or the command center? But the dead, who sacrificed their lives in the service of their country and faith, received a warm welcome at the cemetery, putting my fears to rest. I saw this as Jahan Ara's doing; he had alerted the authorities in Mahshahr. I heard them saying that they would make all the arrangements.

I turned to Hoseyn and Abdollah and said, "Look at these crowds. Have you ever seen so many people in one place at one time?"

They were amazed. Hoseyn said, "During the past few days I had forgotten, but there was a time Khorramshahr was as crazy as this."

The van stopped at the cemetery. The guard who was sitting in front said, "Wait here for people to come. Many are still on their way."

I looked at the men, women, and children in the cemetery; some had picks and shovels in their hands. There were even mechanical shovels, which with their clean wooden handles were obviously new. People slowly crowded around the van and peeked inside. When they saw the bloodied corpses they struck their faces and expressed their sympathy. The women wept and the children, all aged around ten or twelve, gaped. To counter he mentality of mourning I felt I needed to say something about the sacrifices of the dead. Wailing and tears weren't going to solve anything. The dead were dead; it was time to do something for the living. This was a good opportunity for that.

The day before, I had seen a major standing on a truck in front of the Congregational Mosque. He was haranguing the crowd about conditions at the front and trying to mobilize forces. I asked his name and someone said he was a major in the army called Sharif Nasab.

When I saw all officials of Mahshahr gathered there, I started to have second thoughts, but I came to the conclusion that if I didn't speak up, I'd be doing the people of the town a disservice. I remember father telling me that the news of the disasters hadn't reached some of the cities. If the Imam learned of what had happened in Khorramshahr, he couldn't sit idly by.

I asked him, "Who won't allow it? Who would stop the information from getting out?"

Father said, "The traitor Banisadr."

I thought: If I don't say anything about what was happening in Khorramshahr, I would be a traitor, too. But what if talking did no good? Then what?

So I decided to take the bull by the horns. Whatever happened, would happen. The worst they could say is that the girl is crazy. So let them.

I fixed my chador, stood up at the edge of the van, and started speaking, "People! The bodies you see here are those of the poor young men and women of Khorramshahr. They have been killed defending the honor and faith of their country. They remained out in the open for three days because there was no water to wash them or shrouds to bury them in. The bombardments didn't help either. For three days they lay under the hot sun like the martyrs of Karbala."

The tears streamed down as I spoke and at several points a lump in my throat stopped me from going on. But I continued, "People in Khorramshahr have neither water nor electricity; they are even afraid to go to the Shatt for water. Despite this and though they have no weapons, they are fighting tooth and nail to defend the homeland. This is the situation, though soldiers tell me that there's no shortage of guns and ammunition in the country. There was a time when we had a regional gendarmerie, but now the traitors won't let fresh forces and weapons reach Khorramshahr. You people must tell the authorities about the terrible fate of the folks in that city. Everybody must help any way they can. Brother soldiers and guards, whatever weapons you can spare—send them to Khorramshahr. You in the municipality or governor's office, don't let their cries for help go unanswered. The people are desperate...."

As I spoke, Hoseyn and Abdollah reminded me to mention the lack of shrouds and water. And whenever somebody in the crowd started speaking, Abdollah, I was surprised to see, would shout at him, "Listen, brother, these words are meant for you!"

Finally I said, "Each of us is responsible for what he or she does. I felt it my duty to speak to you this way. What you do next is between you and God. Khorramshahr does not belong to me or to these poor martyrs; it belongs to all of Iran. Saddam has come to take the whole country. If we don't stop him today, he'll take Khorramshahr. Tomorrow he'll be here, so there's no choice but to defend the country with everything we've got. We've all sworn to be the Imam's soldiers, now we must show we really deserve the name and do what he orders."

The crowd cried out, "GOD IS GREAT! DEATH TO SADDAM! DEATH TO AMERICA! DEATH TO THE TRAITORS!"

I climbed down from the van, and women surrounded me, some planted kisses on my head and face and expressed their good wishes. They wished they could be in Khorramshahr to help.

Some were curious about the conditions in the city, while others prayed to God for help and praised me, calling me a "lion of a woman."

It was embarrassing; I didn't want to make myself the center of attention. I was in the middle of talking to people when a guard interrupted, saying, "If you don't mind, sister, would you please come with me. The city preacher would like a word."

I was amazed and a little hesitant: What did such a man want with me? What could I tell him? Asking for God's help, I followed the guard to the body washers' where the preacher was standing beside the commander of forces in Mahshahr, the governor, the head of the gendarmerie, and the mayor. As soon as they saw me they stepped forward and greeted me, each introducing himself and thanking me for what I had done. The preacher said, "We are honored by brave women like you. You are putting the message of Zeynab into practice." Then he asked, "What can we do for you? What do need? We are ready to help."

"For now," I said, "nothing. The only thing I ask is that the bodies of the Iraqi soldiers that are among our dead not be desecrated. These poor creatures were killed by their own troops, trying to surrender to our boys."

"You needn't worry; they are Muslims just like us and will be buried according to Islam." Our driver and the guards from Khorramshahr also spoke with the officials. With all my heart I silently thanked God for Jahan Ara's farsightedness.

Then, led by the preacher, we all said prayers for the dead. They wouldn't allow me or the boys to lift a finger in disposing of the bodies. No matter how much we insisted, they said it was their responsibility and theirs alone.

Afterwards they brought a bucket of lemon sherbet drink and served it to us. Though there was a coating of dust on the surface, it was cold and hit the spot in that inferno. After drinking the slushy liquid, I noticed my throat was raw from all the shouting I did at the gas station and my speech to the crowd. I felt bad I couldn't offer a glass of the sherbet to the guys at Jennatabad.

Then they brought us to the guards' building in Mahshahr where there was a full-spread breakfast waiting for us: bread, white cheese, butter, jam, etc. I had to laugh; there was no comparison between here and Khorramshahr. Since I felt I had to get back, I went through the motions of eating and got up quickly. As I was leaving the building, the commander of the guards was just returning from the cemetery. He kindly suggested that we stay and rest a while. I thanked him and said, "I have to get back." We were going to wash the van, but when we got to where it was parked, we saw it had been cleaned thoroughly, and that they had loaded the back with full gas cannisters.

Leaving Mahshahr, I had mixed emotions. On the one hand I wanted to return quickly to Khorramshahr; on the other, I didn't want the van to leave. The feeling seemed like a premonition; something was about to happen on the way back: a rocket attack, a traffic accident, Iraqi mortar fire—something, I thought. But I also realized these things no longer frightened me. So what was it that was causing my indecision? I sat down in the back of the van, vaguely concerned, and had no desire to respond to Hoseyn and Abdollah who were jabbering away at me.

Abdollah said, "You know, sis, if there were this many people in Khorramshahr—all with weapons—the Iraqis wouldn't even get a meter into the city."

"Yeah, that's right," agreed Hoseyn.

Ignoring them, it suddenly crossed my mind that something might have happened to Leila. The car might have overturned or come under attack by Iraqi jets. I also was worried about mother and the kids, who, according to Leila, had taken shelter in the Sheikh Soleyman Mosque. We put Mahshahr far behind us, but my mind was racing. I started to hum remembrances for the Imams to calm myself. Back in Khorramshahr, I decided that the first thing—before going to Jennatabad—would be to stop in at the Congregational Mosque.

9

The Death of Father

We arrived in Khorramshahr around 4:00 p.m. I got out of the van on Revolution Avenue and headed straight for the Congregational Mosque.

It was less crowded than on the previous days; there were no wounded people in the clinic. Contrary to what I had imagined, the girls were busy doing their own work. I said hello, and they greeted me warmly. The reaction was very different from the way they had behaved toward to me the day before. Gone was the familiar teasing: "Here comes the grouch" or "You look like a cadaver." They couldn't have been more genial or endearing, and there was no edge to their voices. This surprised me and I thought something was going on, because, in addition to the warm reception, they kept stealing glances at me and whispering. I also got the sense they were not really working, but pretending to be busy. Zohreh Farhadi was fiddling with a G3. Sabah was preparing cotton swabs. The other one was wiping down the table. I said with a laugh, "So what's up? You seem busy, but nothing's happening? No wounded?"

"We're straightening up," they said. "We want to be ready for them."

Again they seemed affectionate, which made me curious. I had to ask, "Would you please tell me what's going on? How come you're being so nice?"

Zohreh said, "Nothing's going on. It's just that we haven't seen you since morning and we missed you."

"Okay, you've said it and I believe you," I said.

I suddenly heard them calling my name over the mosque loudspeaker. I went into the courtyard. Ebrahimi was sitting behind a table with a microphone in his hand. I said hello and asked, "You called me?"

He got up from the table. Very calmly and respectfully he said, "A man had come here wanting to see you, but you weren't here so he left."

"Who?" I asked.

"He didn't say his name."

"Did he say what he wanted?"

"I can't exactly say," he added. "One of your family has been wounded, it seems."

This was puzzling. If somebody wanted me, they knew where to find me. It was odd that a stranger would have come. I had expected them to tell me that the Soleyman Mosque had been bombed and mother and the kids were hurt or even that father had been wounded. But to have a stranger come and say that one of my family members had been hurt seemed farfetched. "Which member of my family?" I asked Ebrahimi. "Everybody in my family has gone from the city. Nobody's left."

"He didn't say," said Ebrahimi.

I got the feeling Ebrahimi was keeping his answers short to control his emotions. There was clearly something bothering him. As we spoke he kept fidgeting, which made me sure he was holding something back. I was losing patience, but I tried to stay calm. "What did he look like, this man with the news?" I asked.

"He was little pudgy and bald as a coot."

"As far as I know there is no such person in my family," I said irritably. "Tell me the truth. What's happened?"

"Nothing's happened. Believe me," he said feebly.

The quiver in his voice was terrifying to me. I said, "For God's sake tell me what's happened. I can take it. I've seen a lot these days, done a lot of things that I never thought I'd do."

As I spoke, Ebrahimi didn't say a word. He looked down and kept running his hand through his hair. I realized from his stubborn silence that it was very difficult for him to speak, so I decided to ask

Leila, thinking they would have definitely tried to contact her. "I'm going to Jennatabad to check on things," I announced.

Ebrahimi got up and begged me not to go. I ignored him and left. I had wasted enough time. On the way I had a strange feeling, which I couldn't shake. Without thinking I remembered a very disturbing dream I had had a few months before.

I saw that a pomegranate tree had sprung up in our garden. It had new leaves and was full of the bright fruit that shone through the leaves. Two of the red orbs were brighter than the others; they hung from the tree like lanterns lighting up the yard and shedding a mysterious glow. Entranced by the sight, I saw a neighbor woman of ours in the yard. I knew her husband was ill and unable to work. She wanted me to give her the two dazzling pomegranates, explaining that they would be a tonic for her ailing husband. Knowing of my father's generosity and wanting to help the old man get better, I plucked the fruit and gave it to her.

I had no idea why the dream suddenly popped into my head. My gut feeling was that something terrible had happened, someone in the family had been killed and that I would soon have to face that horror. The slaughter at Karbala also appeared in my mind, and I felt I would soon be witnessing the same dreadful thing. I walked faster, and the closer I got to Jennatabad the louder the turmoil in my heart became. I thought about the family. Don't let it be mother and the kids, I told myself. I wish I had looked in at the mosque where they were before going to Jennatabad. I hadn't seen them since the day before. Little Zeynab with her unibrow and big almond-shaped eyes appeared in my mind first. It hardly seemed possible that the last in father's line was now five years old, so spoiled by one and all you couldn't even say "boo" to her. Then I remembered when I said goodbye to father. I had entrusted Leila to Zeynab. Then I thought: Maybe Ali has come back; he's definitely heard news about the war and decided to return. Which one would it be? Ebrahimi is certainly mistaken. But why should I think the news is about martyrdom. Ebrahimi said someone had been wounded. So stop, I told myself. The road seemed never to come to an end, no matter how fast I ran.

I caught myself speaking aloud, talking to God and begging Him for the strength to go on if indeed somebody from the family had been killed. Up to that point we hadn't lost anyone, and I didn't know how I would react. I saw the dramatic ways grieving relatives behaved at Jennatabad, and I didn't want my hysterics to sap the will of the people around me. Ali's advice echoed in my ears: Be like Zeynab, Abbas's mother. Whenever they recited what happened to the martyrs at Karbala, I would sit at the foot of Alaviyeh, a Seyyed woman, who told of Zeynab's composure in the face of tragedy. Ever since those days, the mother of Abbas was my role model par excellence. Alaviyeh would tell us of how Zeynab's heart was etched with grief at the sight of the slaughter of her most cherished relatives; how she endured all the torments of imprisonment and, when finally she confronted her tormentors, stood up and said defiantly, "On the plains of Karbala, I saw nothing but beauty." I admired Zeynab for the way she stood up to cruelty, and asked myself: How could a human being reach such a state of wisdom that she could look beyond the obvious horror and see the blessings in her son's and brother's torments?

When I got to Jennatabad, I looked around but didn't see many people in the graveyard. Several people were standing outside the body washers' building. There was a woman sitting in the yard, wailing and digging in the ground and throwing the loose dirt on her head. Then she keened and clawed her face. It was mother. I could never stand to see her upset; but what, I wondered, brought her to this state? I was afraid of what was in store for me. What was I about to hear?

The suspense was so terrible it kept me from walking further. It was a strange sensation. Though I wanted to go to her, a force held me back. I felt like running away, getting as far from the place as I could. Then I also had the feeling I was having a terrible dream, like the nightmares of the past few nights.

But suddenly I found all eyes—including mother's—turned toward me, and my heart sank in terror. Her wails grew louder, and she walked unsteadily toward me. She had poured so much dirt on her head and shoulders that her face and clothes were unrecognizable. She appeared to be stooping and, after her cloak had slipped from her head a few times, she gathered it up and pulled it tightly around her face and clasped it to her chest.

As if pushed from behind, I stumbled forward, but before we got close, she said in a way that made my blood curdle, "See now, your father's dead. SEE?"

I couldn't believe what she said. A huge lump formed in my throat. I began to tremble and hugged her. All I wanted from the world was some privacy; that way it would be easier to comfort her. Then I began to weep out loud, with my entire being, and I tried to dislodge the lump in my throat before it strangled me, but I couldn't. The soldiers, a few guards, and the rest of the people there had their eyes on me. I had to calm mother. I didn't want anything we did to shake their spirits. While I was hugging mother, I kissed her and caressed her head, saying, "Mom, you have to bear up—dad chose this path for himself. Why upset yourself? Isn't it what he wanted? Wasn't he the one who said he'd end up martyred or in prison or wounded? With his arms and legs amputated?"

After I said this, she started to claw at her face again and tear her clothes. She tried to rip open her chest, but I grabbed her hands and said, "Don't do that. You'll make God angry and his soul will be the worse for it."

She didn't seem to hear me—didn't have the strength to hear me. She only shrieked and beat herself. She had a right to—after all the misery and grief she had experienced in life, she finally experienced some relief, but then everything fell apart. It was as if this woman was fated never to reap the rewards of all that pain. Between fits of weeping she managed to say, "How can you know what I'm feeling now with all that happened in Iraq and what's happening now?"

It occurred to me—how I don't know—I should just worry about her and not myself. I said, "I understand, but you have to manage somehow. Let's go to the children."

I put my arm around her waist and we walked away together, but her tears wouldn't let up. I realized she was putting on a touching show of modesty for the onlookers, but if they hadn't been there, her hysterics would have been much worse.

Nearing the children, we could see that Hoseyn was dragging a stick along the ground, and Hasan, holding Zeynab's hand, seemed pale, even sickly. It was clear from Mansur's expression he couldn't speak, but his pride kept him from crying. Mohsen was standing in a corner and sobbing. I looked around for Leila, who was being comforted by the woman Zeynab. As I looked at them in their grief, I thought about how quickly they had become orphans. Zeynab, Sa'id, and Hasan ran toward us, and to that point I thought they hadn't fully understood the gravity of what had happened. They looked stunned as they crowded around mother and me, but then they began to sob, softy but pitifully. Seeing them around her, mother raised her voice and asked father in Kurdish, "Abu Ali, who will take care of these children? Why did you abandon us?"

This made the children cry even more. I sat down and hugged them one by one and kissed and caressed them, trying to soothe them. Although on the inside I was in a frenzy, I said to them, "Don't cry; father's gone on the same path as Imam Hoseyn, toward God. You remember the children of Imam Hoseyn. The enemy martyred their father and burned their tents." I don't know whether they understood, but since this was how I kept myself calm, I thought it might help them.

The children did calm down, so I went over to mother and brought her to the mosque and sat her down on the ledge by the entrance. Then the woman Zeynab and the other body washers came. They kissed me and offered their condolences. Although I was choked up, I managed to answer them. I sat down next to mother. Several of the soldiers came up and offered their condolences. Some were crying, some were smoking, and others were pacing around. One said, "May God give you strength and may He bless your father—he was a saintly man. He was afraid of nothing and gave us all the will to fight, telling us, 'Don't fear the enemy with all their weapons; we have God.' "

My eyes filled with tears, but I kept them from running down my cheeks. Those were difficult moments. I couldn't decide whether to concentrate on my own grief or mother's or the children's. Ali wasn't there to console us or, at least, to calm mother, who was in agony, striking herself. Whenever she grabbed her collar to tear at it, I held her hands and said, "Don't act like that in front of the soldiers. They're far from home and it'll make them feel worse; they won't be able to stand up to the enemy."

But she wouldn't listen and went on keening until it got so bad I had to scream at her, "Mother, if you go on like this I won't let you be there when they bury him!"

She shouted at me in Kurdish, "Little tramp, you've got everybody looking at you. How would you know what I'm going through?"

"What do you mean?" I shouted back in Kurdish. "I wouldn't know what you're going through? Was father dearer than Imam Hoseyn? Are we better than the blessed Zeynab?" Then I embraced her and reminded her of the miseries Zeynab had to endure.

She cried and said, "I'd die for her!"

Then the woman Zeynab came forward and took mother in her arms, trying to calm her. She kissed her and whispered, "For the children's sake, you have to compose yourself."

In Arabic mother said, "I've lost my protector. How can I get him back?" During the interval, I looked around. Everyone there—my father's coworkers, the soldiers, the other body washers—were grief-stricken as they watched us. One of the older men was sitting by a wall and sobbing. Hoseyn was also sitting by himself and crying, clearly moved by father's death. Not wanting to see him that way, I went over to him and said, "It's not the end of the world. What's with you?"

He looked up and I could see the pain in his expression. I laughed, wanting him to think that I could take the pain of father's death. When one of the soldiers saw me laughing like that, he came over and scolded me saying, "My friend has just been martyred, and you're laughing? What's so funny about martyrdom?"

I didn't know what to say. Obviously he had just arrived and hadn't seen me with mother and the children. In a serious yet consoling tone, I said to him, "No, there's nothing funny about martyrdom. It's a good thing, in fact. But I wasn't laughing about your friend's death. It was about something else." Hoseyn, silent to that point, finally spoke, “What’s wrong with you, man? This friend of yours was the lady’s father.”

The poor soldier was stunned. He looked down and asked me to forgive him. I said, “Don’t give it a second thought. How did you know my father? When did you first meet him?”

He said, “For a few days we were on the same gun, a 106, holding off the Iraqis. But they got our coordinates and started shelling. We didn’t have a chance to shift our position.” He burst into tears. Then he continued, his voice quivering, “The first shell landed behind us, but the second one hit in front of our position, riddling the Seyyed’s body with shrapnel. These Baathists are real bastards.” Again the tears came, making it hard for him to continue, but he managed to say, “Although we were together for only a few days, the Seyyed put me under his spell. All the boys know that he was my spiritual guide. He was immune to despair. When the Iraqis attacked, we wanted to flee, but the Seyyed steadied us. His fighting spirit made us think that we were all heroes like Rostam. He never sat still and was always reminding us if we were careless, even for a moment, the enemy would find the nerve to mount an attack. Nothing kept the Seyyed from his prayers, not mortar shells, not tank fire. Everything he did left me speechless. I envy you having lived with such a man.” Then he handed me father’s velvet prayer mat, a box of Quran tapes, and his tape recorder. I opened the recorder and the soldier said, “The Seyyed’s Quran tape was always playing these past days.”

I didn’t have the strength to stand. Mother seemed to be wailing but I could make out the words: “Wherever you went, you touched people’s hearts. You were a spiritual guide to all those who met you. If only you weren’t such a saint.” Then she repeated in Arabic, “You’ve set my heart ablaze, Abu Ali. Ablaze.”

With this, she pushed me over the edge. I wanted to cry but I couldn’t, which only added to the pressure I felt on my soul. I had to quiet her again somehow, so I shouted at her. This calmed her a bit, but it didn’t last long; her keening and moaning started up and she began to hit herself. Mohsen had gone over to her several times telling her not to stop crying and reminding her we were no different from anyone else.

As the time passed, I ached to see father again. When the soldier who gave me father's prayer mat and the tape recorder said, "The Seyyed's Quran tape was always playing these past days," I couldn't stand it. The only thing I wanted was to see father once more. I turned to the people standing there and asked, "Where's my father?"

"We washed and shrouded his body," they said, "and he's in the mosque."

I knew that there was no water; we'd been dry washing the bodies at that point. So I turned to father's coworkers and angrily said, "Did you use pull to get water for him? The other bodies weren't so privileged."

"That's right," they said. "There was a shortage, but the Seyyed was one of us; we had to give him a proper washing."

I said, "I want to be alone with him; I'm begging you: keep people out of the mosque."

No one said a word, but as I started to walk, mother got up and followed me. I turned to her and, choked up, said, "Mother, give me a few minutes alone with him, will you?"

I went to the mosque and stopped before the wooden door, not daring to open it. I wasn't even able to look inside through the lattice window. After waiting a few seconds I raised my head and looked into the mosque. There was a shrouded body on the floor in the center of the building with the head facing the direction of prayer. Although it was just as dark inside the mosque as outside, I sensed a faint halo of light around my father's body. I was in agony as I opened the door and went inside. I was trembling, and I felt as if my legs didn't have the strength to on. Then I stopped and fell to my knees. I pulled myself forward with my arms, which were shaking terribly. I dragged myself forward, saying, "Father, father," desperately hoping dearly he'd answer as he always did: "My darling."

My face was covered in tears. I was in the grip of a strange terror, not knowing where I'd get the nerve to look at him. But in between all my "father-fathers," I slipped in the name of Imam Hoseyn—after all he was my only source of strength and tranquility.

Although I sorely wanted to see father's face, when I got to where his body was, my hands started to shake more and I found it hard to breathe. All at once I felt everything around me had plunged into absolute darkness. I couldn't see a thing. There was something horrible pressing down on my chest. It was like I was flailing about in a whirlpool. I was about to choke and cried out with all my heart, "Rescue me, O Hoseyn!" Though I had no strength in my arms, I managed to lift father's head and caress it. I began to kiss him through the shroud. I called out to him, "Father, my sweet father, talk to me. Why aren't you answering? Get up and see what mother's doing. Get up and see the children." But this only made me feel worse. I laid his head down gently and, using the last ounce of control in my trembling hands, opened the shroud. I blinked through the film of tears in my eyes and focused on him. How the light shone from his face! He was a handsome man, my father, with his chestnut hair, his eyebrows that joined over the bridge of his nose, and his honey-colored eyes. He looked fit with his lanky and trim body—and now in this pearly light he seemed even more attractive. I bent down, examining him more carefully. Shrapnel had opened a wound in his left cheek, exposing the bone. He had also lost an eye and part of his forehead. It was sheared off, but, thank God, his brains remained in his skull. There was no blood in the wound or on the shroud. I looked at his face again. The right side was intact and the eye with its beautiful color was intact.

I looked him up and down, searching for other wounds. There were tiny bits of shrapnel in the rest of his body; the large piece in his head had finished him off. I put my lips to his eye and kissed it. I remembered it was only yesterday when I had said goodbye to him. I tried to close the eye, but his, unlike the others I had seen, stayed open, which surprised me. "What does that mean?" I asked him. "Are you trying to say that you died with your eyes open?" Then I placed my face on his cheek. I wanted to scream and rip the heart out of my chest. I shook him and pressed his head to my breast and said twice, "Daddy, say something for God's sake!"

I took his hand and put it on my head wanting to have him caress me, but he wouldn't. I couldn't believe he was gone. I placed my head on his chest, hoping to hear his heart beating. I told myself they had probably made a mistake; maybe he wasn't dead, but his heart didn't respond. I was powerless. I opened the lower part of the shroud and knelt down to kiss his feet, those feet that had been tortured with steel cable, bloodying and bruising them, feet that had walked all the way from Iraq to Iran, that had taken him this way and that as he bore heavy loads in the bazaar. Then I took his hands and looked at his fingers—these were the same hands that had held mine as we said goodbye for the last time. I ran my hands over his, noticing how calloused they were. I remembered the times he would go off to work in the fierce heat of a Khorramshahr summer, his tongue rough and dry from fasting. The molten asphalt they were paving a road with burned those hands, which were now motionless but nevertheless scalded my heart, burning my entire being. Nothing, no act of consolation, would quell the fire. I wanted so to use those hands as a pillow and sleep beside him the way I did when I was little, craving to be spoiled by him, hugged and kissed by him.

I reminisced about my childhood and began to tell him of what I was going through. I told him, "I'm seventeen and I still need you, want you forever. For five-year-old Zeynab; for Sa'id, seven; for Hasan, nine; for Mansur; for Leila; and for mother. What is mother supposed to do without you, father? What should I do with all the children? Zeynab, your pride and joy, the one so attached to you…."

Father was very friendly to the neighbor's kids, who didn't have fathers of their own. He wouldn't touch anything mother had prepared, not even the loose greens, the yogurt drink, or sherbet, until he had invited them to sit with us. He insisted on doing this himself, never letting anyone bring the food to them. He paid so much attention to those orphans that we would sometimes get jealous, but he made sure to help them in a private way so as to allow them their dignity. But now father was gone and we were orphaned. I don't know why I started to remember these things, raking over old flames. I remembered how he was the last time I saw him, acting as if he sensed he was going to die and didn't have much time left.

I remembered the last Ramadan, which fell during the summer, and how hot it was. We children were sleeping on the roof as usual and I woke up in the middle of the night to have some water. I saw father in the yard crying and asking forgiveness as he prayed. I tiptoed back to the roof so he wouldn't notice me. Ever since then I would awake at about the same time of night and soon realized this was what he did every night. I would watch him secretly as he prayed and wept until the crack of dawn, when he would call us to breakfast.

Those were wonderful days and nights! We had just begun to feel that things were going our way. We had fewer problems, and it seemed the hardships were behind us. Those were the years father worked as a porter in the bazaar or did plumbing and construction work, but never took money from people he knew were in dire straits—even though we could have used the money ourselves. His word and his work were his bond. People naturally sought him out even long after we had moved from the old place to municipal workers' housing. They would say, "The Seyyed's hands are blessed by God; he's more humane than other workers."

Now the Seyyed was gone, and here I was weeping beside his corpse. It was only yesterday he told me he was entrusting me with the children. I didn't understand exactly what he meant then; but now the full weight of it was dawning on me. I leaned my head on his chest again. I remembered the times he would send me to the head of the alley to see whether the security agents were waiting to ambush him. During those anxious moments how his heart must have been racing.

I don't know how long the memories lasted. I lifted my head and looked into his face, sensing somehow that he would have been upset with such shows of agony. I sensed his presence all around me. His spirit, I thought, was probably not at peace. Then I felt very sorry for myself, enfeebled that I was without someone to turn to in times of trouble. I turned my rage against him and began to scold him cruelly, "Why did you abandon us? Why didn't you give a thought to us? How could you? How?"

But I knew the answers to those questions; he was right to act the way he did. He behaved according to a pact he had made with God. If father hadn't gone to the front, then others wouldn't have either. Who would be left to defend the country in that case?

Then, regretting what I had said, I begged him, "Father, if I wasn't the way you wanted me to be, if I caused you any grief, please forgive me. I'll try to live up to the task you've given me to make up for the past."

While I was speaking I heard them knocking on the door. I sat cross-legged on the floor with my head on his chest, not wanting to leave him. I kissed his breast, throat, face and forehead. I ran my hand through his delicate, soft hair. The strange look in his eye, as if from joy, stunned me. His pallor and general state made him look different from the bodies I had seen during the past days. He wasn't cold at all. His complexion was bright and ruddy; he seemed to be asleep rather than dead. He was even more handsome than he was before his death. Even the crow's-feet around his eyes and the wrinkles on his forehead were gone. The glow from his face was so intense that after I had opened the shroud, I had to wait a moment before I looked at it.

They knocked on the door again and I had to close the shroud, kissing his eyes and begging forgiveness for the last time. It was very hard to say goodbye; closing the shroud was even harder than opening it—as if closing it meant finality: the last look, the last touch, the last time I would smell his scent. I asked God what to do. Help me, I begged Him, tear my heart away. Please God, I said, take my love for father from me, the way You took his soul. Remove the affection for him in my heart. How was I supposed to bear him not being around? I reluctantly tied up the shroud but placed my forehead on his, as if it were a prayer stone, and held his head in my hands, saying "Father, tell God to be patient with us."

Then all at once I remembered what he had said when someone passed away: "I have no use for a natural death. I don't want to give up the ghost in bed."

"Is there such a thing as an unnatural death?" I asked. "Everybody dies naturally."

He said, "A natural death happens when you die in bed or as the result of sickness or an accident."

"So if somebody doesn't die that way, how do they die?"

"They die in a way that is to God's liking. It happens when one is doing something to please Him."

"You mean if they die fighting?"

"Not just fighting," he said. "There are many acts that please Him other than fighting. For example, if you die restoring the rights of someone who has been wronged—that's also a beautiful death. If a man dies trying to feed his family: that's good also. But these are not even the half of it. A person should put his entire heart and soul into something that will satisfy God."

I raised my head. It was time to leave him, and leaving the mosque was much harder than entering it. I had hopes before that the news of his death was a lie and that he was in a coma, but when I put my ear to his chest and didn't hear his heart beating, I lost all hope. Now I was leaving with the certainty that he was gone, and that was very hard. For a moment I thought of the blessed Zeynab. I said goodbye to father and crawled backward to the door. I had no strength in my legs. The life spirit had drained out of me, as if I were stone or wood. I felt terrible when I reached the door and said "Hoseyn" to bolster my spirits. I felt an energy go through me as I got up and looked at father for the last time. Before I left the mosque I adjusted my headscarf and chador and rubbed my eyes and face with my hand. I knew what I had been through with father showed in my expression. I so wanted to run away from everything and everyone, to put the scene far behind me. I didn't want to see anybody, didn't want them to ask me anything, because I couldn't talk. It was as if there was something huge stuck in my throat, which was causing me to suffer terribly. I opened the wooden door and stood back.

As soon as the door opened I could feel the weight of everybody's stares on me. Zeynab, Sa'id, and Hasan came running toward me. They seemed to want to confirm father was dead. Their eyes were riveted on my face. Although I had told them not to cry, it was clear from my face how many tears I had shed. Zeynab stepped forward and asked in a childish voice, "Father's gone, isn't he?"

I felt that all their senses were trained on my face, waiting for a response. Choked up, I nodded and said, "Yeah, Daddy's gone."

They were stunned for a moment. I saw Hasan claw at his hair to keep himself from crying. Sa'id and Zeynab were also visibly in pain, and I felt someone should hug them. All at once they surrounded me, and the tears came. I bent down and gathered them in saying, "Daddy's with God. All of his sorrows are over now. You should be happy for him. He's watching us from above seeing everything we do."

As soon as mother, who had come a bit closer to the mosque, saw how much I had been crying, she started to wail like a banshee. These were difficult moments. I didn't know what everybody had expected—maybe that I would tell them something hopeful, like father really hadn't been killed. Through her tears mother said to me in Kurdish, "You're going to kill me with those tears."

I went over to her, embraced her, and tried to console her by talking about what the blessed Zeynab had suffered. She said, "I'd give my life for her." Then, continuing in Arabic, she repeated what she had said when I first saw her, "I've lost my protector. How can I get him back?" I didn't know whether to stay and look after her or to see to the children—whether to soothe my own aching heart or to lift the spirits of the others, people who at any minute could be killed by a rocket or a strafing.

Father's friends, who I didn't know very well, approached and, by way of greeting, nodded to me, saying, "Good for the Seyyed!" Then they asked me, "What can we do?"

Greeting them one by one would delay things for no reason, I thought, so I said it would be better to get the grave ready.

"We already dug one," they said, "but it filled with water, so we're digging another."

"What difference does it make? He'll have to be buried somewhere," I said.

"Yes, by that time the water will empty out," they said.

"There are still several graves that he dug himself," I said.

"They're also filled with water," they responded.

Then they brought a stretcher and put father on it. Salarvand, Parvizpur, the body washers, three of father's coworkers at the mayor's office, a few soldiers and local militia all accompanied the body. It was a strange sight taking him to the grave. Usually when somebody was lost, the deceased's entire family was on hand for the burial, but today not one of father's many relatives was there. Not even grandfather, which really upset me. It made me think of the funeral of Hoseyn, the Prince of Martyrs. How his body just lay on the ground with no one to accompany him to the grave and, adding insult to injury, the mutilation of his pure flesh and the imprisonment of his family. Father's bizarre funeral was nothing compared to the wicked and inhumane way they buried the blessed martyr.

It was odd, but I remembered the blessed Zeynab and called on her again and again to help me keep my composure, to help me go on. These thoughts and appeals all combined to make me stronger, to withstand the agony without losing control. The private weeping in the mosque had raised my spirits. Naturally I had gone there to see father, but the tears, which came automatically, were a relief.

The sounds of people crying "There is no God but Allah" and mother's moaning and keening echoed in the enclosure. Mother tried to walk in the procession but kept stumbling, only to get to her feet again. She was in a very bad way, bent over with her arms tightly wrapped around her waist, willing herself to move forward. At times I kept pace with the body, other times I went ahead or trailed behind. The tragedy was an unbearable weight, but I felt God had granted me enough strength to get through it.

I looked at the graves of the unknown as we passed by and wondered how many of them had been buried in the last few days. I was ashamed of my grief; at least there were several people to accompany father to the grave, but what about those poor souls? We didn't even know what names to put on some of the graves.

When we reached the gravesite, they put father's body down. As soon as mother saw the site, it was as if she had lost all hope or, as she put it, her house had been destroyed. She fell to the ground beside the grave and poured dirt over her head. In Kurdish she wailed, "My heart won't bear it, Abu Ali, what am to do with these orphans?"

Then she dragged herself close to father's feet and, as she wailed, I could make out her cursing father, "Get up, lying there, go and see what's happened to Zeynab, your little favorite. On your feet, you answer her. You comfort her, keep her from crying!"

Then she threw herself on his corpse. Leila was also hugging it, as Mohsen, Mansur, Hasan, and Sa'id sat around watching. Mohsen and Mansur tried to hug and comfort her. The woman Zeynab also kissed her and whispered consoling words. Maryam told her, "Don't let your grief out like this. Think of the children."

Father's coworkers took the children aside and comforted them. It was strange to see that even the soldiers were sobbing. Some left to have a smoke. Others sat down saying, "God is great," then got up. For a moment I thought it would be best to put father in the grave myself. Although my voice was shaking, I managed to control my emotions and I announced, "I'm going into the grave myself."

The cries of father's coworkers became louder. All of them and the body washers protested, "We're here. We'll do it."

"No, I want to be the one to put him in the grave," I said. I went in and asked them to pass him down to me.

As soon as she saw me there, mother's screeches got even louder. She began to wail, calling on her absent relatives: grandfather, her brothers, to come to her aid and put out the fires in her heart.

Then, turning to father's body, she moaned, "We're burying you like some stranger; there's nobody to see you off."

The effect of the grief became more intense with each moment. She droned on in Kurdish, in Arabic, standing up for a time, and then throwing herself on father's body. I got the feeling that when she sang in Arabic, it was more of a comfort than Kurdish. I could also hear the sounds of the children crying; five-year-old Zeynab's sobs being the loudest. With mother going on like that, the rest of the people also started wailing. Parvizpur and several others kept warning them their grieving only added to the suffering mother and the children felt.

I asked mother, "Didn't you promise me you would try to control yourself? Look at all the people here. They're like family to us, like our brothers. So what's the difference? They're offering their sympathy. Remember the blessed Zeynab, how there was nobody to comfort her. Think of Imam Hoseyn's children; how they were slapped around. Everybody here has treated your children with kindness and comforted them."

Then I repeated, "Pass father down to me."

One of the body washers joined me in the grave. The other men stepped forward and lifted him. Mother shrieked. The children, terrified, clung to her for dear life and cried in a louder voice.

Leila, who had been in my keeping these past few days, was now in hysterics, but I couldn't comfort her, as I was focused entirely on mother. If Ali had been there, I thought, things would have been easier. Mother's shrieks sent shivers down my entire body. My mind stopped working. I didn't know whether to climb out of the grave and embrace her or what. I was at a loss. It was unbearable seeing her like that. There had always been a mysterious bond between us; whenever she was away from home, visiting relatives for example, I wasn't myself until she returned. That was how much I felt her absence. Now that she was writhing on the ground that way, I was coming apart body and soul. My heart was in agony and it was hard to breathe—as if someone had taken all the oxygen from the air. I looked to sky in the hope of finding relief, but the world around me had gone dark. The air was thick with dust. All I could say was: "Mother, I swear for the love of father's soul, calm down! For the sake of the blessed Zeynab, control yourself. These poor children are having a fit seeing you this way!"

My swearing like that turned her shrieks into quiet sobbing. Parvizpur and one or two others lifted the body and handed it to me and the old man. I took father's head, pressed it to my chest and kissed him. But I couldn't take it any longer. I was physically and spiritually drained. My head felt like it was in a vice, while the rest of me was totally lifeless. Unable even to cry, in a husky voice I said, "I can't do it. Somebody help me."

One of the men slid into the grave and took the body by the waist. Then he called on the others to help. Zeynab and Leila grabbed me and hoisted me from the grave, otherwise I wouldn't have climbed out myself. Once out of the hole, however, I felt weak and collapsed in a heap. I still managed to crawl to the edge of the grave, where I had my last look at father, whose face was uncovered as they recited in Arabic over his body. The recitations gave me the feeling Judgment Day had come.

There was a saying from Imam Khomeini that I had seen written on a wall of the Imam Sadeq Mosque: "The red line of martyrdom is the lineage of Ali in the Family of the Prophet." The memory of that sentiment, so full of beauty and meaning, made me for a moment ashamed of feeling so sorry for myself. I pulled myself together. One of the soldiers who had been with father during his last moments told me in a quivering voice how he had sworn to avenge the Seyyed's blood. Even if ordered to retreat, he said, he would not leave Khorramshahr and allow the Iraqis to trample on the martyrs' remains. As the soldier spoke, an old Kurdish poem that father used to recite when I was a child came to my mind: "It's time for war, my belt is full of bullets … let my enemy beware."

Someone in the grave said to mother, "Lady Seyyed, it's time to come and ask the Seyyed's forgiveness."

Mother wailed, "What sins I have committed that I should beg for forgiveness from him? He's the one who should ask me for forgiveness." Nevertheless, she sat by the grave and said, "Seyyed, I have a long list of sins and I beg your forgiveness. I tried to be a partner in all the good times and the bad times in your life. If I failed in any way, please forgive me. Forgive me if I caused you any pain. Whatever goodness or evil we've had, forgive me. Be content with me and, God willing, the Lord will be content with you."

These words pierced my heart. Mother and father—both of them endured so much hardship, having been orphaned as children, which was harder on mother than it was on father; girls feel the loss more than boys.

As they were arranging the gravestones, my heart was in turmoil. I sat by the grave, clawing the earth, breaking up the clods. All the while my eyes, my whole being, were fixed on the corpse.

With the stones finally in place, I had to face the fact that there was no hope of seeing father again. Mother, who had finished her asking for forgiveness, was now staring vacantly in silence. It seemed that the shrieking had taken all the life from her. She would whimper from time to time, though.

All my senses were trained on father until they put the final stone in place and they began to shovel dirt on him. I couldn't stand to be there any longer. I rose with difficulty; my legs wouldn't hold the weight, but somehow I managed to walk away from the grave. But as I got closer to where the soldiers and the others were standing, I felt that what I had done was not right. I returned to the grave and began shoveling earth on it with my hands, saying under my breath, "Sleep well, father, sleep well. It's finally time to rest."

With all my heart I wished Ali and some of his friends were there so they could chant for father the same songs they chanted for the martyred soldiers. But I knew this was impossible; the mourning would have to go on in silence. I couldn't possibly chant something for him myself—not out loud. So I began to recite something I had heard at the recitals for the martyrs at Karbala:

O campsite of father of Abdollah, why do you lament?
They have abandoned us both to everlasting pain
and sorrow.

The men piled earth on the grave and brought a jagged piece of stone on which Parvizpur had written with a marker: "The Martyr Seyyed Hoseyn Hoseyni, Felled by Shrapnel, September 27, 1980."

Then I found myself chanting:

O forlorn, O Hoseyn, O Martyr, O Hoseyn, O Karbala, O cruel to us, O forlorn, O Hoseyn, O slaughtered, woe unto us, O forlorn, O Hoseyn

I neither saw nor heard anyone now. The whole scene was shrouded in mist and dust. I had no idea how they managed to move me from the gravesite and get me back to Jennatabad building. All I heard was the chant asking Hoseyn to intercede for us.

The woman Zeynab took the children by the hand and we got under way. It was getting dark by the time we reached the Sheikh Salman Mosque. People from the neighborhood and those in the mosque came forward gathering around us. All the aunts came by to embrace mother and the children, kissing them and offering their condolences. All of them were weeping. The mother of Reza said, "The last time I saw the Seyyed I had the feeling he was a goner; he had that special glow about him. I could tell by the way he acted he wasn't long for this world."

With tears streaming down her face, the wife of Uncle Gholami agreed, saying with her Bandari accent, "Yeah, that's right; when the Seyyed came to the door of our home, it dawned on me that the man wasn't going to be with us long." She turned to me and said, "Your uncle's hurting badly now that his brother's gone. He felt alone before, but now it's worse."

Mother and the children were seated on some carpeting people had spread in the yard. The neighbors kept on grieving for them, but mother, who was now squatting in a corner, didn't even have the strength to cry. I heard her moan feebly from time to time, but it wasn't clear whether she was mourning or just weeping.

I felt terrible and couldn't sit still. It was like I was choking but I couldn't clear my throat. I remembered father telling me not to lose hope no matter how bad things got. "It's true," he said, "that the Iraqis outnumber us, but we have the Imam. We have faith on our side. Let the whole world come and stand against us. History is about to repeat itself. The Prince of Martyrs also faced overwhelming forces."

His words helped ease the pain a bit for me, but what about mother? I felt very sorry for her and called on God to give her the strength to go on. I recited from the Quran, "You we worship, and to You we turn for help," and puffed air in her direction to try to calm her.

After a time just sitting there didn't seem right, so I rose and said to mother, "I've got to go."

"Where to?" she asked without emotion.

"The Congregational Mosque."

The woman Zeynab asked, "Where do you think you're going, dear? What good will it do?"

She said "dear" so tenderly that I wanted to kiss her face. "We need to get back to work. How long do you think we can sit around here?"

"Don't leave me," said mother almost begging me. "Till now there's been your father, but…."

I didn't let her finish the sentence. "Don't worry, Mom, I'm not going anywhere. I'll be right around here."

The two women, Leila and Zeynab, also stood. Zeynab whispered to mother, “I can’t say how sorry I feel for you. If only a few of your kin were here.” She turned to the neighbors and said, “Don’t let her be by herself, I beg you. I’ll drop by regularly and see how she’s doing.”

The three of us left the mosque together. I separated from them in the alley and headed for the Congregational Mosque. As soon as I got there the women surrounded me, offering their sympathies. I tried as hard as I could to keep calm responding to them. The girls were all choked up as they consoled me. Ra’na Najjar was especially devastated. I turned to them and asked, “You all knew that father had been killed. What kept you from telling me?”

Zohreh Farhadi said, “You’re right, but it was hard, because we didn’t think you’d take the news as well as you have. The way you are coping is helping us stay calm.”

Struggling to keep my emotions in check, I said, “I thank God father got his wish. He said there’s nothing wrong with death, so long as it’s a good one, a death that pleases God. It’s worth it to die on God’s path.”

“You’re almost acting as if your father’s death hasn’t affected you at all,” said one of the girls.

“This was his choice. For years he’s been hoping he’d die that way. By the way, he’s no different from other martyrs; they’re all my father and brothers.”

When the call to prayer sounded I left them, washed, and went into the prayer room. Wanting to be alone, I stood behind a pillar. First I prayed, then I sat down with only God as company. I couldn’t stop thinking about the responsibility father had put on my shoulders. It was weighing on me. I began to cry as I thought: How was I supposed to take his place as the head of the family? I turned to God for help.

But there was no escaping the conflict raging within me. I argued back and forth with myself and finally reasoned that since father had died in a way that pleased God, God would now help us get through this. How could the God who won’t allow a tiny plant in a vast wasteland to perish forget us? If that happened, I thought, then where could we turn?

I felt a bit better after prayers and entered the compound where they were serving people supper. I helped take portions of cheese from the 17-kilo tins and placed them in plastic bags. Then we bundled flatbread and handed the bundles to people waiting in line. We also gave out tins of tuna, canned eggplant, and broad beans to both the soldiers and civilian militiamen who, covered in grime, were in a hurry to get back to the front.

As I worked I couldn't help reminiscing about father: the time when he banged his fist on that sign saying that Banisadr had betrayed us by not sending troops to the front. The more I thought about him the more I hated the traitor.

I was so busy that I didn't pay attention to what was happening around me. Suddenly I realized the girls were standing around me, expressing their sympathy and love. Mrs. Purheydari, one of the more hard-working women at the mosque, kissed my cheek periodically and assured me of her affection. But I found this a bit annoying. Their pity, I felt, was based on the assumption that father had merely died rather than become a martyr in the true sense. This was why I chose to keep my distance. At the same time I was heartsick about mother and the kids. So when there was a lull in serving dinner, I stopped and headed back to the Salman Mosque.

It was now pitch black outside, and anybody who had gone from the mosque was now back safely inside. Several people were standing guard at the entrance. Inside the compound families were bunched in small groups by the wall, which had regular indentations like prayer niches. This allowed the families to have a modicum of privacy.

Still grieving, mother huddled against the wall, resting her chin on one hand while she stroked her head with the other. The children, also still mourning, were gathered around her. The only one not near her was Mansur, who was walking in the yard. It broke my heart to see them like that; it was a scene that I wanted to avoid. When I drew closer, the children got up and I took Sa'id and Zeynab in my arms and caressed them. Seeing this, mother burst into tears. I let the children go, took mother in my arms, and kissed her face. "What am I supposed to do without your father?" she asked between sobs. "What can I do with them with him not around?" Her words struck me to the quick, despite the immense grief I already felt; even so I was able to keep my emotions in check. Mother's show of grief caused the children, whose eyes were now on me, to begin crying again, and I knew I had to keep myself from breaking down in front of them. There was enough pain to go around that day, after all. I said to mother, "Why are you being like this? Would it have been better that father had died in a car accident or from being sick?" All she could manage was a feeble "Praise God. Praise God."

"So why are you going on like that?" I asked.

"Nothing stops the pain I feel in my heart," she explained.

I spoke to her until she calmed down and finally said, "Zahra, I don't know what it is about what you're saying, but your words give me strength."

Seeing her in that state upset me nevertheless. She had lost her own mother when she was a child and had to endure a lot because of it.

From the day they were married, mother and father's problems never stopped, but they were happy together. As she rested her head on my shoulder, I recalled that father was forever declaring his love for her. Even after having eight children, they doted on each other like newlyweds. Whenever father would come home to find mother out, he'd get all wound up and pace up and down until she returned. Whenever he came home from work, he'd sit down with her, and they'd talk and joke. When I was a child, it struck me how much more attractive and how much younger father looked than mother, and I tried to figure out what made him love her so much. But as I grew older and saw how kind and patient she was, I understood that father was right. Mother's understanding and good sense were more precious than good looks.

Father never lost his temper with mother no matter how bad things got financially. Even when he came back from work empty-handed, ashamed that he couldn't provide for the family, mother would comfort him by saying, "So it's not like the end of the world. God will provide; thanks to Him we won't starve." Then she would whip up some dinner to show that the larder wasn't bare. Mother never mentioned our money problems to grandfather or to her brother.

But even when her family did bring it up, she would defend father by saying, "The man's a hard worker who'd never dream of stealing."

For his part father looked after her. Because mother's last name was Shah Pasand, meaning "lantana," father planted the bushes in our little garden, and you have no idea how carefully he looked after them. Whenever Mother's Day rolled around, he would take some time thinking about what to buy her. He gave us money and told us to buy presents for her. I don't know where he got the idea that an expensive necklace would make her happy, because she had never said anything about it. I noticed that he struggled to put a little aside each month in his savings account, and one day there it was—that grand necklace. Although she was overjoyed, she rarely wore it and later sold it to buy a gas-operated cooler that made the summers bearable. Father was very upset but mother insisted.

I stayed there for half an hour as she grieved for this man. When I started to leave, she said, "Stay."

"I've got work to do," I said curtly.

"Don't go away like that," she pleaded. "I know you. You'll just rush some place dangerous. But think of me; I can't go through this again. One death is enough."

"It's not like that," I said. "I'll be working at the Congregational Mosque caring for the wounded. Then I'm going to Jennatabad to look in on Leila. Don't worry." I said this knowing full well I had every intention of going to the front. I wanted to see the spot where father had died.

I hadn't gone far when I saw the Reza's mother, our across-the-street neighbor, who was on her way to our house with a plate of food for the children. I asked her to look after mother and the children. She said, "God bless your dad. When I look at little Zeynab, the one he loved so much, my heart just breaks. Your mother is going through hell; she hasn't stopped crying since last night. God help her, she's had quite a time of it. Wish you could be with her."

I headed for the Congregational Mosque. In the yard I bumped into Mr. Soleymani. Though I was aware of where they kept the food and how much there was, I wanted to get his permission to bring some to Jennatabad. I said, "I'm on my way to Jennatabad. Do you have anything for them?"

He said, "Take some bread and watermelons," and I went to where the food was and grabbed some bread and choice melons, which had come from Esfahan. There were no bags around, so I pulled a woman's blouse from a pile of clothes in the yard and wrapped the food in it. I tied the sleeves together and carried the bundle on my back like a pack. The heavy load dug into my back, and I felt I didn't have the strength to make it. The streets were empty and dark. Not a creature was around. As I slinked along by the walls, I heard the whistling of the mortars. Soon I was good at telling which ones were far away and which were close. I crouched down often and cradled my head in my arms, waiting for a shell to find me. Then I got up and continued walking. The dogs growling in the empty alleys robbed me of the nerve to go on. I saw cats darting in every direction terrified by the sounds of explosions. I was so familiar with the way to Jennatabad that I could find it with my eyes closed. As I passed our house, the thought that father would never return brought tears to my eyes. If I hadn't had my hands full, I would have stopped. My heart beat faster the closer I got to Jennatabad. My connection to the place was stronger now that father was buried there. I prayed to God that I wouldn't see anyone so I could go straight to his grave. My longing to visit him had grown since that afternoon. But as luck would have it, everybody was congregated in front of the body washers'. I called out to Leila, who was sitting next to Zeynab in the pale moonlight. She got up and walked reluctantly to me. Something had changed in her; she was more withdrawn, and, as she approached, I sensed she did didn't want me to see her face. She greeted me and I asked, "Everything okay?" She said nothing. It was clear that she had been weeping. She looked at me furtively. Zeynab came from behind her, and I could sense that she wanted to comfort me, to tell me that I wasn't alone.

I greeted Zeynab and she said, "Hello, little mother. Welcome back. Look at the trouble you've gone to, bringing food for us."

She took the bundle from me and, trying to lighten things, joked, "Watermelons again? How much time do you want us to spend in the restroom? We'll never thaw out with all the cold food you're feeding us!"

Then we joined the others. When I said hello, everyone stood out of respect. Maryam hugged me and said, "Girl, I really miss you when you're not around."

I thanked her and said, "I want to go to father's grave, if you don't mind." But she grabbed my arm and wouldn't let go, demanding, "Sit down. You're tired. You can go later."

I sat on some carpeting that they had put down, not bothering to take my shoes off. Zeynab, Maryam, and the older woman started talking to distract Leila and me from thinking about father. Leila didn't say a word. I knew that she was on the verge of tears, but wouldn't cry in front of me. I thought that if I cried she would follow suit, but I knew I mustn't let that happen. Why inflict that on the poor body washers? They were just trying to relax after hours of preparing the bodies for burial; it wouldn't be right to show them how miserable we were.

I tried to break the silence and speak normally with Zeynab, Maryam, and Khadijeh. The old men would occasionally join in our conversation, analyzing what was going on. The minutes did not pass quickly for me; the atmosphere had become heavy. I didn't want to be there, pretending everything was normal. I wanted to escape from their talk about how things were going. The telephone rang, coming to my rescue. When one of the men got up to answer it, I saw my chance to leave; but just at that moment, the man called out to me saying, "They want you down at the Congregational Mosque. You'd better get there as quickly as you can."

This came as a surprise. I didn't think that they knew me well enough to summon me personally. As I was leaving I gestured to Zeynab, telling her to look after Leila. She nodded, assuring me not to worry on that score. I bent down and hugged Leila and kissed her face, saying softly, "Don't worry. It was an honor for father to be martyred. It's a credit to us."

I said goodbye and desperately wanted to visit father, but they had said I had to get to the mosque as quickly as possible. I walked by the grave just to say a quick hello behind the sign so nobody would see me. Even the sign that father had pounded with his fist had become dear to me. I kissed it and stood by the grave in the darkness. In the past when he had been away for only a few days, I missed father. But now, after a few hours away from him, I couldn't bear it. I recalled the times I played the brat, deliberately not listening to him, and felt miserable for doing it. More than anything I craved his forgiveness. But I managed to put all those thoughts out of my head, paying my respects and berating him at the same time: "Hello, Father. Why did you break your promise? How could you leave us in the lurch like that? How did you have the nerve to abandon little Zeynab? Didn't you promise mother you wouldn't let her suffer any more? She's worse off than ever now. You could have at least waited until Ali had returned before abandoning us."

With tears streaming down my face, I continued, "You wanted to go, but think how long Zeynab will be an orphan. Whose knee will she sit on now? Who will give her piggyback rides? Who's going to get the hugs and kisses you hungered for? Now that you've gone and left us, beg God not to abandon us."

I ran my hand across the sign. There was no more time. "Now Ali's back in Khorramshahr," I said at last, "tell God I want to join you; beg Him to let me be with you."

Then I raced from Jennatabad, which had become mired in grief for me, and headed for the mosque, all the while trying to figure out what was so urgent they had to summon me by name. I hadn't quite reached the entrance when one of the men said, "Sister Hoseyni, they're hysterical again. You've got to do something. Maybe you can get them to calm down."

He was referring to three or four shell-shocked women and their children. In those days people didn't know about such things and couldn't figure out why women were behaving so abnormally. This was why their first thought was that there was something wrong with them mentally, but now it was dawning on people that the blasts were the cause of the problem. The women and children had come in by themselves from various parts of the city, except for one girl blind from birth, who was brought in by her grandfather.

That evening the blind girl began to race around the yard, shrieking with every explosion. I ran out, grabbed her, and asked, "What is it? Why are you screaming? Don't be afraid."

"I'm scared," she said.

"Don't worry. Nothing's going to happen here. Everybody's safe here."

"No, the Iraqis are coming," she said.

"They wouldn't dare take children from their parents. I'm here, don't worry. Go inside the mosque and whenever you need something, tell me." This calmed her and she said, "Please stay with me. Don't go. I'm not scared when you're here."

"I can't stay here now," I said. "There's other work for me, but whenever you need anything, just let me know and I'll be here for you."

Having seen how I had handled the girl before, the people at the mosque summoned me from Jennatabad when they couldn't calm her. When I arrived, I went inside the prayer room. The cries from the yard had the poor people inside at their wits end. The girls tried everything but were unable to calm the people. Zohreh Farhadi, Ra'na Najjar, and Maryam Amjadi were furious. They told me that the first person to start shouting was a victim of shell shock, a young light-complexioned woman who was a few months pregnant. The others started in after her. I looked at the woman and it seemed impossible from her appearance that anything was physically wrong with her, but she was in a bad way nevertheless. She was shrieking and trembling terribly, saying, "They've killed everybody, cut their heads off! Now, now they're coming to get everybody here!"

The girls helped me take her aside. Her body was shaking violently and her mouth was dry. She had no strength left after all the shouting and spasms. The girls brought some sugar water and forced it down her throat. With her taken care of, I had to see to the others. I ran into the yard and got some preserves out of a box. Then I found some bread. As soon as they saw me with the food, they stepped forward and started to gripe. It was a lucky thing I spoke Arabic, because all the hysterical women were Arabs. I talked my head off, assuring them that their safety was my only concern, and I was finally able to calm them down a bit. With the girls' help, I managed to feed them.

We caught our breath, thinking there would be no more trouble from them. For a few hours at least they would rest their heads on the floor. But less than an hour later, the hysterics began again. They were marching around and making a racket. They wanted to leave, but we wouldn't let them. All hell broke loose, and now I was quite furious. After all the Arabic chit chat, it was the same thing, and the worst of it was that being cooped up had made them even stronger. One-on-one we were no match for them. We had to get the medical assistant from the pharmacy to help us contain them.

The assistant, whose name was Khalil Najjar, recommended we sedate all victims of shell shock and isolate them in one part of the mosque. After a few hours, relative peace returned and Ra'na Najjar, who had been horror-stricken by the all the shouting, now couldn't thank me enough, trying to build up my spirits so I'd be ready for the next bout of hysterics. She said, "If it weren't for you, I don't know what we would have done."

Maryam Amjadi's blood was boiling, and Zohreh Farhadi, whom I had seen clawing at her cheeks during the melee, said, "These people are a disgrace. Why don't they do something about them?"

Exhausted, I leaned against the wall and closed my eyes. A woman I had spotted when I entered the mosque was groaning. Her pregnancy didn't have long to go, and the girls had tried to get her to the hospital several times. Despite her obvious discomfort, she refused, saying that this was no time to bring a child into the world. She paced back and forth, occasionally stopping to writhe in the shelter of a wall. They kept bringing in the wounded all through the night, and I did whatever I could for them. During the lulls, I permitted myself to lean against a wall and nap for a few minutes. My ears wouldn't cooperate, however; I would wake with a start at the slightest noise. Father was with me at all times. I saw him beside me and spoke to him. I saw how the pharmacist Mr. Najjar and the girls tended to the wounded, and wondered what would have happened if there had been people like them with father when he was dying. Whenever I asked how he died, all they'd say was: "He was at the front." This made me wonder what was going on at the front. What was it like? Obviously people were firing at one another. I wanted to go there and see for myself. Because they decided to transport the dead to other cities, there would be less work at Jennatabad. Tending to the wounded would take precedence. If they could be treated in time, we would lose fewer people.

I grappled with these thoughts until morning. At the crack of dawn the pregnant woman got worse it seemed, and she was shouting for help. Men went out to find a vehicle, and finally a truck pulled up. Several of us piled into it, and we took her to a birthing center. On the way back I stopped in at the Salman Mosque, where most people were still asleep. I saw mother with Zeynab busy lighting a camp stove. Hasan and Sa'id were asleep. Mansur was out in the yard. As soon as he saw me, he rushed to me with a big smile on his face. I put my arms around his neck and said, "So Mansur, what've you been up to?"

"Nothing. There's nothing to do here. It's boring."

Like everybody else, I had thought then that the firing would stop and we could get back to our lives. I told him, "God will bring this to an end, and you'll be back in school soon."

I walked over to mother and said hello. She looked up at me with those hound-dog eyes of hers and quipped, "So, child, you're here?"

"Yeah. What's happening? How do you feel?" I asked.

"How should I feel? This is a horror."

"No, mother, wrong word; it's an honor," I corrected her.

"You don't understand, girl; you're too wrapped up in this. Wait till the war ends, then you'll get what's happened to you." She teared up and said, "I want to visit the grave."

"You were just there yesterday, weren't you?" I asked.

"What do you mean?"

"Don't you remember," I said, "people normally go to the grave on the third day? Wait a day."

Worried about her health, I didn't want her to break down again.

"What's that got to do with it?" she sobbed. "Did I get a chance to have a proper ceremony for him? So now I have to wait for the third day like normal people? Could things get any worse for us?"

This made me angry. I said sharply, "Mother, everybody's in the same boat. It isn't right for people to give into their grief whenever they feel like it."

Our arguing woke up Hasan and Sa'id, and they greeted me with sour faces. Sensing they were on the verge of tears, I also choked up; I couldn't stand to see mother and the boys cry. I was yelling at mother, I realized, to keep my own emotions in check. A few moments later I calmed down and said, "Mother, just wait a while and I'll bring you and the kids to Jennatabad myself."

She was bent double and had wrapped her simple cloth around her forehead the way Kurdish women do when they are grieving. She also wrapped a dark cloth around her waist. She didn't seem to have the strength to move. I wanted to go and find a vehicle so she wouldn't have to go to Jennatabad on foot. She said, "I'll wait for you; if you come, fine, but it not, I'll go on my own."

"Fine," I said. Then I hugged and kissed Zeynab, who had been glued to me the whole time. To her it was as if nothing had happened. Where the family was now living and what was happening to us didn't seem to register. So it was natural for her to ask, "Are you going to bring that pink dress Daddy got me?"

I looked down at her. Father had just bought the dress for her. She continued, "And don't forget the toys, too: the doll and the cooking pot. I want to play house here with the other kids."

I ran my fingers through her lovely hair and said, "I can't. Maybe some other time."

Annoyed, she said, "Then take me with you, please, please! I really miss you!"

"No, love, I can't. Where I'm going is dangerous."

She squeezed my hand and said anxiously, "If it's dangerous, why are you going there, Zahra? You shouldn't."

I realized what a stupid thing I had said, upsetting the child for nothing, and added, "Oh, don't be afraid, I can take care of myself, but if you come along, it'll tie my hands and I won't be able to do anything."

With Zeynab still clinging to me, I looked down at Sa'id. Those big black eyes of his seemed to be talking for him; he was so quiet and unassuming and innocent. I pried Zeynab loose and sat down by Hasan and Sa'id; but Zeynab had just gotten started, and, with nobody to stop her, she chattered on and on. Out of respect for the people who were still asleep, I kept my voice down answering her questions. When I go up to go, Zeynab having lost all hope that I would be back, said, "Stay!" I repeated that I had things to do, and she threw a tantrum. The tears finally came and she said, "I'm sick of it here. Let's go home. If we do, daddy will come." She had forgotten about his death. I couldn't take any more of this and left the mosque. On the way back I stopped in at the Congregational Mosque to grab some bread and cheese. I stayed there long enough to see how Leila was doing. Her spirits seemed to have improved since the day before. She told me that they hadn't brought in any corpses since the previous night. I said, "Mother wants to come to Jennatabad. If possible I'll arrange for a vehicle so she and the children won't have to come all that way on foot."

I gave the bread and cheese to Hoseyn and Abdollah, who were sitting by the curb, and said goodbye. Abdollah took the M1 from his shoulder and ran after me saying, "Ms Hoseyni, I'm coming with you; there's nothing for me to do here."

We headed for the Congregational Mosque and hadn't quite reached the main road when we heard the sounds of some horrendous explosions. They were shelling the area around the Ordibehesht traffic circle. The closer we got to the area, the more I could hear the sounds of houses being blasted apart and shrapnel striking the metal shutters of the shops. The murmuring of the crowd and cries of Allah Akbar also became louder. I told Abdollah to make a run for the circle, which was under mortar fire. Every ten meters another round landed, and I could feel the thuds from the blasts push against my chest, hollowing out my insides. The explosions sounded to me like death itself, and I envisioned myself bathed in a bloody redness before I died. That kind of death had beauty and dignity, which was why I welcomed the roar of the mortars.

At times the noise and the shock waves were so strong they stopped us in our tracks. The houses in Khorramabad, most of which were made of mud, blew apart, sending so much dust into the air that

I couldn't see my hand in front of my face. The shock waves were so strong some of the houses actually imploded.

Some people were fleeing their homes in terror, while others were running toward the ruins to see if they could help. We got to the lane that had suffered the most shelling, and about halfway down encountered two wounded men propped up against a wall. One of them was an older man with shrapnel in his legs. The other, wounded in the arms, legs, and face, was no more than twenty-five. Neither man's condition appeared serious. Seemingly in shock, the older man cried, "Look! Look! They tried to murder me!" His leg was bleeding profusely from a gaping wound. I told the people who had gathered to find some cloth to stop the bleeding.

The man shrieked at the sight of his own blood. His face, which had been bronzed by the sun, now had the pallor of death. Several men tried to comfort him, telling him that at the hospital they'd take care of him.

I tied some cloth around his thigh to staunch the blood flow, something I had learned the previous night. I examined other places where shrapnel had penetrated his skin. I tried to stop the blood flowing from his calf and arm with the cloth. After I did the same for the younger man, I told the men there to try to find a vehicle so we could get them to the hospital.

One of the men went off to get his motorcycle. I showed Abdollah how to stop the younger man's bleeding. The man with the motorcycle arrived, and we loaded the wounded men on it, first the older one, then the younger. The poor creatures were in terrible pain as they rode off to the hospital. Walking further up the lane, we met two or three men and several children wailing. A shell had hit their kitchen where the two young women in the house had been preparing breakfast, killing both. People helped us retrieve the bodies and pile them into a pickup. One of the men, who held his wife's identity card in his hand, stared helplessly at us and then at her body as they transported it to the cemetery. He couldn't believe how, in the space of a few seconds, his whole life had been wiped out. Time was short so Abdollah and I took a glance at the other homes down the lane, asking those standing around, "Any more wounded?" "No," someone said, and I told people not to stay. "They're going to keep on shelling, and no one will be here to help the wounded," I said. "It'd be foolish to die just from a scratch."

I returned to the Congregational Mosque, where they had placed five or six huge copper cooking pots in the yard. If I remember correctly, the first hot meal was split yellow pea stew. I told the women who had done the cooking to leave the washing up to me. After washing the plates and pots, I sat and cut up slabs of flatbread into pieces to put on the stew. A truck pulled up with a load of dry bread in bags, sacks filled with old blankets and clothes, and cans of preserved food. We carried the food and clothing into the prayer room, and, as I walked back and forth from the truck, I saw Khosrow, the dark-haired boy from yesterday dressed in the work outfit. At the same time one of the women helping to unload the truck emerged from the prayer room. I had seen her around a few times during the past few days. She seemed very good-natured. She helped out at the mosque during the day and went home at night. She reminded me of one my relatives. She stopped when she saw me talking to Khosrow and said, "This is my boy, Khosrow, but it seems you two already know each other."

"Yeah, Mom, we do. This is Sister Hoseyni, the Zeynab of our time. You know she buried her father with her own hands. Do you believe that? It's unbelievable. Could you imagine me burying dad with my own hands?"

The woman's mood changed abruptly and she yelled at the boy, "Khosrow, when you speak of your father like that, you must say GOD FORBID!"

Khosrow, in with his own special accent, said, "That's mom. I tell her that she buried her martyr dad, and she yells at me for not saying GOD FORBID."

The truck was unloaded quickly. I saw Mr. Najjar seemed to be free for a moment, so I took the opportunity to ask him if I could help with nursing the wounded. In one way or another I was going to get to the front—even if it was as a nurse. I didn't know Mr. Najjar well enough to predict how he would react to the request. He was a man of medium height, around thirty, with a dark complexion and frizzy hair.

A piercing stare and a mustache conspired to make him look very serious.

He was Khalil Najjar, but he told the girls to call him Khalili. I decided to take the bull by the horns and walked over to where he was talking to Zohreh and Ashraf, who introduced me to him. It appeared that they had spoken to him about me, because his tone was polite and respectful when he said, "At such times we normally say: 'congratulations,' but I'll offer my condolences. I was amazed to learn from the girls that such a young woman could bury her father with her own hands. I thought you'd be much older."

I thanked him and said, "I would like to help out here, but I'm afraid I don't know anything about medicine. I'm a fast learner, though!"

"Do you have any course work in nursing?" he asked.

"No, what course?" I asked.

"I mean in first aid, meaning do you know how to deal with someone who is wounded or injured?"

"Not a thing."

"What about giving injections?"

"I'd be afraid to; never did anything like that before."

He said, "Not a problem. You can stay here for now and begin with the light chores, things like rolling bandages, stocking the trolley with tape."

"Do you operate on people here?" I asked.

"No, we don't have facilities for that," he said. "We only remove shrapnel from surface wounds, bandage people, and stop their bleeding. This place is not sterile enough for anything more serious."

Then by way of my first lesson he picked up a syringe and a pillow and quickly gave it an injection. He had taught many of the girls to give injections this way, and Zohreh and I took the pillow and syringe from him, bursting out laughing as we punctured the thing.

It was just my luck at that point they brought in a wounded man. He happened to be Maryam's brother, Ali Amjadi, and his foot was badly infected from a cut. Because he hadn't been able to remove his boot that day, the infection had spread. Mr. Najjar told Ali to sit on the floor.

Then he bent down and struggled to remove the boot, making Ali writhe in pain. He bit his lip but said nothing. Before removing Ali's sock, Mr. Najjar poured disinfectant over it, trying to make it easier to pry from the infected skin.

Maryam couldn't stand seeing her brother in agony. She sat on the floor behind him and tried to comfort him by putting her arms around his neck. "Stop that!" Ali barked. "What are you doing?" But Maryam wouldn't stop. Seeing them like that reminded me of our Ali, also a member of the guards. I missed him badly and wished I could hug him the way Maryam hugged her brother. After a few minutes, Mr. Najjar was able to remove the sock and apply pressure to the wound to clear the pus. The pain made Ali squeeze his hands together and mutter prayers under his breath.

I had an idea of what he was going through. It reminded me of the time I stepped on a nail, and my foot got infected. I was nauseous and went into the yard to clear my head. Seeing the women washing rice and beans, I grabbed a tray and got to work. The mosque was a busy place, with people constantly coming and going. As I worked I kept my eye on the entrance to see if wounded were being brought in. After the pilaf was cooked, I began to ladle it out into sacks or pots for the fighters. The oil company had supplied disposable containers for food. As we worked Hajj Aqa Mohammadi, Hajj Aqa Nuri, and another clergyman around fifty with a face darkened by the sun and salt-and-pepper hair led us in rounds of spirited prayers. Everyone within earshot responded in loud voices. Upon learning that I was the daughter of a martyred Seyyed, the dark complexioned man, whose name I don't remember, treated me with great respect.

Seeing the trucks had been loaded with the pots of rice for the front, I made up my mind. I had decided this was the time for me to go to the forward lines. When I saw the lightly armed police out there by themselves, I thought: The Iraqis had tanks, what did our boys have? In a port city like Khorramshahr, there were places to take cover, but out there in the field the police would be defenseless. We had heard rumors of soldiers bleeding to death from simple wounds. Medical personnel at the front could do wonders. I found it hard to believe reports of manpower shortages, what with the crowds at the mosque.

They probably had no training, I reasoned, but then I thought: We would stop the enemy with sticks and clubs if we had to.

Wasting no time, I walked over to the men around one truck and asked, "Brothers, can I come with you?"

"Impossible," they said.

"Why?" I asked.

"We're on our way to deliver food."

"Fine," I said. "I'll come and hand out food."

"We've got enough people. You're not needed."

"I've been working since morning preparing the food," I explained, "now all I want is to serve it to the brothers myself."

"It's dangerous. Tanks and mortars are operating there."

"If it's dangerous for me, it's dangerous for you, too. What's the difference?"

Realizing I had an answer for every objection, they stopped arguing. It seemed they weren't prepared for this. I hopped into the back of the pickup as it left. There were many of them now in front of the mosque, each going in a different direction. The one I was on was heading for Railroad Circle. The driver sped along making my chador fly up. I had trouble keeping my chador in place, while, at the same time, helping the others steady the rice pots. They would spill over when the truck hit a bump in the road. The streets were full of craters from bombs and mortar hits, and the driver zigzagged madly around them. But sometimes he had no choice and the truck went into a hole, sending the pots flying into the air. The streets became more deserted the closer we got to the front. Signs of fighting were etched into the walls of the homes and in the tree trunks, many of which were stripped of their branches or charred by the shelling. Dogs and cats scrambled for shelter. As the shelling intensified, the driver slowed down. It came to a stop at the traffic circle, where the sounds of the two sides firing at each other were unmistakable. The boys on the truck ladled food into the nylon sacks and gave them to the defenders by the stadium wall. I looked at them closely. They were obviously from the city, irregulars without uniforms. They looked dead tired, but only one of them had opened the collar of his blue shirt because of the heat. He was wearing a dark green helmet, which was obviously taken from one of the Iraqis. As soon as he saw me, he asked, "What are you doing here, sister? It's not safe."

His tone, which seemed high and mighty, offended me. I said, "If it's dangerous, what keeps you here? I'm no different from you." Then I quickly got back on the pickup, and we were off. The driver raced ahead about two or three hundred meters, to a place where a number of boys had taken cover. They banged on the cab and the driver stopped to give them some food. While the food was being distributed, I took a closer look at the road. They had ripped out the concrete curbs and covered them with dirt and turf to make a barrier. The trees here were stripped bare. I jumped down from the pickup and went through the alleys around the traffic circle with food; giving it to the few people I met. Most of the fighters had taken positions on the roofs, where they shouted instructions to those on the ground. They were also firing at the Iraqis. Although this place wasn't exactly the front line, we could hear fighters giving orders from above: "Go there and fire! Watch out for the tank! Get that RPG guy! Watch your back!" The shouts sent shivers down my spine. There was no telling what would happen next, and I was scared. The shooting got more intense, seeming to come from all directions. Even though I was surrounded by buildings, I knew that if I had stood up, I would have been cut down by machine gun fire coming from the buildings opposite us. As I went ahead, crouching by the walls, I could hear the sounds of the tank treads like the one I had seen on the Forty-Meter Road.

As I moved forward I wondered how the poor souls were going to eat with all this going on; nevertheless, I gave out sacks of food to everyone I met. Some of the defenders were surprised to see the hot meals but said that this was no time to eat. Others welcomed the food, asking, "What have you brought us?" Some said they had no idea that there would be food and were happy to see that people in the back lines had given them any thought at all.

To them I'd say, "Naturally they're thinking about you. So long as we're here, you won't have any worries on that score." They thanked me, and those who had the time sat by a wall and ate. Handing out food to those who really deserved it was very gratifying to me.

It was important to let them know people behind the lines were concerned about their welfare.

As I was leaving the alley, I asked if there were others who had not eaten. People said there were, so I left sacks for them. I went back to the pickup for more food. As I pulled the pot toward me, I heard someone ask, "What are you doing here?"

"What are *you* doing here?" I repeated.

"Well, I've come to fight, naturally," he said.

"Well, I've come to feed," I said.

"Isn't there anybody else to do that?"

"What difference does that make? We're all the same," I said.

"I meant," he said, "there are brothers who can do it. So long as there are men around to bring food, women shouldn't have to come to the front."

"Why not? Is my blood redder or more precious than theirs?" I asked.

"That's not what I meant. There are Iraqis everywhere here. What if one of them sneaks up on you?"

"Let him," I said bluntly.

"This one's got an answer for everything," he said testily. "What if they take you prisoner, girl?"

"So why are you standing around here and arguing?" I asked him. Then he threw up his hands and said, "Okay, friend, forget it! Do whatever the hell you want!"

I said, "Don't think that only men can fight; women can also. My father said that at times like these it makes no difference who's a man and who's a woman."

The fellows who had come with me on the pickup explained to him, "We've told her the same thing, but nothing we said worked. Now that we're at the front, you want to convince her to go back?"

I picked up the nylon sacks and went through the alleys in the area for a second time. In some places I had to crouch down and, when the firing got too bad, I sat. Then I ran as fast as I could. People I met would snap at me, "Where the hell did you come from? Who brought you here?"

I ignored them and went on, this being no place to argue. Seeing no one in some places, I would call out, "Anybody here!" Hearing no answer, I ran back. Though the very thought was terrifying, I felt like climbing on the roof of a house and joining the battle myself. After the food ran out, I returned to the pickup to find that everything had been doled out. I really wanted to stay behind and said so to my companions.

This took them by surprise, "Stay and do what?" they asked.

Considering just my coming to the front a miracle, I said, "There's always work to be done. I can hand out weapons."

"What weapons?" they objected. "All the arms are already in their hands. Some boys don't even have a gun."

It was very upsetting not to have an excuse to stay, but everybody was against it. If I only had brought a medical bag or a weapon, I could have remained.

Seeing my hesitation, the boys said, "If this is the way you're going to act, we won't bring you along next time."

I thought they were just trying to fool me into going back, and that wasn't going to work; but I sized up the situation for myself and, though it went against everything I wanted, I didn't want my being there to cause a problem for the others. So without another word, I hopped on the pickup and we raced back. I was certain I could find a better way to get to the front. By the time we reached the mosque, the cleanup was over.

Even though servers at the mosque had yet to eat, Soleymani set aside a small pot of it for the body washers. I took the pot and headed for Jennatabad, praying to God that I wouldn't find mother there.

When I got to the cemetery I handed the food to one of the old men by the entrance and went to the body washers'. Leila emerged from the building just as I came. As soon as she saw me she said hello and, pointing at a white bundle she was carrying, asked, "Zahra, will you bury this for me?"

"What is it?" I asked.

"Somebody's remains," she said uneasily.

"What? In that bundle?"

She said, "The people who brought it said this was all that remained of one whole woman."

"Why did you bundle her like that?" I asked.

"What else could we do?" she said. "Zeynab used gloves to scrape her off a blanket. Zahra, I'll never eat meat again in my life!"

I felt terrible for her and took the bundle. The thing was light but carrying it made me weak in the knees. I couldn't feel any bones in it. Probably a mortar blast caused this, I thought.

I gave it back to Leila, who went off to bury it herself; it seemed she had found the strength to do the job now. I trailed behind her as she walked on determinedly. She put it in a hole in the ground we found and used our hands to pile dirt over it. Not wanting Leila to linger there and see such horrors, I suggested we go back to the mosque, where there was more than enough work to do. But she said that she didn't mind and preferred to stay in Jennatabad.

"But I'm worried about you," I said. "You're going to see more gory things."

"It's okay. I feel more comfortable here. The dead are piled up everywhere, in the houses and other buildings."

I realized she was right. Then I asked, "What's new?"

"Since this morning, we have buried a few," she said. "Mother came by with Mansur and Mohsen to visit father's grave."

I said, "I told her to wait until I could come for her. I didn't want her to come all this way on foot, but no matter how much I tried, I couldn't find a vehicle. So, how was she feeling? She wasn't torturing herself, was she?"

"She was, in fact," she said, "crying a lot, wailing all she could in Arabic, in Kurdish. I tried everything, but I couldn't calm her. I showed her the graves of the dead, saying look the people buried here also had families. I said, 'You've got to be strong; you're father and mother to us now.' But it was no use. I forced her to get up and sent her after the children."

I left Leila and went to father's grave, feeling very upset. I knelt down and put my face to the earth and said, "Do you hear me, father?" I so wanted him to hug and caress me. I kissed the place on the stone where his name was written, scolding myself for not appreciating him more when he was alive.

I sat there with tears in my eyes. It was unbearable as I waited for him to take me in his arms.

Sobbing uncontrollably, I poured my heart out to him, and if there had been others around mourning the loss of a loved one like me, I didn't hear them. But I didn't want anyone to see me like that so I returned to the body washers'. Two or three young men had brought in a corpse and were standing in front of Parvizpur's door. I knew he wasn't there. The young men were waiting for someone to record the particulars of the dead person. The door was unlocked. I told them to come in, and I would record the body. I sat behind the desk and took the register from the drawer. I asked them about the deceased and, in tears, they answered me. He was from the Taleqani neighborhood and his name was Abdosattar. As I wrote this, Leila entered and sat in a chair by the filing cabinet. The men left to take the body to the mortuary. I said to Leila, "I had this awful feeling I wanted to go home."

Leila said, "I had the same feeling. Get up. Let's go. At least we can change clothes." We left the office and said to Zeynab, "We're going home."

She got up halfway and asked, "Want me to come with you?"

"No," I said. "We'll be back soon."

On the way home we spoke about what we remembered of father. When we got to the door, I realized I didn't have my key. I looked up and down the alley, but didn't see anyone. I put my foot on the wall and grabbed the edge of the roof to hoist myself up. I perched on the tall fence father had placed around the little garden to keep the hens and roosters in and jumped into the yard.

This was the first time I had set foot in the house since father's death. I said to Leila, "What I really wanted to do was look at the pictures of father I had put up in the bedroom and living room. I thought seeing them would help me feel better inside." I opened the door to the yard and Leila came in. It felt as though I had been away for years. Looking around the garden, I noticed all the plants, the tomato and the okra, had dried up. I thought: Father had put so much work into the garden, and now look at it! When he worked in the garden, father would mumble in Kurdish about the death of his parents and the hardships they had. He not only made himself cry, he brought all of us to tears. Often our neighbor, Mr. Goruhi, hearing father, would knock on the door and come in. Being a good friend of father's he would insist that he sing in Kurdish. At first he refused, but then he would sing like a professional neighborhood crooner.

I opened the spigot in the yard, but nothing came from the hose but a rumbling of air. Whenever father came home he would hose down the yard, wanting it to be clean when we ate outside. As I looked around, I noticed that Leila had walked over to the welding equipment father used to do projects for people. I joined her and bent down to kiss the places on the tools where father put his hands. I imagined they were still warm from his touch. I remembered the look on his face as he worked with the tools, then I saw the plastic tub we kept the New Years fish in. It was in an alcove. I said to Leila, "The fish!"

We both ran to the tub. The surface was covered in a thick layer of oily soot from the fire at the Abadan refinery, which was still raging. Floating in the dusty gunk were the lifeless bodies of the goldfish we had bought for the New Years. I plucked at the fish and glanced at Leila, who stood there crying silently. I knew what she thinking: The 1980 New Year celebration with the table spread and the seven things with names beginning with the letter "s"—it was only six months ago.

That was the second time we celebrated the New Year in the house. Father was not that happy about it, but after he had agreed to celebrate, we went crazy buying the table decorations and setting it up. On New Year's Day we spread the cloth on the floor in the living room and one-by-one decorated it with the things we bought. Mother had made gingerbread; she prepared the dough with sesame and cinnamon and brought it to the baker on the alley to bake for her—it was in a covered tin on the table. Then she made henna paste to decorate our feet and hands. Father appeared to be reading the Quran, but he was hiding the bills he was going to give us as New Year's presents between the pages. To prevent the boys from snatching things from the cloth, Leila and I put the fruit and dried seeds in ceramic and crystal bowls. We told Zeynab, Sa'id, Hasan, and Mansur to come to the table and had each take a hardboiled egg to paint. While the children were busy with this, I cleaned the framed mirror that was a souvenir from our home in Basra and placed it along with the silver candlesticks father had bought at the head of the tablecloth. I placed the mirror in front of the fish bowl so that it would reflect the fish that were constantly swimming back and forth in it. I also brought the rosewater dispenser and the sandalwood incense. Minutes before New Year, I lit the candles and the sandalwood. We all sat around the cloth. Although I was terrified the children would get their new clothes dirty, they did what they had to do without fuss. This was the second New Year that they had bought them new sets of clothing. When I was younger, I saw the other children my age in the alley with their new clothes, but my parents didn't buy any for me and I cried. "Why didn't you buy me clothes?" I asked mother. "How could I?" she said. "Your father doesn't have the money." Then she patted me on the head and asked me not to upset father by mentioning it. "Whenever he has the money," she assured me, "I'll buy some for you."

I just waited until they had some money. When I grew up, I promised myself, I would do whatever it took to buy clothes for my kids.

In my make-believe games, the fathers and mothers had plenty of money and took their kid to the park. The girls in crepe blouses and pleated dresses would play on the swings, and life was good for everybody.

These dreams kept Nuriya and Keyfiya, local seamstresses who were distant relatives of ours, busy sewing clothes for my dolls.

I got up from the tank and unlocked the door. I went straight to the pictures on the wall of the living room. When I saw father's picture the tears started; I was trying to hide what I was feeling from Leila, but I couldn't help myself. It was a picture that was taken by one of the families around New Year's time, and father had it enlarged. I stepped forward and kissed it. I looked carefully at his face with those sleepless eyes and his usual composure. He was wearing the long-sleeved shirt with the three buttons and his green pantaloons, and he had Zeynab, not more than four years old at the time, in his arms. Mother's brothers and few other male relatives were in the picture, but their expressions were nothing like father's. I went in the small room where father kept his work tools and certificates. I collected the Quran tapes and the speeches of the late Kafi and looked at them. Some were missing. I remembered that one of the soldiers had given them to mother the day of father's funeral.

He spent a lot of time in this room listening to the tapes of Ayatollahs Motahhari and Beheshti or weeping as Kafi recited the passion of Imam Hoseyn. He was so moved his face was still red when he left the room. I'll never forget it when he said, "Khomeini is the heir of Imam Hoseyn. We're always saying we wish we could have been there to help the Imam in his hour of need. Now it's our turn to help Khomeini and show we weren't just talking."

I kissed the tapes and took them in my arms and said, "Father, the message of these tapes was not lost on you. You were true to your word."

Then I saw his weights and dumbbells. I had come home hoping to find some peace, but I felt worse. I missed him more than ever. I would give up everything I had for just one glimpse of him, one embrace. Unfortunately, it was not to be, and my heart and soul were in agony. I wanted to tear it from my chest. Nothing could bring me peace of mind?

Managing to snap out of this mood, I noticed we had been there an hour, and it was time to get back. I left the room and called out to Leila, but she didn't answer. I opened the door to our room and found her sitting on the edge of the bed. It was clear she'd been weeping. I sat down beside her, looking around the room with all of its memories—the day the municipality had the lottery and all of us were so expectant, and how disappointed we were when we lost; the second-chance lottery when all our prayers were answered and we got the land for the house. We would visit the site to see how our unfinished house was coming along, waiting for the day we could move in. The day the foundation was poured, the day the house was framed, the day the walls went up.... At each stage we got more and more excited and couldn't wait for the work to be completed so we could take possession. In the end the pressures and headaches of renting made father move us into the structure before it was finished and, with the help of the boys, sped up work on the building.

Now we occupied a fully built home. But where was the owner? I got up and looked for the key to father's wardrobe. I wanted to take his clothes in my arms, but I couldn't find the key. With Leila in father's room I took the opportunity to open Ali's closet and kiss and hug his army uniform. Although they had been laundered and ironed, I breathed in their fragrance. The green color was sacred and had a soothing effect on me. Where is Ali? I asked myself. Has he gotten word of father's death? Is he well enough to come back? Then I prayed he would come. This was how I lightened the burden of responsibility I felt. I left his room and opened the window in the living room that looked out on the yard. I stood where father often stood, staring at the garden, when it was clear something was on his mind. Wishing so much to read his mind at such times, I would look out at the garden from the same angle he would. He had been less talkative recently than in the past. I even asked him outright what was on his mind that time I had returned from Jennatabad. I got the sense that he had a lot to say but wouldn't. It had to be, I thought, about going away and how he'd leave us to fend for ourselves—and what was to become of us without him.

I recalled that when we first came to the house, it was cold, and we lit a brazier in the yard. After it stopped smoking, we brought it inside. We sat around the brazier warming ourselves and I remember father telling me, "From the time I was a child I didn't have anyone to look after me; I tried—and got a lot of help from God—not to go wrong in life. It was very hard for me to get where I am. You've also got to put your trust in God. Don't expect anyone to help you, but that must never stop you from helping others."

Now I understood why he said this; he was preparing us for what was happening now, what had to be done when he was gone. Not to expect anything from anyone except God.

The memories, though very painful, were very vivid in my mind, especially the time we all sat around the brazier. When mother and the children were busy elsewhere, I remember that father whispered to me: "I could have been a better father to you all, could have made your lives easier. It shames me to say that if you had been brought up in another family, it wouldn't have been this hard for you...."

In the pale light from the embers in the brazier I could see the tears on his face. Trying not to get choked up, I said, "What are you saying? It's true things aren't easy but there's no substitute for the serenity you bring to this home. If I had been raised by another family, I would never have been able to see the value of the things we do have and could never have become as strong as I am."

He took my hand and said, "No, you've got to forgive me."

I was shocked. Here was a man who insisted he earn an honest living with his own hands. He even refused to work at the port saying, "There are a lot of things at the docks that make the money you earn there suspect."

I looked him in the eye and said, "That's no reason for you feel guilty. As long as everybody's together, we'll be fine." Then I hugged his head and kissed him. He kissed me back.

I looked around and saw that Leila had changed her clothes and was standing behind me. "Should we go?" I said. She nodded and we were off. It was very hard to leave, but we had to. I told Zeynab that we'd be back soon. We closed the compound door and went away. Because the number of casualties had decreased in recent days, I assumed they probably needed us more at the mosque.

Leila and I separated. When I got to the mosque, there was a pickup parked in front with a wounded man in the back. His body was peppered with shrapnel, and he was bloody from head to foot. Mr. Najjar was busy staunching the bleeding. He handed his serum bag to me and said, "Let's get him straight to the hospital."

He jumped down from the pickup and it took off. The wounded man was hurt badly. I kept one eye on the serum and one eye on him. We hadn't gotten to the bridge when Iraqi planes materialized. The area around the bridge was a madhouse. People were fleeing. Most of the shells rained down on the banks of the river. The planes unloaded their bombs in the midst of the bedlam. I realized that they would hit the bridge next, and it was time for people to jump off. I had always been terrified that I would drown someday. There was that one time I almost went under in the water near Basra. I had gone there to soak the newly born Mansur's diapers. I bent down to retrieve them, but my foot slipped and I fell in. I wasn't more than five at the time and didn't have the strength to pull myself out. I went under several times and flailed about. Nearby people saw what was happening and saved me. That gave me quite a scare; even when I was older I never got over my fear of the water. After some time had passed, we would go with father to Kut-e Sheikh, where people would take skiffs to villages along the water. I dreaded the trips in the small boats, and with each movement I thought I would suffocate. Now I was as terrified as I had been then. From the bridge I could see that they had hit Kut-e Sheikh with rockets, making the water in the Shatt choppy. We managed to cross the bridge. The closer we got to Abadan the thicker the smoke from the recently hit refinery became. The billowing blackness covered the sky and made the air hard to breathe. My nose burned from the fumes from the soot in the air. The driver tried to maneuver his way through the traffic but failed. The injured man went into a coma, and began to moan feebly. I asked the young man who had brought him, "Which neighborhood is he from?"

"He's from around the Mehr Hospital," he said. "I found him near the Ahmadzadeh Circle."

When we got to the hospital, we delivered the man to the nurses, who were dead on their feet and were complaining about the volume of wounded. "Why did you bring him here?" one of them asked. "Take him somewhere else."

"He's in a bad way," I said.

The van dropped me off at the mosque. I entered the courtyard, where there was pandemonium. Everyone who had come to the mosque for shelter was standing around. Some officials were speaking about evacuating the city, while the crowd stared at them in stunned silence. They didn't know where they were supposed to go. I got closer to the speakers to hear what they were saying.

"The authorities have decided to evacuate the population from the city. All able-bodied people must not delay and leave."

One person in the crowd asked, "Where're we going to go? There's no place for us to go."

"That's up to you. There's no telling how long the war will last, but one thing is certain: if you stay you will perish. There's nothing you can do. To remain means you'll die."

Angered by what they were telling the crowd, I shouted, "Why? Why should people have to leave? What's going on here? What's the point of emptying the city? So it'll fall into the hands of the Iraqis without a fight? What good is turning all these people into refugees?"

"What do you mean? You want everybody to remain under fire?"

"No, let's bring everybody to the mosque."

"How long do you think we can look after people under these conditions? Don't you think they'll shell the mosque, too?"

"Haven't we been fighting for a year now anyway?" I said heatedly. "Don't you remember that fracas they started by playing the Arabs-against-the-Persians card? You saw how fast that was over."

"That was just some internal dispute. They got it quickly under control, but this is war. They've attacked us with everything they had."

"We can take care of that. Banisadr's supposed to be sending planes, right?" I had heard the rumor so many times, I couldn't stop myself from repeating it, but a few of the onlookers were chuckling at how gullible I was.

The man I was arguing with said, "You can't count on what the higher-ups say. If they were going to do something, they would have done it by now. It's been a week and there's no sign of them."

"I, for one, am staying," I declared. "Nothing's happened to force people to evacuate. If we do that, we'll just hand the city over to the enemy."

Then I went to the prayer room. The mosque was cluttered with boxes and equipment people had brought in. The girls and I were sorting things when we heard the sounds of explosions and everything stopped. People were shrieking and began to rush in panic from the mosque. Shells were landing nearby, making the building shudder. Now people were running all directions. Most interesting were five or six strange creatures; while the world was coming to an end around them, they seemed to be going about their business calmly. God help them, I said to myself and went to see about the others. Some of the boys and I tried to restore calm. The women and children were utterly terrified, but I managed to reassure them that our forces at the front were giving as good as they got. I was just repeating what I had heard from boys I knew, people like Mohsen Baqalani, Taqi Mohsenifar, Hoseyn Ta'ynezhad, all friends of Ali. I was so worried about what was happening at the front, I threw modesty to the wind and went right up to any soldier I saw and asked, "What's the situation?"

Some would say, "It's bad. The Iraqis are armed to the teeth, while we've got nothing."

Another said, "Today we gave them what for. If only the planes would come and bomb the Iraqi positions, then we'd stop their infantry."

When things had died down a bit, someone called me. I went into the yard where Abdollah Mo'avi was waiting. As soon as he saw me he came over and said, "Sister, you need to come to the Abbasiyeh Prayer Hall—there's quite a crowd there; they're panicking and we don't know what's going to happen to them."

I told the boys where I was going and that I'd be back.

Being a local boy from the Safa Market, Abdollah knew the area well, but I'd never been to the Abbasiyeh. As we passed the market, the changes I saw there made my heart break; a week earlier it was so bustling there wasn't room to move. Now, except for a few dairy places and bakeries, everything was shut down. There were a few people peddling potatoes and onions from carts, but there was no sign of the pre-war throngs. Everything spoke of disaster. Gone was the famous Mashallah stewed meat and vegetable place that was the talk of the town. Gone also were my fellow Arabic speakers who would bring in clothing and perfumes from Kuwait and display them on cloths on the ground. The village women selling cream, local butter, and chickens; the date sellers and fish mongers who would shout out the merits of their catches—all of them had left, robbing the place of its charm.

Putting the market behind us, we headed for the Abbasiyeh. There was a young boy holding an M1 in front of the gate. We greeted him and asked what was going on, what was the trouble. He said, "There are several sick people here. Over all things are bad; everybody's lost their nerve. They say we're going to lose. The Iraqi guns are just across the straits from us, after all. When they start shelling, all hell breaks loose."

I said, "You should tell them that it's not like that. Tell them that our forces are fighting the Iraqis."

"I say that," he said, "but no one believes me. As soon as I try to build up their nerve, somebody comes along and says the Iraqis have gotten closer. Somebody else says their planes are in the air and bombing everywhere. So it seems worse to these people than it did before."

I got the feeling the poor kid had given up himself, and no one could expect him to keep up morale. That morning I had heard from some of the boys that the defenders had managed to push the Iraqis back. Although I knew that they would lose any ground they took, given the lack of personnel, fatigue, and not having enough ammunition, this one piece of good news would be enough to lift the people's spirits. And this was the news I was going to tell the people gathered at the Abbasiyeh.

I climbed the steps of the building and entered the prayer room where they held the passion plays. It was larger than the ones I had seen at other mosques. Light was streaming through its green wood-frame windows. People were sitting on the carpeted parts of the floor. The ceiling was very high, reminding me of our Hoseyniyeh in Basra. I looked over the crowd, trying to gauge their mood. I was determined to raise their spirits no matter what.

It was just as the boy had said. People were demoralized and out of sorts. For want of something to do, some were lying on the floor asleep. Many were sitting with their backs leaning against the walls with their legs stretched out. There was also one person in a corner pouring tea into glasses. I could feel my heart beating madly as I got ready to speak. I was going to tell them what I had heard, not what I'd seen, which was why I was a little shamefaced. But my mind was made up because I knew the only thing that would get them into action and give them some hope was the news of the boys' success. I stood in the doorway and, as my body shook making my voice quiver, I said, "Greetings."

All at once everybody looked up at me. Some responded to the greeting in a formal way.

"Listen, I have good news for you."

"What's that?" they asked. "When is the war going to be over? When can we go back to your homes?" They kept asking questions until one voice rose above the others, "Good news? What's the good news? Let's hope you're going to say the war's over."

"No, it's not over, but it will end. Our boys at the front have pushed the Iraqis back. It will end, God willing."

As soon as I said this, the people who were lying down sat up. Several came nearer to me. I continued, "There's no reason for you to upset yourselves now. You'll be back in your homes, we hope, back in your lives. Khorramshahr will be back to normal, I hope. Do you remember how fast the Arab-Persian thing ended?"

"There were no mortars, no planes then," they said.

"Put your trust in God. The Baathists have thrown everything they have against our boys, but they still held their ground. They won't let our city fall into their hands. Tehran is also supposed to send planes that will take care of their tanks." When they heard this, the women gathered around me and began to pour out what was on their minds. "We're really fed up; these kids are just rotting here. There's no peace and quiet...."

I tried to comfort them and said, "God willing it'll all work out." After they had quieted, I asked, "Is anyone ill here?"

They pointed to an old couple. I took off my shoes and walked over to them. After speaking with them, I realized that age combined with fear and hunger had robbed them of the will to go on. They looked pleadingly at me, and I told them that the hardships were almost over and they would be returning to their homes. They blessed me.

People also pointed out a girl in her teens with a bandaged arm. I went over to her and asked, "What happened?"

"They hit our house with mortars. I was in the yard and shrapnel went into my arm." Her bandage was filthy. I told her not to move until I brought a new bandage.

As I was leaving the building, several people told me there was no water. The children piped up, "There's no water for us to drink when we get thirsty."

This was heartbreaking for me. They thought I knew everything and could do anything. I said, "Okay, I'll tell the boys at the mosque to work something out for you, but you'll have to help one another also. Don't just sit around waiting for somebody else to act—everyone has to pitch in. The prayer room needs a good cleaning, so get busy. Since you're making use of this place, you'll have to isolate the sick so that the rest of you don't become ill. I'll do whatever is in my power to help."

As soon as I was out the door, the boy with the gun said, "Now that you've said that to the people, what do you expect to happen? Why didn't you tell them the truth?"

"It wasn't so far from the truth. The boys are fighting, aren't they? Did you want me to tell them we're losing? That we've been betrayed and that's why so many are dying?"

I didn't wait for an answer and ran toward the mosque. I got a new bandage from Mr. Najjar and told the girl at the infirmary what I had seen and said. One of the men overheard me and said, "Sister Hoseyni, it was good of you to tell people the news so long as it didn't make them want to stay."

"I said whatever came into my head, not caring whether it was right or wrong."

"No. What you did was right, but it shouldn't get their hopes up too high."

I explained the situation at the Abbasiyeh to him. He said, "I'll tell people to bring them water. I've already sent them whatever food was available these last few days, but more and more people are arriving."

"God bless you," I said. "At least they'll have water."

"As soon as we get a delivery, I'll send a truck."

I thanked him and after procuring a new bandage for the girl, I returned to the Abbasiyeh, where I changed her dressing. Shrapnel had stripped away some of her flesh, and the wound smelled like it was infected. I told her to be more careful. I gathered my things and left. It was getting dark when I got outside. As soon as I set foot back in the mosque, I saw that the shell-shocked people had started up again. I had originally wanted to get back to Jennatabad, but I decided to stay on account of them. The war was only six days old, but it seemed like a lifetime to me. Whatever happened, I was going to stay the night.

10

Yearning to Go to the Front

Early the next morning I saw Mr. Najjar washing his hands with a white liquid after each time he bandaged someone. He would also wash the blood from the floor and apply the same white liquid to the spill. Curious, I asked him about it. “This is Dettol, a powerful disinfectant,” he said. Then he went on to tell the girls and me about drugs, their effects and uses in medicine. He also told us about his experiences working in the hospital. I felt I needed to learn all I could from him so I could go to the front and tend to the wounded, and I hung on his every word.

When he had finished, I asked, “Wouldn’t it be a good idea to do something about this place, make it like a real infirmary? Shouldn’t we isolate it from the rest of the mosque? It disgusts people to see all the wounded and the blood.”

Of course, I had something else in mind when I said this. There was a lot of traffic in the mosque, and being in the public eye made me uncomfortable. Then, again, it was dispiriting to see the wounded.

Mr. Najjar said, “I’ve had thoughts along those lines. I wanted to go and get some screens, but with all the foot traffic it didn’t seem like a good idea; they wouldn’t stay in one place. Something more permanent would have to be done.”

“Do you want me to go back and get some tents so we can sew them together and make one big curtain?” I asked.

“That’s a good idea, so long as the material matches. Otherwise it won’t look right,” he said. “Let’s see what we can do.”

Since there were no wounded, I went into the yard. I just couldn't stay idle and was looking around to see if there was something to do when I caught sight of the man who had warned me about spending the night at Jennatabad.

I asked Maryam Amjadi what his name was. "Mahmud Farrokhi," she said. "Why?"

"He's the one who told me not to stay at the graveyard at night. What kind of a person is he?"

"He's a good man. Very solid."

I walked away and decided to ask about the forces that had been promised. Farrokhi was standing by the stairs that led to the second floor. He was busy shifting weapons and ammunition.

"Excuse me, those armed men that you spoke about. Were you able to arrange anything?"

Sheepishly he said, "No, I couldn't. No one wanted to go there. The boys said it was more important to fight the Baathists. Of course, some of them didn't have the stomach to do morgue work at Jennatabad."

"So now you'll admit I was right," I said. "See why I stayed there, now?"

"Yeah, I heard about what it was like myself. They said there was no water or shrouds. But I didn't see it for myself."

He went back to what he was doing, and, taking advantage of his embarrassment, I said, "So now that you're not sending any troops our way, at least give us some weapons."

"What for?"

"You said yourself that we aren't safe there. We're tired of fighting off the dogs with stones. With one shot we can make them go away."

He stopped and picked up a rifle from the meager supply he had and gave it to me. I noticed there were grenades in the pile and said, "Give me some of those, too."

"What are you going to do with them?"

"I want to throw them at the pack of dogs. Or, I don't know, at the Iraqis, the Hypocrites, anybody who attacks us. We want to defend ourselves. I even want to go to the front now."

He picked up a grenade and held it out to me. I begged him for another one and he gave it to me. Happy, I thanked God the problem was solved. Now, I had to find a way of getting to the front.

When Maryam saw me with the weapons, she said, "You must have pull. They don't give weapons to just anybody." I laughed and went into the yard. I leaned against the sack of clothing they had collected. I put the grenades in my pockets and looked at the rifles. They had been in storage so long they looked like they might not be of any use; but they were more than what most people had. At that moment a young cleric entered the mosque from the Fakhr-e Razi entrance. He seemed very strange to me. His cloak was gathered around his waist, and he held the hem in his hands. The lenses of his glasses were so dark in the sun at first I thought he was blind. He was standing and speaking to some people who had entered before him. Now that he was in the shade, I got a better look at him.

His piercing look made him seem like an eagle. He had the sunburned skin of a farm laborer. I sensed a certain amount of pain in his expression, the suffering of a man with his hands full. The people with him were obviously not from Khorramshahr. They were all wearing the kind of woven tunics they wore up north. I didn't sense any defeatism in the little I heard from their conversations about the front. They all had arms, either Brnos or M1s. The cleric, whom they called Sheikh Sharif, had a G3.

I looked at him, wondering what kind of man he was, what he was capable of, whether he would come through if I asked him for something.

When he had separated from his companions and was walking toward Maryam and Zohreh, I followed him. He said hello to them and asked, "Will one of you keep my cloak for me for a while?"

"Sir, there's no telling how long we'll be here," said Maryam. Then she nodded in the direction of the stairway and said, "I'll put it over there beside the weapons. Just tell Farrokhi when you come, and he'll retrieve it for you."

I didn't hesitate, "Do you intend to go to the front, sir?"

He looked at me questioningly and said, "God willing."

"I want to go there myself. Would you take me along?"

"There's no need for you people to go to the front. We're there and, whenever it's necessary, we'll bring you out there. They need you here more because, from what I've seen, what you sisters are doing is no less than what we're doing at the front. Probably more. Saving someone's life is no less valuable than fighting—often it's worth more. We're going there to save lives—you're also in a struggle to keep people alive. So there's no difference. You're acting exactly like Zeynab."

"But sir," I objected, "I don't find the work fulfilling. I want to confront the enemy myself."

Even though I told her not to blab about my father, how he was sacrificed, Maryam said, "Sir, she lost her father recently and buried him herself."

This was so embarrassing to me I couldn't say anything. His tone a mixture of tenderness and sympathy, the Sheikh said, "That's exactly why I feel the sisters should stay behind. No one can praise you sisters enough for fighting like lions. You're the reason why we can hold up our heads with pride. You give us the spirit to fight harder at the front." With that he handed several boxes of dried bread and some canned preserves to his people and rushed from the mosque. I sensed how different this man was from other men, how much he supported the idea of women staying behind the lines.

Still in the thrall of the sound of Sheikh Sharif's voice, I suddenly became aware that Soleymani, one of the city elders who had been active lately at the mosque, was having it out with Mash Mammad, the caretaker. Soleymani was holding some dark blue cloth that had served as a curtain between the men and women's prayer sections. They had gathered up the cloth and some carpet pieces the day people had come to the mosque for sanctuary. Soleymani now wanted to give the cloth to Mr. Najjar, so they could use it to section off the infirmary.

This annoyed Mash Mammad, who snorted, "The cloth belongs to the mosque. You can't let it get bloody. I want to use it as a curtain again."

Soleymani tried to restore peace, "Why get so upset, my friend? If it gets dirty, it gets dirty. They're not going to hold public prayers here any time soon. There's no telling when the shelling will stop.

You should be praying it's over soon. When that happens I'll buy you some new fabric and deliver it myself."

Mash Mammad stared at them as they put up the curtain.

I felt sorry for him. He was around fifty, and the crowds in the mosque had put a strain on his back. The mosque trustees and city elders like Mesbahi, Soleymani, and Farrokhi's father tried to make things easier, but still there was always extra pressure on Mash Mammad. The constant flow of people, military and civilian, and especially the large number of asylum seekers meant that the mosque had to be constantly swept and mopped. It took several men to keep the tank on the roof filled with water from the Shatt. The other girls and I would sweep out the yard and the alleys around the mosque as best we could. The large crowd overwhelmed the meager services we had, and the infirmary had to be sanitized constantly. Adding to the drudgery was a blocked drain in the bathroom that caused the floor to be covered with waste, something that should never happen in a mosque. I was forced to step through the muck to unclog the drain.

Mesbahi and Nuri struggled even harder than I to keep the shell-shocked five under control. It was not easy. Still, I wasn't satisfied and had to keep a watchful eye on them so that they didn't wander into the street. The effort of keeping Genoa in the mosque was driving me crazy. I was fed up and short of breath. They would occasionally go on the attack and scratch and bite. One time the blind girl bit me so hard that I nearly fainted. I couldn't free my hand, but after a lot of coaxing the girl let go. I didn't want to have anything to do with them, but fearing they would get lost or be the cause of some immorality left me with no choice but to keep an eye on them. I said to the men, "If you don't get them out of here, I'll go mad."

"Their relatives might show up any time," they said. "If we send them away, no one will find them."

I don't know why, but whenever one of them started up, the rest would begin to howl. At first it was no more than three, but gradually the pack became larger.

There was only one of them I was fond of: Abbas, the seven-year-old. He was worse off than most. Thin as a rail, he would trip and fall whenever his physical condition worsened. His eyes would go blank, and he would call feebly to his mother, "Yuma, Yuma..."

Seeing him like that brought out the mother in me. He also made me miss Hasan and Sa'id. He sensed my maternal instinct and would come to me whenever he saw me. At times when I was working, someone would take my hand, and I would turn and see it was Abbas. I would pat him on the head and ask in Arabic, "Abbas, what do you want?"

Whenever he would say in that pathetic way of his, "I'm hungry" or "I'm thirsty," I would rummage through the boxes to find some biscuits or cake for hm. When he asked, "Where's my mother?" my heart broke. I didn't know what to tell him. I tried to console him by saying, "God willing, your mother will come."

The girls and I were in the process of straightening out the yard by bringing sacks of clothes and cartons of food into the prayer room. We first separated out the food, then we opened the sacks. We had been told to find all the clothing that would be of use by the defense forces, whose clothes would get blood-stained and torn during the fighting. Men's clothing was hard to find, and we waded through the piles to find the odd scrap. When we found things women could wear we would throw them at Ra'na Najjar or Ashraf Farhadi and laugh until our sides hurt.

Around noon someone announced I was wanted outside. I slid down the mountain of clothing, getting my chador full of lint. After brushing off my chador and straightening it, I went into the yard where Hoseyn Eidi was waiting for me. As soon as he saw me, he walked over and I asked him what was happening.

"They say that the morgue at the hospital is full of bodies, sister. We want to transfer them to Jennatabad. Will you come?"

"Are there any women among them?" I asked.

"There must be," he said.

"Wait here while I tell the girls," I said. Then I went in and said, "I'm going to help with the bodies at the morgue. Anyone want to come along?"

"No," they said.

I didn't insist. There was a white van waiting outside with two people sitting next to the driver and three in the back. I got in and we were off. When we got to the bridge, the driver put his foot on the gas. I thanked God the bridge had survived the Baathist air strikes and artillery. We were a quarter of the way down the ramp when I noticed the driver had to carefully avoid a hole that was half a meter wide. I could see the choppy waters through the hole. The railings along the bridge were pockmarked by shrapnel. My old fear of water returned, but luckily we soon put the bridge behind us.

The van went toward the Taleqani Hospital and stopped at the emergency room. I got out and entered and was greeted by a nurse in a cape, pants, and a kerchief—all in white. I liked the look. I said, "Hello. We've come for the bodies."

"Tell him," she said, indicating a man who was limping toward the end of a narrow corridor.

Hoseyn, who was behind me, ran to him and said, "Sir!" The man, who had thick glasses and a bald head with a fringe of hair, turned around. Hoseyn explained why we were there, and the man asked, "Do you have a vehicle?"

"Yes, we came with a van."

"Good. Go and bring it around the back," he said.

I knew where he meant. We left the hospital and Hoseyn motioned to the driver to follow us. The morgue attendant opened the double doors in the back and said, "Come in."

The young men with us guided the driver as he backed up to the loading dock. We entered the through the small back door. The room was about fifteen meters square with a stone floor and stone walls. There was no light, so we had to grope our way forward using the light from the outside. Although I was used to the smell of bodies, the stench of blood inside the room sickened me.

The dead were just strewn about on the floor. On the left side of the morgue there were three bays with three drawers in each bay; these were the only bodies stored in any particular order. I went around looking at them. Except for three old women and two children, the corpses were men burned in Saddam's fire.

The hospital was running on a generator. Because the emergency rooms had priority, they decided not to refrigerate the morgue and to bury the bodies in it before they rotted. According to the attendant, most of the dead had been found on the streets of the Arab quarters of Kut-e Sheikh and Moharrezi.

I asked him, "Wasn't it decided that no more people would be buried at Jennatabad?"

"Yes," he said, "but it's still better to bury them in their own areas."

I remembered the time when we had arranged to bring bodies to Abadan and Mahshahr. But if we tried to do that now, who would be there to take possession of them? How could we bury them ourselves? There wasn't enough room in the van for them, so we told them we would take the ones lying on the floor.

The attendant said, "It's hot out; none of them should remain here. You have to take the ones in the drawers, too."

"If we take them," I said, "they'll just lie on the ground. There weren't supposed to be any more buried at Jennatabad because there's no water to wash them or shrouds to bury them in."

The young men brought stretchers. I told them to gather the women first and put them in the van. One of the women, around fifty, was terribly overweight. I didn't want to involve the boys, but because I realized I couldn't get her on the stretcher by myself, I asked them to help. They were just as bothered by the prospect as I, insisting that they would only carry men.

"It's not right to leave them," I said. "There are only three of them. Let's all carry them out to the van."

Three of us struggled to get the body on the stretcher and into the van. The two other women were lighter. They were able to get eight or nine other bodies into the van. While the boys did this, I looked at the women's faces. The two thin ones looked alike; they were probably related. Their arms and faces were sunburned, testifying to how hard their lives had been.

They stacked the bodies in the back of the van and told me to sit up front. I said that I would rather stay in back and lean against the railing.

"It's dangerous," they said. "You might fall. We even had a hard time back there."

Hoseyn, who was standing on the fender, said, "Go sister, sit in front. Why cause trouble?" I reluctantly sat in the front, and the van drove off. The heavy load made it go much slower than before, and the motor groaned as the van strained to get up hills. The Abadan-

Khorramshahr roadway was under fire, which made me worry about Hoseyn and the other boys in the back. We watched out the window as mortar shells burst nearby. I was afraid they might be hit by shrapnel. When we got to the bridge, the driver gunned the engine, but the van couldn't make the grade. The boys jumped from the van to lighten the load as the air filled with the smell of exhaust.

We got over the bridge without incident and headed for Jennatabad. I had wanted them to drop me off at the mosque, where there was so much work to be done, but I didn't have the heart to abandon the corpses. I saw Zeynab standing outside the gate, deep in thought. I said hello to her and asked, "What are you doing here, honey?"

She sounded depressed, "Ever since morning, I've had this horrible feeling. I miss my daughter Maryam something awful."

"Don't worry," I assured her. "Wherever she is, she's out of range. We've brought more dead, my sweet," I continued.

"But didn't they decide not to take any more?" she asked.

"These were leftover at the morgue and they said to bring them here so they wouldn't rot."

"Sister, what should we do? Unload them here?" asked Hoseyn.

There was no need to unload the bodies there because we were not going to wash and shroud them, I thought. It would be better to bring them to the gravesite. I told Hoseyn what I was thinking and he agreed.

He guided the driver to the end of the dirt lane. Zeynab and I grabbed a couple of stretchers. I didn't see Leila around and asked Zeynab about her. "There was no work for her, so she went to your mother's with Maryam. The poor thing was so homesick. Afterwards she was going to go to the mosque to look for you."

We got to the martyrs' section where there were only a few empty graves. We had to grab picks and shovels and help the boys do more digging. Many of the handles were broken. It wasn't easy to dig. I wrapped the pick handle in some leftover plastic and got to work. The plastic didn't stop me from getting blisters; the skin between my fingers was especially raw. I tossed the pick away and began to dig the grave with my hands, knowing that the dirt wasn't good for the cuts but at least it didn't sting. My arms were red and swollen, as if they had been scorched. The old men at the body washers' rounded up some other men to help us dig.

Zeynab and I stopped digging and went to see to the bodies of the women. The two thin ones, the young women, slid into their graves easily, but we needed the men's help to place the stretcher with the larger woman at the edge of the grave. Zeynab jumped down into the hole and took the woman by the shoulders, and I slid into the grave and took her legs. When the men tilted the stretcher, the woman's entire weight pressed against my chest. My temples throbbed, and my eyes were about to leave their sockets. This was the worst thing I had ever felt. Zeynab used an expression in Arabic about how the woman must have eaten with blind people, wolfing down their food without them noticing. This made me want to laugh but I hardly had enough breath to giggle.

Before they covered her with earth, I looked at the woman's half-opened eyes and thanked God she had died relatively intact. Shrapnel had hit her in the head and neck. Many of the other casualties with similar wounds would dry out, and no matter what we did to the bodies, they never looked natural.

After the extra help arrived, I told Zeynab that I was going back to the mosque.

"Traitor, leaving us like that?" she joked.

"There's a lot to do, I swear!"

"I know, dear, I'm just kidding. God bless you for all the work you've taken on."

Zeynab and I walked slowly back to the entrance to the body washers'. She seemed very preoccupied and anxious. The situation had thrown her for a loop.

Parvizpur's car was outside, which meant he was around somewhere. Zeynab said suddenly, "Let's see if they've done anything about the shroud fabric. We can't go on like this. The least we can do is ask the mosque people to do something about it."

"I told them what it was like here until I was blue in the face. The poor people don't know which end is up, and it's only natural they would see to the needs of the living first. If they have energy left and time permits, they may give Jennatabad some thought."

"Let's just see what'll happen anyway," she said.

Although I knew going there would do no good, I said nothing. I stood outside the door while Zeynab went to find Parvizpur. After a few minutes they emerged from the building. I said hello and got into the car with Zeynab. We were all silent as we drove to the mosque. Once inside we immediately saw Soleymani, Dr. Sheybani, Farrokhi, and two others. They were all standing in the yard under a small cupola talking. As soon as they saw us, they said hello. Parvizpur told them why we had come.

One of the men not exactly known to me answered, "By the way, the Jennatabad situation bothers us, also. We've discussed the issue among ourselves. The clergy were also involved in the discussion. We have concluded that if there's a shop still open in the bazaar, we'll buy the calico. But if that fails—and we've already asked the clergy about this—we'll take fabric from the closed shops. Under these conditions there's always the possibility things will disappear. By the same token the bodies of Muslims have dignity and should be buried according to proper Islamic practice and customs."

Disturbed by this, I said, "Forgive me, but any shroud that we take without permission has no business on a Muslim's corpse."

The man said, "We didn't say we should steal them. This is an emergency. Besides, you're not going to do this yourself. We'll have one or two of the trusted people from the mosque pick up the fabric and write a receipt. They'll also record the name of the shopkeeper so that when all this dies down, we'll add up what we owe and pay the owner."

At that point he called out to a few of the men, "Come with us." We went to the get into the car. Zeynab and I sat in the back and the men sat in the front next to the driver. One of the men told Parvizpur to drive to the Safa Market. "The shop owner is an acquaintance," he explained. We reached the market quickly, and Parvizpur pulled up in front of the famous Amu Naser Teahouse. Zeynab and I remained in the car while Parvizpur and the two men got out and headed for the covered part of the market where the cloth sellers were. Zeynab said, "Do you remember what it was like here before? There was such a crowd, so much material spread on the ground, you couldn't move...."

I nodded, absentmindedly listening to her, but there was something else on my mind. I was still upset about the way they were getting the material. To me it was neither fair to the shopkeepers nor to the martyrs. In the end I said to myself it was an emergency and if the clergy had okayed it, who was I to object? With that I tried to steer my thoughts in another direction.

I looked around. Thick smoke blackened the sky over the market, making the covered part even darker. The roll bars were pulled down over the shops; some of them were locked. I wondered where all the shopkeepers were. What they were doing? How were they supporting their wives and children? Seeing the cassette store next to the teahouse reminded me of the times I used to come to the market with mother. The shop always had a tape of the Iraqi singer Sa'dun Jaber playing. The shopkeeper played it loud enough to be heard over the roar of the bazaar.

Jaber's lyrics echoed in my mind:

O sacred land of my fathers, how I yearn for you.
My clan and tribe, my family, my birthplace are not far,
  were a person to learn the way.
Not far, the moon knows the way.
Why is it that the heart senses their nearness?
Not far if someone wants to go to them.

I also remembered the tape of the Egyptian poet and singer Abd al-Halim Hafez. His "O my son":

O my son, don't feel sad.
Love is your destiny.
My son, you will certainly die a martyr.
He who sacrifices his soul for his beloved.
Your fate is to ply the sea of love without a sail,
Caught between fire and water.
Despite all the burnings.
Against all happenstance.
My son, my son, love shall endure.
The most beautiful of adventures.

These memories reopened old wounds, and there was no remedy for them with both father and Ali gone. It was two days since father's death. Only two days! His absence still seared my insides. I wept silently, keeping my face shielded from Zeynab, but she was in her own world anyway. A half hour later, the men returned with four or five bolts of white fabric. One of the men carrying a ledger had Zeynab and I add our names to it. The book was open to a page that had the name of the shopkeeper, his address, and the date when the fabric was taken. Parvizpur and the two other men had signed it. Zeynab inked her finger with the pen and made a mark instead of signing. We took the fabric and returned to Jennatabad. Leila had returned from visiting mother, and we all got busy cutting the fabric into shrouds. The work was over quickly. We folded the shrouds and, since there were few female corpses, gave most of them to the men's morgue. Many mutilated bodies had been brought in. Several days before we had decided to wash only those that were relatively whole. This way we'd use less water and there would be less blood from wounds. When there was enough nylon to wrap bodies, we would use it, but when that ran out, separating out the less mutilated ones seemed logical. Nevertheless, this was difficult for me. Thinking that the poor souls were being doubly victimized, it pained me to ignore the mutilated bodies. But there was no choice. As we were leaving the body washers', I noticed a pile of old clothing in the corner. Proper sanitation dictated we put the clothing in a ditch and pour lime over it, but I was too tired to do it. I preferred to have the others do it, but they were just as worn out. I went to get a wheelbarrow and shoveled the clothing into it. One wheelbarrow couldn't hold it all. I had to make a couple of trips before all of it was piled in an empty corner of the cemetery. Then I poured kerosene over the pile and set it on fire. It went up quickly. I stepped back watching the flames devour the clothes. I found myself thinking about how delighted the owners of the articles were when they had bought them and how they felt when they put them on for the first time. All those feelings were turning to ashes now.

Zeynab's voice calling me brought me back to the present. I rose and walked to her. She said that someone said my brother was waiting outside the door. He wouldn't come in, so I had to go and see what he wanted.

For a moment my heart stopped. What's happened now? I thought.

I raced to the door where I saw Mansur with his hands in his pockets looking around. He stepped forward and said hello. I said hello and asked, "What did you come here for? Didn't I tell you not to leave mother and the kids?"

"Yes, but I've brought you some food," he said pitifully.

"Food? Where'd it come from?" I asked in surprise.

"The neighbors cooked supper and gave us some. We were eating and mother said, 'I wish Zahra and Leila were here.' So I secretly put some aside for you, but mother found out and asked me what I was hiding. I told her it was for you."

I was touched and asked, "You came all this way just for us?"

He nodded and took some bread out of his pocket. I took it from him; it turned out to be a sandwich with a couple of cutlets inside. "Why didn't you come into the building instead of waiting outside the door?" I asked him. "Or, why didn't you just give the food to the people who had called me to the door?"

"It wasn't that much food," he explained. "I didn't dare give it to somebody else. Maybe they'd have taken it for themselves, but it was for you."

I bent down and kissed his head. "There was no reason for you to come all this way, baby. It would have been better if you had eaten it yourself."

He snapped his head up to say "No." I invited him inside.

"No, mother said to come back quickly," he said.

The previous times when I had been at the Sheikh Soleyman Mosque, I hadn't seen Mansur. I thought he had to be around, but when he didn't turn up, I asked mother. She said, "I don't know where he is. Maybe in the alley or he's gone to the Congregational Mosque." With this in mind I stared down at him and warned, "Don't keep sneaking off. Don't leave the mosque again. You don't have to come all this way to bring me something. We've got everything we need here. Besides, I'm not always around."

"Whatever you say," he said.

"Fine. Now don't dawdle. Get back as fast as you can, so I won't get anxious worrying about where you are."

"Okay," he said.

As I stood there watching him leave, my eyes filled with tears. The Mansur who had raised such hell at home was now so well-behaved, which seemed strange because he wasn't more than thirteen. Thinking of how he was an orphan now tore at my heart. When he had disappeared from view, I went back inside. I gave the cutlet sandwiches to Zeynab.

She looked at them in surprise. "Mansur brought them," I explained. She offered me a piece but I pushed it aside. The lump in my throat was almost big enough now to strangle me. Leila was also in a bad mood. I guessed that seeing mother and the children had brought her down. She didn't let on, but I could tell what was going on inside her. A few times when I tried to speak to her, there were tears in her eyes. I decided to stay the night with her. That way there'd be enough time to get her out of that mood. We said our prayers in the room, then we left and noticed that they had covered the porch floor with a carpet and there was a tablecloth with food laid out on it. The old men, Hoseyn and Abdollah, sat on one side of the cloth and the women sat on the other. Leila and I joined them. They cut up a watermelon and divided it among us. My mouth watered as I took a piece, but my thoughts were on Leila. She answered tersely whenever I tried to engage her in conversation. After dinner, I got up, put on my shoes, and grabbed my rifle, which ordinarily never left my side. "Where are you going?" asked Leila.

"For a walk. Coming?"

"Yeah," she said and got up.

Sounds of shelling and explosions were coming from the direction of the base, so we decided to walk toward the gate, which gave us a nearly direct view of it. We stood before the gate and looked out at the avenue. It was intimidating to see it so deserted, giving the impression that the Baathist forces were stronger than they actually were. But when I looked out at the base, I told myself that while our forces were around, we were secure. Then I took Leila by the hand and we walked the length of Jennatabad. I tried to get her to speak by bringing up memories of the good times and asking what she remembered of them. She opened up. We stopped at the sign father had touched, and for a moment I wished she had not been there. I so wanted to kiss the spot where his hand had been.

It was hard for me to stay composed, so I kept quiet. We began to stroll again. The moonlit night reminded me of those nights at home in Basra with no electricity. This made me even more heartsick. At that point Leila said, "I wish Ali was here. It's been about three or four months since went away. If he were here, it would be easier to bear this. Mother wouldn't be so hard on herself either."

As we spoke, we found ourselves gravitating to father's grave, and I couldn't control myself any longer. I bawled like a baby. Recalling the good times only made things worse. Leila was no better off than I. Watching hot tears stream down her cheeks was unbearable for me. I made an effort to pull myself together so that I could comfort Leila. I got to my feet quickly and said, "It's late and it's dangerous here. Get up, let's go. Zeynab's probably worried."

When we reached the building, the old men were sitting on the porch having a smoke. As usual one of them was listening to the news about Iran on BBC. Their reading of the situation made him furious, and he started to say foul things and curse at the radio. A little further along the porch Zeynab, Maryam, and an old woman were leaning against the wall napping. Hoseyn Eidi and Abdollah Mo'avi were busy keeping watch over the area. I thought I would ease their burden by taking a turn at guard duty. I told Leila to sleep while I took my shift. Realizing we didn't have much time together, she insisted on keeping me company.

The best thing for us, it seemed, was to take the first shift. I told Hoseyn and Abdollah to get some sleep. They refused at first, but after I put my foot down they gave in. Leila and I walked away from the porch so we wouldn't disturb them. As we surveyed the grounds, we spoke about the war and what we thought was going to happen. "How did it start in the first place?" Leila asked. "Haven't you heard Saddam's speeches? He said he wanted to create a unified Arab nation, but he actually had something else in mind. Otherwise it didn't make any sense to start a war of unification that would kill all these Arabs. You've seen yourself at Jennatabad how many Persians and Arabs have been slaughtered. What he says is nonsense. They really want to do away with the revolution in Iran and get their hands on the oil. They want to turn Iran into another Palestine."

Then she asked, "How long will it last?"

"That's in God's hands. Our boys have put up a good fight in resisting them. If Banisadr would let the Phantoms take off and bombard the Iraqi positions, this would end. We also have to put up a good defense for the resistance to bear fruit."

"Zahra," she asked, "after father who in our family will be the next martyr?"

"Me, God willing," I said.

She got all choked up and said, "God forbid! What will we do without you?"

"The same thing we did after father died: carry on. After me, it'll be your responsibility."

"No, I'm not like you," she objected. "I can't bear up the way you do. The responsibility is too much."

"I know. I didn't want it either, but it was placed on my shoulders. Now I have to manage it as best I can. For good or bad, I have to try."

Then I said, "Leila, pray that I become a martyr. Don't be afraid of the responsibility. Ali will come back and take charge of the children. You'll just have to wait till then."

Mentioning Ali frightened her. "No, I pray to God he doesn't come back or I hope he does get martyred."

I nodded and said, "Yeah, there's no doubt he'll be martyred. He's not the one to return and stay at home. Remember what he said, 'I'm going to put so much effort into the Lord's work I'll die in the process and become a martyr.'"

She broke down at this point. To put an end to the conversation I took her by the hand and said, "Get up. Let's walk around the grounds. Weren't we supposed to keep watch?"

We started strolling in silence, but I couldn't stop wondering what would happen when Ali came back. Had he heard that father had died? I asked myself. When would he be back? Was the news reporting what was happening in Khorramshahr? Even if he did want to return, how could he, what with the operation on his hands? What would he do if he did return? God forbid he had already been martyred. But then I remembered what he said about dying for God, that it was exactly like living. Real living was in self-sacrifice. The Holy Imams were martyred. Look how blessed they were. If we want to live on for an eternity, we'd have to follow their example. By this logic Ali had a right to martyrdom, but where? How? Would he be shot? Hit by shrapnel?

Then the scene of father being hit by shrapnel passed through my mind. I remembered the time when we were all together as a family, when father would tell me to be back home before sundown no matter where I was.

How times had changed. Now the two daughters of the family were patrolling the graveyard in the dead of night with the streets in shambles, and the Baathists at the gates of the city. With the two of us together, the grim atmosphere at the cemetery didn't frighten me. Only occasionally when the wind blew the dry leaves over the ground making a strange rustling noise did my heart beat faster. I took Leila's hand and we walked quickly between the trees to the end of the cemetery. Because Zeynab had asked us not to walk in the section with the older graves, we turned back. "The far end of the graveyard isn't safe," she told us. "The walls are crumbling and somebody could get hurt."

An hour passed this way. To keep Leila from tiring I said, "Let's go back."

When we reached the door of the building, I called out to Hoseyn. Both he and Abdollah answered, which told me that neither of them had gotten any sleep. When they emerged, I told them I wasn't tired if they wanted to get some sleep.

"No, we couldn't sleep either," Abdollah said. "We were talking."

We sat on the edge of the porch and spoke. It didn't take long for the sound of our voices to wake Zeynab, who shouted out, "You've been on your feet from morning to night, dear. You're tired. There's nothing going on now, get some sleep." "Okay," I said and we went into the building and stretched out on the carpet. Leila fell asleep quickly. I had trouble keeping my eyes open, but I couldn't help remembering the bedroom set father had bought recently for us. How much it delighted me to sleep on a bed. Of course, he originally hadn't intended to buy it for Leila and me, but when he saw how thrilled we were, he said it could be ours.

With that I fell asleep only to have a nightmare. There was chaos everywhere. I also dreamed of father. He was wearing a green turban and walking toward a lush garden. No matter how hard I tried I couldn't reach him. I yelled out to him and he turned to look at me and smiled, but all the while he was receding further into the distance. I struggled to reach him but it was as if my feet were bound together. I screamed and cried, begging him to take me where he was going, but he only smiled. When I saw I wasn't going to reach him, I cried even harder, wailing and moaning so loud that I woke myself up. Morning was still a long time away. I looked at Leila, who was also awakened by my cries. "You okay?" she asked. "Yeah," I said. "Go to sleep. It's nothing." I fell asleep again and, once more, there were the same agonizing nightmares. I woke several more times before the morning call to prayer.

I heard one of the old men sound the call to prayer. I roused Leila, Zeynab, and the others. Then I did my ablutions and prayed. I waited for it to get light before I went back to the mosque to hear the latest news and eat breakfast.

Leaning against the wall, I overheard the two body washers talking. They hadn't gone back to bed. One of them was saying, "God Almighty, the number corpses of have I washed in my life! For a while it was like an assembly line, and I noticed that after two hours they had gotten so ripe you couldn't stand near them; but the martyrs that had been around for a few days still smelled like roses." The other man said, "You remember how it was in the beginning? If they brought in a few bodies, how we reacted. It was like it was going to kill us. But God knows how many they have brought in."

The older man said, "It's like the older you get, the more you want to stay alive. But those young ones, they aren't afraid to die; they just rush toward the bullets."

At sunrise I told Leila and Zeynab I was going. I hadn't gotten to the gate, when Hoseyn and Abdollah came running up, saying they would be coming also.

"You were up all night. Why don't you get some rest?" I asked.

"We took turns sleeping."

Iraqi shelling had been going on constantly for about an hour. I said, "You should stay; they may need you."

Hoseyn went back, and Abdollah and I went off. As we walked, I noticed how the Iraqi shells would hit one spot, then hit another spot further along the road. No matter how far we advanced, we couldn't get ahead of it. We could tell where their shells were landing from the smoke, fire, and the earth that flew into the air. First, they hit Amir Kabir Avenue, then they moved on to the Forty-Meter Road. A couple of shells landed about 200 meters from us, where the flour mill was. We ran to the mill to find two people running from it. When we finally got there, we saw they had dragged a third person from the rubble. All three were mill workers. One of them was badly wounded by shrapnel; blood was pouring from his wounds. Another had fine pieces of metal embedded in his face, while the third was in a state of shock. I asked them to find something to stop the severely wounded man's bleeding. The one with facial lacerations said, "There's nothing around here like that."

"Part of a blanket, a piece of cloth?" I offered.

I saw them look at each other. The poor guys were asleep when the shell hit and now they were running around dazed and confused trying to find a rag. "Never mind, I don't need anything," I said. "Just help me get him out of his shirt." They took off his shirt and one of the men whose hands were shaking terribly tried to tear it into strips. Seeing he was unable to do it, I took the shirt from him. He was afraid they would hit the place again. Explosions were going off everywhere.

I tore one of the sleeves along a seam and tied it around the man's thigh. The man raised his head to look at the blood-soaked bandage and asked, "Is it severed?"

"Don't be afraid, it's not severed," I assured him and tied the rest of the shirt around his waist. The man moaned and cried out to the revered Abbas each time he moved. I needed more cloth to cover the wounds, but before I could ask them for their shirts, a car pulled up. Abdollah motioned for it to stop. They loaded the wounded man into the car. As it departed, Abdollah asked the workers, "Was there anyone else here besides you?"

"There was a watchman sleeping on the roof."

With the car gone, I was about to ask the workers to try to find the watchman, but I realized they were still in shock, so I decided to go and find him myself. While they were getting the ladder, I looked around. There were bomb craters in several places, and the brick walls and wooden doors of the mill were studded with shrapnel. They produced the ladder and I climbed up. Standing on the last rung, I surveyed the roof, which was broad and higher in some parts than in others. The old man was stretched out in one of the sections directly opposite me. Shrapnel had bashed in his skull; the wound was a mass of large and small slivers of metal coated in scalp, tufts of hair, and bits of brain. Half his head was blown away, and his face was missing. A few meters away from him lay a red plastic water pitcher mangled by the blast.

I wasn't feeling right, what with my nightmares, and now I had to look at this atrocity the first thing in the morning. I felt even worse. I regretted coming up on the roof and wanted to climb down, leaving retrieval of the body to the others, but looking down I saw Abdollah a few rungs below me, blocking the way. Having no choice, I climbed on the roof. Behind me came Abdollah and another man. I walked toward the corpse, and the horrible sight became even more nauseating. I felt myself gag, but managed to regain my composure. I was careful not to show weakness in front of the men. I stepped back a few paces. As soon as he saw the corpse Abdollah quickly turned his head saying, "God! What a sight to see first thing in the morning!"

The man behind the ladder took one look at the body and decided not to come up on the roof. I told Abdollah, who was still looking away, that I would take care of the body if he found a way to collect the poor man's brains.

"Me?" he asked in disgust. "I can't do it. Don't even ask such a thing."

"Fine, Abdollah, but we're going to have to put him back together somehow. We can't let him stay like this, can we?"

"Do it yourself. I'll see to his body, you scrape up his brains."

Annoyed, I said, "What do you mean 'you'll see to his body.' What's there to see to?"

"Whatever you were going to do for him."

Now I was really sore at him. The past several days he would preempt me in everything I was about to do, but now that I actually needed him for something, he refused. It took a few minutes for me to change my mind. I felt sorry for him. He was no better off than I was, so what right did I have to expect more from him? I looked at him.

During the last several days his face had become sallow. The lack of sleep and food, the impossible workload, and the unspeakable things we saw left us with no energy to take on more. When I first saw Abdollah with that posture of his, it looked like he was stooping, but now with the exhaustion, it was worse and he looked like he was bent in two. I had to do the job myself.

I looked around the roof for something to scrape up the brains, but found nothing. There was some cardboard the old man had used for bedding, but it was no good because it was drenched in blood. I looked at it more carefully. Some of the cardboard, where the old man's legs were, was dry. I could use these sections as a broom and dustpan. I tied my chador around my waist and, fighting the urge to vomit, gathered the bits of brain mixed with scalp and hair that were plastered to the mud and straw surface of the roof. As I picked up the pieces, I was very careful not touch them, but twice small bits sprung into my hand, sending a strange feeling down my spine. I shook my hands frantically. Nerves and nausea made me tremble from head to foot, and the stress was becoming unbearable. Under my breath I called on the blessed Zeynab to give me strength to go on, which helped, but I still felt sick to my stomach from the stench of blood. I gathered the pieces and put them in the hole in the front of the old man's skull. His sockets were so full of blood that you couldn't tell whether he still had eyeballs. Every time I went back to deposit bits of brain in his head, I tried not to look. In the meantime Abdollah searched for something to put the body in so we could get it down the ladder. He yelled, "Nobody has a blanket?"

"No," said the men on the ground.

"Try to find something," he told them.

"There's nothing to find," they said.

"Let's use the blanket that's under his head," I said.

It was drenched with blood. Opening it up, we found it had been shredded by the shrapnel, and not one piece was large enough to hold the body. One corner was torn off completely. Abdollah folded the blanket in half. When I was finished with the brains, I said to him, "Tell someone to come up and help us put him in the blanket."

He went to the edge of the roof and repeated what I had said. A few minutes later the same man who had retreated down the ladder returned, but as soon as he got a glimpse of the corpse, he threw up. He went to another part of the roof and stood with his back toward us. Finally he climbed back down. "Forget about him. Let's do it ourselves," I said.

I had no choice but to take the old man by his legs. His body was heavier than it looked. Abdollah used the cardboard to shovel him on the blanket. We tied up the blanket with some rope we had gotten from the workers. We wound it all around to be better able to control the bundle as we lowered it to the ground. We also covered the head so no one below would see the horror of the man's mangled face. First, we tried to lift the old man but he was too heavy. Then we slid him along the roof, but the ripping sound the tattered blanket made as it scraped along put an end to that. We had no choice but to inch him forward until we got to the edge of the roof, which wasn't all that steady. Shrapnel had loosened the bricks and the adobe underneath it. I wrapped the rope firmly around my arm. Abdollah took one end of the blanket. The body was so heavy that if we had stood up and tried to lower it, it might have taken us with it. I knelt down and, propping one hand on something, held the rope with the other. Abdollah bent down and we slid the body over the edge. His end was heavier than mine so it went down first. To maintain his balance Abdollah stretched out on the roof. We were letting out more of the rope when there was a ripping sound. I had a horrible sense of panic, and it felt like my arm was being pulled from its socket. At that point Abdollah let out more of the rope from his side, and the body folded at the waist. "What are you doing, Abdollah! It's about to drop!" I yelled.

"Faster, sister!" he shouted back in Arabic. "My ribs are breaking!"

The blanket was about to tear open, disgorging the body; but the man who had gone back down the ladder was now perched on one of the rungs and grabbed the rope on my end. Finally, as the workers shouted their prayers of thanks and salutations, adding their own advice on how to manage the rope, the body reached the ground. My palms were horribly chaffed; the rope was so rough it took off pieces of skin. As I climbed down, I noticed that the van that had taken the wounded was back. They quickly loaded the body of the old man into it and went to the cemetery. As soon as my feet touched the ground, it felt like there was no strength in my body. The bombardment and explosions went on nonstop. I asked the mill workers, still in a state of shock, for water to wash my hands.

"There is none," they said.

I looked around and noticed two piles of sand by the yard. I walked to them and rubbed my hands with sand. Then I wiped them off on the earth in the yard. Abdollah followed suit but used more force than I did in trying to rub his hands clean. I got the bloodstains off, but I wasn't satisfied with my efforts. So I went back to the mill and wiped my hands on the bricks; they felt heavy as if they weren't part of my body. Then I left the mill.

As we walked Abdollah and I were strangely quiet. I continued to rub my hands in the dirt by the road. Abdollah did the same.

The further we went, the more the enemy fire intensified, which offered a distraction from the horror of touching the old man's corpse. To take Abdollah's mind off it, I said, "You see where the shells are landing?"

He grumbled in Arabic, "I'm not going with you anymore. I'm going back to the mosque." Then he added in Persian, "We were supposed to go and have breakfast."

"Well, did I stop you?"

"No, but you went after corpses. My nerves can't take any more of this. I'm never going to handle dead people again."

"So don't," I said. "Who said you have to? This is what I do. That's why I stayed in the city." He said nothing.

We continued to walk in silence, but after a while, realizing I was angry at him, he asked, "What are you going to do when we get to the mosque: stay or go?"

"I don't know. We''ll see what happens."

It was clear that he wanted to have a heart-to-heart. "Look, sister, this one was really messed up, don't you think?"

"Yes, he was, but there was no need to say so."

We left Ordibehesht Street and entered Forty-Meter Road. The Iraqis were now targeting the center of the city. Every twenty meters along the road our forces had set up sandbag emplacements: in front of the Quran school, the Imam Sadeq Mosque, on the corner of Forty-Meter and Revolution, which led to the Congregational Mosque.

Along the curbs the sandbags were piled in semicircles, but the emplacements in the roads were fully circular and surrounded by trenches. The shelling destroyed the houses that had remained standing after the first assault. The trees along the avenue were scorched and the city looked even more deserted. We passed several soldiers sleeping in their emplacements; they had obviously been on post all night. The expressions on their faces said one thing: exhaustion.

Before I reached the Quran School, I said hello to the girls who were nearby. The school had been designated as a backup post. Several times when I had passed the school, I had seen them fortifying it.

The first person to answer my greeting was Shahnaz Hajjishah, who was perched on a sandbag. As I got nearer, I said hello to Fakhri Taqati and Mrs. Abedi, the principal. They were sitting on the ground with their backs against the sandbags. "What's the latest?" I asked.

"You're the one who's going around all the time, and you're asking us? We're just waiting for someone to let us know."

I laughed and said, "Well, you've certainly made a nice foxhole for yourselves."

"Yeah. Now, you tell us what's the latest?" they asked cheerfully.

"No news, as usual. We've collected a few bodies and sent them to Jennatabad." Then I gave them a brief description of how the old man at the mill was killed. Everyone was moved. Mrs. Abedi sent up a prayer for me. Then Shahnaz said with a smile, "You're the one who's working; we're just happy to look busy."

"Isn't that something? Just sticking around and doing what you can—What else it there?"

As we spoke, some of the remote areas of the city were being bombarded. But when I said goodbye and headed for the mosque, they started to shell Forty-Meter Road harder.

I found Zohreh Farhadi and Maryam Amjadi sitting on the front steps of the mosque, following the progress of the shelling. I said hello and went inside. Everybody at the infirmary expected a shell to hit the mosque at any time. After the usual greetings, I said, "What's he up to? The shells have been dogging my steps ever since I left Jennatabad."

The sounds of explosions drowned out their answers. The shells were getting closer, and bombs were landing nearby. The whine of rockets and the roar of the blasts seemed to be coming from from all directions at once, and the smell of smoke and cordite filled the air. I ran outside, but no sooner had I gotten to the bottom steps of the mosque and before I could reach the street, the ground beneath my feet jerked. A terrible blast knocked the wind out of me, and the shock wave propelled me a few feet. At the same time several people were knocked to the ground at the crossroads. I caught a glimpse of one of them just before the blast. He was middle-aged and dressed in brown pants and a grey shirt. I wanted to go and see to the wounded but thought I should let the people at the infirmary know what had happened first. I rushed inside and said, "Move it! There are wounded outside."

I didn't waste a second and ran back. Although my ears were ringing from the explosion, I could hear people murmuring pathetically as they stood beside the wounded. One of them announced, "Help is on the way."

I began to examine them. Besides being wounded by shrapnel, they had been slammed to the ground by the shock wave. They didn't respond to anything we said but merely lay limp and lifeless on the ground, which had been furrowed by pieces of shell casing and shrapnel. The man that I had seen running before the blast was covered head to foot in blood. His eyes were open and he stared into space without blinking. I went over to him and said, "Do you hear my voice? Are you alive?"

He didn't respond. I quickly took his pulse. It was very weak. Mr. Najjar came by and said, "He's alive but he's had a very bad shock." His condition was worse than the others. There was shrapnel in his legs and stomach, and the wounds were bleeding heavily. People helped us bring the wounded into the mosque so we could give them first aid until a vehicle arrived. Then we sent them to the Mosaddeq Hospital.

When I left the hospital from the emergency room, I saw two of the girls who had been helping at the mosque running around frantically. I don't recall their names now, but they said, "Have you heard? Two of the girls from the school were killed."

"NO! When?" I said.

"A few hours ago, in front of the school."

In shock I said, “That was when I was there, but there was nothing going on then.”

“If you don’t believe us, go to the morgue and see for yourself.”

I didn’t waste a minute and headed for the bulky gate that opened onto the yard. There was a pickup parked in front. I entered the building and saw Sabah Vatankhah, who worked mainly in the mosque infirmary. She was staring into space. I walked by her and my nose was greeted by the stench of blood.

Shafts of light from the open door penetrated the darkness inside, making the job of identifying the corpses easier. The stone floor was littered with bodies dressed in tattered clothing and scarred by deep wounds. Blood and water from the melting blocks of ice flowed over the floor. Some of the corpses were still on stretchers, which meant that they were so mutilated that the attendants didn’t dare lay them on the ground. People circled the bodies looking for their loved ones and wailing. Other people were busy trying to put the corpses into some kind of order. It was hard to make out the faces of the girls of the school among the mass of bodies. Already reeling from the blast, I got dizzier from turning this way and that. The buzzing in my ears was still there.

I remembered the instant of the blast in detail: how people seemed to fall to the ground like so many leaves, how shards of metal from the bomb dug into the asphalt, and how shrapnel burrowed into the earth for a considerable distance in all directions. I was replaying the scene in my mind, when I heard someone behind me say, “Come, the two Shahnazes are over here.” I turned around and saw the face of a woman, bright in the darkness. “Weren’t you the one who was looking for the girls at the school?” she repeated.

Then she pointed to two bodies near me. I couldn’t believe it. Shahnaz Hajjishah? Without knowing it, I stepped away from her body. I didn’t have the heart to look at her in that condition. Her white tunic was blood-soaked and her chador was wrapped around her body. My head started reeling as I looked around and kept repeating to myself, “Never! Never!”

I bent down to look at her hoping it was a mistake. There was no mistaking the look of kindness on her face. I looked more closely; it was as if her face was radiant. She also had a look of satisfaction, almost delight—no sign of pain or suffering. I adjusted her dark blue headscarf so it would cover her hair, which was matted with blood. Given how much she prized her dignity when she was alive, the last thing I wanted was for her to lose it now. I looked at the face next to hers, which was less familiar; I only knew her name: Shahnaz Mohammadi, one of the girls at the school. I looked at Shahnaz Hajjishah again. We had become friends during the first days of the war. After father's death, we became closer. Whenever we saw each other, however briefly, we would always pour out our hearts or offer comfort by joking or saying a few words. I started to cry silently. A painful lump had formed in my throat. If I had only stayed a bit longer at the school, I could have gotten my wish. I could have joined father. Why didn't I stay longer?

I looked at her through a film of tears, wishing it wasn't so. Why did it have to be Shahnaz? I was so fond of her. I knelt and cradled her head in my arms. Even though death had become an ordinary thing for me, I still couldn't believe she was dead, and the more I looked at her, the less her death seemed real. I lay her head back on the ground and began to shake uncontrollably. I rose and turned away feeling horrible. Unaware of the time, I didn't notice that Mahmud Farrokhi and several others had entered the morgue. The girls went over to the Shahnazes and cried. I heard Mahmud say, "We want to take the bodies."

A man came with stretchers and called on the girls to help.

Looking for someone to help us, I saw Sabah Vatankhah's mother there, which was strange because she normally worked at the mosque kitchen.

I called out to her, "Come and take her head."

She approached me with a look of apprehension on her face. She probably doubted she could do such a thing. Finally politeness overcame her reluctance, and she wrapped her chador around her waist. She bent down and took Shahnaz by the legs. I tried to lift her by the shoulders, but that was impossible. I was forced to take her arms. I looked at Mrs. Vatankhah and signaled to her that we should lift the body together. But her arms were trembling. "Scared?" I asked.

"No, my heart's aching."

"On three, okay?"

She nodded and, after saying "Ali!" I got her body off the ground about a meter, but I saw Mrs. Vatankhah had let go of the feet. All the weight fell me, and I couldn't stop the body from slipping through my hands. Before I knew what had happened, I found myself holding one of Shahnaz's arms in my hand. It had apparently come out of its socket. I shuddered and a horrible feeling came over me as the world went dark. It was impossible to breathe. I dropped the arm and, without thinking, ran headlong into a wall. The thought that I had caused Shahnaz more harm drove me insane. My heart was beating so hard it seemed it was about to burst from my chest. The grief I had felt about Shahnaz apparently was not awful enough; I had to feel guilty about dismembering her on top of it. I turned and looked at the body from a distance. My legs were shaking so much I sat and leaned against the wall. I couldn't stop weeping. No matter what I did, I couldn't keep my emotions in check. I had always been aware of how others viewed me and never wanted to show weakness in public, but now I didn't give a damn about anyone or anything. I rubbed my hands together and began to slap my face frantically and grind my teeth together. Why, I asked myself, why does it have to be like this? What if Shahnaz's mother and sisters were here to see this? Think of how they would have felt. Why was I such a weak sister that I couldn't even manage something as easy as lifting her body from the floor? Was this the way I showed how good a friend I was to her? Then I began to ask her for forgiveness. This was the last thing in the world I wanted to have happen to her.

The psychological pressure on me was beginning to tell for the first time. I wanted to shriek but up until now there was no opportunity. I clamped my hand over my mouth. What I wanted most at that point was for someone to come and embrace me and say, "It's not your fault." But the morgue had suddenly emptied out; even Sabah's mother was gone.

A voice calling me to come outside interrupted my thoughts. "Come and help us unload the truck."

I willed myself back to the present. If you don't have the stomach for this, I told myself, you might as well go back to the city. There's no reason to stay. Even if you could help, wallowing in grief is not the answer. How long do you want to sit around mourning? Get up.

God has helped you get to this point; you'll have to rely on His greatness. These words helped me get my nerves under control a little. I walked to the entrance to see what was happening. There were several people standing by the pickup listening to the driver. I also heard a child crying but couldn't see him. The driver said, "This boy is all that's left of the family." Then he pointed to the bodies in the back and said, "Fourteen people, I've brought them from Taleqani." The crowd looked at the corpses sorrowfully.

I needed help to move the two Shahnazes. There was no sign of anyone—even Mahmud Farrokhi, who had promised to help. I just wanted to get them off the floor. So I shouted to them, "I need help." Several men turned toward me. To the women I said, "If it's not any trouble, could you come with me?"

A nurse and one of the women separated from the group and asked me what I needed them for. I pointed to Shahnaz Hajjishah's corpse and said, "Come and help me put her on a stretcher."

"Why is she on the ground in the first place?" the nurse asked.

This put me back on the verge of tears, but I managed to remain composed. "They want to take her away."

Too ashamed to take Shahnaz by the head, I asked the nurse to do it. To the other woman I said, "You take her by the waist."

I placed Shahnaz's other arm over her chest. Then I took her legs and said, "Let's try to be gentle, okay?"

"What difference does it make?" the woman asked.

"She can't feel anything. Why are you so touchy about this?" the nurse asked.

I managed to say, "Well, she was some mother's darling girl. You shouldn't speak about her that way. Let's treat her the way her mother would."

As we were lifting Shahnaz, I said, "Please be careful, I beg you."

My eyes were wild with fear as we struggled to get her on the stretcher, but we finally managed. I breathed a sigh of relief. I rearranged her chador and placed her arm beside her. I was in the process of straightening her headscarf when the nurse asked, "So why were you so upset? What's she to you?"

I was so choked up I couldn't answer her. Noticing how my lips were quivering, she asked, "Was she family?"

In a tortured voice I said, "A friend. But what difference does it make? Let's just say she was my sister."

After they had left, I cradled Shahnaz's head in my arms and kissed her through the scarf. I caressed her face, expecting her to open her eyes and with that cheery voice of hers ask, "Zahra, when did you get here?"

But it was no use. Shahnaz was gone. Taking her hand in mine, I asked her to forgive me again for what had happened. Then I brought my face close to hers and said, "Say hello to father. Tell him not to forget us."

Now I spoke to her only with my tears. I recalled the first time I saw her. It was at the school during Ramadan, the ceremonies held to mark the time when the Quran was revealed to the Prophet. After the ceremonies were over I saw her running about preparing the meal for the morning breaking of the fast. She worked with enthusiasm and excitement as she laid out the food for the guests. I could tell then she was no ordinary person.

People outside were calling for help again. I forced myself to say goodbye to her saying, "Remember what I told you—especially the part about saying hello to father."

Then I looked at her face for the last time and left.

Several people were standing behind the pickup, helping a man in the back, who was unloading bodies. They put the corpses on stretchers and carried them into the morgue. "Let me help," I said to the man. I climbed up and pulled the bodies of the women forward. I asked the women in the yard to come and help. The bodies were horribly mutilated. Some were hit in the head or chest by shrapnel. Only the faces of a few of them were unmarked. There were people of all ages: men, women, and children. There were several women in Arabic head cloths, their faces stained with mud and blood. The blood-soaked tresses of another woman were coiled around her head. Most of the women had their eyes wide open, as if they were in a state of shock with no inkling they were about to die. What was more horrible to me than anything was the body of a girl no more than ten. The innocence in her face, which clashed with the tattered rags she had on, made me lose my composure. I remember that her headscarf had been opened and her hair had spilled out in every direction. She was wearing hand-me-down, boyish clothing, which was woven from a green, wooly yarn. From the way the sleeves bulged, you could tell her shirt was too small for her. She also wore a skirt and pajama bottoms; it seemed that her family was insistent about keeping her covered up. I had seen the kind of scarf the girl was wearing; it was made of artificial white silk decorated with colorful butterflies. The butterflies were now floundering in the girl's blood. The scene was heartbreaking. What did this girl have to do with war? Had she ever thought about war, even in her wildest dreams? Why didn't the people who started this war give any thought to the women and children it would kill? What crime did they commit to merit the horror of war?

The pressure growing in my chest was again so unbearable I thought I would go into the street and shriek, "LORD! LORD!" until I died.

The lone child survivor of the family in the back of the pickup was still crying, which made me feel worse. I begged the women in the yard to quiet him. They held him in their arms and patted his back, but it did no good. I sensed that he was just hungry and frightened, crying out to his mother. They passed him around in an attempt to calm him, but the child only became more upset and shrieked until he fainted. His head rested on the shoulder of the last person to hold him, but suddenly it popped up as if he had forgotten something or had suffered an attack. He was screeching so much his eyes shown crimson against his brownish face. I remembered how the newborn Sa'id would move his arms and legs in the cradle when he saw father. Unable to take any more of this, I jumped down from the pickup. I walked toward a nurse, who had just begun to hold the baby, and said, "Give him to me."

The woman, who was impatient to be rid of the child, handed him to me without hesitating. I gave him several hugs and kissed him. I looked at his face. He was about ten months old, with sparse light-colored hair and dark brown eyes. He only had two teeth. His face was reddish from screeching, and tears tracked down his cheeks. Dried milk was caked at the corners of his mouth, which told me that he was still nursing. I put my fingers near him and he tried to suck on them. Addressing no one in particular, I said, "Can we get something for this child to eat? He's starving."

"There isn't anything," they said. "He needs milk."

I walked toward a bluish hose lying in the garden and opened the spigot. Thank God there was water. First, I washed my hands of the dirt I had used to get the remains of the old man off them. Then, cupping my hands, I filled them with water for the baby. His shrieks died down as he brought his mouth toward the liquid, but he quickly turned his head away and began to howl. I washed his face and put the pacifier hanging around his neck into his mouth. He screamed and pulled his head back. I got choked up again seeing there was nothing I could do. The baby was in agony; he had no refuge and all the people who could take care of him were dead. I felt helpless with nothing to do but sob. Then I climbed into the pickup and sat looking at the faces of the dead women. Which one was his mother? Was it the one with hair caked with blood framing her face? Or the one whose half-opened eyes still looked out at the world blankly? Then it hit me: What if the child were to see his mother's face? Would that calm him? But then I thought better of it. I took the baby's head in my arms and the lump in my throat burst. Both of us were orphans. The baby's shrieks drowned out the sound of my sobbing.

After a good cry, I felt better. I began to stroke the baby's head and neck and massage his belly and legs. This seemed to work, as his crying jags became less frequent. He was overtired and couldn't keep his eyes open. His head kept burrowing in my chest searching for milk. The futile efforts of his tiny lips tore at my insides. It was clear hunger has brought him to the end of his tether. I wanted to go out of the hospital and find something for him to eat, but I knew there wasn't anything available in the neighborhood. I continued to massage his back and shoulders and managed to get him to fall asleep. I rested my head on his chest and said, "God help us!" The baby's crying resumed. I raised my head and looked through the windshield to see the nurse coming toward us. She wore her dyed brown hair up, and she had biscuits in her hand. I quickly tried to dry my tears. She said, "If it's not a bother, I found these, but I know it isn't what the baby needs. Our newborn ward is empty, otherwise I would have gone there and brought a bottle with some powdered milk." Then she opened the pack of biscuits and gave it to me. I pulled one out and put it in the baby's mouth. It was dry and, unable to chew it, he pushed it away and started to cry. I struggled to keep it in front of his mouth. He sucked on it and quieted a little. But it did not satisfy him, so he pushed my hand away again. I refused to give up and forced the biscuit into his mouth to moisten it, hoping he would be able to get it down. But then I thought it would be better to crumble it and pour the crumbs into his mouth. That didn't work either. He wiped his mouth and nose with his hand. His tears mixed with what was running from his nose, and he cried, spitting out the biscuit crumbs. I stopped trying to feed him. Now, lacking the strength to cry, he was whimpering. Amid the sounds of explosions, ambulance sirens, and the horn honking that never seemed to stop, I had a thought. The child had no one left and nowhere to go. Why not keep him myself? It was true that my own fate was not certain, but at least he could be with me wherever I was going. Like Zeynab and Sa'id he'd have to depend on the goodness of God for his daily bread. The more I thought about it the more I realized that I wanted to stay in the city and work. There was no telling how long the war was going to last. When it was over, I'd give him to somebody. Where was I going to get food for him? Who was going to take care of him while I went about town? God had kept him alive to this point, but if I kept him in the city would he survive the bombings?

My thoughts were interrupted by someone saying, "Sister, give us the child, we have to go." I raised my head and saw it was the same man who had brought the bodies. "Where do you want to take him?" I asked. "You're not going to abandon him, God forbid. He's an orphan now. Take him somewhere safe, somewhere his family can find him." "Don't worry. I'll hand him over to the health center in Abadan," the man said.

I kissed and kissed the boy, who by now was lying limp in my arms. The man took him. I climbed down from the pickup and watched it as it left the hospital compound.

I felt terrible and lacked the strength to stand. I had seen nothing but tragedy that day. As I walked from the compound, I didn't know where I was going. I wanted to flee, go where there were no people, drown myself in my own being. The only thing that would restore my peace of mind would be to see Ali. I could no longer entertain any hope of seeing father. Besides him the only person who could give me the strength to go on would be Ali. He was the only person I could talk to now, and there was so much I had to tell him. I walked dizzily into the middle of the street, thinking I could escape these horrible thoughts by getting lost. I wished the whole thing had been a nightmare, a long period of terror that would disappear. It was no use. I knew with all my heart that all the misery was real. I called on the Lord to send some shrapnel my way and put me out of my misery.

Not knowing where I was going, I reached the traffic circle where the municipality building was. I sat down in the middle of the traffic circle and stared at the building. I remembered that a few days before Banisadr had been at that very spot. Father had convinced me that he was a traitor, and said so openly when arguing with people. A few times when I had brought food to the girls at the Quran school, I repeated the charge, but Shahnaz objected, "That's still not certain and saying such things weakens our solidarity."

The day Banisadr came I had just finished burying bodies and ferrying the wounded to Taleqani Hospital. The nurses had confronted me grumbling that I couldn't keep depositing bodies with them. So I was in a very bad mood when I got to the mosque. I wanted to pour out my heart to someone, tell them that they had to make somebody in charge of admitting wounded to the hospitals and coordinate their activities. I also wanted a decision about whether we should bring the corpses to Jennatabad or deposit them at the morgue or bury them in the cemetery in Abadan. Just finding vehicles and convincing the drivers to cooperate were huge challenges. I had no choice but to dragoon anyone I found into service and make them work so much they would try to run away at the first opportunity. By chance several men were standing outside the door. Annoyed, I asked, "Why can't anyone take responsibility for the dead and wounded?"

More annoyed than I was, they said, "Go and tell it to Banisadr."

"And how am I supposed to get a hold of Banisadr?" I asked in surprise.

"He's at the municipality right now," they said.

At that moment all the heartrending sights of Jennatabad, all the damage inflicted on the city and the people, flashed before my eyes.

My blood began to boil. I asked myself, what prompted the traitor to come here? I was going to go right then and there and spit in his face. If you're man enough, I'd say, pick up a rifle and fight. See how long you'd last!

I went into the street and saw a pickup parked there with some of the people who worked in the mosque on board. I grabbed the rail, pulled myself up, and stood with the girls. The pickup was overloaded and it was just as likely to tip over as reach the municipality. There were also two people sitting on the roof of the cab. To cries of "God is great!" and salutations and prayers, the pickup started to move. Some people shouted their encouragement to the defenders of the city. Others threatened Banisadr, while others said that it was better to be reasonable than start a riot. When we reached the building, we saw a huge crowd gathered there. Everybody from ordinary people to military, defenders, women and men, were all standing by the entrance. At times the crowd would surge against the double doors trying to open them. There were soldiers on the other side standing ready to fire. There were also plainclothes bodyguards in the compound. We joined the crowd. "Let us in," we shouted, "let us have our say!"

From the other side of the door the men asked, "What do you want? What do you want to say?"

I pushed my way through the crowd and screamed, "OPEN THE DOOR! Why are you hiding him in there? Is there a reception or something?"

One of the armed men said, "Calm down. The president is meeting with the governor."

"Meeting?" I yelled over the clamor. "There's no need for a meeting. Bring him forward so he can see for himself what's happening here. We've lost everything. He's got to see what people are going through!"

Someone in he crowd said to me, "Come on, sister, show a little respect. He's the president of the country after all."

"Respect? What for? How many people have to be slaughtered? How many of our young men have to be crushed under the enemy tanks? It's like it makes no difference to this man how much of our territory they take. He's a traitor. We made him president, and now we want him out!"

At once one of the military types behind the door barked, "Watch what you're saying. If you don't change your tone, I'll come out there and smack you in the mouth. Understand?"

"You watch what you're saying, you ass-kisser! If you're man enough, come out here and I'll show you who's going to smack who!"

Then the young people near me said to him, "Shut up! We going to come in there and punch your face!" Grabbing the railing, they yanked themselves up. The bodyguards took the military man aside and shouted, "Stand back!" Then they gave the door a shove, knocking several of the boys to the ground. Several of the onlookers intervened and helped the other boys climb down off the door. They said to the crowd, "Why don't we wait for now and see what happens at the meeting they're talking about?"

The hour we waited there went badly for me. Angered by my own helplessness, I walked away and sat down by a fence. Then leaning on the bars of the fence, I asked, "So, is the meeting over?"

"No," they said.

In the end the only thing we accomplished was to shout. A bodyguard told me to go to the mosque, because Banisadr was scheduled to visit everywhere. They told me I could say what I wanted when he came to the mosque. People said, "Mister, all we want to tell him is send two Phantoms so they can bomb the enemy positions. We don't want anything for ourselves."

"The generals will tell him that," they said

Dejected, we all walked back to the mosque; people rushed up to us and asked excitedly, "What happened? Did you see the president? What did he say?"

"Nothing," I said, "don't get excited. They didn't even let us inside. This clown just came to blow his own horn, not to see what was happening to us."

"What do you mean? What actually happened?"

I didn't feel like saying more. The others answered for me, "Nothing happened. It was useless going there. They told us that Mr. President would deign to visit the mosque in due time."

I was depressed. I went to the back of the prayer room to think. If he's not a traitor and really cares about the people, why doesn't he join the crowd? Why go to the municipality and not the mosque? Why didn't they let anybody see him? Father must have seen something to make him say Banisadr was a traitor. He wasn't the kind of person to say things off the top of his head. But why would the people at the mosque, people I respect, why would they take Banisadr's side? They were decent people with college degrees, who understood politics. Where was I wrong? Why didn't he order the planes to fly and hit the enemy targets, then? Why were his bodyguards behaving like brutes? Why did they speak to me that way?

After giving the matter a lot of thought I concluded that father was right; this man was an absolute bastard. My doubts were due to my own inexperience. I threatened Banisadr in my mind: Come winter, Mr. President, your face will be charcoal black from shame. We're resisting and as soon as we kick the enemy out of Iran, I'm coming to Tehran and telling Imam Khomeini at Jamaran that you are a traitor.

I felt better after this, charged with new energy. We've got to stand on our own two feet, I told myself, with their support or without it, whether reinforcements come or not.

The next day I was even more convinced I was right. They played an interview with Banisadr on the two o'clock news. He presented the circumstances surrounding the war as normal, saying, "The problem is not as dire as has been reported. There was an attack and our forces repelled it." The boys said that day they had been finally able to intercept Banisadr on his route. But instead of expressing his sympathy for their plight and offering encouragement, he said, "Phantoms are not candy that I can just pull out of my pocket." "You're the commander of the air force," they objected. "It would be easy for you to give the order."

"You don't understand the inner workings of the military," he said.

Later when I saw Shahnaz, I said, "See what I mean. So much for Mr. Banisadr!"

"Yeah, God help me. What was I thinking? I wish I hadn't voted for him." It was more painful now to dredge up those memories, so I got up, looked one last time at the building, and dragged myself to the Congregational Mosque. I was dejected, worn out. Though I didn't have the strength to move, I somehow got to the mosque. As soon as I entered the girls gathered around me and I asked, "What happened?"

"Where were you all this time?" they asked. "Have you seen your brother?"

Stunned, I asked, "Which brother?"

"Your Ali."

My heart skipped a beat. Still in a state of shock, I asked, "Ali? You're sure it's Ali?"

"Yeah. A tall young man with bandaged hands stopped by."

"What did you say?" I asked.

"We told him we didn't know where you were. We guessed you were either at Jennatabad or somewhere in the city. You could be at the front, too."

"Fine. He didn't say anything else?"

"He said he was off to Jennatabad and maybe see you there. He gave us a magazine for a gun and a shirt uniform and told us to give them to you."

"When exactly was he here?"

"About two hours ago."

"If I go now I'll probably find him."

"Do you want the shirt and the magazine?"

As I left, I said, "Keep them here until I come back."

I didn't wait to hear the rest of what they said and raced out of the mosque. I thought I would go to see mother first, but I remembered Ali said he would be going to Jennatabad. I tucked up my chador and started to run.

Ali had finally come back! I was delirious. There were chills up and down my spine and even when talking to myself, my voice trembled. But there was also a lump in my throat. Now that Ali was back, I thought, everything would be the way it had been before. I could get rid of all those responsibilities that weighed so heavily on me and finally have a chance to breathe.

I was going to hug him as soon as I saw him no matter who might be looking—hug him tight and cover him with kisses. As I ran I thought about what I should tell him first. It was probably best not to start with father's death, so as not to upset him. I'd let him get settled first before we had a heart-to-heart.

I remembered the last conversation we had. It was hard to call the hospital in Tehran from the pay phone. We kept getting cut off. I went with Leila to the shop of one of our relatives and called from there, but no matter how many times I tried I couldn't get through. In the end I wrote to him, but there was no answer. When he first had gone to Tehran I used to include a letter with the dates and fish we would send him. He answered me and would ask about conditions in Khorramshahr. But there was no answer to my last letter. It probably had gotten lost because I knew ordinarily he wouldn't keep me waiting for an answer like that.

As I ran past our lane, I looked back at the house as I always did. A few months earlier a neighbor's house had caught fire. The flames reached the kitchen and there was the real danger that a gas canister would explode, blowing the neighborhood to smithereens. People gathered outside, but no one had the nerve to enter the house and retrieve the canister. All of a sudden Ali rode up on his motorcycle. I told him the problem. He immediately ran into the yard and grabbed a hose to wet some cloth. Then he entered the house, got the canister, and threw it into an empty lot. It was so hot from the fire that it burned his hands. Relieved, everybody praised Ali to the sky for saving their homes. When the neighbor returned from work, he came by the house and hugged Ali, unable to thank him enough.

I ran and ran but never got to where I needed to be. It was as if the road had gotten longer. Probably there was pandemonium at Jennatabad, everybody gathered around Ali, talking at once. I thought the whole world would be as delirious as I was. But when I finally got there and began to hug and kiss Leila hard asking her where Ali was, she said, "What's gotten into you? Why are you doing that?"

I felt confused and panicked. I was suddenly blind and disoriented. I ran toward Zeynab and began to hug her. "Ali's come!" I said.

"How wonderful!" she said with a smile. "Thank God! You've been Ali-ing and Ali-ing so much he's finally back."

"Where is he?" I asked.

"What's wrong with you? Why are you acting like that?" Leila asked.

"She's got a right to be," Zeynab said. "If I were her, I'd be the same way."

"So where's Ali?" I asked.

"He went."

"Where?"

"To the Sheikh Salman Mosque, to mother."

I grabbed Leila's hand and said, "Come with me."

I sensed she was over the excitement of seeing Ali—she was so calm and quiet.

"Hold on a minute, don't pull me like that," she said.

"No, we've got to run or we'll miss him."

As I pulled her by the hand and ran, I kept saying, "Run, Leila, run!"

I was out of my mind. I couldn't contain myself and with my hands held up to the sky, I whirled around. I took a deep breath and said, "Oh wow, God be praised. Ali's come and all our troubles are over!"

Leila said, "Zahra, don't do that. They'll think you're crazy."

"I am crazy, crazy about Ali; you have no idea how happy I am. You didn't have the responsibilities on your shoulders, but now I'm free!"

The road was empty up to the Ordibehesht Circle, but after that there was a crowd. We started running faster and, with mounting excitement, we turned into Rudaki Avenue and followed Fakhr-e Razi until we reached the Salman Mosque. In my mind I saw Ali everywhere. I opened my chador and let the wind raise it. I ran and whirled about. The world was mine; my worries were over. Ali was going to make everything better.

When I got to the door (how I don't know), I scarcely said hello to the people I knew. I kept saying, "Ali's come back!"

All my relatives said, "Wonderful! Thank God!" I rushed passed them and yelled in the yard, "Mother! Mother, Ali's here!"

This was the first time since father's death she seemed happy. No longer gloomy, she was standing with the other women from the family instead of huddling alone in some corner. I ran up to her and asked excitedly, "Have you seen him?"

"Yes, my sweet, I have."

Her tone said it all. She was overjoyed. We hugged and kissed each other. "Thank God, mother, nothing to worry about now!"

Her eyes welled with tears. I stared into her eyes. I knew mother's moods well. It seemed that in addition to the normal worry, there was a deeper anxiety. I sensed that she was anxious about Ali, who didn't seem able to stay put anywhere.

I was so excited I hugged and kissed mother's neighbors at the mosque. Ali had finally returned. I was beyond happy and wanted to go into the yard and jump for joy, run around making my chador twirl in the air. I turned to mother and took her by the hand. As we looked at each other, I asked, "Where is he?"

It had slipped my mind that he had told Leila he couldn't wait to get to the front. I didn't say anything. Mother said, "Ali said he was going to the military. Pray he doesn't go to fight."

"Don't say that, mother. Is Ali any more precious to you than the other boys are to their mothers?"

She didn't know what to say but tried to justify what she had said, "No, but his hands are not right."

"That not a problem," I said. "God is great. Your son's a lion. You should be proud he wants to go fight the enemy even with those hands. Pray to God to keep him safe so he can fight."

"Trust in God. Put your faith in Him," she said.

The neighbors stood around us and said happily, "God preserve him. May the blessed Imam Hoseyn watch over him!"

"Mother, what am I supposed to do? I haven't seen him yet," I said.

"He'll be back."

Hoping to see him or just get a whiff of the shirt he had left with Sabah, I raced back to the Congregational Mosque. It was dark when I got to the mosque where I saw a soldier from the base stretched out on the ground, his long frame blocking the entrance to the prayer room. There was no blanket over him or pillow, which was strange. I went closer and saw in the darkness he was dressed in army boots, pants, and jacket. I could make out his face in a light somebody had placed nearby. His young face was pale in the dark, but even whiter in the light. "Who's that, sleeping there?" I asked.

Somebody said he was an officer who'd been like that ever since they brought him in. No matter how much they spoke to him, he wouldn't say a word. It was heartbreaking to see him like that on the cold ground. How much must his family, especially his mother, be worrying about him being at the front? I went into the prayer room and got a blanket for him. On the way back I stopped in at the infirmary and, seeing there was nothing going on, left. Then I covered the soldier with the blanket and sat by his head. I couldn't tell whether he was suffering from shell shock, not knowing exactly how it affected people. I began to recite a verse from the Quran, the Throne Verse, and prayed that God would restore him to health. He seemed to be staring at the sky in horror. Occasionally he turned his head, looking this way and that. One or two times he stared right into my eyes so fearsomely it terrified me. I kept reciting the verse. Now and then some of the girls passed by and asked, "Don't you have anything better to do? Forget about him. There's nothing wrong; he's trying to get a medical discharge."

"Nobody here is stopping him," I said. "If he wants to escape, there's nothing to stop him."

I imagined how it had been for Ali in Tehran for months, not knowing anyone, how he might have felt alienated himself.

I tried to flag down Mahmud Farrokhi as he ran around the mosque to help me bring the soldier inside.

He said, "He's in a bad way. We can't bring him in because his screams will wake the others."

After about an hour, the soldier pointed his hand to the sky and held it there. I told him to lower it several times, but he didn't respond. I followed his finger and could barely make out something faintly glowing in the distance. "Spotting enemy aircraft?" I asked.

He showed no reaction and kept pointing. I had hoped reciting the verses would make him feel better, but all of a sudden he went into convulsions and shouted deliriously. Before Mr. Najjar could get there, he had raised himself up and then slammed himself hard against the ground. Several people came running and grabbed his arms and legs, but he was very powerful, and they couldn't hold him down.

Mr. Najjar injected him with a sedative, but it took a while for it to take effect. The young officer finally fell asleep. When I was sure he was out, I got up and went inside the mosque. I sat with some of the girls who were still awake and talking.

The moon was out, and I could see everything clearly now. The girls were stretched out on the carpeting in the infirmary with their shoes off. The curtain around the enclosure gave me a sense of security. Leaning against a wall, I tried to sleep, but although I was dead tired, I couldn't. As I listened to the girls talking, my eyes started to droop.

Around 2:00 or 3:00 a.m. I was awakened by cries of "Hold him! Don't let him hurt himself!" I raced into the yard and saw that Mr. Najjar was already there with a syringe in his hand. I realized they had given the man another sedative. I stepped forward and saw that two of the people around him had his arms pinned. They were trying to get him to lie down. The blood flowing down his face glistened in the moonlight. Startled, I asked, "What happened?"

"He smashed his head against the wall," they said. Mr. Najjar was bandaging the man's head. I was about to help when he said, "You go back inside. It's dangerous; he's liable to attack at a moment's notice."

At that point a few more people came by and headed straight for the officer. He didn't respond to anything they said. The men asked the newcomers, "Do you know who he is?" "Yeah, he's from our town, a friend. We were sent to the front from up north."

"Do you know why he's acting this way?"

They said, "We've been together at the front since morning. We were under constant bombardment, and the blasts have gone to his head. Otherwise he's as normal as any other man. He's the model soldier of our company."

This was clear from his appearance. He managed to remain clean shaven and keep his clothes spic and span despite the lack of water.

I returned to the infirmary, but I was so upset I couldn't sleep. A few of the girls were up and asked what happened.

"Nothing," I said, "just that same officer."

After a while a car pulled up and they took him away. No longer fretting about bringing him in the mosque, I felt I could now sleep. I felt cold a few times during the night and found warm place among some gunnysacks and cartons. I curled up in a ball and, thinking of Ali, fell fast asleep.

11

More Bodies—More Martyrs

On the ninth day I awoke early in the morning to the sound of a man giving the call to prayer in the yard. The explosions and shelling, which had been going on all night, had intensified. The intervals between explosions seemed to be getting shorter; it was as if the Iraqis were using everything they had to grind the city to dust. I woke up the row of sleeping bodies for prayer and went into the yard myself for ablutions. I was still tired and bothered by the cold. Just before sunrise a woman, who had come to the mosque for shelter the night before, called out to me. She wanted me to get her to the hospital. I had heard her moan feebly the whole night. The woman was in the last stages of pregnancy, but whenever we asked her about helping, she would say, "It's still not time for the child to come into the world."

I didn't know why she had no family with her. The girls told the men to get a car ready for her, but they said she had to wait. The woman was in distress and couldn't take much more, however. Having asked the men repeatedly, the girls finally got their attention. At that time of morning they couldn't reach anyone and asked, "Is the patient that sick?"

The girls had no choice but to admit that she was pregnant and that the child was due any moment. Waiting, they said, would put the lives of both in danger.

The men ran around to see what could be done, and then announced that a car was on its way.

Because there was no stretcher, we had to carry her from the mosque. She put her hands around the necks of two of us, while three others had her by the legs. We managed to bring her out that way and headed toward a beverage truck parked outside. In addition to bottles it had a load of potatoes and onions for the mosque. We had no choice but to lay her on one side. I climbed in with her and leaned against the metal bottle rack. As the truck started to move, a woman known as Evil Zahra hopped on and sat at the other end of the rack. I had gotten to know her after father's death. I don't know what kept her at the mosque. She never helped, and anytime anything went against her sensibilities she would shout and argue. During the bombings, she would go rigid with fear, faint dramatically, and pretend to be dumb. Everybody was sick of her antics, and for this reason they called her "evil." I wasn't too happy she had come along.

But what could I say? The pregnant woman was in agony. I cradled her head in my lap, trying to comfort her. Ashamed of having her grief made public, she tried to keep her emotions in check by muttering prayers under her breath.

By now I was fed up with the truck. The motor wasn't right. It chugged along until reaching the bridge and then struggled to make the incline. When the driver gunned the engine, I almost jumped out of my skin. The truck picked up speed after it reached the other side. We were near the gas station when an enemy plane appeared in the sky; the roar of its jets sounded everywhere. Suddenly I feared for the woman's life.

There was a motorcycle twenty meters behind us. Keeping one eye on the sky and the other on the cycle, I noticed a passenger bhe-ing the driver with his head ducked to one side. Like us, they were trying to outrun certain death, but unlike us they had speed on their side. I knew the bridge was the enemy's primary target. I prayed and prayed the two boys on the cycle would make it over the bridge before the jets fired. I covered the woman's eyes with my hands to keep her from seeing the gory scene I feared. Seconds after the motorcycle cleared the bridge, the jets fired their rockets. One of them landed on the Kut-e Sheikh side, and the shock wave sent the two boys flying in opposite directions. Their empty bike skidded along the road and burst into flames. I held my breath. If they were anywhere near the gas tank when it exploded, they would be burned to a cinder. At the sound of the jets, the woman seemed to forget her pain. She stared at the sky in terror and prayed in a loud voice.

Instead of trying to maintain her cool, Evil Zahra went into her usual hysterics. Worried that upsetting the woman might jeopardize her and her baby, I yelled to Zahra to sit down and stop being so annoying. But she was deaf to that.

When the truck reached the birthing center, nurses rushed out and we got the woman inside. As I was saying goodbye to her, the woman thanked me and said she was worried about how I was going to get back.

"God will provide," I reassured her.

Leaving the center, I was more concerned about what happened to the two boys on the motorcycle. I said to Zahra, "I think I'll go to try to find those boys; they must be hurt. If you want to come, by all means. But if you're going to pull those antics, please don't bother. I don't want you around."

"I'm not play-acting. I'm really scared sometimes."

"Look," I said, "you know yourself that things aren't normal. Now's not the time for drama."

She said nothing and started walking with me. Sensing the wounded boys needed immediate attention, I hurried. It wasn't far from the center to the traffic circle. Soon I saw the smoldering remains of the motorcycle. The tires had come off the machine. I scoured the area for any sign of the boys, but found none. I followed a trail of blood leading to a half-built structure with no door. I went inside and found one of the boys lying in a dusty hallway with his legs spread apart and his head against the wall. There was blood all around him. I rushed to him and took his pulse, which was very weak. He had shrapnel in his side and stomach. He was also badly mangled below the belt. He had lost so much blood it looked as if he was breathing his last. He tried to say something but was too weak. I brought my head closer to his mouth but I couldn't make out what he was saying. I tried to talk to him; it was no use as he coughed up a foamy stream of blood. There was nothing I could do, so I said to Zahra, "Let's go find a car. He's gone." We left the building and craned our necks trying to spot a vehicle. None came into view. "Stay put," I told her, "and try to flag down anything that comes along."

I ran back into the building hoping that the boy was alive but fearing the worst. I tugged on his bloody trousers trying to get his attention. "Look," I said. "You're going to be all right. Don't worry; it's not serious. I'll help you." As I spoke, he struggled to look at me. All of a sudden his eyes rolled back in his head, which scared the life out of me. I had never seen that before. Uneasy, I shook him again and said, "Look. Look. You're going to be fine. Don't worry; you've lost some blood is all. I'm going to get some serum and a transfusion into you and you'll be fine."

A low moan told me he had understood what I had said. I ran from the building and asked Zahra to help me get him outside. We couldn't drag him by the legs because they were too mangled. So, despite our disgust, we grabbed him below the waist and pulled him to the side of the road. A couple of cars sped by and Zahra shouted at them, but it was no use. They wouldn't stop because of the jets. Frustrated, she began cursing, "Stop, you bastards! Yellow sons of bitches, we have wounded here!" "Stop that," I said, "They're already gone. Who are you cursing at?"

Finally, a battered red van came to a jerky stop near us. The driver, an old Arab with frizzy hair, agreed to take the boy to the hospital. In the front seat next to him was another man; both appeared to be dockworkers. After we loaded the boy in the van, I went to look for the other one. Following a blood trail that led from the street to a date grove, I found him lying next to a hut. It appeared that he had been able to walk part of the way and then collapsed.

When I got to him, he was making his peace with the lord, saying, "There is no God but Allah and Mohammad is His prophet." The oath was not coming from his mouth but from a large gash in his throat that was also streaming with blood foam. I shuddered in horror and took his pulse. There was a piece of shrapnel in his throat, but when I tried to take it out, I found I couldn't reach it with my fingers. The boy seemed younger than his companion. Transfixed by the bloody gash in the boy's throat, I said, "Brother, brother, you're going to make it. Don't give up. Think of Imam Hoseyn and the blessed Ali Akbar and stay strong." I ran from the grove and called out to the driver. Then I rushed back to the boy. By the time I got there, his head had slumped to one side. I went into a panic and took his pulse again. There was no pulse. I put my ear to his chest. It seemed his heart had stopped. At that point the driver and the other man came; their clothes were bloodstained from carrying the first boy. We lifted the other boy and noticed immediately the wall behind him was dripping with blood. Then I realized that shrapnel was not only in his throat; it had blown off the back of his head. "This one's almost gone," I said to the driver. "He won't make it to the hospital. Let's get him to the birthing center; they're admitting wounded also. Maybe they can do something, which'll be quicker."

"We won't get them there in time in this old crate," the driver said.

My heart told me that it was over for the two boys. I was so upset I couldn't speak, and Evil Zahra was also quiet. We started walking toward the bridge, hoping a car would come by and at least give us a lift across. Hunger and weariness made it difficult for us to get up the ramp. I told Zahra to walk faster so we could be on the other side quickly, but suddenly there was a horrible explosion from the Moharezzi area. The shock wave made everything shake for moment. A cloud of smoke and dust rose in the air, showing us where the shell had hit. We ran toward the spot. It appeared to have landed in the date grove along the Shatt, among the modest mud dwellings. We headed for a place where there was the sound of a woman wailing. The closer we got, the louder her shrieks became. We ran down the alleys past the huts as the cries continued. "Tell us where you are!" we shouted.

But all we heard was the sound of her wailing. We shouted again, but this time there was an answer.

We were faced with a strange sight when we finally got to the spot. The shell had landed in a foxhole beside a hut. The hole was obliterated and the walls of the hut had collapsed. The ground was dug up as if ploughed by shrapnel from the shell. The iron door of the hut was dislodged and was leaning in toward the yard. The horribly mutilated body of a young man lay by the door. I could hardly look at him let alone gather his remains. The force of the blast had torn a hole in his midsection and rotated his pelvis so much his feet seemed like they were on backwards. One of his arms was mashed up to the shoulder. His entire body, in fact, was shredded. I felt as soon as we tried to move him, his bones would disintegrate. More heartrending was the sight of his aged mother and father, who, having come out of their hut, were wailing, "Abd al-Rasul, Abd al-Rasul."

I realized the old woman was blind from the way she got on all fours and crawled on the ground toward her son's corpse. Her husband also seemed to be blind. The woman reached her son and cried in Arabic, "Sweetheart, sweetheart." The old man stood in the doorway saying, "Abd al-Rasul, answer me." The old woman seemed to realize that something had happened and said to her husband, "Go to him. See why he doesn't answer." She didn't want to believe that her son was dead. The old man feebly went forward unable to stop crying and saying, "Dear, dear?"

He fell to the ground and ran his hand over his boy's lifeless body, trying to waken him. The two of them hoped that their son had been knocked unconscious. I couldn't take any more of this. Wishing I was anywhere but there, I cried, "Mother, come here. Leave him." As soon as she heard my voice, she said, "He hasn't been martyred, has he? He's not dead, is he?"

Although I knew he was gone, I couldn't bear to tell them the truth. "We'll take him to the hospital," I lied. "You should pray for him." Hearing this, she hugged the corpse even harder and glued herself to her son. No matter how many times I asked her to leave him, she refused. I went to her and tried to persuade her to let her son go. In tears she pleaded, "Don't make me leave him, I beg you!"

I examined the boy's face. He was around twenty-eight. He wore a bright blue shirt and jeans. His rifle, which had been mangled by the blast, lay near the foxhole. Apparently he had dug the hole himself; it was about half a meter deep and was lined with sandbags.

The old couple's faces put thme in their sixties, and their eyes seemed glassy either from old age or cataracts. The man was tall and thin. He had a ragged turban on his head and was dressed in a faded grey and wrinkled dishdasha. His hands were unusually large, and I could tell from the calluses on them and his stubby fingers along with his sunburned face he had farmed the date groves all his life. Although only one of his eyes was completely filmy while the other seemed clear, he was completely blind. His son had inherited his regular features.

The woman was in no better shape than her husband. Her headscarf and dress were shabby and her feet stuck out from her plastic sandals. When I saw that she wouldn't budge from her son's side, I suggested to Zahra, who was standing to one side like a statue, "Let's go and try to flag down a car so we can remove him." We walked from the grove and sat by the side of the road. There was no vehicle in sight. Worried about the old couple, I couldn't just sit there. "You try to flag down a car, and I'll come back when you do," I said to her.

When I returned to the hut, the old man seemed resigned to the fact that his son was dead, but said nothing. The old woman continued to beat herself and keen, "Hope is lost. Our lives are over." But she pleaded with me to examine him to see whether he was alive. More than anything, this tore at my insides. It was noon and, instead of bright sunshine, a dusty haze hung over the city, probably caused by smoke from the refinery fire. I went to the head of the road several times. The old woman sensed my coming and going and asked, "What are you doing?"

"I want to find a car to take your son to the hospital."

"Wherever you take him, I'm going, too. Don't let him go alone. His father and I are coming, too."

"That's not possible," I said.

"Why not? My son's alive and I want to be with him."

I was sick to my stomach. I realized that it was better to remove all doubts about the son. If they couldn't see what had happened, at least they could learn about it. Taking the bit between my teeth, I said, "Mother, I'm no doctor, but it's clear your son has been martyred." With this they began to beat themselves harder and wail with their voices raised. I didn't wait around and went back to the head of the road. We flagged down a Land Rover and, pleading every way we knew, managed to convince the driver to take the body. He put the car in reverse, bringing it as close to the hut as he could.

The driver got out and followed us to where the body was. I didn't know how we were going to lift the corpse and keep it intact; with any movement it might have disintegrated. "You don't have a blanket we can put under him? We can't lift him like this," I said.

The old woman said to her husband, "I can't get up."

The old man said, "There's one in the room. Get it."

Evil Zahra went inside the hut. With the driver's help we managed to spread the blanket under the body. Then we got him into the car. The mother and father groped their way to the vehicle. When they reached it, they ran their hands along the side, trying to find the door. "Why do you want to bring these two to the other side of the river?" the driver asked. "They're evacuating everybody from that side to this part. What's the point of them going there and becoming refugees? At least on this side somebody may come by and rescue them. It's much more dangerous on the other side."

The driver was right. If the old couple came with us, we'd just have to take them to the Congregational Mosque where conditions were not all that good. If they remained in their home, their chances of staying alive and getting help would be better. Although logic demanded they remain, I couldn't find it in my heart to abandon them. "You should stay. Why do you want to come with us?" asked the driver in Persian.

"Mother, you stay here. We'll bring your son to the hospital," I said to her in Arabic. "If you can, you can come later."

I meant someone would bring them to the hospital and take them back. This way they would learn their son's fate.

They began to wail, saying they wished to come. "Where are you bringing our son? We want to be with him. Let us die also. Our lives are no dearer to us than our son's. There's no reason for us to stay. We've lost all hope. Why should we stay?"

I signaled to Zahra, and we both got in the car. When the car started to move, the old couple, still gripping the side of the car, fell to the ground, but the driver kept going. The old woman was on her hands and knees. Then she got to her feet and tried to lunge after us, but she fell again. This time it seemed that she didn't have the strength to get up. She dragged herself along the ground. The sight was gut-wrenching. I was disgusted with myself. I didn't know which people to curse—the ones who started the war or the ones who betrayed us.

As we drove over the bridge, I kept looking at the couple as they cried and wailed. The old woman beat her chest. She said things in

Arabic and started to move faster, but when the old man, who was following her waving his hands in the air fell, she stopped. After she had gotten her husband to his feet, they disappeared from view. A few moments later we were in front of Mosaddeq Hospital. The driver got out and called out to several people. They unloaded the blanket. I also took one end and got out. A nurse who was in front of the emergency room door administering to the bodies said, "He was gone the minute he was hit."

I said to her, "His name was Abd al-Rasul. We brought him from the other side of the bridge. They lived in Moharrezi; his parents are blind."

The nurse wrote the information on the boy's clothing with a magic marker. Then we took him to the morgue, which served as a kind of cold storage, and laid him on the floor.

I was very upset. I straightened up clumsily, as if struggling with a heavy weight on my shoulders. Thoughts of Abd al-Rasul, whose face was like his father's, also brought those two young motorcyclists to mind. The hair of the man, whose throat was hit by shrapnel, lay on his forehead. His eyes were large with long lashes, and he had a thin mustache. Unlike the other man who had an olive complexion, his face had been white but was now yellow from loss of blood. I didn't know whether they were alive at that point. Sick and tired, I returned to the mosque with Zahra. I had no desire to see anyone, but there was no way I could be alone, as the wounded were piling up as noon approached. I would occasionally leave the prayer room to see what was happening outside. I could see a halo of smoke and dust over the city. The clamor of people mixed with the wailing of sirens. The sounds of one explosion after another echoed through the city like fierce rounds of thunder.

This type of drawn-out attack was unusual. Some said the resistance put up by the boys at the front lines surprised the Iraqis, who were taking their revenge on the young men by slaughtering their relatives in the city. There was nothing we could do for many of the wounded they brought to the infirmary. We could only stop the bleeding, infuse serum, and things like that. A few of the wounded had superficial shrapnel wounds not requiring surgery. We laid them on the floor or removed the shrapnel as they sat. One of these patients was a young girl of four or five with wounds on her arms. As the girls held her down, Mr. Najjar took out the shrapnel. She squealed and cried out for her mother. She became more terrified when her wounds started to bleed. Mr. Najjar told the girl's father, who was hugging her, not to let her see the blood. To try to calm her one of the girls brought her something to eat, but it was no use. Between her cries I heard several people in the yard shouting, "Why isn't anyone paying attention to us? It's a massacre. The Iraqis are advancing. They've kept us pinned down since morning with their constant shelling."

I left the bandaging to the other girls and ran into the yard where a few young men in their twenties were shouting at the top of their lungs. Their heads and shoulders were covered in dust and their hair was all over the place. One of them in particular, tall, dressed in baggy jeans and a button-down shirt that seemed out of place on his thin frame, was the most upset. They were telling the crowd gathered around them about the conditions on the front lines. I stepped forward, and saw the tall boy had raised his weapon to show that there were no bullets in it. "What are we supposed to fight with? There're traitors involved in this. If we had ammunition, we'd be able to push them back. If any of you have weapons or ammo, hand them over. Wherever we go they say there is none. You know what's happening out there. Boys hungry and thirsty are standing up to the Iraqis. They're all being cut down. You can put up with the hunger, but the thirst, no...."

"How far have the Iraqis gotten?" I asked.

"They were at the outskirts of the city by the time we arrived and nothing'll keep them from taking it. We couldn't just stand there twiddling our thumbs while the city falls. We don't have the forces, though."

Hearing that it was like I was jolted into action, and I yelled, "I'm ready to go. Can I?"

The young man exploded like a firecracker and stamped his foot on the ground. Then, still waving his weapoin over his head, he gave me a hard, cold stare and shouted, "Go where? With me and be a millstone around our necks, forcing several of the boys to watch your back? We need men!"

To have him shout like that in front of all the others made me feel terrible. It also hurt to hear that our forces had to die at the front while having to beg for supplies behind the lines. I was even more put out now. Hajj Aqa Nuri said to the young man, "Son, we are trying to arrange reinforcements for you. We're going to send water and food also. Trust in God and try to maintain your solidarity. Militia, military, paramilitary, everybody's got to obey orders."

As Hajji Aqa Nuri spoke, Mahmud Farrokhi and several others were loading two cases of Colt and G3 ammunition and a number of RPG shells in their van. Two others came forward with several canisters of water, a couple of cartons of bread, and tins of food.

I wanted to stay and hear what the young man was telling Hajj Aqa about the situation at the front, but Ra'na Najjar called me and said, "Come on, we've got work to do." I went to see about the wounded lying on the floor of the infirmary, but I was still sick at heart.

The group of angry young men left. Taking their place were several others, who acted the same way, standing in the yard and yelling angrily, "What are you holding back? Get people to the front as fast as possible. Don't let those boys be taken prisoner."

The men in the mosque tried to calm them. They didn't want the shouting cause a panic, but it was no use. These boys were spent. They said, "We've been at it at the front for a few days. By day we push them back, but at night the forces are so tired that they don't have the strength to fight. Then the Iraqis see their chance to retake all of our positions and, what's more, they advance even farther. We have no weapons, nothing the boys can use to stop their tanks."

Mr. Mesbah said, "That's no way to talk. Why scare people like that? We have our trust in God. We don't have weapons, but we have our faith. We have the Imam."

I had wanted to stay in the mosque just in case Ali came looking for me, but Mr. Najjar suggested we leave. Reports came that Heydariyeh had been bombed, and the wounded were piling up.

It wasn't far. A number of people had taken shelter there. We took the road past the Congregational Mosque toward the Shatt and then turned into an alley.

After a brief survey, Mr. Najjar said to some of the less wounded that they would have to get themselves to the hospital. Then he removed shrapnel from the leg of a boy in his late teens and bandaged his wound, while I closed up the incision. He examined the boy's forehead and found only a flesh wound, which we also bandaged. Then it was the turn of a twelve-year-old girl who had a large piece of shrapnel in her thigh. She was crying and wouldn't let us stitch up her wound. She was right not to. The needle did not penetrate her skin easily. Unlike the mother of the boy, the girl's mother remained calm and by soothing her daughter helped us immeasurably. As we were leaving Heydariyeh, a youth entered yelling and screaming. He was talking like the young men I saw in the mosque earlier. "The Iraqis are coming. The city is about to fall and...."

I felt terrible. Everybody was saying that the city was about to fall. A strange feeling of terror gripped my body. The panic was almost instantaneous, as people all began to scream. Some turned to us, asking, "What do we do now? What he's saying, what does it mean? How far have the Iraqi's come?"

I didn't know what to tell them. Mr. Najjar took the boy aside and said, "Why are you saying that? You shouldn't make things worse."

"No, I have to tell them. Everybody's going to be killed. They'll all be taken prisoner. We've got to tell people the truth."

Mr. Najjar repeated what Mr. Mesbah had said, "We've told them the truth. What's the point of filling their hearts with fear? Making the situation worse than it is? It doesn't help. Let people abandon the city in an orderly way. We'll evacuate them, but without panic."

The boy stopped arguing and stood aside. I told people, "Don't worry. Keep calm. The situation isn't that critical. Our boys are fighting at the front. God willing the war will be over, and we'll return to our homes."

As we were leaving, Mr. Najjar asked the boy to come with us. He wanted to bring him to people at the mosque who could decide what should be done.

At the mosque the debate about whether the people should go or stay was still raging. The previous day (September 30, 1980), the Iraqis had advanced to Railroad Circle, and this was exactly what was troubling the military, the clergy, and the mosque elders. Among them were Mr. Mesbahi, Sheikh Sharif, and Major Sharif Nasab, whom I had gotten to know at the beginning of the war.

I stood listening to what the girls were saying and to what they had heard from others. Everybody had something to say.

"We'd best evacuate the neighborhoods before we're sorry we didn't."

"They'll never go. Nothing you say will get them to leave their homes."

"We've got to get them out, even if it's at gunpoint. You've got to scare them. I don't know how, but you've got to do whatever's necessary."

"We have to make a move, while the bridge is still intact. If the Iraqis hit it, then there'll be no way of getting to the other side."

Finally, amid all the arguing it was decided several groups of men and women would be formed and sent out to the neighborhoods closest to the fighting. These groups were to convince people to evacuate the city. In the meantime, they would get trucks ready to ferry people out and get them to the other side of the bridge at least.

At the tail end of the discussions, a truck pulled up in front of the door. They announced all workers without other duties should help with the evacuation. Although I had absolutely no desire to help, I had no choice. I had to convince myself that under the circumstances there was nothing better for me to do. I went to get on the truck where there were three or four other girls whom I had seen in passing in the mosque. A couple of men also got on, and we headed for the Taleqani neighborhood. In the past they had told us not to go there.

The avenues were deserted, and the alleys were full of debris from the homes that had been hit. The truck let us out at the head of an alley. The alleys in the neighborhood were relatively wider and longer than those in other areas. We fanned out each of us going in a different direction looking for people. The area was badly damaged; many of the doors had been blasted off their hinges or peppered with shrapnel. In spite of this, we knocked on every door and, if there was no answer, entered the homes. After making certain no one was inside, we went to the next home. These inspections yielded some very strange sights: large chunks of shrapnel stuck in walls seeming to hold the compounds in place; the corpses of chickens or cats hit in the head or gut by metal fragments; the broken frames of family pictures and women's long cloaks fluttering over the debris; old kitchen appliances that told of the poverty of the neighborhood.

In one of the homes a breakfast spread was laid out near the porch. It wasn't clear how long the home had been abandoned. The butter had melted, dust covered the white breakfast cheese, and the bread had gone dry. Ants were having a field day with the food, though. The spread showed signs of disarray: cups spilled staining the cloth. It seemed the terrified family had escaped during breakfast. I wasn't sure but maybe one of them had been killed.

I also looked in at a couple of homes leveled by the bombing to see whether there were any bodies I could bring out. In these homes, bedding was spread out and pots and pans lay in the middle of the yard. The place was a mess as if it had been struck by lightning. In another home there was an empty cradle, which made me think of the newborn at the body washers'. It also reminded me of Sa'id, who wouldn't sleep unless he was in his cradle. Where was the baby that slept in this cradle?

I couldn't hold back my tears when I saw a framed picture of the revered Abbas by the Aqalama channel. I remembered mother saying in Arabic, "That Saddam is the spawn of Shemr." I reckoned these crimes were the continuation of those crimes at Karbala. The deeper I ventured in the neighborhood, the more deserted it was and the more terrifying the atmosphere. It was not just the Baathists that terrified me, there might also be Fifth Columnists. I set the G3 on rapid fire. Before entering a house, I would shout "In the name of God" and enter cautiously. Most of my focus was on what was behind me. Playing hide-and-seek when I was young, I would always hide behind a door. Remembering this, I would look behind the doors and search the rooms, always expecting a Fifth Columnist or a Baathist to jump out. At such moments I hoped to God they would finish me with a spray of bullets; I had not desire to be taken prisoner. The men with us were also very concerned about our safety, warning us not to go in the homes first. The fear and dread were so real the slightest sound made me jump out of my skin. The most comical things would happen when a dove would suddenly take flight or a cat would dart out or someone would bang his foot. This would draw our attention and make us blast away with our guns. The poor animals would dash off like bats out of hell.

Later I would agonize every time I fired my gun. Suppose one of the bullets killed an Iraqi. Wouldn't that make me like them? Wouldn't I be a murderer then? But then again, didn't they attack us? Weren't they the aggressors?

I remember father saying a few months before, after he had been in one of the border skirmishes, "These people have one goal: killing Shiis. They make people fight among themselves and then take advantage of the turmoil."

This made me realize that many of the Iraqi soldiers were forced into fighting. I wondered what I would do if one of these conscripts appeared before me. I prayed to God that wouldn't happen. If I had to kill someone, I wanted him to be a hardcore Baathist.

The people I met in these sweeps, people who had stuck it out in their homes under such impossible and terrifying conditions, were mostly men who had sent their women and children away. There were also women who stayed out of concern for their children.

Some of them believed us when we told them, "The Iraqi batteries are nearby. Why stay behind and get killed needlessly? Trucks are ready to take you away." Others, mostly the old, would simply not be persuaded. "What good is staying behind here, dear sir?" I would tell them. "There's no water, no food here, just fire spewing from the ground and raining from the skies."

"This is home. Where are we going to go?" they'd ask.

Another said, "Seeing us stick it out here will make the boys at the front fight harder."

"Death is at your doorstep," I said. "It would be a sin to die this way."

They responded by asking, "Why did you stay? You're young; life has just begun for you. We're old; it's the end for us."

I said, "I stayed, well, to help the wounded and bury the dead."

Nothing I said convinced them. I didn't have the stomach to stick a rifle in their backs and force them out. I took an old women by the hand and begged, "For God's sake, leave. My family members are all in the mosque." One old woman with a southern drawl said, "Where am I going to go with my son here? Is my blood redder than his? I spent a lifetime raising him, making him somebody, and now I should just get up and go? He's gone to fight the enemies of the faith, and what about when he gets back all worn out and covered in dust? Shouldn't there be someone here to give him water?"

Another woman, an Arab, was sitting in her yard. She peeked out when I knocked on the door, and then went back to the yard. I knocked again and entered. She was thin with dark skin, sitting in a corner. She had her arms wrapped around her knees and was in pain. "Are you alone here, mother?" I asked.

"Yes, dear, all alone."

"Why are you staying here all by yourself?" I asked.

"What am I supposed to do? I have no one."

"Get up and we'll go to the mosque. Everybody's gathered there."

"Why should I go somewhere I don't know and get lost?" she asked. "This is my home. This is my life. I can't find it in my heart to leave."

"It's dangerous here, mother. They're going to start shelling. God forbid...."

"Let me die right here. Dying at home is better than being a refugee."

I felt for her but kept arguing, "Come with me to the mosque for now, and we'll bring you back and stop in at your home whenever you wish." She stared at me in surprise. I surveyed the many wrinkles in her face, which spoke of the difficult life she had led. She rose and stood before the door, stopping to see what she would bring with her. She turned and said, "Can I bring the hens and roosters?" I wanted to ask her what she was going to do with chickens with the world going to pieces, but I was afraid that she might change her mind about going. "Fine, take whatever you want," I said.

Before I knew it she was carrying a number of small boxes. She also had a straw basket full of chickens in her hand, which I took from her. She wiped the tears from her face with the end of her headscarf and locked the door to her home. Locking it made her feel better. She didn't know the Iraqis would just kick it open when they got there.

I accompanied her to the truck and helped her get in. We walked through the other streets and, when we were certain no one else was left, returned to the truck. I choked up when I saw the garlands of paper flowers hanging from the walls of the homes in the alleys. These reddish blossoms were the only things intact in the area. Even the palm fronds were charred and smoldering.

The happiest passengers on the truck were several children acting like they were going on an outing. The little devils loved having the wind whip through their hair and wouldn't listen when we told them not to stand up in the back of the truck. A few children, uneasy because the truck lacked doors and side panels, held onto their mothers. Most of the passengers, old men and women, reminded me of grandma and grandpa. The men cursed Saddam; one kept saying in Arabic, "May God avenge us."

The old woman zealously guarded her boxes and chicken basket, fearing that someone would take them from her. The chickens would cluck at times, making the children laugh.

One person in the crowd was clutching a prized possession—his television. When we reached the mosque, we helped the passengers off the truck. "Hurry," we said. "It's dangerous outside."

I asked Ebrahimi, "Okay, now that we've brought them, what do you want to do with them?'

"Go and tell the officials," he said.

"I'm going to Jennatabad. I haven't heard anything from them since last night," I said, and as I did I saw Hajj Aqa Farrokhi, Mahmud's father. I knew him before the war; he had a bookshop and a bath in the Safa Bazaar. I told him, "Hajj Aqa, they told us to evacuate people from the Taleqani neighborhood, and we have. Now it's up to you to keep them here or take them out of town."

Then I left for Jennatabad.

Wherever I went that morning I kept one eye out for Ali. I hoped Leila had gotten word about his whereabouts. At Jennatabad I found several people standing around a coffin, spent, it seemed, by all the weeping and wailing. I came nearer and read what was written on the coffin: Hoseyn Mojtahedzadeh. It was my guess that he was the brother of Hasan Mojtahedzadeh, who had been tortured by SAVAK and died a few months before the revolution. I whispered to the women around the coffin, "Is he any relation to Hasan Mojtahedzadeh?" "Yes," one of them said with a pained expression, "his brother."

The woman next to her voiced her grief with the Arabic expression, "May I go blind for them."

How hard it must have been for the family to lose two young men. What's keeping their mother alive, I wondered. I stood around for a moment, saying a prayer and expressing my condolences. Then I left. I saw Leila in the body washers'. She told me that she had seen Ali that afternoon with his friend Hoseyn Ta'yi Nezhad. I left and headed for father's grave, wanting to tell him Ali had come back.

As I was leaving, I helped Zeynab with a stretcher. It felt light, probably because the men had the heavier end. It was the body of a young man. They buried him in a hole dug at the foot of father's grave. When Zeynab looked at the boy's face, her expression changed. I felt her getting worse day by day. Aside from missing her daughter Maryam, the mounting misery was robbing Zeynab of the will to go on. I got her to her feet. "Going to see your father's grave?" she asked.

Not waiting for me to reply, she took my hand and said, "Come, let's go."

We hadn't reached the gravesite when Zeynab said, "Greetings, Seyyed, I envy you your good fortune. You have left us with all this hardship." She continued with tears streaming down her face, "Yes, Seyyed, you're rid of all this hardship. Bravo!"

Her words caused a large lump to form in my throat. We reached the grave, and I bent down to kiss the ground. My tears started flowing. I couldn't speak to father with Zeynab around. She kept on in the same vein, "Intercede for us, dear Seyyed. How about a helping hand?"

The men who had helped us carry the boy sat down by father's grave, said a prayer, and left. Zeynab also said a prayer. She took my hand and got me on my feet, and we walked toward the body washers'. We hadn't reached the building when a military jeep pulled up. Several officers got out. I knew one of them; he had offered his condolences to me and mother when father died. I had seen him going about the avenue or inside the Congregational Mosque getting munitions. He was polite and treated me with respect every time we met. I found his deference embarrassing and hoped he wouldn't recognize me. He spoke so well of me after father's death, I felt ashamed. But he greeted me this time, and I answered his greeting by acknowledging all the hard work the men had done.

They took equipment from the jeep: a tripod, a tube, a box of paraphernalia, etc. They mounted the tube on the tripod. One person remained in the jeep on the field radio repeating the numbers they told him in a loud voice. Another soldier adjusted the tube. I watched what they were doing curiously. I asked one officer, more or less an acquaintance, "What's that? Is it what they call a mortar?"

The lieutenant, who was in his mid-thirties, was supervising the work. He said, "No. This is a launcher for the mortar." He took a shell from the box and showed it to me.

The first time Ali brought his weapon home, I remember father had explained to us the various insignias worn by the officers and their weapons. I touched the shells and asked, "What do you intend to do with this?"

"Word has come the Iraqis have started to advance from the direction of the police station toward the fort. We'll use the coordinates supplied by spotters to shell that area, and maybe we can halt their advance." Then he said, "I want to give you the honor of firing the first shell."

"Me? Why me?" I asked in surprise.

He said, "Because you have lost the person dearest to you. He died in the service of God and defending his country."

I blushed again. For a moment I missed father more than ever. I looked toward his grave, feeling him looking back at me wherever I went, watching over me.

They fiddled with the tube until they had the coordinates they wanted. Zeynab, who was not feeling well, didn't stay. Two or three of the men came to watch. The lieutenant ordered the soldier handling the shells to give one to me.

He said, "Hold it at an angle and then drop it in the tube, but not until I tell you."

It seemed heavy to me. The only thing I knew about mortars was what it sounded like when they hit, sending pieces of shrapnel shooting out. How much damage does this little thing cause, how many young men can it take it from us? I wondered.

Preoccupied by these thoughts, I forgot to tell the soldiers I was about to load the shell. I got close to the thing and peered down the tube. All at once the munitions soldier sitting on a box saw me and yelled, "What the hell are you doing, you idiot?"

I was startled. What did I do to deserve that? I felt very bad. He bellowed again, "Just what do you think you're doing?"

"What did I do?" I asked innocently.

"Nothing!" he said. "You want the shell to hit them or your head? Standing over the thing that way, your head will go flying as soon as you fire it."

I couldn't have been more embarrassed. The lieutenant and a few other soldiers who were busy with the radio looked around fearfully to see what was going on. I held the shell out to the soldier and said, "Please, take it."

The lieutenant said, "No, sister, it's only natural. You lack experience. The fault is ours; we should have been more careful. Now fire it. God willing we'll avenge your father and all the other innocents the Iraqis have slaughtered."

Seeing how the lieutenant treated me, the munitions soldier said, "Forgive me. I just happened to look up and saw that you were about to blow your head off."

This made me feel a little better, nevertheless there were times when I just got furious with myself. The soldier explained again how to load the shell into the tube, saying I should only have my hands near it. Then he raised his voice and said, "To the good health of Imam Khomeini and prayers to the blessed martyrs!"

The soldiers and the men standing nearby echoed his cry. I fired the mortar exactly as he had told me. Then the men said, "God is great!" The blast was so loud it made my ears ring. Despite this I felt something novel and strange. I had never felt this way before. Wanting to know where the shell would land I watched as it flew through the sky. "Do you want to fire another?" I heard the lieutenant ask.

Although it was something I wanted to do, I knew I had no business there and said no.

I said goodbye and walked toward Zeynab. I saw them fire a few more rounds from a distance, and then they moved the mortar further in the other direction. I realized I hadn't said my evening prayers yet and went inside to pray. Toward the end I heard the sound of people talking outside. I finished the prayer and went to see what was happening. Three men and two women were standing near the office talking to Zeynab and the others. As soon as she saw me, she pointed to them and said, "That's her. Go and ask her yourself."

They turned to me. Their faces were red and raw from crying so much. "What's the matter?" I asked.

They surrounded me, all speaking at once. Finally, one of the men who was older than the others said, "They say our brother has been killed and they brought his body to the hospital, but when we went there they wouldn't give him to us. They said they would only give the body to the person who brought it. We've been everywhere trying to get an answer. We went to the Congregational Mosque and they told us the people at Jennatabad handle the dead and the wounded. Your colleague told us you did that sort of thing."

"That's true, but why didn't the hospital hand him over? It's strange."

At the hospital they normally recorded the details of every corpse in a ledger and would hand the body over to anyone who could identify it. That's why what they said was odd to me. As I thought about it, a woman who seemed older than the others said in a thick Arab accent, "Come with us. It'll count as your good deed for the day. My son is missing. They say he's been killed. Come and find out what's happened to him." Then she began to wail and hid her face in her cloak.

"Why didn't they give you the body? You gave them a detailed description, didn't you?"

The man said, "Sure, and they said they had somebody like that, but they wouldn't give him to us. Let's go, God will reward you for it."

"What was the description you gave?" I asked. "Sixteen year-old boy, tall, thin...." he said.

Since I had been running around constantly, I couldn't remember. I asked for more details. I remembered then we had brought someone of that description to the Mosaddeq Hospital.

"I'm going with them," I told Zeynab.

"Are you coming back?" she asked.

"God knows."

"If you can, stop in at the photographer's and see why he hasn't come."

"Sure. Please keep an eye on Leila for me, will you?" I asked her.

"Go, don't worry."

Seeing I was about to go with them, the woman blessed me in Arabic.

Their car, a white Arya, was parked outside Jennatabad. I sat in the back with the women, and the men sat in front. The woman whimpered and muttered as we drove. Another woman, thinner and shorter, who might have been the wife of one of the men, was sobbing quietly. From what the mother of the missing boy had said, I sensed she hoped the news her son had died was a mistake.

When we got to the hospital we first went to the nurses' station. I told one of them the situation. She told us to see the person in charge of the morgue.

I went to the morgue, but the person in charge was not there. We asked at the emergency room and the other wards. Finally somebody said, "He's gone out." We waited in the yard for him to come back. He was a man over forty, tall with glasses, olive complexion, in a white coat and boots. We knew each other well. As soon as I saw him, I went up to him and asked, "Where were you? We've spent over an hour searching."

"Everything's okay I hope. What do you need? Have you brought us more dead?"

"No," I said, "I've come to find somebody from this family they say is dead. According to them, you said the person who brought him must take possession."

"Yeah," he said.

"Is this a new law?" I asked.

"Not a law, but they instructed us not to hand a body over until we're sure it belongs to the family. This is because a number of people have come and taken possession of bodies in the names of the families, stealing them in effect. Later we found out that they were Hypocrites, who want to claim the bodies as martyrs to their cause and stage burials for propaganda purposes."

Then he asked, "Are you sure about the family?"

"Do you think they have nothing better to do than to turn the hospital and Jennatabad upside down looking for a body? The name and particulars that they gave match."

We accompanied the man to the morgue. The women waited outside while the men entered with me. The place was littered with bodies, some on stretchers, others on the wet floor, some covered with sheets, others without them or wrapped in blankets. Row upon row of women, men, and children. I began to search for the boy. Armed with the particulars, the man in charge began looking from the side opposite me. The two men stood to one side, stunned and saddened at the sight of all the corpses. It appeared the hospital generator was working; the overhead lights in the morgue were on. I stooped in the glow of the lamps and pulled aside the sheets from the faces of corpses. The sight of the lacerations and various other wounds on the bodies of the dead tormented me. Eyes open, eyes fallen from their sockets, tranquil stares, each spoke to me of their suffering. I thought: Here am I bringing in bodies like this, but there's no telling how they'll bring me in when it's my turn. Will I be whole? My face recognizable? Decapitated? I had heard of someone running frantically when shrapnel suddenly took off his head, while the rest of his body went on going.

I pulled the sheets back over the faces of each corpse I passed. I noticed the men sighing each time in relief and intoning again and again in Arabic, "Hope we don't see him here. Hope we don't find him here."

This made me feel worse. Not finding him on the floor, I went to the drawers. They had put a rather chubby man in the first one. Opening the second drawer, I saw it was the boy, thin, wheat-colored complexion, a bit of thick frizzy red hair on his forehead. He was dressed in a white shirt and jeans, not blood-stained, his body apparently whole. "Come here," I said. "It's him."

One of the men slapped his hand and said, "Oh, no!"

That confirmed it; this was the boy they were looking for. The older man approached the drawer and put his head on the feet of the corpse and started to wail. The other rushed out to the where the women were. A few moments later I saw the boy's mother in the doorway. She cast a hurried glance at all the corpses, shrieked, and then ran to the boy. Striking herself in the face, she came forward, her shrieks echoing in the room. "Momma's here, my boy. I'm here." She pushed aside the man who was kissing the corpse and screeched, "My boy's just asleep. Why did you put him in a drawer?"

Then she threw herself on the body. With tears streaming down her face she said, "My darling boy, my big, strong boy, my pride. Why didn't I die so I wouldn't have to see you like this? How can I live without you, my sweet boy?"

She shook the drawer as if trying to yank it out. She was in a horrible state. She began to run around the morgue among the bodies, staring wildly at them. Then she went to her son again and hit herself. She also cursed Saddam, "Goddamn you, Saddam. You love Arabs, do you?"

Seeing her beat herself and tearing at her face that way, I tried to calm her but couldn't. She kept shouting and wailing. The man responded to her lament with tears of his own. The younger woman, who was faint from seeing the boy or weakened by the sight of the bodies lying there, was standing in the doorway crying. I took the old woman by the arm and stroked her head and said, "Don't hit yourself. It's sinful. It's not right to torment the boy's soul this way. The Lord gives and He takes away. Thank the Lord the boy died a martyr and not the victim of some accident. May He grant you patience and serenity."

This did not comfort her and she said, "You have no idea what's in my heart, what's going inside me."

"I do, my heart has also suffered like this," I said.

She became less hysterical, looked me in the eye, and asked, "Who have you lost?" Choked up, I said in Arabic, "My father."

"May God also grant you patience. May the Lord strike Saddam dead for slaughtering all our young men!"

She began to whimper, "O, father, my heart is on fire. Inside I am ashes because of my boy." Her words went through me like a knife—I wept as if I were mourning the blessed Imam.

Her moaning didn't last long. She got up and, out of her mind, began to run about screeching. Then she returned to the boy's corpse and stroked his face. The fire that raged in her breast seemed to spread. The men bellowed at her to calm down, but it had no effect. I found this so stressful I didn't have the strength to watch. I told the men, "If you have no further need of me, I'll leave."

They thanked me. I passed the young woman as I left. Crying pitifully, she said, "We've been a lot of trouble, forgive us."

I nodded and went out. I thought I'd visit the photographer's before I returned to the mosque. He had said his shop was on Imam Avenue or Saheli Avenue, in the fishmonger's bazaar.

I reached Saheli Avenue from the Forty-Meter Road and stopped before the fishmonger's bazaar. I scanned the signs but didn't find the photographer's. Instead my attention was drawn to the bazaar itself. I had fond memories of the place. Mother and I would often shop here. It wasn't far from the Safa Bazaar. With memories of those days in mind, I entered the bazaar. It rested on pylons driven into the Shatt bed. The bazaar was a pavilion lined on both sides with cement benches, in front of which there were metal tables and platforms of various heights. The fish mongers would lay out a variety of fish—javelin grunters, pomfret, pampus, wolf herring, flame tail snapper—on round metal trays or in reed baskets. Iranians of every stripe living in Khorramshahr and working at the Customs House or the port were regular customers at the bazaar.

Some of the mongers would gut and cut the fish the way their customers wanted. There also were Arab women in nooks and crannies, selling fish on trays. As we passed them they would call out to us in accented Persian. Everything combined to make the bazaar a pleasant place: the smell of fresh fish, the bright sheen of their skin in the lights; the expressions on some of the fish, especially the pampus, which always seemed to be smiling. The sharp teeth of a few species protruded enough to seem threatening. The fish were fresh, seemingly alive with their tails flapping. Most of them were caught in the Arvand and the Bahmanshir rivers. The mongers would fish with their nets at night and in the morning present their catches to the customers. The ever-present gulls flapped their wings and made a racket as they feasted on the trimmings the mongers threw into the grated openings in the bazaar floor.

It was painful to remember the wonders of the market at that point. There was no sign of them now. The place was dead quiet. No fish, no mongers. The stalls were a shambles. A few straggly fish lay on the cement slabs. The place had received its share of shelling through the roof, and the walls were dotted with shrapnel. I left the place and sat on the metal stairway by the water. After regaining my composure, I started to walk.

12

The Death of Ali

In the early morning of the tenth day of the war word came that Iraqi tanks had advanced to Railroad Circle and the Slaughterhouse Circle. There was a fierce battle going on and the wounded they brought in by droves kept us extremely busy. I worked, but my mind was on other things. I was busy with bandaging and taping, but my eyes were fixed on the door. I had been expecting Ali since morning. Each time the city was shelled, we got into cars and went searching for wounded, ferrying them back to the infirmary. When I got back, I would ask about Ali. At around 10:00 they brought in another load of dead and wounded; a few had been severely wounded by shrapnel. Mr. Najjar ordered a vehicle for them so they could be quickly brought to the hospital.

I wanted to accompany them, but Mr. Najjar wouldn't permit it, saying, "Today it's really busy. I need everybody here. As many as possible." He hadn't even finished speaking when the Iraqis began to pound Fakhr Razi Avenue. Then they went after Twelfth Circle. That must have been a sensitive target. Every two hundred meters dust and smoke would shoot up into the air, and there would be the chilling sounds of explosions and whizzing shrapnel. A few minutes earlier I had seen an army van race by the mosque toward the front. One of us said, "Hope to God they haven't been hit." I wasted no time and ran toward the circle with a few of the girls trailing behind. When I reached the circle, I saw that our worst fears were realized. The van had been hit, and the blast had knocked out a rear tire. It had skidded along, leaving long black marks on the asphalt. The passengers had all been thrown from the van and were moaning on the ground. Some hadn't been hit by shrapnel but were groggy from broken limbs or blows to the head. I thanked the Lord that the back of the van had not exploded; otherwise they all would have gone up in smoke. There were a few passersby lying on the road in bad shape. We wasted no time getting all the wounded into another van. Those who could sit took the seats. Not one was ready to give up his weapon, cradling them so tightly that you would think they were their newborn children. After the van went, I ran back to the mosque.

Mr. Najjar weeded out the severely wounded and attended to them himself. Under his supervision we hooked up the others to serum drips and bandaged their wounds. A couple of boys who had been with us during the past several days helped with transferring the wounded to Abadan. We were able to send about eight of them by coordinating with Ebrahimi and convincing the drivers of passing cars to take them. Earlier the occasional Red Crescent ambulance had been going to Abadan, but at this point there weren't any around. The situation at the front was on everybody's mind. The large numbers of wounded showed how intense the fighting was. I asked each person they brought in from the Railroad Circle and Slaughterhouse Circle how it was going. To a man they said, "Their tanks advanced, and we stopped them." No more than that. I insisted on hearing more, promising them that I would keep it to myself. They didn't have to worry. But they would just say, "The situation is good. Nothing out of the ordinary." Only when they were sure of the person they were speaking to, did they open up. The higher-ups had ordered them not to say anything that would weaken morale. "No one is to say anything about what was happening at the front," they instructed.

The psychological and emotional pressure on everybody was intense. Some of the soldiers couldn't take it; they were so terrified that they would pound themselves on the head. Just back from the front, they would stand in the yard of the mosque and howl. Sometimes we had to sedate or evacuate them from the sector.

I wanted desperately to ask the wounded they had brought in about Ali, but they were in no shape to answer. I would, though, ask those in better shape, "Ali Hoseyni wasn't with you, was he?"

There was one, a soldier in the Aqajari Division, who said, "I saw him at the Railroad Circle."

"What was he doing?" I asked.

"I only saw him for a second." I sensed he knew more but wouldn't say it.

My patience had run out. I couldn't keep still any longer. I went back to Jennatabad that morning, but again there was no word of Ali. I raced back to the Congregational Mosque. A van was parked outside the door. Several people were in the back loading boxes of ammunition and water jugs into it. Mahmud Farrokhi was showing them where the ammunition was stored in the mosque. I knew some of the boys. I went over to Farrokhi and asked him, "Where are they taking the ammunition?"

"The front," he said, "for the boys." I asked him, "Which front?"

"The area around the police station."

"Can I come along?" I asked.

"What for?" he said.

"Just want to. Maybe there's something I can do."

When he hesitated, I quickly added, "Maybe I'll see my brother there, too."

He turned to me and said in surprise, "You haven't found your brother yet?"

"No, haven't seen him."

Everybody at the mosque knew that Ali had returned and that I had been searching high and low for him.

Despite his rigidity, Farrokhi seemed to soften, "I don't know whether they'll take you or not."

"If you give them the order, they might," I said.

"Fine. I'll talk to them," he said.

"Just let me run and get some medicine," I said. I dashed into the mosque and asked Mr. Najjar for medicine and supplies.

"What do you want them for?" he asked.

"To take to the front," I said.

"Why do you have to go? In any event, we don't have that much in the way of supplies for you to take to the front."

"The truth is I want to go and find Ali," I said. "So far I haven't been able to find him. Maybe he's out there."

"Be patient, he'll be turn up. The word is that he's coming."

"Yeah, but he hasn't shown up yet. If I go I'll probably see him sooner."

"Okay," Mr. Najjar said and then told me what things to bring. I took scissors, bandages, Betadine, syringes, sedatives, and a variety of disinfectants and put them in a box. As I was leaving the infirmary, he warned me, "Don't do any surgery out there. Just bandage their wounds so they don't bleed to death, then send them back here. Okay?"

"Fine," I said and ran out.

One of the girls—her name escapes me—followed me and asked, "Should I come with you?"

"No. I'm not even sure they're going to take me, let alone someone else."

I went to the van where the boys were still busy loading the supplies. Realizing that they were the same ones who had refused to take me before, I began to plead, "For God's sake, it's been months since I've seen my brother. He is in Khorramshahr, but we keep missing each other. I beg you, let me come! I have to see him." They were not more than twenty years old and were in no mood to bargain, but I was so insistent that they finally gave in. "Come, but don't do anything unless we say it's okay. You're going to have to listen to us and not go wherever you want."

"Okay, don't worry. I'll just follow you."

They took an ammunition clip and a G3 from a box and handed them to me. "Do you know how this works?" they asked.

"Yeah."

"Keep it with you then and use it when necessary."

Delighted, I got into the van. I sat down on one side of the hump and held onto the panel. A couple of armed boys were in front; others were in the back. The van started with a jerk, sped away and sent me sprawling over the boxes and the equipment. After falling several times, I had no choice but sit on the floor.

The driver took Forty-Meter Road, and we passed Jennatabad. I peeked out but saw no one there. I said hello to father, telling him that I was on my way to find Ali.

We passed Jennatabad and entered Ring Road. Near Taleqani Avenue there was heavy fighting. Bullets, shells, and RPGs were flying in all directions. Shells landed in the desert to our right, in the asphalt, and on people's homes. I ducked and rolled myself into a ball, but I was still dying to see where the firing was coming from. It was impossible to make out the enemy positions. Opposite the homes on Taleqani where the road widened into something like a traffic circle, a mortar round had hit an electric pylon, knocking it to the ground. If it had been a live wire, we would have been fried in the explosion. In the past when there was a windstorm in Khorramshahr, the electric lines would break and wires would slither in the sand like snakes.

As we got closer to the Ahvaz-Khorramshahr Highway, the firing became fiercer and the van sped up. The blasts reached the vehicle, smashing a side mirror. Bombs whizzed above us, making me duck again and cover my head with my hands.

The driver stopped for a moment at the end of the Ring Road. He seemed to be debating which way to go on the highway: right to the killing fields or left to the police station? As we waited, the firing seemed to focus on the van. This sent the driver into a panic, and he floored the gas pedal, making the van lurch forward with terrifying speed. It flew off the road and rolled down the dirt embankment. The panic-striken driver lost control by stepping on the accelerator rather than the brake. We were hurtling toward a cement wall, and I felt it was all over, but the driver found the brakes and we stopped short, sending me sliding along the floor until I banged my head against the cab. I ended up squeezed between the cab and the boxes of ammunition I had been leaning against. Dazed, I heard someone ask, "Nothing broken, I hope?"

I pulled myself together and said, "No, but I'm pretty banged up." The pain shot through my body, and I couldn't straighten my back. Water was gushing from one of the canisters that had overturned. I bent over and righted it. Half the water had spilled. I couldn't find the lid. One of the ammunition boxes, which had been open, was on its side and all it would have taken was one shell to send everyone to kingdom come. Several boys came by to view the wreckage. When they saw me, they protested, "Why did you bring this woman with you?"

"We didn't bring her, she came by herself," the boys in the van said.

"Don't worry," said another. "She's as tough as any of us."

This sort of talk did not give me a good feeling. I gathered myself and said, "What's it to you? I came on my own."

After I had answered the first group, another bunch showed up and asked, "What's she doing here?"

I said, "I wanted to come. Aren't you here to fight? Well, I know how to fight."

"Sorry, Ma'am, that isn't what we meant," said one.

During a lull, I asked, "Do you know the military boys around here? Seyyed Ali Hoseyni is one of them. Do you know him?"

The boys, who were mostly gendarmerie or the civilian forces, said, "No."

They unloaded the ammunition and the water and said, "God bless you. You've done us a real favor bringing water." I asked, "Any wounded here? I have medical supplies with me."

"No, there were a few, but we evacuated them. There are probably some at the front, but too much is going on up there to bring them back."

"Let me go and see," I said.

"No, stay here. You promised that you would listen."

I was afraid that if I didn't do what they said, they wouldn't let me come again. Besides, two of them were responsible for the daily mess run to the front. Two-by-two they grabbed the ammunition boxes and followed the soldiers, who made a mad dash zigzagging across the road. Then they ran along the row of truck-weighing ramps and shops on the other side of the road. Those not carrying anything strapped their ammunition belts to their bodies and, spacing themselves, ran across the road. I watched them until they were of sight, then I looked around. There were prefabricated houses behind me, the police station to my left, and the gas station at Dieselabad to my right. The thought that a shell would come whizzing over my head and hit the van made me move away. I thought I would take shelter in the prefabricated houses but changed my mind.

I could clearly hear the dreadful sound of tanks as they ploughed through the sand. I could also make out the voices of the boys trying to stop them. They were shouting, "Make sure you have them in your sights. We are out of RPG ammo. Take care when you fire." They were trying everything they could to stop the Iraqis from taking the Ahvaz-Khorramshahr Highway.

I also heard voices coming from the direction of the police station, but I couldn't make out what they were saying. At times I saw boys bent down zigzagging their way across the road. They would run, then roll on the ground, get up, and dive to the ground on the other side. I prayed to God not to let anything happen to them. Any moment, I thought, they could have their brains blown out because the Iraqis would concentrate savage machine gun fire on whatever moved on the road. Everything around me was damaged or completely destroyed by the wild strafing. It seemed that they had taken up positions on the second story of the police station, which allowed a good view of the area. I can say with certainty that the volume of rifle fire, RPGs, and Kalashnikovs, which I later learned to distinguish, was so great it sounded like a rainstorm. The bullets strewn over the road or embedded in it shone so brightly in the sun I could actually count them. The Iraqis must have had all the ammunition in the world to be so generous with it. I got up and took cover by a cement wall. I felt like I was burning up and fanned myself with my headscarf and chador, but, unable to sit by idly, I decided to move ahead. Now that I had come this far, I thought, I had to do something. The whole idea was to find Ali, but now I was pinned down.

The boys showed up a half hour later to collect the ammunition clips strewn on the floor of the van. They gave them to a soldier. "What next?" I asked.

"Nothing. There's no more for us to do here. We've got to go back."

"But I have all these medical supplies," I objected.

"Yes, but there were no wounded," they said.

"Not here, but definitely up front," I said.

"No," they said, "no way are you going forward."

"So, why did I come here in the first place?" I said angrily.

"Your being here has been a morale boost. Maybe you don't realize it. All the men here know how much the sight of a woman at the front makes them feel like real men and helps them fight the enemy. Your presence has raised spirits tremendously."

That was no consolation; I was still upset, having come all this way with no word of Ali. I felt it had been useless for me to come.

I didn't know whether to leave the supplies or bring them back with me. I separated out some of the bandages and disinfectant and said, "Give these to the soldiers to take to the front lines." One of the soldiers who had taken the ammunition across the road said, "Give them to me and I'll handle it." He took the box, bent down, and hurled himself to the other side of road. Waiting for him to return, the others began to talk about how we were going to escape the shelling. Finally the driver said, "God will take care of it. Everybody get in, we're going back."

They told me to lean against the cab; it would be less dangerous that way. Everybody else found a corner to huddle in. The driver put the van in reverse and drove along the dirt path by the prefabricated houses. We hit so many potholes we had our guts in our mouths. Backs aching and bones bent out of shape, the boys protested, "We're dying back here." Another shouted, "Step on it!"

The driver floored the accelerator right at the Ring Road cross-roads, sending the van up the embankment and straight onto the road. The gunfire began to concentrate on us again. One of the boys lay flat on the floor, while the rest of us were curled up into a ball. Once out of range, we all breathed a sigh of relief. The driver went back the way he came. When we pulled up in front of the mosque, I got out and once again asked about Ali. No one had seen him.

A couple of hours later I went with the girls to find mother. Entering the yard, I saw the wife of Uncle Gholami was crying like a baby. "What happened?" I asked.

In her Bandari accent she said, "Your uncle says we have to leave Khorramshahr. I don't want to go."

"God is great," I told her. "Maybe before you get ready to go, He'll settle His accounts with them, or maybe He'll end the war some other way."

Still bawling, she said, "From your lips to God's ears. Pray that we don't have to leave. How can I leave my home? It's impossible."

The neighbors stood around and comforted her saying, “Don’t worry, if things go on like this, we’ll all have to leave.” I wanted more than anything to send mother on with them. They had pounded the area around the Sheikh Salman Mosque several times, and a mortar had even landed in the yard. Once, when I saw that shrapnel had hit the wall, I asked mother about it. “The children had gone into the alley to play and I went after them. When I got back, I saw that it had been hit. Several people were wounded also, one of them so seriously they took the person to the hospital.”

Another time, when everyone was asleep, a mortar landed in the yard and they woke up terrified. Even after seeing all this, mother still refused to talk about leaving. Every time I spoke to her, she would say, “Where am I going to go? Aren’t you here?” I said, “I need to be. You should go. It’s a sin to be here with the children.” She said, “Are my children’s lives any less valuable than other people’s children? We’re staying. So long as everybody else is here, we’re staying.”

But everybody didn’t stay. The crowd at the Sheikh Salman Mosque was always coming and going. A number of people would leave and then another group would take their places. Many of our neighbors—like the wife of Uncle Darvish, the wife of Ali Salari, their daughter and her husband, Naneh Salimeh and others—had gone. Mother was the only one stubbornly refusing. I passed by the wife of Uncle Gholami and walked toward mother and the children. Zohreh Farhadi had Zeynab in her arms. The rest were talking to mother and the boys. Embarrassed, Hasan and Sa’id had their heads down and were turning colors. As soon as she saw me, mother said, “What good friends you have! How kind they are. When you’re not around they come and look in on us.” I saw Mohsen, who was looking very down and upset. “What’s up?” I asked.

“What’s up?” he repeated sarcastically. “There’s nothing to do. This sucks.”

“What with all the work in the mosque? Why don’t you find something and do it?” I said.

“Sweeping. Fetching water from the Shatt. That’s work? I want to go to the front. I want a gun.”

I knew Mohsen hadn’t made any friends despite his time in the mosque. He had no military training, so it wasn’t likely that anybody would give him a weapon. I said to him, "You don't know how to handle a gun. With all the shortages, do you expect somebody's going to hand you one? Come in the mosque and do some work. The people at the front need the support of people behind the lines." When I finished with Mohsen, I asked mother about Ali. She said, "Nothing new."

It was time for the call to prayer, and the general uproar and shelling of the city made me worry about Leila. I raced to Jennatabad. She seemed very happy and, when she saw me, said, "Zahra, Ali came back again."

"Really?"

"Yeah, I swear. He came back."

"When?" I asked. "I've been running after him so much, I don't know what to do. Where has he been between yesterday and now?"

"The front, Railroad Circle. He came and I gave him your message. Then he went to mother. I was so happy."

"Thank God, Ali's okay," I said, adding, "When did he leave, Leila?"

"Just before you came," she said.

"Then I'm going."

"Wait for me."

"I can't."

I began running as fast as I could. As soon as mother saw me, she ran to hug and kiss me. "Where's Ali?" I asked her.

"He just left."

"Well, what did he say?" I asked.

"Nothing. Just that tomorrow the kids and I should leave."

"Then, Ali said so and you're going, right?"

"Yeah."

"What do you want to do now?" I asked.

"Nothing. Tomorrow I'm leaving. Ali told me not to worry about you and Leila. He would be here for you. He said to take the children and go. To stay here would be dangerous. It would be sinful for the kids to die."

I thanked God that Ali had convinced her to go. Wanting to hear more about Ali, I asked her, "It's the right thing to do. What else did he say? Where did he say he was off to?"

"He didn't say much. Said he was going to the army. He was with that friend of his, Hoseyn Ta'i Nezhad. He said he had gone back to the Congregational Mosque, but you weren't there."

I felt sick. I looked at mother, wanting badly to tell her not to count on him being around much longer. But seeing her in such good spirits, delighted by his visit, I couldn't bring myself to spoil her mood. But that was impossible; I had to tell her what I felt. I looked at her and said, "Ma."

"Yes, darling, what is it?"

"Ma, make your peace with Ali."

She didn't take her eyes off me. I continued, "Tell him you forgive him for anything he did to you."

"What do you mean by that? What do you mean 'make my peace'?"

"Ma, Ali isn't long for this world."

She got angry and said, "What do you think you're saying? It's like you hope to God something happens to him."

"No, Ma," I said. "I swear it's not that. But everywhere I went today I couldn't find him. I've been looking high and low for two days, but couldn't find him. That must mean something. Ali's a hothead. He's come back to say his goodbyes."

She hated what I was saying, and I could tell that on top of that she couldn't stand me either. She looked me straight in the eye and through clenched teeth snarled, "I'm warning you. Don't ever speak that way again, you little louse!"

"Ma, you can say whatever you want to me, but tell your baby boy you forgive him."

I couldn't wait any longer. I tried to swallow my tears, and before they spilled out, I said goodbye and ran. I couldn't imagine how she felt then. The last thing I wanted was to upset her. I didn't know what made me say Ali was not long for this world, but I was certain he was about to die.

Ali, with all his injuries, had managed to get back to Khorramshahr. Even though no one expected him to fight, he had made a beeline for the front, leaving behind his magazine and a shirt as keepsakes. And there were other indications he was destined for martyrdom. As soon as I got to the Congregational Mosque I made a beeline for the things he had left for me on top of the armoire. I took them and went to a corner where I could be by myself. I hugged and kissed them, breathing in his odor. I said, "Where are you Ali? Why did you disappear? Why is it that wherever I go to find you, you've just left?" Later as I searched for him, steadily losing hope of ever seeing him again, I would console myself by smelling his shirt. This reminded me of the story from the Quran about Joseph and his brothers that Grandpa used to tell us.

When he got to the part when Joseph's brothers gave Jacob the bloody shirt and lied that a wolf had eaten him, he would cry and say Jacob knew they were scheming. Joseph hadn't been eaten; he was alive. In the end Joseph's shirt opened Jacob's eyes so he could see the truth.

The tenth day, a very busy one after all, finally was coming to an end. But even in the dark of night, the Iraqis continued to shell the city, particularly the streets around the mosque. The shelling was so intense I said to the guys, "If I'm not mistaken, it looks like they're honing in on the mosque. What'll we do with the wounded if they hit it?"

I even posed that question to the higher-ups at the mosque. "What can we do?" they said.

"At least," I said, "find a vehicle so we can send them away."

Gradually we managed to evacuate all the wounded to hospitals in Abadan. Then we cleaned the floor of the infirmary. It had been days since, except for prayer time, we had taken off our shoes. Dead on my feet, I prayed the dusk and evening prayers. It was pitch black inside. We had put out all the lamps. I removed my shoes and lay down on the floor next to Sabah. The shells seemed to be landing farther from the mosque, making us feel safer, but the Iraqi artillery never let up.

They had evacuated a number of others from the mosque. Even Genoa and the shell-shocked people were gone. The only one I missed was Abbas; the others had gotten on my nerves. The day before I had told Mr. Mesbah and others I was fed up and had little patience for their antics. Pondering where they had sent them, I closed my eyes.

As Maryam, Zohreh, Ashraf, and Sabah talked, all I could think about was Ali. No matter how hard I tried, I couldn't fall asleep. I kept wondering where he was and what he was doing. Would God ever let me see him?

I didn't know how much time had passed, when I finally drifted into a kind of sleep. But even then, Ali would appear before me, jolting me awake. I opened my eyes wanting to run toward him, but he wasn't there. I was on the verge of going back to sleep when I heard two horrifying explosions. They were so powerful I felt the ground shaking beneath me, and the windowpanes shattered. A few minutes later, screams echoed in the yard, "Please help us! They've killed the boys. They've killed the guards. They hit the army base...."

As soon as I heard the word "guard" I sprang into action. I was shaking from head to foot. I hiked up my chador and groped my way through the dark, stumbling over some of the people on the floor. I ran barefoot into the yard. In that pitch black I was able to see a young man bending up and down and grabbing at his legs. He was clapping hands and shouting repeatedly, "They've killed the boys. They've massacred them!"

Frozen with fear, I asked him, "Brother, where did the shells land? Who was killed?"

"They hit our base and killed everybody!" he said in tears.

"Where is your base?"

"Darya Bod Rasayi School,[1] behind Hezb-e Jomhuri."

I wasted no time. I knew no matter what, I had to get to the base. Ignoring the Iraqi forces or the Fifth Columnists that might be operating in the area, I just ran. The streets were deserted. Still barefoot and unable to see the holes made by the mortar shells, I tripped several times. But I was in such a hurry I didn't care. There was a storm raging in my heart. Could Ali have been there? I asked myself. Then I reassured myself: No, he wasn't there. He's at the front. But then I would scream at myself, Zahra, don't the other soldiers have sisters, too? Their brothers are as precious to them as Ali is to you. What's the difference? That second I came back to the present and saw a large ditch in front of me. I had forgotten there were foxholes in the

[1] A boys' school, now called Martyr Fahmideh Konuni.

area. I leaped over it and after a few minutes I was on Hezb-e Jomhuri Alley. I looked around for a second but saw nothing, only thick smoke and dust that burned my throat. I rushed on as broken glass cut into my feet, but that didn't bother me. I wanted to find out what had happened as quickly as possible. Where was Ali? The school was at the end of the alley on the corner of a three-way intersection. Light from the lamps soldiers were carrying gave me a vague picture of the scene. The boys carrying the dead from the school didn't seem to be in very good shape themselves. They were crying. Some were screeching and writhing in pain. In the chaos I saw Jahan Ara, the commander. He was silent and calm, but grief was etched into his features. Amid the howls and wailing I made out some of the troops calling to him, "Mohammad, what should we do? Mohammad, the boys are gone."

I felt sorry for him. Everybody was looking to him for support. Even I had become as crazed as they were. I passed Jahan Ara. If it had been any other time, I would have stopped and said hello. But now everything was a blur to me. I felt dizzy. I started to walk backward and bumped into an obstruction. There was a red Blazer parked where the three streets came together. I saw them trying to load the bodies into it. With the back seat removed, it had as much room as an ambulance. I approached it and looked into the window, but it was dark inside, and I couldn't see anything at first. Then somebody held up a flashlight. It was Jahan Ara, with one hand on the car and the light in the other.

I could now see into the Blazer. Five or six people were piled on the floor. I looked at them carefully. None were moving or moaning. They were all dead. One who was near the side caught my attention. There was a piece of cloth wrapped around his head and his eyes and mouth were half open. Some of his upper teeth were also visible. His beard and eyes were so covered in dust I couldn't make out his features. It was only because of the cloth and his teeth that I could tell how much he looked like Ali. Ali had a habit of tying a cloth around his forehead when he would weld or work in construction. At that moment I shuddered, wondering whether it was Ali. Then I thought, no, everybody said Ali had been at the front.

The resemblance was very upsetting just the same. I didn't bother looking at the others and ran into the schoolyard. Though the light was fading, I could see parts of the school were in ruins. I felt broken bricks and other debris under my feet. A half hour had passed since the attack. The soldiers had retrieved as many of the dead and wounded as possible from the rubble and laid them out in the yard. I looked for Ali among the wounded men. I wished then I had looked at the body in the car more carefully. I had to be sure it wasn't him.

The chaos and the psychological pressure I felt stopped me from going back to the Blazer. The din was horrible. The crying didn't stop for a moment. At once dazed and frantic, I could neither cry nor stay calm, frantically looking for someone lost. If I found him, there would be true peace for me. With the arrival of the vans I helped load the wounded. I saw the Blazer move out with one of the vans. I jumped on the bumper and clung to the side. The van was full. I remained perched on the bumper all the way to the mosque. As soon as the van pulled up, people ran out of the building to help. Everyone was up and the lanterns were lit. We emptied many people from the van. The infirmary was full of men. The badly wounded ones were laid out. Others were sitting with their legs stretched out. Hoping to find Ali among the wounded, I began to walk around saying, "Ali, Ali, where are you?"

When there was no answer, I gave up. As the van that had brought the wounded was about to go back to the base, I hopped on. We returned to find the scene more chaotic than it had been the first time. They weren't letting anyone into the building. "There may be an unexploded missile or mortar shell," they warned. "I've come to remove the wounded," I said.

They pointed to three wounded men and said, "That's all there are for now. We'll have to wait. If there're others, we'll bring them out." We loaded the men and went back to the mosque.

I didn't feel like myself anymore. My head was swimming. I didn't know what to do. Mr. Najjar was so busy he didn't have time to think. He asked me for an instrument, but my mind wasn't on the work, which made him ask me what was wrong.

I didn't know what to say. No matter how much I tried to get my feelings under control, I failed. I didn't know what I was doing and didn't have a clue why he was yelling at me, "What is wrong with you? What is this game you're playing! Keep your mind on your work!"

It made no difference to me that he was angry. I searched among the wounded for any of Ali's friends. The only ones I knew were Taqi Mohsenifar, Mohsen Baghalani, and Iyad Helmizadeh, but none of them were there. Then I was shocked to see Hoseyn Tayinezhad sitting on the floor with his legs stretched out. He was Ali's close friend and was with him at Jennatabad and the Salman Mosque. I asked him whether he had seen Ali.

He raised his head and said, "Ali? Your Ali's at the front. Ali was never with us."

The first thing that went through my mind was that, God forbid, he didn't want to tell me the truth. But then I thought: What reason would he have to lie? I gave up and went back to work.

The floor of the infirmary was covered in blood; the area was filled with the combined odors of gore and fresh earth. The floor was littered with so many bodies there was no place to walk, so we had to hop over them. The mosque and the infirmary were getting more congested by the minute. The soldiers arriving at the mosque, upset and listless, would ask about their comrades. About Jahan Ara. They were worried that with him gone the entire defense of the city would fall apart, which was true. The most critically wounded person they brought in was Mohammad Javad Golshan. A mortar hit the front of his ankle and his foot, looking as if it were on backwards, was hanging by a thread from his shin. Before they could stitch up the wound, he had lost a lot of blood. He was pale and didn't have the strength to speak. Mr. Najjar examined him and said, "We can't do anything for him here. The foot has been severed. We have to get him to the hospital quickly. Who'll take him?"

I jumped up and said, "Me. I'll take him." Mr. Najjar gave me a sharp look and said, "There's no need for you to go." I looked at him and said, "I'm looking for Ali anyway. He might be at the hospital."

He looked down, saying nothing. A couple of soldiers lifted Golshan from the floor, which was puddled with his blood, and laid him in the back of a pickup. I got in and the pickup went off. Mr. Najjar said, "We'll get Golshan to the Oil Company Hospital where the more critically wounded are."

As we drove a few of the soldiers began to talk about what had happened at the Darya Bod Rasayi School. They said, "The Fifth Columnists gave the coordinates of the base. Because it was only a temporary military position, they hadn't been able to locate it." They also said they had evacuated Mohammad Reza Rosta'i and two or three other amputees to Abadan. As I listened to what they were saying, I had my eyes on Golshan, whose condition grew steadily worse. I didn't know what to do for him. My feelings for Ali made me see him in all the boys. Golshan was like Ali's brother now. I wanted to take his head in my lap, but I knew it would upset him. On the other hand, I was worried he'd go into a coma. To help him breathe easier I took his head in my hands and raised it, but I also noticed his foot was still bleeding. I gently lowered his head back on the floor of the van and raised his leg to lessen the flow of blood from the wound. After we cleared the bridge, we were flagged down at a guard post. They were conducting night inspections of those going in and out of the city looking for Fifth Columnists. The van came to a halt, but the guards did not approach. From inside the van the soldiers confirmed our identity and said we had wounded, but the guards said, "Get out." Fearing Golshan was breathing his last, I said, "Go and see what they want. This one's almost gone."

They got out, walked away, and didn't return for a long while. Hearing them argue, I called out to the boys, "What's going on? What's keeping you?"

One of them returned and explained, "They've seen some suspicious people in the building. The guards haven't been able to flush them out and asked us to help. If it's okay, they want you to help them, because there are two women with them."

I jumped out and walked over to an unfinished home where several very young boys had their guns trained on two mean-looking men. When they saw me, they said, "Sister, there are two women inside and no matter what we do they won't leave. We got the men out by force, but we can't treat the women the same way. We don't know them. Can you do something?"

"We've got somebody half-dead back here," I said.

"These are probably Fifth Column, and if we leave them, they'll kill even more."

I entered the yard and saw two hefty women almost twice my size. They were going back and forth with the boys, "What the hell do you want from us? What did we do? They threw us out of our home and now they won't allow us to take cover here."

One of the boys said, "You think it's very safe here? If it's really refuge you're after, go somewhere else."

I said, "Why are you being so stubborn? We have wounded who are dying. If it isn't too much bother, why don't you just move on? What's the point of arguing?"

They ignored me, so I took a G3 from one of the boys, cocked it, and set it on automatic. I drove the barrel into the neck of one of the women, actually more a young girl. The G3 was heavy and the girl was tall. I don't know what made me come unglued—seeing the wounded at the base and thinking about Ali, knowing the Golshan was about to breath his last—all these things had put me on edge. I had had it, and I held the gun to her neck saying, "As God is my witness, if you don't leave I'll shoot. The hell with you both! I can't take any more of this. You damn well better leave this place before I kill you!" The woman uttered a filthy curse in Arabic.

It was so vile I got beet red, and several of the boys, who apparently understood what she had said, looked away and left. I angrily grabbed her hair from under her head covering and, clenching it in my fist, said, "Watch your mouth you worthless.... What were you doing in here half the night? Go on, get out. If you don't, I'll kill you right here!" Then I kicked her in the shin and shouted, "Get the hell out!" To the other woman, who was around forty or fifty and hadn't stopped swearing the whole time, I yelled, "Out!"

I poked her harder with the gun barrel. Then the soldiers entered the building and returned with several Kalashnikovs, some Colts, and a radio. This convinced me they were spies, and, when they were confronted with the guns, they began to beg for their lives. First they pretended that they were just poor folk dressed as Arabs, and that, terrified by the Iraqi attacks, they'd taken refuge in the building. After they saw pleading was useless, they started cursing again. Then they returned to begging, "Honest to God, we didn't do anything. Let us go. We've got kids. Homes."

"When you holed up here planning God knows what, why didn't you give them a thought then?" I asked.

A guard placed one of the men in the front of the van. One of the boys sat next to him holding a gun. The three others they put in the back and the van took off. By this time Golshan had lapsed into a coma. The floor of the van was full of his blood. To the women, who were staring at him, I said, "See what you've done to our boys? What did they do to deserve this?"

It wasn't far to the Oil Company Hospital, but the road leading to it was in range of Iraqi fire, so the driver had to go all the way around the city to get to it.

After we pulled up to the hospital, male nurses put Golshan, now unconscious, on a stretcher and took him to the operating room. We followed them to the operating room door. They told us that it was too early to know about his condition.

As we left the hospital the soldiers said, "Get in. We have to hand these people over to the Revolutionary Court." I was about to board the van when that same red Blazer pulled up. As soon as I saw it I froze. The soldiers kept telling me to go, but I told them, "No, I want to stay and find out about the boys who've been killed."

They said, "That's fine, but you can do that later. Who else will take you back to Khorramshahr this time of night?"

"No, I'm really searching for my brother. I've got to find him."

"You mean your brother is among these?" one of them asked.

"I don't know. My brother was with the army boys. Maybe he's one of them."

"Okay. What should we do?" they asked.

"Nothing." I said. "Go and hand these over to the court. Then come back for me."

"Fine," they said and left.

I wondered why the Blazer, which had left before we did, was just arriving. I stood there wondering whether I should wait until they unloaded the dead or open the door myself.

The moon was out. The air smelled like gas. They covered up the hospital door and windows with sandbags so no light shone through the cracks. There was no noise, no sounds of traffic. After a few minutes, several nurses and workers showed up. A door opened and a ray of light escaped. I went to the door. It seemed they wanted to put the dead there. I went in and entered a large room with a floor and walls made of stone. There was a raised slab in the middle and a large number of utility sinks on one side of the room, which meant this was where they did autopsies. I stood to one side as they brought in the bodies one by one. I went over to them. The first three were boys from Aghajari with bodies mangled by shrapnel, but with faces still intact. Their olive-colored uniforms were now stained black from blood. As the nurses and workers had finished bringing in the stretchers, a strange fear gripped me. My heart was racing. A voice inside me kept asking: Who was that dead boy? Why can't you stop thinking about him? The fourth body they brought in had a torso but no head. Shrapnel had torn his shoulders apart and the lower part of his body was missing. The corpse was nothing but a lump of meat with innards draped over the stretcher. What was left of the boy's hair and the relative bulk of his upper body told me that the corpse was Taqi Mohsenifar. Taqi had frizzy head of hair after all and was on the chubby side. Seeing him in that state turned my stomach. I remembered how modest and reserved Taqi was when he would visit us. He would knock on the door and ask, "Is Seyyed Ali home?" I mumbled to myself, "God help your mother, Taqi...."

As I spoke to his corpse, I saw that they had brought in the next body. I ran to the stretcher and looked at the face. Stunned, I couldn't help blurting out, "Oh, but this is Ali!"

One of the nurses turned to me and asked, "Why are you shouting, ma'am? Who's Ali?"

"Ali!" I said, "Our own Ali. You mean you don't know him?"

She looked at me, not knowing what to say. I was in shock. I flung myself at the body and lifted Ali's bandana from his head. I looked at him carefully. It was him, Ali himself. I didn't know what I would do. I began to kiss him, breathe in his scent, caress him.

I was in tears complaining to him: Why did you do this to me? Why did you get me to come here? Why don't you get up and speak to me?

I cradled his head in my arms. His eyes were open, and there was a beautiful smile on his lips. I cleaned the dust from his face. One fist was clenched around his bandage. I took it and opened the bandage. His fingers were separated. How soft his skin was. I showed the hand to the others. Look, I said, how beautiful the skin is, how soft; it was in plaster after all.

I examined his body. Shrapnel had torn through his left side, which was drenched with blood. A large piece of shrapnel was lodged in the gash in his chest. A bone protruded from his mangled arm. Pieces of shrapnel were also embedded in his legs.

I didn't know how much time had passed, what I said, what I did. For a moment it felt like my cheeks were on fire. Two or three people took me by the arms and lifted me off the body. I didn't know what was happening. Then they slapped my face, and I heard someone plead, "For God's sake, that's enough. Stop, will you! That's enough; this is murder for us."

They dragged me out to the van and made me get in. It was clear they also had been crying. I heard the nurses say, "We can't keep them here a long time. You have to come soon and take him."

I said, "I beg you for God's sake don't let anyone take Ali. I'll come myself and get him early in the morning."

"Fine," they said, "but make sure that you come before our shift is over. If not, our colleagues might not know about it and hand him over to someone else."

The van drove away. Wind blew in my face, making my skin tingle. I was silent. The soldiers were talking to me, "The radio we found belonged to the mother. There's no doubt they were Fifth Column." Then they said, "Sister, you kept us waiting for you a long time, but seeing you like that, nobody dared come near. Your grief paralyzed us."

I didn't answer them. I had only one thing on my mind: Hoseyn Tayinezhad had lied to me. I wanted to get back to the mosque and take out my feelings on him. There would be no question of standing on ceremony; I was going to let him have it. We were there before I knew it.

I jumped from the van before it stopped and ran into the mosque shouting, "Hoseyn! Hoseyn! Hoseyn, you lying bastard, Ali had already been martyred when you told me that he was at the front."

All at once I noticed it was dead quiet. There was no sign of all those wounded people and the hubbub they caused. Mr. Najjar jumped to his feet and said irritably, "Hush! Quiet! What's the matter with you? What do you think you're doing? What's all the noise about? Everyone's asleep. They're exhausted."

I told him, "That lying Hoseyn told me Ali was at the front. Ali's dead."

With that he stopped being angry and said softly, "Okay, calm down. Everybody's asleep. They're tired after being awake since sunup."

The noise woke up the poor guys, and realizing what had happened, they stood around hugging me, saying things that would comfort me, and wailing. There was something raging within me, and I couldn't stand still. Mr. Najjar told them to inject me with a sedative, but I wouldn't hear of it and started to struggle out of their arms. Several people were now holding me down. I couldn't move. Afraid of tearing an artery, they had to remove the syringe from my arm several times. I begged, "For God's sake! Don't make me fall asleep. I've got to go and get Ali. I swear to God, there's no one else. I have no one. I can't go alone; you've got to come with me." They said, "Fine, we'll go with you, but why don't you get a little rest now?"

I didn't sleep despite the sedative. I flailed my arms and legs in a nightmare. I screamed and awoke suddenly. Everyone was looking at me and speaking at once, trying to calm me. I got up all at once and said, "I can't wait longer. I've got to go and get Ali."

"Wait for the call to prayer," they said.

I stretched out, but with the sudden sound of the call to prayer I was fully awake. It was coming from a loudspeaker and made me feel strangely calm. I rose and asked the girls to use tweezers to remove the bits of glass making my foot ache. Then I went to wash my legs for ablutions. I came to the prayer room, stood by a pillar, and prayed. After completing the normal prayers, I did two extra ones, gifts to the revered Zeynab, begging God to grant me strength. I wanted that saintly woman to help me go on. My tears flowed as I said, "Don't let the calamity make me lose my faith. I leave mother in your care. The grief will surely kill her."

If I had been able to let my emotions show, if I hadn't been afraid of robbing the others of their will to resist, I would have torn myself to pieces. The horror of Ali's death itself was hard enough on me, but trying to keep my emotions in was harder to bear. I wanted to tear open my breast and pull my heart out and shred it to keep myself from feeling. I went through this when father passed away. But this time it was worse, much worse. I was already carrying the scars caused by father's death; now a new agony was added to that. I hadn't seen Ali for three months and, after all that searching, I was suddenly confronted by his corpse. All that made it even more painful, like a burn that never stopped throbbing. Why go on living? I asked myself. What good was this world? Life without Ali was meaningless. Better for me to die also. I wanted mother to stay in Khorramshahr and meet whatever fate had in store for her.

I felt lost, adrift, flailing madly in a vast ocean but getting nowhere. There was no one to hear my screams. I couldn't feel more alone, even in a crowd. After a good cry, I found a quiet place and unloaded my feelings to God. The lump in my throat was gone; it felt as if a weight had been lifted from my chest. But this was no comfort; everything seemed dead to me, shrouded in grief. I saw the world as grey. Little by little the sun was rising, brightening the air, but for me the morning was ruined and agonizing. The roars of the shells were still there. I put my shoes on and, before leaving the mosque, I placed a call to Jennatabad. I wanted to ask Zeynab whether Leila knew about Ali.

But it was Leila herself who answered the phone. This surprised me, being so early in the morning. "What's happened? Is there's news of Ali?" she asked.

"No. No news, but Ali did get a chance to tell mother to leave the city. If you can manage to find a car, get her out of the city."

"Fine," she said. Then she said, "Zahra, for God's sake, you'll tell me if something's happened, won't you?"

I didn't want to say anything at that point. I wanted to tell her in person. I knew the news would be impossible for her to bear, so I didn't say anything. I put the phone down. I felt I was at the end of my tether. I didn't know who would come with me to Abadan to retrieve Ali's body. Then I remembered that Salim, mother's brother, was with her. He had returned in the last couple of days because the army had called up military men who had left the service in 1977. He had been loading the giant copper rice pots into vans or wheelbarrows and fetching water for the mosque. But I wondered what I would do if I tried to contact uncle and mother saw me. She'd ask about Ali. Should I tell her he had been killed and remind her that I told her to make her peace with him? At that point she'd have a heart attack. Then they'd all be gone: father, mother, Ali. I was nearly certain she wouldn't survive seeing Ali's corpse.

A few months earlier, before Abbas Ferhan Asadi and Musa Bakhtur were killed in the border skirmishes with the Iraqis, Ali with his native command of Arabic spoke to the Iraqi troops. He tried to explain the nature of the Baathist regime and convince them that war between Iran and Iraq was a conspiracy to sow dissent among Muslims. But the Iraqis responded by firing at our defensive positions. Repeated attempts to raise the issue only led to Baathist snipers taking aim at Ali or others like him who were propagandizing against them. The next night there was a fierce battle and our positions were overrun. The next day Ali and his friends were busy shoring up the foxholes with sandbags, when a snake lunged out of its lair and bit his hand. Ali's friends rushed him to Mosaddeq Hospital. It was the crack of dawn when one of the neighbor's boys knocked on our door. I opened it and he said, "I happened to be at the hospital and saw Ali there." Shaken by this I asked, "What happened?" "Don't worry," he said, "it's just a snake bite. But Ali told me not to tell anybody but you. You'll have to tell your mother and father."

I had no idea what to do. I wrestled with what to tell my parents. Finally I said to them, "Ali was jumping over a water channel and fell, breaking his arm." But father wouldn't let me finish telling them, "No, there's no doubt the boy's been killed. I heard that there was heavy fighting last night on the border." With that he turned green and fainted. Mother, for her part, began to keen and go into her lamentations. They raised such an uproar the neighbors gathered, each trying to say something that would calm them. "Why don't you believe me?" I managed to ask finally. "Let's go to the hospital so you can see for yourselves." The whole family went. When we arrived, I asked them to stay by the door while I went inside first to find Ali. After some searching, I saw Ali lying in a bed in the emergency room. They had undressed him and placed a blanket over him. His face was extremely yellow as he lay listlessly. Soldiers were standing around the bed. I greeted them and bent over to kiss Ali's face. "What happened, Ali?" I asked. "Everybody's worried sick because of you."

"It's nothing. Don't tell Ma."

"Don't tell Ma? It's a little bit late for that. There's an army gathered outside." This made him angry, "Didn't I tell Faramarz not to tell anyone except you?"

I said, "Now there's no reason for you to get upset. Just pull yourself together so father and mother won't get scared when they come in."

I left the room and said to my parents, "See how you've upset yourselves for nothing? Ali's in the pink lying there resting. There's nothing wrong with him." Despite this they rushed in and started hugging and kissing him, all the while tears were streaming down their cheeks. Ali spent two days in the hospital and, after his release, went to see grandma and grandpa, whom we hadn't brought to the hospital. He told them not to worry and headed straight back to the border.

If this was how mother would react to a snake bite, it was obvious what would happen if she heard of his death. I took the bull by the horns and started out for the Sheikh Salman Mosque. The nurses had warned me that if we were late, the body might be handed to God knows whom. My fear was that he would be buried in Abadan. I wanted him to be next to father. I didn't know where I got the strength even to think these thoughts. I didn't know why I was still alive and walking around. If it had been up to me alone, I would have just succumbed and waited for the Angel of Death to take me. That "I" could not go on, but it was as if there was another person inside me, moving me along mechanically. The only thing I was conscious of was reciting dirges for the Holy Imams, calling on them to help me. The last thing I wanted was to have mother guess the truth from the expression on my face or from my mood. But when I got to the yard, I saw that she was awake and, with uncle helping, was packing her things in a reed basket. The children and most of the others were still asleep. I went into the alley wondering whether I should stay. I prayed that God would give me an answer.

I did the difficult thing and went back inside. I went up to mother with a pretend smile on my face. At that point, it was difficult and painful. I said hello. As soon as she saw me, she became terrified and asked, "Baby, what's wrong?" I said, "What? Nothing's wrong. Should something be wrong?"

"Any news about Ali?"

Her mentioning Ali turned my whole being inside out. I wanted the Angel to come and take me right then and there. "No. Ali was with you. When was I supposed to have seen him?"

"So, why are you here?" she asked. "What's up?"

"Ma, where is it written that I have to have news?"

"They called up the soldiers who left the service in 1977. I've come to tell uncle to report to the Congregational Mosque. They need him."

This was the best I could do on the spur of the moment. Uncle just looked at me, not knowing what to say. "Come, uncle," I said "Let's go to the mosque. They said everyone must go. They're waiting. I need to return also and arrange breakfast for Jennatabad."

This was the excuse I used to get uncle out of the mosque. When I stopped in the dead end next to the mosque, he asked, "What are you doing?"

"I lied, uncle. The mosque doesn't need you. I do."

"What do you mean?" he asked in surprise.

My voice quivering, I said, "I came to tell you that Ali's also gone, too; he's been martyred."

Uncle slammed his palm against his forehead, then he sat and broke into tears.

I didn't expect him to react like that. He shouldn't have cried. He should have been above that. I expected some sympathy from him. I wanted him to comfort me, take me in his arms and soothe me, saying, "Don't be upset. Ali is with God, but I'm here for you. Everyone else is here. It's okay. You're not alone." But he did nothing of the sort. Instead, he clawed his face and pounded his arms with his fists and said, "Why? Why did Ali have to go? He was so young, only nineteen.

I'm his uncle, I'm old. Why not me? He had just come back to Khorramshahr."

I kept saying to him, "For the love of God, uncle, don't be like this. Mother will find out. Instead of crying, you've got to think of something."

"I can't," he said. At that point I saw the woman Zeynab coming down the lane. She took one look at the state we were in and guessed Ali was dead. She began to wail and moan like uncle. When she hugged me, I couldn't hold back my tears and said, "Baby, not you, too. I let you know about Ali so you would think of something to get mother away from here. I don't want her to find out. I've got to go and get the body."

Uncle said, "Zahra, I can't get over this. Is this really you? How can you be so calm?"

"I don't have a lot of time, uncle," I explained. "I've got to go and bring his body back. Think of something. If I don't get there soon, it'll be too late."

Zeynab said, "You go and get Ali. I'll find a way to get your mother away. Don't worry. Whatever it takes, I'll make sure she leaves the city."

"Can I be sure of that?" I managed to ask despite the lump in my throat. She hugged me and said tearfully, "Don't worry."

"I don't want her to be around when Ali comes."

"Don't worry about it," she said.

Then she wiped the tears from her eyes. It was impossible to get uncle to pull himself together. Afraid that mother would appear at any moment and see the state he was in, I was losing patience with him. I kept on saying, "For God's sake, uncle, that's enough. Dry your eyes. Mother's liable to come out any moment, which will ruin everything."

"I can't," he said again and again.

"Get up. Get up. Tell mother to go with the kids. I'll come in after you."

He rose and walked a few steps up the alley and returned, apparently trying to gain control of himself. He kept wiping his eyes, trying to make his face seem normal. Then the three of us went inside.

Zeynab greeted mother with her usual cheerfulness and asked how she was feeling. "We came for you," she explained.

"Fine, but to go where?" she asked Zeynab in surprise.

"Didn't Ali tell you to leave Khorramshahr?" Zeynab reminded her. "I came to get you into a car."

"You've actually got one?" mother asked.

"The good Lord will provide," she said. "Now gather your things and let's go."

As if unsure about it, mother asked uncle, "What was all that before?"

"Nothing, I just have to go to the mosque."

Mother asked, "When will you come back?"

"I've got to go now to see what they want," he explained. "You go and I'll join you later."

"Better get moving," I said to him.

Even though this might be the last time I would see them, I couldn't bear to look at the children who were now up. With Ali gone, I didn't want to stay alive much longer. If I hadn't considered suicide out of bounds, I would have killed myself somehow or thrown myself into the Shatt. The only way I was going to join father and Ali was to be present at the front lines. I had to get myself there and, perhaps, while tending to the wounded, a bullet or a piece of shrapnel would come my way.

Uncle started to weep again as soon as we left the Sheikh Salman Mosque. "What are you going to do?" he asked me tearfully.

"We've got to find a vehicle to go to Abadan and bring Ali back."

I saw Ebrahimi in front of the mosque. The news about Ali had greatly upset him. I said hello and asked, "Do you know where we can find a vehicle? I want to bring Ali back."

"I don't right now, but I'll try to arrange one for you."

"I need one now. Later will be too late."

"Okay," he said.

I entered the mosque. The girls were up and Sabah and the others had decided that they would come with me.

"No," I told them. "First, because there's no vehicle. Second, what if they bring wounded? You've got to stay here."

Sabah said, "I'm coming with you."

Hoseyn Eidi, who was in tears, said, "Sister, I just heard. I'm coming also."

It was decided that uncle, Sabah, Hoseyn Eidi, and Abed, the brother of Yunes Mohammadi,[2] whom I had met at the mosque, would go to Abadan. There was an ambulance parked by the curb when we left the mosque. Hoseyn said, "Tell the driver to take us."

"No," I said. "It's for the wounded."

Everyone then ran in a different direction to find a vehicle. I went as far as the head of the Forty-Meter Road. All the running around was no use. We gathered again in front of the mosque. The boys said, "Now tell the ambulance driver. There are no other vehicles to be found at this time of morning."

We approached the ambulance. The driver, who was a slim, young man, had his window down. I said to him, "Brother, pardon me. We have a martyr at the Oil Company Hospital in Abadan and we want to bring him back. Can you take us there?"

"I'm sorry, but I'm parked here in case there are wounded to be carried to Abadan," he said.

I said, "Yes, but there are no wounded now, thank God. We can go and be back in no time." But he wouldn't budge no matter how much I insisted. Choked up, my voice quivering and trying hard not to cry, I said, "Look, I've always tried to get the wounded to the hospital as quickly as possible. I'm well aware of what your job is. I'm begging you now, for the love of God; all I want to do is bring back the body of my brother. If I don't act soon, it's possible that they'll bury him somewhere else. That can't happen, because I want him laid to rest next to my father." With that he looked down and said, "God Almighty." Then he rested his head on his hands, which were clenching the steering wheel, and said, "Okay. Get in."

I motioned for the others to come. Everyone except for Abed climbed in the back of the ambulance. Unlike the other ambulances I had been in, this one was spic and span. I curled up in a corner and rested my head on my knees, speaking silently to Ali. I paid no atten-

---

[2] At the time Yunes Mohammadi was a parliamentary representative from Khorramshahr.

tion to the route we took; all I knew was that we got there. I didn't know who went to get Ali, but I do remember not crying. There were no more tears left. I felt weak and was unable to straighten my back so I stayed seated.

I remember one of the nurses giving me a hug and, with tears in her eyes, telling uncle and the rest about the events of the previous night. She said to me, "You made it unbearable for us last night. You threw yourself on his body and said, 'For three months I hadn't seen Ali. I was thirsting for him, thirsting to see him.' You spoke of the kids. Praised Ali. You showed me his hands. I've seen a lot of them, the ones who lost their fathers or brothers, but I never saw a scene like the one last night. What you said, what you did, set our souls on fire. The whole place was crying. In the end it took three people to pry you off the corpse."

With Ali inside, the ambulance took off. I embraced his head and started pouring my heart out to him. I complained as much as I could as the tears poured out of me, "Father said that I was to be in charge of mother and the kids until you came back. What made you just go and leave me in the lurch like that? What am I supposed to do with the children? How am I supposed to tell mother, who had all those hopes? I convinced myself that you would come back and be a father to Sa'id and Zeynab."

I caressed him and ran my hand through his hair. I spoke to him as I brushed the dirt from his head. Like a mother with her child, I held his head against my breast. Although the blood on his wounds had long since dried, when I touched them, the blood came. His tattered uniform was bloodstained. This was the very uniform that made us so excited the first day he put it on. From that moment I began to think about his impending death. I was certain it was only a matter of time. Just as he had said, we would put that framed picture of him in the room where he would spend his wedding night. At that point I told myself that we would be strong when the news came. We wouldn't cry because he wanted us to act like Abbas's mother. But then when I gave him my answer, Ali would say something convincing. But how could I remain calm if something happened to him? The moment when he died, I also had to be dead. This was why I was so tearful those days. Each time he would come home, I would breathe a sigh of relief and thank God he hadn't been killed. But each time he left the house, the old dread would return. Even father, that powerful man, would get all choked up when Ali left the house. Tears would well up in his eyes. None of us dared tell Ali we were all worried about him. He'd get aggravated. One time mother said to him, "Ali, why don't you leave the army? Everybody in the army dies. You should leave; join the Construction Corps or something else. Just don't stay in the army. I'm always stressed about you."

Ali became upset immediately and said, "Abbas's mother wasn't worried about him? Musa's mother wasn't in a state? Didn't those boys have families? I'm staying in the army until I die."

Then he charged out of the house. Mother sat down and wailed. When I remembered those scenes, I cried my eyes out. All the people in the ambulance followed suit. Uncle grabbed my hands and pleaded, "Zahra, enough! I'm dying. Don't let yourself go like that. I can't take any more."

When we got to Khorramshahr, I said, "Everybody go into the Congregational Mosque."

I had wanted to telephone Jennatabad from the mosque to make sure mother had left the city. The girls said they would call, but I was afraid they'd botch it and blurt out that Ali was dead. The ambulance stopped before the mosque. Uncle helped me get to my feet because I didn't have the strength. It felt like my back was broken, it was so hard for me to get down. Mr. Ebrahimi dialed the number for Jennatabad and gave the receiver to me. Leila was on the line. She said, "Zeynab, Mr. Salarvand, and I took mother and the kids. Mr. Salarvand had brought his car and took them as far as the Station Twelve of Abadan. Zeynab got mother on a minibus on its way to Sar Bandar." Then she asked, "Where are you? Are you coming this way?" It was clear she was upset that mother had left.

"I'm coming," I said.

"You seem different today. Your voice is strange."

"It's nothing. I'm tired."

"You never say you're tired," she said bewildered.

"Well, I'm saying it now," I explained. "I'm worried about mother and the kids."

With that I hung up and left the mosque. The girls, Mr. Farrokhi, Ebrahimi, and many others were standing by the ambulance looking at Ali and crying. It was difficult for me to keep from breaking down. I went to get into the ambulance. I said to them, "Why are you crying? I'm the one you should be comforting, not standing around in tears. This is Ali's wedding day. He said himself, 'The day I'm martyred will be the day I become a groom.' So, you have to rejoice; Ali's gotten his wish."

But this only upset them more, and they started to bawl and scream. The ambulance took off. The mosque people followed. Once again I cradled his head in my lap. I thought about mother. With Ali back in town, where was she? Did she know that her heart and joy was in such a state? Did she know that she would never see him again?

We were soon at Jennatabad. Hoseyn Abedi opened the door and I saw Zeynab, who had been waiting for us, running toward the ambulance pounding her head and chest with her fists. She was crying and shrieking, "What joy! Dear Ali! Blessed be your wedding day!"

All at once I was terrified. "Leila! Where's Leila"? I asked her.

"Don't panic. She's not around here. I didn't tell her anything." Then she started beating herself. She squatted down and clawed at her legs, struck her face, and screamed. I said to her, "Don't act that way, I'm begging you. What's the point? You're just making it more unbearable for me! If you keep carrying on like this, I'll never heal."

They brought a stretcher and put Ali on it. Zeynab helped me. I noticed that my legs and hands were bloody from his head wounds, and my heart shattered. This told me the back of his head was also hit by shrapnel. Several of the army boys and some of the civilian forces from the mosque had gotten to the cemetery before we did. I saw some of the people from the mayoralty among them. They carried Ali to the body washers'. "Where are you taking him?" I asked.

"We want to wash and shroud the body," they said.

"You can't. There is no water, no shrouds," I said.

"We've gotten a shroud and have some water," they said.

"Why the special treatment?" I asked.

"What special treatment? There simply was water and a shroud. We want to wash him."

With that they brought Ali inside the body washers'. At that point everything went blank. Unable to stay any longer, I walked away—where I don't know. Upset and confused, I just walked and walked. I didn't know how much time passed. Someone called and I went to the door. It may have been Mr. Parvizpur or Salarvand who asked, "What do you want to do with your brother's clothes?" "I don't know," I said. My mind wasn't working. I was afraid to bring them home. Somebody might throw them out. The Iraqis would probably occupy the house, and I would never get them back.

I hesitated and finally said, "Give them to me." I took them and kissed them. Then I decided to bury them the way I buried the clothes of the other martyrs—except I buried those clothes to get rid of them. Ali's I would bury in a safe place so I could find them again, and they wouldn't be destroyed. I found a plastic bag and then gathered his clothes, boots, and even the leggings he used to attach them to his trousers. The army boys asked me, "Sister Hoseyni, what do you want done with those things? Just tell us what you want and we'll do it."

"I want to bury them myself. No one should follow me," I told them.

I had no idea what I was doing or how I looked. It didn't matter that I was making people stare and break into tears. I went to stand under one of the trees in a small wood, one of the places where branches through no fault of their own had come crashing down. I sat under the tree and hugged the clothes. I put the boots into the bag, but I couldn't bear to put the clothes in. I brought them near the bag, but then thought better of it and pressed them to my breast. I remembered grandfather and called out to him. He loved Ali so much. I called out to him, "Where are you?" "These bloody clothes belong to your Ali, your Joseph. The wolves, it's true, have eaten him this time."

I finally managed to let go of the clothing and put them in the bag. I marked the tree and buried the clothes in a hole nearby. It was clear from what people were saying about the front, how the Iraqis were advancing, how there were no weapons or reinforcements, the city would soon fall. So Jennatabad, a place that I knew like the back of my hand, would be the best spot to hide the clothes. We didn't bury people under the trees, so they would go unnoticed.

I returned to the body washers' and sat with my back against a wall. I was worried Leila would appear. I didn't know how to tell her about Ali without shocking her. Mr. Parvizpur came by again and gave me two cartridges and Ali's watch. "The cartridges were in his shirt pocket," he said. Both the bullets and the watch were bloody, and shrapnel had torn the metal watchband in half. The watch had stopped at ten minutes to ten. I put the things in my pocket and got up. I told uncle and the others around me, "Let's go and prepare the grave." Hoseyn said, "Sister, we've already dug one. It's over there." I looked where he was pointing; it was very far from father's grave. "No," I said, "that's too far away. I want him next to father."

We walked to father's grave, and as if God had willed it, there was an empty space next to it. It was odd given all the bodies that had been buried in the last five days since father's death. This was the very grave that had been dug for father originally, but it had filled with water and left to dry.

Hoseyn and two others removed the loose earth people had thrown into it to soak up the water. I sat down on father's grave and peered into the empty hole that would soon hold Ali.

A short time later they put Ali's body into a coffin and brought it to the grave. I didn't have the strength to stand. I wanted desperately to be alone so the fire raging in me could come out. At the mosque I saw how the soldiers whose friends had died or been wounded agonized over their losses. Their words and actions had a terrible effect on the others. Despite the torment I felt, I was determined not to behave like those soldiers. When the pallbearers reached the end of the dirt path, I rose and went to greet Ali. The bearers made way for me, and the whole time I kept running my hand along the coffin. Then I took hold of the underside.

As we neared the grave, Ali's words to mother when she asked him about his marriage echoed in my mind: "My wedding day will be the day I'm martyred. My first night with my bride will be in the grave. My blood will be my wedding henna." Although these words set fire to mother's soul, he was sincere. The memory made the moments I spent by his grave unbearable. Then again, when I realized they were the best moments in Ali's life, the time when he was on his way to the One he worshipped and adored, I told myself I ought to share in his joy. Paying no attention to my surroundings, I spoke to him as we neared the grave. I was oblivious to everything around me, and occasionally tripped over my useless feet but managed to maintain my balance.

They laid the coffin beside the grave. I wanted to open it so I could see his face, but the people standing there wouldn't allow it, saying that decorum had to be observed. I sat there clasping the wooden box. Uncle Salim was not himself. He would sit by the body, then get up and move about, all the while crying out, "Ali, you were younger than I am; you should be burying me. Why me? Why should I be the one standing over your grave? What am I supposed to tell grandpa? Grandma? And what can I say to your mother? Shah Pasand, where are you? Your son has gone on without you!"

I raised my head for a moment and was about to say something to uncle, when I saw Leila coming from a distance. I tried to pull myself together. If she saw me in that state, so close to the body, she would immediately realize that the martyred one was a relative. I didn't want that. I got up and walked some distance from the grave. Leila came closer and, when she saw me, said cheerfully, "Hi. Mother's gone away." "Hello," I said. She studied my face and asked, "What's wrong?" I said nothing.

"Have they brought someone?" she asked.

"Yeah."

"Who is it?"

I hesitated and said, "A soldier." Leila craned her neck to look at the people standing around the grave. Realizing that all of them were familiar faces, she asked, "Do I know him?"

"Yeah," I said. "I think you do."

"What's his name?"

I couldn't open my mouth but only stared at her. I struggled to find a way of uttering "Ali," when she asked, "It's our Ali, isn't it?"

I nodded and said quickly, "For God's sake, Leila, I'm begging you, watch what you do. Ali always wanted it to be this way."

We sat down across from each other. Leila was looking up at the sky and keening, "Hoseyn!" Then she covered her face with her hands, and the tears poured down.

In a quivering voice, she repeated the Imam's name again and again, so much her entire being seemed to be in flames. This made the people nearby cry even harder. Zeynab arrived at that point and tried to comfort her with hugs and kisses. Now Leila was silent, but her body shook and her tears flowed. She looked down and pulled her headscarf low on her head so no one could see her face. Only her tears were visible as they trickled down. Uncle came near. He was worse off than Leila, constantly beating himself in the face, pounding his arms, wailing. All this was even more heartbreaking to me. "Uncle, uncle," I repeated, but he was in such agony he didn't hear me. I got up and said, "Uncle, you're the man here, you should be comforting us. Do you really think it's right for me to the one to calm you down?" "I don't know. I can't help it," he said.

Seeing they had taken Ali from the coffin and laid him next to the grave, I left uncle and Leila and moved toward him. Apparently they had to put the body a short distance from the grave to remove the large amount of earth in it. I took advantage of the opportunity to take his head in my arms and open the tie in the shroud. Although they told me not to, I ignored them and pulled the shroud aside exposing his face. It was free of grime, almost glowing; they had washed it. His complexion was so natural, ruddy almost, that it seemed he was sleeping and nothing had happened to him. He was only a little gaunt and there were hollows under his eyes due to the operation. I pressed his head to my chest and went on kissing his face and stroking his beard until they took him from me. This was exactly how I would greet him after he came from being away for a time. I would kiss and hug his head and stroke his beard for a while.

Uncle could take no more of this. He swore to me he would come to grips with it, but said, "That's enough. It's killing me. Stop, I beg you." But I couldn't let these moments slip through my fingers. I no longer cared how it looked to the others. There were times I could control myself, but there were others when I was so weak I would welcome the inevitable. It didn't matter anymore. Finally Zeynab pulled me aside and began to hug and kiss Ali herself. She spoke to him so fondly and naturally you would think she was his own mother. This made my heart break for mother, who would never see her Ali again.

I was staring at Ali's half-open eyes and the smile on his lips, when Hoseyn said, "Let's have the body." I stepped back. Hoseyn, an old man who was reciting the Quran, and one of the body washers were in the grave. I said to them, "I want to put him in there myself." Hoseyn got out and I took his place. Zeynab changed places with the body washer. They lifted the body, and I took the head, while Zeynab took the feet. It felt like my back was about to break, not from the struggle to support his weight but from the burden of losing him. I thought I would never get up again. I no longer wanted anything from life. That bitter feeling was with me once more. I wanted to rip my heart from my chest and tear it to shreds so I wouldn't feel anymore, not grief or joy, warmth or cold, nothing.

In tears, uncle said, "You should bring her out now, this is too painful for her. I beg you. Out of the grave!" As if he hadn't said a word, I went about the business of putting Ali in the grave. I managed to sit down and hoped I would never leave it. I hoped to die and be buried with him. Although the sun was shining, I was flailing about in an unholy darkness. It was as if the world was frozen solid and Ali's body was the only source of warmth. Afraid I would go to my death if I left his side, I kept bending down and kissing him, fondling him. I wanted nothing more than to stay with him and speak to him.

Zeynab had already climbed out, and she and the others were urging me to leave the grave. They were saying "Come out!" so much I got fed up with it. Finally Zeynab and uncle took my arms and pulled me out. The old reciter began to say the two oaths and other verses. When he mentioned the names of the Imams, I thought I heard Ali joyfully respond, "Hallelujah."

Now I was lying in the dirt at the foot of Ali's grave. Having completed his recitation, the old man began to arrange the gravestones from bottom to top. Although I never took my eyes off Ali's face, I can't express how hard it was to lay these stones. With each stone it seemed the end of the world grew nearer. I felt that a giant storm would come and crack open the earth after the last stone was laid. With me now was that same bitter, incredible vision I had when they buried father. I half expected Ali to rise and tell me it was just a nightmare, but with the final stone in place, my eyes went blank. I couldn't see a thing. I wanted to flee but didn't have the strength to run. My entire body became a solid block, and all of a sudden I was torn from the face of the earth and hurled into the air. I was in a blackness, hurtling toward the bottom of a deep well, and all around me the dark walls reaching up to the sky raced by. I had felt from the way Ali's hand was cramped that it had broken when they washed his body. While I was flailing about in the blackness, the sound of his bones breaking echoed in my ears. I put my hands over them. The bitterness in me grew by the minute.

I remembered when Ferhan Asadi was martyred, I felt truly happy for his mother. How much does God love this mother, I thought, that He has taken her son while on His path. Her sacrifice has been accepted. After that I prayed that God would enroll us among the martyr families. And now this was indeed true; nevertheless it was still hard to have a loved one taken, very hard.

When the old man got up from the grave, I don't know what I did to keep them from putting earth over it. But all of a sudden I came to and noticed that everyone's eyes were on me. "What's wrong?" I asked. "What are you waiting for?" They looked at me. I began to fill the hole with dirt using my hands. Hoseyn asked innocently, "Sister, should we start shoveling?" "Yeah," but as soon as I said this I wanted to go and lie down on the slabs of stones once more and be buried.

I remembered the dirges mother would sing at the women's gatherings on Ashura mornings. She sang of Ali Akbar and the women would beat their chests. When she got to the emotional parts of the passion, she would lose control and tear at her collar and beat her breasts. Where was mother now, so she could recite the passion for her own Ali Akbar?

They smoothed the top of the grave and Zeynab poured water over it. They had written on a part of a cement block:

The Martyr is the Heart of History
Seyyed Ali Hoseyni
Martyred 10/2/1980

This they put at the head of the grave. Leila sat by the grave hugging it and moaning. I remained kneeling at the foot of it. I bent down and put my head on the earth. In my heart I wanted all the young soldiers to gather at the grave the same way they did when Abbas, Musa, or Seyyed Ja'far Musavi were martyred. That day the boys circled the graves singing anthems and renewing their pledge to their ideals. It was too bad they weren't there to be a source of comfort for me.

Still crying uncontrollably, uncle didn't stop kissing me, kissing my hands, and saying, "Get up. Let's go. I can't take more of this. I'm begging you, let's go." As I rose to leave, a van pulled up with five or six Iraqi dead. Two of them were burnt badly and deformed. One of the boys in the van seemed to know me (how I don't know) and said, "Sister Hoseyni, rejoice! Your Ali did not die for nothing. He got rid of a number of Iraqi's. The ones you see here serviced the tanks your Ali destroyed with an RPG." It annoyed me that he had said "rejoice," especially when I saw there were several barking dogs circling the van. I said, "Seeing these bodies is no consolation. We don't know who they were, how they came to be in the war. They were probably also draftees."

The bodies were horribly mutilated, and several of the boys were sickened by the thought of burying them. "They were the ones who attacked us, after all," they said. "Let's dig one hole and stick all of them in it."

"That's not right," I said. "They may have been Baathists, but they were Muslims—even if only in name. We have to bury them separately. I'll do it myself."

"No, not you. If that's what you want, then please let us," they said.

Leila, uncle, Hoseyn, Zeynab, and I returned to the body washers'. The old men and Maryam were sitting in a corner smoking. Their eyes and faces were puffy from crying. As soon as they saw us, they got up. Maryam came forward and hugged me. Then she took Leila in her arms and consoled us.

At uncle's insistence, Leila and I returned to the Congregational Mosque. We sat in silence leaning against the glass doors, facing each other. Neither of us could endure seeing anyone or anything. We were in such as state that if we didn't have to speak, our silence would last several days. While we remained listlessly grieving, I noticed a short soldier with light colored hair was sitting with his back against the opposite wall and just staring at us. This irked me, but I tried not to take notice. Finally uncle broke the silence and asked, "What do you want to do? Are you coming with me to see your mother?"

"No," I said. "I want to stay right here."

Uncle looked at Leila, but she also said, "I'm here as long as Zahra."

"I'm going to your mother." Uncle said, "What should I tell her if she asks about you two? If she asks about Ali? Why do you want to stay, anyway?"

"Uncle," I asked him, "it should be obvious why we stay. To help. From now on that's the only reason."

"That's enough. Why torture your mother more? She can't take it. I can't take any more, either. What's the point of making it unbearable for us?"

"Whatever happens, happens. It's up to God," I said.

He continued to try to convince us to go, and though I lacked the strength to argue, I had no choice but to answer him. To top it off, the soldier's immodest staring was now adding to my grief. He looked at me as if he was searching for something or he wanted to read my thoughts. "You're not going to say anything to this fellow?" I asked uncle.

"Forget about him, darling," uncle said. "He'll get fed up and go away."

I couldn't just sit without saying anything. I went up to him and said, "Why are your eyes on us rather than on the ground? Aren't you ashamed? What are you doing here, you creep?"

Without taking his eyes off me, in a thick Azeri accent he said, "Your recompense is with the blessed Zahra."

This was a shock. "What do you mean?" I asked.

"I was there when you were burying your brother," he explained. "Even though I had wanted to leave the city because of all the chaos of the last few days, when I saw what you all did, it made me want stay to the end."

"You'll have to excuse me," I said. "I thought you had something bad in mind."

"You must forgive me, but I couldn't help staring. What kind of people are you? Where do you get the strength, the patience?" he asked.

I didn't know what to say and went back to where I was sitting. Uncle, who still had his mind on us but had heard what the soldier said, tried to get us to leave with him. I said nothing. Leila said, "When Zahra leaves, I will too."

Uncle realized it was no use trying to argue. He said he would leave around noon. We came out of the mosque together and stood by a place on the wall fortified by sandbags for a minute. Uncle tried again, saying to Leila, "You, at least, should come with me." She looked at me and said, "No, I don't want to leave Khorramshahr. Uncle turned to me and said, "Zahra, don't be stubborn. Why are you so intent on doing only what you want? Have some pity for your mother. How much does my sister have to suffer?"

"I'm not coming," I said. "But if Leila wants to go, I won't stop her."

I looked down at some bottles they were using for Molotov cocktails and continued, "Better if Leila does go with you, then I wouldn't have to worry."

"No way. I'm staying on my own accord; nobody's going to tell me what to do," she insisted.

At that point uncle, who had been holding back his tears, began to weep. He shook his head and said, "I don't know how I can make you go. No matter how many times I beg you to think of your poor mother, your little sister, your brothers, you don't listen."

"Where are you going now, uncle?" I asked.

"To find my sister and see where she's found shelter."

After he left, we went back inside and kept ourselves busy with work. Khosrow's mother came by regularly to console us. A short time later Leila said she wanted to return to Jennatabad. "You go," I said. "I'll come by later. I want to help with dinner." The mosque was no longer a suitable place for cooking. Around the eighth or ninth day, I had heard they wanted the infirmary and the kitchen to change places. Since the building was becoming more of a target, the windows would break from time to time, shrapnel would plough into the walls, and bits of glass and dirt would spill into the cooking pots. In addition, more and more people were coming to the infirmary. The sight of the wounded, so terrifying to the crowd in the mosque, was making the place unhealthy psychologically. Moving the infirmary also made sense from the point of view of hygiene. Mr. Najjar rightly said, "Space is pretty tight here. I'm not happy being right in people's faces." With all the pressure of work, we couldn't take a break. We spent the nights behind the dividing curtain, while Mr. Najjar remained in the yard and managed to sleep despite the racket made by people coming and going.

If I remember correctly, that day at dusk Mr. Najjar announced, "I have spoken with Dr. Sheybani and he has agreed to put his offices at our disposal. We should go there today and put it into working order. Undoubtedly it's filthy."

Several of the girls and I volunteered, and we went to the clinic armed with brooms and water canisters. Dr. Sheybani, a dentist, had his offices opposite the Congregational Mosque on the south corner of Fakhr Razi and Enqelab Avenues. It was only a few steps away from the mosque, and this was a big plus because the defenders who brought in wounded would know exactly where to bring them. In addition, we could stay in touch with what was happening at the mosque. When we got there the door was open. Sabah, Zohreh, Ashraf Farhadi, Maryam Amjadi, Hosayn Eidi, and I went down the step of the entrance and entered a relatively narrow hallway with rooms on the left and right side. The hallway led to a foyer with two other rooms. After that there was a largish, empty yard without a shade cover but with good sunlight.

The dental equipment and the doctor's library were in the first rooms. We needed to brush and scrub the office floor, pack up the books in the library, and gather all the equipment in one room. This would allow us to arrange our store of drugs on the bookshelves. The cleaning took around two hours. We removed the dust that covered the mosaic tiles of the clinic and washed them. We put a bed in the main room so that the wounded could be examined there first. We made the library a dispensary, and one of the other rooms became a place where the girls could rest. I had absolutely no desire to do the work. I just wanted to get it over with quickly, then creep into a hole where no one would find me. It was completely dark when we finished. Happy to have a safe place to themselves, the girls wanted to spend the night there. I said goodbye to them and went to Jennatabad. I wanted to be near Ali.

Although I went there with the idea of being near Ali, I couldn't bring myself to visit his grave. Every time I got up, Zeynab stopped me, saying, "What's wrong with going during the day? It's dangerous now." When she saw me get all choked up, she comforted me and said, "I know you don't want him to be alone, but it's not right to go now."

As long as I was awake, she didn't leave my side. She tried to keep Leila and me from sinking into a depression by encouraging us to talk. It was very difficult to be with other people during those moments. I didn't want anybody to see me and realize from my expression what I was feeling. Late at night, when everybody was sleeping, I sat up against the wall and wept. I knew Leila was also awake and like me was mulling over the past. I tried to bring Ali's shining face to mind. I hadn't seen him for three months. I wanted to remember the most recent image I had of him, but the flood of other memories broke my concentration, and his face disappeared from view. The only thing that came to mind was how he looked as a corpse—his half-open eyes and his smile. At the same time I wondered where mother and the children were at that time. What had happened to them? Had Uncle Salim reached them? Did grandfather and grandmother know about Ali? What were they doing? Finally beset by questions on all sides and with tears in my eyes, I fell asleep.

After the morning prayer, I set out for Ali's grave. No matter how much Zeynab tried to get me to have a bite of something, I refused. When I saw Zeynab and Leila were following me, I asked, "Where do you think you're going?"

"Well, we just want to come along."

"No. You stay here. You can come later. I want to be alone and talk with them by myself."

Leila looked at me with a hurt and questioning expression, as if to say, "Aren't I part of the family, too?" I went but I didn't stay long. I had a good cry, said my peace, and got up. I knew we had to move to the new clinic. Even though I had hurried back, when I got to the Congregational Mosque there was no one at the infirmary. They had gathered up the curtains and equipment and took them to the new place. The mosque seemed deserted to me. They had also moved the kitchen to another location. Most of the people had been evacuated.

No one could deny things were becoming more ordered. I went to the clinic where the work really began. They had brought empty boxes and with some boys began to clear the metal shelves of books and put them in the boxes. I thumbed through some of the books as we packed them. They were thick, large volumes written in English. Although I had left school early, I wouldn't allow any newspaper, magazine, or book to slip through my fingers. Aunt Salimeh would buy me many newspapers and magazines, and I was her most faithful customer. This was why I was so well informed about many things. I would solve the crossword puzzles in record time and would wait impatiently for aunt to buy the next editions of the magazines. When I saw Dr. Sheybani's English language books, the reading bug got me again; unfortunately I didn't know the western alphabet.

We were about to finish the work when they brought in the first wounded person, a young man of some bulk with a piece of shrapnel lodged in his left soldier. His friends were very worried about him, because of the shrapnel near his heart. They brought him into the examination room and took his clothes off. Mr. Najjar called me. I entered the room. As he looked at the wound, Mr. Najjar said, "We can't touch the shrapnel here. As soon as we remove it, there will be severe bleeding. If he is moved the shrapnel will cut through his arteries. All we can do here is stabilize his arm and chest."

Then he said to me, "Bring the bandages and splints." Unlike his friends who were upset, the young man was laughing and said, "It's nothing. Don't worry. Don't be afraid." But when we started to work on him, he got woozy and, because of the bleeding, he fainted. Mr. Najjar lined the wood planks with cotton and wrapped gauze around them. Then he put them around the shrapnel. He put one of the splints under the wounded man's side so that his arm stood at an angle from his body. Then he tightened the splints with pressure bandages. He hung the bandaged arm around the wounded man's neck, warning him, "Don't let yourself get jostled in the ambulance. Sit up straight." He told the driver, "Get him right to Mahshahr."

Almost immediately afterwards, they brought in another wounded man who had been hit by a lot of shrapnel. Mr. Najjar furiously cleaned the man's wounds. He inserted a pair of tweezers into them and asked us, "Hear that sound?" as the tweezers made contact with the pieces of metal. He extracted a piece of shrapnel and immediately stitched the wound. He didn't touch the shrapnel lodged in the man's side, saying, "These have to be seen to at a hospital. They may have reached his intestines." To get me involved, he asked me to help with the work. Not desiring to be found wanting, I madly tried to follow his instructions. The wounded man's bleeding wouldn't stop. Mr. Najjar continued to stitch the wound while I cleaned around it so he could see its dimensions. Mr. Najjar's face was covered in perspiration, which would occasionally drip into the wound. Although, out of modesty, I didn't want to do it, I wiped his face with gauze. The boy was writhing in pain and trying will all his might not to scream. When the strain got too much, his features told me what he was really feeling. My fears increased. Dead on his feet, Mr. Najjar kept asking the man, "Are you okay?" He would always answer, "Thank God." At one point during the treatment, Mr. Najjar gruffly demanded, "Sister Hoseyni, inject him with a sedative."

I wanted to ask him, "Why didn't you put it in his drip?" Instead I only said, "You want me to give him an injection?"

His tone said I couldn't refuse. I was afraid he would throw me out of the clinic. For my part I was afraid I would make a mess of it, and he'd get so angry he'd tell me that I had no talent for that kind of work.

I stepped forward and swabbed the man's arm with disinfectant. Then I inserted the needle halfway into his muscle. Mr. Najjar, who had his eyes on me, came near as I nervously put the rest of the needle in and injected the sedative. I extracted the syringe and said, "I did it."

When it came time to deal with the shrapnel in his leg, I was feeling queasy. The suture needle was not going in easily. I held my breath each time Mr. Najjar inserted it. It was as if he was putting it into my heart. As he extracted the needle, I found it hard to breathe and my heart felt like it was being pierced instead of the boy.

With all the mangled bodies and amputated limbs I had seen at Jennatabad, I didn't know why this scene had such an effect on me. I tried to keep myself under control, not wanting the slightest sign of weakness or distress to show. In the last several days, people had been pointing me out saying, "That's the Hoseyni girl whose father and brother were martyred." Then some would approach me and ask, "Where do you get the will to go on? We're amazed; it's almost like you haven't lost your father and brother. Like your heart hasn't been seared. The way you go around with a smile on your face!"

I put on such a brave face no one would guess the horrible effect the deaths of father and Ali had on me. I forced myself to show people I had the strength and will to go on. Even though I was dying inside, I said nothing. The pressure of keeping up a brave face was ruining my health. My hands started to tremble. When I had lost track of what Mr. Najjar wanted, he shouted, "Stop daydreaming, Sister Hoseyni! You can't do that in here if you want to stay. This place is all work; no one's going to coddle you. You won't get away with feeling faint. Anybody who wants to stay has to have the guts of a lion." Fear of Mr. Najjar made me keep my emotions in check. The suturing finished, I heard him say, "Come and bandage him."

My eyes went blank. I felt very weak in the chest, and then the feeling spread to the rest of my body. I was spinning in a dark hole, spinning and spinning, then everything went blank.

When I came to, my face was burning. The girls were standing around me. I heard them say, "We were worried about you. What happened all of a sudden?"

I made out Zohreh Farhadi kindly saying, "She had the right to faint. Who could stand up to all that pressure?"

Ra'na also sympathized, "Poor thing."

I opened my eyes, still not knowing where I was. "Where am I?"

"In Sheybani's office," they said. "You weren't feeling too well."

I slowly became more alert and tried to get up. "Lie there," they said. "It's still too soon for you to get up."

"The wounded man. Mr. Najjar said to bandage him."

"We did that. He's gone. Don't worry."

"Where's Mr. Najjar?" I asked apprehensively. "Did he say anything?"

"Don't worry. He was also very worried about you. He blamed himself for shouting at you."

I stretched out and looked around. There was a drip in my arm. They put curtains around my bed. The toll that working at Jennatabad took on my nerves, hunger, lack of sleep, the deaths of father and Ali, and, finally, the scenes of open wounds, all of it put me in this state. Of course I had sensed from the second day at the body washers' that I wasn't feeling well. It felt like all the veins in my body were dry, emptied of blood. My joints creaked when I worked. My eyes lost their brightness, and I always felt dizzy. But now with the drip, I felt much better. I got out of bed. "Should we bring you something to eat?" they asked. "No," I said. "I don't feel like eating anything." Mr. Najjar's words really offended me. I left the clinic and told myself I would prove to him I wasn't spoiled.

That same day a team of five doctors from Tehran and Isfahan arrived at the clinic. The poor men were not used to the sounds of explosions and bombardment. They cowered in a corner with every whine of a mortar shell. During those initial hours when talk turned to the Komala Groups and the Demokrats, the new arrivals defended them. By doing so they passed themselves off as progressives. Despite all their pretensions to equality, the way they acted toward Mr. Najjar was not at all appropriate. They couldn't believe an ordinary health care worker was capable of doing things on the level of a specialist physician. They made it obvious that they didn't respect what he did, but Mr. Najjar ignored them and went about his business.

The next morning I was shocked to see that there was no sign of the team sent from Tehran. Late the night before, when the shelling got intense, they decided that flight was the better part of valor. But very soon another team came to the clinic. They were specialists from Tehran, ranging in age from thirty to forty-five. Their names, as I recall, were Dr. Sadeqi, Dr. Habibollah, Dr. Torabi, and another doctor Habibi or Habib Nezhad. They also disappeared after the first day, but they returned a few days later with their heads covered in dust, which told me that they had been to the front lines. It was clear they hadn't slept in the last few days. Their pale faces were drawn, and they didn't have the strength to talk. Despite this, after a few hours rest they gathered their possessions and equipment and went back to the front. I remember Dr. Sadeqi best, because whenever he saw us at work he would thank us. He was a man of sympathy and energy. Although exhausted each time he got back from the front, he'd take a turn working in the clinic.

13

Where Ali Died and the New Clinic

It was the morning of October 5, 1980. I went with Hoseyn Eidi and Abdollah Mo'avi to the Congregational Mosque. We got some bread and cheese and returned to Jennatabad. On the way we were passing Islamic Republic Lane when I had the idea of looking in at Darya Bod Rasayi School. I said to Hoseyn and Abdollah, "Let's visit the place and see what's happening." They agreed and we turned into the lane. The door was open and we went in. It was just like the day of the accident; the place was a shambles. Mortar shells had hit the compound, and it looked like the ground had been ploughed. The windows were broken and bits of brick, stone, and metal littered the area. A bomb had landed in front of the entrance, leaving a deep crater. We passed through the door. There was a relatively large foyer and then two classrooms on the right and left, followed by a wide hallway onto which other classrooms opened. There was a stairway that, after six or seven steps, became a spiral staircase that led to the second floor. The sides of the staircase were glass to allow light to come in. A bomb had smashed through the right corner of a class, creating a large hole in the wall and finally burrowing in the floor. The door of the room was knocked completely off its hinges, but some broken bricks kept it from falling to the ground. We passed by the class and entered the hallway. The floor was littered with earth, broken glass, unexploded bombs, etc. The destruction was so great one would think a truck had dumped a load of dirt on the floor. Piles of debris were everywhere. The burn marks on the walls indicated something horrible had happened.

As we went further we saw more blood on the ground than there had been in the hallway. In several places, the blood was dry but in others it was smeared and appeared fresh. At one point, I was not watching where I was going, and I slid across the floor. I began to feel unwell, as the smell of dirt, blood, and powder filled my nostrils. Though I felt dizzy and was about to faint, I walked on because I wanted to see the whole place, the place where Ali was taken from me. I waded through the rubble, looking everywhere. The walls were dotted with the skin and flesh of children. There were even pieces of brain, which, after two nights, having lost their sponginess, were dry and brownish. Worse still was the scene in the part of the building where a great deal of munitions had gone off. The walls in that part were covered in blood to the ceiling and so thoroughly plastered with bones, brains, hair, and shrapnel there weren't any bare spaces. I pointed to that part and asked Abdollah, "What do you think caused this?"

"It appears that a shell entered the classroom through the yard and hit the wall."

Then I said, "Let's go to the first class and see what happened there."

The three of us went back down the hall. The door of the classroom was open about twenty centimeters, and, although it had been pulled off its hinges, it wouldn't open. It was as if someone were holding it closed. Hoseyn and I tried and tried, but we couldn't budge it. "Hold on a second, I'll fix it," Abdollah said.

After managing to enter the class through the hole made by the shell, he said, "It's blocked by a mountain of dirt and debris."

As we pushed on the door, he cleared the dirt on the other side. Suddenly Abdollah in a terrified voice shouted, "One's in here! One's in here!"

Hoseyn and I pushed on the door and, with some effort, entered the room. There was a toe sticking out from the one of the mounds. "Don't be scared," I told Abdollah. "It's nothing." Then I sat and pushed the earth aside. It wasn't an entire corpse, just a severed leg emerging at that point from under the earth. The three of us grabbed the leg by the ankle and managed to pull it out. It was heavy, apparently the foot of a fairly large person. We were sick to our stomachs. Without food for two days, my stomach was in my mouth. I asked Abdollah, who was as white as a ghost, to help me lift the leg. In a crazed voice, he said, "No way am I touching that thing."

"Abdollah," I insisted, "come and help. It's very heavy."

He came forward grudgingly, and the three of us dragged the leg into the hall. "Let's go back in. Maybe we'll find something else."

Hoseyn said, "Come on, sister, leave it. Let's go."

Thinking that the leg belonged to Taqi Mohsenifar, I said, "It makes no sense. These are the limbs of martyrs and must be buried." We began to search again everywhere: in the debris, the blankets, the RPG rounds, the uniforms, the boots, the loose earth. We found a hand so mangled it looked as if it had been chopped off with a cleaver. We didn't give the second floor a look, worried there might be an unexploded mortar round up there.

Hoseyn picked up the severed hand and Abdollah slung the leg over his shoulder. We went out into the yard, where we found a nylon sack. "I'll wrap the leg in this, and you find something for the hand," I told them.

Hoseyn went back inside and returned with a leg severed from the knee and an army shirt. He put the leg on the ground and said, "Look, I found another one."

I put the severed hand and the newly found leg in the shirt and tied the sleeves together. Abdollah asked, "Sister, what's the point of making us heave our guts out the first thing in the morning?"

"Abdollah," I said, "if these things remain here, the dogs will get a whiff of them and eat these poor souls."

"But why wrap them up now?"

"To keep people from seeing them before we get to Jennatabad," I said. "Say an 'In the Name of God' and let's go."

Hoseyn pointed to the nylon sack with the leg and said, "Abdollah, you take that and I'll take the bundle."

I saw them hesitate and said, "Give it to me. I'll help carry it."

Their male pride hurt, they said, "Are we dead or something that you have to carry it? We'll do it."

"Fine," I said. "So each of you take one now, and you can switch when we're halfway there."

Then I went to clean my hands by rubbing dirt on them and picked up the sack containing the breakfast food. Finally we left. As we walked Abdollah pretended to shout like one of those peddlers who go door to door. "Severed legs and hands!" he bellowed

Hoseyn laughed out loud. Although I was really upset, I had to laugh, too. When I saw them dragging their feet and fumbling with their loads, I grabbed the bundle from Hoseyn's hand and said, "You two take the sack."

But this didn't stop them from arguing. Abdollah said, "Come and take this end, it's heavier."

Hoseyn laughed and in his thick accent teased, "I got the easy part." They kept on joking and laughing until I said, "It's not right. Allow the dead some dignity. What's gotten into you two? Carry them the right way."

"Lord forgive us," they said, but soon they were joking again. The funniest thing was to see several stray dogs and cats had joined our caravan, stopping whenever we did. I had a very bad feeling when one of dogs began to bark. I turned around and shouted, "You keep that up and I'll strangle you!" As if he understood the threat, the poor animal lowered its head and whimpered.

The sound of shelling and mortars scattered the dogs. I kept looking back toward the end of the street, hoping a car would appear and give us a ride. But nothing came by. So we continued walking until we reached Jennatabad, where the dogs ran to the graves. Then they went into the wooded area to sniff the ground, as if looking for something. At first I wasn't paying attention to them, but then I remembered Ali's clothes. I was suddenly afraid they had gotten wind of them. Luckily they scattered a few moments later. My mind at ease about the clothing, I went back to the rooms.

The body washers had just woken up and were groggily waiting for breakfast. With obvious concern in her voice, Zeynab asked me, "Are you okay, sweetheart? You're looking a bit better today, God be praised. Run and throw some water on your face. Then come back and have a bite to eat."

Seeing the dismembered corpses had robbed me of my appetite, so I said nothing.

As soon as she saw the bundles, she said with a laugh, "So what's new in your bridal trousseau today?"

"Nothing, just a hand and some legs," Abdollah said.

"What?" Zeynab gasped. "Hands and feet? From where?"

"The Darya Bod Rasayi School," I said. "There was a base there."

Looking surprised and hurt, Zeynab asked, "Why did you go there? Without me? You could have said something."

"We didn't intend to go initially, but when we passed Hezb Street, I thought let's stop and see what happened there."

Zeynab gave me an understanding look, and then she brought some tea. I had no idea where Leila was or what she was doing. I said to the boys, "Go and wash for breakfast. I'm going to visit father and Ali."

When they began to follow me, I said, "Don't come with me. I'd rather be alone."

Before I got to the graves, I greeted them, "Nice to find you two so happy together without a thought for us."

Now at the site I didn't know which grave to sit by. Because father was the older, I thought I would sit by his grave first. I bent down and kissed the ground saying, "Had a good night with Ali by your side, didn't you?"

I crawled over to Ali's grave and kissed the ground saying, "You shouldn't have bothered to come back, Ali. It only incinerated my soul is all. I waited and waited for you to come so I could loosen the knot in my heart. But now all you've done by dying is to make it tighter."

"God! Why did you leave me behind?" I said bitterly. "How much more do I have to take? What else do I have to bear? I called on you to give me patience and on the blessed Zeynab for strength, but now I can't take any more. How long are you going to test me with all these calamities? She was the blessed Zeynab, after all. But me? I am nothing compared to her."

I stopped talking; the more I complained the more it stoked the fires inside me. I could no longer find solace in logic. I even lost interest in Leila and, the truth be known, began to dislike her, and, jealous, even started to hate her. Why, I asked myself, should she have been the one to see Ali and not me? Was she better? I so desperately hoped to see him. Just one look would have been enough to raise my spirits and, perhaps, help me endure his passing.

I put these thoughts aside and lay down to rest between the two graves. I stared fixedly at the sky and said to father and Ali, "The least you can do is show yourselves to me. It's the only thing that would comfort me."

I waited in vain. At that moment death to me was the most important and inviting thing. I hoped it would come calling. I closed my eyes and said, "I'm tired of living. I want to die."

I don't know how long this feeling lasted. As I lay there I felt someone kiss my forehead and cradle me in her arms. I opened my eyes. The lump in my throat burst. It was Zeynab. In tears I said, "Where did you come from, dearest?"

"I was worried about you from the start. When I saw you leave, I followed you, but I didn't want to disturb you. But seeing you lying on the ground like a corpse, I couldn't stand it."

"I want to die, love," I said to her.

I pressed my head against her chest. It was as if I had been waiting for a chance to do it, as if I had needed to do it. Then, still weeping, I yelled, "I want to die!"

Zeynab caressed me and said, "Don't say such things. You've got to take the place of your father and Ali for your mother's sake and for your sisters and brothers. Your father and Ali left them in your care."

"Why me?" I asked. "Why did they have to place this burden on my shoulders and go? How much can I stand after all?"

Zeynab said sympathetically, "Girl, it's not like you to give up. Weren't you always the one to give us the strength to go on? Didn't you always tell us we had to learn from the blessed Zeynab? Have you forgotten?"

"No, I haven't. But who am I compared to her?"

"You've got to be strong. They've placed a burden on you, and you've got to go on. If you want your father to be proud of you, hold his head up high in the next world, you've got to show strength."

"I don't want to," I said. "How can I be strong? There's no one to prop me up. How do you expect me to show strength when there's no one behind me?"

"Zahra," she reminded me, "you have always called on the blessed Imams for help, haven't you? They're the sources of blessing and grace. What's worrying you? Besides, the most precious thing a person can have is God. When you put your trust in Him, you won't need anybody else. God Himself will become the head of your household."

After pausing, she continued, "If you're okay with it, I'm willing to take on any role, be a mother, a sister, whatever support you need from me. Now get up. Don't let it bother you. God is great. He'll never leave you. Do you imagine you've suffered all these hardships on your own? All of this was the hand of God at work. And don't you dare forget it."

"I know," I admitted. "If it hadn't been for God, I would have died a thousand deaths by now. But it's still impossible."

"I agree, but if you put your faith in Him, the difficulties will disappear."

I had never felt as close to Zeynab as I did then. I had seen how she had acted as a mother toward Leila, but this was the first time we had been so close. When she meekly asked to be a loving mother to me, in my heart I realized what she had said was true. Although there was nothing particularly special about her, Zeynab was a so kind and innocent that for the first time I was able to surrender myself completely to her embrace. The last the thing I wanted was to leave her side. I had been too reticent, too proud to show how torn up I was. Here I was, so fed up with the world that I wanted to die. Now, after a good cry, I felt relieved. A weight had been lifted and the fires raging in me had cooled somewhat. I was certain that had Zeynab not done what she had, I would have gone mad. She was a true comfort to me. Even mother couldn't have improved on what Zeynab had done for me. Mother needed someone to lean on herself. I was certain she didn't understand me. I was sure the news of Ali's passing would so upset mother she'd lose all sense of reality.

I wanted with all my heart to stay in Zeynab's embrace. With my head resting against her chest, I looked up at her face. Her olive skin and dark eyes told me she was from a village in the southeast, Jiroft or Hormezdegan, but I couldn't be sure. There was something special in her look that people people found attractive, though she was not a particularly attractive woman. She just had pleasant features. Even when the pressure at work got too much and she became annoyed or started shouting, the love and kindness never left her face.

From the very first day we started working together at Jennatabad, something told me that she would be a friend.

Sensing I had calmed down, Zeynab caressed my face with her hands, which were rough and ragged from work. She communicated a special warmth and kindness to me. Her hands were the hands of a true mother. The maternal feelings she had for me radiated through my whole being.

Before we got up, Zeynab recited the opening of the Quran and, addressing the graves, said several times, "Blessed be your good fortune. Lend us a hand."

I sensed the extraordinary sorrow she felt in saying this. We returned to the rooms. At Zeynab's insistence, I washed my hands and face. She poured some tea for me. "I don't feel like tea," I whispered. "My dear girl," she said, "you'll just have to put up with it. If you want you can go and wash the kettle and brew some yourself." "Forget it," I said. "I don't feel like it." Then I looked at Leila, who, contrary to me, never lost her appetite. She was sitting happily eating and drinking tea. I managed to get down a little bread and cheese. "I want to go to the mosque," I announced.

"Go," said Zeynab, "go, but keep in touch."

After I got up, I saw a motorcycle entering Jennatabad. As it got closer, I recognized the photographer with, as usual, a camera slung around his neck. He also had his film case with him. He parked his motorcycle near the rooms and got off. He was very upset. "They hit the laboratory," he said. I let out a deep sigh and asked, "What do you mean?"

"I mean everything was blown to smithereens."

On the day Ali was martyred, he had taken pictures of his body and scenes of the burial. Those pictures were some consolation. At least mother, who was not at the funeral, would believe that her son was actually dead. But now? This was all I needed—one more sorrow to add to the mountain of suffering. I stormed out of Jennatabad and went to the mosque. I explained what happened to Zohreh Farhadi, who also became upset. Then I decided to look in again at the Darya Bod Rasayi School. Zohreh also wished to see the place. Together we walked out and, seeing Abdollah and Hoseyn along the way, the four of us went to the school. After rummaging around in the hallway and the classrooms of the school, we couldn't believe that we found a Samsonite briefcase. Hoseyn said, "Let's open it to see who it belongs to." Without waiting for an answer, he sat down in a corner and fiddled with the combination lock until it opened. The minute I saw the contents, I was shocked; it was Ali's.

The first clue was a piece of wax inside the case. I was sure he used it to exercise his fingers. I had a strange feeling as I took the case and pulled out the contents one by one. A bandana lay under a towel from the Mithaqiyeh Hospital, a last will and testament, and, most importantly, an envelop full of pictures. It is hard to describe how happy I was to find them. I greedily took in the pictures one by one, unable to stop crying. These were pictures of him on separate occasions during his hospital stay: giving the call to prayer; unconscious, being taken from the operating room; sitting in a wheelchair. Many of the pictures were of various public figures visiting Ali and the other wounded men: Ayatollahs Khamene'i and Beheshti, Mr. Falsafi, and others. There were also picture of Ali at the Behesht-e Zahra cemetery and at the Congregational prayers.

While I was looking for him, I was curious to know about his time in the hospital and other events. The pictures told me everything—what he had done in Tehran, where he had gone, whom he had seen. Many of the snapshots showed Ali and the other wounded men fooling around, shoving their wheelchairs and aiming their canes at one another. The pictures were so clear and vivid that it was as if they were speaking to me, making me laugh and cry at the same time. I felt I wasn't myself, seeing the pain on the patients' faces, and I was uncomfortable being with Hoseyn and Abdollah. I said to myself: I wish I could have been there with you and taken care of you. What a difficult time you had. I picked up his skullcap, which still had his scent. He must have had it with him when he was traveling. It made me happy to smell it. Then I opened his will. It had been written quickly, on the road, I guessed. He wanted us to give his books to Hojjat, one of his dear friends in the Construction Corps. To me he gave his camera. There were a number of debts that he wanted us to pay out of his pocket. Because of his surgeries, he had been unable to fast during Ramadan, and he wanted us to hire someone to atone for it.

I went out of my mind reading his will and breathing in the scent of his clothing. My tears upset Hoseyn and Abdollah, who left the room, but a few moments later Hoseyn with his usual strength and maturity returned saying, "Sister, think of me as your little brother. I'm begging you. Don't upset yourself like this." Zohreh Farhadi also tried to console me. I closed the case, which Hossein took from me, and we went to the clinic.

I placed the case on top of one of the armoires so, given the opportunity, I could get back to it.

The flow of doctors coming and going went a long way in putting my mind at ease about our stock of supplies and drugs. People could come and help themselves now, whereas before Mr. Najjar had to go to the hospitals and drugstores to get what was needed. When we told him not to go himself and send one of us instead, he would say, "It's not your job. I'm the man. I'll do whatever it takes, even if it means getting into a fight to get what we need. You can't do that."

The Bustani Drugstore, which was across from the Congregational Mosque, put all its drugs at our disposal. The other drugstores made it known that they would do likewise. Although we worked with the new medicos, we still considered Mr. Najjar our supervisor. When the first team of doctors left, we asked Mr. Najjar, "What should we do now?" "What we have to do: cooperate," he said. "These people have made a tremendous effort leaving their homes to come here."

It was easier for us to work with Mr. Najjar, given how well we had gotten to know him, but this familiarity had no effect on how he treated us, of course. He cut us no slack and sometimes during work he would warn us, "Watch it, now." That gave us a scare, not knowing exactly whom he meant. He would say, "You know who I mean. You're dawdling and if you want to work like that, don't stay here. Leave now; this isn't your grandma's house. You'll have to be better than that to pull a fast one on me."

I was hugely interested in treating patients and, fearing Mr. Najjar would tell me I wasn't cut out for the work, I tried to learn quickly. Mr. Najjar had also noticed how serious I was about the work. He said, "Thank God. How sharp you are. You get everything so quickly." Even though he didn't know it was out of fear, I was happy I was learning the latest medical advances and the use of medication. Lidocaine intrigued me the most, anesthetizing a wound with just a one or two percent injection. The deeper the wound, the higher we made the concentration. Mr. Najjar taught us when to inject around the wound or in it.

We got more work done at the Sheybani clinic than at the mosque. In addition to not having panicky people around, the environment was better; it was easier to reach the patients and see to their needs. Gradually we gathered the equipment and paraphernalia in one corner. We filled the empty spaces with beds so that if the number of wounded increased, we wouldn't have to put them on the floor. Still we could only perform the kind of simple surgeries we did in the mosque. If people needed longer-term care, we would transfer them or they would come and go, and we would change their dressings and give them injections. No one stayed overnight. Ambulances and vans regularly ferried the wounded to Abadan or Mahshahr. This allowed things at the clinic to run very smoothly. But in my heart of hearts, I still wanted to go to the front lines. Whenever there was no work at the clinic or during the bombardments, I would leave and go around the city or the places that had been hit looking for the dead and wounded.

14

Refugees and Evil Zahra

After the death of Ali, almost all my memories faded. Thoughts of Ali occupied my mind so much that my attention to other things dwindled to nothing. Time and space collapsed for me. I went on working out of habit. This is why my memory of many things is not that reliable. Time erased many of the events. I was like a sleeper who awakes from a dream with a start and only remembers a few things about it.

The mosque was still very busy. The crowds there swelled with people we pulled from their neighborhood homes. Groups of people were constantly leaving, and others were coming to take their places. Families had their own particular problems. The food situation was not good. The adults could tolerate it, but the little ones, especially the children who were on powdered milk or the ones feeding on a solution of sugar water and dissolved biscuits couldn't get their fill. On most nights the sounds of their crying echoed in the mosque, driving everyone to the limits of their patience. The men were worried most that a shell would hit the mosque directly, causing mass casualties. Once, when I was not at the mosque, this actually happened.

When we told people there was no point in staying, they would ask, "Where should we go? We don't have cars. How can we get to other cities without them? Abadan is also being shelled. You have to do something for us."

Which was what happened. Once someone called me out of the clinic, saying a vehicle was coming and I should help them get people.

I would ask, "How? With what? If they hit the car on the bridge, then what?"

"There's no way we're taking the bridge," I was told. "We're going on the Shatt by boat and dropping them off somewhere above the bridge."

"From where?" I asked.

"The Khombeh side, where the Forty-Meter Road ends. It's safer there."

Khombeh meant the part of the Shatt by the Mosaddeq Hospital. At that point the Karun River entered from the northeast, then changed course flowing to the center of town. This was considered the easternmost part of the city. The other girls and I got busy rounding up people from the prayer room, telling them they had to be ready to leave the city.

This made quite a few of them angry at us. Although we had been warning them from day one it was not wise to stay, they still hadn't cut ties with their old lives and villages. "Where should we go?" they asked. "The war's going to end. We'll wait it out here until we can get back to our lives and homes. Where are you going to make us live like refugees?"

Even the children were complaining, "We want to go home. We want to go to school."

By contrast, there was another group of people ready and eager to leave. They had every right to be fed up with the shelling and not knowing what was going to happen to them. These poor people were always with their bundles of possessions by their sides, ready to flee at a moment's notice. At night they would untie their things and in the morning repack them, expecting something to happen.

With the news a truck was at the door, we asked the people to get up and bring their things outside. We helped the armed civilians and the guards at the mosque see to the needs of people. Everybody loaded what they had lugged to the mosque: large boxes, old metal trunks, cardboard cartons, even televisions.

Some people helped us move their possessions aside, because there wasn't room for everything in the truck. We loaded women and children first. There were no young men in the crowd. The elderly and those who were unable to fight and were in the mosque stood to one side. The truck filled with women, children, and old ladies, some sitting and some standing, then it started to go, traveling from the Forty-Meter Road in the direction of the Farmandari Circle. The driver stopped at the end of the avenue that led to the Shatt. People got out and made their way to the water. I always liked this part of the waterway. So many reeds had taken root on both sides of the avenue it was now a beautiful, green meadow. The water level along the Shatt was high, and the water was murky. Skiffs, small launches, even rowboats crowded around taking on passengers. To get people in the boats they had to put planks in the water and, despite my fear of the water, I tried to help several of the women with small children board.

It was difficult to walk because my feet sank deep in the soft mud. In addition to the people we had brought, there was another crowd waiting to cross. People already on board stood up in the boats to make room for more, though the boats didn't have far to go to get to the other side. During the move, a corvette-class warship came through the Shatt, and several of the sailors shouted their greetings and encouragement to the people on shore. The people waved back at them. Although the corvette was moving slowly, the water turned choppy in its wake. The small boats rocked, terrifying the passengers and making it difficult for those on the narrow planks to maintain their balance. The poor things thought they would fall in. The panic caused by the choppy water combined with the roar of enemy planes and bombs, terrorizing them even more. The crowd on the banks and the corvette made a tempting target for enemy fire. Suddenly all hell broke loose. The people on the banks started to run in all directions and then dove to the ground. The people in the boats looked up at the sky in fright, at a loss as to how they would get to the other side. At that moment I caught a glimpse of a young boy who had lost his balance and fallen into the water. No one else saw him. I ran into the water shouting, "Get him! Grab him! He's fallen in! There's a boy in the water!"

No one heard me in that din. Terrified that the innocent child might drown, I dove in even though I couldn't swim. Thank God it was not that deep near the boat, but deep enough for a five-year-old to drown. After I went in, one of the men on the banks also rushed into the water. I paddled with my arms and feet for five or six meters until the water was up to my chest. I became frozen with fear. Then everyone, noticing what had happened, began to scream, calling on the sainted Abbas Abol Fazl for help. The boy continued to flail about, as I got closer to him. I grabbed his arm, but he went under and I tried to pull him up. At that point, the man who was right behind me dove down, caught hold of the boy, and lifted him out of the water. The people on the boat took hold of the boy and slapped his back to get him to spit up the water he had swallowed. I tried to get back to shore as my chador bobbed up and down on the surface of the water. I emerged covered in mud and slime, but just as I reached dry land jet fighters appeared in the sky above me. There was nowhere to take cover so I dove to the ground and covered my head. Everyone was terrified; a number of people wouldn't stop screaming, while others tried to calm them by saying the planes were only for reconnaissance. Fearing the planes were on a bombing run, most people didn't listen. The planes headed for the corvette, which had disappeared among the reeds. They dropped two bombs; the first didn't go off, landing with a splash. The second exploded in the water, sending up jets of spray. We remained motionless for a few minutes.

Evil Zahra, a young woman who had come with me from mosque, was white as a sheet. Fear made her eyes bulge from their sockets. She wouldn't let go of me. Soaked to my skin with my clothes all muddy, all I wanted was to find some privacy so I could wash, but, feeling sorry for the girl, I stayed by her side. I said to her, "Don't be scared. It's nothing. Try to control yourself." After it was over, I got up but this Zahra stayed on the ground. She pretended to be struck dumb with fear. Familiar with these antics, I knew she was faking. "Enough drama," I told her.

I walked away angrily, leaving her by the shore. Fear had scattered people in all directions; some even ran as far as the Mosaddeq Hospital. I went to retrieve them and, just as I reached the hospital, the sound of planes breaking the sound barrier froze everyone in place. My nerves were shot now. I didn't have a chance to duck down, but as soon as I bent over to dive I caught a glimpse of the caretaker at the municipal motor pool making a mad dash from the yard. I kept my eyes on him. He was around forty and wore a blue shirt that seemed to be part of a uniform. His sleeves were rolled up to his elbows. He kept running until he was clear of the place.

The sound came nearer and nearer. I fell to the ground as the fighters struck the motor pool building. The explosion was truly horrifying this time; it shook the area like an earthquake and sent thick clouds of dust into the air. The blast, followed by the demolition of the buildings at the end of the compound, the smashing of glass, and the whine of the shrapnel as it burrowed into the walls was so deafening I felt like my eardrums were about to tear. I still had water in my ears from diving into the Shatt to save the child. This magnified the sounds even more. The shock wave from the explosion cascaded to the ground. When it broke, the pressure was so great it felt like my chest would crack open.

Lying on the ground as dust, dirt, and bits of brick shot toward me, I looked around for the caretaker. In the seconds it took for me to dive to the ground, a piece of shrapnel had decapitated him, but his headless body, mangled and bloody, continued its mad dash until it ran into a partially open double door and hit the ground. The sight petrified me. Anxiously looking around, I saw the nearest person to me was a soldier from the base, whom I knew slightly.

"Come, let's help him," I said.

"What do you mean, help him?" he asked. "He has no head."

"Maybe something can be done," I said.

Over the roar of more jets, he shouted, "Take cover! There're about to blast this place!"

Then he ran toward the hospital and dove into some box trees behind a metal railing. The soldier, whose name was Abdol Reza, made me angry. He and his friend Nemat were at father's burial. They came by Jennatabad often. Although they were friends and came from the same town, Abdol Reza and Nemat could not have been more different. Despite his bulk, Nemat was quick on his feet and smart, without an ounce of fear. I had heard from his friends that he was not right in the head. He would just charge right at the Iraqis. They even said he would loot their bodies. One time I saw Abdol Reza without Nemat and asked, "What do you know! You're by yourself? Where's your friend?"

In a thick Lori accent, he said, "The boy's as stubborn as a mule. All by himself he took a broken-down Iraqi tank and drove it to Ahvaz for repair. The turret cannon was broken, but he insisted, 'We've got to get the thing fixed.' I don't know what to do with him. There's just his mother. If he goes on this way, he'll wind up dead. What'll I tell his mother, then?"

I waited a few minutes for the sound of the planes to die down, then I got up and walked over to the caretaker. He was in horrible shape. The shrapnel had entered through the back of his neck, mangling it so much that he didn't look natural. But even though the back of his head was crushed and his brains were matted in his hair, I could still make out his face. The last time I had seen him he was prone, but now he was lying on his side. It seemed he had tried to turn over. I took his pulse. He didn't have one. He was killed instantly. There was shrapnel all over his body, and a lot of blood still flowed from his neck. His legs were braided like a pretzel. Everything was blood red. I felt sick, without an ounce of strength left, and started throwing up. It was one of those times I just wanted to die, end it all, so I wouldn't have to see such things. I couldn't stand any more of this. I called out to Abdol Reza, but I didn't want to be too loud because people would have run toward me and be forced to see this sight. Abdol Reza didn't come. He probably had gotten a glimpse of the body. "I'm not coming there," he said. "You come here. All of these people, they'll crowd around, you know."

"What does that mean?" I asked angrily. "Come on now."

I didn't know what the matter was. He was probably terrified or maybe he was as unhappy with me as I was with him. He said, "The planes will be right back. Understand? You want to die, fine, but you're going to get everybody else killed along with you. Girl, why are you acting like such a big shot? You're young; act your age."

I didn't answer him and started to think about how I was going to gather up the caretaker's body. I thought I would get a stretcher from the hospital across the way. At that point two men, who had been by the Shatt, appeared. They were also affected by the state the body was in. Although they had seen ugly things like this before, they were not prepared to handle the body—and rightly so, I thought. As I searched for a way to carry the body, another worker from the municipality came with a wheelbarrow from the direction of the Farmandari Circle. I thought I would use that. I ran forward, pointed to the body, and asked him for the wheelbarrow.

He stared in horror at where I was pointing and immediately gave me the wheelbarrow. He also joined me and the other two men in lifting the body. The bulk of it fit inside, but the legs dangled from one end and from the other what little was left of the head with blood seeping from the severed arteries. After the men had wheeled the body to the morgue, Evil Zahra returned from the Shatt. There was no sign of enemy planes, and the process of loading people on the boats was running smoothly now. I was about to go back to the mosque, but before I got to the circle, she asked, "If you're going, why don't you come home with me?"

"I'm not feeling well. You go."

"I'm not going alone. You come, too," she said.

"What's the problem?" I asked, "Forget how to go?"

"When that kid fell in the water, I got a bad feeling. Let's go."

"No," I said.

She pleaded so much I had to give in. We passed the circle and turned toward the bridge. A car gave us a ride to the entrance to Kut-e Sheikh. The bombardments had left the neighborhood in ruins, driving most people from their homes. Zahra negotiated alley after alley in silence, and soon it seemed to me that it was taking too long to find her house. Knowing her, I became a little afraid. She had said so many contradictory things in the past that none of the girls trusted her. By now I was worried this was some kind of trap. I started mumbling prayers and, trying to stay calm, I asked, "We haven't reached this house of yours yet? What's the problem?"

She didn't say anything. "Do you actually know your way home?" I asked again. "Or are you just leading me down the garden path? I'm going back."

"Don't. We're almost there," she said.

We reached a brick house decorated with thin white stones. Zahra pounded and pounded on the blue, metal door of the compound, but no one came. The noise brought several people from their homes. When one of them saw us, he said, "Most people have gone since the bombardments."

He turned to Evil Zahra and said, "Your family is in the date grove across the way."

I said, "I'm going back, then."

"No," she insisted, "let's go to the grove."

The man's words put my mind at ease about Zahra telling the truth, so I decided to accompany her. As we were leaving, the man said to her, "Your child was really acting up. Where were you?"

"What child?" I asked in surprise.

Ignoring the man, Zahra said, "Let's go."

"Why don't you answer him? Does he mean your sister? Your brother?"

"Let's go. I'll tell you later," she said.

We walked from Kut-e Sheikh to the date grove across the road. It was extensive, large enough to accommodate quite a crowd. If I hadn't just been through a bombardment at the Shatt, I would have said that it was the beginning of the spring New Year, the time when people came to picnic in the grove. The ground was covered with grass, wild flowers, chamomile, and clover, which perfumed the air. Here and there the palms still had dates, some of which were ripe, on the ground by the trees. The families had taken shelter there and spread carpeting and blankets in the dry irrigation channels that separated one row of palms from the next. They had hung swings from the boughs for the children. Here and there clothes were drying on the ground. Everything was there for a picnic: gas canisters, thermoses, water pipes, cups, plates.... We soon found Zahra's family in the crowd.

As if of two minds, Zahra stood to one side before showing herself to her family. I watched them as they sat in the channel. It was a large family with a number of men sitting around talking and smoking. Several women were looking after the children. A woman who seemed older than the others sat a bit apart, deep in thought. There was a scrawny child with a pale yellow complexion sleeping on one corner of the carpeting. Everything about the child said it was very ill. The poor thing's belly was distended, and his arms and legs were limp and giving him pain. If it weren't for the child's moans, one would think it was dead. After a few moments of indecision, Zahra, looking ashamed and fearful, walked toward her family and said hello.

I also greeted them. At once everybody turned toward us, but it seemed no one was glad to see her. They hesitated before saying hello, then they grudgingly answered and turned away. After a few minutes of silence, she whimpered, “What’s new?”

The woman who was older than the rest said, “What could be new? Your child there is about to die. Go and see what it’s going through. We’ve reached the end of our rope with that child.”

Evil Zahra went to the child and picked it up. Too weak to notice, the child’s head flopped to one side. It amazed me to learn that she was a mother and had abandoned her child like that. There was nothing motherly about her. It was as if she had no feelings for the baby. She didn’t even hug or kiss it. It seemed to me that the baby was about to die. Although the child was one year old, in that weakened state the poor thing seemed no more than six months old. Even I was wilting under the family’s angry stares. I stood by a woman who, I gathered, was Zahra’s mother-in-law. The woman asked, “Was she with you?”

“Yes,” I said.

“What do you do?”

“The truth is that I help out at the Congregational Mosque,” I explained.

“What about her? Is she with you there?” she asked.

“Yeah, in the mosque.”

“Listen, I beg you,” she pleaded. “Her kid is about to die. It’s driving us crazy. The child never enters her mind. She never comes around to see what’s happened to us with all firing going on.”

“Why?” I asked astonished.

“Don’t know,” she said. “You’ll have to ask her that.”

I didn’t ask about her husband, what he did. Whatever the case, it seemed that life was not going well for Evil Zahra. She couldn’t have been that indifferent. Thinking that she had found someone willing to hear her troubles, the mother-in-law said in a thick Lori accent, “Is this any way to live, I ask you, dear? How long do you think we can go on like this? These past few days all the children have come down with something. When is this war going to end? How far have our forces gotten? When are these damned Iraqis going to go back into their holes?”

I didn't know what to tell her. I told her, "Pray, mother. God has to help us." Then I said, "I've got to go."

"Wait," Zahra said. "We'll go together."

"You don't need to do that. Stay with the child."

I said goodbye to them and left the grove. When I got near the bridge a van pulled up and gave me a lift to the Farmandari Circle. Then I walked the rest of the way to the mosque. As I passed the public library and the Ettehad High School, I recalled some schoolboys making a commotion. I imagined that they were playing football or playing piggyback, chasing one another. Now a lot of those boys were at the front.

15

The Girls Beg to Stay

On October 1, 1980, with Iraqi tanks having advanced as far as the Railroad Circle, the men started to think about evacuating families, women, and girls from the city. I heard rumors at that time but didn't attach any importance to them. Things had become so critical that Commander Jahan Ara said the women should leave.

When I heard this, I thought: Let them go. Why should we have to?

Sheikh Sharif Qonuti, the same priest who had given his cloak to Maryam Amjadi, was the only one who thought it was necessary for women to be in the city, as they were vital to getting things done behind the lines. The day after we left the mosque to set up the clinic, another message came demanding women evacuate. No one paid any attention to it. We were busy disinfecting the clinic when Mahmud Farrokhi and several other men, whom we recognized from the mosque, entered. They said, "Sisters, pack up your equipment right now and leave the city."

This made me very upset. Mahmud Farrokhi said, "It's better for you to go. When they tell you to, you have to leave. It's definitely the right thing to do."

We all said the same thing: "Why do we have to go? The Iraqis aren't here yet. When they get near, we'll leave." I motioned to the girls and we stepped forward. I told them, "Look, I'm not going anywhere. Anybody who wants to stay has to stand up to them. If you show any weakness, they'll take us away. But if we show strength, they won't dare lay a hand on us and take us from the city. The upshot is that if we sit tight in the clinic, nobody can force us to go."

The girls agreed, and we told the men. Then they told us Dr. Sheybani wanted his clinic back and we'd have to leave.

"No way," we said. "Where was Sheybani when he said this? If that's true, he can come and tell us himself."

They left and we went on with our work. Less than a half hour later we were busy mopping and sweeping the hallway when the men returned with Dr. Sheybani in tow. "Here he is. Now what do you have to say?" they asked.

I was dumbfounded. How did they find him so quickly? Dr. Sheybani, a quiet, reserved man, said, "I want my clinic back. I want to take the equipment away and lock up and leave the city."

"Fine," we said, "take the equipment. We don't need it. With everything taken away, what difference does it make if the door is locked or not? We want to work here."

The poor fellow hesitated, not knowing what to say. He knew we were right. As he looked at us, the man with Sheybani realized his dilemma and gave him a look, which forced the doctor to say, "No, really, I want to take possession of the clinic."

At that point, I thought the situation called for something drastic. I said, "Okay. You want the clinic back. Take it. We'll just set up another one in the middle of the road, which belongs to no one. Either you let us go on using your clinic or we'll just set up shop where mortar shells will kill us."

The girls backed me up saying, "Yeah, we'll just sit in the middle of the road and take our chances."

We left the clinic and just sat at the corner of Fakhr Razi Avenue, right across from the mosque. They told us to get up, warning us about the shelling.

"We're not budging until we know what's happening," we said.

They kept coming and going, arguing that the middle of the road was no place to sit. The traffic! The danger! We had to wait inside the mosque so we could be evacuated….

When they left we kept saying to one another: Don't back down. If we show the slightest weakness, they'll take us away. Even if they promise we can set up elsewhere, we shouldn't believe them. It would just be an excuse to evacuate us. We weren't leaving Khorramshahr and that was that.

We spent a couple of hours sitting in the heat after the midday call to prayer. I was exhausted after running around all morning evacuating the wounded. The sun was merciless. Noticing some of the girls were weakening, I said, "We just have to hold on a little longer. Otherwise they'll think they can force us to leave any time they want."

For their part the men merely watched us stubbornly, not saying anything. Concerned about us sitting in the traffic, they redirected it around the spot.

Finally, after seeing that they were no match for us, they brought in Sheikh Sharif, who had become quite a figure among the people at that point. They valued his words and actions, and I particularly respected this tireless man of action.

They said that although he had come from Borujerd, he knew all about Khorramshahr and served with the forces in defending it. It was because of these efforts I held him in such esteem.

Once I saw the Sheikh walking the yard at the mosque hitting his leg with a piece of shrapnel. I asked why he was hurting himself like that.

He said, "My daughter, I'm doing it so I'll always be mindful of my physical being, and not allow the Devil to lead me astray. It's not punitive, it's curative."

Now we were face-to-face with the Sheikh. In this past, he had said women should be allowed to stay in the city, but now he appeared to have changed his mind. "Sisters, you have done your duty to this point. We thank for all your efforts, but now it's time to let the brothers take over and for you to go."

I stood up and asked, "Sir, what color is your blood?"

"Red, of course."

"Our blood is the same color as yours," I said. "Why must you stay while we have to go?"

"It's for the best, of course," he said.

"How is it for the best? The situation is not that critical. We're not surrounded or anything like that. I know you are concerned we will be taken prisoner, but we swear it won't happen. We don't want to place a burden on you, but do you imagine if we go the men will do the jobs women do? Shouldn't the men reserve all their strength and energy for the front? Sir, our presence here is necessary. Besides, weren't there women fighting alongside the Prophet in the beginning of Islam?"

"Of course," he said, "but times are different now. Today the enemy is acting inhumanly. You aren't aware of all the facts. You don't know how these godless Baathists are breaking every standard of decency."

"Sir," I said, "since when has the enemy ever behaved decently? They have always acted cruelly. That logic won't win any arguments. We're not leaving. We'll sit right here and won't drink or eat until it's clear what's going to happen to us—no matter how long it takes."

The words I used at that point came from movies about political actions or strikes or out of something I had read in the book *Women Heroes*. Sheikh Sharif asked me, "Why be that way, sister? Why don't you listen to reason?"

"If you recall, you were the one who, during the first days of the war, had said our presence here was necessary. Without the sisters, you said, nothing would get done. Now what's changed to make our being here such a bother?"

I was boiling mad, almost beside myself, burning with rage. I wasn't ready to leave the city under any circumstances. I firmly believed in women working. I saw there were tasks to be done and that women were genuinely capable of doing them. I felt in war men and women both were obliged to defend the country. Besides, it irked me to have men think that we didn't know how to fight, that we would just give up. Surely we were far more sensitive, our pride stronger than that when it came to those things. That was why I was so insistent. The men at times tried to interrupt or speak over me to create confusion.

Finally the Sheikh saw it was no good and asked, "What's your final position on this?"

I said, "We'll stay here until we determine the work we're doing is no longer of use and our presence here is doing more harm than good. Then we'll go. Don't worry. We won't let the Iraqis take us prisoner."

Sheikh Sharif said, “Very well. Now that that’s settled, I don’t want you coming around every day saying you want to go to the front. You have to compromise. When they tell you you can’t go, don’t argue. It’s got to be arranged ahead of time. I’m going to see to it you can stay, and I’m asking the doctor for permission for you to be allowed to work in his clinic. Now get back the work; the clinic will be under your control. God willing, I’ll last long enough to see us drive the enemy from our land.”

This made me so happy I didn’t know what was what. Laughing, we went back to the clinic. Everyone agreed the settlement was the result of our solidarity, and we had to keep watching each other’s backs.

From that day on the Sheikh made sure we had something to do. They brought sacks of weapons around and dumped them in the clinic yard. Most of them were old, worn-out M1s or G3s that came, I suspected, from the base, because there was no word about new weapons entering the city. Many of the boys were fighting without weapons and munitions. As soon as anyone with a weapon fell, they immediately retrieved it.

From the day of our sit-in onward, when there were no casualties to see to or other work at the clinic, we would venture out into the city in search of wounded people. Other times we would sit down with the old weapons and try to fix them. Initially they gave me detailed instructions on what to do. We took apart the guns that appeared to be in good shape. They gave us chains with small brushes on the end to clean out the barrels. We oiled the cocking mechanisms and shined the barrels. Then we put the guns back together. If a gun had a problem that was reparable, we would fix it. With a pair of pliers we straightened cocking mechanisms bent from use. We hammered softly on crooked magazines to straighten them and get them to load easily.

Sometimes instead of fixing the weapons we made them worse, so much so nothing could be done for them. After the weapons were repaired, we loaded the magazines, which saved time for the defenders at the front. A few days of jamming bullets down the magazines with my thumb put blisters on my fingers and made my hands bleed.

From that day on reloading magazines became one of my regular jobs. The boys would come by and carry off the sacks full of weapons and magazines. They would return with loads of empty magazines, worn out weapons, and ammunition for Colts, G3s, and M1s, as well as some RPG rounds all mixed together. While doing this mind-numbing work, the girls and I would and laugh in the quiet of the yard. We asked one another: How many in your family? What are the names of your sisters and brothers? We made it a point that we would visit one another and get together when the war was over.

When we got tired, we snoozed in the dentist chairs. Sometimes the girls would take a spin in the doctor's swivel chair and pretend to be medical authorities. What a kick it was to be a doctor, they thought.

Two other girls joined us: Mehrangiz Daryanavard and Belqis Malekian, who, it seemed, were from Abadan. Despite an obvious limp, Mehrangiz was very active and quick on her feet. Belqis was a quiet, modest girl with an olive complexion and large glasses. Most of the time she carried out her work in silence.

Once when I was busy repairing and reloading the arms, I heard someone speaking with a megaphone. Curious, I wiped my hands with a cloth, got up, and went outside. I saw Major Sharif Nasab in front of the mosque. He was standing on the roof of a pickup addressing the civilian and military forces crowded around the mosque. He was calling on them to accompany him to the base and empty it of weapons and munitions. "We can't let them fall into the hands of the enemy," he said. "Before the base goes, we've got to salvage everything we can from it." But the troops, who thought that orders to take weapons from the base had to come from the high command, were not listening to him. They either remained silent or said that they didn't have permission from the brass.

Delivering messages was the major's almost daily task. I had seen him around. He was a military man around thirty or so with fatigue written all over his wheatish face. There was a nobility and seriousness about him that invited people's respect. Ordinarily he started each day with enthusiastic pep talks to the troops, calling on them to listen to Imam Khomeini and resist the enemy.

He answered the soldier's rejection of his suggestion by saying, "We cannot, with all due respect, let the weaponry we so desperately need fall into enemy hands."

I was astonished to see a woman jump up out of the crowd and grab the megaphone out of his hand. She stood before the crowd and said, "You are soldiers. You're trained especially for such days as these. At this time there are men at the front fighting without your training. Now you're refusing to take action just because there isn't some higher-up standing over you, issuing an order? Your basic training was all about defending your homeland, the honor of the nation. Now that's in danger…."

The woman's brave words had no effect. The poor men had been trained to obey the orders of their superiors and had been punished for disobeying them. Now the situation called for them to act against the dictates of their training, which unsettled them. The most disoriented were the soldiers, whose faces told a story of despair and fatigue.

I felt very sorry for the major. I had criticized him myself once. It was several days before Ali died. Around noon on a scorching day, I saw several military men beside the mosque surrounded by civilian forces and ordinary soldiers. From their epaulettes I reckoned that they were officers of some rank. One of them was Major Sharif Nasab. Another man of about thirty or so, who appeared to be a lieutenant, had a nametag on his uniform that read "Aqareb Parast." The situation at the front and the solders' lack of purpose had made me angry. I felt I had to say something to the officers. I wanted to wait until they were finished talking, but I was afraid they would race away. I stepped forward, greeted them, and said, "Excuse me, are you from military command?"

Major Sharif Nasab smiled and answered in all humility, "I'm military, just a simple soldier."

"Why aren't you doing anything about these soldiers?" I asked. "The forces at the front need these men. They've had training just for times like these. The boys fighting now know nothing about guns and war, while the troops with training are just sitting around. Why don't you do something about mobilizing them and send them forward?"

The poor guy didn't know what to say. Finally he told me, "We're doing our best. These troops are not under one command. They're from different units."

I said, "This time the situation is different. What you say is true ordinarily but not for what's going on now. It makes no sense today to speak about units. Anybody calling himself a self-respecting man has got to fight and defend his country. Why else did they receive the training? Why was the money spent on them? What good is a soldier who doesn't fight?"

Major Aqareb Parast said, "I wish everybody thought the way you do. If only the commanders showed the kind of pride the civilian militias are showing. Then things would be different. But you have to agree, sister, force is not the answer."

I was now in front of the clinic, witness to how powerless Major Sharif Nasab was and feeling sorry for him. I wanted to go and do something but realized it was pointless. I just stood there watching. Then I heard the girls who had stayed behind to work in the city say, "We'll help you empty out the base." I glanced at the major, who was moved to tears. He said, "I thank you, proud sisters, revolutionary sisters. I hope the sight of you at work will make the others act."

There were about ten or twelve of them all climbing into the back of the pickup. The major got down from the roof and, with another man, joined the driver in the front seat. The men around the mosque just stared at them, not knowing what to do. I really wanted to join them, but the need to repair weapons as quickly as possible kept me at the clinic.

The truck started to move, but it hadn't gone far when Afsaneh Qazizadeh, who had been perched on the side with her back to the crowd, found herself dangling halfway out. The other girls quickly grabbed her legs and held on. Suspended over the road, she struggled to right herself. The girls laughed as they pounded on the side of the truck for the driver to stop. The truck halted, and the girls pulled Afsaneh back in. Humiliated by having women do their jobs, the soldiers ran after the truck saying, "Wait! Wait! Get down!" "No," said the girls, "we're going. There's no need for you to come." "Please," begged the soldiers, "get down." One of them joked, "Haven't we been punished enough?"

The major jumped down from the truck and pleaded with the girls to get off. They agreed. After the soldiers took their place and the truck sped off, we all laughed our heads off. These were a very nice bunch. If I hadn't been in mourning, it would certainly have been fun to be with them. But, though I was smiling on the outside, inside I was still in agony. The girls, of course, all had problems of their own.

Most families were against having their daughters stay in the city. The evacuee families even went so far as to send messages to the girls telling them to leave Khorramshahr on their own or they would come to get them themselves.

The first one forced to go back was Ra'na Najjar, who resisted for a couple of days. Others also couldn't overcome their families' objections. The whole the time she waited for her family to come for her, Ra'na was in tears. She'd choke up and say, "I'd love to stay."

"When your family wants you to leave, Ra'na, you don't have any choice," we said.

She cried and said, "I know my being here won't make that much difference, but I want to be with you and do whatever I can."

The day they came for her I wasn't at the mosque. When I came back and saw she wasn't there, I got depressed. The girls told me, "Ra'na was weeping. She sent her regards and told us to say goodbye for her."

Elaheh Hejab also was able to persuade her family a few times to allow her to stay, but finally they took her away. During this period we had become very close. Those who knew their families were coming for them said their goodbyes ahead of time. We comforted one another by saying that Khorramshahr would soon be back to its old self again.

Sabah Vatankhah's family insisted on getting their children. I remember one morning when I was going from Jennatabad to the Congregational Mosque, I saw Fowzieh Vatankhah leaning against a wall, crying. Fowzieh, Shahnaz, and Saleheh were Sabah's sisters. All of them were active in one way or another. I had gotten to know them during these past days. Being from the Mowlavi neighborhood, which had been shelled heavily, they moved to the mosque. Their father had been wounded several days before the move. At first I thought that something was wrong with her. I stepped up to her and asked, "What happened?"

She didn't answer. "Are you upset about your father?"

She cried even more and said, "No, my uncle came and wants to take me away."

"That's not so bad. Go. What's the harm?" I asked.

"You should talk. You can stay and nobody bothers you. Enjoy it while you can. If you were in my shoes, you'd do more than cry."

"Fine. There's still Sabah. They didn't tell her to leave."

"Sabah's on her own; she's got nothing to do with me."

I touched her neck and said, "Don't cry. Come with me to the mosque." "No," she said. "My uncle is there. I don't want to see him."

"How is it his fault, the poor man?"

"It is. He's come with a truck to take me away," she said.

She had said her uncle, who owned a truck, lived in Borujerd and was probably going to come for the sisters. But none of them were ready to go. Their brother was in the army. The sisters loved their brother and wanted to stay in Khorramshahr on account of him.

I took her hand and pulled her to the mosque. Seeing her uncle made Fowzieh cry even more. I said hello to him and asked, "Can't she stay?"

He said, "If Fowzieh stays, then they'll all want to stay. What did I come for, then? Who should I take back? Their mother will be beside herself without her daughters."

Having to get back quickly, I comforted Fowzieh. I kissed her cheek and said, "God willing, you'll be back soon."

I left her standing there and left the mosque. By the time I returned that night, Fowzieh and Shahnaz Vatankhah had gone. Only Sabah and Saleheh, who was helping the army reserves, stayed behind. Having put my own thoughts about the girls aside, I saw the others were busy reliving their own memories. We worked late into to the night under the dim light of the pressure lamp.

That night a team of four or five doctors arrived from Behbehan. The next morning they took some weapons and went to the front. Before we had come to the clinic, there was a doctor/pharmacist there called Sa'adat, who also had come from Behbehan to help. He ordinarily remained at the clinic. He was a tall, thin man with greenish eyes and frizzy hair. He was soft-spoken and a stickler for rules and regulations. The doctor even brought pajamas to the fight and would change into them every night. His bedside manner was so calming and suave he made us look like clumsy barbarians by comparison. The girls would say, "It's clear he grew up in an upper-class family. He's never experienced what we have. Wait till the shelling gets bad, then we'll see what he's made of." The doctors who had come to the clinic the first day were supporters of political splinter groups. Although they were not as chic as Dr. Sa'adat, they didn't stay long. We waited to see how long this new group would last before they quit.

The more we got to know him the more amazing Dr. Sa'adat seemed to us. He was so humble that, if we didn't know better, we would have taken him for a nurse. After he finished with work, he would go to an empty room, close the door, and pray and chant blessings. His chanting was so beautiful that we, listening from behind the closed door, would break into tears. Dr. Sa'adat's spirituality had an influence on all of us. I came to conclusion that the calm Dr. Sa'adat showed in his work at the clinic was a result of his benedictions and prayers. This was contrary to the general feeling that the care and precision in his work was as a result of his aristocratic upbringing. Unlike Mr. Najjar, whom we respected and feared, we got along with Dr. Sa'adat easily. He was respectful and patient with us. We always saw him as an elder, a person we could confide in. I recall on the day of Ali's burial, he asked me, "Where were you, Sister Hoseyni? Haven't seen you all morning." I choked up and started to cry. My voice quivering, I said, "Didn't you hear last night my brother Ali died. I was at Jennatabad for the burial." His face reddened and his eyes filled with tears. He looked down. When I said Ali, like father, had left us on our own, he burst into tears. He then walked from the room with his hands covering his face.

I asked him why he did that. After all, I said, I had come to him for sympathy.

In tears, he said, "No, Sister Hoseyni, that's not in me. Unlike you, I lack the strength." With that he went to his prayer room, and I heard him crying from behind the door. Unable bear any more tears, I left the clinic.

16

The Desert Hospital

I think it was now around October 6 or 7. I was busy working in the clinic when Hoseyn and Leila suddenly appeared. I was startled or, actually, anxious. "What happened?" I asked. "What are you doing here?"

"Khalil told us that his brother Abdollah Mo'avi had been wounded," they said.

I got very upset and asked, "How? Where?"

"We don't know exactly, but he was at the front."

"Where is he now?" I asked.

"We don't know. Even his brother doesn't know."

I didn't have the patience to wait to find out. "Let's go," I said.

The first place we went was the Mosaddeq Hospital. It was deserted. It had been hit once or twice during the heavy bombardment of the bridge and the municipality. When I entered, it seemed abandoned. I tried to find Abdollah, and they told me they were no longer admitting patients and were about to move the ones already there.

I went to the maternity ward. He wasn't there. Then we went to the Taleqani Hospital, which, unlike Mosaddeq, was packed. People there said, "There was a patient by that name here, but they decided to transfer him to Mahshahr."

"Is he in Mahshahr now?" I asked.

"No telling," they said. "The ones who were scheduled to be evacuated they sent to the desert hospital." I had never heard of such a place. I asked them about it, and they said, "It's in Darkhovin, around Shadgan."

It was already afternoon, so I said to Hoseyn and Leila, "We won't make it today. Let's go back and wait till tomorrow morning."

Early the next morning Leila, Hoseyn Eidi, Zohreh Farhadi, Zeynab, and I left Khorramshahr. There wasn't a car to be had. We walked and caught the occasional ride to get to Station Twelve of the Abadan Road. We got a ride on a military vehicle from the station toward Darkhovin. I was very concerned about Abdollah. I had gotten very close to him; he and Hoseyn were like Ali to me.

It was a long way. None of us had ever been to Darkhovin. Hoseyn said, "Desert hospital—the name sounds like it's the result of some crash program."

Eventually the driver dropped us off at the head of a dirt road leading to the desert hospital. A bit down the road there were some containers and a number of tents. There was also a large metal super structure with canvas roofing and a steel door. They had placed barriers fifty meters from the hospital to control traffic. When we reached one of the tents, a guard emerged from it. We told him why we had come, and he asked us to deposit any arms we had with him. We would get them back when we left.

Hoseyn took the M1 from his shoulder and gave it to the guard. I had given the grenades and the G3 to Farrokhi and only had a couple of bullets. These were the same bloodied bullets I took from Ali's pocket. The guard gave us a receipt for the weapons.

We entered the hospital compound. Sandbags were piled high around the containers and the tents. We looked around blindly until someone said that Abdollah Mo'avi was in bed 3 in a large hall where there were about fifty or sixty beds, each with a wounded soldier. We examined their faces. Most of the soldiers were in bad shape. All had dark complexions, meaning they were from the south. There was also a scattering of military from the base among them, but no matter how hard we looked we didn't find Abdollah. We left the hall, and I told the nurse, "We didn't find him. Are you sure he's here? You haven't sent him elsewhere?"

The nurse said, "Go and look again, ma'am."

"Believe me," I said. "He wasn't there. My friends looked also."

"How is that possible?" the nurse asked. "I just visited him myself. How could you have missed him?"

"We missed him. That's all," I said.

The nurse entered the hall with us. When we got to bed 3, she stopped and said, "See—bed 3, Abdollah Mo'avi."

It was unbelievable. Could this be him? So weak and thin? His face was so changed we didn't recognize him. His head was wrapped in so many bandages it looked like he was wearing a turban. Tubes emerged from the bandages, draining blood from his wounds into a bottle beside the bed. Although his eyes were wide open, you could only see the whites. He was very pale. All sorts of monitors were attached to Abdollah's bare chest, and he was breathing oxygen. They were also pumping serum and blood into his veins.

Zeyneb went over to him. Obviously choked up, she struggled to hold back her tears. She bent down and tenderly kissed his bandaged head. Seeing him like that upset me greatly. My eyes filled with tears. I wanted to sit down in a corner and weep. I remembered the way he would make us laugh by messing things up. He did this, I thought, as a way of calming his nerves after he saw something horrible or when something pained him. He was very protective of Leila and me. Whenever a stranger came to Jennatabad, he would stop them and ask what they wanted. "Tell me what you want," he would say. "I'll get it for you."

He always had been all skin and bones, so thin it seemed his stomach was attached to his spine. It didn't feel right to make him do any heavy lifting. But when he saw us doing it, he would get upset and say, "What are you doing? Let me to do it. What am I? Dead or something?" Then he would look down and with his hands motion us to go away. As we got to know him, he became a true brother to Leila and me. He was also especially close to Zeynab, treating her like his mother. When we went to the Darya Bod Rasayi School, the sight of the massacred boy was too much for him. "There's nothing to do at Jennatabad," he repeated. "I want to go." Since his brothers, Hasan and Khalil, were at the front, he thought he should go. We told him, "That's not necessary. We need you here now. Wait." But he left that day, which was the last time I saw him.

"How is he?" I asked the nurse.

"He was hit in the head by shrapnel. He lost a lot of blood and went into a coma."

"What does that mean?" I asked. "What'll happen to him?"

She said, "There's not much hope. The helicopters are ferrying patients who have better chances of survival to Mahshahr. The ones like him we'll send on later."

"When is the next flight?" I asked.

"There's no telling," she said. "Whenever there's a helicopter, we evacuate patients." Then she asked, "Are you family?"

"No. Abdollah was with us in Khorramshahr," I said and briefly explained how I knew him.

She said, "Go now. This is no place for a disturbance. If you want to visit him again, go to Mahshahr. He'll be evacuated there."

We left the hospital but, after handing the guard the receipt, they wouldn't give the weapon back. No matter how many times we asked why, we didn't get a good answer. We got fed up with him and said, "We handed our weapon over to you. You've got to give it back now."

I didn't know whether it was because we looked young or something else. Finally he said, "We won't give you the weapon unless you come with a letter from someone in authority."

We left and had a very hard time getting back to Khorramshahr. As luck would have it Yunes Mohammadi, the representative in parliament, was at the mosque. We got a letter from him, and the next day Hoseyn and I went back to Darkhovin. This time we had no trouble finding Abdollah's bed. It was empty. I asked a nurse where the patient was. "He passed away," she said.

All of a sudden everything went blank. I felt sick, as if I was in shock. Dismayed, Hoseyn asked, "He's dead, fine. What did you do with his body? Give it to us so we can take it to Khorramshahr."

At that point one of the doctors in a crisp uniform passed by. When he saw the state we were in, he asked what had happened.

"Nothing," I managed. "There was a wounded man here we knew, hit in the head by shrapnel. They just told us he's gone."

"What was his name?" the doctor asked.

"Abdollah Mo'avi."

"Mo'avi? Mo'avi was sent off yesterday," he said.

I couldn't think of a better gift than these words. I asked, "Are you sure, Doctor?"

"Yeah. Was he your brother?"

"Yeah, just like a brother."

"Let me check the evacuee list just to make sure."

He went to get the list and said, "Yes, ma'am. Here it is. He was evacuated to Mahshahr."

Our spirits restored, we thanked him and left the hospital. We gave the letter to the young guard. He went to get our M1. "What about my bullets?" I asked.

"Those we're not giving back."

"What do you mean?" I said. "We willingly gave you our weapons and ammunition. I didn't have to tell you they were in my pocket, but I trusted you. It's not right."

This had no effect on him. I got choked up and felt I had to say, "Look, sir, those bullets had my brother's blood on them. I want to keep them to remember him."

He looked down and, after a moment's hesitation, he went into the tent and emerged with the bullets. I took them from him and, miserable, we were on our way.

17

Life Along the Shatt

Ever since I started working in the clinic, whenever there was nothing to do, I would go to the new place where meals were being prepared. They had transferred the kitchen at the Congregational Mosque to a bank compound. To get there I walked toward the Shatt. The glass building was located on the corner of an alley, on the left side of the road just before Ferdowsi Avenue. I turned into the alley and entered the partially covered compound through the back door. Among the mosque women already gathered there and cooking were Mrs. Pur Heydari, Mrs. Fuladi, the mother of Yusof Ali, the mother of Yunes Mohammadi, the mother of Khosrow No'dusti, and others. All were there always working away whenever I visited.

As always, there were sheep in the yard, some of which were donated by people to feed the defenders or had been found wandering in the city and would have died anyway. Religious authorities were questioned about the propriety of eating sheep abandoned by their evacuee owners or felled by hunger or shrapnel. The ruling was that it was permissible to eat them until peace was restored and their owners could be recompensed or that alms be given with the intention of compensating them.

The atmosphere at the kitchen was nice and friendly. Passionate about their work, the cooks would chant and send up prayers to heaven as they prepared food. People treated me with great affection whenever I came by. They tried to draw me out of my shell and restore my spirits after the death of father and Ali. Khosrow's mother, a thin, sharp, quick-witted woman, was devoted to me. She would tell me, "I wish God had made you my daughter." I was very fond of her. She was a knowing and sympathetic person. When we were working in the mosque, she noticed every time I caught my arm on something, I couldn't help groaning in pain. Since my skin was very rough and sensitive, a thread or a button from the clothes we were sorting would tear it open and cause bleeding. The burning and itching were driving me crazy. Khosrow's mother told me to rub sheep fat from the tails of the donated animals on my hands to make them feel smoother.

They slaughtered the sheep in the avenue beside the mosque that faced the bazaar and brought the carcasses to the mosque. One day I asked the butcher if he would give me some tail fat. He cut off a piece the size of my palm and handed it to me on the point of his knife. "That's too much," I said. He cut a smaller piece, which I took to the dispensary. There I sat behind a divider and rubbed my hands and forearms with the fat until my skin was soft and smooth. From that day, every time I saw Khosrow's mother I would say, "God bless you."

Men usually did the outside work at the mess. They loaded the large rice pots on handcarts and brought them to the Shatt. One man would climb down to the shore and fill a bucket or a smaller pot with water and pass it to the men above, who would fill the larger pots. Several times when I was there, the men came back empty-handed. Planes had strafed the shore, and the men had fled leaving behind the pots, which floated away. The look on the poor men's faces was a sight. Embarrassed and ashamed, they were looking to be forgiven, but the women spoke up, "It's one thing you didn't come back with water, but losing the pots is another!"

Once or twice when there was no water, one of the women and I put pots in a wheelbarrow and went to the shore. The first time the sight of the waterway gave me a chill. Enemy planes had hit the tankers and their half-sunken hulks jutted out of the water.

Then I remembered how it was before the war. The scene was firmly etched in my memory. Both sides of the Shatt were lined with trees so lush and leafy that walking under them was like entering a tunnel sheathed in green. The sounds made by passing ships' horns were a reminder we lived in a port city. When the tide was high and the water muddy, gulls and other fowl gathered to hunt fish swimming near the surface. My favorite thing was watching the green dragonflies whizzing among the reeds along the banks.

It was so hot during the day, the samosa, falafel, roast liver, and stewed offal sellers had to wait until sunset to set up shop. Peddlers would spread blankets with expensive foreign goods, clothing, toys … things that people out for a stroll in the cool and refreshing air along the Shatt would buy. Back then people rented rowboats, and boys would fish along the shore. A few meters out to sea, men sat in boats waiting for fish to catch in their nets. Ships from abroad docked at the jetty; the ordinary act of unloading cargo took on a certain grandeur especially in the dark of night. Their lights sparkled on the water, adding to the allure of the waterway. The whole thing made a person want to hole up somewhere comfortable and just drink in the beauty.

We went down the steps leading to a part of the shore where there were no scrub bushes or trees and fetching water was easier. Beaches farther down the shore were clogged with the bodies of fish and the well-fed sharks killed during the shelling. The water stank. The guys said they had seen the corpses of Iraqis there, too. That day the water level was low, and it seemed cleaner, almost glassy. But, despite that, the taste was off. Added to the stench of the rotting fish, which the locals call *zefr*, there was the smell of loose earth and a hint of fuel oil. Trash of all descriptions was also in the water. On previous days, when the level was high, we could easily taste a combination of oil, diesel, and grease, which made it impossible to use the water immediately for cooking or drinking. At the kitchen they would fill large pots and wait for impurities to settle to the bottom. Then they would remove leaves and branches floating on the surface and use the water for washing.

With my thoughts on how the Shatt had changed since those pleasant summer nights, I absentmindedly watched as planes returned to strafe the shore. Several bombs landed in the water, causing it to rise. To keep myself from being dragged in, I had to dive through the filth along the shore. After the planes had gone, I struggled to free myself and emerged from the muddy mess covered head to foot in slime.

18

Eggs

I don't remember what day it was, but it was around 11:00 a.m., and I was busy sweeping the mosque with the long-handled wicker brooms they had recently brought. They were always telling us the mosque was the house of God and to let it get dirty would be a sin. We took up the carpets in the prayer room and swept everywhere. It was difficult to handle the new brooms because we were used to the Arab *sa'af*s, which were made with date palms. We hadn't quite finished with the cleanup, when Mr. Mesbah asked me to come into the yard.

I put the broom down and followed him. He showed me a man in the yard and said, "Gather some sisters and go with this brother. There's work for you in Kut-e Sheikh."

"Do you think it's necessary?" I asked him.

"Yes."

Having complete trust in Mr. Mesbah, I went back to the girls and said, "Let's go. There's work to do."

"Where to?" they asked.

"On a mission" I said with a laugh.

We quickly spread the carpets and left the mosque. As usual Maryam Amjadi stayed behind. Ashraf, Zohreh Farhadi, Sabah Vatankhah, a girl from Abadan, and I got in a waiting pickup and we drove off over the bridge.

The truck pulled up in front of a factory at the end of Kut-e Sheikh and we got out. When we entered the building, we saw it was an egg farm. Two women in work uniforms approached us. One of them asked, "Have you come to help?"

"We don't know exactly, but they told us there was work to be done here." One of the women explained, "Many of our workers have left. During the past few days the eggs have piled up, and if they're not boxed and sent out, they'll spoil."

The girls and I walked around the factory. One of the halls contained white chickens in cages with food and water in front of them. In another hall were eggs spread out on conveyor belts. They told us to put them into cardboard beds, crate them, and tape the tops of the crates. Because of the lack of personnel, eggs for breeding hadn't been separated from eggs for eating. We had to hold the eggs up to the light, and, if there were no embryos in them, we put them in the beds. As we worked I began to regret coming to the place. The other girls also seemed to feel the same way, and I don't know who it was who told one of the workers, "It seems strange to be doing this, given what's going on outside."

"We want to provide eggs for the people in the city or to those who've taken shelter here from surrounding areas."

Around 3:00 p.m. they stopped work and told us to wash up for lunch.

They had spread some carpeting on the floor and unbundled flat bread. Lunch consisted of hard-boiled eggs and the bread. Seeing embryos in some eggs reminded me of the aborted fetuses at the body washers'. The thought made me queasy, but the idea of having eggs for lunch made me feel even worse. I stood aside as the girls greedily peeled the eggs and wolfed them down. They kept insisting I join them, but I refused.

They offered me bits of bread and egg, but not wanting to tell them the reason why I wasn't eating, I could only say I wasn't able to keep it down.

They laughed and said, "For the last few days, it's been bread and cheese. Now that we've got eggs, come and eat. It'll do you good."

"No," I said and walked into the lush flower garden. Seeing lantana there reminded me of mother. Father always planted many kinds of flowers, especially lantana, in the months before the New Year.

With the first day of spring they bloomed, filling the air with the perfume of roses and snapdragons. Just before the New Year, when the weather turned warm, father dug up all of the plants except for the multi-colored lantanas. Because I adored flowers, I cried and asked him why he did this. "I want to plant tomatoes, eggplants, and broad beans," he said.

"So why not pull up the lantanas, too? Is it because mother's maiden name is Shah Pasand?" I asked.

He laughed and said, "Because lantanas eventually grow into bushes, but the other flowers will wilt and die after a few days in the hot sun."

I strolled in the garden thinking about this quiet little refuge from the war. Luckily the Iraqi batteries had not found this spot, but the devastation wreaked on the homes told us the area had not been spared the shelling and rocket attacks.

My thoughts were interrupted when the girls called me back to work. The factory closed at five. The vehicle that had brought us was waiting to return us to the mosque. The driver arranged to take us back the factory the next morning.

I had decided not to return but didn't say anything. With all the work at the mosque, why was it necessary to gather eggs?

Back in the mosque I telephoned Jennatabad to see if someone had brought them dinner.

"No," they said.

I picked up some tins of fish and bread and took off. Not wanting Leila to leave Jennatabad for food, most of the time I brought it to them myself. Naturally, with everything going on, the women sometimes forgot to set aside food for Jennatabad. Sometimes there wasn't enough, so I would bring them something else. On days when there was nothing but bread and cheese, Leila would let it get to her and complain to me, "You couldn't find anything else? I'm dopey from all the bread and cheese I've eaten. You pass a watermelon patch on your way. Couldn't you have brought one of those?"

When she saw the tinned fish, she said, "Amazing!" She had a right to be sarcastic. Before coming to Jennatabad she had always been plump. Often she wouldn't wait for mealtime and, whenever she felt the urge, would prepare something for herself. Now with all the work and the lack of food she had slimmed down; her face was especially drawn. There were dark circles under her eyes. Often, when I was busy working, I found myself worrying about her mental state. I could only imagine the kinds of things she was seeing at Jennatabad. How would she react? After father and Ali died, my relationship with her changed from sister to mother.

Leila did not speak about her own inner turmoil, the pressures at work, or the aggravations at Jennatabad. Once or twice, when we were standing by father's grave, she said to me, "Zahra, the faces of some of these corpses are really terrifying. They're so mangled that I'm afraid to look at them." I didn't know what to say. The only thing I could think of was to invite her to leave the place and come to the clinic. She refused. "At least come to the clinic so we can sleep near each other," I suggested. "No," she said. "I'm not that friendly with the girls there. I'm closer to Zeynab."

For the most part she put up with the psychological stress at Jennatabad, but there were times when she would let it get to her. I would ask her to take the head of a corpse, and she would refuse, saying that she had had it. "From morning till night," she said, "it's been nothing but washing or shrouding or burying."

"Isn't that what you wanted from the beginning—to work at Jennatabad? No one forced you to come. It's not as if you're working for me. You don't have to lift a finger again. So leave," I said.

"It's true. It was my choice, but I'm only human, and I'm dead tired," she said.

She had a point, but there was no other choice. We were drowning in work, and if we broke our word, what would become of the corpses? I was skin and bones compared to her but managed to race around without getting as exhausted. Leila would gasp and break out in a sweat whenever we lifted a heavy coffin. If I moved too quickly for her, she would complain, telling me to slow down.

"Hurry!" I would say. "There's work to be done." Sometimes I would joke, "Leila, I'm not the one in a hurry. It's this martyr; he can't wait to get into heaven."

19

Visiting the War Room

Beginning October 6 or 7 onward, I made it a point wherever I was to get to the food distribution around noon. Hitching a ride on one of the food trucks, I thought, was the best way to get to the front. Sometimes when I asked Mr. Najjar for drugs and medical supplies, he would joke, "Someone take you for a doctor?"

I would laugh and say, "Never pretended to be one."

He would set things aside, telling me to take them along when I went to the front.

With the passage of time, the need for first-aid people at the front became clearer to me. In the beginning I had heard that some boys had died on account of needing some minor surgery. But one of the front-line soldiers told me a story, and then I knew I could no longer stand quietly by. He said, "One of the boys defending the city was hit in the stomach by shrapnel, causing his intestines to fall out. He gathered them with his hands, stuffed them back in his stomach, and started to walk back. He lost consciousness a few times on the way and, after a few hours, died."

One day I picked up the first-aid materials and left the clinic. There were trucks waiting in the alley near where they prepared food. They put the food and the large pots in the truck. When I tried to climb in, they asked, "Where're you going?"

"I want to go and hand out the food," I said.

"What are we for, then? You're a woman. You can't come with us," they said.

With each change of personnel it was the same tug of war. I kept locking horns with them until they finally gave in and brought me along. "What medicines do you need?" I asked them. "I'm a nurse and I want to help with the wounded."

I picked up the sack with the supplies and showed it to them. Then I climbed on and sat by the large pot as the truck started to move. The wind blew the lid off, and I saw they had cooked a kind of stew with white beans. I put a tray over the pot and kept it in place with my hand. The driver went toward the Slaughterhouse Circle from Forty-Meter Road. When we passed the Chasbi Bazaar, I stood up and got a glimpse of the house Uncle Nad Ali had rented two or three months before. It was a beautiful home, and we had put a lot into getting it clean. I wanted nothing more than to see uncle standing outside at that point. We hadn't had any news of them for two weeks. I sat down. Around the Slaughterhouse I saw a young man limping along on the side of the road. He banged on the truck and the driver stopped. They offered him some food. Noticing a wound on his leg, I said, "Come with us. After we hand out the food, we'll return to the mosque and bandage your leg."

He agreed and the truck went on its way. The streets became emptier and the explosions increased the closer we got to the front. The driver would constantly speed up and slow down, making stew and grease slosh over the side of the pot. I kept one hand on the truck and the other on the pot. To keep from being hit by shrapnel each time I heard the whine of a mortar shell, I would drape myself over the pot. All at once the truck slowed, and I raised my head.

Several men with guns standing in front of a Quonset hut motioned to the driver to follow them. The driver put the truck in reverse, leaving the road and moving toward the structure. A few shabby-looking defenders in grubby clothes emerged. As usual, as soon as they their eyes fell on a woman, they began to protest, "It's not safe here. Iraqis are liable to crawl out of their holes any moment now."

I ignored them. One of them, who seemed to be the commander and had a radio, said to the driver, "You can't go further. From this point on you're in range from the air."

"So what should we do?" one of the boys asked. "We've got food for the front."

He said, "Let us take it in for you. The situation is no good at all. The forces are tired. We don't have many people left, and, if we don't get reinforcements, the boys won't be able to resist them. Go back and tell them we must be rotated out."

I asked, "How far away are our forces? You mean we can't get there ourselves?"

"No," he said.

"So, how are they are getting there themselves?" I asked.

"With difficulty," he said. "The Iraqis are spread out all over the place. We're here to make sure the Iraqis don't cut them off, but there's no telling how long we can hold out."

While the boys unloaded the stew, water, and munitions, I was busy bandaging the boy's leg. The driver said, "We're going toward Railroad Circle."

He said, "Don't go by way of the Slaughterhouse otherwise you'll definitely be taken prisoner. They may even grind you to dust with their tanks, which are all over the place. Go another way."

As the truck started moving, the boy jumped down, saying he wanted to stay. "If you put pressure on that wound, it'll start to bleed again," I told him.

"You've bandaged it. It's fine. I'll go to the hospital if I have to."

The driver took the route suggested by the man. He stopped a few times on the Forty-Meter Road to see what was going on. He asked the boys in the back whether to go or not. The soldier's warnings had made them cautious. They told me to get out because of the danger ahead.

"I'm not leaving until it's over," I said. "Wherever you go, I'm going."

"It's not safe," they said.

"If so, it's dangerous for everybody not just me."

The driver turned from Naqdi and headed toward Shahram Avenue, which ran behind the stadium. Then the driver changed his mind and went on the Moqbel Circle toward the Railroad Circle. The firing grew louder. We saw personnel carriers, jeeps, and fire engines moving up and down the street. We asked the soldiers in the jeeps coming from the direction of the houses at the municipality if they wanted food.

"Sure," they said.

"Do you have a container?" I asked.

They handed us a metal can with handles like a jerry can. We dished out the food and made sure each person had a piece of bread. Then we passed the neighborhood where the engineer Behruzi's house was. I had been here several times looking for wounded. The shelling had destroyed some of the homes. The trees along the avenue were also burnt. I remembered the good times we had, and, despite the hardship, I was in a good mood.

Just before the Railroad Circle we had to stop because of the explosions. The driver switched the motor off in front of the Ibn Sina School. We got out to look for defenders. Then the air got heavy with a mysterious silence. We couldn't find our wounded no matter how hard we looked—there was only the sound of distant shelling.

There was no sign of schoolboys chattering or shouting "Allah Akbar." The quiet was even more unnerving than the explosions. It didn't seem normal to me; maybe it was a trap. They told us not to get separated and not make a sound as we walked.

They told me specifically, "Sister, watch your back." Then they formed a phalanx around me and we went forward.

We were all unarmed. I don't know why I hadn't grabbed the G3 from the clinic. I kept my hands on the grenades in the pockets of my chador. I was gripped with fear from head to toe. This was the perfect place for an ambush. Always longing to join father, I wasn't afraid of death, but I didn't want to be taken prisoner. The idea tormented me. I took one of the grenades out of my pocket and squeezed it so I'd be ready at a moment's notice to pull the pin. Sheikh Sharif's words echoed in my mind. Responding to the boys' questions, he said suicide was not permissible under any circumstances; pull the pin only to kill the enemy. The blast will destroy you, and it'll also keep you from falling into their hands.

I thought about the boys. What would they do if I were taken? It would drive mother to her grave. I had to make sure that it would never happen. Then I asked myself if I could do what Sheikh Sharif said: Take out the enemy as well as kill myself? In that case I had to use both grenades. I'd pull out the pin of one with my teeth and throw it at the enemy; then I'd quickly pull the pin on the second and finish myself off. Thinking more deeply about it, I asked myself if I really had the nerve to kill myself? I had heard from common people and defenders that despite what Saddam and his forces said about the Arab character, they were nothing more than criminals. Our boys said, "Come and see what happened to the women and children in places they have captured. They think nothing of attacking women and don't even show mercy to the Arab villages."

Imagining the shame and humiliation of prison camp, I concluded I would pull the pin. It was a difficult decision. I told myself it was inevitable, and there was no point ruining my nerves thinking about it.

We proceeded quietly and cautiously and entered a narrow alley, seemingly a dead end lined with high walls that gave it a somber air. We kept our eyes pealed and ears open to any sign of wounded. Suddenly a young person stepped from a doorway and, at the same time, a mortar round hit the wall to the left of us. The blast slammed me to the ground. Terrified, my first thought was to get up immediately. I struggled to spread my arms. My eyes weren't working, and my ears were ringing with the sound of the explosion. I felt very groggy and couldn't get my hands to stop trembling. This lasted several minutes. I heard the men asking, "Are you okay? Are you hit?"

"Just dizzy. I can't get up. Help me."

"It's not serious; you were caught by the blast," they explained.

After I felt a little better and could stand on my own two feet, I looked around and saw a wounded young man, the same one who had emerged from the doorway. I wanted to run to him, but my feet got tangled. One of the boys was worse off than I and was unable to get up. He started foaming at the mouth, and his eyes bulged from their sockets. I got very frightened. The driver and the other man with us took him under the arm and carried him aside and leaned him against a wall. He didn't respond to what they were saying and didn't even move.

I went to another wounded person. Debris from the explosion littered the alley. The man was lying on his side and blood was spurting from the veins in his neck. I was terrified, but, trying to staunch the wound, I put my hand on the bleeding without thinking. My hand became covered in blood, but the bleeding didn't stop. His flesh was torn in several places. When I put pressure on it, the young man moaned. "Bring the first-aid," I screamed.

The driver ran to get it. "Betadine," I said.

He opened the bottle and handed it to me. I poured all of the yellow disinfectant over the wound. "Gauze," I said.

Holding the wound together with one hand, I put gauze on it with the other and applied pressure. I still felt woozy and couldn't work rapidly. I was afraid that the other young man had lost consciousness and might die. I asked the driver to help. He raised the man's head while I wrapped a bandage around his neck. The gauze and bandage became all bloody. I put down several more layers of gauze and wrapped the wound again. The young man's eyes were half-open, staring feebly at some point in the distance. His green jacket turned blackish with blood. The jacket told me that he was an officer. I said, "Let's take off his jacket so he'll breathe easier."

I got to my feet. There were five soldiers, all armed, standing around us. Some were also wearing military caps.

The sounds of shooting and artillery exchanges got closer and closer. One of the soldiers hoisted the wounded man on his shoulder. "It'll be harder for him to breathe that way," I said.

He put the man on the ground. Several people came forward and carried the man to the truck. They also helped the shell-shocked boy sitting by the wall to his feet and led him slowly by the hand to the truck. Then they unloaded the pots and told the other soldiers to distribute the food.

The soldiers laid the wounded man in the truck and put the boy at the other end. I sat on the edge of the truck with my legs dangling. We had yet to move when a mortar shell landed between the truck and the soldiers who had taken the pots. There was the sound of earth breaking open, and I saw and heard shrapnel going in every direction. This is where my head comes off, I thought, and it took less than a second for some to whizz by me and burrow into the asphalt. I looked at it. It was the size of my palm. A soldier, who was returning with us, was standing in the back of the truck. He said, "Ma'am, if you sit there, you'll be thrown off. Let's change places." I gave him my place and went to where the wounded man was. The driver stepped on the gas, and we raced off as mortar shells exploded around us. As the truck jerked up and down on the hilly road, I kept my eyes on the wound in the young soldier's neck. The bleeding had slowed, but his condition was getting worse by the minute. I prayed to God the shrapnel that kept striking the truck chassis never found the tires, otherwise it would be all over for us. Suddenly the shell-shocked boy, who had been sitting with his legs stretched out, quietly, not troubling anyone, started to foam at the mouth and his eyes went back into his head. He began to shake. I looked at him. His gaunt and lifeless body told me that he hadn't eaten for days. His cheeks were sunken and his bony face spoke volumes about how it had been for him. He seemed to be the dockworker type. The men on either side of him tried to hold him still. His mouth foamed up again, and his olive complexion turned yellow. Going back the driver retraced the way we had come.

After we were out of range, he stopped on Forty-Meter Road. He stuck his head out the window and asked, "Where to, ma'am?"

"Taleqani," I said. "His condition is so serious we won't be able to do anything for him at the clinic."

"Can he make it?" he asked.

"That's up to God," I said.

The truck moved so fast it didn't take long for us to reach the hospital. Before the driver could turn around and back up, one of the men had jumped down and returned with several nurses and a stretcher. They lowered the man out and brought him at a run to the operating room. Then they helped the shell-shocked young man out. In that state, the poor kid was ready to do anything they told him. They transferred him to the emergency room.

The driver drove me back to Khorramshahr and dropped me off at the mosque. Though still groggy, I could tell things weren't right there. It was as if an autumn wind had blown everything away. The road to the mosque, which was always the busiest in the city, was empty. There was no sign of the usual hustle and bustle in front of the entrance. The few people I did see were in their own worlds. I assumed shells had hit the area causing casualties and emptying the place. I asked someone, who was coming out from the mosque, "Has something happened? Why is it like this?"

"Don't you know?" he asked. "They executed some people."

The word "executed" sent a chill down my spine. I was terrified by the word. Once, before the victory of the revolution, father had bought a newspaper that reported several terrorists had been executed. Angered by the headline, father said, "The Shah's regime—there's the real terrorist! And they have the nerve to call people fighting for freedom 'terrorists.'"

Father stared at the faces of the executed people and cried silently. He was depressed and withdrawn for a few days and wasn't able to eat. Now the word "terrorist" conjured up "Fifth Column" in my mind. "Who was executed?" I asked. "What did he do?"

"You haven't heard?" he said. "A guy was going through the pockets of the dead and wounded."

"How come?"

"They caught him and Mr. Khalkhali set up his court, declaring him a 'sower of corruption on earth.' Then they tied him to that tree over there and shot him. Afterwards they took his corpse away."

I looked at the tree he pointed to. It was in front of the mosque at the corner of Fakhri Razi. Then he added, "People say that in court, when they asked him why he had done it, he said nothing to defend himself and accepted the verdict."

I left the yard and walked to the tree. It was a large, harmless thing, its trunk studded with bullets. A branch had fallen from it. Its leaves and broadbean-looking yellow seedpods lay grieving on the ground. Seeing the blood on the ground at the base of the tree made me sick. From that time on I always had a bad feeling about the spot.

I went back in the mosque. It puzzled me that, given the conditions, a person would do such a thing when death could come any time. Nevertheless, I didn't feel good about them executing the man.

After my nerves had settled and the wave of gloom, which had broken over me when I heard about the execution, had passed, I went to find Ebrahimi and report what I had seen at the front.

"More things to tell me?" he asked.

"What can I do? Who else is there?"

"Sister," he said. "You've got to tell the commanders and the people in charge. They need to know the situation. They're the ones who can give the orders to change things. What do you expect me to do? What are you telling me for? I'm just a flunky who answers the phone and coordinates things at the mosque."

"Where am I supposed to find the commanders?" I asked. "Let me know and I'll tell them myself."

Afterward I told Ebrahimi several times that I wanted to go to the War Room. "No way," he said.

"There's always a way," I replied.

It was like the first days of the war again, when I wouldn't give Ebrahimi a moment's peace. Finally, I was in the yard and Ebrahimi called me over and said, "Come, you want to see the commanders. These people are going to the War Room this afternoon. You can go with them."

Terrified I asked, "Who is going?"

He pointed to a few young men and said, "Those standing by the car." Then he said to one of them, "This is the Sister Hoseyni I was telling you about."

I stepped forward. There were about eight young men, but the one in a military coat appeared to be in charge. The rest of what he was wearing was ordinary. He asked me, "Why do you want to go to the War Room?"

"Because of the situation we're in."

"Do you think," he asked, "we haven't told them what's going on? That they don't know it in the War Room?"

I looked down at his sneakers and said, "Fine, but I want to tell them myself. Maybe it'll do something."

He rolled a sheet of paper he was holding into a tube and, after a few minutes of silence, said, "Yeah, not a bad idea. If they see that sisters are also raring to fight, maybe they'll give a thought to the war. Maybe this'll wake them up a little."

Happy now, I asked him, "So how are we going to meet up and go to the War Room?"

He said, "It's not that simple. First I have to say something. Our commanders go to the War Room, but nothing gets done. You think you can just go there and turn the whole war around? No, sister, nobody buys anything they say. That's the problem."

"Fine," I said. "What you say is true, but I feel I must go there and say something. It might make them think. Maybe if I stand my ground and press the issue, it'll make them follow up. Everybody's waiting for orders from above. Even if orders don't come, at least they'll know where they stand."

"I keep saying it can't happen," he said, "and you keep insisting it can. I say don't go, you say let's go."

After half an hour of bickering with his companions, he got fed up. The others were saying, "It can't happen, sister. Happy? It's not something you can do just like that." "Come and see what it's like yourself," he shouted over them, "and stop pestering us!"

"Please, give me the address," I said.

"What address? You think that this is like visiting auntie? This afternoon or tomorrow morning I'll come for you at the mosque."

"I'm always around here somewhere. If I'm not, tell Mr. Ebrahimi and he'll get word to me."

I said goodbye and went back into the mosque. All afternoon I kept my eye on the door, waiting for them to come. But I soon got tired of that and said to myself: Maybe they'll come tomorrow or some other day. Fearing they would come when I wasn't there, I didn't dare leave the mosque area or the clinic. I wondered who would be in the War Room and how I should start the conversation. The day that Banisadr came to Khorramshahr, I tried everything I could to reach and speak with him. I don't know which day of the war it was. After burying the dead, I brought the wounded to Taleqani Hospital, where the nurses confronted me grumbling that I couldn't keep depositing wounded with them. This put me in a foul mood when I entered the mosque. I searched for someone to see if they could do something. They had to take responsibility for the dead and wounded and make the hospitals coordinate their work. Each had its own quota. There shouldn't have been arguments about taking in the corpses. Eventually we would bring them to Jennatabad or they could keep them in their morgues until they could be taken to Abadan for burial. Finding transportation for the bodies and convincing drivers to take them were other problems. I had no choice but to force anyone I found to work.

That day I hung around the mosque until late afternoon. I had heard that the War Room was outside of town. I thought if the visit lasted into the night, it wouldn't be right to go alone. I didn't know the people. I said to Zohreh Farhadi, "Will you come with me somewhere?"

"Where?" she asked.

"I'm going somewhere. Just tell me whether you'll come."

"I'm coming," she said. "But tell me where."

"It's not a bad place, Zohreh," I said.

"I know it's not a bad place. I know you're not a member of any of those groups."

I said, "Zohreh, I want to go to the War Room, but don't tell anybody. Okay?"

Her eyes opened wide and she asked, "The War Room?"

"Yeah. Just keep your ears peeled; they'll be around any time to pick us up."

Not long after this, as it happened, they did come for us, saying, "Get in the truck, ma'am."

Zohreh and I left the mosque. As we were about to get in a young man left the passenger seat by the driver and, in a way that Zohreh couldn't hear, said, "Just you, sister. This other sister cannot go into the War Room. It'll do no good to argue. So don't. Okay?"

I was so anxious to get there as quickly as possible, I said, "Fine. Fine."

"We first have to get passes," he said.

Zohreh and I got into the Toyota and we left. To get the passes we stopped at Farmandari and several other places. Finally we had five passes with our names on them. Beside Zohreh and I, there were three young defenders sitting in the back of the truck talking among themselves. They didn't seem like ordinary soldiers. From the bits and pieces of what they were saying, I could tell that they didn't speak about the war the way simple soldiers did. Their seasoned analysis of the conditions told me that they were military intelligence.

Zohreh and I spoke while, at the same time, we listened to the young men, hoping to learn something about what was going on at the front. "Do you think you have enough nerve to go and talk to higher ups?" she asked.

"Of course. Why not? What else should I do?"

"What do you want to say?" she asked.

This made me think. Actually what did I want to say? How should I begin? All of the bigwigs would be there. I hoped to God there would be a familiar face, someone to keep up my spirits, to make it easier speak freely.

We went over the bridge and from a place on Behruz Alley or Arya the truck entered a military compound and stopped in front of a building. It looked to me like one of the naval headquarters' buildings. We got out of the car and entered the hallway. Metal plaques on the doors identified the offices: Logistics, Command.... The head of the group stopped in front of a door and said, "Wait here." He went into the room. I heard him presenting our passes one by one. He came out, turned to me, and asked, "You're the Seyyedeh Zahra Hoseyni?"

I was amazed he knew my name. "On my ID, my name is Zohreh, but my real name is Zahra," I explained.

"They won't need a copy of your ID. Come in for a minute," he said.

I entered with him. There was a soldier in civilian clothes behind the desk. He asked, "Zahra Hoseyni, that's you?"

"Yes."

"Wait outside," he said.

I sat beside Zohreh on a bench in the hallway. The young soldier came out and said, "Stay here until they give you permission to enter." Then he went away. I had butterflies in my stomach. I looked myself over. I was dusty and shabby looking. I got up and went into the yard to shake off my clothes. I beat my chador against a column to get the dirt off. Then I went back inside and waited. There were lots of soldiers and runners going back and forth. I was on the verge of getting what I wanted. I had heard so much about the War Room and was curious to see what went on there. Were they really at work on the war? If they were, why were we in the situation we were in? What was it like in the War Room? There was probably a large round table in the middle with freshly minted colonels sitting around it and stacks of maps and equipment. I got more nervous the longer I waited. After all the sarcasm about how it was useless for me to go, I was afraid to come back empty-handed. People wouldn't take me seriously after that. This made me so jittery that the things I had planned to say were slowly slipping from my mind.

I called on God to help me tell them about the pain we were going through, about the injustices inflicted on the boys at the front lines. These boys without weapons, without aid, without food—how long could they hold out? We waited behind the door about three quarters of an hour. Finally, a soldier opened the door and said, "Come in, please."

I got up. I was in a strange state. There were butterflies in my stomach. I said to Zohreh, "Stay here until I come out."

"You have to convince them we need weapons badly. Tell them to send reinforcements from other cities. Don't forget to mention the state of the dead and conditions at the front lines," she said.

"Pray for me," I said and went in.

Another door opened, and I entered the War Room. No one noticed me at first. I looked around the room. I was shocked by what I saw. The War Room was not what I had imagined. It was a large room lit by a fluorescent light. The walls were papered with maps, and there were two people sitting by radio sets at the end of the room listening to the scratchy voices coming from them and taking notes. Then they showed the notes to officers sitting in chairs or standing around a table. Nearer to the door several uniformed people and civilians were seated on the floor around some carpeting, talking to one another. A couple of them seemed very young. The rest appeared over fifty. I was surprised at how young the commanders were. It appeared that one of the older men was not doing that well; his face was pale and he was shaking visibly. I guessed he must be Colonel Rezavi. I had heard that he had recently come down with typhoid and was in bad shape. The poor thing was forced to stay at the front with a fever in command of his troops. They said he had close cooperation with the army. I felt ashamed, standing in front of all these men, but it hadn't been easy getting here so I couldn't waste the opportunity. I sensed if I didn't make my presence known, they would go on working without noticing me. "Hello," I said in a loud voice.

The sound of a woman's voice made all of them turn their heads toward the door and stare at me. Then a colonel, who was older than the rest and was leaning on the table, said, "Hello, dear, welcome."

I removed my shoes and stepped on the carpeting. The same colonel asked, "Tell me, dear, what is it that you want?"

Hearing the word "dear" made me choke up. His tone was affectionate and fatherly. I got the sense they had told him I was coming. I entered and, with a lump in my throat, started, "I came here to…."

I couldn't continue and had to wait a few moments for the lump to go away. The strain in my voice and my hesitation made them more attentive. I began again, "The truth is I've come to talk about conditions in Khorramshahr. I don't know how much you know what it's like for the people. What it's like at the front. I want to tell you about it. The people have had it. They are losing their homes, their possessions, what they've worked for all their lives. The forces at the front—there are so few of them. They don't have an ounce of strength left to fight. As is well known, they're short on weapons and equipment. It's gotten to the point the boys are firing bullets at tanks. Tell me: Is it possible to stop a tank with a G3?"

"How do you know the situation at the front?" the colonel asked.

"I went and saw for myself what's going on," I said.

"You went and fought?" he asked.

"No. I didn't fight. I brought food, water, and munitions. I went to help with the wounded. I'm an aid worker. My father told me about the front."

I couldn't go on. At the mention of my father, the tears started flowing. I fought them back and I continued, "My father was not military, but stood like a man before the enemy for five days until he was martyred. He didn't retreat. My brother escaped from a hospital in Tehran and fought here for two days before he was also martyred." I hiked up my chador and held out my arms and said, "I buried both with these two hands. Now there's only me and my sister. Like everybody else, we help in any way we can—burying the dead or seeing to the wounded. But I've seen soldiers running about, not knowing what to do. Why don't you get them organized, give them weapons? They're waiting for orders from above. So give them some so they can go and fight. I've spoken to a number of them who say that some commanders have run away. How should we fight, then? Why should we? Gentlemen, many of us know the person who calls himself president is a traitor. Banisadr and many of the bigwigs around him are traitors. Those of you who've remained have to do something. You're the commanders. We don't have the power to change things, and we don't know what else to do."

I looked up several times to see if they were listening. Most of them were shaking their heads in sorrow. It seemed like some were in shock, staring at me with tears in their eyes. Others were whispering, which heartened me. So I went on, "We have been waiting for the army from Quchan. When will it get here? They keep promising the front-line fighters that reinforcements are on the way. So where are they? If there are no reinforcements, at least give us women weapons so we can defend our homes." One of the two men bent over a map looked up and asked, "You mean there are still women in the city?"

"Yes, of course," I said. "And a lot more than a few. I'm sure if they were to get their hands on weapons, they wouldn't have a problem going to the front."

Some of them responded by saying, "Bravo! Bravo!"

That made me mad. It seemed like they were just trying to pacify a child. "Look," I said, "I've come here to tell you about this so you'll tell the upper ranks. No one listens to what we say. No one knows who we are, but everybody respects you as the commander."

Although I was bursting with more to say, I realized I had stopped. Then the colonel said, "The presence of sisters like you is good for our morale. If it weren't for you, many tasks would be neglected."

Another man said, "God bless your father! Bravo! I mean it."

The colonel continued, "Daughter, you may be young, but you're fearless and you speak very well. Your analysis is quite good. But you've got to realize this is not the time and place for such talk. We know a lot about what's happening ourselves, but in today's conditions, it's not right. You can't say everything you want with impunity. You've got to watch it. We're all friends here, but in other places such talk might cause problems for you."

I said, "What I said was not untrue. I'm telling you what I saw. I'm not making anything up."

"I know you're right," he said, "but you can't say everything. We've got to maintain our solidarity. What you say will cause dissent and duplicity."

"You mean," I asked, "I should close my eyes when I see treachery? Isn't treachery itself the cause of dissension? That's worse."

He insisted that I shouldn't speak so openly about Banisadr's treachery, but I wouldn't give in on this one point. "Even if they put me in front of a firing squad," I said, "I'm going to stand by what I say. He won't let the army defend Khorramshahr. We're not blind. We see how the soldiers are serving their country, but we also see the traitors. We know who they are and won't stop saying so. You should go to the front yourselves and see how the army, the guards, and the civilian forces are fighting side by side. Any self-respecting people realized they must stay and defend the city. Some don't even know which end of a rifle is up, how to load it; but they've gone to the front anyway and become target practice for the enemy. Come to the city and see the soldiers running about, not knowing what to do. Major Sharif Nasab stands in front of the mosque and talks till he's blue in the face, but some soldiers don't listen to him, because they have to get orders from their own commanders. It's like talking to the wall."

"God willing, things will be straightened out. You should pray for that. We will do what we can. We'll be around to support you and won't hesitate to do whatever we can. Where is your family now?"

"I sent them out of town a few days back."

In the end I said, "So long as there are people in the city, you here can do something. The higher ups may be traitors, but you have the backing of the people. You should use this to try to bring some order to the situation."

The colonel along with a few others said, "Will do."

I didn't know what else to say, then, but goodbye and left the room. I was still trembling. I never thought I could say as much as I did. Although I had to stop a few times to choke back the tears, I thought that my voice was forceful and clear.

As soon as I emerged, Zohreh came running over and asked, "What happened? Why is your face so red? Did you tell them what you had wanted? What did they say?"

"Yeah, but let me tell you later."

Zohreh took my hand and sat me in a chair. Then she brought me some water. We waited there for the young soldier to come. Gradually I calmed down and told Zohreh the story. She said, "Thank the Lord. I hope they take it seriously and do something."

Even if they don't, I thought, saying what I said was more important than remaining silent.

On the way back to the mosque the soldiers made a few stops. "We have to follow up on a few things," they explained. I said nothing, not wanting anyone to pester me with questions about what was said.

I didn't even want anyone to see me with my face red like that. I prayed to God I wouldn't see Ebrahimi.

It was dark when we reached the mosque. After getting some dinner, I went to Jennatabad.

The next day when Ebrahimi saw me, he said laughingly, "Word is you made a shambles of the War Room."

"Who told you?" I asked.

"It's not important how information gets to me. What's important is that I get information."

20

Abadan

It was, if I'm not mistaken, the sixteenth or seventeenth day of the war, around 1:00 p.m. I was at the clinic busy repairing and loading rifles when somebody said that they'd brought in wounded. I hastily grabbed a stretcher and went out. A wounded man lay on the floor of a fire truck. Shrapnel had hit him in the knee, and he was in agony. We called out to Mr. Najjar, who came and examined him. "The knee's probably shattered," he said. "Bring him down."

I brought Mr. Najjar's medical bag. As always, we first closed the wound and set up a serum drip. The wounded man, a member of the fire brigade in a blue uniform, was groaning in pain. Terribly weakened from the loss of blood, he was perspiring and shaking. Mr. Najjar gave him a sedative. Then we bandaged the wound and put a splint on his leg. We told the men with him to keep his leg stable in the van so he would not feel more pain. I held the serum bag.

On the way to the hospital, I said hello to Hatem, the fire truck driver, who told me how sorry he was to hear of father's death. Long ago I had gotten to know Hatem and his Arabic-speaking family. They were neighbors of grandfather and Aunt Salimeh. Hatem's wife was very close to Salimeh. Any time they had a Persian-speaking guest she asked Salimeh to join them to help greet the guests and cook Persian food. On the holidays important to the Arabs, Eid-e Fitr and Eid-e Qorban, Hatem's family would visit us, and father and mother would go to their house for the traditional rounds of visitation.

Hatem was driving fast, which made the low moans of the wounded man turn to sharp cries whenever the truck hit a bump in the road. Since the start of the war, I had traveled this road so often I knew every dip, rise, and pothole by heart. The surface was cratered by mortar shell hits, and dug up even more by bulldozers collecting earth for sandbags. There were ornamental date trees in the median, which, because they were sterile, were dubbed "Abu Lahab." Although they weren't very tall, the tops of the trees were charred. I also knew where all the unexploded mortar shells were and the two or three burned-out hulks that littered the sides of the road. All of these things were so fixed in my mind I thought I could navigate the road with my eyes closed. The most difficult part of the route, after going over the bridge, came when we turned left from the gas station and headed for Abadan. At that point the geography put us in range of the Iraqis stationed on the other side of the Shatt. What frightened us even more was the possibility that they would hit the gas station, causing everything around it to go up in smoke.

They brought a stretcher to the door of the emergency room, and the nurses placed the wounded man on it gently. I handed the serum bag to one of them and entered the hospital with Hatem. I saw a couple of the boys from the mosque there. We greeted one another and they asked, "Did you bring in a wounded man?"

"Yeah," I said. "The man on the stretcher."

"You have a way of getting back?" they asked.

"Yeah. That red truck outside the door," I said.

"Then we'll come with you. The car that brought us didn't wait."

Hatem came by and the boys said hello. A fireman colleague of Hatem's sat with the boys in the back of the truck, while I sat with my back against the cab.

On the way back to the mosque, the firing was much worse than it was in the morning. Several mortar shells landed. Poor Hatem was at a loss; he would floor the gas and race ahead, then he would slam on the brakes, sending us careening into the sides of the truck. At the dangerous turn in the road, Hatem screamed, "Get out, get out! The truck's about to fly into the air!"

"Stop! Stop!" the men shouted.

"I can't. They'll hit us. Jump out and take cover!"

Mortar shells were flying everywhere. When we first heard the awful whining sound they made, we were terrified they would find the truck. Hatem slowed a bit, and the boys from the mosque jumped out and rolled down the embankment next to the road. The other men also immediately dove from the sides of the truck, leaving me wondering what to do. I first thought I would jump down, but it seemed too far to fall and I changed my mind. I managed to reach the door and held on tight to my chador. I looked down at the asphalt and then at the dirt embankment beside the road, trying to figure out how I would jump out and not get too hurt. Hatem kept shouting, "Jump, girl! Quickly!" I had to jump and roll down the hill, I told myself. I'd probably break both legs if I jumped feet first. These calculations took but a few seconds. I closed my eyes and, with a cry of "Ali!" flew into the air.

As I was suspended for a moment between heaven and earth, a mortar shell went off about four meters away, burning my leg. Although I'd done my best to land on the dirt beside the road, my left arm hit the asphalt, making it feel it was on fire. I rolled immediately and came to a stop on the slope of the embankment. My arm ached terribly, and my right leg was scorched above the knee. I rubbed it gingerly. I realized from the wetness on my hand that I'd been hit by shrapnel. I gently felt the wound but found no sign of the shrapnel. I tried to turn over on my stomach and look down the road, but I was unable to roll on my left side.

In the midst of all the explosions and tremors beneath our feet, one of Hatem's fellow firemen shouted, "Isn't there anybody out there to help us? Damned heathens, that's enough! O Abol Fazl, HELP!"

The boys laughed and said, "Don't worry, uncle, this is nothing. It's about to stop." Then when they saw me lying on the ground that way, asked in loud voices, "Are you hurt?"

"No," I said.

I raised my head a bit. Hatem had abandoned the truck in the middle of the road and run to the desert. We waited for a direct strike on the truck or for a piece of shrapnel to hit the gas tank and send it flying. I asked myself: If the shrapnel that had hit me in the leg had hit the back of the truck, would I be nothing more than ashes now? If God didn't will it, not even a leaf would fall from a tree. I looked at my leg; there were two holes in my jeans. The denim prevented the wound from being larger than it was. We stayed flat on the ground for about twenty minutes, after which the firing moved away and concentrated on Taleqani Hospital. We got up and walked to the truck. Shrapnel had turned it into a sieve, and one of the front tires was punctured. It would never work again, I thought. To that point the only good car I had been in was the ambulance that brought Ali to the hospital. This truck had been the most well-kept, soundest vehicle I had ridden in.

We got in and left. The flat tire made going on the road hard and going over the bridge even harder. The boys and the firemen had become friends by now and were talking. The one that made such a fuss during the shelling was now joking about panicking. "Strange how much we're attached to our own souls!" The others were describing the bruises they had gotten from flying off the truck at that speed.

When I got back to the clinic, the first thing I did was go into one of the rooms and closed the door. I rolled up my sleeve and looked at my arm. My skin was all red and raw, the veins on the surface having run dry. The pain in my arm was getting worse, and each time I tried the arm, I groaned. It was much worse the next day. The redness gave way to black and blue bruises and as I worked, it bothered me so much I almost fainted. I took some painkillers, but they didn't help. I told Mr. Najjar about it and he gave me Novalgin, which Belqis Malekian injected in my arm. I didn't have a change of pants, so I went to the Shatt and washed the soiled ones. From being submerged in the Shatt and dragged through the dirt, my chador was a filthy mess, dotted with white blotches. Every time I went to Jennatabad, I would take it off and bang it against a tree, hoping to at least remove some of the dirt. Under these conditions, however, I didn't dare part with it. But, despite that, something would happen that made me take it off.

Once, when I was in Jennatabad, a truck pulled up. The first time the driver brought in the dead, we wouldn't leave him in peace. Every time we saw him, we begged him to help us. "Your presence is essential," we said. "We cannot work without a vehicle." He would say, "God knows, I have no objection, but I can't find fuel. If there's fuel, then I'm at your service."

This time he brought in a body. As we were taking it out of the truck, he said to me, "They told me there was a body that had been with the police for three days, and, given the state it's in, it can't be moved. What should we do?"

"Do you know where it is?" I asked.

"Yeah. They showed me."

"Then let's go. Maybe we can pick it up."

As we were about to get into the truck, an old woman who had come to Jennatabad a few days before put on a white chador and plastic sandals. She asked if she could come along. Although I knew the police were in a bad spot, I couldn't say no. She was staying at Jennatabad hoping to find her son among the bodies coming in. I gave her a hand, and, with some difficulty, she climbed into the truck and sat in a corner. From her craggy face I assumed she was quite old, but, despite the wrinkles, she looked lovable and charming.

The truck took off. Knowing that the police were under fire, the driver stopped on the Ring Road.

There were several people from Jennatabad with us in the truck. We all got out. The path we had to take to get to the spot the driver showed us was under fire. The Ring Road was slightly elevated, nearly two meters in places above the surface of the land, and we had to climb down an embankment. The road ran through swampy land, which flooded when it rained. They had installed large cement drainage pipes under the road to allow water to flow from one side to the other. We went as far as we could on the embankment. To get to the body we had to reach the other side of the road, which was under fire. I gathered my chador around me and crawled through one of the pipes. Now in range of Iraqi shelling, when at any moment a bomb could find me, I thought I was going to die.

Going through hell, I finally reached the body. It was face down in a mass of dirt soaked in all the blood the man had lost. I tried to turn the man over but couldn't. I looked behind me and saw the boys crawling on their chests toward me. "Come on," I said. "Give me a hand."

"We're not going to touch it," they said.

They had a right to say that. After three days in the broiling sun, the body had become something no one would want to touch. I put my hands under one side of the corpse and tried to lift it. It made a dry rasp as it separated from the ground. Finally, it rose and then settled back on the ground, making things worse. The innards had spilled out. Shrapnel had severed the man's throat. It was clear that after being hit, he had thrown up some bread and cheese.

When the boys caught a glimpse of that, they said, "Leave it. We can't possibly touch that thing the way it is now."

"Guys, don't you see we're in range?" I asked. "You can't keep sitting on your hands, can you?"

"There's no way we're lifting that corpse given the state it's in," they repeated.

They turned away as they said this, refusing even to peek at the body. I became annoyed and said, "So what's it to be? We've come all this way, gone through hell to get here. What do you want to do?"

"Fine, but can you just cover the thing somehow?" one of them asked.

"How on earth am I supposed to do that?"

"I don't know, but we can't touch it if it's like that," he said.

I didn't know what to do. I didn't have the heart to leave the poor soul in that state and return empty-handed. There was nothing in that wasteland that would do the trick. Then it hit me: cover the body with my chador. But that would be difficult for me. These days, even during the worst conditions, I managed to keep on my chador. Without it I didn't know what I'd do. The girls were always urging me, "Come on, you can take your chador off."

I ignored them. Wearing it, I told them, was a comfort to me.

This time I had no choice. Whatever it took, we had to remove the body. Underneath my chador, I was wearing a turquoise terry cloth shirt with long sleeves and silver stripes father had bought me for New Years that year. I also had on a black headscarf and blue jeans. I took off my chador and drapped it over the corpse. Then I said to the boys, "Okay, now? Help me pick him up, will you?"

Together we managed to get the body on the stretcher and dragged it along behind us. When we got to the truck, I breathed a deep sigh of relief and got in. After the truck started moving, I asked the old woman who was crying over the corpse whether she would lend me her chador.

"There's nothing wrong with the way you're covered. What do you want with a chador?" she asked.

"I've always worn one. I can't now just appear in public without it."

"Put that out your mind," she said. "Who would possibly give a thought to your chador in the middle this mess?"

I kept nagging until she finally gave in. She wasn't all that happy about removing it as well. We took the old woman and the corpse to Jennatabad, and I, now dressed in the floral print white chador, went on to the clinic. The girls kidded me about it mercilessly. "For God's sake," I said, "does somebody have a black chador they can loan me?"

"No," they said.

All my clothes were stiff as if starched with dirt, grime, and dried blood. So I finally settled for a loose-fitting coat. As luck would have it, Elaheh Hejab, whose family had taken her out of the city the first week of the war, came back to Khorramshahr. On a visit to the clinic to see me, she said she would get me another coat.

While her family was away inspecting their home, she ran from the clinic and quickly came back with a crepe coat. I put it on and said it to the girls, "For God's sake think of something. Let's go to the public bath in Abadan. I can't stand myself any more."

Almost everybody was filthy. We didn't give the matter much thought while there was work to do, but when we had time to sit around and check one another out, we noticed how horrid we looked. We were covered in sores and we stank, and, if we didn't do anything about it soon, we'd all come down with skin infections. Having spent so much time wallowing in the dirt and the blood of the dead, I was worse off than the others. My skin was dry as paper. My hair was so filthy I couldn't stand it myself. Those first days, my scalp itched so much it drove me crazy. I scratched and scratched it until it became a mass of welts. But this became the norm gradually, and the itching bothered me less. My hair automatically formed dreadlocks, which I didn't even try to untangle. The first week the runners had told everyone to cut their hair short to avoid lice. They were afraid the large number of corpses rotting under the rubble would cause a typhus epidemic. This reminded me of what I had seen in World War II movies, but I didn't believe the war was going to go on long enough for that to happen.

I often went to the shore either to evacuate people or to get water from the Shatt. I would sink knee-deep in mud and become covered with diesel oil. I tried as best I could to wash it off and shake out my clothing, but that only made matters worse.

One time, before Ali's death, all of us girls decided that we should go to the bath. We left the mosque together, telling Mr. Najjar that we had something to do.

"You're all leaving? Where to?" he asked in surprise.

We had to admit we were off to the bath.

It wasn't easy to reach Abadan, and when we got there, we realized it was a mistake. We had no money, nor did we know where a bath was. None of us had the nerve to knock on someone's door and ask if we could use the shower. I had once asked Zeynab about washing, and she kindly said she would arrange something. Zeynab kept herself very clean. She regularly went home to change her clothes and would bathe at the body washers', which was something I couldn't bring myself to do. The place still gave me the creeps.

Zeynab finally told Abdollah about the bath situation. He and his brother Khalil drove Sabah, Leila, Zohreh, and me to Abadan. We went to their home and Khalil opened the door for us, saying, "We're going to the bazaar to get something to eat."

After they had gone, we went into their bathroom one by one and, in a clumsy haste, washed our hair and clothes with laundry detergent. As there was no time for the clothes to dry, we put them on wet. Abdollah and Khalil returned a little later having bought bread, tinned fish, and eggplants. We warmed the food on the stove and ate. The glass of hot tea we had after dinner perfectly completed the joy of feeling clean again.

Now several days had passed, and there was no telling where Abdollah had been sent or what disaster had befallen him. We had all agreed to find a place to bathe, but no one knew anybody in Abadan. Despite this we went. When we got there we explored a bit, but no one was brave enough to knock on a stranger's door. We decided to go back, but since we had come this far, we figured we should at least have something to eat. We were starving.

"I don't have a penny to my name," I said.

Everybody was in the same fix, nevertheless we pooled the last of our funds, which didn't amount to more than a few tumans. We went to the Kafesheh Bazaar, and to our surprise several shops were open. First, we bought fresh bread because we didn't have enough money for anything else but half a kilo of pickled vegetables. We mixed the bread in the bag containing the vegetables and wolfed it down. I said to the girls, "The vinegar in these things is going to upset our empty stomachs."

"No way," they said, "our stomachs are bullet-proof."

As we were speaking, I noticed a boy of about seventeen approaching. He had been leaning against the wall of the Abadan Construction Corps building. "Excuse me, sisters," he said. "I don't want to interrupt, but are you waiting for someone?"

We looked at one another and said, "No."

"So why are you standing here?" he asked. "I've been on guard duty for a couple of hours."

We didn't know what to say to him. Finally one of the girls said, "We've come from Khorramshahr thinking maybe would could find a public bath, but we don't know where to go. It's embarrassing to go and knock on some stranger's door."

The boy, whose sunburned face was innocence itself, said, "My aunt's house is right near here. Everybody's gone away, leaving me the key. I'll go and get it, and you can take a bath there. You can bring the key back afterwards, and if I'm not here, give it to one of the Construction brothers."

We looked at one another uncertainly. "I swear to God," the boy said, "it's my aunt's house. You don't have to worry."

We nodded and the boy ran into the building to get his bicycle. It took a long time for him to return. In the meantime a truck pulled up with some of the mosque boys and runners who knew us. One of them was Maryam's fiancé Yaddi, who scolded us, "Why did you come here?"

I thought to myself: Now the great poet Hafez, Master of Mysteries himself, will be the only who doesn't know we're in Abadan to take a bath.

The girls had no choice but to say nervously, "We've come to have a bath."

"So why are you standing here?" asked Yaddi.

"Well, we don't have anywhere to go."

"Get in," he said.

I didn't know whether I should have been happy or upset by that show of male pride. "Where are we going?" the girls asked.

"The home of one of my relatives," Yaddi said.

We got in the truck. Just as we were leaving, the boy who went to get the key showed up at the end of the street. When he saw us in the van he held up the key and shook it. He tried desperately to reach us shouting, "Stop. Stop."

I felt really sorry for him. We waved and said goodbye. Somewhere along the way, the mosque boys got out, and Yaddi and his runner friends took us to the home of an old man and woman. They were very happy to see us. The old woman said, "You go and wash, while we get the food ready."

We hurriedly doused ourselves with water and, emerging dripping wet from the bathroom, went to dry in the sun. After about a dozen days without showering, this was a real luxury. I could finally run the comb I had brought from home through my hair, which had been impossible before. The other the girls used the same comb.

They called us to lunch. The old woman put a small pot of lamb meat and split pea stew she had made for her and her husband on a tablecloth spread on the floor. The food was both a delight and a blessing for the dozen or so of us sitting around the cloth.

On the way back, still not dry, we began to shiver in the chilly wind. To take our minds off the cold someone suggested that we sing. Everyone began the song that went "Boy oh Boy! That night the Imam's words were joy!" It was so uplifting. As soon as it was over, I sat in silence and thought about Abdollah's kindness. How gracious and respectful he had been when he showed us to his aunt's home, saving us from wandering around like refugees.

I also remembered the time his antics in the back of the truck had us all in stitches. I don't recall the exact day, but I remember it was dusk on one of those days I was in the mosque. They hadn't sounded the call to prayer yet. I was passing Ebrahimi when a skinny boy with an olive complexion said in a thick Arab accent, "There's no sound coming from it. Nobody's home, and we didn't have the nerve to go in. You're here. You go and get him."

Ebrahimi said, "Who can I send this time of day? Wait till morning."

This made me curious and I asked, "What's up?"

"It's nothing," said Ebrahimi. "He says that there's a body in Abareh and we should come and get it."

I asked the boy, "Why didn't you bring it yourself?

He said, "We weren't up to entering the house. No one's home. They're all gone. The old man had been lying in bed sick, and now it's been a while since we've heard a sound from him. We think he's gone."

I said. "So, what do you want us to do?"

"Nothing. I just came here for help. We have no way to get him out."

"You mean," I asked, "there's no one who can help take him out?"

"No."

"What do you think we should do?" I asked Ebrahimi.

"I don't know. It's too late now to do anything."

"Too late? Just arrange for transport and we'll go and get the body," I said.

"This time of night? Impossible. We don't know whether he's got it right. It's dangerous. Besides, it's a long way from here to Abareh."

"If somebody will come with me," I said, "I'll go."

Ebrahimi was against it. I called out to Hoseyn and Abdollah, who were in the mosque and explained the situation. Abdollah asked, "Is it really necessary that we go now, sister?"

"Well," I said, "they say they haven't heard a peep from him since morning. He's definitely dead. We've got to get him out before he starts to rot or some animal happens by and eats him."

They agreed to come. While we were waiting for transport, Zohreh and Sabah said they wanted to go also. Ebrahimi and a couple of the other boys were dead set against it. "It's dark," they said. "This kid may be lying. It could be a trap."

I said, "Abareh is not in Iraqi hands. When there's work to be done, it makes no difference what time it is. Besides, there are several of us now."

Hoseyn and Abdollah found a pickup, and we all got in the back. The boy who originally brought the news sat next to the driver to direct him. He went from the Farmandari Circle to the Asha'er Circle. We passed the Pars Avan Company and left the road for the desert. The truck hit a number of bumps, slamming us against the sides. The farther we went into the desert, the more Ebrahimi's words rang true in my mind. I was afraid it was a trap. The boys seem to feel the same. We looked at one another and mumbled some prayers. They removed the safety on their weapons to be ready to fire at the slightest sign of something out of the ordinary. After a while a remote village appeared on the horizon. The driver made his way through the alleys, passing the mud brick homes until the boy told us to stop in front of one. We jumped out. The boy pointed to a house next to the one we were standing in front of and said, "That's our house."

"Good," I said. "Now open the door of this house from yours."

"I'm scared," he said.

"You're a man. What are you afraid of?" said Hoseyn.

"I'm just afraid. If not, I wouldn't have come all this way to get you people. I would have gotten him myself. I'm afraid his ghost will come after me at night."

"Why are you talking nonsense? Go and open the door," I said.

He refused. I said, "Okay, we'll do it ourselves."

Hoseyn and Abdollah said to me, "You shouldn't come."

"Remember, I'm a nurse. If he's still alive and needs attention, I may be able to do something."

Hoseyn climbed over the door to the compound. Abdollah and I went up the stairs of the boy's house to get to the roof of the man's house. Then we went down some stairs, which led to the entrance hallway. A door to a reception room opened onto the hallway. This was traditionally where nonfamily members would stay to keep them from intruding in the private part of the home. We went down the hallway and into the yard. Another door opened onto it. Hoseyn and Abdollah went to look at the rooms at the other end of the yard. I turned on my flashlight and, with a prayer, went to the other door of the reception room. I was gripped by fear in that pitch darkness, and scolded myself for not waiting outside the door. What if is was an ambush? What would I do then? The answer was obvious; it would have been unconscionable to let Hoseyn and Abdollah go in alone. If something happened to them, I would never have forgiven myself. Shining my light into the room, I saw that there was someone lying directly opposite me. I moved the light around and found no one else in the room but the old man. I called out to Hoseyn and Abdollah to come.

They came running. We entered the room. The old man's mouth and eyes were open, seemingly frozen dry in the light. I put my hand on his carotid artery. There was no pulse. In the hope of finding a faint heartbeat, I bent down and put my ear to his chest. Nothing. It was as if his heart had never worked. I felt all around his teeth, which jutted out from his mouth because it had been ages since he had eaten. Even though I was used to handling bodies, this one affected me. I scanned the room with the flashlight. There was a bowl of water near the corpse, and a prayer mat with a set of rosary beads on a shelf.

Abdollah went to open the outside door and the others entered the compound. The driver removed the blanket from the old man and spread it on the floor. Then they lifted the body and placed it on the blanket. Seeing them carrying the body out of the house, the boy retreated. "Don't be afraid. This miserable old corpse won't eat you," I said.

Drawn by the noises we were making, several of the neighbors emerged from their homes. "Where's this old man's family?" I asked.

They said, "All of them left. No matter how hard they tried to get him to leave, the old man refused. God bless him. He kept saying, 'I'm not leaving my home.' "

"There's no one else in this neighborhood?" I asked.

"Sure," they said, "everybody's around farther down."

"You have to leave, also," I said. "The Iraqis are coming from the Ring Road. In a few days, this place'll be under fire."

While the driver was turning the pickup around, more people from the neighborhood showed up. The boys urged all of them to leave the village. It was quite dark now, and on the trip back the truck landed in more ditches and hit more bumps than it had on the way there. We couldn't help falling on the hapless corpse. Abdollah joked, "If anybody had doubts about it before, the old man's sure as hell dead now, and we killed him!"

We delivered the corpse to Taleqani Hospital and returned to the mosque. I had barely set foot in the place when everybody started yelling at us. First it was Mahmud Farrokhi; then the rest of them joined the parade of blame. "Why did you go out there this time of night without permission? Without clearing it with anybody, you just up and left? What were you thinking? Are you saying that you're not responsible to anyone? You can just act on your own?"

Mr. Mesbah and Haj Aqa Nuri also came down hard on us. Most of their anger was directed at me. I said, "Nothing happened. There actually was a body, and we went and got it."

"What if," they said, "there were Iraqis? Then what? What if Fifth Columnists had done something terrible to you?"

They really let us have it and said, "You're not allowed to go out late at night. Don't think you can do whatever you please. Remember!"

"Fine. From now on we'll tell you. Whatever you say."

21

Suspicious Characters

I didn't find working at the clinic, gathering the dead, and tending the wounded in the town all that satisfying. The weapons they gave us to fix were useless, which was even more infuriating. I felt that none of these tasks was vital. What I really wanted to do was to go to the front. I knew that there'd be more work to do there. Zohreh Farhadi was like me, restlessly expecting something else to do. She once told me, "There's a detachment known as Abu Zarr on its way to the front. Come on, let's try to go with them."

"Joining up with some group or band is not something I want to do," I said. "We can't be independent that way. I want to be able to go where I feel I'm needed and not take orders from somebody."

Zohreh said no more on the subject until one day an Abu Zarr pickup pulled up for her. I so wanted to be at the front, I went with her. I believe Maryam Amjadi was also with us.

Several of the men in the truck had weapons, but although they were an armed unit, there was but one machine gun among them. They spent an hour going around the city, picking up several others and stopping in at a few places. I soon got fed up. We had scarcely left Naqdi Avenue when I said to the driver, "Mister, stop here. I want to get off." Zohreh and Maryam, already members of the detachment who had gone to the front several times, said, "Be a little patient. We'll get there."

"I can't. Stop, please."

I got down and returned to the clinic. A few hours later Zohreh returned. "Well, what happened?" I asked.

"We got to the crossroads. There was heavy fighting there. The truck stopped and dropped off several of the men, but they sent us back."

From the time that Sheikh Sharif had vouched for our presence at the clinic, putting himself on the line for us, we had to be super careful. The clinic took in anybody who wanted to work, and if somebody didn't do his best, we had to take the blame. The men and boys at the mosque kept their eyes on the place and, without appearing too nosy about it, checked up on us. Mahmud Farrokhi and Mr. Mesbah were especially protective. At dusk they would come around and sit in the clinic. If they didn't see one of the girls, they would ask after her. "She had something to do. Why do you ask?" we'd say.

"It's nothing," they said. "We just need to speak to her." Or they would ask about things in general, about any problems.

If we suspected someone or something, we would let them know. For example, one of the men who had come the first time with the medical team that had disappeared even before the day began, showed up at the clinic a few days later. He was a hefty man with a handlebar mustache, who spoke Persian with a Kurdish accent. He said that he was from Sanandaj.

This time he wasn't doing anything in particular. He hung around the medications and kept busy, he told us, by rearranging them. He talked a lot about the Komala Groups and the Demokrats, defending their view of things. Knowing these groups well, I would stand up to him. Ali had told me that in Kurdistan they made people's lives miserable in the name of defending their rights. The man brought in posters showing the bombardment of the Dowlehtu Prison and the torture of revolutionary guards and Kurds.[1] He would

[1] The Dowlehtu Prison was set up in a secret location in a forest between Sardasht and Baneh by order and direction of the Komala Groups and the Demokrats. It was built by the inmates. The physical and psychological torture of the people imprisoned by the separatist groups is beyond description. On May 9,

say, "See how bloodthirsty they are and how they muzzle the people?"

Given this background, I didn't have good feelings about him. In addition to his politics, he was always trying to sow dissent and said bad things about Mr. Najjar behind his back. He would also make up things that I had supposedly said and tell them to the others. Once I confronted him directly about this. He knew I was Kurdish, yet asked, "Aren't you a Kurd? You should be defending their rights. Why do you call the Komala and the Demokrats deviant groups?"

He had heard me labelling these groups "deviant" in front of the other girls. I said, "Are you saying that anyone who's Kurdish has to be a traitor as well? First and foremost, I am a Muslim; second, I am a Kurd."

He defended the groups, calling them the saviors of the Kurdish people. I mentioned the horrors that they were responsible for. He said nothing. That evening Mahmud Farrokhi came to the clinic asking if there were any problems. I told him what had transpired and was astounded to learn that he already knew the whole story. "Don't worry," he said. "We have him under surveillance. We realize ourselves he isn't really here to work."

That man wasn't the only one of his type I had to deal with. Around the same time we had come to the clinic, a young man in his twenties named Jownshan would pop in every time his travels took him that way. Although he made a great show of being religious and a zealous enforcer of the law, none of us had anything good to say about him. Mr. Najjar also didn't like him and would tell us, "This guy isn't what he appears to be. Don't let him in."

But he wouldn't leave us alone and unbeknownst to us would show up while we were working. He would say, "We must form a

---

1981, at a time when this place had become insecure for the Demokrat groups, it was bombarded with the collaboration of the Baath Party and about seventy prisoners were massacred.

group. We must act independently. If we act on the orders of the other forces, then nothing will be accomplished."

Besides that, whenever he saw us he would tell us to mind our morals. "You girls have to be strict about modesty," he said. "Always keep your heads down when you're walking."

None of us took him seriously. More than anyone else I was aware of the gap between his words and actions and told the others about them.

He would say to me, "You're very forward." I would reply, "Do you imagine you're our guardian, that you have the right to interfere in our lives like this? We don't need your advice." I wasn't his favorite person after that, and I heard he warned the other girls not to associate with me because I was "headstrong and cocky."

He would say things like that, but then he would try to get around my opposition and bring me over to his side. He told me that the judiciary had appointed him as a special agent to identify and arrest Fifth Column forces. With each passing day, I grew more aware of his lies, and I had my heart set on catching him in one of them.

One evening the girls were talking and readying the medical equipment for the trolley, when he entered the clinic and said, "We caught a suspicious character among the naval forces. I want to put him on trial, and I want you to come and see it."

"Who are you that you can put someone on trial?" we asked.

"I am an officer of the court working under the prosecutor," he said.

"Okay, but why is it necessary for us to be there?" I asked.

"It's not necessary. I just want you to see what I do, because you've made so much about it," he said.

No matter how many ways we tried to get out of it, he wouldn't stop pestering us. "Let's get it over with once and for all," I said to the girls. "Either he's lying or telling the truth. But watch out; he may try to pull something."

Zohrah agreed to come along and the three of us went to the avenue along the Shatt. From there we turned right, went to the corner of another street, and stopped in front of a two-story white building. "We're here," Jownshan announced.

I looked at the building carefully. It seemed abandoned with no sound or light coming from it. "What are you waiting for?" he said. "Come on in."

"I don't see any reason to," I said. "This your courthouse, isn't it? Please, you go in first."

He shrugged his shoulders, went up a few stairs, and entered the leafy green yard of the building. He walked around a bit and returned to say, "It seems they haven't brought the accused in yet. We'll have to wait."

Now, certain that the man was a shifty character, I said, "There's no reason to stick around. Do you take us for children? You think we have nothing better to do? We have absolutely no desire to see this court of yours." A little anxious now, Zohreh whispered to me, "Now what do we do?"

"Nothing," I said. "We'll go back. There's no telling what this man has cooked up in his sick little mind. I hope I'm mistaken, but maybe he's got something going with the Fifth Columnists. Let's go."

Just as we were about to leave, he said, "Hey. Hold on a second. They're about to come any time now."

"You stay," I said. "We're going. The trial is your show. It's got nothing to do with us."

We went back to the mosque and found Farrokhi and Mesbah and told them what happened. We asked them to do something about it.

Just as before, they told us that they were aware of the situation and that we should keep on doing our work but keep him under surveillance without letting him know we were doing it.

When we got back to the clinic, I told each girl to be on her guard. Ever since that day no one was friendly to him. Jownshan himself soon realized how we felt, and after a while he disappeared.[2]

---

[2] Several months later I heard they were looking for him, and there was an order to shoot him on sight. According to what people said, he was a member of the Ferqan Group and all his documents were fakes.

22

Iraqi Prisoners

We were in the area around Arya Lane in a truck with three wounded we were taking to the Taleqani Hospital when we saw a man standing beside the road waving his arms. The driver stopped and the man stepped forward. I knew him vaguely. He worked at the Jennatabad mosque. "We found a body here," he told us. "We were bulldozing and it came up in the blade."

"We've got wounded. Let us get them to Taleqani, and we'll be right back," I said.

We delivered the wounded and returned. The man and two others had been working the bulldozer and filling sacks with loose dirt and sand. They explained the sacks were for protecting the hospital. I walked to the bulldozer and saw the body of a soldier in the blade with his torso and the head hanging out. The corpse was skin and bones and dried up as if it had been mummified. The skin had turned violet and was singed in places. Clearly it had been there for several days. Despite multiple shrapnel wounds, there was no blood. There was a smell, but it wasn't strong enough to drive people away. To me it was strange that it hadn't disintegrated. The soldier, I guessed, was part of the invading Iraqi forces coming by water from Minu Island and had been caught in our mortar fire. He tried to take cover in the pile of dirt, but then died from fatigue and hunger.

"Did you go through his pockets?" I asked.

"We didn't dare touch him."

With disgust I pulled an ID, a family photo, and some crumbled cigarettes from his shirt pocket. The ID was illegible because it was wet and the ink ran. The only word I could make out was the Arabic *al-naqib*, which seemed to be his rank. I looked at the picture, which showed several women, children, and men standing next to one another. Their faces and clothing said that they were Iraqi Arabs.

They loaded the body in the truck and it drove off. While we waited for the truck to return, we took a stroll in the area looking for a radio and other equipment. We crossed the road, and about 150 meters away a barrel caught my eye. I suggested to the people with me that we look inside.

One side of the barrel was dotted with bullet holes. To my surprise, we found the body of another Iraqi soldier in it. From the pool of fresh blood at the bottom, I assumed he had been killed that day. The body was crammed in the barrel making it hard to get out. As it emerged blood spilled to the ground, and the stench turned my stomach.

I wondered if there was a connection between the two men. Had they come to spy or were they trying to surrender? I went through the man's pockets but found nothing. The body was in pitiful condition. There was a lot of shrapnel in the back, and the area around the kidneys was completely butchered.

The poor driver returned only to be confronted by yet another body. They put it in the truck. I got in, and we delivered the corpse to the Taleqani morgue.

In front of the hospital I saw that an ambulance with the Oil Company insignia had pulled up with more wounded. The driver told the nurses, "We've got many burn victims at the Oil Company Hospital. There's no room for them, so we brought them here."

I walked over to the ambulance. I had heard that during the first days of the war, they had bombarded the refinery at Abadan. Forty people had died, and between 120 and 140 were wounded. The fire fighters who had come to put out the blaze also fell victim to the disaster. Every day would bring word of new horrors. Seven firefighters had been burned. One person had fallen into a pit so fiercely on fire they couldn't retrieve his body.

When they opened the door to the ambulance, I saw there were two wounded inside. One was badly scorched, a blackened piece meat. There was no way of telling whether his skin was naturally black or whether it had been charred. The man's face was in relatively good shape, but strips of flesh had been torn from it. Blood flowed from the wounds on his arms and face. The man didn't groan when they put him on the stretcher. They put a blanket over his face and quickly took him away. The second wounded man seemed to be in better shape. He had burns on his arms, hands, and back, and some of his skin was hung loose from his body. His burnt hair and blistered face made him look quite scary but, apart from this, his condition was not that bad. Because of the burns on his back, they put him on a stretcher and carried him away.

After all this time, they still hadn't managed to put out the fires in the big oil storage tanks. They stopped traffic from going on the avenue that led to the refinery. When we were in Abadan, we could feel the heat of the blaze and see flames shooting up several meters in the air. The temperature was higher than normal, and in several parts of the city people were finding it hard to breathe.

I had seen burn victims before. Once I was bringing bodies to the morgue with the help of a couple of the boys. It was dark, and I got to the door of a home before the others to open it. As soon as I turned the handle, I saw a man squatting on the floor with his hands over his head. The man was black from head to toe. I figured that, having come to be with one of the dead, he was in his own world. It was dark, and I couldn't see clearly. I said hello but heard nothing. I figured he was so grief stricken he hadn't noticed I was there.

The boys brought up the corpse, and I opened both parts of the double door. Since the man was in the way, I said, "Would you mind getting up? You're in the way." Again, there was no response. I shined a flashlight in his face. All at once I saw this charred body. I began to tremble and my heart leaped from my chest. Terrified, I ran outside. The boys told me that the body was probably that of a helper on a tank, who had been burned alive while in a sitting position. Since we didn't have tanks, they reasoned, he had to be a Baathist.

And there was the time I saw one of the Iraqi prisoners. It was during those first days when we moved into the Sheybani clinic. They had shifted a large number of people from the mosque, clearing it out considerably. They closed the prayer room, and the foot traffic became mostly military.

That morning the girls at the clinic said they had captured prisoners at the front.

When I went to Jennatabad, they said the same thing, adding that all sorts of people were among the prisoners—English, German, and Iraqi. This surprised me, and I asked, "Well, how did they end up here, I wonder?" I wasn't aware that the rest of the world was backing the Iraqis and supplying them with materiel.

On the way back to the mosque, I heard they had captured a jeepful of foreign reporters. They had also taken many Iraqi's prisoners. They also said that there had been women in the foxholes. These reports made me curious to see the prisoners. I wanted to see for myself if there were actually foreigners among them. Toward evening the boys said that they were bringing prisoners to the mosque. When I got there, I saw that a lot of people who, like me, wanted to see them and had gathered in the yard, making quite a commotion. After a quarter of an hour, several young men brought in a relatively heavy-set, tall man who seemed around thirty-five. He was a good-looking man who bore no resemblance to an Iraqi. His light-colored eyes, sandy hair, and fair skin, which had gone red either from the heat or fear, said that he was non-Iraqi. He was wearing a fresh uniform, but there was no indication of rank on his shoulders. Contrary to what I expected, his hands were free and his eyes were not blindfolded. He sat immediately in a corner of the compound, stretched out his legs, and put his hands behind his head. He had a horrible case of the shakes. He kept repeating rapidly in Arabic, "Help me. Help me. I'm your prisoner."

The people standing nearby were yelling at him. A few were cursing and wanted to beat him up. The others stopped them. One of the boys said, "Son-of-a-bitch comes here begging for help. But when he was at the front, his shooting was making life hell for us."

Then he held up the badges of rank worn by the prisoners and said, "He's a captain. He tore off his epaulettes. I found them right where we had taken him."

This enraged the people even more. When the prisoner saw this, he started to act strange and said, "This is a sanctuary. The house of God. I'm Shii. I'm Shii. Give me water. I'm thirsty."

The boys began to tease him saying, "Don't be afraid. We're not cannibals like you. We're not Baathists. Your people are the savages."

I was just as anxious to see the prisoners, so I could let them have it myself, but when I saw how low he had come, how abject, how he expected to die, my heart went out to him. I stepped forward and said in Arabic, "Don't be afraid. We won't harm you."

He looked at me and said in Arabic, "You're Iranian?"

"Yeah," I said. "I'm Iranian. Where are you from? Baghdad or Basra?"

"I'm not Iraqi," he said. "I'm Jordanian."

"If you're Jordanian," I asked, "what are you doing here? Why have you come to fight us?"

"I didn't want to. They forced me."

"That's what they all say, but, given the chance, you fight us till the last bullet. When that's gone, you surrender and say they forced you. If that's true, why do you keep fighting until you run out of ammunition?"

He looked down. I continued, "Just look who you're up against. A handful of women and some defenseless boys. Our forces are just like your kids. They're the ones standing up to you."

Although I was fighting back tears at that point, I went on. "What do you want from us? What did we ever do to you? Why don't you let us go on with our lives?" The man quickly repeated, "Forgive me. Forgive me."

"Don't worry," I said. "We follow the Prophet's example. We treat prisoners kindly. Whatever you need, tell me and I'll get it for you. No one will harm you here. You're a prisoner and will be treated according to the dictates of Islam. Islam, not the Geneva Convention." The man calmed down a bit and said, "I want water."

I told one of the lads to bring some water.

"How about a cigarette?" I said.

From the way he said "Yeah!" you could tell he was dying for a smoke.

He took a drag on the cigarette they gave him, and my emotions got the better of me again. I said, "Look, I've stayed in the city so I could stop your troops. I buried my father and my brother with my own hands. You people killed them. You make war on us, but we don't know the slightest thing about war. We also have no equipment, but we do have God. It's our faith that gives us the strength to fight you."

After I told him they had killed father and Ali, his cigarette went out. He kept his eyes pinned on me until I had finished. Again he asked for forgiveness. I stood beside him, waiting for them to bring the other prisoners, but there was no sign of them. They had taken the rest directly to Abadan.

23

Sar Bandar

Several days had passed since mother and the kids left, but I still had no word from them. I didn't know where they were or what they were doing. I was very worried about mother, especially because she might have heard about Ali. This was always on my mind. If she found out, I thought, she'd definitely have a heart attack or go mad and run off into the wilderness. What would become of the children, then? Who would look after them once they became homeless?

The anxiety and the nightmares were constant, never giving me a moment's peace. Ever since they had left the city, I had intended to visit them, but the opportunity never presented itself. My plan was that as soon as I had seen mother and the kids, I would stay just long enough to make sure they were all okay and then go back to the city.

The War Room had been moved to Mahshahr, increasing the traffic to and from the city. Sar Bandar and Mahshahr were not far apart. I would tell anyone going in that direction to relay the news to mother that Leila and I were fine and not to worry about us. The few people who had gone and come back told me the refugees were all spread out, so they hadn't found mother.

This increased my anxiety. Night was when I worried about them most. Where were they? What were they doing? Did they have enough to eat? At times I felt guilty about not telling mother about Ali's martyrdom. How could I have denied this grieving widow the opportunity to mourn him properly? From now until judgment day, she'd regret not having seen his corpse. Blaming myself for this, I wept. After I calmed down, I would comfort myself by saying what I had done was not wrong. Mother couldn't have taken it. She was so attached to Ali. How could mother have absorbed the blow, especially after the death of father? What if, after she heard the news, she decided to stay in Khorramshahr? What would I have done if she and the children were taken prisoner or had died in the shelling? So, I felt I had done the right thing.

One day I saw Ra'na Najjar's family in the mosque. I had gotten to know them during the first days of the war. We said hello, and I asked about Ra'na. They said she was in Sar Bandar, where they had a house and waited out the war. They had come to the city to look in on their former home and then return to Sar Bandar.

"If there's room in your car," I said, "could I come along? I want to see about mother. I've had no word from her for five or six days now."

"Sure, come with us," they said amiably.

I told the girls at the clinic and quickly returned to the mosque. I don't know whether they had a Toyota or a Galant. I joined two of Ra'na's sisters in the back seat, and we were off. There were some pedestrians and cars on the road, but compared to the day we had brought bodies to Mahshahr, it was deserted. I stared silently at the desert landscape on either side of the road. The last time I was on this road I had yet to hear about father's passing. That day all my thoughts were on the bodies in the truck and the refugees. I didn't give a thought to the rain water that had pooled at various points in the desert. The supports for the huge pipes carrying crude oil to the petrochemical plant at Mahshahr were submerged in water that collected in the hollows. Seabirds flew over the puddles. The weather was warm and a heat haze hovered over the road. The closer we got to Mahshahr, the more arid and barren the landscape became. Around Mahshahr the road broke off for Sar Bandar. We reached the town around 10:30. It was a strange place, more like a suburb or a village than a town. The houses were different from the ones in Khorramshahr. Most of them were uniform, small villas with low ceilings and walls. Saddam's artillery had reached this place, destroying homes by the bazaar.

I got out at the head of the avenue. Ra'na's sisters kept insisting that I come home with them, but I refused. "Come," they pleaded, "have something to eat, take a shower, then go. We'll go with you to find your mother." "No. I've got to find them now, so I can get back this afternoon," I said.

I thanked them and started walking down the avenue. The whole town consisted of a small market with a several rows of homes. I walked around the place a few times and asked several people where the war refugees were. They told me there was no specific area for them in Sar Bandar.

The place was beginning to depress me. It was hot and dry everywhere, all salt flats and baked earth. I felt like a stranger among those people and started to have more sympathy for mother living all by herself. Everyone I asked about the refugees would just say, "Don't know. They're scattered around."

I lost all hope of finding mother and the children. Maybe they went to Mahshahr, I thought. After asking directions several times, I finally got to the place where there were minibuses for Mahshahr. I waved one down and got on. I hoped to find the home of Mr. Bahramzadeh, one of our relatives who worked at the petrochemical plant and was devoted to mother's brother. I was certain he would help me. I went all over Mahshahr asking various people if they knew Mr. Hamid Bahramzadeh. I gave the address and described how he looked, his demeanor, where he worked, but nobody knew him. I even asked women sitting in front of their homes, but they had no knowledge of him and would ask suspiciously what I wanted with him.

When I explained I'd come from Khorramshahr looking for mother, they brightened and invited me into their homes. "Come inside," they said, "and rest from your journey. Have a nap and then go and look for her."

I refused, explaining I had to get back to Khorramshahr.

The women were anxious about the city, and they peppered me with questions about the war and conditions there. An old woman from Khorramshahr, who had taken shelter with her daughter, asked, "Do you think we'll ever go back, my dear?"

Not knowing the answer myself, I said, "Yes, mother, don't worry."

Mahshahr proved to be another dead end. I felt drained and exhausted but kept walking. Sunlight reflecting off the salt flats blinded me and scorched my skin. My brains felt like they were cooking in my skull. I was about to die from hunger but had no money to buy food. Now in addition to the heat, I had to put up with hunger and poverty. I was desperate with no place to turn. I was on the verge of crying several times, but swore I wouldn't give in to tears.

I returned to the road that led to Sar Bandar. A minibus pulled up in front of me, and the door opened. I debated what I should do: get in with nothing in my pockets or not. Just at that point, I saw someone about to get off and give the driver money. The driver told him there was no fare. He told the passenger to offer a prayer instead.

Satisfied, I could ride now with a clear conscience. From Sar Bandar, I got a ride on an Oil Company truck.

When I got on, the two people sitting next to the driver said, "Sister, we'll go in the back and you sit up here where it's cooler." I thanked them and said, "I'll sit back here."

"It's hot out, you'll roast," they warned me.

"No, thanks," I said.

The truck drove off and I sat in the back, leaning against the cab. The floor was burning hot. The wind scorched my face and all over my body. A little farther ahead, the truck picked up a few more passengers and we all rode to Abadan. From there I was able to find a truck going to Khorramshahr.

As soon as I set foot in Khorramshahr, I felt like seeing Zeynab. She was like a real mother to me. She even wanted Leila and me to call her "mother." When I reached Jennatabad, the body washers, as usual, asked, "What's new? How far have the Iraqis gotten? We don't know whether to go or stay." The poor men were worn out and really wanted to know where they stood. They hadn't received any instructions from the administration. As long as there were dead, they had to stay. There were times I thought that there were only two types of public servants who accepted the risks of operating in the war zone: the firemen and the body washers.

Maryam would occasionally go home and come back, but the old man and woman had nothing to do with their homes, Jennatabad being safer and more comfortable for them. I went to look for Zeynab. They said that she was out scouring the town for dead and wounded.

Zeynab hadn't been in Jennatabad for a time. As the number of bodies brought in decreased by the day, it was difficult for her to stay there, so she went into the town looking for them. From time to time, after an area had been hit, my crew and I would arrive and see that Zeynab had also been there. The first time I saw her was when they hit Naqdi Avenue. The bombs had completely leveled 230 homes. Luckily, they were empty and there were no casualties. I was with a couple of girls from the clinic when I saw Zeynab arriving in a pickup. We kissed and hugged each other. "So you've come here, too, mother?" I said.

"I came to see what I could do."

Then she continued, "When I don't see you, even for several hours, I miss you. It doesn't matter whether the war ends or goes on, eventually we'll go our separate ways. How are we going to see each other, then? I've grown very close to you and Leila; you're like my daughter, Maryam, to me."

I laughed and said, "God is great." It was embarrassing to say what was in my heart. The special love I felt for Zeynab kept me coming back to Jennatabad just to see her.

24

A Needless Death

One afternoon seven or eight of us left the clinic and headed for the front lines. Dr. Sa'adat was with us. We walked to the end of the Mowlavi neighborhood and ran into defense forces scattered here and there in the alleyways. A little farther away near Sentab, the fighting got heavier. Our forces would fire from one section, then run to another position and fire from there. As soon as we appeared, a couple of them told us, "There's a wounded man behind the wall of that house. It's been quite a while since we put him there. We keep looking in on him to see whether he's still alive."

Dr. Sa'adat and I went to where they were pointing. Because they had simply deposited the boy behind a wall, I imagined his wound wasn't critical. When we got there, I saw that the boy, who was no more than twenty, lay with his back against the wall with a severe shrapnel wound. His thigh had been ripped apart, and he had fallen on his side. He had lost a tremendous amount of blood, and it seemed he would lose the leg.

Dr. Sa'adat got to work immediately. He found a vein and attached a serum drip. He added some medications to the drip. There was nothing else we could do. The boy's comrades had torn strips from their own clothing and used them to bandage him. Then they went in search of a vehicle, but with the heavy fire it seemed to take ages for a truck to come. I asked the boy, who was too weak even to open his eyes, "What's your name? Are you a Basiji? Army?"

He said nothing. Occasionally he managed to pry open his eyes, but they would soon close again. What he was mumbling under his breath from time to time was a mystery to me.

A truck arrived and I held the drip while Dr. Sa'adat loaded the wounded boy. At one point, he began to flop around like a fish out of water, as though he was having a seizure. With panic in his voice Dr. Sa'adat said, "Hurry up! Let's get him to the hospital."

I had the feeling that the boy was breathing his last. I couldn't look at him any longer. I handed the drip to one of the boys and jumped down from the truck.

The truck drove off. G3, sixty caliber mortars, and the RPG fire forced me to crawl on my stomach and take cover by a wall. I was a mess. I knew the young man would not make it to the hospital because of all the blood he had lost. Why did he have to wait that long for someone to help him? Of course, that was precisely why I insisted on being to the front—to prevent such needless deaths.

Then I remembered Uncle Shanbeh's son-in-law. A few days before, when we were bringing wounded to the Oil Company Hospital, I was surprised to see uncle Shanbeh's wife there and asked her why she was there.

"Our son-in-law was wounded."

I had met their son-in-law. He was an officer in the navy and a devout and honorable man. She told me where he was, and I went to visit him. Mahin, their daughter, was by the bed, fanning her husband with a piece of cardboard. I said hello and asked her about him. "He's got shrapnel in his leg," she said.

He didn't seem all that good to me. He was feverish, constantly begging for water. They would merely wet his lips and fan him as he moaned helplessly. I left the room and asked the nurse about his condition. "At first it wasn't that serious," they said, "but he's got an infection and has lost a lot of blood, which is why he mustn't have water."

I went back into the room, but didn't say anything to my aunt and her daughter. I hung around a bit and then left the hospital. The next day I happened to go to the hospital to deliver some wounded. I asked the driver to wait while I ran to the son-in-law's room. The bed was empty. I asked one of the nurses about him, and she said that he had passed away the night before.

Shocked, I said, "He didn't seem that critical yesterday. It's true he was moaning and parched, but it didn't look like he would die from the wound."

It was on account of the infection, they told me. It got into his bloodstream. I started to cry. The man was not that old, not much over forty. He had five or six kids. Very upset, I went back to the truck and sat, thinking how the lack of proper care had taken the life of a fine officer, a father, and a loving husband.

They were calling my name, and I stopped thinking about uncle's son-in-law. The girls and I remained there a while, tending to the wounded. When the shelling intensified, the men told us to go back.

Feeling worn and battered, we walked back the way we came. A truck going to the city center pulled up and gave us a lift. We had yet to leave the Mowlavi neighborhood when it came under fire. The driver headed toward the houses. We could hear the sounds of men and women wailing and shrieking in the distance. Before the truck came to a halt, we jumped out. The way the people were shrieking, we imagined one of their children was being dismembered before their eyes! A wall in front of two homes had been hit, making dirt and dust rocket into the air. To make people aware I was there, I said "Yallah" and entered the compound. There were a few men and women standing around. The women were beating themselves and crying. The men were yelling, trying to get the women to stop.

I came closer, expecting to find the bloody body of a loved one. Instead, there was the carcass of a cow on the ground. A large piece of shrapnel had entered its flank, and smaller pieces had penetrated its legs. The worst thing was that the cow was on the verge of calving. The women were standing around the cow crying their eyes out, and the men, with terrified looks on their faces, were shouting in Arabic. They wanted to cut open the cow's stomach and save the calf, but no one had the nerve to do it. Meanwhile the poor animal was struggling to get up; it would get up, bellow, but then fall to the ground. Occasionally it tried to lift its head and opened its terror-filled eyes. The men were beside themselves, seeing the cow in such pain and watching their wealth go down the drain. One of the boys from the truck, who had entered the compound with me, said to the men, "Why are you just standing there twiddling your thumbs? It's suffering; this is sinful. You've got to put it out of its misery."

Another asked, "Is there no one around to butcher it?"

This made the women shriek even louder. The memory of the death of the young man by the wall still fresh in my mind, I couldn't take any more of this and started to walk back down the alley. Many of the houses had been hit, but, luckily, they had been evacuated. I expected at any moment to hear the sound of one of the boys putting the cow down. I put my hands over my ears and walked on, but I could still hear the women shrieking, especially the older one, who appeared to be the mother of the family. A bit later the boys came back and got in the truck. The driver went off and picked me up at the head of the alley. I didn't ask the boys what happened.

25

Evacuating Arab People

Most of the city's inhabitants had been evacuated, but there were still some holdouts. The boys in their travels would come back, reporting that, unlike most other areas in the city, in the Arab neighborhood of Mowlavi many people had remained behind.

They said folks in the neighborhood stayed because they thought the Iraqis wouldn't harm fellow Arabs. Iraqi radio propaganda promoted this idea, constantly telling them that they should stay in their homes. The radio said Iraqis were battling the Zoroastrian Persians not their fellow Arabic speakers, whom they were going to liberate from the Khomeini regime.

Of course, this incitement didn't have much effect on our Arab fellow townsmen, who were smarter than to fall for such lies. In the past the Iraqis had tried to foment separatism by spreading this poison but got nowhere. Among the army boys, there was a revolutionary unit with a large number of Arab guards. Of course, the people who had stayed in the neighborhood generally had nothing to do with the government or politics. They would say, "We just want to lead normal lives and not get involved with other folks."

When the boys were leaving to evacuate people from the Mowlavi neighborhood, Mr. Nuri and Mr. Mesbah told me to go with them to translate. I was to try to get the women to leave, even by force if necessary.

One of the men gave out weapons saying, "This time you've got to be ready to get them out even at gun point. Threaten them. Fire your weapons in the air."

I said to him, "These folks aren't even afraid of canons and tanks. What makes you think that they'd be scared if we fire a few bullets in the air?"

Someone else suggested, "If firing in the air doesn't do it, then what if we fire at their feet?"

"No," the others answered him in unison, "that wouldn't be right."

It was around 10:00 a.m. when we got underway in a pickup. Mowlavi was one of the old neighborhoods; most of its inhabitants were among the downtrodden. There was one main avenue with many secondary streets, lanes, and alleyways branching from it. The avenue ended in a date grove, the customs area, and the port. All in all, it was once a densely populated, noisy, and bustling place, made even livelier because of the traditional fruit and vegetable market as well as shops on either side of an old, run-down gateway, and the peddlers selling their wares from cloths spread on the ground. They called the market Satan Bazaar.

At the end of the avenue where it reached the railway, there was an extensive date grove that went back a long way. Over the years it had become somewhat smaller because of the expansion of the customs area. The people living in the mud and straw houses in the grove grew greens, tomatoes, and okra, which they sold at the market.

When the driver stopped the truck he said, as he had done many times before, "Don't get separated. Go in small groups."

We divided ourselves into two groups, one patrolling the end of the avenue, the other the head. We knocked on door after door. Most of the homes were empty. When no one answered, one of the boys would climb the walls and look inside the compounds from there. When they were satisfied there was no one home, they would jump down. Occasionally someone would open the door and say, "No one's in this alley" or "One family just left" or "The people in that house evacuated the very first day."

We would ask them to come out, but they refused.

When we were loading them into the truck, they cried and cursed Saddam in Arabic. I would tell them in Arabic, "We're Arabs like you. Remaining here will result in one of two things: either you'll add to the number of casualties or you'll be taken prisoner. What good is staying here? If the enemy attacks, you've got nothing to defend yourselves with."

After going through several alleys, we realized some people had remained behind because of their livestock. They had nothing to their names but their cows, water buffaloes, and sheep. As they boarded the truck, they begged us to let them bring their livestock.

We told them, "The truck isn't even big enough. With the bridge under fire we have to cross by boat. There's no room for your animals and even if there were, the water would spook them, and they'd capsize the boat."

Some suggested, "Bring the animals to the mosque and slaughter them there for food for the troops. If they stay here, they'll be blown to bits by mortars, or fall into the hands of the Baathists. We don't want that to happen."

In one of the alleys, there was a partially open door. I knocked and said a warning "Yallah." In both Arabic and Persian I asked, "Is the landlord around?"

There was no answer. I peeped in and saw a young woman by the reflecting pool washing a pot and a middle-aged woman by the oven. She appeared to be about to bake bread. As soon as they saw me, they both stopped what they were doing and ran into the rooms at the end of the courtyard.

I stepped into the yard and asked again, "Is the landlord here?"

A voice said, "What the hell do you want from us? We're not coming out."

I walked over to the rooms and said, "Please let me in."

When I got to the door, a voice said, "Please, come in."

I knocked on the door and opened it. The room was pitch dark. Light streamed in when the door opened, but I still couldn't make out what was in the room. It was made of mud and straw and smelled damp. There was a faded multi-color floor covering in the middle of it and, shoved in a corner, a bunch of futons and random household items. The ceiling was covered in plastic to prevent leaks. Now used to the darkness, I said to the women, "Do you know how dangerous it is for you to be here? Don't you see the fire raining down on us from the sky? Why be so stubborn? Why did you run away? We haven't come here to take you by force. We are requesting you leave. It's not safe here. To Saddam there's no difference between Persians and Arabs. What they say about him not harming Arabs is a lie."

One of the women said, "We've got nothing to do with Saddam. To hell with him! We just don't want to leave. We prefer to stay here and live in our own homes."

"You can't live here," I said. "They won't let you go on with your lives. If you stay, you'll be killed. Is that what you call living?"

I spoke to them until I was blue in the face, but the women said, "We can't go now. Our men aren't around. If they come home and agree to it, we'll go, but we can't go without permission."

"Where are your men?" I asked.

"They went out to find work."

"We'll come back around noon for you. If not noon then we'll come in the afternoon. Tell the men what I've told you. Take whatever you like. We'll come for you."

When we left the compound, I saw two boys standing in front of a house at the end of the alley; one had his gun pointing at a gaunt but tall old man. As I approached them, I heard one of the boys saying, "If you don't leave, I'll shoot you."

"Go ahead," said the old man. "You're just like Saddam. I've got to die anyway. So fire away. I'd rather die at home."

It was heartbreaking to hear this. "Don't treat him that way," I said to the boy. "It's sinful. These people are attached to their homes. This place is their whole world. You can't strong-arm them. Step aside and let me see if I can convince him."

The boy with the gun said, "Fine. I swear: we're only doing it for his sake."

Then he turned to the old man and said, "Don't take what I said seriously, gramps. But it's your fault. Why do you have to be so stubborn?"

"Father," I said, "will it do you or anyone else any good if you die? Isn't this a kind of suicide? Staying in your home means only two things: you will die or you'll be captured. Why do you want things to end that way? Leave the city and when we drive the enemy out, God willing, you can return to your life."

The man gave me a hard stare and said, "You weren't around to see how the English took Khorramshahr before. Now these Baathists, stirred up by those same English, have come to take the city from us. It's the Sheikh Khaz'al story all over again."

"No, God willing, that won't happen. That was the time of the Shah, who was the lackey of the English and the Americans. That's over."

Hoseyn Eidi, now standing behind me, confirmed what I was telling the old man and tried himself to win the man over. We finally persuaded him to go. Although convinced we were right, the old man still had a hard time coming to grips with leaving his home. He lingered in the doorway, which was made of wooden beams and covered by sheets of metal from oil drums. Staring back at his home, he said, "I don't have the heart to leave. I built this place with my own hands. It wasn't easy."

The mud and straw structure was in very bad repair. The wooden beams supporting the ceiling of the rooms at the end of the yard were exposed. The garden was covered in dust. The old man had planted a few date palms in the untended garden. A small channel carried wastewater from the reflecting pool to the alley. There was a shed for animals by the door. From the straw and animal waste strewn in the yard it was clear he had kept a cow. The old man had nothing beside this home. He wore a faded blue jacket over his dishdasha, which was worn and full of holes. He wound a white kafiyyeh around his head and, when he slipped his sun-blackened feet into a pair of torn plastic sandals, it made them look even more ragged.

I kind of liked the old man. Not only was he able to maintain a measure of personal dignity, he also understood to an extent what was behind the war. I examined his grieving face more closely. It showed all the signs of the pains and hardships of his life—like the faces of the hard-working people who by the dint of their own labor managed to get through life.

A bit farther along the alley was another scene that I found very upsetting. This was unlike the other places where there were only one or two people. Here were several families—young men, their young brides, and grandchildren with their grandparents. They had refused to evacuate. We talked and talked until finally convincing the men to leave. I signaled to the driver, who brought the pickup forward. The people walked to the truck, carrying bundles with their possessions.

But no matter what we did, the old man and woman in the group would not come with us. The old woman, who appeared to be very attached to her husband, refused to be separated from him. The old man said to her, "You go with our sons. Don't worry about me."

The woman was crying. Her chubby face was red. The man said to her, "Don't cry. Why are you crying? I'll come for you later."

This failed to calm her. I hugged and kissed her, trying to reassure her that there was nothing to worry about. In Arabic she asked, "How can I just leave him and go? I'm everything to him. I've always been by his side, cooking for him. His favorite is fish. Who's going to make fish for him?"

"Mother," I said, "will it make any difference if he doesn't have fish with what's going on here? Besides, where are you going to get fish nowadays?"

The old man spoke to his wife and sent her over to her children. He wouldn't abandon their two cows. The old woman hesitated getting in the truck because of the strange men. She kissed her young son, who was single and wanted to remain with his father, and said, "Look out for your father. Make sure he takes his medicine on time. Don't run about or you'll be hit by a mortar. Stay by your father."

The grandchildren and the young women came forward to kiss the old man's hands and feet. He caressed them and kissed them on the head. The brides pleaded with him to come with them. "Leave the cows. God will look after them."

He suddenly became angry and barked at them, "What do you know? My whole life is wrapped up in these cows! How can I leave them? Aren't these the same animals that gave you milk and the whey that you drank? They're the ones that kept you going, aren't they?"

The men and their wives gathered around him again and said, "Take care of yourself."

As we neared the last part of Mowlavi, the place became more deserted. Bombs and mortar fire had knocked holes in the walls around many of the homes. We could see children's clothes still hanging on clotheslines through the broken walls. Their pink, red, and blue plastic sandals were also visible. This made me think of Sa'id, Zeynab, and Hasan. I worried about what had happened to them. I saw a doll buried in the debris. I felt its blue eyes staring at me. With each step I expected to see Iraqis or to be ambushed by them.

A breeze whipped up dust in the alleys and sent garbage blowing from one side to the other. At times it was so quiet the whistling of the wind made me imagine all kinds of frightening things. The silence brought memories of the long days of summer before the war, when everybody would gather by the gas coolers and sleep with the ceiling fans going. But we didn't have the means of keeping cool. When it got very hot and dry, father would go to the marsh and wet some straw. Then he would put the wet straw in front of a fan to make the air cool and damp. Sometimes he would wet a cloth for the same purpose, but it would soon dry, losing its effectiveness. Not used to sleeping during the day at all, I would go by the door and peek out into the alley. Nothing was moving in that heat, not even the birds. The silence and the emptiness of the alley frightened me, and I would quickly shut the door. Mother was always frightening us with stories about kidnappers lurking in the deserted alleys. It was like that now. I don't know how long we had been working, but the boys were very tired, and when the truck, which had been ferrying people away, returned empty, we climbed in and headed for the mosque.

I was wondering what to do next, when I heard someone shouting. I raised my head and saw a slim young man in the doorway of the mosque trying to draw people's attention. He was saying, "Our forces have no water at the front. It's so bad they've been forced to drink marsh water. You have to do something."

I had the feeling I knew him. As I was trying to recall where I'd seen him before, I asked myself: How does he know they need water at the front? Then it suddenly hit me. This was Behnam Mohammadi, one of Uncle Shanbeh's relatives. Whenever he visited them, they would warn the neighbors what a devil he was. He'd sneak peeks into their yards from the roof and play with a dog chained there. I was amazed to see him looking so thin, so battered and worn. He was very sunburned, and his long hair needed combing. "What are you doing here, Behnam?" I asked.

He just stared at me in silence, as if he didn't recognize me. "Don't you remember whenever you came to uncle's house, you'd appear on our roof and drive us crazy with your monkey business?" I said.

He smiled, seeming to remember. "What happened to your dog?" he asked.

"Nothing. No doubt he's a refugee like everybody else."

Then I asked, "What's happening? What did you say about the front? Were you there?"

"Yeah. I go to the front with the defender boys. A few days ago we were surrounded all day and couldn't get water. With me being so wiry and strong, they said I should try and get some. That's the reason why I went through hell to do it. Even though the water was filthy, I had no choice. I brought it back but after the boys had drunk some, they all started puking."

"Around evening we managed to get away from the Iraqis, but we were dying of thirst. I went everywhere, knocked on every door to find some water, and finally I ended up by the pool at the mosque. But is that what you call water? There's scum all over it, it's been in the pool so long. I pushed the scum aside and shoved my head under so I could gulp down some of the swampy stuff. But I couldn't help swallowing some of the scum and got sick to my stomach. All of us were like that, everybody throwing up, but because we were still parched, we went on drinking."

I got upset and said, "That shouldn't happen. I'll tell everyone I can to get them to bring water to the front."

After that wherever we went, I tried to make sure that we carried water jugs with us. We would fill them at the Shatt where the water was boiling hot and had fuel oil and gasoline floating on it, but it was still better than marsh water.

26

Fed Up and Unnerved

After father's death, working at Jennatabad was no longer a priority. The number of corpses had decreased, and to me keeping the living alive was more important. Nevertheless, whenever I did stop by and there was a body to attend to, I would do what was necessary. The searing pain caused by the death of father and Ali had made it more difficult to tolerate the work. I no longer had the patience to slave away at the body washers'. In the past I would stay from dawn when I entered the building until perhaps the evening call to prayer. But now I couldn't sit still. Seeing those mangled faces and bodies or hearing the bombardments had eroded my patience. I had seen things that were beyond imagination. Shrapnel hitting children in the stomach, making their intestines spill out. A few women, in addition to having stomachs torn open, had their kidneys come out as well. There was one case so awful it made even me want to get away from the patient. The head and legs were so badly crushed we couldn't tell how old the person was. It appeared a mortar had blown off on his head, leaving no part of the body intact. They didn't wash it, just rubbed it in earth and shrouded it; but so much blood flowed from the corpse that the shroud became soaked. They said, "Place it in a corner to let the blood dry, and we'll shroud it again."

When I first saw that corpse, my heart broke, but I couldn't go near it. Eventually, as I dragged it to where it would dry, I managed to speak to it directly: "Why did you stay in the city only to suffer like this? Why didn't you let them evacuate you? Where were you going? Wherever it was, there was no escaping the hand of fate! It's a good thing that you left this world as a martyr, so now you'll be buried as one." My rage was now coming to a boil, and I shouted: "Goddamn you, Saddam! May God strike you dead! Why did there have to be war? Why do I have to be here now? How long do I have to bear this? How long do I have to go on seeing these things?" Suddenly my ears and face felt like they were on fire. I stop dragging the body and, in tears, declared, "I'm fed up. I can't take it any more in this damned morgue. I'll never set foot in here again."

I pounded the door open and stormed out of the building. Zeynab went with me. I ran where no one would find me, but Zeynab followed. She took me by the arm and pulled me toward her. I tried to push her away, but she wouldn't let me and hugged my head and kissed me. As she caressed me, she said, "You have every right to be fed up. We're all tired and have had it. Anybody in your shoes would be worse off, but, Zahra my dear, what else can we do? I have an idea. Stay away for a while. Don't come to work." Then, after a short pause, she said, "I'm sure you won't be able to keep away. But it would be better now if you do."

Sobbing, I said, "No. That's impossible."

"So, what then? What should I do for you?"

I was ashamed of the way I acted toward Zeynab. I promised myself I would try to keep my emotions in check, but that was impossible. I believe it was around the October 12, 1980, one of those days at the body washers' like the rest when my emotions had gotten the better of me. My nerves were shot. I remember having a bowl or a length of cloth in my hand and throwing it across the room and leaving. Again it was Zeynab who followed me out, but this time she didn't catch up to me. I ran so fast I was short of breath. I stopped and, after calming down, started to walk. I asked myself: Poor thing, who do you think you're running away from? From yourself? From the martyrs? Who? I started crying again, bawling with my eyes closed. When I opened them, I found myself in front of our home. I unlocked the door and went inside the yard. I wanted with my whole being for father and Ali to be there. Seeing them would restore my composure. I wanted to embrace and kiss them, insist they take me with them. But entering the yard, my hopes were dashed. Of course, there was no sign of them. I didn't want to go inside the house. I looked into the hall through the window. Our things were where we left them, but there was a layer of dust on everything. Seeing the furniture reminded me that every once in a while, we dragged it all, huffing and puffing, out into the yard. We beat the dust out of the carpets and the furniture with sticks. I would be in a cleaning frenzy until the whole house was spic and span. Then, with the house full of guests and so much noise I couldn't hear myself think, I relaxed.

I stood by the garden. All of the flowers and shrubs had died. Even the Shah Pasands, denied water, withered. All of a sudden I thought of what mother was going through. I had no idea where she was, which made me feel worse. I stood in that deserted and hushed place until I couldn't stand it any more and left. There was no one in the alleys. Not even a bird was stirring. It was getting dark, and everything was bathed in the reddish light of sunset. I passed grandfather's home and peeked in. As I surveyed the house, I realized how much I missed him and grandmother.

I didn't have the strength to walk all the way down Ordibehesht Avenue to the mosque, so I took a shortcut through the date grove behind the flour mill, hoping to emerge at the Mohammadi florist on the Forty-Meter Road. I could hear whispers in the fearsome silence of the grove. It felt like I was about to have a heart attack. I listened intently. It appeared to be the sound of two or three people speaking softly, but I couldn't hear what they were saying. I tried to control my fear, telling myself that I was imagining things. Nevertheless, I began to run.

A little farther on, I saw several uniforms lying at the base of some trees. I was certain they were Iraqi uniforms because of the dark green color. The boys said that they were Israeli. I had heard that when the Iraqis entered the city, they would change their uniforms and go around the city gathering information in different uniforms or dishdashas. Seeing these uniforms, I was certain the whispering I heard hadn't been my imagination. Upon seeing me, they got to their feet and continued to whisper among themselves. I thought to myself: The thugs would soon have me surrounded.

With these thoughts swirling in my mind, I was gripped by a fear I had never before experienced. I wanted to run away, but didn't have the strength. It was as if my feet were nailed to the ground. I took a grenade from my pocket and got ready to pull the pin the moment I saw anyone. I began to run and pray at the same time, like someone chased by wolves. I cut through the grove to Ordibehesht Avenue and kept on running until I reached the mosque. Afraid the men would start in on me again for going out alone and putting myself in danger, I didn’t tell anybody about what had happened.

27

The Iraqi Encirclement Grows Tighter

I was in a strange mood these days. I was lost to myself. Everywhere I went, whatever I was doing, father and Ali were always with me. More often than not it was Ali's face that appeared before me. I didn't know why. Maybe being more recent, the searing pain of his death was more vivid to me. I was beside myself missing him. I had no desire to eat or rest. Nothing seemed important to me. I worked and went about the city out of habit. In my mind, I would hold conversations with them. I imagined them answering me. I felt the weight of their footsteps.

Seeing the city, which had now completely taken on the face of war, distressed me even more. Conditions had become worse, more critical. Traffic in the area away from the mosque was even lighter. Wherever we went we could see more signs of destruction. Very few houses were intact. Vehicles abandoned in driveways or by the side of the road because of the lack of petrol had become burned-out wrecks. The behavior of animals I saw here and there in town had also become erratic. Before, when they saw people the creatures would follow them in search of protection. Now, they would freeze in terror and then run away. Walking around, we would see the carcasses of animals that had fallen. The wind whipped dust and tumbleweeds from one side of the empty alleys and streets to the other. All the devastation conjured up the nightmare of the city falling.

Planes had no trouble flying at low altitudes. There was no sign of the antiaircraft batteries that had been operating in the first days. The enemy pilots maneuvered in the air, breaking the sound barrier, and, if they didn't drop bombs, the roar of their engines shattered the few windowpanes that were still intact. The sound barrier booms also brought on horrible migraines.

There were now fewer girls working at the clinic. Only Zohreh Farhadi, Sabah Vatankhah, Maryam Amjadi, Belqis Malekian, Mehrangiz Daryanavard, and I were left. We no longer ventured out into certain streets and alleys. Even the Taleqani neighborhood, which I counted as a good area, had become a terrifying place to me. Only the sounds of enemy mortars and artillery broke the fearful silence. I had my heart in my mouth as I went to Jennatabad, expecting at any moment to fall into an Iraqi ambush. Word had it that the Iraqis had fanned out in the Taleqani neighborhood; it wasn't far from there to Jennatabad. I was very worried about Leila and Zeynab. There was talk the Iraqis had taken a number of people in Taleqani and Qezeli prisoner, and they had raped girls in front of their parents and brothers in the Hizan neighborhood.[1] Then they killed the men and released the women, who were in a crazed state. It was said that when our forces reached these women they begged for death.

After hearing this, I couldn't speak for a few days. I retreated into a shell. I didn't even have the nerve to put myself in their shoes. It was insane to see how naïve people were to think the Iraqis wouldn't harm them. How could they be so gullible? For a moment I feared for us, Leila and me. But then I asked myself: Didn't you know how it would be from the start? Besides, this incident happened on the eighth day of the war, and I was just now hearing about it. I thought back to those days and realized the men at the mosque had a good reason to be hard on us about going out alone. They never came out and said it directly, but that was why they pressured us to leave the city. So it was not for nothing that when we had said that we wanted to go to the front to help the wounded, the men retorted, "With men not having died at the front yet, you women want to go there?"

There were no more fighting men in the mosque. They had all left for the front. Even Ebrahimi was gone. They had closed up shop

---

[1] The details of this incident were narrated by Iraqi Second Lieutenant Khaled Salman and published by Soreh-ye Mehr in the book *Fire and Blood in Khorramshahr* (*Atash va Khun dar Khorramshahr*).

on coordinating things from there. I didn't see Mr. Mesbah and the others. Sheikh Sharif was mostly at the front and was working with even more conviction than before. The boys said the Sheikh's son had been wounded and was in the hospital, but he didn't even have a chance to visit him.

It was clear to everyone the war was a very serious matter, and the Baathist regime of Iraq—with all the forces, arms, and equipment they had brought to the battle—had more in mind than just taking Khorramshahr.

The situation at the Congregational Mosque had become very critical. Soldiers were coming and going in greater numbers. Groups of people, who couldn't bring themselves to leave town, had taken refuge there. The rifles of our forces couldn't force them to leave, nor could the deadly fire of the Baathists drive them from the city. Heydariyeh and Abbasiyeh were deserted. I had heard that the bombing had reached those places. The kitchen was closed, and all the women cooks had gone. Even if they had stayed, there was no food. We were out of everything. We made do with bread, watermelons, or tinned food, the same rations the troops had. Sometimes there was nothing but dry bread, which we dipped in water and ate.

The body washers also left in the end. Maryam took her son-in-law, and only Zeynab remained. Jennatabad was not immune to the heavy Iraqi attacks. A bomb landed the old section of the cemetery, destroying many graves. Shrapnel struck the stone slabs, shattering them. I was petrified that the graves of father and Ali would suffer the same fate. I tried to monitor what had happened to them, even if it was from far away. Their resting places had changed slightly. The earth around them had lost its freshness. In the beginning when I watered it, it would give off a certain fragrance. That was gone now. The earth, which at first tended to be a reddish color, had dried and was a salty white. The level of earth around the graves had gone down, and every time I visited them, I would brush off debris brought by the wind and smooth out the surrounding earth.

Worried an animal had dug up Ali's clothing, I visited the place I had hid it. With all my heart I wanted to take his clothes out and see them, but I never had the opportunity. I consoled myself by promising to put it off until the war ended.

I knew the situation was getting more desperate by the day. The Iraqi noose around the city was getting tighter, and they had brought their artillery closer. Compared to the first days of the war, the shelling had gotten worse. Their forces were advancing, while our diminished troops were falling one after another, resisting them. No munitions were coming to us from outside, and what we had was running out. Our own weapons were becoming useless. The Ahvaz-Khorramshahr Highway was generally closed. The shelling around the roadway was so intense no one dared set foot there. It was said the Iraqis had such a tight grip on it they could strike anything that moved.

Word from places farther up the Shatt had it that the Iraqis were approaching Ahvaz from the Hamid Base, and it was just as likely they would take Ahvaz as they would take Khorramshahr. It was also reported they had entered Dehlaviyeh and Susangerd.

Scattered and irregular forces, having heard about the clashes and the emergency conditions in Khorramshahr, had come on their own to defend the city. Among them were Mr. Sadeqpur and his friends. They had come at the request of Ahmad Shush from Rudsar (who was martyred). The poor souls didn't have the temperament to withstand the heat of the south. In my comings and goings, I saw both locals and outsiders so exhausted they didn't have the strength to walk. Unable to carry their weapons on their shoulders, they held them in their arms and dragged the magazines along the ground. It was obvious it had been several days since they last slept, and they couldn't keep their eyes open. Some of them were stranded at the front for several days, but no one could get close enough to provide them with food and water. They themselves couldn't get back behind the lines because the Iraqis had them pinned down in the alleys and lanes. The slightest misstep meant they would be slaughtered. Without food or water for a few days they were sick with hunger and thirst. At the hospital we saw people bedridden only because of physical exhaustion, but these problems also had an effect, more or less, on the defenders' morale.

In the beginning everyone was hopeful that the war only last days. But now they were talking about the large size of Iraq's arsenal and her supply of troops. Many had lost hope for our forces. But, when everything pointed to the Iraqis taking the city, others proudly and stubbornly proclaimed, "We're not that far gone yet to let the Saddamites to take the city. Our trust is in God."

Like them I couldn't wrap my mind around the idea of the Iraqi's taking the city. But, then again, I would ask myself: How long can our boys last? How much did we have left in the way of munitions? How many defenders are left? What is their strength? Is it realistic to hope for reinforcements from other cities? For that reason I asked the military types about Iraqi strength at the front. Almost to a man they said, "They've sent in three divisions of infantry and one of tanks."

Following up, I asked, "How many in each?"

"It's different with each country," they said. "From eight to thirteen thousand. The Iraqis have between ten and thirteen thousand. Other countries have been helping them."

I knew about the aid they got from states in the region and from America, but I didn't know the extent of it. Many nations were involved in the conflict. This was at a time when we didn't have more than three tanks total. I had heard this from the soldiers. I often asked the soldiers at the base, "Why can't you stop the Iraqi tanks?" They answered, "With what? We only have three of our own."

I saw myself that one of the tanks was stranded in the mud by the police station. They said it had been under fire and one of its treads sank in the mud. Another had been out of commission by the wall at Jennatabad since the tenth day of the war. Later I heard they had taken this tank to Ahvaz for repair. The only working tank we had was forever going this way and that—sometimes to the police station, sometimes to Railroad Circle or customs—laying covering fire for the front-line fighters. Recently they had taken a tank from the Iraqis. It was new and fast, clearly not one of ours. It had a different shape than ours. Unlike the Chieftans, which tended to be green, it was khaki color. They paraded it all over the city, letting everyone know it was booty liberated from the Iraqis. This, they thought, might breathe new life into the forces defending the city. But seeing how the port and customs had been looted, no one took any joy from a single liberated tank.

During our forays around the city, we visited the port area several times. It was full of goods. They said that those responsible for customs originally intended to clear it of all goods, but since it was the first spot that had come under heavy Iraqi shelling, they couldn't. Again I heard that they wanted at least to take out the airplane parts that had been purchased, but even that wasn't practical.

One day they brought burn victims to the clinic, explaining there had been a fire at the port. Mr. Najjar applied vaseline and gauze to their wounds and I, along with a couple of others who had secured a vehicle, went to the port to find more victims. We entered through the Sentab gate.

The port area was so vast we couldn't tell where it began or ended. There were so many pieces of equipment, so many goods, it was easy to get lost among them. I didn't see many people. The place where unrefined cooking oil destined for the factories was stored had caught fire. The oil was burning producing a thick, foul smoke. Workers were trying to smother the fire with dirt. We found only one person with burns on his arms and legs; fortunately they weren't severe. He continued to work in that condition, and, no matter how much we insisted he come with us for treatment, he refused, saying, "I've got work to do. I'll come later on."

We scoured the area in the car for wounded we could bring back to the clinic. The imported machines, large containers, boxes, and voluminous bales were evenly spaced, forming avenues and secondary roads. The boxes contained all sorts of goods—from screws and bolts, toys and sewing machines, to machinery and parts for factories and airplanes. Some of the boxes were the size of a large room, and it took a crane to move them. A large number of brand new cars imported from Japan and Germany were parked in a vast area at the port. The brand new Toyota passenger cars, pickups, Mazdas, Mercedes, and BMWs sparkled in the sun. Our own exports took up another part of the port: hand-woven carpets, dates....

In several spots goods were stored in warehouses and steel structures. Most of these were state-owned. Another set of goods was destined for trading companies and factories in other cities. These had been ordered by foreign companies and duly sent to them. Most of this commerce was carried on by post.

Now all these goods—all this wealth—were burning. Several of the ships bearing goods had no chance to unload their cargos, and having come under fire, were smoldering by the jetties. The flames were so intense porcelain pots burst from the heat. Crates had been hit by mortars, their contents destroyed. Large containers of clothing like jeans, high-quality cotton shirts, electrical equipment, bicycles—all were reduced to ashes. Large boxes of imported fruit were left rotting.

It made my blood boil seeing all these goods bought with the wealth of the nation now being consumed by flames or wolves, and it broke my heart there was no way to get them out of the city. At the very least we could have moved them to safety with the cars.

The scene made me even more furious with the treacherous few, who had brought all this misery upon us. In the last few days, the boys returning from the front reported the Iraqis now had the port. They said they were looting the area by crossing over the Shatt or coming through Shalamcheh.

28

Heavy Fighting, Paralyzed, Evacuation

Conditions had become so dangerous and the Iraqis had advanced so far there was no longer any need for me to beg to be taken to the front. Our front lines were falling one after another, and more and more of the central parts of the city were becoming battlegrounds. Because it was too hard to transport the wounded by car, aid workers who could were asked to go to the front and treat them there. I believe Dr. Sadeqi made this suggestion in hopes of saving lives.

The night before October 12 the battle at the port reached a climax. After this several new fronts formed. Our side was badly in need of personnel, which meant every able-bodied person was asked to leave the clinic and to go to Sentab.

Early the next morning, we filled empty munitions boxes with everything we could get our hands on: tape, bandages, scissors, needles, blood clotting drugs, xylocaine, and a variety of sedatives and salves. Well supplied by the visiting medical groups, we were very generous with our supplies. We also filled two munitions boxes with magazines, weapons, and RPG rounds.

When the pickup arrived Sabah, Dr. Sa'adat, and I loaded the boxes. Two young men who had been bringing wounded to the clinic joined us. To prevent the clinic from being completely devoid of personnel, Mr. Najjar kept a few of us behind. Sabah and I sat up front, and the boys found room in the back. Dr. Sa'adat in his white coat sat on boxes and held onto the side of the truck.

The truck started off, and to avoid being hit by the shells the driver took a circuitous route, safer but more difficult to negotiate. He went around the Congregational Mosque, the Forty-Meter Road, Naqdi, Gate Circle, Mowlavi Avenue, and finally through the alleys, lanes, and date groves behind the Mowlavi area. From there we entered the Satan Bazaar. In the last several days, the Iraqi fire had intensified and gave the city an awful pounding. It felt like a replay of the tenth day when they hit Darya Bod Rasayi School.

We arrived at 9:00 or 9:30 and got out of the truck in the grove. We then unloaded the boxes. I picked up a knapsack with RPG rounds and grabbed one handle of a box. One of the boys took the other with one hand and with his other got a box that Dr. Sa'adat had. They piled some other equipment on the box. The other people carried the remaining boxes.

It wasn't far to the area around the railroad tracks, which was under heavy fire. As we got close to the tracks, the soldiers who had taken cover there poked their heads out and asked, "Where are you going?"

The boys answered, "We're following the tracks to the to Sentab gate."

"You can't," they said. "That place is under heavy fire. It's almost impossible to get to that end."

"What should we do, then?" asked the boys.

"If you want to reach the gate, you'll have to cross the tracks. Then you'll have to go from one alley to the next alley on that side. You can't go directly. The Iraqis have set themselves up in the customs area and are firing at us from there."

"Tell us what to do," the boys said.

"We'll lay down covering fire, so you can cross quickly. But don't raise your heads, or they'll shoot them off," they warned.

The tracks and the avenue alongside it were higher than Mowlavi Avenue, giving the Iraqis a clear shot at anything that moved on them. We decided to cross two-by-two. We took some things out of the boxes so they'd be easier to carry. I had three G3s on my shoulder, an ammunition belt around my waist, and held a box of medicines in my hand. "You won't be able to run like that," they said.

"Sure I will," I said.

Although I nearly died carrying all of those things, I was too proud to admit it. I was afraid of not bringing enough supplies, and thought we wouldn't be able to go back for more. Dr. Sa'adat picked two knapsacks and the box I had been carrying. The rail line and the avenue were a total of around eight meters wide. We had to cross it crouching down, because if they hit the explosives, all that would be left of us would be ashes.

The signal came in a flash, and the doctor and I started to run. Our forces lay down covering fire behind us to keep the Iraqis pinned down. By the time the doctor and I reached the sloping roadside, we were breathing hard. The rest of our party, also ducking down, came running, and once again we were off. Before us was a barren field and, beyond that, some mud village houses and the date grove.

At the head of one of the alleys we saw a sandbagged bunker, in which a young soldier was talking on a radio. Seven or eight soldiers and some civilians were gathered around him. I came closer and saw that on the floor of the bunker were other radios, which the military man was operating constantly. On closer inspection I noticed he was wounded. He was pale and obviously fatigued. They had propped up his bandaged right leg with a cement block. He was wearing slip-on sandals, and his bluish and swollen toes were sticking out from the bandage.

The boys said, "This is Lieutenant Aqareb Parast."

A soon as he saw Sabah and me (we were standing in front), he got red in the face and said, "What are you doing here? You think this is a game? The Iraqis are here!"

Then he turned to the boys and said, "Why did you bring these sisters with you? Where do you think you're going?"

"To the entrance to Sentab," they said.

Dr. Sa'adat said, "Well, they told us to come here. They wanted medical help, so we've come to help."

"Very well. You can stay," he said. "But the sisters'll have to go back."

As soon as he said this, I said, "We won't go back. Do you think you're some kind of general to order us around like that?! We're here, and we know what we are doing."

"Sisters, you've got to listen to me," he said. "What do you think you're doing being here without orders?"

"We didn't just come on our own," I said. "We're nurses. They told us to and we came. No one can tell us to go back."

During the heated discussion, a reporter showed up—from where, I do not know—and said to Sabah and me, "Wait a second. Let me take your picture."

This made me furious, and I yelled at him, "Get out of here, man! What the hell good is our picture? You should have a gun, not a camera!"

The lieutenant kept insisting that Sabah and I not go with the group. I was so angry at his attitude I began to scream, "No one has the right to stop us, and I'll shoot anybody who tries."

The poor man looked at me and then at the rest of us and said, "You go and you'll be taken prisoner. Iraqis are everywhere."

"Fine, I'll be captured. But I've got to do something."

"You'll be killed," he said.

Dr. Sa'adat and I started speaking at once. I said, "That could happen anywhere in the city. The difference is that here we're moving against the enemy, standing up to them. At least here a person can die defending himself."

Dr. Sa'adat added, "Whatever happens, sir, we're ready for it. These sisters aren't afraid of anything. They're aware of the risks and have come to the front willingly."

Sabah backed him up on that. Then I said, "We know the risks: being wounded, martyrdom, or capture."

I felt the grenades in my pocket and said, "These are for the time when the enemy is about to take me prisoner."

The lieutenant gave in and said, "You know best. I don't know what to tell you. You don't know where the Iraqis are, so at least wait. There's a group about to go to Sentab. You should join up with them."

We stood there waiting for the group to form. I heard from the military boys that Lieutenant Aqareb Parast was the ranking officer. They told me that even though he was wounded, he would never retreat himself.

I now remembered meeting him, a young man of around thirty, when he was standing in front of the mosque with Major Sharif Nasab.

We didn't wait long. Suddenly a group of armed men emerged from one of the village houses. There were all sorts among them, from soldiers to civilian forces of various ages. The twelve of us joined them. Before we left, a young soldier who was the leader of the group conferred with Lieutenant Aqareb Parast. I tried to overhear what they were saying, but didn't get much. Most of the jargon they used seemed like military code. Then the commander addressed the group, "As soon as we move out, there'll be no more talking. You have to walk in absolute silence."

As we left, Aqareb Parast said, "Sisters, be very careful how you go. Try not to get separated from the brothers. Walk in the middle of the column; do not trail behind or go ahead. You're not allowed to break ranks."

Then he addressed the men, "Look out for the sisters, and, God willing, they'll come back safe and sound." Then he turned to me saying, "You don't have to have so many weapons with you."

I kept a G3 and gave the other weapons to the boys. I stood in the middle of the column with an ammunition box in each hand. As we walked we constantly changed places to relieve the strain on the middle person who was holding a box by himself. We were headed for the now familiar date grove and the mud huts that stood isolated here and there or arrayed in crooked rows along the alleys and roads. As we entered the grove, there was the sound of firing everywhere and bombs going off all around us. The grove was in a terrible state. Many of the palms had been hit; some were burned and stripped of their fronds. Others were uprooted by direct mortar hits. Some of these had not quite fallen to the ground, seeming to be resting as they leaned against trees that were still upright. Dates littered the ground and birds' nests, especially nightingale nests, lay ruined among the dry, scorched weeds.

No one spoke along the way, but they signaled to one another to be careful so often it scared me to death. Worried my footsteps on the dry grass and leaves would make too much noise, I tiptoed as I moved with the column. At the head of each alley we reached, the soldiers would signal us to stop while scouts reconnoitered. Then they would signal us to take turns crossing the open space, while maintaining separation. This became the routine at alleys and crossroads.

As soon as they heard a sound, the Iraqis would rake the area with machine gun fire. We had to stop or change directions when that happened. We didn't see them but expected them to jump out of the grove or from the roof of a house at any moment. We finally came out of the grove and reached the wall of the customs building. I had originally thought we were going to reach the entrance of Sentab by going down Mowlavi, which ran parallel to the tracks; but we were forced to cross the tracks and head straight to customs and then follow the wall to the entrance.

As we went forward, we encountered a number of bigger and newer homes. Suddenly all hell broke loose. They were firing at us from everywhere. We were so dumbstruck we couldn't tell where the Iraqis were firing from or how they had found us. The only thing we were conscious of was the commander and his subordinates barking rapid orders, "Retreat! Get back on the double! Move!"

The sounds of Kalashnikov rounds, machine guns, and RPGs came from everywhere. Dazed and confused, I didn't know where to run, where to take cover. This was the first time that I found myself in the thick of battle. I followed the boys wherever they ran, but bullets were coming in every direction, forcing us to crouch and stay close to the ground. We remained motionless for a while. Then they signaled for us to crawl forward on our bellies. The boys took the boxes from us and dragged them along the ground, making a terrible racket. Snaking my way along the sandy ground was very hard. My shins and knees started to ache, but I had to go on. At several points, I felt I didn't have the strength to continue. I sat up to straighten out my legs for a few seconds.

Our situation was nothing to brag about, but at least we had gotten out of range of the Iraqis. We took cover behind a house to catch our breath. I was bathed in sweat and my heart was racing. The commander appeared, looking ragged and on edge. One of his subordinates said, "God was very merciful. Two of our scouts were leading us straight into the heart of the Iraqi forces. If we had listened to them during those last moments, we would certainly have been captured."

My heart sank. We had been about to be ambushed by the enemy and weren't even aware of it. I had admitted the possibility of capture to Aqareb Parast and was prepared for it; but now that things had reached this stage, accepting the reality was difficult. It tormented me to think I could be captured without putting up any resistance or firing a shot at least. I always thought I would fight back if surrounded. As the enemy's hold got tighter, a person was expected to resist and, eventually, die. But thus far I hadn't done anything; I hadn't fought, nor had I provided help to the wounded.

As we were taking a breather, someone said, "It's impossible to go any farther this way."

Having gone halfway, we had to retrace our steps. After conferring with a couple of the soldiers, the commander chose another route, and we slowly and quietly got underway. We passed through some of the village huts and areas where the downtrodden lived and reached a half-built structure near customs. The building was two or three stories and overlooked the interior of customs, giving us relative control over our surroundings. The commander asked us to divide up quietly and take positions on the different floors of the building.

It was decided that three of the six nurses would be on the lower floor, three on the second, and the rest who were to do the fighting would occupy the roof. As we took up our positions, they told us to walk on the steel girders because the ceiling of the unfinished building might cave in.

We went inside. Sabah, Dr. Sa'adat, one of the young men, and I were to go up to the second floor. The "stairway" consisted of loose bricks piled up, which made the going very difficult. The boxes we carried were heavy and there were no decent footholds. Finally, after much slipping and falling, we reached the second floor and sat on the girders. From that vantage we could see the first and third floors through the unfinished floor and ceiling. We also had no trouble hearing the Iraqis. They were at the port. The commander believed one of them was spotting for their artillery.

We had just sat down and were looking around when one of the boys on the roof started shouting, "Death to Saddam! Death to the Iraqis!" Then he began to fire. It was the same young man who had lost his nerve when we were first under fire. He was so enraged he couldn't say more. His colleagues had been trying to calm him, but he had apparently become unglued at the sight of the Iraqis. Maybe the looting of the port had sent him over the top.

By opening up on the Iraqis, he drew all their fire on us. They hit the building with so many RPG rounds that it shook. One shell managed to penetrate the floor we were on, hitting a wall a nearby wall and exploding. We jumped up in a panic. Dr. Sa'adat asked me whether we should run downstairs.

"Yes," I said. "You go first."

I grabbed a box and retraced the wobbly brick stairway we had so carefully negotiated on the way up. As soon as my foot reached the sloping surface, the box began to slide down ahead of me. I realized that if I didn't let go, it would pull me down with it. I let go and the box tumbled down the stairs, coming to a stop on a pile of sand at the bottom. The box was shut tight so the contents didn't spill out. I began to slide down myself and made clumsy landing on the floor, covered in dust, scrapes and bruises. The building was still under fire, and I thought the buckling iron beams could come crashing down on our heads at any moment.

They told us to drop everything and run.

Almost everybody raced from the building, exposing themselves to gun fire. We gathered by a mud wall, apparently part of a animal pen, and took cover there. "What damned fool fired?" we asked one another.

Somebody said it was the same boy who lost it when they had first begun to shoot at us. When he saw the Iraqis looting the port, he couldn't stand it and started firing. Then he jumped from the roof.

People were certain he had died. To make sure we got up and ran behind a wall, which wasn't all that high, and took cover. The firing was so intense we didn't dare raise our heads; nevertheless, the boys managed to sneak peeks and shoot back at the enemy. All we could hear was Iraqi gunfire. They must have had us under surveillance from the Port Administration Building and customs. From there and from the containers piled up in the yard, they had control of the high ground. We were stuck. The seconds ticked by with no improvement in our situation. All the soldiers were riled up by the boy who had thrown himself from the roof, saying it was his idiocy that put us in this fix, killing himself in the process. He was the one who gave our position away to the Iraqis so they could fire on us. The commander signaled the men to be quiet, but some of them continued to grumble.

In front of us was an open area with houses in the distance. The leaders insisted we shouldn't make a move until the fire died down, so for two hours we didn't move a muscle. Finally the firing died down, and we were about to make a move when we heard a sound. Thinking the Iraqis were advancing toward us, one of the boys peeked around the wall and yelled, "He's alive!"

"What are you talking about?" asked the others. "Who's alive?"

"The one who threw himself off the roof, and he's moving toward us," he explained.

I listened carefully; it sounded like he was dragging his foot. I snuck a peek at him. He was covered in straw as he sidled in the dirt toward us. Still under fire he would sit up at times and then crawl. Noticing where he was headed, the Iraqis began to rain down more fire on us. The boys motioned to him to keep coming. It seemed to me his leg had been broken, and he was in a great deal of pain as he tried to cover the distance to our position. He fell down a few times but got up again. After he finally reached the wall and sat down, they asked him, "Why did you do that? How did you survive the fall?"

"I couldn't come down the stairs. I saw a load of straw and dove into it. I almost suffocated."

After he had calmed down a bit, they told him, "That was not the right thing to do. You almost got us all killed. Do you have any idea how long we've been pinned down here?!"

Upset at himself, the boy said, "When I saw how easy it was for them to enter the port, saw them rushing in without a care, it made me sick. I couldn't stand it."

The boys said, "We've probably seen worse, and if this was all about taking it, then we'd never have come to the front."

With all the soldiers worn out and some even reluctant to go on, we decided to go back. The commander said, "Let's return so we can say our prayers and renew our forces. We'll get back to the front using a different way." We retreated along the same path we had so painstakingly taken. Aqareb Parast was no longer in the bunker. His forces had evidently gone forward.

We crossed the railroad tracks and, after leaving the alleys and lanes of Mowlavi, entered a small mosque. The courtyard of the mosque was bustling. A squad of reinforcements was there. Most of the men were soldiers, but there was also a sprinkling of civilian militia from the area. People were running back and forth. They had placed some food and munitions in the rooms opposite the prayer room. The doors to the prayer room were closed, forcing all to mill about in the courtyard. In one corner was stacked all kinds of materiel covered with tarps. I didn't try to see what was under them. The crowd was making such a racket I couldn't make out what was being said.

With the water cut off, medical services were in bad shape. There was an awful smell everywhere. A tanker was parked by the latrines, but I didn't know whether it had water. Despite this, Sabah, a girl who had joined our group at some point, and I managed to find a strip of sheeting, which gave us some privacy. We used the water from the ablution pool in the center of the courtyard to wash for prayers. Not having been replaced for a while, the water in the pool was fetid and murky.

The three of us prayed, sheltering behind the materiel stacked in the corner. The others also prayed and began to eat bread and tinned fish. They offered some of the tins to us as we sat by the boxes of medical supplies. We politely declined.

The commander said, "Eat. You'll need your strength because you're coming with us to the front."

We opened a tin and began to eat. Our already filthy hands became covered in grease. We dipped chunks of dried bread in the tinned food. The bread had been dried to keep it from molding. Back at the Congregational Mosque I would always soak the bread before giving it out.

After we finished eating, Dr. Sa'adat, ever concerned about us, walked over and said, "Sisters, if you're still hungry, let me get some more food for you. Don't be shy." We said, "No, we're fine."

He left and returned with half a watermelon. Not having a knife to cut it, they had slammed it on the ground. Some of the soldiers used empty tins as spoons to scoop out the fruit.

While we were eating it, Sabah said, "I'm not going back there again. I want to leave."

Before, when we had been pinned down by the wall, she had told me, "What we're doing is insane. If I get out of this alive, I'm not coming back." I thought at the time she was kidding. But now she was repeating what she had said. "Why?" I asked. "We went through hell to get them to bring us to the front, and now that we're here you want to go back?"

She said, "It's just a mess. We don't even know where the enemy is or who we're fighting. They're just firing at us, and we can't see them. We shoot back to kill them, but it's just as likely we'll be taken prisoner. I don't want that. You should come back with me."

"No," I said. "I came here to be at the front, and I'm staying until it is resolved."

I didn't try to change her mind. She had to decide for herself. Several commandos standing nearby were speaking with raised voices. I didn't know what they were arguing about, but, motioning with the machine guns in their hands, they announced, "We'll give one of these automatics to anyone who can work it."

Sabah, who had longed for a weapon when they were in short supply, said, "I can."

I asked the soldiers about the differences between an ordinary G3 and the fully automatic one. I also wanted to know about the effective ranges of the two and how to cock them. They told me everything I needed to know. If I'm not mistaken Maryam Amjadi, who was also interested in this, made extensive notes. I said to Sabah, "Don't even think about it. They're just pulling your leg. Why are you taking them seriously? Those G3s are heavy and have a powerful kick. You've definitely got to fire them using a stand."

Sabah didn't listen to me. She put the machine gun on single-fire and pointed the barrel at the sky. I said, "You're going to fall down and embarrass us all."

"No, I can do it," she said.

As soon as she fired, she fell to the ground. I quickly reached for her hand and took the weapon. I was livid, but Sabah couldn't stop laughing.

Suddenly they ordered to us to move. Addressing the troops, the commander said, "Whoever wants to can go back from here, but those who are coming will have to observe the silence and maintain order. If you think you won't be able to keep your cool when you see the Iraqis, you'd better not come."

Several people, including Sabah, decided to return to the city. But a new group joined our band, making twenty-two altogether. As we got underway I jokingly said to Sabah, "If I don't make it, you should definitely get Leila out of Khorramshahr at the first opportunity. Keep an eye on my mother for me also."

I knew that if I hadn't made a joke of it, it would have been impossible to keep from crying. Mother's grief-stricken features would appear before me and I'd lose it. As we headed out, I thought about what Sabah had said. The situation seemed critical to me at that point; the front lines were in dire need of forces and medical supplies. This was why it was necessary for us women to be there. Under ordinary circumstances, with enough men fighting at the front, there would have been no need. I put my trust in God, the G3 on my shoulder, the grenades in my pocket, and the Colt one of commandos had given me in a belt under my chador. The Colt was in case the Iraqis took me prisoner, but whenever I had to jump or bend over, I was worried the thing might go off accidently and put me out of action.

We followed the old path until we reached the railway, but after crossing the tracks we took a different route. The column walked on steadily without a sound, communicating only with hand signals. A couple of people would leave the formation regularly to keep order at both ends of the column. We crossed the open alleys one by one.

Finally, passing by the narrow lanes where the port housing was, we reached the cement wall of the jetty and kept moving forward until arriving at the entrance to Sentab. Afraid our forces would get into the port, the Iraqis were firing blindly. They themselves didn't dare leave the safety of their positions in the port during the day. The Iraqis had taken possession of all the territory within range of their tanks, armored personnel carriers, and helicopters. Our people explained it this way: "First the helicopters soften up our positions, and then the tanks move in with infantry behind them."

When we got to the front of the building the two giant doors were ajar, apparently yanked from their frames by force. A cement pillar one meter wide divided the two doors. Entering through one side of the huge doorway was a rail track; the other side was a paved roadway for heavy machinery, trailers, and articulated trucks. This gateway, which was known as Sentab, was one of three main entrances to the port. The other two were Filiyeh and Dowrband.

Our forces had fortified their position behind the pillar with sandbags. Around the area they scattered their munitions, everything from grenades, rifles, pistols, and small arms ammunition to rockets for the RPGs. There were no more than five or six soldiers around the cement column. They were overjoyed to see us. Their faces were lined with fatigue; clearly they hadn't slept for days and had to force their eyes to stay open.

The commander of our group divided up the personnel, assigning each person a task. He stationed a number some distance from the entrance and told a few others to stand on the cement jetty of the port. A couple of those who met us at the building were so tired and hungry they didn't have the strength to stand. With our arrival they returned to the back lines. They said small and scattered bands of our boys had managed to penetrate the customs area and repel the Iraqis' advance.

The commander stationed me and the other woman next to the jetty, ordering us to feed RPG rounds to the boys on the wall. The troops very smartly scampered up the three or four meter jetty. The thick branches of the trees lining the wall provided cover for them from the Iraqis. They would either sleep on the jetty or run along the top, changing their positions regularly to make it harder for the Iraqis to draw a bead on them.

From where we were sitting we could see the road and railway and, farther away, the scattered huts of the inhabitants. One of the soldiers who had arrived the day before told us ambulances had been stationed behind the huts to be ready to speed the wounded away.

The other woman and I rapidly fixed charges to the RPG rounds and put magazines into the G3s, handing them to the two or three soldiers standing on the jetty near us. When they ran out of ammunition, the soldiers had no trouble throwing the empties to us on the ground. But it was difficult for us to hand ammunition back up to them. It was too far to reach the top, and were the tip of an RPG round to hit the ground or were a trigger to jerk forward an inch, we'd be finished.

To speed up the process I concentrated solely on loading magazines and bullets. One of the boys frantically replaced the empty magazines with full ones. They would also run into the Sentab gate to retrieve more magazines and bullets, which they had put on the ground. Dr. Sa'adat, no longer showing his customary grace and good humor, now had a weapon in his hand and was firing furiously. From time to time he would declare, "Fighting is such hard work!"

I was dying to know what was happening at the port. I could hear the Iraqis' shouts and cries plainly, but when I peeked around the wall, I saw nothing. The Iraqis were firing on us from behind pieces of equipment and containers in the customs area. The commander and others warned us not to be in front of the door. At times when the shooting intensified, the other girl and I would fire from along the wall to provide cover for troops entering the port or going to the other side of the door. As time went on the firing in this section increased. Some of the boys took shrapnel, and Dr. Sa'adat bandaged superficial wounds.

With the shortage of troops, they asked us to join the group firing on the enemy. Soon my ammunition ran out. I asked the soldier near me, "I'm out of RPG ammunition. What should I do?"

"There's more over there," he said, indicating the sandbagged position between the double doors of the building.

I got up to go to that position. The shooting was so intense he said, "Not you. Cover me and I'll go."

It bothered me that the men were still trying to keep us out of the fighting. Their lives were just as precious as ours. I said, "No, let me go myself. I've gotten this far. What difference is there between us? There's no 'me' or 'you' when it comes to taking fire. You cover me. Your RPG is still loaded, so use it."

Then I strapped the G3 around my waist, put it on automatic, and ran the three or four meters to the sandbagged position, firing all the way. The weapon jerked, and I lost control of it. I thought this was the moment I'd get my head blown off. A few seconds later, I reached the cement pillar. Grabbing the sandbags, I vaulted into the bunker. In the confusion I could make out the blurry image of the soldier, whom I had seen before, standing above me. The pillar shielded his body from the enemy, but he was holding his RPG out with his arms where the enemy could see them—as if he wasn't aware of doing it. He asked me irritably, "What were you thinking?"

He passed me without waiting for an answer, and, as soon as he took one step away from the sandbags and reached the tracks, he blew up. I was on my knees, and the shock wave flung me to the ground and made my head ring. Now everything I saw and heard seemed like a dream. The sounds I were plain enough: the man detonating, the noises made by bits of his bone and flesh falling to the ground, and especially the crack made when his skull burst apart. After the flames and smoke cleared, everything went crimson. My eyes only registered the color of blood, as if the whole place were painted red. The air was thick with the stench of burnt powder and scorched hair and flesh.

The soldier, most likely a first sergeant, had been blown to bits. In the exact moment before the blast, I had seen a bullet whizzing by. That bullet had struck the RPG he had in his hand, sending him to his death.

I got up. Everything was a blur and still felt like a dream. All that remained of the soldier were smoldering bits of flesh. It was as if someone had dismembered him and strewn the pieces on the ground. The sight of the blood and singed body parts stunned me. My eyes were fixed on the ground, but eventually I focused on the spot where he had been standing and felt sick. I looked back at the pillar and the sandbags. Parts of the wall were perforated, and one side was totally gone. Somehow I had avoided being hit by shrapnel.

I don't know whether it was the effect of seeing the carnage or of the blast that threw me to the ground, but my mind wouldn't work. I was numb. How long I remained there, I don't know, but after a while I absentmindedly put a few rounds under my arm and started moving away. I crossed the road and returned to where I had been and sat down. I looked back at the torn pieces of the corpse a number of times. From that distance it looked as if a gummy mess had been left there.

From the time we had arrived at the Sentab entrance and I first saw that man, I had been thinking about father. He looked a lot like father. I even pointed out the resemblance to the woman who was with me. Maybe it was his long face or his unibrow or the way his hair was brushed upward, but he reminded me of dad. I was unconsciously drawn to him, imagining he was father. The only difference between them was that the man was at least seven or eight years younger. More than his features, his character made me think of dad. As he ran with the forces he spoke words of encouragement to them. It was clear he was a man of faith, sure of his aims. "Bravo!" he had said. "You're a real soldier." Having forgotten the way he spoke and acted, without knowing it, I said to myself: "I'll be damned! I've thought so much about him being like dad, now he's gone and joined him."

I couldn't help saying that sentence over and over again, so many times that the woman who was bandaging the wounded with me suddenly shouted, "That's just about enough of that! I'm going to slap you silly if you don't stop! You're driving me crazy!"

I thought it was all in my head and hadn't realized I had been repeating the sentence out loud, but I couldn't help it. I was so dazed and confused I still felt like I was in a dream. To make sure, I stared at that horrid scene again, only to find it was real. I was crazed, not knowing whether to laugh or cry.

The rest, like me, were nearly out of their minds. The incident with the soldier attracted a crowd to the spot where we were. Other forces arrived, drawing more enemy fire with them—so much it prevented people from gathering what was left of the man's body. It just lay where it was. The Iraqis were pounding the other side of the wall from the port so hard it began to shake, and I thought at any moment it would collapse, burying us. The intensity of enemy fire forced the RPG men down from the jetty. The commander had told them before the action not to stay in one place for a long time, so the Iraqis couldn't get a bead on them. Despite that they had located our position and were bombarding it with mortar fire and RPGs.

I wasn't myself under these grim conditions. I moved sluggishly, as if weighed down by something. My arms wouldn't move easily. Gone was my old speed and agility. My ears were still ringing. Any moment, I thought, a mortar round would tear me to pieces. It felt like I was glued to the spot, unable to move this or that, and was now doing things out of habit. Our forces were trying hard to answer the Iraqis' fire. There was a horrid wall of sound around me. A few of our soldiers seemed to have gotten back on the jetty and, running back and forth, were raking the enemy with G3 fire. I couldn't tell how much time had passed or what actually had happened. The only thing

I recall was one of the boys on the wall handing his weapon down to me, saying it had jammed.

I stood up and took it. Leaning against the wall, I tried several times to free the bolt but couldn't. As I was doing this, there was an explosion, and I was slammed face down to the ground. Now even dizzier than before, I couldn't hear a sound. I could only feel my legs shaking. The last thing I remember seeing was Dr. Sa'adat and the other woman bandaging one of the wounded. My voice trembling, I cried, "Dr. Sa'adat! Dr. Sa'adat!"

There was no answer. I yelled the other woman's name, which I can't recall now. Nothing. I tried to get up, but couldn't. My back and legs felt too heavy to move, and I was sure the cement wall had collapsed on me. It was impossible to look back and see what had happened. There was no feeling in my back and legs. I cried out for help again. "Somebody, pull me out of here!" I shouted. "The wall's fallen on me! Help me, somebody!"

Finally I saw Dr. Sa'adat standing over me, holding his arm. Blood was streaming from it. I couldn't hear what he was saying, though his lips were moving. I thought he had lost his voice or couldn't raise it. Unable to make me understand, he got up and left. I called out to him again. I tried to use my arms to raise myself but was only able to raise my head. After a few moments, my field of vision cleared, and I could see Dr. Sa'adat and the other woman running this way and that attending to the wounded. I couldn't understand why no one was trying to get me out of the rubble. My hearing was coming back gradually, and I realized there had been nothing wrong with Dr. Sa'adat's voice.

He stood over me again. He held up his arm and, in obvious pain, explained, "You see, Sister Hoseyni, I've been hit by shrapnel."

It wasn't clear whether he wanted to comfort me or, because of his delicate constitution, to show he couldn't stand being wounded himself. "Don't worry, doctor," I said. "I'll bandage it for you."

I reached out and he handed me the bandage he was holding. I did everything I could to get up and bandage his arm but couldn't. He didn't have the slightest idea how badly I was wounded, thinking perhaps I had merely been knocked to the ground. He was looking around in a daze, horrified perhaps by the sight of so many wounded.

I said, "Doctor, no matter what I do, I can't get up. My legs are shaking."

He was shocked when he looked down and said, "Sister Hoseyni, you're wounded, too! Your back is drenched with blood."

I reached around to where it felt wet. Then my fingers sank into soft, warm tissue. Part of my back, I realized, had been torn open, but even so there was no pain. The thought that they would take me back in this state terrified me. "What should I do?" I asked Dr. Sa'adat. "I don't want to leave. I want to stay right here. What I am supposed to do?"

He said, "It appears all of us will have to go back. Everybody's wounded."

Then he rushed away to help another person crying in obvious pain. The doctor said, "Hurry! This man's got to go to the hospital immediately."

I tried to move again and managed to raise my head and chest a little, but my spine ached so much I was forced to lie back. I was determined to move my legs and though I thought I had been successful, when I looked down I saw they hadn't budged. I called out to the doctor again and asked, "Can't you just patch me up here? I'm not in pain."

"No. It feels like nothing's happened to you, but it's really serious," he said.

I strained my memory trying to work out what had happened to me. I remembered the wall wobbling and being thrown forward, and then the shrapnel going through the wall and entering my body. Then I recalled thinking about the size of the shrapnel and wondering how a mortar shell could penetrate a wall thirty or forty centimeters thick.

Shortly people came to carry me away. I heard the commander calling for help on the radio. He was saying fifteen or so of his twenty-man detail were in a bad way.

When the two men arrived to take me away I said, "No, no. Don't touch me. I'm not going back."

"We've got to get you to the hospital," they said.

"No," I said. "Tell the woman over there and the doctor to come and patch me up right here. There's nothing the matter with me."

I heard Dr. Sa'adat shout, "What do you mean there's nothing wrong with you? You can't get up. You've got to be evacuated, Sister Hoseyni."

"No, doctor, I don't want to."

"All of us have to go," he said. "We can't stay here. We're all wounded."

Then he said, "Take her away."

"No," I yelled. "Nobody touch me!"

"How are we supposed to lift you then?" they asked.

"I don't know. I don't care how you pull me across the ground, but I wouldn't let anyone but a close relative near me."

"We don't have enough stretchers," they explained.

With no other choice, I took hold of their weapons, and they dragged me along. We hadn't gotten but a few steps when a mortar went off nearby, and shrapnel entered my arm, causing me to let go one of the weapons. One of the men took off his overcoat and wrapped it around his arm. I grabbed it. But before we could get going again, the mortar fire became so intense the two men dove to the ground, letting me drop. We stayed like that for half an hour.

During that time, I remembered the scene from my childhood when we were coming to Iran from Iraq, and I saw father at this very port. I hadn't seen him for a year. Now it was fifteen days since he had passed away. That day at the port was the most beautiful and sweetest day of my life, but today.... I recalled as our boat traveled across the Shatt, the closer we got to Iran, the happier I became. It puzzled me when they said we were nearing the border. Where was the land? I wondered. I had no idea the boundary could be in the water, unmarked by a sign or a flag. At a certain point the boat stopped, and they transferred us to a larger one. Petrified by the water, I almost died each time the boat lurched.

As the Iranian boat began to move, I thought about what I would do when I saw father. After all that time, it would be embarrassing to jump into his arms. Then as always I began to think about Iran.

Uncle Hoseyni had gone to Iran from Basra to raise a family when I was a year old. Sometimes he included pictures in the letters he sent to the grandparents. The stylish clothing he and his family wore seemed stunning to me. They weren't dressed in the dishdashas we wore. Even at that early age I could tell that life in Iran was very different from life in Iraq. Mimi and grandfather would say such endearing things about uncle, wishing that no harm came to him. I longed to see him more than anything. Finally we reached the port, and I saw father and Uncle Hoseyni. Father tried hard not to react, but he couldn't decide which of us to take in his arms first. When he got to mother, tears welled in their eyes. I remember clearly how they stared at each other. They didn't say a word; their looks said it all.

The firing died down, allowing the men to bring stretchers, and they laid me face down on one of them. As they shifted me around, I still couldn't feel anything in my legs. There was only a pain, bad but tolerable, in my spine and, later, in my head and neck. Still questioning why I had to go back, I thought: I still had all four limbs after all.

A beat-up ambulance—its windows shot out—was parked behind the line of mud huts. Other wounded had been loaded into it before me. They put me in the front seat. I couldn't sit up and leaned uncertainly on the seat. Sitting next to me was a girl who had taken shrapnel in the knee. Unable to control my movement, I slid closer to the steering wheel each time the ambulance lurched. The lack of space made the driver keep his door open, forcing him to have one hand on the wheel and the other on the door.

Sitting at an angle, I could see the face of a severely wounded man in the back of the ambulance. He appeared to be in a coma. His eyes were rolled in his head, and his throat was making a gurgling sound, which was slowly stopping.

My headache got worse as time passed. I felt the pressure building until I thought my head would burst. I didn't know what route we were taking to get back. When we reached Dr. Sheybani's clinic, everybody rushed from the building. I wanted to get out myself but couldn't budge without help. Mr. Najjar examined the seven or eight wounded in the back of the ambulance and said, "All of them have to be taken to the hospital."

He took a look at me and concluded, "You're also in bad shape."

Then he gave me a knowing look. I felt he wanted to say, "See what you've gone and done to yourself!"

The girls crowded around me. I felt my head was exploding. I couldn't take in much of what was happening. The only thing I remember was Sabah, after seeing how much blood was on the seat and floor of the ambulance, saying, "Didn't I tell you to come back with me? Look at the mess you're in. If you'd returned then, you could have avoided this horror."

It wasn't in me to answer her. Zohreh and Sabah got in the back of the ambulance. They closed the door, and we were off. I felt cold. Some time had passed since I had been wounded, and I had lost a lot of blood. With each passing minute I became weaker.

I wanted to sleep. I felt around my legs and found my clothes were wet with blood, as was the seat and door I was leaning on. This made me feel weaker. The blood loss was actually frightening, but I comforted myself with the lie that it wasn't serious. Hadn't I tried the same thing with the wounded? Saying it would be all right? Now I knew why they didn't have the strength to answer me when I spoke to them.

The ambulance pulled up in front of the birthing center on the other side of the bridge. Everyone was concerned about the severely wounded man, wanting to get him to a specialist immediately, but as soon as the nurse opened the door and took a look at the man, she said, "Take him to the morgue."

I don't recall anything after that. I blacked out. When I came to, I found Zohreh Farhadi standing over me, holding up the drip in my arm. Her expression told me how worried she was. "Are you in pain?" she asked when she saw my eyes open.

"No," I said.

Looking around, I noticed they had placed me in a noisy ward full of wounded. Sabah and Zohreh called out to the nurses, who were working frantically, "Come and see to this patient, will you!"

After a few nurses passed by, a woman stopped and said, "No need to shout. Quiet! We'll get to her."

Sabah said, "We're not shouting. It's just that her condition is worsening."

"It's nothing," I managed to say.

The woman, who wore a white mask and black head covering, came forward and caressed me. She kissed my forehead and asked gently, "Where were you wounded?"

"Sentab."

"Where's Sentab?" she asked.

"It's one of the entrances to the port," I said.

"I thought the Iraqis had taken that?" she asked. "What were you doing there?"

"Well, we were also involved in the fight. I was a medic."

"Okay," she said. "We're going to x-ray you now. There's nothing to worry about. You'll be able to get a good rest."

"I can't," I said.

"No matter," she said. "Just remain the way you are."

Then she left. She returned and while we waited for the x-ray machine, she comforted me, explaining, "They're x-raying the other wounded. They'll be here any minute now."

Her show of sympathy took me by surprise. Soon they wheeled in the huge machine and with the help of a man put it in place. The machine had all the signs of overuse; it was soiled, bloodstained, and covered in handprints and tape.

When they were positioning the machine over my body, the visitors of the patient in the bed next to me, whose body was broken in many places, complained, "You should x-ray our patient here first. That lady's not badly wounded."

I looked at the man. He was covered in grime and blood and seemed semi-conscious. The radiologist said, "On the surface the lady doesn't seem in a bad way, but her wound is in a very critical area."

They took five or six x-rays of me from different angles. Each time they arranged the machine, the nurse would hold my hand or give me reassuring pats on the head. I wondered why she was so maternal in her treatment of me. That reminded me of mother, which made me miss her even more.

After me they x-rayed the man in the next bed. It took no more than ten minutes to develop the pictures. In the meantime they put fresh gauze on my wound and poured Betadine on it. The bleeding quickly seeped through the gauze, and they had to replace it. They brought more serum, and injected me several times intramuscularly. After determining my blood type, they also hooked me to a transfusion bag. Zohreh and Sabah helped the nurses and tried to comfort me. The x-rays having been reviewed, the nurse said, "The shrapnel is in a very delicate area, so you mustn't move much. There's not much we can do for you here. You've got to be evacuated, but don't worry. We'll send you to a better place with more facilities."

Still thinking it wasn't serious and I would heal after a few days, I said, "I'm not worried. Just pray I'll be back in Khorramshahr soon."

"I'm going to pray you'll get well soon," she said.

The loss of blood and the drugs again made me weak and sleepy. But I soon realized I was at the Oil Company Hospital, which was in better shape than the emergency room at the birthing center. The hubbub there almost drove me crazy. There was more breathing space in the ward, which held about twenty or thirty wounded men. Sunlight streamed through the windows, and there was no smell of blood. Zohreh and Sabah were not around, and I was very uncomfortable being among the men. When the nurses noticed I was awake, they notified the doctors. All at once there was a commotion around my bed as they began to examine my kidneys, sides, and legs. "No pain?" they asked.

"No," I said.

They inserted a needle in the bottoms of my feet and asked, "Do you feel that?"

"No. The only thing I feel is the weight of my legs. I have no idea where my knees or toes are," I said.

They prescribed a series of drugs and injections and left. It was upsetting to lie in bed with so many men around. I kept saying, "Get me out of here."

"There's no room," they said.

"If there's no room, put me in the hallway," I blurted out. "It's torture being in here. At least put a curtain around my bed."

No one listened, though; they didn't have time. Body and soul under tremendous pressure, I fell asleep. I didn't know what time it was when the sound of a woman carrying on awakened me. A young girl in a wheelchair was screaming, "I'm not staying here! It's filthy. I'll get an infection! Get me out of here!"

She irritated the nurses, who were telling her, "Why are you behaving that way, Miss? This lady and the others here are in far worse shape than you, but you don't hear them complaining."

She said, "What's that to me? I am a reporter. I'm spending the night here. Send me to Tehran."

Then they brought a bed and placed it next to mine. They took her under her arms and said, "You've got to help us get you onto the bed."

As they moved her, she yelled, "Ow, my leg hurts!"

She sat up in the bed and stretched her wounded leg. The two people with her stood by the bed. A short time later a doctor came and asked, "Who's Zohreh Hoseyni?"

The woman and I both said, "That's me."

We looked at each other and realized we had the same name. The doctor said, "The one with shrapnel in her spine?"

"Me," I said.

After the doctor examined me, he left and the other Zohreh asked, "Are you from around here?"

"Yeah."

"How were you wounded?" she asked.

"I'm a medic. I was wounded at Sentab."

"I know where that is," she said. "I'm a reporter from Tehran. I'm preparing something for the news and taking pictures to send back."

Then she asked, "It doesn't upset you to be here? Why haven't you been evacuated with that wound?"

I said, "I don't want to be evacuated. I'm not upset, either. I want to return to Khorramshahr as soon as possible. The only thing bothering me is being in this ward."

"In any case, given your condition you've got to tell them to evacuate you to another city," she said.

"I want to be treated just like the rest of the people here," I said.

She said, "That's very optimistic for somebody with shrapnel in such a dangerous spot. The doctor just said so."

"Look," I said. "If it was up to me, I wouldn't stay here. I'd be back in Khorramshahr at Sheybani's clinic."

"I know where you mean. I visited it," she said.

She wanted to continue the conversation, but I didn't have the patience for it. To be truthful, I wasn't at all fond of her yammering. I told her several times, "Try to put up with it a little more; there are so many people here worse off than you and I. The doctors and nurses are all dead tired, and the wounded keep streaming in. All of them are on their backs, too."

"No," she said. "If a person doesn't raise a stink, no one will pay attention. It's true that I've only got a small piece of shrapnel in my knee, but it still hurts."

The doctor examined her knee and said, "We have no way of evacuating you now; we've got to wait for transport."

"Just fill out the evacuation form for me, and I'll find a way out of here," she said.

With the help of the two men with her, she got back in a wheelchair and rolled out of the ward. I could hear her arguing with the nurse at the front desk. Finally she got her transfer, and they left the building.

My arms had been in the same position so long, it seemed they couldn't move. My stomach was so empty it seemed the walls were rubbing together, but the nurses said I couldn't eat.

At that point I wished I hadn't stood on ceremony when Dr. Sa'adat offered the tinned fish at lunch. If I had eaten my fill then, I wouldn't be so weak now. Then I fell asleep again. I suddenly opened my eyes and saw a wounded young man with bandages on his legs praying. That reminded me I hadn't said my prayers. At that point the nurses arrived with a portable curtain for my bed, and I breathed a sigh of relief. It was getting dark. Without knowing the direction of prayer and drenched in blood, I registered the intention of performing my ablutions and prayed. I felt better after that and, with the curtain shielding me from view, I slept. Every time I woke up, I felt lost in space, as if I had lost all sense of my surroundings. Shielded by the white curtain, it took me a while to realize where I was and what had happened. I spent a difficult night. When I woke, I thought I had only closed my eyes for a few minutes, but, having asked the nurses, I learned hours had passed.

The nurses spoke to me a few times during the night, and because my wound wouldn't stop bleeding, they had to keep changing the soaked sheets. They put coagulants in my drip and replaced the transfusion bag. The wounds on my arms didn't hurt except when I touched them. They wanted to cut away my clothes, explaining,

"They were contaminated with dried blood," but I wouldn't let them. They insisted on cutting my leggings and replacing them with hospital pants. The catheter was bothering me, but no matter how many times I complained it burned, they said, "We're not removing it."

Finally I asked to go to the bathroom. They removed the catheter and put me in a wheelchair. With the help of a nurse, I went to the bathroom. My urine was thoroughly bloody. Afterwards the burning decreased a bit. Next they wheeled in an apparatus attached to a monitor. They lay me on my side and attached electrodes to my arms and legs and put a hat-like thing on my head. I didn't understand what they were doing. I don't recall how the next day passed. It was morning, then afternoon, then night. I had no sense of what was happening to me and wondered why I was sleeping so much. At times I jerked awake, afraid the sheet was slipping from my face. Other times I would open my eyes and see the doctors standing around. They peppered me with questions and stuck needles in my legs again. One time they sent electric shocks up and down my arms and neck. This burned and I cried out in pain. But all the while I felt nothing in my swollen legs.

The morning of the second day (actually the twenty-second day of Mehr), I woke in terrible pain, after—it seemed—I had been sleeping forever. But I was no longer groggy, fully aware of everything around me. I was still on my stomach. The general numbness was replaced by a severe pain in my back and my legs, especially the right one. My legs were shaking, which made the rest of my body tremble, and I felt cold. At times the pain was so bad I was bathed in sweat. It got so excruciating that I put the hem of my veil in my mouth and bit down on it. I tried steady my legs with my hands, but it did no good. I called out to the nurses. They explained, "It's only natural. You've been unconscious until now and have felt nothing. We'll give you a pain killer. By the way, we're transferring you tonight."

"No, don't, I'm begging you. I don't want to go."

I began to cry. The image of Ali all alone, bedridden in some hospital came to mind. Or the time when father was working at the dock and a load of lumber fell on his leg, crushing it. They didn't give him the right treatment in the hospital. His leg became infected, and he developed a fever. I remembered clearly how much pain he was in, so much he passed out when they rubbed his leg with ointment. He didn't make a peep, though. I was four years old then and noticed mother using some excuse to go to a corner and cry. When the crying stopped, she would join father.

Recalling these things made me miss Ali and father even more. I wished they were with me. All other miseries seemed trivial to me compared to what they went through. It made me angry to have to leave the city just because of a minor wound. I found myself saying, "God, why now? You let me drive out the Iraqis. Then You rob me of my arms and legs."

Again I said, "Martyrdom was all I wanted from You. Look what You've granted me instead? I can't take it."

Next I let the invader Iraqis have it, shouting, "Goddamn you to hell! Why couldn't you have used the 230 mm mortars instead of the 60s and finished me off?"

The good-natured nurse broke into my reverie. "My, my! Look how alert we are! Today we're feeling much better than yesterday."

Then she detached the serum and transfusion drips from my arm. I was no longer bleeding, but my toes were blue and swollen. I wanted to roll up into a ball and would have given anything for a bite to eat, but I was ashamed to admit it. "Are you here to give me another drip?" I asked.

"No," she said. "You can have solid food now."

She got a biscuit and handed it to me. I was chewing it when Zeynab, Leila, Zohreh, Sabah, Hoseyn, and Abed Mohammadi entered along with the man who had driven me from Sentab. Zeynab ran to me first. She took my head in her arms and kissed it. She asked me, "Girl, what made you go and bring this calamity down on your head? What am I going to tell your mother? Didn't you think something like this would happen when you went to the front? How much does that poor woman have to endure?"

"It's not so serious," I said. "Look! Still feeling fat and sassy, all in one piece."

She gave me a motherly hug again and, pressing my head to her chest, repeated, "Thank God. I was very worried about you." After she stepped aside, the other girls came forward one by one to kiss me. Though Leila seemed calm, I could read the anxiety in her features. I whispered in her ear, "It's nothing, believe me. Just a piece of shrapnel, a tiny piece."

Hoseyn Eidi, as if he were responsible for what had happened, blurted out, "You shouldn't have gone, sister. It was my duty to go."

"No one forced me to go. Besides, are you a nurse?"

He said, "First Abdollah, now you. One after another everybody's getting wounded. It's embarrassing for me to still be intact."

"Who says everybody's got to be wounded or martyred?" objected Zeynab. "Who's going to fight the enemy if that happens? If God loves us, He'll call everyone to Him in the end. If He's not happy with us, we'll just have to wait until we can win His affection. For now He's content that we stand our ground and resist the enemy. God willing, Zahra will get better, and we'll all stand up to them together. You can be sure of that."

Then she asked, "Your condition, what is it? What are they going to do with you?"

During the time I was drifting in and out of consciousness, I had gathered I was to be evacuated. Afraid they were going to send me to Mahshahr, I made up my mind I would go back to Khorramshahr with my friends. That was the reason I said to Zeynab, "It's nothing. I've got to go back to the city. They said I could go."

"Really?" she said in surprise. "You can go back to Khorramshahr in that state? Is that possible?"

The girls said, "Let's go and ask what we've got to do. What made them say you're dismissed?"

I said, "No need to bother them; they're extremely busy."

They wouldn't hear of it, but I persisted and convinced them. They helped me sit up in bed, and I felt a terrible weight in my legs. "Take me under my arms," I said. Zeynab and Leila got my legs, over which I had no control, to dangle over the side of the bed. Then I put my arms on their shoulders, and they walked me forward as my feet dragged along the ground. After walking a few steps, I saw my leggings were hiked up and asked Zohreh to throw a sheet around me.

There was so much noise and confusion outside the ward no one noticed me leaving. Even so I was so nervous leaving the foyer I thought I would die. I kept praying no one would notice. Although relieved to get through the foyer, my heart stayed in my throat until I was out of the hospital building. After I was certain no one had noticed us leaving, I began to kid the girls, "Sweet of you to think of me and take the trouble to visit!"

"We had stopped in several times before, but you weren't conscious," they said.

I asked about the Sheybani clinic. When we reached the gas station, I managed to raise myself using my arms and look out the window. I was so happy I blurted out, "Wow! We're in Khorramshahr!"

Zeynab laughed and said, "You sound as if it's your first visit, you goose!"

It felt great to get across the bridge and smell the Shatt—like there was a tune playing in my heart. I thanked God again and again. But this was when the absence of father and Ali hurt the most. Whenever I visited their graves, I sensed they were speaking to me, watching me from above, listening to me. Though mother and the kids were not around, I didn't worry about them, knowing they had moved out of danger. In another way I was glad mother was far away, because I wished to join father and Ali. That way it would be easier for her to get used to not having me with them.

The closer we got to the clinic the happier I got. I missed the place. As soon as we arrived, everyone crowded around the ambulance. Belqis Malekian, Mehrangiz Daryanavard, Mr. Najjar, Dr. Sa'adat, Maryam Amjadi, Ashraf Farhadi....

The girls took me under my arms, and we struggled to get up the front steps. They held up my legs, and I managed to get me inside. This was very embarrassing, but the joy of being back and staying in the city eased the embarrassment. I couldn't stand—not even for a second. My legs were still shaking. Terrible pain shot through me, reaching my head.

Doctors who had been sent in from outside the zone stepped forward to greet me. We were talking in the hallway, when a doctor emerged from the vaccination room. He wore a military uniform and was around thirty-five or forty. As soon as he laid eyes on me, he asked, "Where was she hit?"

"Her spine," the girls said.

"Why did you lift her and bring her here in that condition?"

"They dismissed her."

"Fine, but in this state she has to have as little pressure on her as possible. Take her somewhere where she can be absolutely still." The girls carried me to a room with carpeting over a sheet of cardboard. When he saw me lying on my stomach, the same doctor asked, "Who said she was dismissed?"

"She said so herself," they answered.

"The hell she did!" he shouted. "She's got to be evacuated. Who said she could come back?"

He marched over to me angrily and pulled the sheet aside. He examined the wound, which had started to bleed heavily again. The girls showed him the x-ray of my back. Now even more furious he barked at them, "You haven't mentioned she'll have permanent spinal chord injury, be paralyzed for the rest of her life, and forever be a burden to everyone?!"

The girls didn't know what to say. I looked so normal they couldn't believe him. "We really didn't know it was that serious," they said. "She told us she was better and insisted on returning."

He said, "She can say whatever she wants. Didn't you see the location of the wound? She can't diagnose her own condition, and if she becomes paralyzed, it'll be your fault!"

"There's nothing wrong with me," I said. "I'll be fine. It's only superficial."

"Who's the doctor here?" he snarled. "You or me? Can you get up by yourself and walk?"

"No."

"So why do you want to stay here?" he asked. "If they were to bombard this place, would you be able to run to shelter with the others?"

I didn't know what to say. "God is great," was all I could think of.

"What's that supposed to mean? God is rational. Are you deliberately trying to get yourself paralyzed? As an orthopedist, it's my opinion you must leave this zone and go directly to Mahshahr."

I became very upset. If I had been able walk I would have gone to the Congregational Mosque, and if not there I would have gone to Jennatabad where I had started. There no one could say anything, but it was just my luck I was flat on my back unable to move.

The doctor said, "Change the dressing on her wound."

The girls washed and rebandaged it. The doctor himself injected me with Cephalexin, a strong antibiotic, and said, "There's no hope of healing this wound here, and if it becomes infected, she'll definitely be paralyzed."

"Give me the shot in my arm," I said.

The injection burned my arm so much the fire spread throughout my body. I had to fight to keep from crying. As I twisted in pain, I thought to myself: This doctor is just making this up, trying to get people to feel guilty. He doesn't want them to treat me here; that's all there is to it. I'll be well in no time and walk again.

When Hoseyn entered, saying the van was ready, I couldn't bear to look at him. The girls gathered around me, and one of them said, "You tricked us. If we had known how badly you were doing, we'd never have brought you along. You're definitely going back, and you have only yourself to blame."

It was very hard to hear this. I started crying. With tears in my eyes, I pleaded with the doctor, "Let me stay. I beg you. I'll be better tomorrow, I promise. Don't send me away."

The doctor was chuckling now and said sympathetically, "Do you think it's in your hands whether you get better? I don't want any harm to come to you. I'm not your enemy."

"I won't be a bother, I swear," I said. "I won't blame anyone else if something happens to me. I'll do whatever you say."

"There's nothing for you to do. Don't talk nonsense!"

"I can prepare cotton swabs lying in this position, and I can clean weapons."

Addressing me now as "daughter" and "sister," he said, "I'm telling you for your own good. You have to go. It isn't a problem for us having you here, but it's going to cause you all kinds of grief. Stay and you'll be paralyzed. But if you go, you'll be able to recover and return to the city. By that time, God willing, the enemy will have gone the hell away."

I knew he was telling the truth, but in my heart there was still this nagging doubt driving me crazy that I'd never see Khorramshahr again. This would be my last visit. Leaving, coming back; it made no difference. I didn't give the slightest thought to paralysis, believing it wouldn't happen if God didn't want it to happen. Wasn't He the only one helping me during these difficult days? Every minute of life I saw as a sign of His help. This was why I kept begging to stay. Ashraf Farhadi had opened a can of pears and insisted I have some. Before she could put the spoon to my mouth, I started bawling, stopping me from swallowing a thing. All the veins in my neck and muscles in my chest were aching. I wanted to scream but modesty prevented it.

They loaded me in the van. I said goodbye to everyone and begged forgiveness for being such a burden. My voice shaking, I said tearfully, "Take care of Ali's pack for me; I wouldn't want it to disappear. Don't forget to stop by and visit me."

The girls, who were in tears themselves, consoled me, "God willing, you'll be back. You'll get better. Don't worry." Ashraf, who was weeping more than the others, patted me on the head. Zeynab and Leila got in the ambulance. Hoseyn and two other men, one of whom may have been Khalil Mo'avi, the brother of Abdollah, came with us. Khalil sat on the roof of the van, and the other two stood in the corners. I was on my stomach, and Zeynab held my head in her lap and covered me with a blanket.

The van started to move. I was so distressed I didn't even look at the Congregational Mosque. I covered my face with my hands and kept crying. These were very difficult moments. The thought that it might be the last time I would see the place forced me to raise my head and look out. We were at the Farmandari Circle. I saw that there was no sign of the flowers in the middle of the circle. The road signs had been obliterated, and the pedestal in the middle of the circle, which once supported a statue of the Shah, was pockmarked by shrapnel. I also glanced at the Mosaddeq Hospital. I recalled the times seeing Shahnaz's body; the child who had lost everyone; the horrid noises made by the man who had lost his wife and child; and the sentry, his head severed from his body by shrapnel. Do Ali and father know they're taking me away? I wondered.

The thought they were just standing by and letting it happen made me want to scream, "Father, come and bring me back, I'm begging you! Don't let them take me away! Ali, you were always my rock, why won't you do something for me now?"

I also imagined them saying goodbye to me. I want to join you, I said to them, but, it seems, you don't want me to. You've both abandoned me, and now you're driving me away.

Tears flooded my eyes, blinding me. On the bridge I spoke to the waves below, "Why didn't you swallow me up the time I came to fetch water?"

I saw myself a tree with deep roots, resisting being pulled from the ground. How could I allow myself to be uprooted? Although born in Basra, I felt no attachment to the place. I loved Iran, so I learned Persian almost as soon as I had come to Khorramshahr. I had the feeling I had been here before and knew every place in it. I grew up in Khorramshahr, and all of my emotions, feelings, and attachments belonged to the city. My heart ached for the kindness of neighbors, who with all their own wants and poverty put others above themselves. I shouldn't have left. Those who wished to send me away were not from the city and would, in any case, be returning to their own home ground. They didn't realize my city was on the verge of enemy occupation. They didn't understand my city needed me. It was as if the whole town had its eyes on me. I felt myself a fish out of water, struggling for breath, dying to get back into it—a struggle going nowhere. I was exactly like the fish I had seen at the market—alive, flopping in a basket or on the fishmonger's stand, floundering about frantically to the point of self-injury. I would stare at them struggling like that, but, afraid of what the fishmonger might do, I didn't throw them back in the water.

Leaving the bridge was like having all the familiar doors in my life slam shut. I wanted to hurl myself from the car but didn't have the strength. I finally had to admit that the doctor was right, but my love for Khorramshahr overwhelmed all reason and logic. To the piece of shrapnel I was hosting in my back I said, "I wish you had hit me somewhere else, cutting my leg off rather than taking my feet from under me."

Hearing the sounds of the bomb blasts, mortars, and bombardment, I hoped for death from the air. I prayed and prayed for them to say the road was closed and no one could leave the city. These wild thoughts to some extent dulled the pain, which had died down for a while. We passed Taleqani Hospital, and I hoped someone would say,

"Find a bed for her. She can get better here." But no one said anything. We were nearing Station Twelve of Abadan. Seeing the Seyyed Abbas Shrine in the distance, I turned to him for help, "By your blessed grandfather, I'm begging you to send me back to the city."

I was crying so much I couldn't open my eyes. Noticing the state I was in, Zeynab asked, "Are you in pain, girl?"

To keep her from asking more questions I said, "Yeah."

She said to the nurse who was with us, "Can't you give her a shot? She's in a lot of pain."

"No," she said. "She just had a sedative. Not now. This one's fighting it. Given the dose we gave her, she should have been asleep by long ago."

As we passed Station Twelve, I became convinced there was no turning back. We drove by refugees on their way out of the city; they were pitiful—as I was—shuffling along carrying as many of their belongings they could. Children were wailing, and people besieged any passing vehicle begging for a lift. Fearing he would cause further injury to my back, our driver was forced to go slow, which let people we passed take hold of the side of the van. They said, "For God's sake. We're human, too. Can't you at least take us out of the city?"

When they saw a wounded person in the back, the people stepped aside without complaint. At one point jet fighters appeared overhead, flying so low their shadows fell on me. People screamed and ran away. I heard several say to Hoseyn Eidi and Khalil Mo'avi, "You've got weapons. Why don't you shoot at them?"

They started firing, and the fighters fired back with their cannons. One person said, "Shoot! You can shoot them!" Another said, "Forget it. Stop shooting."

The driver also tried to escape the firing by speeding up and leaving the paved road or coming to a halt on the shoulder. The air filled with the screeches of women and children and the shouts of men, which combined with the sounds of bombs exploding and jets flying overhead. My head was bursting with the noise, and the chaos made me feel worse. Nothing could console me now, and I began to sob. I thought: Leila would definitely want to return to Khorramshahr, but I couldn't let her stay there by herself. Gradually I went to sleep.

29

Almost Executed

I don't know how long I had been sleeping when I was awakened by loud noises and realized we had reached Mahshahr Hospital. The van stopped before an old brick building. People brought a stretcher and placed me on it. Then two well-built men lifted the stretcher and whisked me off to the operating room. They made Zeynab and Leila wait outside the door. I could hear Zeynab saying, "You're in God's hands now, love. Let them remove the shrapnel so you'll get better."

Everyone wore green in the operating room. Large lamps lit the room from above. A nurse threw a gown on me and said, "They're going to examine you here and decide about operating."

She introduced the neurosurgeon, the orthopedist, and the general surgeon. While they cleaned the wound, the doctors conferred about the x-rays taken at the birthing center and the Oil Company Hospital in Khorramshahr.

Afterwards they examined my legs by inserting needles in my knees, my calves, and the bottom of my feet. There was no pain, but I did feel a tingling where they inserted the needles. I felt nothing in other places. The toes on my right foot had no feeling, and it felt like the rest of the foot was asleep. They bandaged the wound. The leader of the surgical team said, "The shrapnel wound is tiny but in a very critical place. It would be better to send you to one of the big cities—somewhere like Tehran or Shiraz."

He asked me to describe my condition at the time the shrapnel hit and the days leading up to it. I told him about my problem urinating and my legs. The team spoke among themselves, using a lot of technical terms so I couldn't understand much. The only thing I did get was that the operation would be very tricky. After they had finished, I asked the doctor "Am I going to get better?"

Sensing my fear, he said, "God willing, you'll be fine soon. But you'll have to go to another doctor for examination. We can't operate on you here because the shrapnel is lodged very close to the spine. Whether to operate or not has to be decided elsewhere."

It was 2:00 p.m. when they brought me from the operating room. The people waiting for me outside escorted the stretcher to the ward. Entering, I saw it was wall-to-wall beds with a wounded person on each. There was no room for my stretcher, so they placed it on the floor. My friends stood around it. Not seeing Zeynab among them, I figured she had gone back to Khorramshahr. After about a quarter of an hour, I heard the voice of Uncle Nad Ali's wife say, "Nadi, she's over here."

As they came toward me, I don't know what made me get so choked up. I kissed them. Uncle's wife, visibly upset, said, "Girl, what made you do this? Why didn't you come here with your mother? Do you think this horrible thing that happened to you is good? For God's sake, hasn't your mother suffered enough? Her heart is already shattered. How's she going to feel when she sees you like this?"

Uncle also seemed very depressed and couldn't speak. His wife asked about conditions in Khorramshahr. "The radio says nothing," she explained. "How far have the Iraqis gotten and…?"

We were busy talking when mother suddenly came through the door, spotting me immediately. My heart sank. A strange fear gripped me. I thought she'd ask about Ali.

What would I tell her? I prayed and prayed she wouldn't ask. I wondered: Who told her I was here? I didn't want her to know I had been wounded.

Seeing me like this, I worried she wouldn't let me return to Khorramshahr. I also missed her and wished no one else had been around so I could throw myself in her arms and let the tears flow. I wanted to tell her about what I had endured and about every moment I was with Ali—from the time I picked him up from the hospital to his burial. It would have been good to get if off my chest, to lighten the agony I felt in my soul, but I didn't say a thing. I said nothing even to Uncle Nad Ali, who kept asking about Ali.

Mother held and kissed me as if I were a little girl again. I had grown up quickly, but mother, who always had young children to care for, didn't have time to pay much attention to me. But that time I was sick, she paid more attention to me and hugged me. I enjoyed being in her arms so much I never wanted to get better. But it was different now. The fear she would stop me from returning to the city tore at my insides. "Who said I was here? How did you know?" I asked sharply.

No one spoke. I asked her directly, "How did you find out? Who told you to come?"

Suddenly I heard Zeynab's voice. "The very idea! This is your mother! She's got to know what's happened to her own child!"

"What's happened?!" I asked. "There's nothing wrong with me. I'm doing better than all of you."

Zeynab laughed and said, "Yeah right, you who can't walk without us holding you up. You're okay, all right."

Mother said irately, "You little brat! You're an orphan all of a sudden? When did you get so independent? Did you think I was totally in the dark? I grilled anybody coming from Khorramshahr about you. I asked: Have you seen my child? But you never asked about me. You've all made me sick to my heart: your father, Ali, and now you! How much grief can a person stand?"

When she mentioned Ali, I tried to lighten the mood and began to laugh. This only made her angrier. She said, "Look! Look at her. She's giggling like it's her wedding day!"

Then she broke into tears. I felt sorry for her and said, "Mother, why are you crying? There's nothing the matter with me. I was hit by a little piece of shrapnel. I'll be better in a day or two, and I'll go back to Khorramshahr."

Hearing I intended to go back was infuriating to her. In tears, she said, "I swear to God. If you set one foot out of here, I'll break both your legs!"

Uncle tried to calm her, but Zeynab piped up, "Have no fears about the ones in this ward—heroes everyone of them. They've done it all. This one you see on the stretcher can move mountains if she wants. Good God Almighty! She's so fine, so noble, it's a wonder we can stand it. Don't worry on her account."

Mother's mood changed after hearing that. Now she apparently realized that I was hurt badly and she should stop arguing. She sat down on the bed and, cradling my head in her arms, kissed me. "You said she was wounded in the arm," she said to the people around me. "Why is she on her back like that?"

"There's a piece of shrapnel near her spine," they said.

Fighting back the tears, she asked me, "What have you done to yourself?! God, let me die now! What if you're paralyzed and have to spend the rest of your life cooped up in some corner. What am I supposed to do, then?"

"Don't worry," I said. "You know me. There's nothing wrong with me."

"Yeah," she said sarcastically. "You lead such a charmed life; nothing bad's ever happened to you."

Then mother got up and hugged Leila, showering her with affection. As she kissed Leila, who hadn't stopped crying since her arrival, she kept saying, "God strike me dead! Look how skinny you are. Didn't they give you anything to eat? You've slimmed down to nothing!"

Mother herself had also become quite thin, having lost ten or fifteen kilos. She was no longer the spirited and merry mother of old. Although she had quarreled with me, she now was very hushed and calm, and a great sadness rippled across her features. She put up a show of behaving normally, but the pain and weariness in her eyes betrayed her true feelings. I sensed she was much more emotional and quick to anger than before, otherwise she wouldn't have lost control like that in front of others. Ashamed to look at her, I kept my eyes on Leila. Although I had instructed Leila several times not to say anything about Ali's martyrdom until the whole family had gathered, I was afraid she'd let it slip out.

With the arrival of Mr. Bahramzadeh and his wife, the situation improved. Mother stopped crying. Mr. Bahramzadeh was an amazing man. The respect he showed me for what I had done was embarrassing. After asking how I felt, he went with uncle to consult with the doctors. They said I had to be evacuated to another hospital, but there were no flights until, perhaps, that night.

The pandemonium at my bedside did not keep me from getting very drowsy. The sedatives they gave me were having an effect, but I couldn't sleep with mother and the others there. I asked her, "What's happening with the children's education?"

She said, "Nothing. The schools are closed. They're bombing here also."

Then she asked, "Zahra, why didn't Ali come with you? Doesn't he know you're wounded?"

Not sure what to say, I hesitated until Zeynab came to my rescue, "Don't worry, Ali's in a place better and more comfortable than the one we're in." I thanked her with a look, but the idea mother might catch on made me panic. I quickly asked uncle something and spoke with his wife, all in the hope of distracting mother. Soon a nurse came and requested all visitors leave the ward. Everybody but mother left. She wanted to stay, but Zeynab was able to get her to leave. "Why stay?" she asked. "There's nothing for you to do. If it's necessary for someone to stay, I'm ready to look after her. But you see they're not permitting anyone to remain."

Mother went, leaving me alone with Zeynab. About to go, she started kidding me, "You picked up so many wounded and delivered them to the hospitals, the poor things started to yowl, demanding you do something for them at the clinic. But you didn't and look where it's gotten you—stuck in a hospital yourself."

"I made a stupid mistake," I said, "and I'll never do it again. I told them they had to go to the hospital."

"How come you can't fall asleep?" she asked. "Don't you know any lullabies? With everybody telling you to stay in the hospital, you still won't listen!"

"Lay off, woman, will you!" I said. "Now what are you going to do? Stay or go?"

"They won't let me stay, otherwise I would. I'll go back to Khorramshahr."

Then she asked, "Zahra, how long are you going to keep your mother in the dark about Ali?"

I said, "For now I am not saying anything. Later on, God knows. I've got to get back on my feet."

"I feel so sorry for your mother. It's like she had a premonition. On the way here, she constantly asked about Ali and made me swear to tell her if anything had happened. If I wasn't going to tell her, she asked me to take her to Khorramshahr so she could find out for herself."

"What did you tell her?" I asked.

"Thank God, I told her nothing bad happened, and whatever it was it wasn't serious. But, Zahra, believe me it was impossible to be with her for that hour or two, she asked so many questions. God help you. What *are* you going to do?"

I shook my head and said, "I don't know."

"Fine. If there's nothing else you need, I'll go now because I won't find a ride later. Any messages I can relay to your friends?"

I fought back the tears again, and Zeynab started kissing me. I began to cry and Zeynab said, "I'm off. Who knows when we'll see each other again."

Then she laughed and said, "Maybe I'll go and get martyred, but, imagine, me a martyr! Maybe all those martyrs we buried will intercede for me, and God will forgive all my sins and admit me to His court."

Her joking cheered me up, and I had already begun to miss her. To keep me from getting emotional, she said, "If you're ever martyred, don't pretend you don't know me. Put in a good word for me with God."

I said, "Count on it. I'm not going to be a martyr. You're the one going to Khorramshahr."

"Martyrdom doesn't happen just in Khorramshahr. Nowadays it can happen anywhere in Iran. God just has to help us reach it."

Then she said kiddingly, "So, I'm off now, on the trail again of bread, cheese, and watermelon."

She tried several times to get up, but I kept grabbing her arm. "Wait, for God's sake. Stay a while," I pleaded.

"Girl," she protested, "I've got to go sooner or later."

I felt ill at ease, as if my insides were on fire. I had a feeling we would never see each other again. She seemed free as a bird. To comfort me she said, “Try to stay calm. God willing I’ll stop by again.”

Forcing a smile through my tears I said, “This whole time you were like a mother to Leila and me. You were always there to help whenever I needed it. And what did I give you in return? So much trouble.”

She said graciously, “I did nothing for you. You had the guts of a lion the way you took care of yourself. More than that, you made it easier for me to get over missing my daughter.”

“Tell father I didn’t want to leave Khorramshahr; they forced me to leave.”

“There’s no need to say so. He knows,” she said. “He knows it all. To be a martyr is to be alive; he’s more alive than the likes of us. We don’t see the martyrs, but they have no trouble watching us.”

“If that’s the way it is, why don’t they do something?” I asked.

“How do you know they haven’t? Maybe they asked God to make it happen like this.”

“Well, if that’s the case, then those martyrs are real bastards,” I said.

“Don’t say that. God thought it best you be wounded. It’s definitely to your benefit somehow.”

This made me angry, but, given the way she acted toward me, I couldn’t say the harsh things I was thinking, namely: You’re the one who’s only thinking of herself, pretending to be my friend, acting like my mother. If you hadn’t been so selfish, you wouldn’t have let them bring me here.”

It felt like father and Ali also had no pity for me, and Zeynab was now acting the same way. They only were hurting me.

Zeynab bent over and, cradling my face in her hands, kissed me. I took her hands and covered them with kisses, saying, “Don’t leave me, I’m begging you. Stick around. Maybe, God willing, I’ll be able to come with you tomorrow. It’s night now and there’s nothing you can do anyway. What’s the rush? Stay the night and leave in the morning when there’s no problem getting a ride.”

"No," she said. "It's better for me to go now. You're right there's nothing for me to do at night, but I can at least get some rest and be ready for work in the morning."

I tried to keep her from going. I loved her and hearing her speak of going shook me to the bottom of my heart. I felt I would never see her again. She wouldn't be back. I had the same feeling when father said he was leaving for the last time. I begged her to stay and help with the tons of work at the hospital. I said, "At least wait till they evacuate me, then go."

She said, "I know there's a lot to do here, but there's no one there. Not anybody can go there and work. I'm a local; I've got to stay. I can't leave Khorramshahr. That's where I've got to make a stand. We can't let it fall to the enemy just like that. Either we drive them out or we die trying and leave this world as martyrs. In any case, I'm never abandoning my hometown."

"So why are you telling me to leave?" I asked her.

"Because if you go back, not only won't you be able to do anything, it's possible you'll be a burden to others. Stay in the hospital, get better, and then return. God willing, by that time the Baathists will have gotten the hell out of the city." With that she got up, and I started crying harder. I grabbed her arm and pulled her back. As she said things to console me, she pried my fingers from her arm. She stepped away, and I cried even more. This made her stop. She turned around and said, "Don't cry. I'm leaving you in God's hands. If you go on like this, I'll be very upset."

I covered my face with my hands so I wouldn't have to see her go. I bawled even more, though deep in my heart I said: You're a rat, just like the others. Traitor, I hope you don't find a ride. It'll do my heart good to see you come back!

After she had gone, I felt completely abandoned. I didn't have the same feeling when mother and uncle had left. But with Zeynab's going it felt like I was an outcast, the loneliest creature on earth. I hated where I was and asked myself: How could Zeynab have left me like that, taking flight like a bird?

I cried myself to sleep and, again, was visited by the same nasty nightmares. Scenes of bedlam plagued my thoughts, and a horrible din in my ears. Terrified, when I tried to pry my eyes open, I imagined there was a bright light shining in them. I kept my eyelids shut. I wanted to scream but my voice got stuck in my throat. I saw myself flailing about, bucking to get free. Finally I jerked myself awake and stayed awake to avoid the torment of the nightmares. It was clammy in the room. Though the ceiling fans were working, I was sweating buckets. My wet hair clung to my neck. I felt there was a great weight on my chest, keeping me from moving. I could see nothing in the darkness. They had covered the windows with heavy black plastic; the only light came from the fluorescents in the hallway. The nurses used flashlights to look in on patients. Several times bombers flew overhead.

In the middle of the night, the nurse woke me to give me an injection of Cephalexin and change my dressing. In the morning the nurses came to say, "Evacuees should get ready; helicopters are on their way." At around 9:00 I heard the whirr of a helicopter. It appeared to land in the area behind the hospital. The nurses went to get a glimpse and carry out the comatose patients. Several people declared themselves to be transfer patients.

I said nothing and remained quiet even when they asked, "Are there any more evacuees?" Suddenly one of the nurses passed by and, very surprised by my silence, said firmly, "You're to be evacuated, aren't you? Why didn't you say something?"

I hesitated, not knowing what to answer. I said, "There's no one to come with me. My family hasn't arrived yet."

"You don't need an escort," she said.

"But at least somebody in my family should know where I'm going," I protested.

"Fine. We'll let them know later," she said.

"How will you do that?"

"Whatever. The helicopter isn't going to wait. If you don't get a move on, it'll leave without you."

"Exactly," I said. "Let it."

"What do you mean 'let it'?" she asked. "Do you think this is a game? You're one of the evacuees, you've got to go."

"There are a lot worse off than me. Start by evacuating them, at least till my family comes. I'll go on a later flight." This made her angry, but she tried to stay calm on account of my condition. "There's no telling when the next helicopter will come. In any case there's nothing we can do for you here. If you stay you'll get infected, and if the shrapnel severs your spine, the infection will paralyze you. It's also possible you'll die. Understand?"

She went away. I heard the sound of the helicopter. It seemed to be hovering. I prayed and prayed it would go, and I was thrilled when it took off. Around 10:00, uncle and Mr. Bahramzadeh came. The nurses told them, "Your patient refused to be evacuated."

Uncle was furious with me. He said, "This place is filthy, chock-full of germs. You have no choice. What if the wound becomes infected? What do we do then?"

He was right. The floor of the ward and the hallways were full of dirt and grime. The ground was splattered with blood. It had rained and people were tracking mud and grime into the hospital. The more the staff tried to wash it, the more they spread the mud around. Being on a stretcher close to the ground I was in greater danger of infection than the others. Uncle and Mr. Bahramzadeh went to find the nurses again. They returned and said, "The nurses told us there is no knowing when the next helicopter will come, when the next evacuation will happen. It might take a week. We suggested to them that if they didn't need you here for treatment, we might as well take you home. They had no objection but they said we had to wait for the doctor to come out of the operating room, because he's got to give the okay."

The specialists didn't appear until afternoon. I was dying of hunger. They gave me serum. My kidneys weren't functioning properly; despite all the serum they had pumped into me, there was no urine. My body had swelled up badly, and I could occasionally feel the weight of my lower parts, but I couldn't make out the legs themselves. My arms hurt from not moving for so long. "Do you want us to hook up a urinary catheter?" the nurses asked.

"No."

They tried to give me an injection, but because of the swelling the needle couldn't find the vein. It was very painful.

"I don't want an injection," I said.

"What a wonderful patient you are!" they declared. "Why are you so headstrong?"

I was in terrible shape until late afternoon. I imagined my head had gotten heavy and larger. When I closed my eyes, the nightmares and dizziness returned. I had become fed up with being on my stomach for days. On top of all that there were the groans from the patients they were constantly wheeling in and out of the ward. My heart went out to them, and, if I had been able to, I would have gotten up to help them.

The nurses were weary from overwork. There were too few of them to handle the volume of wounded. You could hear them grumbling at times. I kept my eyes on the door, waiting for a doctor to come and release me from the place. I felt extremely weak, and I craved a warm cup of tea. At home I would have had several cups by the late afternoon. Several times I begged the nurses to help me lie on my side, as my arms had fallen asleep.

They said, "We can't. The danger is the shrapnel might move."

Just as I felt I was about to die, the doctor came. When he saw me he looked puzzled and asked, "Why is this one still here?"

"She didn't want to go," said the nurse.

Enraged, he asked me, "Why didn't you go?"

"She hasn't urinated yet," the nurse added.

"Why didn't you hook up a catheter?" the doctor asked.

"She wouldn't let us," she answered.

"What? Do you mean we're leaving treatment up to the patients now?" he barked. "We do whatever they want?" Then he turned to me and asked, "Why are you interfering with your treatment?"

Afraid of making things worse, I didn't say a word.

Uncle said, "If you let us, we'd like to take her home."

"If you do, see that she gets her medicine and her shots exactly on time," he said. "And keep her in a germ-free room. Although this is not the cleanest place in the world, we have had some success. Under no circumstances is she to get up. Is there someone who can care for her there?"

Mr. Bahramzadeh said, "Yes, we've got family visiting, and there's a nurse among them who'll see to her needs."

While Mr. Bahramzadeh was gathering my medicines, mother and Leila arrived. They arranged to have an ambulance come for me.

Mr. Bahramzadeh sat in front beside the driver, and mother and Leila sat in the back with me.

Mother began to cry even before the ambulance got moving: "O my God! You poor little orphan, you're so swollen."

"Why are you crying?" I asked.

"I miss Ali. The poor thing, nobody knows where the poor thing is. Right? He's stubborn like you. When he was in that hospital, he wouldn't let me do anything for him. He was in a lot of pain, but like you he never let on. And when I did visit him, he'd ask, 'Why did you come? Don't, you'll just cry.' You keep asking me the same questions. You're exactly like him. You don't listen to me. I wish your father were here. I wish he'd only been wounded. At least I got to see him for a few days before he was martyred."

It tore at my soul to hear her speak this way. I said to myself: The poor creature doesn't know where Ali is. If she did, she wouldn't have brought up the time he was in the hospital.

I wished I'd been able to take her head in my hands and caress her. I knew full well how to calm her. I'd been giving her advice since I was a child and, having gotten the better of her intellectually, I was able to change her mind on certain things. Now, given the way she was carrying on, I was glad I had kept the news about Ali from her.

When we pulled up in front of Mr. Bahramzadeh's, I said, "I don't want to go in on a stretcher; take me under my arms." Up to that point every part of me had been in agony. My neck and arms felt like petrified wood. But while I was in the hospital, I didn't dare show the pain, fearing they'd evacuate me.

Several of Mr. Bahramzadeh's kinfolk, who had been driven from their homes in Khorramshahr and Abadan, came out to greet us when we reached his house. Among them was a young army lad named Sa'id (later killed), who was visiting his relatives. He stepped forward, greeted me and mentioned he knew Ali.

My heart was in my mouth, as I was terrified he would say something. Then what would I do? As usual, mother, who loved anybody and anything military, started to shower him with endearments. Luckily he didn't mention Ali's martyrdom.

As soon as we got inside, a cheerless woman, who had been squatting in the corner of the living room, jumped to her feet. She said, "Goddamn this Saddam! He's made our lives miserable. He's killed off all our young."

Mr. Bahramzadeh explained in a whisper, "This woman's son is missing. We haven't been able to get any news about him, which is why she's in such a mental state."

I felt bad for the woman. The commotion in the house and the presence of all the guest refugees were making me uncomfortable. Maryam, Mr. Bahramzadeh's wife, brought me to a room, and the relatives lay me face down on a floor cushion. The woman followed us into the room, wanting to ask about my condition, but Mr. Bahramzadeh said, "Please leave her alone so she can rest."

The poor woman left the room. Seeing mother wanted to get back to the children, I said, "Mother, stay with me for a bit." On the verge of tears, she nodded and sat down. "Where are you staying?" I asked.

"At the refugee camp," she said.

"I went to Sar Bandar and Mahshahr, but I didn't know where to find you," I said. "So I just wandered around."

"I waited and waited for you to come," she said. "I gave Uncle Gholami a message saying we were at the camp."

Uncle Gholami worked for the municipality and, after getting his wife and child out of Khorramabad, he returned to the city, but I didn't see him after that. I told this to mother and she said, "I've got to go look in on the children. There's nobody watching them."

"What do you mean no one is watching them, mother? There's always God."

I asked her about how the children were doing. She wasn't that happy with them. She said, "Zeynab is constantly pestering me about her father. She's become very willful and annoying."

Mother left but Leila remained in the room with me. It had been some time since we had been under the same roof without having the rest of the family around. Things were looking better now. I tried to turn on my side to sleep, but Leila insisted I stay on my stomach.

"I'm tired. Leave me be. I'll be fine," I said.

We started to speak about Khorramshahr. There was no news about the war. We were in the dark about the city and how far the

Iraqis had advanced. We were also worried about Abdollah Mo'avi, whether he had recovered. But, given his wound, there was very little hope he'd still be alive. Nevertheless, we didn't have the heart to admit he was gone. My soul yearned for Khorramshahr. It felt like it had been years since I last visited father and Ali. I wanted with all my heart to see them resting in peace.

That evening one of Mr. Bahramzadeh's relatives, who was a nurse, came by. She had a friendly manner, and behaved like family toward Leila and me. She gave me my shots and left. When the call to prayer sounded, Mrs. Bahramzadeh came by with a pitcher and a washing bowl. I did my ablutions and prayed. She also spread a tablecloth in the room so Leila and I could have some stew for dinner. Then she offered us fruit. I realized it had been a month since I'd last eaten such food. I stared at the fruit and tried to imagine what the girls at Dr. Shaybani's were going through. Mansur, Hasan, and Sa'id also entered my mind. It made me sick to think of what was happening to them now and how long it had been since they had had a square meal. They were surely having a hard time. With such thoughts going through my mind, I could hardly eat the fruit.

Mrs. Bahramzadh kept coming by, offering more in the way of hospitality. I was so upset and grief-stricken I told her I'd rather sleep.

I don't know how long I stayed at Mr. Bahramzadeh's. I think it was five or six days. He had given the hospital his phone number so they could call as soon as a helicopter arrived. He also called them regularly. His wife, Maryam, took on the extra housework our stay caused without a word and wouldn't think of accepting help from her guests. She told Leila, "You just look after your sister."

Maryam also pestered me about taking my medicine when it came time. She brought food and carried away the dishes. Her food was delicious. Just the aroma was enough to stir my appetite, but when she put it in front of me, I would start to cry and, except for a few bites, I was still unable to eat. At one point she laid down some plastic sheeting and with Leila's help I managed to bathe my head and arms. Then, using a washbowl, they sponged down my body with a damp cloth. To be naked like that in front of others was humiliating, but I had no choice.

Mr. Bahramzadeh's family was like him: very disciplined and organized. They pulled out all the stops for us. Not only did they have a lot of respect for Seyyeds in general, father's martyrdom and the fact we stayed in Khorramshahr caused them to admire us in a way that was embarrassing to Leila and me.

The nurse also regularly looked to my needs, and for the times she was not on duty instructed Leila how to give injections. Leila massaged my legs according to her instructions. She was very worried my spinal chord would be cut. After a while, I was able to urinate again due to her ministrations and the exercises. The swelling went down little by little, revealing how thin and feeble I'd become. I had changed so much that when mother visited with my little sister Zeynab, the five-year-old was afraid to go near me. She hid behind mother, and I kept assuring her I was her sister.

She would peek out from behind mother only to hide again. Leila tried to make her feel more at home by hugging her. It took a while for her to settle down, but she finally came to me, putting her head on my breast and rubbing my face with her hands. I stroked her hair and kissed her cheeks. She gradually began to talk, and soon we couldn't stop her. "I missed you so," she kept saying. "Where were you? Why did you send us away and stay behind? Why didn't you let us stay with you? When are we going home? I can't take this anymore. When is father coming home?"

Every answer was greeted by another question. Zeynab had also become skin and bones, and she clearly wasn't her old self mentally. She looked wilted. Her hair was a mess and there were bruises on her arms. The old Zeynab, always in bloom, the little doll in the colorful clothes father bought her, was gone. Instead, the child was dressed in a long cloth shirt and striped pajama bottoms too big for her. In the cold weather, she wore a green sweater over her shirt. Covering her head and neck was a three-corner headscarf made from netting material. It was so unsettling to see her dressed this way. The worst thing was her hair, which was matted and felt like a gunnysack. With tears in my eyes as I kissed Zeynab's face, I asked mother, "Why does she look like that? Why is she so filthy? Look at her arms; they're so rough and calloused."

"What can I do?" she said. "There's no damned water to wash her with. You don't know what I had to go through just to get her to the public bath. What do you expect? I can't even stand myself."

I shouldn't have said that. It was obvious she was at the end of her rope, and it depressed her. She still wore her shawl fastened at the back with the hem over her forehead as a sign of mourning.

The only thing keeping her alive, I felt, was the hope of seeing Ali. If it weren't for that, her grief about father would have finished her off. Proud woman that she was, she didn't show how much she loved her husband. I even remember father joking to her, "I'm still in the dark about your love for me."

Now I realized how much she actually did love him.

As I spoke, Zeynab, who had gotten used to me again, began to lean on me. Mother said, "Not so close! Your sister's been shot."

She looked at me in surprise and asked, "You were shot?"

"There was this blind mortar shell. It didn't see me and landed nearby. A piece of shrapnel hit me." Then, to divert her, I asked, "Have you made any friends at the camp?"

"I play with the kids, but I'm not friends with any of them."

After a few hours, mother rose to go. She was very upset by the thought I was such a bother to Mr. Bahramzadeh's family. This was why she didn't visit as much. After she told Zeynab to get ready to go, the child said to me, "You come, too." Mother said, "She can't move."

Zeynab burst into tears and wouldn't let go of me. Mother forced her to her feet. Zeynab rubbed her eyes and said, "Let me stay, mother."

After they left, I started to cry. I felt more homesick. Seeing Zeynab made not having a father even more painful. To keep people from seeing how upset I was I put my head under the blanket and pretended to sleep, all the while sobbing my eyes out. Mother didn't bring Zeynab to see me after that.

I got more irritable as time went on. Mr. Bahramzadeh for his part tried to keep anything from getting on my nerves. The doctors told him and uncle to keep me from hearing about the war. When I asked, "What's the latest?" They would say, "Nothing special. We're also in the dark."

At times I would hear the sounds of the "guests"; the number would vary as they found houses to rent in Mahshahr or left the city altogether. Everybody was talking about Khorramshahr. Although I kept my ears peeled, I couldn't hear what they were saying. I pestered visitors for news, but in my heart I knew it wasn't good. This was why I had so desperately wanted to stay in the city. I was certain it would be the last time I saw it. The idea of the Iraqis advancing as far as the cemetery and destroying the graves of father and Ali was driving me out of mind. The hours lying around with nothing to do gave me ample time to think about the places I had been during the days of the war, about the people, the times, and the scenes I had witnessed. I even missed Genoa, the hysteric whose behavior was so repulsive I did everything I could to avoid her. I found myself praying to God to get me back to Khorramshahr and let me work again. After twenty days of frantically running this way and that, I was now lying motionless in a corner with no news of the war.

The agony weighed heavily on my heart. I felt I hadn't done any good while I was in the city. I had to return and try to do more. Now nothing satisfied me, but I couldn't speak openly to anyone.

One night while I was lying in bed, Leila asked, "Sis, do you remember Sa'bari?"

"Yeah. You mean Esma'il, right? We took his body to Mahshahr."

She said, "His older brother, Ebrahim. Do you remember him?"

"Yeah," I said. "Has something happened?"

"The day you were wounded at Sentab, the Iraqis advanced as far as the base. The forces there retreated. As I was walking around Jennatabad, I happened to see Ebrahim lying by the gate. I went to him and saw shrapnel had shattered his jaw. He was barely breathing. Blood and foam were coming from his mouth. I guess he died."

"May God have mercy on his mother," I said. "What pains she took raising the two boys."

Leila continued, "When I got to him, Ebrahim was dying. Even so, he managed to mutter the two oaths to God and His Prophet. I was at a loss until I saw a jeep full of soldiers driving on the Ring Road from the direction of the base. I started shouting and waving at them to stop, but they sped past me. I was enraged and screamed, 'Cowards, can't you see there's a wounded man here! And you're running away?' But I hadn't finished ranting when I saw some soldiers coming from the direction the jeep had gone. I waved my arms again, and suddenly the jeep came speeding back toward me. I wondered what had made them turn around. Then two of them jumped out of the jeep and, with Ebrahim in their arms, said anxiously, 'Hop on fast! The Iraqis are right on our tails!' "

The story petrified me. I felt sick and, horrified, I just stared at Leila. Just the thought of her being taken prisoner was enough to drive me mad. I managed to ask her, "What happened next?"

"Nothing. I really didn't believe the Iraqis had come that far, but jumped in the jeep anyway. After we got going, an Iraqi military car showed up. Had I stayed in Jennatabad, I definitely would have been taken prisoner. I have no idea what happened to the folks who did stay. Zeynab was not there at the time, thank God."[1]

On the verge of tears, I asked, "What would I have done if you were taken prisoner?"

"Nothing. I'm just like everybody else. What do you think they did? Don't you think the Iraqis broke into other people's houses and took them prisoner?"

"Enough! Not another word!" I said.

I took her hand and squeezed it. The more I thought about it, the less I could stand the horror of the thought; it broadened and became more agonizing in my mind. I blamed myself for abandoning Leila, and there would have been no way to atone for it if she had been taken prisoner. What would I have told mother? Father had made me

---

[1] Later on I spent a lot of time and effort tracking down Zeynab Rudbari, the woman who mothered us during those early days. One day Leila saw one of the resistance boys in Khorramshahr. He was sure that Zeynab had stayed in Khorramshahr until the city fell. Then she was severely wounded, and they evacuated her to Tehran. I visited the office at Behesht-e Zahra countless times and went through all of the old registers with the names of the martyrs and the deceased. Her name was not in the registers, nor was it in the computer. I wasn't able to find her daughter Maryam or her husband in Khorramshahr. I am on the lookout for her everywhere. I still miss her. Looking from the outside, she appeared to be just a body washer, but God knows what she actually was.

promise to take care of my siblings. What would have happened if I failed his trust? I looked at Leila, and even as I blamed myself, I thanked God, comforting myself with the thought she was here now, safe and sound. Then again, I thought, I would never have forgiven myself if she had been harmed.

Seeing the state I was in, Leila laughed and said, "Nothing happened. Why make yourself sick about it?"

But I couldn't stop fretting. Without her noticing, I clutched at her clothing to regain a sense of security from her presence. I would also glance at her when she was sleeping and weep. The thought she could have been captured stayed in my mind for a number of days. I would tell myself, "Never be that careless again. Never make father regret he put his trust in you. Don't ever let Leila leave your side for a minute." This was how I passed the time while we were at Mr. Bahramzadeh's.

Gradually I got better. The swelling went down considerably, and I regained some feeling in the toes on my left foot. With help I was able to stand on my feet, but I couldn't feel the ground. When Mr. Bahramzadeh's home became too crowded for comfort again, I asked uncle to take me away.

Mr. Bahramzadeh was against it but finally agreed. After a week's stay, uncle came with a car at around 9:00 a.m. to take me to the refugee camp. Camp B had been the preserve of the Japanese, Chinese, and Korean workers at the petrochemical plant. With the outbreak of war, they were evacuated. The camp was about twenty minutes drive from Sar Bandar.

Uncle brought a folding bed to the camp for me. It felt good being in the open air, but it was embarrassing to sleep that way in public. Mother and the kids appeared a few minutes after our arrival. Zeynab ran to me, but, being shy, the boys stayed back, merely staring at me. "Come here," I urged them.

I remember mother saying they were always playing and wouldn't listen. I said, "I heard you've become little devils."

They laughed. Several families from uncle's side resided in Nad Ali's lane, which was almost at the far end of the camp. They came to visit and gathered around me. The poor things didn't know Persian. It had only been a year since Saddam had kicked them out of Iraq, and they wound up in Khorramshahr.

Around noon Mr. Bahramzadeh came to look in on me saying, "The hospital called to say a helicopter had come."

"I'm not going," I said.

Both uncle and Mr. Bahramzadeh were not pleased and asked, "Why not?"

"I can go by car," I said.

Having seen so many people in far worse shape than I, people severely wounded, in comas, and amputees, I decided I had no right to take up space in a helicopter. Why should they have to stay behind, while I get to go to another city?

"Being jostled in a car could cause you problems," said uncle.

"Nothing's going to happen," I assured him.

No matter how much they tried to change my mind, I wouldn't listen. Uncle got very upset with me. Mr. Bahramzadeh left.

That night the pain returned. My wounds itched, which was a sign of infection. The next day uncle called the camp ambulance. We managed to convince poor mother not to come. The doctor at Mahshahr Hospital quickly wrote an evacuation order. There was an ambulance on its way to Shiraz, and they forced members of the family of one of the wounded to give up their spaces to take Leila and me. Leila sat on the hump, while I stretched out along the side. After a doctor and a nurse got in, we sped off. It wasn't comfortable squeezed in between the door and the hump. The ambulance had no side windows, but wind blew in through a broken pane in the door, at times blowing cold, at times hot.

The driver stopped once to have the motor checked. The nurse pulled up my blanket and the doctor, whose name was Mostafavi, bought a little food and shared it with us. While we were stopped, the doctor said to the people who had gathered around the ambulance and were peeking in, "Come and see what has happened to the people of Khoramshahr. Here they are: those who resisted the enemy."

I heard reports that inhabitants of a certain city had swindled and harassed refugees. They taunted them saying, "You're cowards for surrendering to the enemy. Traitors, get out of our town!"

It broke my heart to hear such talk. At first I didn't want to believe it, but later I heard some Khorramshahris had refused to leave the city. "Why go away?" they explained. "We wouldn't be able to take what they'd do to us. Haven't you heard about how they treat refugees?"

What the doctor said made the onlookers curious. "What's going on in Khorramshahr?" they asked. "How far have the Iraqis gotten?"

That was my cue to tell them what had happened to the city. They became very upset. Some of the women broke down. Others, out of sympathy, asked if they could bring us anything. They even invited us to their homes. The crowd remained around the ambulance until it went away. People looked in through the door with the broken window, offering words of sympathy.

Such scenes recurred several times along the route. Leila gave a very good account of the state of things in Khorramshahr to onlookers.

I was in a great deal of pain on the ride to Shiraz. I napped and the next thing I knew we had arrived at Nemazi Hospital. The ambulance backed up to the emergency room door. A number of doctors and nurses eventually came out with a stretcher and carried me into what seemed like a staging room for patients undergoing operations.

The place seemed very neat and orderly. The nurses were very kind. They quickly x-rayed my back, placed a green, double-thick bandage on my wound, and examined me. Most of the doctors were brain- and neurosurgeons. They stuck pins in my legs, pushing deeper in places where I had no feeling. They pounded my back and … I failed to respond to any of these tests. It felt as if my legs were frozen. Then they said, "The wound is infected and under no circumstances should it be taped." I didn't understand much of what was said. The only thing I got was that there was no question of operating before they knew what Dr. Faqih, the hospital head, thought. Then they asked me question after question about how I had been wounded.

Finally I asked, "Well, how am I?"

The doctor in charge said, "There doesn't seem to be anything wrong with your legs, but the explosion may have affected your nervous system. We'll have to rest while you're under observation, and your system gets back to normal."

They cleaned my wound. They removed the heavy bandaging and placed gauze over my wounds. After about two hours, they notified the ward they were wheeling me down.

I stayed for a week or ten days at Nemazi Hospital. Dr. Mostafavi, who knew me from the Sheybani clinic, told the nurses in the ward about Leila and me. Despite this celebrity, I didn't feel good being there. It was impossible to ignore the large number of wounded crammed in there. I felt that healing didn't have to mean occupying a bed in a hospital. They could bandage wounds and inject sedatives and antibiotics elsewhere. When I voiced my unhappiness, they said, "You have to stay here until the treatment is over. We have to control the infection."

Over time the numbness decreased, but the pain got worse. The fever and burning from the infection increased. The size of the wound also got bigger. I had to remain lying on my stomach. When I tried to lie on my side, the tremors in my legs became worse. My kidneys functioned once every few days. Apart from all the physical problems, seeing the wounded ferried in from Abadan and Khorramshahr made me more irritable. I wanted to get up and find out more about the situation from the newcomers. Sometimes I would ask people in the hallway. More or less they all said, "The Iraqis have advanced, and the city is about to fall."

Later people confirmed the rumors. They said, "The city has fallen, and the enemy has massacred everyone." But I wouldn't accept it. It was unbelievable; hearing the news just made me feel worse. Words can't say how I felt. It was like a nightmare. It meant Khorramshahr, like the former Iranian cities of Herat, Ganjeh, and Qarabagh, had been dismembered by one of the country's enemies. The thought of it drove me out of my mind. The dearest people in the world to me were there. I sobbed and sobbed in the privacy of my room and stayed awake late into the night as the thought the city had fallen stoked my tears.

Seeing me in this state, poor Leila tried to do more for me. From time to time she would put me in a wheelchair and bring me into the yard. But the peace and greenery in the garden did nothing to soothe me; the sight of all that beauty made being there even more agonizing. The date palms in the garden reminded me of the trees of

Khorramshahr. The flowers packed in their beds conjured up the floral pathways and lawns of Farmandari Circle and the roads leading to it. The hospital gardens were the last straw. I needed the Shatt and Khorramshahr with its heat and humid breezes. It felt like years since I'd been there.

One day while I sat in the garden lost in thought, a young man passed by. He walked on a few steps, then turned around and said in surprise, "Sister Hoseyni. Is that you?"

"Yes, and you are?"

"I'm one of the boys from Khorramshahr. I saw you a lot at the Congregational Mosque. I also knew Ali."

"When did you get here?" I asked. "What's the situation?"

"A week ago. When did you get here?"

"The twelfth."

"I heard you'd been wounded," he said. "It's a good thing you didn't stay to see what happened. What they did up on Forty-Meter Road! The asphalt is paved with the skin of the guys and their brains. They finished off our wounded with a bullet to the back of the head. They didn't even take pity on their miserable corpses, blasting them with RPGs. They pillaged the houses and even violated the sanctity of the mosque. They blasted the city to bits. People who saw it said it was a blood bath."

The tears kept pouring down the young man's face as he spoke, and, though I tried to control myself, I too couldn't stop crying. He went on, "After the base fell, they went on to Abadan. They want to surround it from the north and take it. Ahwaz is also in danger from that direction. They're attacking from the direction of the Hamid Base. But what to they expect us to do without arms? With no weapons, no ammunition? There's no way can we fight like that."

The boy was in despair. I tried to console him, "Don't lose hope. We were fighting the enemy for God, and for Him we will defend ourselves. After all, we didn't start the war. Trust in God."

The boy, who was wounded somehow, calmed down. "Do you know what happened to Sheikh Sharif Qonuti?" I asked. His demeanor suddenly changed, and he began to moan, "The Sheikh was martyred in the worst way possible."

"Meaning how? What did they do to him?" I asked.

"On the sixteenth the Iraqis reached the Forty-Meter Road. They fired at the Sheikh and several others sitting in a car, wounding all of them. One of the boys with the Sheikh was shot no less than sixteen times. Then they came and finished off the rest of his companions. They pulled the Sheikh from the car and tried to get him to curse the Imam. The Sheikh wouldn't, so they urinated in his mouth and then emptied their guns in it. After he died, they cut open his skull and ran around the street crowing, 'We've killed a Khomeini!' The boys who had witnessed this are in a bad way. I found it hard to believe it myself. How, I asked myself, could people be so criminal and cruel?" After he left, I could scarcely breathe, but somehow I managed to clear the lump in my throat and cry my eyes out.

Three or four days later the radio and television announced the fall of Khorramshahr. The television announcer said, "Despite all the sacrifices made by the youth and people of Khorramshahr, regretfully 'Blood City' has fallen to the enemy."

"Blood City" (*Khuninshahr*) was the name Imam Khomeini gave to Khorramshahr. He said, "I wish to express my sympathy to the families of the martyrs. Khuzestan has repaid the debt it owes to Islam and…."

I could no longer stand being in the hospital. The doctors finally gave in to my demand to be released, providing I return regularly for observation. Dr. Mostafavi, who was familiar with my case, said, "You have to be under constant care. So let me invite you to my home, where you'll be more comfortable with my mother and sister."

I had absolutely no desire to accept the doctor's hospitality, and declined his offer. But he went on and on, trying to convince me by reminding me I had no money to go back on my own. I'd have to wait for an ambulance or for uncle to come and get me. Left with no other option, I accepted. The doctor got a car and drove me himself. Members of his family, who had been notified, were there to welcome us. They had readied a room in their two-story home for Leila and me. It looked out on a green yard with plenty of trees. Dr. Mostafavi's relatives, having heard he was back from Khorramshahr, came by to see him. While he was in Khorramshahr stationed at Dr. Sheybani's clinic, he always went to the forward lines with a rifle. That was the reason I had seen him only rarely. Now I appreciated how much his family and relatives respected him. Having heard Leila and I were in his home, his guests came to visit us. They asked us about Khorramshahr, showing great interest in what we had to say. I wanted more than anything to get well quickly so I wouldn't be a burden this honorable family. For their part they tried to make our stay as comfortable as possible. As soon I showed signs of dizziness and started to shake, the daughter would run and get some preserves for me. Mrs. Mostafavi made kabob and forced me to eat.

Once I said to Dr. Mostafavi's father, "Please forgive us for putting you out like this."

His was very noble in reply, "Don't speak like that. The way I see it, we have three daughters now."

After repeated visits to the hospital, they altered my medications. When I was feeling slightly better, the doctor's mother took us to the shrine in the city at Shahcheragh. What I saw along the way fascinated me. The food stores were open and well-stocked. People went about their business without a care in the world. "Look," I said to myself, "life goes on. It's true that father and Ali are no longer with us, but we'll all be part of a loving family again."

We reached Shahcheragh, and for the first time I set eyes on the dome and forecourt of Imam Reza's brother. It gave me a strange feeling, and my body was tingling all over. I became choked up, sensing here was the one place where I could speak freely and unburden my soul. The shrine was devoted to the person who could well understand what I was going through. The sight of all the war refugees in the bustle of the crowd at the shrine—especially the ones dressed in Arab chadors—gave me a good feeling, but, at the same time, their presence made it harder to fight back the tears. I would have liked to throw my arms around them and tell them I shared their suffering. I spent several moments watching them as they sat grieving in a corner by the wall. Then I entered the shrine. I walked gingerly, said my benedictory *ziyaratnameh* to the Prophet and his Holy Offspring, and walked toward the metal grate around the tomb. My whole body shook. As I bent forward to kiss the bars of the grate, the tears wouldn't stop. I wept and wept without uttering a word. Gradually I began to feel more at peace, unburdened. I stood in prayer. I didn't have a chador, and my coat was torn. The lining of the sleeve was also frayed. I covered the hole with my headscarf and prayed. Again I sought refuge by the grate, this time fully emptying my heart of the grief and discontent I felt. We stayed for a couple of hours, and I became so relieved by being in the calm of the shrine, when I emerged I felt like flying. I was in less pain and was even able to walk more easily. We also stopped in at the traditional Vakil Bazaar, and I could now say I was much better. It was only when I stood that I felt a strong current shoot though my back and take my breath away. After it ended, my legs went weak, and I could only hobble along.

On my last visit to the hospital, the doctors told me, "The infection has healed nicely." They gave me a prescription and said, "You can go back."

As we left the hospital, I asked Dr. Mostafavi to have the ambulance that brought me take me back to Khorramshahr. "That ambulance is not always in service," he explained.

"What do you think we should we do?" I asked him.

Dr. Mostafavi's wife and Sonia, his teenage daughter, urged us to stay.

I thanked them, but after I insisted on going, the doctor finally drove us to central bus terminal in Shiraz and bought tickets for Mahshahr. The next day, accompanied by the doctor's family we set out for the terminal. Having business in the area, the doctor joined us on the bus.

We passed the night in the dry cold of the bus. Unable to lean back in the seat, I had to rest my head on the seat in front of me. I had already begun to miss mother. I prayed to God she remained in the dark about Ali. The fall of Khorramshahr and the things I had experienced in the past weeks had made me more aware of how people suffered. I was afraid if I saw mother, I would lose control and blurt out everything. I begged Dr. Mostafavi to take us to Uncle Nad Ali's home. I didn't want to encounter mother first thing. As I expected, uncle was up at that early hour. His wife came to the door when we knocked. He was overjoyed to see me standing, albeit feebly. He begged Dr. Mostafavi to join him for breakfast. The doctor declined, saying he had made sure we arrived safely, but had to go.

Although I thought I would fall fast asleep when I arrived, the excitement of seeing my family again prevented that. The rest of uncle's wife's family came and said how happy they were to see me better. One person sent word to mother, who appeared several minutes later with Zeynab. When she saw me standing there, her eyes sparkled. She seemed in better spirits than the old, battered woman who had visited me in the hospital. She kept shooting glances at me and saying, "You're so thin. There's hardly any color in your face."

Zeynab would not climb down from my arms. Even though she was more unkempt than before, she was still pretty. This reminded me of father, who used to say, "The Prophet adored His daughter. If we are to call ourselves Muslims, we have to love our daughters the way he did."

This was the reason the girls—especially Zeynab, who was his favorite—were so important to him. Mother didn't remain with me for long. She said, "I've got to go." She was anxious about the boys. "Let Zeynab stay," I said.

After mother left, I asked uncle's wife to give me a comb.

She said, "It's shameful for the child to look like that. She's starting to be a public nuisance."

I ran the comb slowly and with difficulty through Zeynab's tangled hair. It seemed like it hadn't been combed in weeks. Combing her, I noticed she had head lice, which made me sick. My eyes teared up, and I said to uncle's wife, "It's not a problem. We'll just cut her hair."

She left and brought back one of her relatives who was handy with scissors. She gave Zeynab a boy's haircut. Uncle's wife also heated up some water and gave Zeynab a bath in one of the side rooms. The next day I sat outside uncle's add-on room, removing lice from Zeynab's head. She didn't complain.

I gradually got used to life at the camp. The first thing in the morning the women would go off with pots on their heads. "Where are they going?" I asked some people.

"They're going to wash dishes, but because there aren't enough spigots, people cut in line and fights break out," they said.

Around noon there was a commotion coming from the area where uncle's house was. "Again? What going on?" I asked.

"This time it's coming from the kitchen," explained uncle's wife. "People are running to get food before it runs out."

Not wanting to take food from people in need, uncle used his savings to buy things from the market. "Right now we can manage on our own," he said. "Let the others have it."

Using the few pots and pans she got from relatives at Sar Bandar, his wife would cook outside, picnic-style, over a camp stove.

I spent time shuffling around Camp B, which consisted of trailers and pre-fab homes big enough for one to four people. The refugee camp was about fifty kilometers from Mahshahr. The main camp roads were paved, while the secondary ones were covered by sand. The camp was surrounded on all sides by a fence, parts of which totally disappeared under the bedding and laundry people hung over it. The small camp was now home to some 200 to 300 families, and, naturally, facilities for hygiene and medical care, water, and food were overtaxed.

The demand for water was so great the tanks emptied frequently. The sewers couldn't keep up with the waste, which pooled by the medical treatment facilities. The stink of stagnant water and waste was enough to drive one crazy. Because there was no one to collect it, the refuse piled up. The bins overflowed, and hordes of mosquitoes added to the misery of the inhabitants. Rats were everywhere.

Such sights gave me the feeling that the place was teeming with germs. The reality of this was seen in the clinics, which were filled with people suffering from dysentery, diarrhea, and eye infections. Many children were in such a bad way surgery was needed, but the hospitals were overflowing with the wounded needing operations. At times the landscape would be engulfed in frightening sandstorms. The winds proved excellent vectors for camp epidemics.

After several days, mother said, "Come home already."

Ever since returning to Sar Bandar, I nurtured the hope of going to Abadan and therefore chose not to spend much time with mother. I feared if I stayed with her, responsibility for the children would fall on my shoulders and keep me from going back to the region. Having read my mind, mother said, "I won't let you go. Stay until Ali comes back, and you can return with him. I can't let you go just like that."

I didn't know how to break it to her Ali was no longer with us. One day I finally went with uncle's wife to mother's trailer. It was almost at the beginning of the camp, some distance from uncle's house. Mother had gone to the market and bought a chicken. About to enter the house, I saw an old man who lived with his son and daughter-in-law in the next trailer cutting the chicken's throat. "What's this all about, mother?" I asked.

"I vowed if you got out of Khorramshahr alive I would make a sacrifice." I entered the one-room trailer. The floor was carpeted in green felt. On both sides of the room were two bunk beds, which took up most of the space. A metal cabinet and a device for heating and cooling were the only other furnishings in the room. A small window let light in. Uncle's home was the same type, only with two rooms. I didn't like it there either, but it was even harder for me to call this home because it was now mine. I felt I had entered a cell in a prison camp. The limited freedoms we had were the only differences. I became very depressed. It was not the size of the place, of course, that annoyed me; I just couldn't feel at home there. I wanted our old one, the home that became ours after enduring so much pain and bitterness, the home we built with our own hands. "Why," I asked myself, "do I have to be a refugee? Whose fault is it?"

As I hunched in a corner in a daze, mother came in with a skewer of chicken kabob. "Eat," she said. "You're very anemic."

The skewer was a straightened length of wire. With the children around, I didn't want to keep the kabob all to myself. Seeing me hesitate, mother figured I was reluctant to eat meat roasted on a wire and said, "Don't worry. After the boys gave it a good washing, I got it red hot over the fire. It's clean."

"It's not that, mother," I objected. "The thing is I can't eat. Give it to the children."

"How much do you think there is that I can it give to the children?" she asked.

"I don't want it, mother."

"Get up and leave," she ordered the children.

Upset, I said, "If you act this way, mother, I won't have a bite."

Finally she gave in and divided the skewer among us. Then, using a makeshift wood stove behind the trailer, she spent the morning cooking a stewed chicken dish with the rest of the bird.

She substituted chickpeas for the required split peas and added potatoes without frying them. She also made rice. At noon, explaining it was part of a vow, mother gave most of the food to people she had become friendly with at the camp. I was finally able to have one of her home-cooked meals again.

Soon after lunch the boys went to their bunks, while the others stretched out on the carpeting so I could rest. The boys liked their bunks. They seemed to settle down for a time but, secretly, the little monsters remained what they had always been. Nevertheless, they were curious about was going to happen to them and paid careful attention to what the adults said.

As we rested I felt Hasan watching me. "When are we going back home?" he asked suddenly. I was tired. It was strange to hear this from the mouth of the little devil.

Optimistic that the war would be over soon, I said, "We'll be back in no time." Then I added, "I'll probably be there before you."

Anxious to be back in school, Sa'id, believing I was going back to Khorramshahr, asked, "When you're there would you bring me my school books? Would the Iraqis let you?"

He meant his first grade books. "They wouldn't dare stop me," I said. "We'll go and get them out ourselves, and you can bring them to Khorramshahr so we won't have to bring them here."

The next day I decided to supervise the boys myself. Because the trailers faced one another, and some of the neighbors didn't maintain privacy, we always kept our door shut, which made us feel even more like prisoners in our own home. The boys wanted to roughhouse, and it was impossible to keep them cooped up in one room. But I was also afraid they would wander on the grounds. The poor sanitation, the questionable morality of some of the inhabitants and … made me worry. This was why I went with them when they went out to play. Hasan, Sa'id, and Mansur climbed the fence and the cement pedestal of the water tank and jumped down for fun. For two weeks this was how I spent my days.

Sometimes when I was depressed I would leave camp. I would stand under the sun beside the road, wondering how far it was to Abadan. Could I reach it on foot? People were saying the Iraqis had taken the Mahshahr-Abadan Road, so I decided to get to it from the desert side. Realizing this was impossible was hard on my nerves. Mother knew not to bother me when I became sullen. I had become very irritable. One word was enough to make me burst into tears. Leila was equally grumpy, but she was better able to put up with the conditions. To comfort me she said, “Zahra, we can also work right here. We’ll go to the camp clinic.” But yearning to go back to Khorramshahr with all my soul, I wouldn’t hear of it. I felt like a bird with its wings clipped. I couldn’t sleep at night. Scenes of what happened in Jennatabad, the Congregational Mosque, the Sheybani clinic, and the front lines appeared before me, driving sleep away. Thinking a picture of Ali or father would give me some peace, I regretted not bringing my photo album with me. I didn’t let mother see me during these bouts of depression. I wouldn’t let her see weakness in me and was always fending her off by saying, “You have to have patience and try not to break down.”

Even in worse shape than I, mother was always breaking down. She would sing in Arabic and Kurdish, with tears streaming down her cheeks. Modesty prevented her from mentioning father’s name. It was agonizing to hear her sing of Ali’s absence. At night it got worse, and there were times when I became very stern, telling her not to cry. At other times I would soften and hug and kiss her, saying, “Stop torturing yourself. Ali will come back and become the man of the house. We’ll be back on track then.”

Deep down I didn’t want to give her false hope, but what could I do? This was the only way to calm her. I had no choice and knew that although they were pretending to sleep, the boys were awake and sobbing in their beds.

Several times I returned from my walks to the road to find mother in tears, telling the neighbors what kind of man father was. The people were very moved in sympathy for her. I heard them saying behind her back, “The war has ruined her. She has lost her home, her whole life, even her husband....”

“Why, mother,” I scolded her, “are you squandering the rewards of father’s martyrdom?”

She would say nothing, seemingly agreeing with me. But then I found her doing the same thing. Seeing me coming, she would get up and say, “There’s going to be an argument now.”

Then her mood changed rapidly, so I wouldn't say anything. She would laugh and say, "Is that you, sweetie? Anything you need? Is there anything I can do for you?"

It hurt me the most when she got like this. Apart from our finances, uncle had problems of his own. He helped mother with the expenses and would never let her starve, but how much could he do? A short time later, instead of warm, cooked food, they started distributing dry rations. Seeing mother having to wait in line for the rations was painful. I felt the loss of dignity and suggested she not go and stand in line herself.

"What?" she said. "Who's going to fill these kids' stomachs?"

"So why don't you let them go themselves?"

"They don't give food to children," she explained.

Once Uncle Hoseyni came from Khorramabad and found us in the camp. Mother insisted he take us back with him. We refused, and he gave mother some money and left.

Conditions grew worse for people by the day. The complaints became louder. "What is this all about?" people grumbled. "Why have they dumped us here? Why don't they hear what we're saying?"

Like the family of Uncle Gholami, whose presence was such a joy to us, many people wanted to leave. In the beginning, everybody thought the situation was temporary, but with the widening of the war and the news that other cities were under attack, they realized they would have to escape the misery of the camp and go to safer cities.

Official organizations had yet to look into the plight of the families of the martyrs and the missing in any systematic way. Only in Mahshahr was something set up called the Force for War Victims, which administered the camp. With the mounting numbers of refugees, the conditions naturally became more dire and chaotic. They even cleared out storage facilities and wrecked vehicles to house people. Trucks would come occasionally and distribute sacks of used clothing for men, women, and children—one sack for each family. This was so disgusting to me I started cursing Saddam, the instigator, and hoped for his death; I also reviled those on our side who failed to do their duty. People objected, "What good are these clothes to us? We don't have children. What are we supposed to do with them?

What do they expect us to do? We have our pride. What's the point of treating us like dirt?"

I once accompanied uncle's wife to the food distribution place. She wanted powdered milk for her daughter, who had just turned one. She told the man distributing the food, "This isn't enough for my daughter, and there's none on the bazaar. Would you give me another tin?"

The man said, "What can I do? Teach your daughter to eat less."

Finding that very hard to take, she fought back tears. I was also very put out and felt like messing up his little setup. I managed to control myself and said to uncle's wife, "This is useless. Let's go. They're treating us like we're poor and unfortunate creatures, and are giving us charity out the goodness of their little hearts. They also probably think we're going to hoard the food."

Seeing how upset we were, the man regretted what he had said. He explained, "No offense, but our supplies are limited. They have to be stretched so everybody can get a share."

"What was your point when you said that, though?" I asked.

"Orders are orders. If it was up to me, I'd give everybody everything they wanted," he said.

"You should have said that in the first place rather than rubbing salt in our wounds," I said.

"I swear I have been locking horns with people so much since this morning my head is about to explode. I don't have the strength to argue with you," he said.

"Fine," I said, "but can't you go and see if you have just one extra tin back there you can give us?"

"You're right. What I said was wrong."

It was toward the middle of November, ten days since my arrival at the camp. I was at my wits end. To keep myself occupied I sought out the aid workers at the camp. The Force for War Victims set them up in a tent. One of them directed me to the kitchen, where I saw things were going on as they should, and there was no need for my supervision. I went to one of the large rooms in a storage area where old and new clothes were strewn about. Volunteers were culling bedding, blankets, sheets, and clothing. I spent several days sorting clothing. Later it became necessary to take an accurate census of the camp according to gender and age. I limped from home to home, trying to get an exact count, but failed no matter what we did. Every day a number of people, who had the means or who had sold some gold, would leave for Isfahan, Shiraz, Behbehan, etc., while another group would arrive and wait for places to open up for them.

The areas around the camp were not immune to attacks by enemy planes. Once a rocket landed in the stagnant water in the nearby desert, terrifying people. Despite all the psychological pressures I felt at the camp, deep down I didn't want to leave it for faraway cities. The camp was close to Khorramshahr. I forced myself to come to terms with the conditions so they wouldn't bother me as much. Around noon I would go home where the boys would bring lunch from the kitchen or mother would rustle up something. Her simple, spare meals tasted better than the camp food. When we sat around the floor cloth, the absence of father and Ali weighed heavily on me, and I had to choke back tears. Father always insisted we eat together because it was healthy for us. The harmony, he said, made the angels happy.

Mother didn't eat much; apparently these gatherings had opened old wounds. She seemed to be lost in thought. Often she would sigh and say, "Ali, it kills me not knowing where you are now, whether you're eating or not."

A few times Hoseyn Ta'i Nezhad stopped by with other army boys. I had seen Hoseyn once in Khorramshahr and asked him never to tell mother about Ali. When she mentioned him, Hoseyn said, "Ali's busy. He's in a good place. We've tried to get him to take leave and come by."

But the boys were not happy with me for forcing them to lie.

One day around noon I emerged from the aid tent to see several women in chadors coming toward me and waving. They seemed familiar. As they got closer, I saw they were the girls from the Sheybani clinic. I was so happy to see them I nearly jumped for joy. I shuffled rapidly toward them, as Zohreh, Saffah, and Ashraf ran toward me. I hugged and kissed the three of them. Everybody was crying. As usual Ashraf Farhadi, who was the most tenderhearted, shed the most tears.

I also saw Abed Mohammadi and Dr. Mostafavi a little farther way. They had all come together. We went home, and mother was overjoyed to see the girls. Her first question, of course, was about Ali,

"I don't know why everybody but Ali visits; there's no a word from him. He's never come by."

After pouring tea, she went to prepare some food. The men left the trailer to walk the grounds, giving us the chance to gossip in earnest. "What happened after I left?" I kept asking. "What about so-and-so…?"

"Wait, will you. One at a time," they said. "On the sixteenth the Iraqis reached the Forty-Meter Road, driving all of us out of the city."

"So, where did you go?" I asked.

"We went to our homes. We've come back here now to be able to go to Abadan."

They spoke of how hard it would be to go to other cities without any money. We talked our heads off until mother brought the food. We also joked around and kidded one another. It made me very happy they had come. It put me in a better position to carry out my decision to go to Abadan. Dr. Mostafavi and Abed left after lunch. The girls and I stayed and continued to talk and discuss the different ways to reach Abadan.

We all had ideas. The most important thing would be arranging some kind of permit or pass to go through the war zone. Because of Fifth Column elements in the region, getting such a permit involved a lot of questions.

None of us had any hope of helping the Khorramshahr boys now trapped at an export-import company in Sar Bandar. The girls said, "The enemy is advancing, and there's no telling what'll happen to them."

I said, "There's a number of military men living in a part of the camp. Some are acquaintances. We saw them around the mosque in Khorramshahr. Maybe they can help with the permit."

"It would be better to start at the municipality," they said.

Mother, who had been listening, said, "I'm coming, too."

Eyes wide in surprise, I asked, "Where, mother?"

"With you—I want to find Ali."

"What about the children, mother? What will they do?" I asked.

Her eyes filled with tears, and she left the room.

That night Zeynab, who had been listening and learned I intended to leave, stretched out beside me and, as usual, asked, "Where's father?"

"He's with God," I said. "Because God liked him, He brought father to live with him. God brings everybody He likes to the next world so they'll suffer less. Father was one of those very good people who had a very hard life in this world."

"So, doesn't he miss us?" she asked.

I shook my head. "Zahra," she asked, "will God let father come back to see us?"

"No. Father is not coming back, but he is always with us. When we do something good, he's watching us from above, and it makes him happy."

"So," she asked, "why doesn't God bring us to Him? Are we bad people, then?"

"No, but we aren't as good as father yet."

"What do we have to do to be that good?" she asked.

"We have to do good things, help people who are doing good things, and don't do things God doesn't like. We have to be so good we'll be martyred and be with God."

She asked, "So only martyrs can be with God?"

"No. Any good person, even if he's not a martyr, can be with God," I said.

"So, who is God anyway? Why do we have to listen to Him?"

I spoke and spoke until she seemed satisfied, but there was no end to the questions—so many I got fed up and said finally, "Wait till you're gown up and you go to school, then you'll understand."

It was very difficult for me to hear her speak about these things. I got emotional and irritated by her impatience to know. Many times she didn't ask directly about father, but I knew very well her questions were just an excuse to hear about him. She missed him very much. I had to hide my feelings and soothe her by being calm.

The next morning as I was about to close the door, I said to mother, "It's not clear when we'll be back. We may go to Abadan today." I asked her to keep the children from running wild in the camp. As I said this, I looked at the children, who, awakened by the sound of our talking, were peeking from beneath their blankets. I told them, "It might be a long time before I'm back. Try not to annoy mother. Don't go about with just anyone, only with people you trust."

Zeynab, who as usual was full of questions, jumped up and ran toward me. She put her arms around my neck and asked, "Why are you going? Don't go! I'll miss you. Father's gone. Ali's gone. If you go, Leila will also leave."

I was trembling all over, beginning to have doubts. Wouldn't it be better to stay and mind the children to keep them from going astray? But I knew if I stayed I'd get so fed up that the camp would become intolerable again, and I would end up destroying their morale as well as my own. I said to Zeynab, "Look, darling, I have to go to keep the wounded from becoming martyrs and keeping their children from becoming orphans."

With that I took her arms from around my neck and kissed her. Mother's face was wet with tears. I kissed her and said, "Don't just sit there crying; you'll break the kids' hearts. You're their mother and father now. Living under these conditions is depressing enough. You don't have to make it worse. I know how hard it is for you, but the least you can do is not to show your sorrow to the kids. Crying saps their will to go on. Father and the other martyrs have gone to their rightful places. That's nothing to cry about."

"He left and dumped me in this misery," she sobbed.

"Don't blaspheme," I said. "Father chose the path he always loved. He made us proud by going the way of his grandfather. Do you think crying will bring him back?"

She said, "No. I know he's not coming back. But maybe it makes my heart ache less." Then she sighed and added, "I know one day it'll be all over for me, but the pain will go on."

I kissed her head once more and said goodbye.

We left the camp, hoping to get a pass. We called on everybody: the Red Crescent, military command, the army, the municipality, the navy, and the Force for War Victims.

We told them we wanted to go to the war zone.

"Impossible," they said. "Do you think this a game?"

"Well," we said, "we're nurses and we were there before. Besides, the *games* our boys played kept the enemy from taking Khorramshahr right away."

Finally, after exhausting every avenue, I said, "Guys, I went to the War Room once. They must remember me. Let's go there to see if something can be done."

After repeatedly asking directions, we found the War Room, which was located in one of the military encampments. We were stopped at the door and grilled about what we wanted. "The men in the War Room know me," I said. "I've come to get a pass for the war zone."

Hearing that, they said, "You're dreaming. They don't give out passes to anybody. Go about your business."

But we were persistent and managed to get in the building. We saw some commandos whom we had run into at the Congregational Mosque inside. They knew me well, especially the two stocky men I had quarreled with at the clinic. Mahmud Farrokhi and Mr. Mesbah had told us not to admit to the clinic anybody without business there. Once when I asked the two men to leave, they started to argue. Afterwards, whenever they saw me and the other girls, we could tell from the way they acted, we weren't their favorite people. They were part of a squad trained abroad and, very taken by their own military skill, didn't expect to have run-ins with the likes of us. Unlike the other commandos who went to the front and fought alongside regular soldiers, they stayed behind and went around constantly carping about the war. They declared, "This is an asymmetric conflict and doesn't conform to any military equation…."

As soon as they saw us, one of them asked, "What are you doing here? Who said you could come in?"

I said, "The men in the War Room know me. I want to get a pass from them." They chuckled and made cracks. Knowing I was about to ignite, Zohreh Farhadi grabbed my arm and gestured for me not to react. We walked away from the commandos and waited to speak to someone else.

But unlike us, the men wouldn't let up. Knowing exactly what buttons to press, they began to insult the Imam. They started to mimic the authorities, saying idiotic things to us. The quieter we got the louder and more insulting they became. Pride made it impossible for me to ignore these taunts, especially when it came to Imam Khomeini. They had the nerve to say he had sent the youth of the nation into harm's way while staying safe in Tehran. I broke the vow I had made to myself not to get into fights with such people and yelled, "You don't know what you're talking about! Nobody sent us; we took on the enemy's guns ourselves. What happened is the fault of somebody else."

The largest and bulkiest of them asked, "What does a bunch of brats like you know about war?"

"These same brats kept the enemy at bay in Khorramshahr for thirty-five days," I said.

"So it did your heart good to last it out, did it? But what'll you do from now on?"

I said, "If the traitors let them, the boys who've made it this far will, with God's help, stand and fight."

"What do you mean by 'if the traitors let them'?" he bellowed.

Provoked now, I said, "It doesn't take a genius to realize the key to Saddam's victory over us and the fall of Khorramshahr was our own treachery. Many people from the very top to the lower echelons committed treason."

Although I tried not to mention any names, he seemed to know whom I had in mind, because he asked angrily, "What are you afraid of? You don't have the nerve to say what you mean!"

"You're the chickens, you and your buddies who left when the going got tough. Each one of you found a safe spot where you could hide. I'm not afraid of anything. The biggest traitor to this country is Banisadr."

"Shut the hell up! You don't know what you're talking about!"

"You shut the hell up. How dare you insult Imam Khomeini? Whatever he may be, he's no traitor. He's the one who made men of you; otherwise you'd now be just provincial cops doing the bidding of the Americans!"

One of the others shouted, "You're the traitors! You're the Hypocrites who are trying to bring down the Revolution. We're going to hand you over to the desert court. They'll try and execute the lot of you."

Shaking with rage, I said, "Don't waste your breath threatening us with kangaroo courts. What have we done? We're not the ones who should go on trial!"

They suddenly cocked their Uzis and pointed them at us. It was a strange scene. Seven or eight towering soldiers, well-muscled and imposing, dressed in dark camouflage pants and boots, their caps cocked, and their shirtsleeves rolled up to the elbows with colts, bayonets, and canteens hanging from their belts, confronting a handful of young women.

After they barked at us to move, I asked, "Where to? We're not going with you. We don't trust you."

I said this because when they came to the clinic, they would try to get friendly. At that time we behaved in a way that would make them understand we were not interested, nor was the clinic the place for such things.

"If you don't move, we'll shoot you right here!" they snarled.

The argument got so heated it made those passing by ask, "Why are you all standing around here? What's the racket all about? This is no place to fight, is it?"

A couple of commando friends of the ones confronting us emerged from a room and tried to get their buddies to leave us alone. I heard them say, "What're they to you? Let'em go."

But they wouldn't listen, and the girls for their part kept shouting, "We're not coming with you!"

An officer emerged from a room and asked irritably, "What's going on? Why are you standing here shouting like that? Is this the place for that kind of thing?"

One of the commandos said, "We caught a bunch of Hypocrites."

I said, "You're the Hypocrites, you lying cowards!"

Another man poked his head out of a door and said, "That's enough, mister! What's all the shouting about?"

I rushed forward and said, "Sir, we've come here to get a pass for the war zone. We're medical workers from Khorramshahr. We were there before it fell. All we want is a pass, but these men have been calling us every name in the book."

The man, his face sober and lined with experience, turned to the commandos and asked, "What's this all about? What did you say to them?" One of the commandos said, "Sir, they insulted the commander in chief."

The man, whom I regarded with a mixture of fear and respect, looked at me sideways and asked, "Is that true?"

I didn't know what to say. I thought: If that's what the commandos are like, God save us from the commander! What was I thinking bringing the girls here? I wish I hadn't. Then I had my answer: How long were they going to cover up Banisadr's treachery. Sooner or later the people will have to find out why Khorramshahr fell. Why must we have to hear from every quarter that we failed? I had heard people in Shiraz blame the refugees for running away. They asked the poor people why they had surrendered their own city to the enemy and then come to their town, causing headaches for everyone. They blamed the refugees were for the disruptions, the long lines. I was fed up with that type of insulting talk. Whatever happens, happens, I told myself. Now if we were to go before a military court, at least I'd have my say, and people would know they executed me for revealing Banisadr as the traitor he was. This was what was going through my mind at that point. After a brief pause and although my heart wasn't in it, I asked bluntly, "Sir, isn't Banisadr a traitor?"

That caused an uproar. Every enlisted man and officer surrounded me. My head began to ache horribly, my heart pounded, my lips dried shut, and there was a burning deep in my throat. I worried about what would happen to the other girls. They had backed up what I was saying, and now things were out of hand. They looked terrified. I said to assure myself: These men can't execute us. They don't have the authority for that. Besides, we were only saying what we truly believed, so God won't abandon us. The only thing remaining to be decided was how long the confrontation would last and what the men would do. But what if it kept us from going to the war zone?

While the men continued to rant at us, I caught sight of a man whose calm demeanor marked him from the rest. I got the sense he understood what I had said. He seemed familiar and seeing him calmed me. The next thing I knew, the commander was addressing me. "You mustn't confuse the issues. What you say is not in the interests of the country."

"So," I said, "it's in the interests of the country for Khorramshahr to fall, but not to say Banisadr is a traitor?"

The words burst the lump in my throat, and tears began to flow. I couldn't take all the pressure on me. Seeing the state I was in, Ashraf said, "You have no right to treat us like this. You call us traitors when we did everything in our powers to resist. This woman you are attacking buried her father and brother with her own two hands. She was wounded badly and is just out of the hospital."

The commander changed his tone after hearing that and said gently, "God have mercy on all the martyrs. We know what happened in Khorramshahr, but we still have to maintain unity. We can't say things the enemy will misuse."

"Why don't you tell your own soldiers this?" I said through my tears. "When they stand here and insult Imam Khomeini and the authorities, doesn't that undermine unity? I'm just saying what Jahan Ara has said. He wanted to let people know how Khorramshahr and its youth were victimized. Wherever he goes, he tells the same story. You're the commander of these men, but my commander is Jahan Ara; I follow his orders."

With that Ashraf, Zohreh, Sabah, and Leila burst into tears. This apparently cooled the situation, and the men stopped yelling.

The calm face in the crowd belonged to a man in khaki with a spark in his eyes that shone through his glasses. He came forward and asked with a smile, "How long were you in Khorramshahr, sisters?"

"Almost to the end," we said.

"Were you with them?" he asked me.

"No."

"Then when did you leave?" he asked.

"Around the beginning of November."

"Were you wounded?"

"Yes, on the day of the battle at the customs building."

There was a odd look in his eyes, a mixture of pride and exultation. He said, "Bravo! You have done the Imam proud, but for now you should be with your families. The war's going better; it would be best for you not to be in the zone."

The girls said, "We'd rather be back in our own city helping in any way we can to win the war. Our families know all about what we're doing."

He said, "May God reward you. You've shown true devotion. Your fighting spirit will strengthen our resolve. You're needed here; there's a lot of work to be done, work that is often more important than what's being done at the front."

Then he turned to the rest and said, "These women are our dear sisters. Let them return to their homes."

The man's magnetic gaze and the serenity in his voice left a deep impression on me. I believe the other girls felt the same way. His works caused the commandos, who had been silenced, to look to their chief. They were waiting to see how he would react. Finally he said, "Men, you're dismissed."

Then he addressed us. "Both the men and I are fully aware what's happened, but in order to keep the enemy from taking advantage of any show of disunity, we can't say anything."

Fed up with this passive attitude, I turned to the girls and, without raising my voice, I grumbled, "We'll do what Jahan Ara says and won't bother with what these men think. Let's go."

The commander, who realized our silence meant we disagreed with him, said goodbye and left. The men dispersed, talking among themselves. I thanked the man with the friendly face, who was still watching us protectively and asked him about a pass. He said, "It's not possible now. Besides, we have more than enough medical help. The hospitals are active, and there aren't that many wounded. The enemy has taken up positions on the other side of the water, while we have stationed men along the lines. As long as there are no serious plans for operations, things will stay quiet. The enemy attack has stalled. We've got them stymied."

We said goodbye and walked past the commandos with our heads held high. The way they stood seemed to say: See, we made you cry after all. We stormed out of the building and were very put out, leaving empty-handed. Catching our breath, our nerves kept us from speaking, but we soon all broke into laughter. As we laughed, I looked at the red and swollen eyes of the girls. Zohreh said, "God knows what would have happened if they had taken us away! They're real heathens!"

"We shouldn't have cried," Sabah said. "It let them think they could bully us." Despite the pessimism, we felt good we hadn't backed down and had said what needed saying. Then one of the girls shouted, "Thank God for Chamran!"

"That was actually Chamran?" I asked in astonishment.

"Yeah," she said. "Where were you? Didn't you hear them calling him Dr. Chamran several times?"

"No. I didn't notice. I don't know why."

I knew Dr. Chamran was the Imam's representative on the Supreme Defense Council. Whenever I heard his name or saw his face on TV, it caught my attention. It was good to have actually seen him in person. I felt he understood everything I had said.

After walking a bit, we decided to go to the jetty at Mahshahr. We had heard there were launches taking people to Abadan there. There were also helicopters ferrying fresh forces to the front and the wounded back from it. We caught a ride part way with a pickup heading for the refinery. Now it was around 5:00 p.m. and we were hungry, so we decided to take a short cut.

We left the road and soon got lost. There was nothing to mark the path but the occasional oil pump or pipeline. We were so tired and hungry continuing seemed impossible, but the worse thing was the heat. Sweat poured down our faces. The scorching ground made it even hotter. Water from the seasonal rains had gathered in places but quickly evaporated into salt flats under the brutal sun. We were soon knee-deep in the swampy terrain. We laughed our heads off as we tried to pull one another from the mud and slime. Towering over the rest of us, Sabah should have been more help, but she was laughing so hard she was useless. The girls complained, "Here we are going through hell trying to get back to the front on our own while the army has to use force to get boys to go."

The jetty gradually came into view. When we saw the tall masts of boats docked there, we gladly spent what we had left running to them. There was a large open area along the jetty strewn with crates filled with bundles of clothing and other goods. Blue barrels sealed with wire were stacked neatly in another part. A collection of stackers and lifts were moving the crates and barrels. Several ships and launches were moored by the jetty. To get inside the area we passed through a number of checkpoints. When we said we wanted to go to Abadan, no one barred our way.

Two air force helicopters stood in another part of the area. One of them took off as we entered, raising clouds of dust and debris. Not knowing where to go or whom to ask about a pass, we stood by like little children gaping as people and machines went back and forth.

It wasn't long before a pickup appeared carrying commandos we knew from the Congregational Mosque and the clinic. Among them was Yaddi, the son-in-law of Maryam, my coworker at Jennatabad. I walked up to them and said hello. The way they reacted showed that the sight of some girls standing by the jetty had wounded their manly pride. "What are you doing here all by yourselves?" they asked.

"We've come to see if somebody would take us to Abadan."

"Don't you think you've done your bit? Why don't you go home and let the rest of us get on with our jobs?"

"We still want to do more at the front, help the defenders, aid the wounded. We don't feel right staying behind," I said.

"They won't let you go to Abadan without a pass, you know," they said.

"What should we do? We've tried to get one at the War Room, but it almost landed us in jail."

"You're determined to go, then? You won't change your minds?"

"No."

After a pause, Yaddi, who was doing most of the talking, said, "Tomorrow we're going to try to get to Abadan ourselves. If we can arrange a pass for you, we'll let you know. Go back to the camp and wait."

Missing Zeynab terribly, I asked Yaddi, "Any news of Zeynab?"

"No," he said.

I asked him about Maryam, his mother-in-law. He said, "We got her out. She's with us."

After Yaddi finished what he had to do at the jetty, he drove us back to the camp. That night, after a dinner of potato omelet mother cooked and greens she had bought at Sar Bandar, our small room became wall-to-wall sleeping cushions. As there was no room for Mohsen, we sent him to Uncle Nad Ali's. My back was killing me and I paced most of the night, trying to deal with the pain. I eventually was able to fall into a peaceful sleep.

Before dawn I awoke in a fright and called out to the girls. It was difficult to wake up Sabah, who was still tired from the previous day's exertions. We got dressed and, as we were leaving the house, mother was coming in with a kettle and a flask of water. Seeing us dressed and ready to go, she asked, "Where to?"

"We want to see if they're going to send us to Abadan."

Obviously annoyed by our departure but not wanting to show it, she said, "Sit down now and have some breakfast. You can't go just like that."

Sitting around breakfast, we told her—leaving out the details—about almost getting executed and had a good laugh. Zohreh Farhadi, the youngest, was afraid something bad was going to happen. She insisted we watch what we said. Sabah said, "Yeah, whatever we do we have to keep from getting into arguments." Raising my voice, I said, "Since when is it a law we have to say 'yes sir' to everything others say? If we're telling the truth, we mustn't back down."

Busy pouring the tea, mother looked up and said, "Zahra's just like her father. Her mouth's going to be the death of her."

I remembered this was what she always told father. Once he said about work, "It makes no sense. The boss was bullying some of the workers. None of them had the nerve to say anything. I couldn't just stay quiet while this man bullied them. So I talked back." Mother got upset, because father had just found that job. After going through all that misery and poverty in the past, she was afraid he'd be fired again. She mumbled in Kurdish, "Your mouth is going to be the death of us."

Father laughed and said, "Don't worry, nobody's going to come after you."

I repeated what he said, adding, "Don't worry, I won't let anybody harm you. If anybody's life's going to be ruined, I'll make sure it's mine."

She looked at me and said angrily, "You should be ashamed of yourself, mimicking your father that way!" As we were leaving, she said, "Fine, leave, but why are you forcing Leila to go?"

"I not forcing her to do anything," I said. "She wants to come."

But as we were walking, I said to Leila, "Go back. It's not right to leave mother all alone. She can't manage the children by herself.

She's still in agony over father and will need someone who'll listen to her. Any minute now somebody'll knock on the door and tell her about Ali. If you're with her, you'll be able to manage the situation better and look after her."

Leila said, "If that's how you feel, why don't you stay instead of trying to talk me into going back?"

"Well, I can do more at the front than you. I've learned how to be a nurse."

She said, "Fine, but just like you I can learn nursing, too."

"But it's going to take a long time."

"Since when did I know how to shroud and bury corpses? But I learned how in a day and got over my fears."

"Whatever you say, but it would better if you stay with mother."

We had had it out over this before, but every time I said I would go back, she would say, "I'm coming with you. Wherever you go, I go." She was so stubborn at times she made me want to spit, and I yelled at her, "What about mother and the kids?"

We went to where the busses for Mahshahr were, but the area was such a madhouse we changed our minds and started to walk. On the way we got a ride on a pickup to the town and from there a truck loaded with workers took us to the jetty. By that time the sun was high overhead, and we were feeling the heat. As we searched for the previous day's commandos, a khaki-colored Toyota pulled up next to us. We turned around to find two Revolutionary Guards sitting in it. I immediately recognized Jahan Ara, and my face lit up. I don't know why I thought I was seeing father; Jahan Ara was not that old, but you could imagine he was father to us all. His face for all its sternness invited trust and confidence. He got down from the driver's seat and we said hello. He responded and glanced along the jetty, which was teeming with workers and soldiers, and asked gruffly, "What are you doing here?"

Since we spoke on the telephone, I had the impression he was a straightforward and measured person. I was shocked by his present tone. I saw the girls looking at one another, at a loss as how to respond. Finally I said, "We want to go to Abadan. We came here for a pass."

"What do you want to go there for?" he asked.

"We're nurses," I explained. "We want to go to the hospital and help with the wounded."

"They have all the people they need right now," he said.

"We'll do anything they ask," I said.

Suddenly he turned to me and asked, "You're Seyyed Ali Hoseyni's sister, aren't you?"

"Yes."

"The one who was wounded?"

It amazed me he knew about it. "Yes."

"How can you possibly want to go back, given your condition? There's absolutely no need for you there. Your family has paid its debt to the war effort in full—you've made your share of sacrifices and you yourself have been injured. You're all refugees. Could anyone be more deserving? If the Imam were here, he'd say the same thing."

I was upset and insulted. Until then I had thought of Jahan Ara as a father. I grumbled, "No, I will go. I have my father's permission. No one's going to stop me." The girls said, "We only want to be of use in Abadan; we're rotting staying here."

Everybody started speaking at once. Suddenly the other passenger in the jeep, a guard who until then had been staring into space, turned and glared at us. The look, which showed he was beyond annoyed, was truly terrifying to me. I retreated a little and, standing by Zohreh Farhadi, whispered, "Who could that man be?"

"Reza Musavi, Jahan Ara's deputy," she said.

Jahan Ara went on, "Don't stay here. It's not a good place for you. If we need you, I'll personally issue a pass so you can go to the front."

Then he stopped talking. We looked at one another wondering what to do next. It was a standoff: Jahan Ara waiting for us to go, we waiting for him to leave. After a while, I came to the conclusion he was not going to back down until he had sent us from the jetty. "Let's go, guys," I said. The girls looked at me in surprise, as if to say: How can you back down so easily after insisting you wanted to go back to the front? Resigned, I repeated, "Let's go, it's time. Didn't you hear what he said?"

About to go, I had second thoughts and asked, "You'll really let us know?"

I had to know if he actually meant to call us or whether he had just said so to get us to leave.

"At present there is no need for you, and I don't expect there will be one," he said. "Right now we need fighting men, but if nurses are called for, I'll let you know."

This made me think he was being honest. As we walked away, the girls asked, "What did he say to satisfy you about leaving?"

"The way they were stopped there told me they would never back down," I said.

"So now if those commando friends of ours arrive and see we're not there, where are we going to get our passes?"

I said, "Guys, we aren't really going. We're just pretending to go. We'll wait for them to leave, then we'll double back." We walked along the side of the road for ten minutes or so, but every time we looked back, we saw they were still there, making sure we were actually heading home. At the same time we kept our eyes peeled for any vehicle with our commando friends so we could tell them to wait for us by the jetty. After a while, Jahan Ara and Musavi's Toyota passed by us and stopped. Jahan Ara stuck his head out of the window and asked, "Would you like to wait while I get a car for you?"

"No," I said. "We'll go to the main road and get a lift."

"Where are you headed?" he asked.

"Camp B."

If there had been enough room in his jeep, I was certain he would have driven us himself. Fortunately there was no room. We walked on for a while and, after I was certain they had gone and couldn't see us in their rear view mirror, we doubled back, running and laughing all the way to the jetty. Zohreh said, "It's a good thing the commandos from the War Room aren't here. They'd remind us about saying the only orders we followed were Jahan Ara's and about how traitors caused the fall of Khorramshahr. They'd ask us why weren't we following his orders now!"

I don't know who answered her by saying, "It's all right for Jahan Ara and the others to be at the front, but, when it come to us, all of a sudden there's no room there?!"

We came back to the jetty and for an hour stood to the side, watching the nonstop confusion of new forces arriving by truck. We were afraid of doing or saying something that would get us thrown out. It was so hot our heads and the soles of our feet were baking. Finally the friendly commandos arrived in a white pickup. We ran to them eagerly, but our mood soured when we heard they couldn't get passes for us. "Something's supposed to be done about it, because only five of the eight of us were able to get passes," they explained. Then, pointing at the building where they arranged helicopter passes, Sabah said, "So let's go and do it on our own."

"You shouldn't," the commandos said. "We've been tasked to go to the navy base at Khorramshahr and remove papers and documents there. We've added your names to the list of names on the mission. If you say you're nurses, they'll want proof. There's no point waiting here. Come back in the afternoon when we'll definitely have passes for you."

Sabah said, "We shouldn't go. No doubt we'll run into somebody who'll be able to do something for us."

There was a lot of arguing back and forth, but we finally returned to the camp. After a meal and a nap, we went back to the jetty in the late afternoon with the sun's fury gone. Five of the commandos in Yaddi's group had already flown off on the noon helicopter. Two of the commandos told me Yaddi and another man stayed behind trying to get passes for the rest. As we were standing there, I noticed the commandos who had fought with us at the War Room were on the jetty. When they saw us, the men we were supposed to surrender to took the others aside and spoke to them. I couldn't hear what they were saying, but from the expressions on their faces I assumed they were going to pull something on us. I said to the girls, "They're ratting us out."

Zohreh said anxiously, "I hope to God the other commandos don't believe them and decide not to take us."

"Meaning what?" I asked. "It isn't like this is the first time Yaddi and the others have seen us. They know us from before. Besides, if all it takes is one word from them to keep us from getting passes, we might as well not get them. God willing, we'll find a way to go to Abadan."

Several minutes later the two commandos returned. Although we were dying to know what the others had said about us, we remained quiet. They were the ones to speak first, asking, "Do you know those two?"

"No. We saw them for the first time yesterday."

"How did you get to know them?" they asked.

We explained what happened. They looked at each other and laughed. "Do you know what they told us about you?"

"No."

"They asked what we were doing with you. They said you're Hypocrites trying to bring down the Revolution. You were under surveillance and you'd be arrested and tried in some desert court. You had insulted the leader of the country."

"What did you say to them?" we asked.

They laughed and said, "We're not children. We didn't believe a word!"

We all had a good laugh and said, "They're happy now, but if they stick around they'll really get a surprise!"

Yaddi returned happily with a handful of passes, but told us we would have to go to Abadan by hovercraft at night, so it wouldn't be seen. This was the first time we had heard the word "hovercraft." We thought it was like "Chinook" or "Cobra," a kind of helicopter. The commandos explained it was a vehicle that goes both on land and water at high speeds, so fast it sometimes flies over the water. I was so happy I didn't know what to do. We were going back to Abadan—as soldiers! Yaddi explained the hovercraft was only for military.

We had a long, boring wait until 8:00 when the hovercraft was due to leave. To kill time we walked along the jetty, which was surrounded by water on three sides. We stood facing the Gulf. The water stretched out to where the horizon met the sea. To our right the setting sun was a red ball with a dazzling reflection on the water. At Khorramshahr the level of the water was much lower than the shoreline, but here the waves lapped over the land. It was only at sunset that the level went down, revealing the sandy banks along the jetty. But it didn't take long for the water to rise again. With the call to prayer we went into a building on the jetty. We did our ablutions and said our prayers on a blanket spread on the floor. Then we returned to the staging area.

Personnel, most of whom were military, kept coming on the jetty. Among them were some regular army people. There were about two or three hundred of them. Most of the incoming groups carried munitions boxes of various sorts, which they stacked on the jetty. I knew cartridges and pistols were in the wooden boxes, and mortar shells were in the metal ones. I asked one of the commandos what was in the large wooden crates the size of coffins. "Those are for rockets," he said.

It was now past the time they had promised the hovercraft would leave, and I got more nervous the later it got. Five girls in a military zone stuck out like a sore thumb. Everybody was astonished to see us there. We tried to act in way that blocked all conversation, but I still had a strange feeling of uneasiness. "How could we be sure," I asked myself, "the hovercraft operators were not Fifth Columnists delivering us right to the Iraqis?" I had heard stories about a number of traitors turning their fellow countrymen into prisoners of war. Living under wartime conditions and having to deal with strangers had made us extremely wary. I wished Leila had stayed with mother and not with me. Then, if something were to happen, it would happen to me alone. That would have been easier for mother, and give Leila a chance to live out the rest of her life, but she refused.

At 10:00 the water got choppy, and there was a faint buzzing sound. The monster hovercraft gradually came into view, and the closer it got, the more imposing it became in my eyes. It didn't have an identifiable, geometric shape. Rather, it was a square-ish brown or black blob with round edges. It was about the size of a Chinook helicopter. Two things looking like locusts were on the roof. It docked very gently at the jetty. In the darkness I couldn't make out what it was made of. A few powerful military-issue spotlights lit up the area.

They told people to step aside while munitions were being loaded. Men formed a chain and put the boxes on board quickly. Then a uniformed man read the passenger list, which was compiled from the passes issued at the jetty office. For some reason my hopes were not high. Were we ever going to get to Abadan? Then they read out our names, and we boarded. They led us to a corner of the hovercraft where there was a bench and, next to it, soldiers' packs. We sat and examined the interior, which was darker in color than the outside.

It didn't take long for the entire craft to fill up with the rest of the passengers sitting on the deck. I felt as if we were in a military tent. The concave sides of the hovercraft kept us from leaning back. I looked at the girls, who were as happy as I to be aboard. Then I thought of mother, how she would be concerned about us by now. At that point, Zohreh, as if reading my mind, said to Leila and me, "If only one of you had stayed behind with your mother."

"I couldn't," I said.

"I didn't mean you," Zohreh said.

"So, I should have been the one to stay?" asked Leila very put out.

"God knows," said Zohreh with a laugh.

Zohreh's comment only made me more upset about mother. It bothered my conscience to leave her and the kids alone. I felt I had behaved rottenly, ignoring what was their due and only considering what I wanted. But then I thought, "Father had left them, and Ali took his path. Why should I be the only one to stay behind with the kids? If martyrdom was a good thing, why shouldn't I want to be a martyr too?" Seeing no end to the self-criticism and justification, I left it up to God. In my heart I said, "Lord, if I'm doing the right thing, help me. If You're not pleased, just let me come back alive."

Putting my trust in God was some relief. While we waited for the craft to leave, the men prayed out loud and repeated, "God is great." Then the personnel in charge of seating announced there was no more room, and they closed the doors. Due to the lack of space, it was standing-room-only for many. The rumble of the motors gradually got louder, and I wondered how the craft would be able to move loaded as it was with all the personnel and munitions. Contrary to my expectations, it slipped off very easily. The only hitch came when the things rose and started to hover.

The thrill of gliding over the water didn't last long, however. The air suddenly filled with acrid smoke, burning our throats. There was some anxious talk, as people wondered what was happening. One fellow with an earpiece said, "Everybody stay calm. We've got to go back. It seems one of the motors is on fire."

Panic surged through the crowd. Terrified, someone screamed, "It's going to go up any minute, and we'll be burned to death with all this ammunition on board!" Someone else said, "Why should it catch fire? I hope to God they didn't fire a torpedo at us!" The other one said, "Do you really think this is some kind of submarine they would torpedo?"

Frankly, I was a little afraid. "See what happens?" I said to myself, "How God punishes you for upsetting mother? He won't let you leave. And now you're going to die without even getting to Abadan. You're going to have to explain why you went without permission. Explain why you broke your mother's heart. Worst of all, you'll have to tell father why you broke your promise to take care of the kids." This wasn't the afterlife I had in mind, spending eternity ashamed to look father in the face.

As the smoke got thicker, we kept our eyes fixed on the munitions. The hovercraft returned to the jetty in less time than it took it to reach the open water. Men charged the door before the gangway opened and the craft docked. From all sides people were shouting, "Don't panic. We're putting it out now. Let the women off first. Don't push." They opened a path for us, and we saw several people with fire extinguishers rushing toward the cabin. We jumped from the hovercraft, landing in water up to our waists. Several soldiers were wading toward the bow of the craft. Locking arms, we trudged through the water and mud and, giggling all the way, managed to get out of the water; but we were still unsettled by what had happened. Safely on shore everybody had something to say. Sabah, who had suggested we wait for a different and better way to get to Abadan, said, "What did I tell you? We shouldn't have been in such a rush. But you wouldn't listen and look what happened!"

I got sore at Leila and said, "It's all your fault. If you had stayed behind with mother, this wouldn't have happened!"

I also let Sabah have it, "You and your bellyaching jinxed the whole thing."

"Get off it, will you. Why are you always starting fights?" Sabah said.

Zohreh said, "What bad luck! After all that running around to get passes!"

After finally agreeing it was God's will, we went to help unload the munitions. They didn't let us get too close to the fire, so we just waited in the background. We couldn't see the burned part of the hovercraft, only the reflection of the flames on the water. After the fire was out, engineers got busy repairing the craft. We couldn't go until it was fixed. It was now past midnight, and the hovercraft that had arrived when we had gotten underway was being loaded. It wouldn't be going back that night.

They ordered everyone off the jetty and told us to return before daybreak when the craft was rescheduled to leave for Abadan. Soldiers got into their vehicles and left the jetty. We were at a loss as what to do. When we saw the commandos and Yaddi, we asked them, "What should we do? They won't let us stay here. We have no way to getting back, and even if we did, we couldn't get back here soon enough." They said, "That's true. It won't be long before daybreak. If you have to leave, why don't you come to base with us?"

We stared at one another for a minute, debating whether to stay or go. Could we trust them? Where was their base? We didn't know what to say. If we said we weren't going, they'd conclude we didn't trust them. Naturally they'd ask, "If you didn't trust us, why did you ask us to get you passes in the first place?" If we didn't go with these men, who had never done us any harm in the past, what were we going to do? We couldn't go back to camp, but we couldn't remain where we were. We debated what to do. One girl said, "Let's go with them." Another said, "We can't. We don't know these men." I agreed with her. I said, "It's true Yaddi is Maryam's son-in-law, and we've never seen him do or say anything inappropriate, but we still don't know him well enough. But how do we know staying here won't be more of a problem for us?" Having guessed what we were talking about, the men said, "Do whatever you think is best. If you'd like us to give you a ride back to camp, fine. But we won't be able to come and pick you up at the crack of dawn."

In the end, we put our trust in the Lord and got in their pickup. Two of the men sat next to the driver, the other went in the back. As the truck drove through the empty darkness, I didn't say a word but, fearful, took Leila's hand. I was confident I could take care of myself if something happened, but I worried about Leila, who was younger and more vulnerable. I was concerned about the others, too. It seemed without knowing it I had taken responsibility for the group. As the spokesperson in so many of the conversations with officials when it came time to act, I was the one they turned to. I knew their hearts were pounding as hard as mine, but they wouldn't let it show.

Each time the truck entered an alley my fears increased, but, when we joined the main road again, I relaxed. We finally entered a military encampment, and, immediately after clearing the guardhouse, I said to myself: For God's sake, this is the same place where they almost hanged us! I whispered, "You see where we are, guys?"

"Yeah," they said. "What are we going to do?"

"Nothing. We've no choice. We'll just go in and answer any questions they have." I sounded brave but inside I was afraid. To buck up my courage I told myself I was strong, and there was no reason to be afraid. But the words of those commandos when we had been in the building were still fresh in my mind: "You just wait. We're going to hand you over to the desert court. They'll try and execute the lot of you."

The truck stopped and we got out. They ushered us into the same foyer as yesterday. Outside the building was dark and all its windows were blacked out. Yaddi went to speak to someone about allocating a private room to us. Then they led us to another hallway leading to four or five rooms. They opened the door to one of rooms, a large and tidy place furnished with a few beds. Yaddi said, "You can stay here. Lock the door from the inside. I'll come and knock when it's time to leave."

Before he left he turned and said, "I'll go and see if I can find some food for you."

We were in the process of thanking him when the door to another room suddenly opened and two or three of the commandos from yesterday came out. Curious about what was going on, their eyes fell on us, and they asked Yaddi in surprise, "What are they doing here?"

"They're supposed to come with us to Abadan," Yaddi said. "Last night we had gotten underway in the hovercraft but it caught fire and we had to return. It may be possible to go again in the early hours, so we're all gathered here waiting."

It was irritating to hear him explain to them what had happened in such detail. In the meantime one of the commandos had gone back into their room. Several moments later their commander emerged along with the rest of the group from yesterday. They pulled Yaddi and his men aside and began talking to them in the hallway. Yaddi looked at us and said, "No. You're wrong. They're not antirevolutionary Hypocrites. We got to know them very well in Khorramshahr. The sisters have done all they could. They even went to the front lines. How could they be Hypocrites?" The commandos whispered something, and Yaddi and his men gave them a sharp reply. The girls and I stood at the door listening. I peeked out from time to time and saw them trying to get Yaddi to agree to something. Enraged now, he said, "That's impossible! The sister you're calling a Hypocrite buried her father and her brother with her own two hands!"

This just made me even angrier. I felt helpless as those men spread lies about me, but, at the same time, I was glad Yaddi and his men came to my defense. How can you just stand here, I asked myself, while they humiliate you? Then I spoke up, "Yaddi, if our being here is a problem for you, we'll leave."

The girls looked at me stunned and said, "Where are we going to go this time of night? What are you saying? In a couple of hours at most we'll be off to Abadan!"

"We'll just have to break our pledge to go to Abadan if it means having to put up with this rigmarole for a couple of hours."

Yaddi said, "Don't you worry. We'll stay here and sort it out."

"What," I asked him, "is it you have to sort out?"

"It's nothing," he said.

"Why aren't you talking face-to-face like men instead of hiding in a corner and whispering like that?"

One of the commandos from yesterday said, "You don't know what you're talking about! Keep you trap shut!"

Sabah, Ashraf, Leila, and Zohreh all spoke up, "Who are you to be telling us whether we can stay here or go? You call yourselves men, acting like somebody's old aunt?"

A loud argument broke out again, bringing people out of their offices. Yaddi and his men stayed in the middle of things, telling people, "Quiet! Why are you shouting?" Everybody had something to say.

The unfriendly commandos, knowing our sensitivities, dragged Imam Khomeini into it, slandering him again and making accusations against Ayatollah Beheshti. They seemed to think this was the right time to vent their feelings. One of the most serious charges was that the Imam caused the war.

"Why do you say that?" I asked. "You've been at the front. It's obvious who started the war. It's strange people like you who claim to be trained in Israel can say such things. What's clear as day is that the revolution cooked America's and Russia's goose in Iran, so they got Saddam and the Baathists to make war on us."

Their response to this was very weird. They thought so little of themselves they said, "Who are we that America would have Iraq make war on us?" This sort of defeatism and stupidity made my blood boil, and I said, "We knew the war didn't break out over of the likes of you. The enemy invaded the Islamic Republic to destroy the Revolution!"

The commander bellowed, "Didn't I tell you these people are saboteurs? Get your weapons. I'm going to hand them over to the military court."

Men came running with weapons. Now most of the commandos were armed. The surliest of them drew his Colt and pointed it at me. I was very glad I had gotten his goat, because it hurt when he insulted the Imam. It did my heart good to see him enraged, and my indifference to his threats was now driving him mad. He said, "Orders for your execution have been issued. Now do you know who you're dealing with?"

I looked at him. He was thirty-something years old with a brownish complexion. His hair was combed upward, and his heavily decorated chest swelled. He held his arms slightly away from his sides. This, it seems, was his way of asserting himself, bullying people with his fierce looks. I don't know why his voice got louder with every stupid thing he uttered, but it only made him seem more pathetic to me. He told the underlings in the group, who had gathered around him, to take us to the wall and body search us. We all said, "Don't you dare come near. You've no right to lay a hand on us!"

We said this with such authority they started to argue among themselves. One of them said, "We've got to go back." Another said,

"Back off! This isn't right." As they argued, the commander said, "Go and start the bus." One of them rushed out. They pointed their weapons at us and said, "Get going!" "What did we do?" we asked. Then we said to ourselves reassuringly, "We've done nothing we should be afraid of. Let's go and let them flounder the way they did yesterday." Yaddi and his men were very agitated and offered to come with us, but the other men stopped them. As we got closer to the bus I could see the other girls were terrified. They were white as ghosts, like sparrows caught in the talons of eagles. When they saw Yaddi and his companions weren't going to help, things got very serious. I was comforted by the thought we were standing up to their insults to the Imam, and that was what God would have wanted. I slowed down, letting the others catch up to me and said what I was thinking.

When we reached the bus, they said we'd have to turn around so they could bind our hands and blindfold us.

Horrified, Zohreh said heatedly, "Never! I won't let you!" and she turned toward me. Things now had gone too far. I began to tremble all over. Then I yelled, "Are we the enemy to be treated like this? You're worse than the Baathists! You have no right to lay a hand on us! Shoot us now, right here by the bus! But we'll never let you come near us!"

Sabah and Ashraf also objected loudly, forcing the commandos to back off. We got on the bus one-by-one and sat in the back seats. We noticed Yaddi and his companions getting into their truck. I took advantage of the lull and whispered to Sabah, "They're trying to break us so we'll beg for mercy. Don't back down. They have no idea what they're doing."

Having noticed us whispering, the commander barked, "Hey! What are you saying? Get up and move to the other side!" I didn't listen, but he signaled to one of his men who came behind me and, pressing the barrel of his gun against the back of my neck, forced me to my feet. They had us all sit apart from one another. Ashraf, her blood now on a thorough boil, shouted, "What's this?" She added sarcastically, "We're your prisoners now?"

The bus started moving, and they began to taunt us again. We said nothing, wondering where they were taking us. I'll never bring

Leila with me again, I said to myself. We drove a long way in the darkness. My nerves were shot, and the pressures of hunger and lack of sleep were agonizing. The predicament was wearing me down badly. I couldn't wait to be free of these madmen, even at the price of a hanging. But the more I thought about it, I was convinced these men had no evidence that would convict us of treason. We finally arrived wherever it was we were going. They let us out one-by-one and took us into a building. After pausing briefly in the hallway, they led us into a large room where several officers in camouflage uniforms and green berets were seated around a table. After we entered, the green berets told the commandos to wait outside. One of the officers, who appeared to outrank the rest, asked, "What's the story here? What are these men talking about?"

We all started speaking at once, and the officer ordered, "One at a time!"

As usual I was the one to speak, "Ever since yesterday these gentlemen have been accusing us of being antirevolutionary Hypocrites and saying they want to try us."

"Why?" he asked.

"Banisadr's treachery is the issue here. These men are confused."

This made them all sit up straight and look at one another. They said, "What are you talking about? Don't you know Mr. Banisadr is the president and commander-in-chief?"

"That's no excuse. Isn't the Imam the leader of the country and all the Muslims of the world? Where do these gentlemen get off insulting him and disparaging our sacred beliefs? Why can't they accept a reality as plain as day to everybody else!?"

The officer said, "This is dangerous talk, especially in a place as isolated as this."

"We heard them defy the Imam and insult him," the girls said. "But the only reason we mention treason is because we are from Khorramshahr, and, with Banisadr in command, we have lost everything: our city, our young people, our homes, and our lives."

After a full round of questions and answers, one of them asked, "How old are you?"

Fed up, I said, "Why is that any of your business? If you want to put us in front of a firing squad, go ahead!"

They laughed and said, "What firing squad? Who said anything about an execution?"

"So what are you going to do?" I asked. "We're dead tired, and we need to know now what's going to happen to us. In the last three days we've been running around like crazy trying to get to Abadan."

"We don't execute people. Your fate will be decided elsewhere," they said.

Then one of the officers stood up from the table and called out to someone. He gave him a number and said, "Make contact and let them know we're sending over several suspicious characters."

After a few minutes they piled us into a white Wagoneer and began to lecture us: "You don't have a clue about politics and government. It's still far too soon to understand the roots of this thing."

The Wagoneer drove away escorted by a van full of armed men. We were so exhausted we kept yawning, and all we wanted was to crawl into a corner and sleep. It was well past midnight when we pulled up in front of the large door of a building that seemed familiar somehow. I looked at the plaque over the door: Army of the Guards of the Islamic Revolution of Mahshahr. Seeing it gave me a sense of security, and I relaxed. I said to myself: Thank God. Somebody's got to know me here. They'd remember the day we brought the bodies of the martyrs. The guards at the door took custody of us and, perplexed, showed us into the building. They led us to a room and said, "Wait here." Soon another guard entered and politely asked us our names. "Where were you this time of night? What made them arrest you?" he asked.

"No one arrested us," I explained. "We went with them of our own free will."

They asked us questions about our families, which we all answered. Finally I said, "The girls are with me." Then another person entered and asked more questions. From what he said, I gathered they wanted to take us to their commander. After he left, we couldn't help slumping in the chairs and falling asleep. A bit later the commander entered. He said hello and immediately went through the door of an adjoining room. I was the first person they called into the room. I rose and went in. "Sit down," he said.

I sat in the chair opposite him. Another guard began to question me. "What's your name? When did you leave Khorramshahr? What were your activities there? Who do you know from the army in Khorramshahr?" Then he said, "Put whatever you're carrying on the table." I took the two bloodstained IDs belonging to Ali from my pocket and put them on the table. The interrogator picked them up and asked, "Where did you get these?"

"They're my brother's."

"What does you brother do?" he asked.

"It's on the card. Can't you see?"

Another man said, "Just answer the questions."

"I am answering the questions," I said.

"What does your brother do?" he asked again.

"My brother was a soldier."

"Was? You mean he's no longer in the army?"

"He was martyred," I said, my voice cracking.

I felt persecuted and alone, because Ali, had he been there, would never have allowed them to behave like that to me. It was all I could do to keep from crying. One of the guards showed the cards to the commander. It seemed he was pointing out the difference in the dates of birth on the cards, as if he were trying to catch me in a lie. As the guard looked at the cards, he said, "I know the guards in Khorramshahr, but I never saw him."

I got more agitated and said to the guard, "Just because you didn't see him doesn't mean he wasn't in the army. The reason why the dates of birth are different is because they had underestimated his age. Later on he corrected it, and they gave him a new ID. Our Ali was nineteen."

After saying this, I could no longer hold back my tears. The commander, a man of about thirty, started speaking, "Why are you upset now? Why are you crying?"

"This man is trying to make me out a liar. That's why," I said.

My nerves were in a horrible state. I couldn't control myself. I said, "They've been giving us hell for two days now. This bunch of antirevolutionaries have been harassing us, threatening us with a court-martial, saying they'd set up a kangaroo court and have us executed. Why aren't you asking why these sell-outs are insulting the

Imam? Are we the antirevolutionaries, the traitors, or are these men who have nothing good to say about the Revolution while, at the same time, they're defending the real traitor?"

"Why do you go around telling everybody Banisadr is a traitor?" asked the commander.

"If it weren't for his treachery, people wouldn't have been driven from their homes and forced to wander in the desert."

"How do you know he's a traitor?" he asked. "My father said so," I said. "He saw it with his own eyes. He said, 'Banisadr's the reason why the enemy got up the nerve to invade our country.' "

"What does your father do?" he asked.

"My father was a city worker, but when the war started he couldn't sit by and watch the enemy occupy our land."

"Where's your father now?"

"He's a martyr, too," I said tearfully.

The commander turned pale suddenly. His eyes filled with tears, and he bowed his head. He remained silent for a few minutes. My sobs were the only sounds in the room, but I couldn't stop them. The commander raised his head and started to console me, "Let me congratulate you on having such a father and brother, on their martyrdom, and let me express my sorrow for your losses. Why didn't you say you were from a martyr family in the first place?"

"Suppose I had. What would have been the point? You would have brought us here anyway," I said.

"No, sister. You're mistaken. We wouldn't have treated you like a suspect. They sent you here, and it was our duty to interrogate you and find out the truth."

Then he said, "Tell the other sisters to come in, please."

When they entered, I looked up at them. All of them had been crying their eyes out. I realized they had overheard what we were saying, and they went to pieces. They sat down, and the man began to question them but not harshly. After learning Sabah's brother was army and now a POW, and her father had been wounded, and Leila was my sister, his manner improved. There was talk of my activities in Khorramshahr, and the commander all of a sudden declared, "You must be the same sister who brought the bodies of the martyrs to Mahshahr?"

"That's me!" I said.

"Why didn't you say so in the first place? There would have been no misunderstanding then, and could have avoided a lot of trouble. We know Banisadr is a traitor, but we can't say it publicly on account of the crisis the country faces. We have to show unity now more than ever. Discord only helps the enemy."

Then he said, "It's an honor to have you sisters as our guests. If you wish, we'll take you all back to the camp or you can spend the night here, and go where you like in the morning."

Given how worn and weary we were, we decided to spend the few remaining hours until morning there. Seeing our faces at that point, so tired and grim, would have been the last straw for mother.

They led us to a room with carpeting on the floor, and brought some army blankets and cushions. We locked the door and spread the blankets. Though delirious from lack of sleep, we started talking. Sabah said, "That went well, thank God." Zohreh and Ashraf asked, "Zahra, didn't we agree we would not say anything till we got what we wanted?"

"I can't keep my mouth shut when someone bullies me. Didn't you hear the rubbish they were spouting?"

Again they started pleading with me, "For God's sake, whatever happens tomorrow—even if they beat us—nobody say anything! At least not till we get to Abadan." Sabah said, "Let's get there first and then we can tell the guys we know all about these traitors. They'll give 'em what for. And we'll get 'em to screw up!"

I don't know what else was said. Even though I was dead tired, I had the same nightmare all over again: they were insulting the Imam, and I was stewing. It wasn't long before the men woke us for prayer. We forced ourselves to get up and did our ablutions. After prayers, around 7:30 or 8:00, they knocked on the door with breakfast: flatbread, white cheese, butter, preserves, a kettle of hot water, and a teapot with tea. After twenty straight hours of ranting and raging on empty stomachs, we were finally having a proper meal. But, though I was famished, I had no appetite. I blamed myself for making things so hard on the girls. "If I had only kept my mouth shut," I told myself, "the girls wouldn't have had to endure what they did." Leila and I were in places mother would never have approved. I felt guilty because she trusted me to take care of my sister and now, unbeknownst to her, we were in God knows where. I felt so guilty I couldn't swallow a thing.

As they ate, the girls discussed whether we should go back to the jetty or somewhere else where we could get a pass. I didn't say anything. We finally decided we would go back home. We handed in the breakfast things and thanked the soldiers. We turned down their offer of a ride. Instead, we got on a minibus heading for Sar Bandar. Once there we started to look for the home of Sabah's aunt. No one was able to help us. My legs and back ached so much from all the running around I could no longer stand or walk. More often than not I sat and rested. In the end I told Sabah, "It makes no sense trying to find the house without the address. I couldn't do it the last time I looked for mother and the kids."

We were about to start out on the road to camp when a jeep showed up with the same commandos, thirsting for our blood. They were just as stunned to see us as we were to see them. They pulled up, blocking our way and, asking nobody in particular, "How come they're out?"

One of them asked, "What are you doing here? Didn't we hand you over last night?"

Sabah said, "What are you doing here yourselves? Shouldn't you guys be at the front instead of cruising around town?"

"Still mouthing off, huh?" he said.

"Didn't you know? They executed us yesterday," I said. "We're ghosts, you see, looking for revenge. Now mind your own business!"

Fearing another flare-up, Zohreh and Ashraf tugged at my sleeve and pulled me away. At the same time, they shouted, "Why don't you leave us alone? What do you want from us, blood? You've had your fun, so now go about your business!"

I started to walk away and the other girls followed, but the men wouldn't stop their taunts, trying to provoke us into defending ourselves. Finally they said, "Yellow-bellies, how come you're sitting here behind the lines?"

I turned around and said, "There's only one answer for fools: silence."

We reached the road and got a ride to camp. I was shamefaced, walking home. What would I tell mother if she asked where we had been the previous night? I prayed she wouldn't be home and shared my worries with the others. They said, "Tell her the truth. We were supposed to go by hovercraft, but it broke down. They told us to wait till it was fixed. We stayed there till morning, but it was still broken. Then they told us to go home, and promised to let us know when to return." This way we wouldn't be lying but, at the same time, we wouldn't be telling the whole truth.

Luckily mother wasn't home when we entered. The boys said she had gone to wash dishes. All the same it bothered my conscience to have to keep part of what happened the previous night from mother so she wouldn't get upset. On the other hand, I knew if she felt it was dangerous, there was no way she'd give us her blessings when we wanted to leave again. She had only to say something like, "You make me regret nursing you when you were a baby." This never failed to get me to cave in.

Mother was surprised to see us. I explained what happened the way the girls said. She said nothing. I considered it a good thing to have the girls around for several reasons. First, it increased my chances of going to Abadan. Second, mother had to be hospitable to them. But they sensed what was going on between her and me. After lunch when they tried to leave, I made them stay. I told them I was certain Yaddi would arrange something for us.

In the evening we took a tour of the camp. Again we saw families being turned away from the aid tent. Women were wailing and begging pathetically for God's help. Seeing the crowds and the chaos in front of the tent we felt we had to do something. We walked to the tent that served as a makeshift clinic, and said, "We want to help." We wrote down the names of the sixty or so people waiting there, and assigned them numbers. That way they took turns rather than trying to rush inside. We took advantage of being there to speak to some of the refugees. They opened their hearts to us. With people taking turns, the work at the clinic went more smoothly, and we soon went back home.

That night we waited and waited for word from Yaddi and his comrades, but none came. The next morning, the girls said goodbye, and I walked with them to the road. It was very distressing to think we might never see one another again. I could barely speak. Sensing how choked up I was, they tried to cheer me up by joking. Finally they boarded the minibus and left. I stood by the road until the bus was out of sight and cried. I felt abandoned in a world of suffering, and, on top of that, my back and legs began to give me trouble. I hadn't given them a thought to that point. I wanted to sit in a corner somewhere and cry my eyes out. I felt I had to get to Abadan somehow or I'd be stuck in the camp forever. The more I thought about it, the more I held onto the hope of going back.

I wandered around the camp and found myself at the aid tent. There was a crowd as usual. I told the same man we had spoken to the day before I would do anything to help. I handed out numbers until 4:00 or 5:00 p.m. and monitored the coming and going of patients. I also translated for Arabic-speakers and explained the prescriptions to them. There seemed to be no end to the flow of patients.

As soon as I got home, I sprawled out on a cushion. "Where were you?" asked mother.

"At the aid tent."

"Does your back hurt?" she asked anxiously.

"No. I went there to help out. They fed me." As we sat around having tea, mother's expression told me she was happy having Leila and me around. It had been quite a while since we had tea together. I looked closely at her face. She seemed demoralized, as though she never smiled any more. I got the feeling if it weren't for the children, she wouldn't do any housework, not even prepare meals.

After tea I played soldiers with Hasan and Sa'id, and I gave Zeynab a piggyback ride, which made her roar with laughter. The boys followed us, laughing as I limped around the room with her on my back. Distressed by this, mother said to me, "Put her down before you injure yourself." But seeing Sa'id, Hasan, and Zeynab so happy and giggling, I didn't have the heart to stop.

Just before sundown, one of our neighbors popped in to say two soldiers had come looking for us. Mother, Leila, and I went out and saw Yaddi with one of his runner friends. The neighbors thought they were bringing news of Ali's death. They stared at us anxiously, waiting to see what would happen. Once, when mother was out fulfilling a vow she had made to be charitable in father's name, I had told some neighbors about Ali. Word of his death spread around the neighborhood. After the usual greetings, Yaddi told me he was only able to get two passes. The next morning two of us would be able to go to Abadan by helicopter or launch. When he asked about Zohreh, Sabah, and Ashraf, I told him they had left. Then I asked, "What time should Leila and I be at the jetty?"

"You don't have to bother coming on your own; we'll pick you up." Then he added, "For God's sake, if you see those other commandos, keep your distance. They're up to no good."

Mother asked Yaddi about Ali. Uncomfortable with lying, he looked at me and then said to mother, "God willing he'll be back. Don't worry. But it's war. He can't just drop what he's doing and come."

After they left, we went back inside. Leila and I were hugging each other deliriously. Mother growled, "So the enemy did us a favor by destroying the family, killing your father—you two are so happy about going back to the front. God knows how joyful you'd be if they hadn't done it."

That night I stopped in at Uncle Nad Ali's to say goodbye. He was against our going back, saying, "There's work for you in the camp and, besides, if you stay you can look after your mother and the kids." But I was determined to go and help with caring for the wounded. In my travels, I had gotten to know the nurses at the Taleqani and Abadan Oil Company hospitals.

They would definitely welcome an extra hand. Zohreh and Sabah confirmed this when they said, "After the fall of Khorramshahr, the nurses went to Taleqani Hospital."

The next morning after prayer, Leila and I got ready. We kissed the sleeping kids; I didn't have the heart to wake them. Even before sunrise mother had breakfast prepared. We were busy eating when we heard the sound of a jeep pulling up. We jumped to our feet. I hugged mother and rapidly repeated the instructions I had given her before. She barely managed to get a word in edgewise, but pleaded, "I beg you, tell Ali to come." "Sure. Sure," I said and kissed her goodbye. Walking to the road, I kept looking back at her. Seeing her cover her mouth with her scarf, I realized she couldn't stop crying again. Having the girls and the two of us with her for the past days had kept her emotions in check, but now she was drowning in grief. But having nearly gotten myself killed for a chance to get back to the front, I wasn't about to let it slip through my hands now.

It was fully light when we got to the jetty. Soon a Chinook landed, and people boarded in the order that their names were called. Next, they loaded the munitions, medical supplies, and stretchers. After a tank entered the hold, the helicopter took off, sending up a cloud of dust and debris and putting a chop on the water by the shore.

Our turn to board came around 10:00, when an air force helicopter appeared. Around forty people crammed into it, sitting on two rows of benches or on the floor. Among the passengers I saw seven or eight women army nurses. Leila and I were the only civilians. Others were mostly military, oil workers, or hospital personnel. The helicopter wobbled a bit before gaining altitude. The sound of the motors and whirl of the blades drowned out everything. I looked out the window. Though we weren't far from the town of Chu'ebdeh, there was water as far as the eye could see. The pilot had chosen to give a wide berth to enemy radar and antiaircraft. Under ordinary circumstances, he would have taken a route over land. He also varied his altitude during the flight. In addition to the pilot and co-pilot, a flight engineer and two attendants were in the crew. The engineer and the attendants sat with us and were in touch with the pilot with headphones. When the helicopter jerked sharply, causing us to lose our balance, they said, "Don't worry. It's just turbulence." I whispered to Leila jokingly, "Was this a good idea getting on this helicopter, or what?"

When we arrived in Abadan, my first thought was to get in touch with a unit called Warriors of the Southern Front. When I had been at the Nemazi Hospital in Shiraz, I heard that Mr. Mesbah and some others had formed the unit at the Congregational Mosque. They arranged courses in guerilla warfare for people on their way to the front. It made me very happy to see the word "warrior" in the name. Previously we had referred to them as "urban militia" or "defenders." "Warrior" seemed far more fitting under the circumstances.

Leaving the helicopter, we saw water on one side of us, and a desert flat with a road running down the middle on the other. Launches were moored by the shore where many people were waiting to board them. They were carrying as many of their household belongings as they could. Most were from families that had already been evacuated but had returned to rescue their possessions from the fires and falling debris. We started walking with Yaddi and his companions down the deserted roadway. Our throats were parched not just from the heat, but from the dust stirred up by the helicopter. Vehicles speeding by added to the grit we had to swallow. It took only a few minutes before we were covered head to foot in dust, and our throats were raw. Yaddi and his companions had large duffel bags with them to carry the documents they had been ordered to retrieve. "Will you and Leila come with us to collect the papers?" they asked. "No," I said. "We're going to the hospital."

They flagged down a white pickup near a traffic circle and we got in. The driver stuck his head out the window and asked if we had passes. "Yeah," we said. "I don't mean just a helicopter pass," he warned. "There's a checkpoint up there, and they'll want to see your permits for Abadan."

"Just take us there and leave the rest to God," we said.

They stopped us at the first checkpoint, but after a little pleading, they let us pass. They warned us we would never be able to get past the next checkpoint. We went another kilometer, and Leila and I got out by the Abadan gate. Having been instructed never to let us out of their sight, Yaddi and his companions also got out. They spoke with the guards, trying to convince them to let us come with them, but to no avail. Yaddi told them, "Don't worry. We'll get passes for them and be sure to bring them to you." "That's impossible," they said. Finally Yaddi said, "If they don't come back with passes, you can detain us. Here's the address of our base." I was embarrassed to be such a nuisance to Yaddi and his companions, but I found their support gratifying. In the end, two things convinced the guards to let us through: Yaddi's guarantee and my teary speech about having come this far, only to be denied entry. But even then they warned, "There's another checkpoint up ahead. They'll never let you stay in the city on your own."

"I don't know what to do. We came to work in the hospital," I said.

One of Yaddi's companions said, "If you think it's all right, I can take you to the home of my wife's family. We had decided I'd bring them back to Mahshahr when we went back. You can wait there while we try to get passes for you."

We had no choice but to accept. They brought us to the house, which was in the Ahmadabad neighborhood. An old man opened the door. His daughters, who were around thirteen and seventeen, were dressed and ready for their brother-in-law to take them out of Abadan. In addition to the bundles of possessions, one of them had—of all things—a birdcage. Yaddi's companion asked his father-in-law, "Can these sisters stay here until we come for them?" The old man politely offered them lunch, but they said "Thank you. We'll eat at the base." We sat on the old man's porch, which overlooked the rear compound. I had a nagging sense of being out of place there. I was also upset we had intruded on the family at a time like that. The several hours we spent there seemed to go on for ages. Finally because Yaddi and his men failed to get passes for us, we only had to go back to Chu'ebdeh.

We boarded the helicopter. During the return trip, the pilot, who had traveled back and forth between Chu'ebdeh and Mahshahr several times that day, testily said to Leila and me, "There's a war going on and you two are taking helicopter rides? This isn't a taxi service, you know!"

"What choice do we have? It's not our fault. They wouldn't let us into the city," I explained. The commando's family members were also on the helicopter. The two girls, who weren't happy about leaving Abadan, were still carrying the birdcage. "It'd be a sin to leave the poor birds there to die," one of them said. During the flight I kept thinking, "Why is it that no matter what we do to get to get back to the war, we fail?" Later I comforted myself, thinking it was what God intended. After reaching Sar Bandar, we went to the camp clinic and got back to work.

30

Visits with Leaders

The clinic was nearly at the end of the main road of the camp. It was actually a shipping container, ten by five meters—perhaps more—with a bluish tile roof. The walls were painted white inside and out. The container was divided into two rooms. The larger of the two was also divided in two; on one side was an examination room and on the other a room with two beds used temporarily for patients. The other room was for injections and bandaging patients.

The Red Crescent had done a good job of equipping the clinic. Doctors had been sent from Tehran, Shiraz, and other cities around the country to attend to the medical needs of the refugees. They also brought victims of the bombardments in Sar Bandar and Mahshahr there. Despite the good treatment at the clinic, diseases were rampant—especially eye infections, diarrhea, and vomiting. Children could be heard crying in and around the clinic. The rains had started and patients, most of whom wore plastic slip-on, plastic sandals, tracked dirt and mud into the container. During off-hours we would sweep the floor, but the carpeting made it difficult to keep clean. After sweeping it, we tried to wipe it down with a damp rag to get the mud out, but the rains made the job impossible. At one point we hosed down the floor of the clinic and stationed someone outside the entrance to tell the patients to remove their footwear before entering. Despite our best efforts to get people to observe basic hygiene, the general health of the camp was poor.

Water for the camp was stored in two large tanks that would run dry from time to time. The number of latrines and places for washing was limited. Communal toilets contributed to the rapid spread of disease. When the clinic was crowded, older people were forced to wait hours outside for treatment. They would gripe to us, "What kind of a set-up is this you've got here?"

We told them, "We're all in the same boat. We're doing the best we can. Why take it out on us? If you've got a complaint, you should tell the people in charge."

Ordinarily this would satisfy them, and they would wait patiently for their turn. The crowds and noise around the clinic, though, didn't prevent us from pumping people for information about the war. We put more trust in what they said than the news on the radio, which, we knew, couldn't be trusted. Most of the talk was speculation about when the war would end and when people could stop being refugees.

"It won't last long, and we'll be back in our homes soon. After all," they said, "Arabs and Persians have always been at each other's throats." Language didn't seem to make any difference: Arabic or Persian—war was terrible on everyone. Everyone believed Saddam's call to liberate the Arab nation was just a ploy for gaining power and territory.

We eagerly listened to what they said, and tried to finish our work quickly so we could hear more. To keep things orderly one of us made a list of the patients' names. The doctors sent from the cities didn't speak Arabic, so even though I had my hands full giving injections, I also had to act as translator.

In addition to Leila and me, nurses from the Red Crescent helped at the clinic. Brother Echresh was in charge. Sisters Karimi, Raziyeh, and Marziyeh Alizadeh (who actually were sisters), Shahnaz Kabiri and her cousin, along with several nurses from the Ministry of Health worked in two shifts: morning until noon and noon until evening. The women nurses did not stay at the clinic at night, but attendants were around day and night.

One day Ali Echresh asked, "Sister Hoseyni, do you remember me? I was the one who transported your brother Ali's body from Abadan." "No," I said. "You don't remember?" he asked. "I was the driver of the ambulance waiting in front of the mosque for wounded. When you said you wanted to bury your martyred brother next to your father, I couldn't refuse. You were in an extraordinary state that day. On the way back to Khorramshahr, I watched you in my rear view mirror as you wept and spoke to Ali as he lay in your arms. What you said touched everyone beyond words. I was crying so hard I could barely drive, and it took hours to get to the cemetery. May God give you strength."

One member of the medical team sent from Tehran was a large, slightly overweight doctor wearing glasses with thick lenses. He seemed around forty-five. He didn't introduce himself to us, so we dubbed him "Dr. Esteemed Sir" because he would use this formality whenever he spoke to other men. After a while, it dawned on him this was his nickname. He was a humble, self-effacing man. It was strange; the moment I saw him he reminded me of Dr. Sa'adat. He prayed with the same feeling and devotion as Dr. Sa'adat. At night, when there were fewer patients, the attendants would take turns manning the desk and alerting the rest of us if someone came in. We would sit on the floor of the large room and listen while Dr. Esteemed Sir explained verses from the Quran. Poor eyesight made reading from his pocket holy book difficult for him. This prompted me go to a book exhibit in Sar Bandar and get a larger print version, which he gladly accepted.

On Thursday and Friday nights we would turn out the lights and say special prayers (the Tavassol and Komeyl) by candlelight. Most of the time Dr. Esteemed Sir acted as prayer leader. I found being in the presence of people who had remained decent despite the horrors going on around them gave me peace of mind.

Part of my arm had been itching me for some time. One day I noticed a lump there. I told the examining room doctor about it, and, after seeing me, he asked, "Have you ever been wounded? I believe this is shrapnel." "Yes," I said. "I was hit, but the shrapnel passed through me." He said, "No, it didn't. The shrapnel entered the muscle and has worked its way through your bloodstream toward your heart. This is what's bothering you. You've got to be operated on." Then he wrote out an admittance slip to Imam Khomeini Hospital in Mahshahr. I had no intention of being laid up because of a little piece of shrapnel, so I went to Mr. Esma'ili, the assistant at the clinic. Despite not being an MD, Esma'ili was an experienced surgeon; I asked him to take it out. The flow of patients had stopped for an hour, and they put me in one of the temporary beds. The two nurses from the Red Crescent, Misses Karimi and Alizadeh, prepared me for surgery. Mr. Esma'ili opened my arm and extracted a piece of shrapnel from it the size of a coin.

The whole time I was at the clinic, I reminisced about helping patients at Dr. Sheybani's. I still hadn't given up the idea of returning to Abadan. Work in the camp was satisfying, though, and I justified it to myself by saying people here needed me to make it easier for them somehow. One day they brought in a boy of about six, who, while playing, had been struck in the face with a stick. The three-pronged gash in his cheek was large and dangerously close to his eye. One of the doctors, a recent arrival, said, "Send him to Mahshahr."

Knowing how busy they were at that hospital, I thought it would be better to treat the boy at our clinic. As the boy sat patiently in a chair, I told him to close his eyes. I sprayed the wound with a little anesthetic and very deftly stitched up the gash. Then, delighted, I led him to the doctor's room and showed him the stitches. He immediately started to berate me in front of the patients: "I gave you specific instructions to send him to Mahshahr. Why didn't you?"

I said, "There was no need, doctor. By the time he got to Mahshahr the wound would have bled out. I stitched him up, and that was the end of it."

This didn't satisfy him, and he continued to shout at me. Some time later the boy's mother turned up to say, "You did a great job. There's hardly any scar."

In time, even the doctor admitted, "I was too harsh on you. Between you and me, it was a very fine job; but I didn't think you had it in you."

Patients at the camp often came in with similar wounds. A six-month-old, who was just able to sit up, had a metal door fall on him, making a triangular gash in his head. It took forty stitches to close. His mother brought him regularly to the clinic to have his bandage changed. Everyone was worried that the serious blow to his head might make him feeble-minded.

Worse than this was the case of an eighteen-year-old with a severe burn on his leg, which never healed properly. His callused skin had gotten as hard as a rock and was infected from the knee down.

The burn was so disgusting it hurt just to look at it. Nevertheless, we forced ourselves to wash and disinfect it by extracting the pus with a fine pincer. After two months of treatment, the doctor concluded the leg had to be operated on. Otherwise, they would have to amputate.

Some of the patients exhibited hysteria. They acted sick but the doctors couldn't find anything wrong with them physically. Once a newlywed came in saying she was ill and pretended to faint. The doctor examined her and concluded it was nerves. He ordered her to be sedated, but, as we were about to inject her, she jumped down from the bed and started running around it. We had to catch her to give her the sedative.

One night Evil Zahra came to the clinic. I was in one of the rooms when I heard her voice in the hallway. She was acting up, as usual. "What's the fuss?" I asked smiling. "Causing trouble, again?"

She pointed to her son and said, "He's got diarrhea and can't stop vomiting. They're telling me to take him to the hospital because they can't do anything for him here."

We took him to the hospital, where Zahra argued with the doctor so much he refused to see her son. I stepped in and explained to him that she wasn't right in the head. After they got the boy settled in bed, I returned to the clinic.

A few times when the doctors were not around, I was forced to do things for which I had neither the training nor the nerve. One night an Arab man came to the clinic saying his wife was so ill he thought he would lose her. The assistant got an ambulance and drove to the man's house, which was near the camp. She had been in labor so long without help at home she was at the point of giving birth when he got her in the ambulance. The assistant said we would have to deliver the baby there. Nobody was willing to assist him. This was to be the first time I saw a birth, and, naturally, I expected it to be embarrassing and frightening. But the assistant needed someone to help him.

First, we suggested the man's mother, who was standing by the ambulance, but she seemed incapable. Though it was the last thing I wanted to do, I volunteered. I would never have forgiven myself if the woman had died giving birth. Once inside the ambulance, I noticed the woman was very distressed to have a man see her naked.

The assistant injected her with a sedative, and told me, "You've got to try and learn what must be done, ma'am. In a war situation, you've got to know how to do all kinds of things, so when the time comes you can act."

Afraid the woman would die, I turned my back. I stood by silently, responding only when the assistant asked for something. Despite her miserable condition, the poor woman never complained, only squeezed my hand tight when she was in pain.

The baby eventually emerged, but didn't make a sound. It was blue in the face and seemed to be suffocating. The assistant said to me, "Quick, cut the cord."

"I can't," I said.

He turned to me and shouted angrily, "So, when do you plan on learning?" Terrified, I asked, "Which part do I cut?"

Shaking with fear, I cut the cord. The assistant turned the baby upside down and smacked its behind. He cleared the mucus from its nose and mouth, and the baby began to howl. The girls, who had been standing outside the clinic, came in with a sheet and blanket and wrapped the baby—a roly-poly little girl, cute and cuddly.

The assistant was shouting again, "What's going on in here? You think this is a nursery or something? Out!"

The girls and I managed to help the miserable woman get inside the clinic, and we attached a serum drip to her arm. Because she wasn't up to nursing the baby, we spooned sugar water into the infant's mouth. The father was very put out to learn his second child was another daughter. He didn't give a damn, it seemed, that he had almost lost his wife and baby. The poor woman seemed to be more afraid of her husband than of dying. The man angrily demanded we let him take the woman and baby home. We explained to him his wife's condition was serious and she needed hospital care, but it did no good. After the serum had run out, we transferred the woman and the baby to the clinic at Sar Bandar. The nurses there demanded to know why we hadn't taken her to their clinic in the first place.

We explained that we had no choice because she had been in labor, which didn't assuage them, but they reluctantly admitted her. A few nights later, something similar happened. It turned out women in the area preferred to have their babies at home rather than at a clinic.

Only when there were difficulties did they think of calling a doctor. The woman in this second case was also in distress. After giving birth, she lost consciousness. We put her in the ambulance and brought her to the Sar Bandar clinic. This time there was a real brawl, and they told us they would try to have our clinic closed.

We said, "You're free to do what you want. We've done as much as we can, not being midwives or having any training. The two women were on the point of death when we reached them. Suppose we had tried to take them to your clinic. By the time we got there, they would have died. Which is better—to have them brought in like this or as corpses?"

Another medical team from the cities arrived at our clinic and stayed the night. They slept in the room used for patients, while local staff slept in the room used for injections. Mr. Ateshkadeh, recently made head of the Red Crescent in Abadan, inspected the clinic regularly, supplying us with drugs and equipment. The head of the new team was called Dr. Hoseyni. The first thing he did was to draw up a schedule of specific tasks for each staff person—even the most menial things like washing utensils or cleaning the clinic, which, until that time, had been done by the girls. We told him, "Medicine is your job; let us take care of the other things."

"What difference does it make?" Dr. Hoseyni asked. "Work is work. Doctors are no exception. We came here to work, after all, and, if necessary, we'll get guns and fight. We've got to do something when there are no patients. You did pledge to keep this place sanitary, didn't you?"

In spite of all the complex problems of practicing medicine, he remained faithful to the schedule. I found it humiliating to see Dr. Hoseyni eat at the camp kitchen and, after dinner, scrupulously sweep out the clinic or wash dishes. I insisted he let me do those things for him.

"No. It's my duty," he would say. "You should go and do your own work."

The days went by, but the pain in my back and legs wouldn't go away. The doctors in the hospital in Shiraz had advised me to go to Tehran for more examinations and treatment. With the help of a soldier I knew I got in touch with brother Jahan Ara and explained the problem. Jahan Ara promised to send a letter of introduction, which I could present at the army hospital in Tehran. When it arrived, I didn't know what to do. Never having been in the city I didn't know a soul I could stay with there.

At that time Yunes Mohammadi, the representative of Khorramshahr in parliament, happened to be making a site visit of refugees at Camp B. I managed to speak to him about going to Tehran for treatment.

Mr. Mohammadi said he would help me, as he was about to return to Tehran. But first he had to go to Behbahan to visit with refugees from Khorramshahr. He asked me to accompany him. "As a woman, your presence in the group will make it easier for the families to say what's on their minds," he said. After talking it over with mother, I accepted Mr. Mohammadi's offer. A few days later, Mr. Mohammadi and his brother Abdol Azim, Khosrow No'dusti, a few others whose names I don't recall, and I went to Mahshahr by minibus. Because there weren't any vehicles going directly to Behbehan, we patched together a series of rides with anything going in that direction. On our arrival Khosrow No'dusti took us to his home. No'dusti's mother shouted for joy when she saw her son. I remembered her from the time we were working at the mosque. She had her eyes on a girl with blue eyes, also a worker, for her son. She was always saying how devoted she was to the girl and hoped the war would end soon so the she and her son could be married. The mother gave me a warm welcome.

Later we went to visit Hoseyn Fakhri, the noted eulogist of the revered Imams, who rented the house next to No'dusti's mother. Familiar with my financial situation, he told me, "I'll speak with my nephew to see if it's possible to get a plane ticket to Tehran for you."

Apparently his nephew was the governor or mayor of Behbehan. We spent the few days we were there visiting the refugee families. I asked the women from Khorramshahr to tell me about conditions in Behbehan and about their needs and relayed what I had learned to Mr. Mohammadi. When that was over, I went to Mr. Fakhri's nephew to ask about the ticket. He said, "Getting you a ticket without your being a relative presents a religious problem for him."

Now I had to figure out how I was going to get to Tehran. I had no money. To that point Mr. Mohammadi had been helping me with my expenses, but he wasn't all that flush either.

In the end, people managed to raise enough for a bus ticket. Mr. Mohammadi remained in Behbehan to continue his work, while his brother, one or two others, and I set out for Tehran by bus. Before I left, Mr. Mohammadi suggested I visit his family, who had moved to Tehran after the war had heated up. When we got to the south bus terminal in Tehran, we were at a loss, as no one in our party knew the city. We decided to chance it and head for the center of town. We asked a man where that was, and he said, "Artillery Square."

This was the first time I had heard the name, which seemed so ridiculous to me I checked with several people there to see if that really was what it was called.

It was very cold, and I was still dressed in the same overcoat torn by shrapnel. The only thing keeping my body from showing through the rips in the coat was the short-sleeved blouse given to me by the girls at the clinic. The cold sent shivers up and down my back, and my voice shook. Everyone felt the same way, and we tried to stay in the sun as we walked. I didn't have anything else to wear, so I couldn't wash the overcoat and wait for it to dry. I never liked to ask for help—not even the time when Sabah Vatankhah and I were on our way to Abadan and we were waiting for a lift at a place near an aid station. We were really stuck, not knowing what to do. Swarms of people had come for food, and it was a madhouse. One of the aid workers noticed how long we'd been waiting and asked, "Sisters, excuse me, did you want something?"

"No," we said.

"Food, clothing? Something you need?"

Although we were famished, we refused.

He went and got us food anyway. It was a warm pilaf, which we ate and blessed him thoroughly for it.

He came back and said, "If you need clothing, let's go to storage, and you can take whatever you want." "No," we said, "people need it more than we do."

At Artillery Square we stood at a bus stop in the shadow of the communications building. Freezing cold, I begged my companions to cross to the sunny side of the square.

While we were standing in the sun, a lone bicyclist stopped to stare at us. But after one look at the weapon in my hand, he began to pedal madly toward the communications building.

I wondered what made him stare at us like that. The G3 I had belonged to Mohammadi, who insisted I keep it with me because, he said, the young men in town were headstrong and might cause problems. A few moments later the bicycle rider returned with an armed guard. He pointed at us and said, "That's them. They might be Hypocrites. They even have a weapon!"

The guard asked what we were doing there and how we'd gotten a weapon. I showed him the gun permit Mr. Mohammadi had given me. He read it, and I explained why we were there. After a moment, he wished us Godspeed and left.

My first thought was to go to the hospital they had mentioned at the camp. Unaware the name had been changed, I asked where the Misaqiyeh Hospital was and how to get there. Naturally, no one knew, but finally one person told me the new name was Martyr Mostafa Khomeini Hospital.

I won't say what we went through to get there. Not having much money, we had to walk most of the way to Italia Avenue. When we finally arrived, I stood in the entryway not knowing whom I should see. Would anyone know me there? I had no choice but to go up to one of the brothers from the army and take my chances. But as soon as I went to the reception desk and introduced myself, everybody started saying, "Sister, where have you been? We've been waiting for you a couple of days now. Brother Jahan Ara had gotten in touch with us, saying you'd be favoring us with a visit."

They introduced me to the nurses, who gave me such a warm welcome you'd think we'd known one another for ages. The hospital workers showed great respect for me, saying I reminded them of Ali. Seeing me was like seeing the martyr himself. It was clear in the three or four months Ali had been there, he'd made quite an impression on them.

I asked the nurses to show me his room. They told me to wait until I had been admitted formally.

I said, "I can't wait. I just have to see where he spent those months."

They agreed. We went to the second floor, and, stopping by a door, they said, "Here's his room. He heard the war had broken out and wanted to leave, but the doctors wouldn't release him. So he tied bed sheets together and climbed down from the window, landing in the avenue below. That time he didn't make it because the attendants had gotten wind of it, but later, on a visit to the graves of the martyrs at the Behest-e Zahra cemetery, he managed to escape."

I entered a kind of vestibule leading to the room but didn't go farther. Standing beside a small refrigerator they had installed, I looked around. There were three beds in the room. The one in the middle was empty, but the other two were occupied. A nurse pointed to the bed closest to the window and said, "That was your brother's."

All I could think about was how much I missed him. It was too much to bear, and I burst into tears. I ran from the room as the wounded men stared, not knowing what to make of it.

The nurses explained the situation to them. I tried to pull myself together in the hallway, and asked if I could go back in the room again if I promised not to upset the patients. It was an effort to remain composed and quiet. The wounded man in Ali's bed said to me, "It's an honor to sleep in the bed of a martyr."

The nurse said one Thursday night the hospital Islamic association held a remembrance ceremony for Ali and invited Mr. Falsafi, a well-known preacher, to speak. The nurses put up flyers and hung posters about Ali's martyrdom throughout the hospital. They showed them to me, along with pictures of Ali that his brother soldiers had taken. The announcement for the ceremony was on red paper with a picture of Ali dressed in hospital clothes. The title read: "Brother Martyr, Seyyed Ali Hoseyni, a fearless warrior in the lineage of Abel." There was an explanation of how he had gotten to Khorramshahr and was martyred. I kept one of the flyers.

The specialist was not in that day, so they made an appointment for me. As it had been quite awhile since I was wounded, I didn't have to be hospitalized. The doctors only wanted to know where on my spine the shrapnel was and gauge the likelihood of paralysis if it were to move.

From the hospital we went to Mr. Mohammadi's family home, which was located at the end of Tehran-e Now. The Cultural Revolution was going on, and all the universities were closed. This allowed the authorities to house refugee families in the building of an officer's college, which was protected like a military base with soldiers everywhere. Everyone had to pass through a checkpoint before entering and exiting.

Each family was assigned one of the large college classrooms. Mr. Mohammadi's family, his wife's father's family, and his father's family were all living at the college. While in Tehran I stayed with his sisters in their mother's room.

Those days were frigid. The rooms had heaters, but they didn't work because of a fuel shortage. There was no hot water, and, unaccustomed to the cold, my hands swelled. Because I was shivering and always speaking about the cold, Mrs. Mohammadi gave me a black knitted woolen sweater. It was so tight on me I couldn't button it. One corner was singed and had turned brown. Part of the sleeve had unraveled and the rest was moth-eaten. People from the Refugee Aid Committee supplied the sweater and other clothing, which, however shabby, were better than nothing. The sweater, which I wore under my chador, truly came in handy in the cold when I found myself constantly shivering.

A short time later, Mr. Mohammadi returned from Khuzestan. A little while after that he took his brother Abdol Azim and me to parliament.

It was not as hard to visit parliament then as it is now. With him we were able to enter without formalities. He introduced us to Mr. Rafsanjani and Mr. Karroubi and gave them a rundown on my activities. Mr. Rafsanjani said, "We are honored to have such brave sisters and daughters at the front." Mr. Karroubi was very kind and consoling to me, and then he gave me a letter of introduction. He said, "Take this to Mr. Mazandarani at the Martyrs Foundation."

The next couple of times I went to the parliament, I saw Mr. Khameneh'i, Dr. Dialameh, Dr. Ayat, and Hojjat al-Eslam Montazeri and spoke to them about the war, the sacrifices of the people, and the conditions in Khorramshahr. They said, "The people who ought to tell Imam Khomeini about these things are not doing their jobs. It's people like you who should give him the news." Mr. Khameneh'i and Dr. Dialameh seemed to be strong personalities with gentle souls. Dr. Dialameh's obvious humility and modesty put me to shame, speaking to him. There was a certain innocence to his features. He never raised his voice. People said he was on the faculty of the University of Tehran, and he was the first in the city to hold a public Komeyl Prayer and Supplication.

I witnessed an ugly scene at one of the sessions of parliament. That day the members were discussing relations with America. Those opposed said, "America could have shown its good will by returning the Iranian funds it seized, but it didn't even take this first step. All of the policies it devises are against its own best interests."

A number of other delegates Mr. Mohammadi called "nationalist" were strongly opposed and wanted to resume relations with the United States. Owing to a painful wound he had received in a terror attack, Mr. Rafsanjani was not presiding at this session. In his place was Mr. Sahabi, a nationalist. The debate had become very heated, and one of the supporters of resuming relations with the West attacked Hojjat al-Eslam Montazeri by grabbing his collar and shaking him as he screamed at him. The Hojjat al-Eslam showed no reaction, nor did he speak. He merely stared at the man. Then another nationalist suddenly got up and boxed the Hojjat al-Eslam's ear.

All he said was, "So this is nationalist logic?"

All the while people in the balcony, who had come to parliament with high hopes of disrupting the proceedings, were fanning the flames. It upset me to see how easily people were able to enter the parliament building and disrupt the legislative process. I said to myself: We are at war. Decisions made here affect the people of this country's lives and property. Why do they allow a few—if not Hypocrites, certainly ignorant and shortsighted people—to make a mockery of the proceedings?

Finally, after a series of attacks by the Hypocrites, especially after the terrorist attacks of June 28 and August 30, 1981, and the resulting loss of all those top individuals, it occurred to the authorities to beef up security at parliament by setting up checkpoints. The representatives of the people in those days were an uncomplicated and trusting lot. People had easy access to them at all times and could speak their piece. I ate at the parliament several times. The food was simple, ordinary fare. The representatives came and went without drivers or bodyguards.

One time, as I was leaving parliament with Mr. Mohammadi, Dr. Ayat drove up in his own Peykan and parked in one of the alleys near the north corner of the building. All at once some Hypocrites, who had apparently been waiting in ambush, attacked him. Moments later people rushed from parliament to stop the attack. Many representatives during that period were attacked like this, and many of them, including Dr. Dialameh, perished in the explosion at Islamic Republican Headquarters.

Mr. Mohammadi's home life was very spare. During my visit to his home, all the family had colds. They didn't have a drop of heating oil to their names. Even though they put carpeting on the cold floor and spread coats over that, his wife felt so cold she couldn't nurse their infant. Seeing the authorities in the same boat as us common folk during that week made my problems seem simple and bearable by comparison.

Mr. Mohammadi was also quite a card. One time when we were walking from the parliament to Revolution Square, he asked his brother and me, "Do you know, guys, what SAAAR stands for?"

"The Society of Armed, Active, Avant-garde Revolutionaries, the Maoist group?" we guessed.

"No," he said. "The Shah's Armed American Agents on the Run."

One day I went to see Mr. Mazandarani at the Martyrs Foundation with the letter of introduction Mr. Karroubi had given me. I didn't know why he had given me the letter. After I spoke with Mr. Mazandarani, he led me to another section. The head of that section placed three overcoats and 15,000 tumans in cash in front of me. It was a startling sight, but I refused the offer, saying, "I didn't come here for charity."

"Given your financial state, you've got to accept," he said.

"I don't want them," I said. But he kept insisting.

It was embarrassing for me to take the coats and the money. Although I needed them badly, it was not in my nature to beg. But he justified these "gifts" in so many ways I reluctantly accepted them.

With money now in hand, I decided I'd better get a proper overcoat for myself. I went to a men's tailor on Imam Hoseyn Square and ordered two overcoats: one in my size and a smaller, looser one for Leila. Leaving the tailor's I realized I didn't have a chance to have a chador made, so I returned to the shop and told him to make my overcoat loose-fitting.

A few days later I picked up the overcoats. He had done a fine job: two dark blue overcoats costing all together 400 tumans. I finally took off the overcoat someone had given me and kept it as a souvenir.

A few days later, it was time for my medical exam. I went to Mostafa Khomeini Hospital where the specialist examined the shrapnel near my spine. It was decided to bring up my case at the physicians' meeting. They said an operation was out of the question. With that I decided to go back to Sar Bandar. As I was saying goodbye to the hospital staff, they gave me Ali's effects: a suitcase I had packed for him with his personal items, his clothes, a Walkman, and a camera. There were a number of photographs of important figures who had visited Ali and the others in the hospital: Ayatollah Beheshti, Dr. Chamran, and Commander Abu Sharif. There were also a number of photos of other wounded men with Ali at Friday prayer.

One of the brothers working at the hospital, also a soldier, asked me for the Walkman and a tape of Ali giving the call to prayer as a keepsake.

While in Tehran, I had asked Mr. Mohammadi to get me an appointment to see Imam Khomeini at Jamaran, but it turned out to be impossible. During the last few days, I went to the Behesht-e Zahra Cemetery to visit the graves of the martyrs. The Freedom Tower on Freedom Square was quite a sight. I took many pictures of what I saw in Tehran with Ali's camera. Mr. Karroubi insisted I visit the Martyrs Foundation again. He was intent on keeping me in Tehran and bringing my family to the city, but I wasn't keen on the idea. Being in Tehran meant being far from Khorramshahr. Staying in Tehran for only a short time put me on edge, as it seemed nobody in the city had even heard of the war. They were so immersed in the pleasures of daily life that they complained about not having certain favorite things. Having gone to Revolution Square several times to buy books the children wanted, I saw it for myself. This convinced me I didn't want to stay in Tehran.

People argued otherwise: "There's more opportunity here. Your brother and sisters have to continue their educations. There's no telling when schools will be open again there." Since the outset of the war, refugee children had been left on their own. All the schools in Khuzestan had been blown to pieces. Planes regularly bombarded the southern town of Ahvaz, Dezful, Andishmak, and Sar Bandar.

A letter arrived for me from the Martyrs Foundation saying they had reserved a room for me at the Kushk Building.[1] I decided not to tell mother about the offer and, out of fear of her finding out about Ali, stored his things at Mr. Mohammadi's. I said goodbye to his family and took a bus to Ahvaz. From there I went to Sar Bandar by minibus. The only thing of Ali's I had was his camera.

Upon entering camp I saw mother was cooking fish over a wood fire. As was usual when she was alone with her thoughts, she was weeping and whimpering to herself in Kurdish. Zeynab was standing nearby. I readied the camera and said, "Mother!"

As soon as she saw me her expression changed, and she started to smile. The picture I took was of her smiling and crying at the same time. We talked about my trip to Tehran for a time, and then she brought the conversation around to Ali. She insisted on seeing him and had gotten ready to go out the next morning to find him.

I objected, "Ali's at the front, on a mission. He can't come." She refused to listen. In the end she sat and cried her eyes out. I didn't know what to do. Finally to calm her I had no choice but to fake a letter from Ali myself. I had heard from some soldiers that they were sending a number of the boys to Bushehr for scuba training, so I wrote, "I'm in Bushehr and cannot come."

Mother was so overjoyed to get the letter she went out and bought congratulatory candy for all her neighbors at the camp. She

---

[1] The Kushk Building, located on the avenue of the same name, formerly housed the Bureau of Budget and Planning. The avenue, which links Sa'di with Ferdowsi, is now called Martyr Taqva.

told them she had received a letter from her son. The letter worked for a while, but she was soon asking repeatedly, "What's happened to Ali?" Uncle Salim and Seyyed Abbas, the husband of Aunt Salimeh, would stop by from time to time with Uncle Nad Ali. Uncle Hoseyni also visited often. I don't know how he got hold of the letter from Mr. Karroubi, but he told us, "Get packing. We're going to Tehran."

Leila and I opposed moving to Tehran, and we had kept the offer a secret. One night Ms Azam Taleqani, who at that time was a representative in parliament, visited the camp. She brought some medical supplies and books. In answer to her questions I told her briefly about conditions at the camp and added my belief that the refugees didn't need books to occupy their time. What they needed most were food and clothing. Instead of books, I said, she should have brought more medicine. Then I told her about Mr. Karroubi's letter. She asked, "Why do you want to go to Tehran? It's so noisy and crowded—no place for you. Staying here and guarding this land would be the best thing."

"You don't have a clue about what's going on here, do you?" I said. "If you had to put up with what people here endure, I doubt you'd last a day. Don't get me wrong. We're not dying to go to Tehran, either. I just wanted to hear what you thought!"

She clearly didn't like what I had said, but I couldn't help speaking my mind. That night after giving the supplies and books to the head of the infirmary, Ms Taleqani left the camp.

The subject of moving to Tehran came up again. Leila, the kids, and I were not happy about leaving. We were afraid of being far from Khorramshahr and Abadan. I was waiting for a time when I could go back to Abadan and aid the wounded at the hospitals. But Uncle Hoseyni insisted we go, and, since we owed him so much and he was our elder, we had no choice. But my heart wasn't in it. When he saw how upset I was, he said, "You can be of help to the front from Tehran, also."

In addition to my work at the clinic, I also canvassed the needs of the refugees. The directors had me go around and identify families needing financial help. During my conversations with them, I gathered information about their circumstances and was able to prioritize the relief efforts. Many faced truly serious problems. Some even lacked bread for the night. A number of refugees had relatives in Mahshahr and Sar Bandar and with their help managed to get through this period. Others, who worked for the state, were transferred to other cities and received their monthly wages. The government was now allocating funds for the movement of refugees.

The paramilitary corps, the Red Crescent, and the army ran the camp. Sentries were stationed in various parts. They also established a library and a mosque. The clergy visited regularly and conducted communal prayers and delivered sermons.

A refugee camp, of course, had other problems, some of which stemmed from impropriety and bad behavior. The resident population was large, and not everyone was mindful of basic health and sanitation. The baths were communal, and skin, eye, scalp, and yeast infections were common. The flea infestations were so bad we feared an outbreak of typhus. As a result, we went to people's homes and sprayed them with disinfectant. We shaved children's heads and applied antiflea powder to their scalps. Some families objected to having their children's heads shaved—especially their daughters—and refused to give permission. We went ahead anyway.

Even with all these problems, Uncle Hoseyni still forced us to go to Tehran. We didn't argue with him and got ready to move, still hoping he would change his mind.

31

Move to Tehran

Early one morning in December 1980, Uncle Hoseyni came by to bring Leila and me to Sar Bandar to buy chador material. He returned us to camp while he went to Mahshahr, where Mr. Bahramzadeh's wife was to tailor chadors for us. During the last months we didn't have the wherewithal to buy chadors. That night uncle returned with them and said, "Gather your things. We're leaving first thing tomorrow. Before we go to Tehran, we'll go to the Molavi Camp to see your grandparents." Aware of how upset we were to leave the region, uncle said to us, "You have to consider your sister and brothers. Camp life makes no sense for them. What crime did they commit to have to grow up in such a place?"

He was right. I was very worried about the children myself. Father had entrusted them to me, and, to keep an eye on them, I would bring them to the clinic while I worked. Mansur was an adolescent, and the chances of him going astray in that environment were great. I stuck Sa'id, Hasan, and Zeynab in a corner while I worked. My colleagues and I kept them busy with little chores. Hasan was very mischievous. I had to watch him like an eagle in case he did something that would get him thrown out of the clinic.

Unable to go against uncle's wishes, but scowling in protest just the same, we left for the city. Leila and I were despondent, sitting next to each other on the bus. We got underway late in the afternoon. Our first stop was the Molavi Camp. Located between Pol-e Dokhtar and Khorramabad, it was a broad explanse along the river, which had been leveled by bulldozers. Refugees were housed in two facing rows of tents. Everybody was gathered there waiting when we arrived: Uncle Nad Ali, grandfather, Aunt Salimeh, my father's cousins, and the family of uncle's wife. We were overjoyed to see one another. The day was devoted to eating and talk—mostly about what was happening in Khorramshahr and how father was martyred. We stayed up all night discussing these things.

Uncle Hoseyni had heard about Ali's death from Uncle Nad Ali and that same night told grandfather about it. Grandfather cried in his tent until morning. Besides Uncles Salim and Nad Ali, no one else knew about Ali; the others thought Uncle Hoseyni was mourning the death of father. Mother stayed the night in Uncle Hoseyni's tent, while I spent the night with Uncle Nad Ali, his wife, and Aunt Salimeh. The camp assigned each family a tent with enough room for four to six people. Uncle Hoseyni's tent was near the entrance to the camp. Four tents down the line was Nad Ali's tent, and next to that was the one assigned to grandfather. Because the refugees arrived with nothing to their names, the camp supplied them with basic things like blankets, utensils, and a kerosene lantern and stove

Early the next morning around 5:00 a.m. grandfather's mournful voice sounded the call to prayer. The way he said "I affirm there is no God but Allah" you'd think he was complaining to the Almighty. Grandfather's grief-stricken voice during the wee hours of the morning brought all of us from our tents. Uncle Hoseyni's wife said, "I think my husband told grandfather about Ali." That was when I realized grandfather had known about Ali but kept it to himself the whole night mother was with him. Having finished his strained call to prayer, grandfather gave a full-throated recitation of how the Prophet's grandson Hoseyn was martyred at noon on the tenth of Moharram. Grandfather's voice, normally calm yet firm, rose with the mention of every calamity. He recounted the names of each of Hoseyn's companions and how they were martyred on the battlefield. He also described what Hoseyn's sister Zeynab did. We stood outside the tents crying. We didn't know how grandfather was going to tell mother about Ali's death. Mother thought he was giving the recital in honor of father's martyrdom. When he got to part describing the martyrdom of Ali Akbar, Hoseyn's older son, he recited beautifully, "When Ali Akbar was martyred, Imam Hoseyn's back bowed." Immediately after that he said, "The revered Imam

Ali, Hoseyn's father, was martyred like Ali Akbar." Mother realized what he meant and she immediately broke into an anguished wail, bringing all the neighbors from their tents. Suddenly a crowd gathered around grandfather's tent. I went inside the tent. As soon as she saw me, mother turned white. She shrieked and then fainted. When she opened her eyes, she asked me, "Why didn't you tell me? The whole time why didn't you say something?"

She glared at me and raved and ranted so furiously I couldn't take it and left. The moment I had been dreading had finally come. I went off to say my morning prayers. Grandfather stood in prayer, while the rest of the relatives and the neighbors moaned and wept. Uncle Hoseyni urged them to get up and say their prayers.

With this the crowd went to pray. After prayers, uncle's wife prepared breakfast, but no one could stop crying long enough to eat. For my part, it was as though I was hearing the news afresh; the searing wound caused by Ali's death had not healed after all this time. Each day I woke knowing father and Ali were gone, there would be the same old grief and anguish.

Now two things tormented mother: the death of Ali and my having kept her in the dark about it. She kept saying, "Ali had been dead for four months, and I didn't know it! Why didn't you tell me? Why did you lie?"

She stared at me, fuming. All of a sudden she yanked a hefty limb from a tree that had fallen nearby and began to beat herself over the head with it. This opened a gaping wound on her scalp, which bled and bled. One of the nurses from Khorramabad, who helped at the clinic, came to grandfather's tent, but no matter how hard she tried to stitch the gash she couldn't get it to stop bleeding. Wracked with grief, mother wouldn't lie still. Her hair became blood-soaked. I saw it was no use, but we couldn't just leave her on her own—she might have bled to death. I knew I had to do something. I got down and sat on her shoulders, pinning her arms with my legs. Then I quickly shaved the hair around the gash and, without an anesthetic, I started to sew it up. Mother tried to buck free, leaving me with no choice but to work even faster on the wound. I poured disinfectant over it. My hands were shaking but there was nothing I could do about that. I was very worried about her. Zeynab stood by watching in terror and sobbing. Sa'id and Hasan were in shock. In the end I managed to put five stitches in her scalp. I covered them with a large piece of gauze and tied a scarf around her head. During those frantic moments, I wasn't aware of what I was doing; it all happened so fast. Mother was unconscious from the loss of blood, but uncle's wife forced sugar water into her mouth, while I gave her a fortifying shot of vitamin B12.

Uncle Hoseyni had previously told others in our families living in Darreh Shahr and Zarrinabad about Ali and invited them to the Molavi Camp for the bereavement. They arrived around noon and began the special ceremonies the Kurds use to mourn the dead. They all sat around keening, reciting elegies, and crying. Some mourners raised their voices in piercing, solo laments, which the others repeated. Women were beside themselves, clawing at their faces. The residents of the camp joined us in mourning Ali.

Uncle Hoseyni went to a roadside restaurant near Pol-e Dokhtar to arrange lunch. Two cooks from the place brought the fixings for kabob, and the women provided the greens. The relatives from Darreh Shahr and Zarrinabad went back to their homes that afternoon.

During the week we spent at the camp, groups of family members, having learned about Ali, kept coming and going,. Camp people also visited us regularly to mourn. Officials helped with conducting the ceremonies. Despite the many expressions of sympathy and the mourning rites, grandfather remained inconsolable. He dearly loved Ali and was stricken by his passing. Ali was his favorite. During the mourning period, he kept repeating: "I swear there is no God" and "God is great." Time and time again we heard him ask why he head lived long enough to see both Seyyed Ali and Seyyed Hoseyn dead.

Then he would take me in his arms and kiss my head, saying, "You were so brave, my girl, to take on such a heavy burden! You're an honest to God lioness! You honored our family," which was his way of comforting me. Grandmother was upset beyond words. Both she and mother lost the will to go on. Mother was now totally broken, visibly older. With this going on, Zeynab—no more than five at the time—was passed from woman to woman, who caressed and kissed her. Sa'id, however, came and sat by me in a quiet, pitiful state. When I got up he would follow me.

Adding to our anxieties, Uncle Salim was called up to fight at the Allah Akbar hills.[1] With the week of mourning over uncle told us to get ready to go to Tehran. Saying goodbye was not easy, given the critical state of the country. It wasn't likely we would see one another again.

Tearfully we left grandfather, grandmother, and the others and went to Khorramabad. From there we got a bus to Tehran. In those days some bus drivers were overcharging for trips to Tehran, forcing people to haggle with them over the fare.

We arrived in Tehran in the late afternoon. Leila had been in the city before and had been given a letter from the Martyrs Foundation with the address of where we had to go. She had lost it, however, and couldn't remember exactly where it was. All she recalled was "it faced a square"!

Thank God she remembered the name of the avenue. After asking several people, we found the place. With our bundles in tow we walked from Artillery Square to Ferdowsi, and then we backtracked to Manuchehri Avenue. We asked passersby where Kushk Avenue was, but no one knew.

Though it was dark by then, we managed to find the place. Having seen the building once before, Leila recognized it. There was a guard stationed at the entrance. Uncle explained to him why we were there, and the guard contacted the Martyrs Foundation, after which he let us in. He led us to a series of connecting rooms at the end of a hallway and, pointing to one, said, "This is yours."

The seven-story Kushk Building previously housed the Bureau of Budget and Planning and had many interconnecting rooms. The building from top to bottom was filthy with smoke and grime. The rooms were carpeted. The heaters—except for the one in our room—worked, and there was hot water. We wanted to clean the room but lacked supplies. We didn't bring any of the things they had given us at the camp—only the necessities. Uncle borrowed a broom and dustpan from the room opposite ours and got to work himself. Knowing Leila and I still resented having to come to Teh-

[1] The Allah Akbar Hills, an important and strategic objective, were the site of one of the forward lines on the heights of Dasht-e Azadegan.

ran, he did everything he could to make us happy. Eventually we joined in and cleaned the walls. The room was freezing, so cold our teeth chattered. "What are we going to do without blankets and floor cushions?" we asked uncle.

"Nothing's open now," he said. "Let's go get some supper and see what happens." Uncle and Mohsen went to get flatbread and kabobs. It was the first time I had the flatbread called "barbari." We were tired and hungry and ate a lot, but there was still the brutal chill. The wall facing the street was all glass, which allowed the cold to penetrate the room. Uncle went to the neighbors across the hall asking if they any spare blankets to keep the children from freezing.

A woman named Khorrami, who lived in the building with her husband, gave us a thick covering used for the low heated tables people sat around during winter months, two blankets, and some cushions. We spread one of the blankets on the floor, and everybody but uncle slept on that. Then we crawled under the thick covering. Uncle made do with the other blanket. Even though the covering was large enough for everybody, we pulled and tugged at it all night. The children slept between us, because we were afraid they get uncovered and catch cold. In the morning we joked it was a good thing our struggles with the blanket hadn't ruined it. Uncle said he and Mohsen would go back to Sar Bandar to fetch our belongings. Leila and I kept on badgering him about being shanghaied to Tehran. What we were supposed to do, we asked, if the children got sick?

With Uncle Hoseyni and Mohsen gone, how to get lunch became a question. Mansur, Sa'id, and I went out to buy food. Not knowing the area, we went to the end of the avenue but didn't find a shop or restaurant. We weren't too sure about how wholesome the sandwiches sold on the street were. We turned back and went to Revolution Avenue. At Lalehzar Avenue we found a basement kabob place. Sa'id and I waited at the street-level entrance while Mansur went down to buy food. He came back with five portions. But now, because of all the twists and turns, we didn't know how to get back to the building. We asked somebody where Ferdowsi Square was and were told to follow the avenue until we got to Ferdowsi Street. When we got back, we realized how mixed up we'd gotten.

The sleeping arrangements that night were the same as the previous one.

A few days after coming to Tehran, mother got very ill and became completely bedridden. She was so sick we were afraid she wouldn't make it. The news of Ali's death had been a great shock to her. During this time a relative told her she had read a newspaper interview with a wounded man named Seyyed Ali Hoseyni. Mother thought it could be her Ali. I told her the relative was mistaken, because I had buried Ali myself. I asked her, "Wouldn't I have known my own brother?" I told her the Martyrs Foundation had lists of people with similar names.

It turned out the wounded man with my brother's name spoke Turkish and was from Tabriz. Despite this mother still nurtured hopes that her Ali was alive somewhere. Now I felt even guiltier about not telling her immediately. On the other hand, I knew if I had told her she would have remained pinned to his grave forever, making leaving Khorramshahr impossible—she was so emotionally tied to her son. Every word he spoke was scripture to her, which was why when Leila told mother it was Ali who said to leave Khorramshahr, she did.

Around this time, Mr. Mazandarani and two others from the Martyrs Foundation came by to ask us to make a list of things we needed. I had warned mother if anyone asked if there was anything we wanted, she should say nothing. We hadn't given two martyrs to the cause to go on the dole here. That was why I told Mr. Mazandarani we had everything we needed.

"Take the clothes," he said. "The kids will catch cold without them." I said, "We don't need a thing." "My dear sister," he said, "you don't even have the basic necessities." "We'll buy them ourselves," I said. "You can't," he said. "Your legal status is still not clear. Don't be so pigheaded." "We don't need a thing," I insisted. Mother also joined in, "Whatever my daughter says. It's not easy to hear somebody say he'll provide for us. It's the worst thing in the world for us, I feel. It's insulting." Mr. Mazandarani kept at it, saying, "God forbid you think it's charity or you're under any obligation. Perish the thought! We're the ones who owe you a great debt."

He was so insistent I finally gave in and took a few little things. After uncle and Mohsen came back, they went with Mr. Zeyn al-

Din, the building manager, to the foundation to get a full set of blankets, utensils, plates, bowls, etc. Seeing Mohsen drive up with a van was very upsetting. Mother said, "Darling, there's no way around it. You've seen how we're freezing to death at night? If things go on like that, we'll all be sick."

After they unloaded the supplies, I returned the covering and the blankets to Mrs. Khorrami. Then I went to the superintendent and said, "You said there would be another family in addition to ours in these rooms. Apart from its being small, our room is connected to the other one. There's only one way of getting in and out of it. How is the second family supposed to go to their room? You've got to do something for us."

The superintendent moved us into a room directly opposite the stairway. It was very large and had two doors, one at each end. The room was partially partitioned, which created two separate living spaces. We cleaned it and settled in.

There were several other refugee families on our floor. One was a Khorramshahri family, who lived with their daughter and son-in-law. They had commandeered the only kitchen in the building, stocking it with their own utensils, a gas stove, and a refrigerator. They didn't allow us to use it. Our other neighbor, Mrs. Akbari, had her own hotplate so she didn't have to fight with them. The Khorramshahris claimed they had a right to the kitchen because they had been in the building before everyone. Some time later, when that family's circumstances improved, they left the Kushk Building and moved to a rental home. After they left, the superintendent said no family had the right to appropriate the kitchen; it was to be for common use. It was first come, first served, which meant everyone now had to wait their turn.

Each floor had only two working bathrooms, one of which they had closed. As the number of residents increased, crowds waiting in line for the bathroom grew. Little by little the carpeting in the hallways was pulled up because it was getting ratty and full of germs that might cause infections. There was no place to shower in the building, so we had to go out to the public bath.

It took some time to get used to life in Tehran. Apart from the annoying things I mentioned, what I found most irritating was the idiotic talk I heard on the street. In Tehran, I took a bus back from the hospital to Mr. Mohammadi's house. One day around sunset, with no bus in sight, I heard people in line saying, "It wasn't smart for the people of Khorramshahr to run away from home like that and pitch their tents in cities around Iran and in Tehran." Suddenly an air raid siren sounded, and everything went dead quiet. Antiaircraft guns started firing, terrifying people. Several women in line fainted, and everyone else was anxious. I thought this was the perfect moment to say something. "See how easy it is to cower or pass out at the sight of one enemy plane. You're all looking for a place you can hide. So why blame the folks in Khorramshahr for fleeing? There're under enemy shelling day and night. Do you think you would have been able to put up with what they had to?"

The ones who complained about the refugees in their midst didn't know what to say. Others agreed with me. Then I added, "Don't take it out on the refugees. Saddam is to blame for the suffering. There's no need to make it worse. Right now the people of Abadan are in the same boat, surrounded by the enemy with no hope of getting help from the outside."

I couldn't help speaking out. It hurt me to hear them blame the refugees for fleeing. Having seen boys mowed down at the front, I found myself getting into a lot of arguments with city people. It was my impression they didn't know the first thing about the war and what was happening in the region. In the beginning, of course, the news had not been reported well or extensively, but in time people became more aware of the problems the war caused.

Not everyone was like that. There was a man, Hajj Aqa Talayi (now deceased), who went out of his way to help the refugees in the Kushk Building. A very decent and pious person, he owned a trading house on Manuchehri Avenue and was a trustee of the Qa'em Mosque. He would visit our building regularly to see if he could do anything for us or to know if there was something we needed. "Being of service to you is only my duty," he said.

In addition to the refugee families and victims of war, living in the building were a number of poor people from the city, who had no connection to the war. They were officially known as the "oppressed." In time the atmosphere and character of the building changed for the worse. We asked the Martyrs Foundation to do something for the young children. The seventh floor of the building, formerly the cafeteria and assembly hall of the Bureau of Budget and Planning, was converted into a preschool and cultural center, which offered classes on carpet weaving, the Quran, and sewing. They also set up an infirmary on the third floor and invited physicians and nurses to staff it. I was made responsible for giving injections. The infirmary soon caught on, and people from neighboring buildings started to use it.

The new classes and recreational activities at the center took a load off the minds of residents with children. The school eased concerns about the young ones getting into mischief in the hallways.

As part of the Ten Days of Fajr (January 29-February 8, 1981), the celebration of Imam Khomeini's return to Iran, the Martyrs Foundation put on a terrific program. In the morning they brought the martyr families to Freedom Stadium. Going back and forth to the stadium, I saw many old acquaintances from our town. They put on various athletic and cultural events in the convention center, which held about 12,000 people. The learned cleric Mohammad Taqi Jafari came to speak. A very unpretentious, plain-spoken person, he lectured in a way everyone could understand.

On one of our visits, Leila and I saw Abdollah Mo'avi at the stadium. He had come along with a number of wounded convalescing in Tehran. It was a joy to see Abdollah, and we rushed over to say hello. I noticed he recognized Leila but not me, which was upsetting. I said, "It's me, Zahra, Seyyed Ali's sister. You remember Seyyed Ali, don't you? I was working at Jennatabad." "I don't know you," he said. I was bewildered and tried to jog his memory by mentioning what happened in those days. "Remember the time, Abdollah, we were walking from Jennatabad to the Congregational Mosque, when a dog started following us, and nothing we did made him go away?"

"No," he said.

I went into detail about it. Zohreh Farhadi, Sabah Vatankhah, Leila, and I were walking from Jennatabad to the Congregational Mosque. Hoseyn Idi and Abdollah were with us, walking a few paces ahead. Because of the heavy Iraqi shelling, even the animals in the town sensed the city was unsafe. As we walked along, the dog started following us, and each explosion brought the poor thing closer to us. Suddenly a Peykan appeared. Abdollah flagged it down and told us to get in. When the back door opened, the dog hopped on. I went out the other door, and the dog followed. We all chuckled. Abdollah asked, "Why don't you get in? What are you waiting for?"

We pointed to the dog. Abdollah blocked its way, and we got in. He and Hoseyn sat in the front seat. The dog followed the car all the way to the mosque.

Abdollah didn't remember any of it. I went over to his companions and asked them what was wrong with him.

"He's got amnesia from being hit in the head by shrapnel," they said.

I saw him several days later, but this time he remembered me not Leila. We visited Abdollah several times. Later I learned from his friends he had succumbed to the head wound.

Though I was in Tehran, I never stopped believing I'd go back to Abadan and help the wounded at the hospital. I set my mind on either taking a course in nursing and returning to the zone armed with a degree or volunteering at one of Tehran's hospitals. I applied to the Red Crescent but got nowhere. They told me, "Because the instructional material contains terminology in English, only people who know the language can take part in the classes." Not having completed my education, I didn't know any English. I kept promising to learn the words, but the teacher wouldn't let me in.

Dr. Kamarizadeh and his team regularly visited the building to check on victims of the fighting. Dr. Kamarizadeh knew me because he was one of the doctors at the infirmary at the Sar Bandar camp. I invited him, a very kind and committed older man, to our room. He was very impressed by how clean it was. The old carpeting we had laid was swept so often it had no pile. He said, "You keep this place as sanitary as you kept the infirmary."

"Well," I said, "this is where we live." Then, given our acquaintance, he insisted I come to work at his clinic. "The secretary at the clinic," he explained, "is a Hypocrite supporter and always arguing politics with the patients." He planned to use this as an excuse to make a personnel change.

I went to visit his clinic in the city of Rey. It seemed a long way to commute. Besides that it was a private clinic, which was not for me. I wanted to work with the wounded, so I had to turn him down.

Though the many chores at the Kushk Avenue clinic kept me very busy, I couldn't help thinking how much I detested Tehran. Everything about the city was so unbearable living there almost killed me. I felt desperate and wanted to take the kids to Sar Bandar or Molavi. They weren't in school, so they had free time. On top of that, we had come in the middle of winter, when they gave the trimester exams, so the kids had already fallen behind that year.

Afraid the kids would be led astray or have some other calamity befall them in that monstrous city, I made them come with me on errands. I drew the line, however, on the trips I made to Sar Bandar due to the heavy bombardments. There I went to the home of Mrs. Barati, a nurse I had visited several times before while we were at the camp. Her husband worked at the petrochemical plant, and they lived in company housing. I no longer saw any familiar faces among the workers at the camp clinic; even the refugees were new to me. Many of the old families had left for Shiraz or Behbehan or were renting homes in Mahshahr and Sar Bandar. The only people I knew were one who had stuck it out, hoping to get back to Abadan some day.

I felt comfortable leaving mother on her own when I went back. Because of the heavy shelling, Uncles Hoseyni and Nad Ali had been transferred to Tehran and were now living with us. A few times bombs landed so close to Uncle Hoseyni's home that he was forced to move. But every few weeks or so, they would visit their families in Khorramabad, which the Iraqis were also bombarding regularly. Having the two uncles in Tehran gave me peace of mind. Nevertheless, mother was saddled with the burden of being the only parent to the children. She had to feed and cloth them on the meager allowance from the Martyrs Foundation.

My brother Mohsen, though the eldest, didn't feel ready to take on the responsibilities of the older son. His mind was badly affected by the fall from the roof. He liked to work, but only preferred the heaviest kind of labor. That was why he didn't last long answering telephones at the Kushk Building. He was so stubborn about this mother finally had to give in and allow him to take father's old job at the municipality in Khorramshahr. The Iraqi occupation had forced them to move the town administration south to Kut-e Sheikh. Even though father had been with the municipality for a short time, they were willing to hire Mohsen as a member of the team extinguishing fires set off by the bombardments. Fearing he might be injured, mother at first withheld her permission but in the end gave in.

What was happening in the war was still not clear. No one on our side ever imagined it would go on so long, which was why no thought had been given to the fate of the refugees and victims of the fighting. As the conflict dragged on, the Martyrs Foundation began to set up programs and pass laws dealing specifically with refugees. They allocated living expenses to martyr families. After a couple of years the municipality took over the expenses for the families of martyred municipal workers. We would no longer receive support from the Foundation, so to arrange our allowance from the municipality mother had to become the family's legal guardian. We went to the local police station to fill out a form, after which several people from the police came to inspect our room and, in their words, "take inventory" of our possessions. We tried to convince them we were refugees from Khorramshahr and had nothing to our names when we arrived. They wouldn't listen when we told them we had bought all the things in Tehran.

They made a list of the things in the room: blankets, a kerosene stove/lamp, utensils, and plates and bowls. They handed back the application for aid and said, "You have to get written confirmation of the father's death from Behesht-e Zahra Cemetery before the paperwork can go through."

We didn't know the way to that cemetery so Seyyed Abbas, the husband of Aunt Salimeh, accompanied us. It was the middle of the week, which meant we had to wait ages for a ride. We finally arrived at around 2:00 p.m., just as the office was about to close. I had mother sit outside, while I went in with Seyyed Abbas. A man sitting behind a desk opened a large black register. He took the IDs belonging to father and Ali and recorded the information in the register as the afternoon sunlight illuminated the page. He stamped "invalid" on the last page in the IDs and returned them to me. I started to weep, which was a first for me in front of strangers since the death of father. It was impossible for me to watch the last vestiges of father and Ali declared void, to accept that the two of them—albeit officially—no longer existed. Their IDs had been tokens of their continued existence; but now they were "invalid." Now there was no escaping the fact that father and Ali were no more.

The trip back was a somber one for the three of us. We had been running around like mad since morning, but now it was over, and we were in no hurry to get back. We left the cemetery with our heads hanging down.

Later on, when we visited the graves of Jahan Ara[2] or Hoseyn Hamzeh'i[3] at Behesht-e Zahra, the black register reminded me of what had happened on that awful day.

---

[2] One of the army commanders, a very brave man, killed at the beginning of the war.

[3] A member of the regular army from Khorramshahr. Before the war he worked as a welder in a shop on Ku-ye Farshid. I would see him working there many times on my way back from school.

32

Run-in with the Hypocrites

The political situation in Tehran was unsettled. Everyday the Hypocrites appeared at some new location to spread their propaganda, hold meetings, agitate, and debate their opponents. Unable to defend their views with logic, they used force and smacked their opponents silly. Laleh Park was one of their regular meeting places. After the meetings, fights would ordinarily break out. I tried to take part in the debates, but it was no use debating them with words; they would run roughshod over anyone who tried.

During this time the Hypocrites would ambush the revolutionary kids in deserted alleyways and try to beat them to death. They thought they were—to use their words—"undermining the enemy."

On March 5, 1981, I attended a speech by Banisadr, which Hypocrites disrupted with their shouts and chanting. As I walked home, I sensed three very weird-looking figures—two girls and one boy—were following me. I told myself they weren't after me, but one of the girls, wearing Adidas sneakers, raced up and kicked me hard in the back of the leg. I was no match for them; there were three of them and they were armed with probably more than just a box-cutter. I started to run and disappeared into the crowd when I reached the avenue, where they didn't dare show themselves.

There was a revolutionary committee stationed on Ferdowsi Avenue. They asked the guards at the Kushk Building give them the names of trustworthy women to work with them. The guards recommended Leila and me, but because I wasn't going to be in

Tehran much longer, I gave them Sabah Vatankhah's name. She was living in the building with her family at the time, and we renewed our friendship, which had started with the war, there.

Whenever the brothers on the committee caught a female Hypocrite fighting or planting a bomb, they would send for us to do a body search of them. These types tried to get rid of a lot of their paraphernalia before they were taken before the committee. But sometimes they failed. They seemed a very strange lot to me. Sometimes, searching them, we found salt or pepper in their pockets, and I would ask them why they carried such things. They didn't plan on cooking, did they?

Some were brazen enough to admit, "To rub in your wounds."

"So making us feel worse would make you feel better. Is that it?" we asked.

"Yeah. Why not?"

33

Audience with Ayatollah Khomeini

Although I never found Tehran a very agreeable place, for the longest time I was gripped by the idea of visiting Imam Khomeini, who lived in Jamaran in the northern part of the city. Leila, the Vatankhah sisters (Sabah, Saleheh, and Fowzieh), and I would set out at 6:00 a.m. every Monday and Thursday when the Imam held public audiences, which generally took place at 8:00 and 10:00 in the morning. It was bedlam at Jamaran on those days. No matter how early we arrived, we always found others waiting to be admitted ahead of us. It was easy to get swept up in the crowded streets leading to his residence.

The Imam would appear, wave, and leave. Sometimes we would sit with visitors waiting for his next appearance, but the women guards would remove us. We'd beg them to let us stay for one more look at him.

We saw the Imam several times this way, but that never satisfied our longing for a private audience. No matter how much we insisted they just wouldn't let it happen.

The Vatankhah sisters and I had long ago decided to return to Abadan. The sisters and several other Khorramshahris worked at the Taleqani Hospital there. One day at noon, with time before our departure growing short, we found ourselves in front of the Hoseyniyeh Hall at Jamaran and noticed Mr. Karroubi there. We stepped up to him and said, "Please, Mr. Karroubi, is there anything you can do to get us a personal audience with the Imam?"

"I have to force my way in myself. What makes you think I can get you in?" he said.

"You can," I insisted. "We're about to return to the front. It would be cruel to make us go back without seeing him."

"You're the same sister Mr. Mohammadi brought to parliament, aren't you?" he asked.

"Yes."

"Okay," he said. "I'll write a letter, but no promises. Understand?"

Then, right there in the street, he rummaged through his bag for a piece of paper. Not finding one, he wrote on the back of an envelope, "These sisters are Khorramshahris and will be returning to the front soon. Please allow them to meet with the Imam personally."

The security detail around the residence saw Mr. Karroubi give us the envelope. We got our hopes up but still were not sure we'd be allowed to see him. A guard came forward and asked, "Why are you here?"

We explained. "You're really from Khorramshahr?" he asked.

"Yes."

"Come tomorrow morning and I'll arrange it personally."

"Can we bring others?" we asked.

"Yes, but not a crowd," he said. We agreed.

We were so excited we didn't notice Saleheh Vatankhah had gotten lost in the crowd. Only after two bus trips and reaching the building, did we notice she was gone.

We were exhausted. We thought of going all the way back to the residence to find her, but realized it would be useless. The poor girl didn't have a ticket or money. After a long walk in the heat of the afternoon sun, she came back on her own dead tired. She began to give us the what for: "I didn't know how to go, and just walked down Vali Asr Avenue from Tarjrish. When I got to the square, I made a turn toward Ferdowsi."

"So why didn't you borrow some money?" we asked.

"I was too ashamed."

Early the next morning, excited beyond words, we went to Jamaran so they could arrange a time for the audience. It was Thursday and we got mother and the kids ready. I invited Mohsen, at that time eighteen, and the Vatankhah family to join us.

We set out at 6:00 a.m. When we arrived at Jamaran, the place was deserted. We waited. Moments later I saw one of the people at the Foundation with whom I had previously had words. At that time I said, "I'm going to complain about you to the Imam."

"Since when do they let the likes of you see the Imam?" he asked.

The man had come with his fiancée so the Imam could read them their vows. I had to laugh when I saw him. I said, "See, we're going to get to see the Imam after all! So what should I do? Should I make my complaint?"

He chuckled and said nothing. We waited in line for our turn to enter the small yard of a house by the Hoseyniyeh Hall. The Imam was seated on a balcony overlooking the yard. He was dressed in white and on his head was a skullcap. His legs and hands were covered by a blanket. The men took their turns first, followed by the women. All of them kissed the covering over his hands. My eyes were fixed on him, and I had a lump in my throat. The moment I put my hands on his, I thought of father and Ali—Ali especially, because it had been one of his dreams to see the Imam.

I also remembered the first picture I had seen of him when I was five years old. Father had nailed it to the wall in our house in Basra. The last thing I wanted was to let go of his hand. Feeling his hands through the blanket, I sensed I was in touch with the holiest thing in the world. I cried. I kissed his hand and raised my head. I was giddy, as if I had left this world and was sailing through the clouds.

I remained lost in thought until Mr. Eshraqi, the Imam's son-in-law, said, "Don't trouble him so." I stepped away and stood before the Imam, unable to utter a word. The brothers introduced us to the Imam as the family of martyrs.

He looked at us, smiled, and said a prayer. I couldn't hold back my tears, and I wasn't the only one who lost control. Mother was also weeping as she kissed his hand. The Imam consoled her by muttering a prayer. Then we went into Hoseyniyeh Hall to see him once more. This lifted mother's spirits. Although she didn't speak to him, I got the impression she had finally resigned herself to Ali's death.

As far as I was concerned, that was the best day of my life. Ever since the start of the war and subsequently having to leave Khorramshahr and move to Tehran, there had been this odd feeling of disquiet in me. Nothing would cheer me up. I tried to put on a happy face, but there was always this gnawing sorrow in my heart. That day I felt the pain had been removed from my chest and I could breathe easily again.

Shahnaz Vatankhah had a friend named Nasrin who lived on Jamaran Alley. Seeing us all together at Hoseynieyeh Hall, she invited us to her home. We ate lunch at her house regularly on Mondays and Thursdays. Nasrin and her family took it upon themselves to host people visiting the Imam. I admired the simplicity of what they offered visitors: bread, cheese, greens, butter and jam, pickled vegetables, and rice. What impressed me most was that they prepared all the food themselves. The greens were from their garden; the jams and the cooked food were all homemade. Their doors were always open to visitors, who would come to pray, rest, and have a bite to eat.

After a time, the Imam's health worsened, and his doctors stopped the public visits.

34

Assassination of Dr. Beheshti

Whenever Tehran got too much for me, I would go to the Molavi Camp and spend time with grandfather and Mimi. The folks at the camp were very decent to one another. People from Andishmak, Shush, Dezful, Khorramshahr, and villagers from places like Abbasabad, which was between Andishmak and Shush, were all spending their days in tents. The villagers said, "The enemy is constantly firing their long-range missiles at us to destroy the batteries our side has positioned there."

Ringing the Molavi Camp were the Zagros Mountains. In the spring they became carpeted in green, forming beautiful vistas. The camp itself was landscaped with two rows of large palm trees, which in effect formed a kind of wall. One row artfully ran along the river. You could do almost everything with river water—bathe in it, swim, wash dishes, but not drink it. At the end of the camp was a spring with very clear, cool water, which people collected using plastic jugs. Or having hollowed out a shallow pool, they would dip their bowls in it to fill their jugs with drinking water.

The Refugee Aid Committee supplied newcomers with bare essentials like utensils, pots, blankets, etc. They also gave them basic staples, which the families cooked themselves. The aid, however, gradually dried up, forcing families to buy what they needed in Pol-e Dokhtar. Next to the administrative tent in the camp was a clinic where medical aid workers from the Red Crescent and several women and men medics treated people. Many patients came to the clinic because they had fallen prey to the snakes, scorpions, and tarantulas in the camp.

When the refugee population grew too large for the original camp, people pitched tents on the other side of the road. To minimize the snake and spider bites, the tents were set up on cement slabs. Because it had been hastily constructed, the original camp didn't even have a public bath. It was worse than that: the latrines were shielded from public view by sheets of canvas instead of a proper wall. The new camp, by contrast, had much better facilities. I felt at peace there. It reminded me of the good times we spent in Khorramshahr with grandfather and Uncle Nad Ali. It was easy there to visualize my childhood in Basra, when grandfather would tell us good stories from the Quran and explain their moral lessons. In addition to reciting some verses of scripture from memory, he would illustrate his talks with lines from the *Shahnameh*. Uncle Nad Ali took after grandfather. Often I would see him walk to the river early in the morning and find some cozy spot where he could be alone and recite lines of soulful, emotional poetry to himself. Sometimes he would fish. I wouldn't approach him when he was in this solitary state. Once his wife and I took a picture of him, but he was clearly upset because we had intruded on his solitude.

In the spring of 1981, after the Now Ruz holiday, grandfather and Nad Ali were transferred to a camp five kilometers from Borujerd. I visited them a few times there. The occupants were for the most part like me, refugees from the war, but the camp was a big improvement on Molavi. It had a communications center and minibuses that ferried people to and from Borujerd. That year Ramadan fell in a very hot summer, and we had to spend long, scorching days of fasting and cold nights in the tents. Often, to break the fast we would drink a cold, delicious yogurt drink from Borujerd.

To relieve the summer heat, they set up two large Quonset huts, one for the men and the other for the women. Water from a spring near the huts flowed through pipes to a basin in the center. The cold spring water cooled the air inside the hut. Around noon, when the temperatures in the tents became unbearable, everyone transferred to the huts.

Three clerics from Qom came to the camp to lecture on the laws and logic of fasting. They also oversaw the camp's cultural programs. One of the clerics was Sheikh Mojahed, an Iraqi by birth who had been driven from his homeland. He was fluent in English and a gifted speaker. Although a clergyman with a degree from the theological seminary in Najaf, he had also been trained as a helicopter technician in England.

It was a first for me to meet a cleric with such a background. In addition to lecturing and leading communal prayers, he also gave Arabic and English lessons to the children, who had fallen behind in their studies.

Even though I had to leave school early because of the issue of coeducation, I was very interested in continuing my studies. I thought as long as I was in the camp I would take part in the classes.

They took place in a large, roofless hall where communal prayers were held. Most of the students were Persian or Luri speakers; very few knew Arabic. Mr. Mojahed was fluent in Arabic and English, but struggled with Persian. In English class he would write words on the board and try to explain them. Often not knowing the meanings in Persian, he would say the Arabic words. For example, once he wrote the word "apple" on the board and tried to define it in Persian. Unable to do so, he rounded his hands and said *toffah* in Arabic.

"What is *toffah*?" asked the students.

Although it was embarassing to get up and make a spectacle of myself in front of everyone, I raised my hand and told him I knew Arabic and Persian. Then I explained to the students, "In Persian *toffah* means *sib*."

Another time Mr. Mojahed called a good math and language student to the board. The student, normally very well prepared, failed to answer his question. Mr. Mojahed said to him in Arabic, "Before you were a help (*shater*), but now you aren't."

Misunderstanding the word *shater* ("baker" in Persian, "helper" in Arabic), the boy said, "No, sir, I'm no baker. That's my cousin." I explained the mix-up to the boy in Persian, and the whole class roared with laughter. The helper/baker mix-up became a kind of joke among the students. From that time on I translated for Mr. Mojahed.

One day the wife of Uncle Nad Ali asked me, "Have you heard the news?"

"No."

"Dr. Beheshti has been killed by Hypocrites in a terrorist attack."

Everything went dark before me. I couldn't believe the news and thought she had made a mistake. I ran to grandfather's tent, where he had a small radio brought from Khorramshahr. Salimeh's husband was in front of the tent, and his eyes were red from crying. Once I heard the news on the radio, I realized it was true.

I should mention here that Seyyed Abbas, Aunt Salimeh's husband, would scour the mountains for dried branches and twigs and bring them to grandfather. Though his eyes were failing him and he had undergone two eye operations, grandfather used an axe and a knife to turn the wood into simple things like cutting boards, spindles, spools, rug hooks, sugar cone hammers, pulleys, etc. Mother and Aunt Salimeh would use the spools and spindles to weave woolen skullcaps and loofahs.

The news of Dr. Beheshti's death made me recall the time some months before when he had visited the Molavi Camp to inspect the refugees. During his tour, Dr. Beheshti was delighted to see a man of grandfather's age and physical condition still at work. He spoke with him, and, for his part, grandfather was so taken with the simple way Dr. Beheshti interacted with refugees he kissed the man's hand. Grandfather always remembered his conversation with Dr. Beheshti fondly.

That day the loudspeakers announced we were all to go to Borujerd and participate in mourning ceremonies for Dr. Beheshti. There was a large demonstration during which the people shouted slogans against the Hypocrites and America.

The Hypocrites continued with their atrocities. I was at the camp at the time of the assassinations of Raja'i and Bahonar and the attempt on the life of Mr. Khameneh'i. The people at the camp held ceremonies in their honor.

At the end of the summer of 1981, Uncle Nad Ali and grandfather left the camp near Borujerd and got a house in Khorramabad. With their departure I lost my refuge from Tehran. Now I was in the city for good. For a time I worked in security for Friday prayers. Once I saw Mozhdeh Onbashi at them. Friends told me that on the October 16, 1980 (the same day Sheikh Sharif was killed), she had been hurt while getting a wounded man to the hospital. I hadn't seen her since that time. She was struck by shrapnel in the head and arm, and her leg was paralyzed. This didn't stop her from getting married, though. Seeing her again made me very happy.

35

Marriage and Liberation of Khorramshahr

The issue of my marriage came up in the fall of 1981. This wasn't the first time, of course. It had come up often before the war, at the Molavi Camp, in Tehran, and even in the chaos at the beginning of the conflict. Each time I strongly objected.

At the time we were in bad shape financially. The burden of supporting us as well as several other family members had fallen on Uncle Hoseyni's shoulders. Meanwhile Jahan Ara had assigned several of the brothers from the army with the task of going to various cites and seeing to the martyr families. Mr. Mohammadi, brother Behnam Mohammadi,[1] Mahmud Zamani, and (once) Seyyed Saleh Musavi along with his wife Batul Kazeruni visited us. I knew none of them except Mr. Mohammadi. I asked mother about them, but all she knew was they were army and had been friends of Ali.

One day when mother had gone out and Uncles Hoseyni and Nad Ali were at work, two brothers from the army visited us. Only Leila and I were at home. Though it was burden to have these strange men in our home, we made them feel welcome, and, during the course of the visit, I heard one say to the other in Arabic, "So, tell them."

---

[1] Behnam Mohammadi was a young man of thirteen who was so small his G3 scraped along the ground when he patrolled the neighborhoods, alerting the defense forces about the presence of the enemy. He died when shrapnel entered his heart during the last days of the resistance.

The other one said, "There's nobody home. Whom am I supposed to tell?"

Thinking it had something to do with our funding, I thought to myself: So give me the money. Who are you waiting for?

I didn't know what was keeping mother. When the two men got up to leave, out of politeness I offered them lunch; but all the while I wished mother would come back to take the money from them. There was one good thing about having them in our home, though; it brought back memories of Ali.

One of them, Habib Maz'ali, had almost lost a finger when an RPG round he was carrying went off. They reattached it at Taleqani Hospital in Abadan.[2] His finger was still bandaged. After I made the offer of lunch, he said, "No. I have to go and have my bandage changed."

"You can stay, if that's not a problem. I have everything necessary to change the dressing."

"If you're sure it won't be a bother, I'd really appreciate it," he said.

I went and got my medical kit. Then I removed the bandage and cleaned the wound. After his companion left the room, Habib began to speak about Ali, and telling me he knew about what I had done at the front and how I was wounded. It was my modesty, decorum, and decency that impressed him the most. He said, "Before the war, I had intended to start the ball rolling toward marriage, but the war came, and I had to put it off." Then he asked me for permission to talk to the family.

I was so unnerved by what he said my hands started to shake. Struggling to rebandage his finger, I said, "I actually have no intention of getting married. As far as I am concerned, it's a dead issue."

After we were married, Habib told me, "The way you reacted to my proposal I nearly ran from the room."

Habib didn't take my firm "no" for an answer and continued to pursue the matter. After talking to friends and checking on Habib's character with people I trusted, I began to have second thoughts about

---

[2] To this day he does not have full use of the finger.

marrying. One of the people I consulted was Hoseyn Ta'i Nezhad, a close friend of Ali's and, for several months, Leila's fiancée. Worried about what mother and the kids would do without me, I hesitated. Father had made me responsible for them. What would happen to them if I got married and moved away?

After several months of paying the customary visits to us, Habib came by one day to have a serious talk about my terms. Habib had no preconditions; his only real issue was my faith. "I am not concerned about your cooking or whether you'll work or not," he said. "I will accept your terms to the extent I am able."

"I have two conditions," I said. "One: I won't be separated from my family. Two: You won't prevent me from going to the front."

He seemed to take this in stride and said, "I don't have a home right now, and we can live with your family. I'm off to the front, and you can join me whenever possible."

"Don't say this just to humor me," I warned him. "I'm serious about going to the front. Don't say later it makes no sense for women to be at the front."

With that our engagement became official. Several days later Jahan Ara, commander of forces in Khorramshahr, died in a helicopter crash.[3] Everyone was grief-stricken. Several months after that, in the winter of 1981-1982, Habib returned from the front, and with his family we made arrangements for the marriage. There was some dickering about the bride price. "It should be enough," insisted Habib, "to protect the interests of the wife."

In the end Uncle Hoseyni offered a volume of the Quran and 100,000 tumans, which all parties accepted.

On January 2, 1982, there was a small reception held in the Kushk Building. Members of my family formed a small army, while Habib's side was represented only by his father and brothers with their families. (His mother had passed on in 1979.) My relatives in-

---

[3] On September 30, 1981, several days after the breaking of the Iraqi siege of Abadan in Operation Somen al-A'emeh, the helicopter carrying Jahan Ara and several other commanders crashed on its way back to Tehran.

cluded Uncles Nad Ali, Salim, Aunt Salimeh, and all their families. One of Uncle Hoseyni's friends by the name of Mr. Qaruni also came. Finally, a cousin of mother's, Seyyed Jafar, came with his family. Some neighbors from the building also attended the ceremony. Abdollah and Khalil Mo'avi came with a basket of flowers, which was especially dear to me.

The number of guests, nevertheless, was limited; grandfather and Mimi didn't even come. We had invited many others but conditions at the time kept them from coming. In any case, there wasn't enough room to accommodate more people. I wasn't all that happy with the celebration in the first place and insisted on economizing on the trappings. Habib didn't agree, saying, "It's true there's a war going on and expense is an issue, but things aren't completely dire."

"With the war going on many things have lost their meaning for me," I said. So what we spent on the traditional nuptials amounted to 500 tumans for the ring, 800 tumans for the mirror and candelabra, 13,000 tumans for the wedding dress, the reception, etc. Three days later Habib was back at the front. We had agreed he would find a place so we could begin married life in the region.

After he had gone, uncle's wife asked me, "You're not upset, are you?"

"No, why should I be?"

"You don't realize it now, but soon you'll see how hard it is to be alone."

"It's not all that unpleasant. God's alone," I said.

A month after my marriage, Mohsen and I decided to go to Abadan to participate in the ceremonies marking the Ten Days of Fajr, which took place on January 31, 1982 at the Persian Hotel.[4] The master of ceremonies was Behruz Moradi,[5] a gifted orator, who transfixed

---

[4] The Persian Hotel was the temporary headquarters of the Khorramshahr army after the fall of the city. It was located on the Abadan-Khorramshahr Highway.

[5] Behruz Moradi was a powerful and active member of the Khorramshahr army. He studied at the Arts College. The pictures he took of the war and his diaries

his listeners with his booming voice. That day he spoke of the Hypocrites, the antirevolutionaries, and those who were on the sidelines. He also mentioned the saboteurs.

The ceremonies that night lasted a long time. Mr. Hosam al-Din Sarraj along with a vocal group gave a beautiful rendition of "The City is a City of Blood." When they sang, "The house is blood, so is the lane; The eye and the heart are blood from all the pain; Headless lies the brother's sacred gore; The sister's, the mother's eyes fixed on the door," all my grief and pain returned, bringing with them a flood of tears.

Mr. Kuwaiti also performed the dirge "How Like the Dispossessed Have the Friends Left Home."

The shrapnel in my back kept me from sitting still for long periods of time. I also had trouble standing. The injury chose that particular point to act up terribly, so much so I couldn't even stand. My kidneys hurt like mad. Not seeing anyone I knew at the celebration and separated from Mohsen, I didn't know what to do. Toward the end of the program I happened to see Tahereh Bandari Zadeh.[6] Although we had been friends since primary school, we were always arguing. We would get mad at each other, but our disagreements never ripened into feuds.

I called out to her. "What's wrong?" she asked after seeing the state I was in.

"It feels like my sides are made of stone. I can't get up."

Tahereh left and alerted a few of the other sisters, and they called for an ambulance. Two medics came with a stretcher and carried me to the ambulance, which took me straight to the Oil Company Hospital.

---

give some idea of his transcendent personality. He was killed in 1988 during Operation Shalamcheh and is buried at Jennatabad in Khorramshahr.

[6] Tahereh Bandari Zadeh was a classmate and friend of mine in elementary school. Her sisters were in the army of Khorramshahr.

This was the second time I was hospitalized after Ali's death, and it brought back painful memories of his martyrdom. The examination indicated that my kidneys were badly infected. Surprised, I said to the nurses, "You must be mistaken. I've never had kidney problems."

They decided to take x-rays. After examining them, they said, "There's a foreign object on the x-rays. We have to take another set to be sure." The object was visible in the second set.

"What could it be?" I asked. "I took my clothes off and put on a gown. Maybe it's something that stuck to me when I was asleep."

I had completely forgotten about the shrapnel in my back. The third time they took x-rays, I said to the nurse, "The foreign object is a piece of shrapnel."

I was hospitalized for about eight days, being injected twice a day with penicillin. Mohsen had no idea what had happened to me. I had told Habib I was coming to Abadan with Mohsen, but I wasn't able to contact him for several days. Habib was responsible for a district in the city called Moharrezi.[7] When Mr. Jabbar Beygi came to visit me, I asked him to tell Habib I was in the hospital (at the time he didn't know we were married).

Habib came at night and was shocked to see me in bed. I explained what had happened, and he got word to poor Mohsen, who had been desperately trying to find me.

After I was discharged from the hospital, Habib moved Mohsen and me to a place assigned to him by the army. It was a two-story house on Line 1 in Ahmadabad. Two other soldiers lived there with their spouses. Habib had scrubbed the place clean before our arrival and stocked it with the things he had received as a marriage bonus: several blankets, a kerosene light/stove, four plates and spoons, two pots, and one pressure lamp.

According to Habib, the place had been vacant for a year and a half and only recently had the army allowed him, Seyyed Mozaffar Musavi, and Rahim Eqbal Pur to move in. The house had a small

---

[7] Moharrezi was the southeastern corner of Khorramshahr, which was in Iranian hands.

front yard. The door opened to a narrow passage that led to a foyer. On the right of the foyer were two adjoining "sitting" rooms. On the left were a bedroom and a relatively small kitchen and a bath. Then came the stairway to the second floor. The first floor was carpeted. Each couple had their own bedroom.

Although I was settled in Ahmadabad, it didn't feel like home because the family wasn't with me. Habib could only get away once a week, arriving around noon and leaving the next morning, but Mr. Musavi and Mr. Eqbal Pur were there more frequently. Even when there was a call-up, at least one of the men was present. Being back in Abadan brought memories of what had happened to me during the defense of Khorramshahr. It seemed as if I was reliving all the pain and suffering of those days. That was when I missed mother most; I needed her emotional and spiritual support. Having Habib around was a joy, of course; it took my mind off the negative thoughts for a while. When he left, I tried to pretend I wasn't affected by all of that—but I was. My own crises of nerves, on the one hand, and my worries Habib would be killed, on the other, were tearing me up inside. I tried to take comfort in the thought that everybody in the sector was in the same boat. I had to be ready for the worst. Each time Habib and I said goodbye I imagined it was for the last time. "Just get word to me you're safe," was all I'd say.

He closed the door and I would remain behind it, listening to him get in the car and start the ignition. Then I would open the door again and wait in the doorway, watching as he disappeared down the road. He drove toward the police station, turned left at the traffic circle, and headed for the Persian Hotel. Feeling I would never see him again, I tried to keep the car in sight as long as possible, so I wouldn't be sorry later on that I hadn't. Afterward I learned he was also watching me in his rear view mirror, but he'd never admit it.

Making friends with our housemates was one way of taking my mind off the morbid thoughts. We'd go shopping and cook together. The yard had a small garden, and we bought some bulbs from a druggist in the bazaar and planted them in it. I was very fond of plants and would sit by the garden remembering the times when father planted lantana, and we kidded him about how the name of the bush was also mother's last name.

One of the women, Mrs. Eqbal Pur, had a small radio, and we'd pass the time listening to the news and other programs on it. Some days after we arrived, Mr. Musavi brought home a television. At one point a guest, Sakineh Hurosi, a friend of Mrs. Musavi, came for a visit with her six-month-old baby Mehdi. The baby was a welcome diversion from the war for everyone—especially since none of us had children of our own.

One of our biggest headaches was an infestation of rats. In the lane beside the house was a wastewater channel where they bred. They had no trouble finding their way from the channel to the nearby alleys and homes. They even nested in the sandbags piled up by the windows to shield them from mortar blasts. The worst thing was that they got into the house from the sewage pipes by gnawing holes in the grating over them. Whenever I stepped outside our room, I would see rats scatter in all directions.

I was terrified of them; they were so big even the cats didn't dare go near them. One time a cat came into the yard, and so many rats attacked it, it let out a howl and went flying over the compound wall. The rats ate all the food that had been stored in the house. They even gnawed on onions and potatoes. You could see their half-eaten leavings in the stairway. Whenever I opened the door to our room, a dozen rats would jump up and scamper away. I would scream and slam the door. Even when I was in the room with the door closed, I could hear them munching on the gunnysacks. The idea of them eating their way through the doorframe and coming into the room terrified me. We tried and tried to get rid of them but nothing worked. There was no poison to be had on the bazaar.

Habib and Mr. Eqbal Pur tried to kill the rats. They blocked up the places were water entered, but the rats would gnaw through everything. Fortunately my neighbors, especially Mrs. Eqbal Pur, weren't as terrified of them as I.

One day I was horrified to see Habib come home covered in blood. "I'm not hurt," he assured me. "One of the boys took some shrapnel, and I brought him to the hospital."

Habib also felt the blast. The wounded boy, Ayad Baramzadeh, lost his sight as a result of his injuries. Habib would often come home in this state. Whenever one of his comrades was hit, he would ferry him to the hospital, ending up soaked in blood in the process. Although I was thankful to have the neighbors around, living under these conditions was not pleasant.

The Hypocrites and the Fifth Columnists were a constant threat to families in the sector. To guard against these people our husbands devised secret ways of letting us know it was they who were outside the door. Mr. Eqbal Pur rang the doorbell three times, Mr. Musavi knocked twice, and Habib honked his horn and knocked once. From time to time we would change the codes.

For added protection, Habib kept a G3 at home and took us for target practice at the army garage. He would tell us, "Suppose you're face-to-face with the enemy. Now fire."

One by one we sat taking aim with the gun while our husbands held our shoulders to keep us from being jolted by the recoil. With Habib propping up my shoulders, I took aim at the wall and blasted away. Apparently the wall had been coated with tar, because it suddenly burst into flames. Men came running to put the fire out. Habib said, "Thought you were killing Iraqis, didn't you? But that wall was government property!"

Because the G3 proved too heavy, they added a Kalashnikov to our home arsenal. Whenever anyone came to the door, one of us would stand in the foyer with the weapon, while the others asked who was there. Then we would slowly open the door.

One day when none of the men were at home, someone knocked on the door. "Who's there?" we asked.

"Open the door," a voice said. "Something's wrong with the electricity."

"There's nothing wrong with our electricity."

"There is; the whole neighborhood is out."

Pretending our husbands were home, we said, "Wait for us to go and wake the men."

The voice said, "No need to bother them. Turn on the light in the passage, and we'll fix the wire from the outside."

"We can wake them up, if necessary," we repeated, and that was the end of it. We had heard many such stories about the Hypocrites and the problems they caused inside the country, while, at the same time, we were under constant attack from abroad. Being bombarded by enemy planes had become a regular feature of our lives. Explosions were so routine that when they stopped for half an hour, we felt there was something missing.

In the past the Iraqis would use intelligence supplied by the Hypocrites' spotters to identify inhabited parts of the city and bomb them. In time things got back to normal, and people were less wary of returning to their homes. During our first days in Abadan, there was no activity in the bazaar to speak of, but soon Arab women would come to sell dairy products made with milk from their flocks. A soup person and a kabob place soon joined the bakery that had been operating. Once I was at the bazaar with Mrs. Eqbal, and we saw a shopkeeper selling sweets and okra. We asked him for a kilo of the sweets. He didn't have a box so he grabbed a plastic bag and used his hands to fill it. Mrs. Eqbal asked, "You're using your hands?"

"What should I use, my feet?' the shopkeeper asked.

"But your hands aren't clean."

"Where am I supposed to get plastic gloves? If you want them take them, if not, don't," he said.

Water presented another challenge. At times there was too little, at other times none at all. The public bath didn't have enough hot water to shower. We had to heat some at home and bring it to the bath. I was terrified to go there because of the rats, which would jump down from the walls, landing on our heads and shoulders. To avoid that I was forced, despite my aching kidneys, to stand in the yard fully clothed and wash with cold water. On windy days I was chilled to the bone. After showering so many times in cold water, my skin became very sensitive to chills. My entire body ached, and my arms became chapped and started to bleed.

On April 1, 1982, the army of Khorramshahr invited all the martyr families to Abadan to celebrate Islamic Republic Day. The ceremony and reception, which were attended by many of the families, were held at a building the city called Martyr House. The ceremony also brought mother to Abadan. Not having seen her for months, I rushed to greet her. As we hugged, she whispered endearments in my ear. I laid my head on her shoulder and cried my eyes out. I was so overcome with emotion I couldn't speak.

After spending a few hours with mother, I got up from the floor and was about to do my ablutions before evening prayer, when I overheard people talking about a family bereft of a father and a son, who now had just lost another loved one. They didn't say the name. Dumbstruck, I stared at mother. I didn't know how we would go on. How was I to break the news to her if it turned out to be one of us?

At that time Mohsen and Habib were at the front, and naturally I thought one of them had been killed. After prayers, I sought refuge in the Quran. It opened to the Throne Verse, which I recited and, at the same time, poured out my heart to God, begging Him to help me endure the agony of having to tell mother she had lost another child. Some of the sisters in the army came by to comfort me; Sima Bandari Zadeh was especially sympathetic. Trying hard to appear calm, I sat with mother on the floor, eating supper. The kids' eyes were on me, but I was in my own world, oblivious to what was going on around me. I tore off a bite of food for mother. During the meal, I frequently put my arms around her and kissed her, saying how wonderful it was to see her, but my heart was in turmoil. What would I say?

That night passed without any news. The next day I found out the grieving family's name was indeed Hoseyni, but they were not related to us. Afterward Sima Bandari Zadeh said, "I was watching you the whole time. Your composure was a sight. How you held up like that I don't know!"

All I could say was: "My heart was in shambles. I had to call on the blessed Zeynab."

Two days later they arranged to take the martyr families on a trip. The other sisters and I chose not to go. After the evening prayers, there was a knock on the door, and I was asked to come down. I found Habib standing there covered in blood. "Are you wounded?" I asked.

"Not me. One of the boys was hit."

"You've got blood all over you."

"I grabbed the boy and took him to the hospital, but he died before we got there. I just stopped by to tell you Mohsen is with me and not to worry. Last night there was heavy fighting, and they gave the sector a good pounding. Two of the boys were killed and a number were wounded."

Mother stayed on with us after the ceremonies ended. Habib told her I was pregnant. She was so overjoyed she kissed me many times and said, "It's not right for you to stay here with the shelling and all."

"I'm used to it. Besides, I like this place and wouldn't be able to tear myself away."

We argued back and forth—she telling me to go, me insisting on staying. I took advantage of mother's visit to go to the bath a few times. She would sit behind the cubicle door on the lookout for rats. Her visit lasted a week. When it was time to say goodbye, it was like I was losing part of my body. I can't say how much I missed her. She took Mohsen back to Tehran with her.

Despite all the problems of life in the town—the water shortages, the frequent power cuts, the limited means of communication—people went on with their daily lives. They even celebrated the Return of Ayatollah Khomeini and the Triumph of the Revolution holidays under enemy fire. With danger all around and folks rightly fearing death, many many souls were willing to sacrifice their wealth—even their lives—for others.

During the first months of our marriage, Habib would get leave from time to time and buy things we needed at home, but not everything was available in the area. At one point I had this craving for sour pickles, and we happened to be in the Amiri Bazaar when I got a whiff of them. I asked Habib to get some for me.

"Where are they? I don't see pickles," he said.

"There's this strong smell."

We went around the bazaar until we found a shopkeeper who had boxes of them hidden under other boxes. Habib asked him if he had pickles. Holding a bag filled with them and so as not to be caught in a lie he said, "We had some but these are the last ones."

"So would you give us two of those, please," said Habib.

"They're for somebody else," the shopkeeper said. "They asked me to put them aside."

But then he took out his hidden stash and gave us two kilos, explaining, "So many people have asked for them, I just tell them there are no more. I hide them so as not to disappoint people."

As soon as Habib got the pickles, I wasted no time and finished a whole kilo before we reached home.

Around the time of Operation Fath al-Mobin,[8] Habib and I were returning to Abadan from Tehran. With the bus on the outskirts of Andishmak, the driver wanted to stop for morning prayers. I suddenly heard Habib say in his sleep, "Mamad, Mamad."

I woke him and asked, "What? Who's Mamad? We're in a bus."

Habib woke up and said, "I was dreaming I was sitting in a room with Mohammad Jahan Ara and the other boys who were martyred. We were joking and laughing. I was teasing them. Sitting behind a table, Mohammad Jahan Ara said to me, 'I've come back to take the boys with me. No teasing now or I won't take you.' Then I pointed to the sandwiches and cool drinks on the table and said, 'Give me one of those drinks.' But Mohammad said, 'Take this sandwich.' I took the sandwich but kept on teasing the boys until Jahan Ara threw Farhad Mola'i[9] and me out of the room."

I laughed and said, "You should have had the drink; it was the sherbet of martyrdom."

When we got to Abadan, they told Habib the sector wasn't safe because of the on-going operations, and he shouldn't have brought me. I stayed in Abadan only two weeks and then returned to Tehran. One day the guard at the Kushk Building came to our room saying I was wanted on the phone

I went downstairs to the telephone and heard Habib's voice on the other end of the line. I wondered why he was calling, because I

---

[8] Operation [al-] Fath al-Mobin ["Holy Conquest"] began with the code word "O, Zahra," on March 22, 1982, in the area west of Dezful.

[9] Farhad Mola'i was one of the guards from Khorramshahr.

knew that during operations they cut off communications. "Where are you?" I asked.

"Tehran."

"How did you get here?"

"I didn't come on my own. They brought me."

Startled, I asked, "What do you mean?"

"I'm flat on my back. It seems I took a bite of Mamad's sandwich after all!"

The squad evacuating the wounded said they wanted to take Habib to Dadgostari Hospital.[10] Not knowing Tehran, Habib told them to take him to Molavi Hospital. Uncle Hoseyni, mother, and I went there to see him.

Habib was resting in a large ward along with eight others. They were praying when we got there, and we waited for them to finish. Habib seemed fine on the outside. He had taken a lot of shrapnel on the right side of his body, especially in his leg. "This hospital being so far way is very hard for us to get to," I said to him.

"It's fine. They originally had wanted to take me to Dadgostari, but that's even farther away," he said.

"What do you mean? It's almost next door!"

Habib insisted they release him. We spoke to his doctor, who said, "Impossible. There's a good chance of infection. Some of the shrapnel is near the nerves. He's got to stay here."

The next day he was even more determined to leave the hospital. The doctor said he had to stay. They needed to operate, fearing pieces of shrapnel might be dislodged and get into his blood stream. In the end they had Habib sign a release before we could bring him home where I would look after him and change his bandages dressing. As I was cleaning his wounds, Habib said, "Use a pair of tweezers to take out the shrapnel so it won't be a problem."

"I can't," I said.

I explained I only knew how to give injections and change bandages. I had no experience with surgery. All the shrapnel I had re-

---

[10] Dadgostari Hospital was on Pars Avenue not far from Ferdowsi Square.

moved in the past had been from superficial wounds and that was under the supervision of a doctor or specialist medic. But Habib insisted. The pieces on the surface were easy to get out, but extracting the deeper ones was torture for me. I don't know whether it was because I was pregnant that I had become so sensitive, or whether it was because it was my Habib who was the patient. It was very hard. My body trembled as I dug into his leg with the tweezers, and I cried and cried as I took out pieces of shrapnel. I cleaned the wounds and rebandaged them. Habib was laid up at our place for two weeks, after which he returned to the front.

With the military operations over, I returned to Abadan and resumed married life in Ahmadabad. Some time later Mr. Musavi and Mr. Eqbal Pur went on leave, taking their wives with them, which left me very much on my own. Habib, who was often away at the front, spoke to one of his friends, Mr. Masbubi, and asked if I could stay with his wife at their home. I stayed with them, but once a week Habib would return and we would go home together. The next day I would return to the Masbubis.

As we were going back and forth, something occurred that told me Habib's eyes were not quite right. He had been driving in the war zone with his lights off so long he had trouble with his night vision. "Something seems to be the matter with your eyes," I said.

"No, my vision is fine," he said as we drove. "I'm okay driving in the dark, thank God."

At that point we were approaching a traffic circle, and I could tell he didn't see it because he didn't slow down or veer toward the entrance. "Careful!" I warned him. "We're going to hit the curb."

"Impossible. We not at the circle yet."

No sooner did he say that when the front wheels climbed the curb. "Evidently the circle is not in the right place tonight," I said.

Once we were driving home when a mortar round or a shell—I don't remember which—hit our house, destroying a good part of the second story and collapsing the ceiling of the first. The house was a shambles with dirt and debris everywhere. We had to find another place to live.

Mrs. Musavi and Mrs. Eqbal Pur had gone to Ahvaz, but I was left homeless in Abadan. We found a place in Braym, a spacious neighborhood with a desert feel to it, where workers for Abadan radio and television had been housed. There were seventeen houses in all: eight pairs of attached duplex villas and one home larger than the others, apparently the residence of the network head.

Each pair of houses was separated from the next by an open triangular area. The homes had three entrances and raised terraces lined with flowerpots. There were tables and chairs on the terraces. The homes had roomy, green backyards, and there was a large park in the neighborhood with a playground for children. Rows of boxwoods ensured privacy. The English-style homes stood on asphalt lanes that branched off from the main road. On the first floor were a kitchen, storage closets, a large hall, a living room, and a full bath. The living room opened onto the terrace. Steps led down from the terrace to the lawn. On the second floor, over the kitchen, was a bedroom. A hallway led from the bedroom to a bridging walkway to another full bath. The homes had been abandoned since the outbreak of the war. The residents had carted away all their personal possessions, leaving behind only large pieces of furniture. We arranged to have our things moved to the new home. The place was filthy, but were no rats—they probably hadn't been able find anything to eat. It was teeming with geckos, though. The first time I saw one of these creatures, I jumped on the hall table and stayed there until Habib killed it. Then he went after the others and managed to get rid of about eight of them.

With a lot of effort we managed to clean up the place. Shock waves from the bomb blasts had shattered all the glass in the picture windows lining the place. Habib replaced them with thick black plastic sheeting, which gave us privacy and protected us from the rain and wind. The front door had been knocked off its hinges by a mortar round. We replaced it by nailing a sheet of waterproof canvas and a blanket to the doorframe and made the kitchen door the new entrance to the house. Every once in a while, a mortar shell would knock out the power. Repairmen would come and restore it, and then there would be another round and then another.

Water trickled from a faucet at the side of the house. The pressure was so low it took an hour to wash the pots. When people in the adjoining house were using water, ours would stop completely. Soon even the trickle from our spigot ceased. We were told the main supply had been shut off. Every few days, tankers from the army came around to fill the cisterns. After they hooked up the pipes from the central source, water flowed by itself again, but since the well in our kitchen was blocked up and we had no way of unclogging it, water backed up regularly, and the house filled with sewer gas. The kitchen stove didn't work, and there was no refrigerator.

A few months after we moved in, I became a mother, which under normal conditions was difficult, but under these was almost impossible. It was the height of summer, and by 8:00 a.m. temperatures would reach 135, leaving me with no choice but to cook outside over an open fire on the lawn. Habib would say to me, "There's no need for you to work like that and put so much pressure on yourself."

"I'm not doing anything here to help. You're the soldier. At least allow me to look after you."

But he wouldn't listen, and on days he was home he did all the washing, even my clothes. Nevertheless, when he wasn't home, I tried my best—hard as it was—to do housework. There were times, however, when the pain in my back was so bad I couldn't move; it felt like I had a needle in my spine. Often I had to sweep the house crawling on all fours.

Our house was located on the edge of the development. It wasn't the safest place because Hypocrites were always prowling around and knocking on doors to see if the men were at home. They were particularly curious about the houses in the raido and television development because they knew military families were living in them. In time I knew all the women in the neighborhood. Either we had been friends before or we had been introduced through our husbands. We visited back and forth regularly.

Among all these friends, the person I would say I was closest to was Batul Kazeruni.

We met one day when Tahereh Bandari Zadeh came by, saying, "Come, let's go to Batul's house."

"Who's Batul?" I asked.

"Saleh Musavi's wife."

"I've heard of her, but I don't think we've met."

I put on my chador and we walked to Batul's house, which was in the middle of the development next to the Bandari Zadehs'. To the best of my memory, it was April around the time they were going through initial stages of Operation Beyt al-Moqaddas. As we walked mortar rounds went off everywhere, peppering the area with shrapnel. Tahereh and I would stop and point to the places where the metal landed. I looked up and saw Javad Kazeruni standing at a window, making gestures and angrily shouting at us to get out of the way.

We paid no attention. "Let him shout," Tahereh said.

When we were inside, Javad growled, "Are you two tired of living, or what? Didn't you notice it was raining mortars out there?"

Ignoring him, we went to Batul's room, and, the minute I saw her, it hit me: she and I had gotten into an argument back in Tehran. It happened before I was married, during Moharram. I had gone to Mr. Mohammadi's apartment for a visit. They had been moved from their place at the officer's college to a building across from Laleh Park. The building had two sections: one for the martyr families and the other for refugees.

Since all the residents of the building were Khuzestani, they were holding the mourning ceremonies the way they did back home. I had gone to Mr. Mohammadi's building to take part in the ceremonies. It was the eve of the tenth day of Moharram, and I saw a good-looking young woman with a lively sense of humor talking and laughing with the women around her. Offended by seeing someone telling jokes on such a solemn occasion, I was furious and yelled at her, "You think this is funny? We're supposed to be mourning the death of the Martyr. If you want to make jokes, go home and let the other people mourn his death."

Things got out of hand, and they called in security. We went to the guard office, where the matter was settled. Now I found myself the guest of the same woman with her lively sense of humor.

Batul was in a bad way. She was at her wits end with her baby Hajar. She said, "She won't sleep, so I have to stay up with her all night." Weak from lack of sleep, she fell behind in her chores. Although neither of us brought up the incident, it was embarrassing to be in the same room with her. I tried to make up for it by doing housework for her. Our friendship dates back to that time. One day we were talking and joking, and Batul, a very blunt and straightforward person, asked, "Do you remember that night?"

"Yeah, may it rest in peace!"

"You were really serious, huh?"

"Yeah, but you just wouldn't stop carrying on."

With preparations for Operation Beyt al-Moqaddas in their final stages, Habib begged me to go back to Tehran.

I said, "I'm staying." Faithful to the vow he had made to let me be with him wherever he was, Habib didn't pursue the matter. He only said, "Whatever you think best, but I feel it'd be safer if you went away."

Leila had gotten married shortly after I did and had moved to Isfahan. A few days before the operation, Leila's husband, Hoseyn Ta'i Nezhad, came to our house and asked Habib, "Why is she still here?"

"She's intent on staying."

"Meaning what? She's said she's staying, and that's that?"

"I can't convince her she should go."

Turning to me, Hoseyn said, "It's not right for you to stay. Habib'll be worried about you. There's nobody to look after you. The sector is very dangerous. It's not just your life that's at stake here!"

We went back and forth like that for a while, but, knowing I couldn't say no to my brother-in-law, I finally gave in. Hoseyn said, "Go to Isfahan and spend a few days with your sister. She's all by herself. But don't go anywhere for now. Wait until we come for you."

Habib's duties prevented him from taking me to Isfahan himself. After a few days Hoseyn came and drove me there. I hadn't seen Leila in five months, but since I was only able to stay with her for a few days, I soon found myself stuck in Tehran again.

With the start of operations, they stopped all nonmilitary traffic in and out of the war zone. My exit and entry permits were revoked, and I couldn't even get through by telephone or by mail. Every once in a while, I got an inkling of what was happening from soldiers convalescing in the hospitals.

Khorramshahr was finally liberated on May 24, 1982, at 2:00 p.m. It was difficult to express what we felt hearing the news. Cries of joy echoed throughout our building, and people hugged and cried. Passersby and neighbors from Tehran congratulated us. Everyone was delirious. We left the building and saw that office workers had left their desks and taken to the streets to celebrate. There was pandemonium. I stopped a van in the street and hopped on with the kids in tow. I told the driver to go to Jamaran, but we weren't able to see the Imam because he was meeting with officials. They wouldn't let us in no matter what we said. We weren't the only ones; many people had come to congratulate the Imam and express their joy. We went back to the city in the same van and went around the streets. Tehran was a madhouse. Wherever we went, people were handing out sweets and offering sherbet. Drivers drove with their lights on and honked their horns. Many people were waving Iranian flags. During those moments, memories of the martyrs came to mind, and when tears of sadness mixed with cries of joy it was a thing of beauty. The feeling of what it was like to be in that special moment is impossible to describe.

The day of celebration came to an end, but we still didn't have any word from the front. I kept cursing myself for being persuaded to come to Tehran. I wanted to be there to celebrate. The first thing I said to Habib when I finally made contact was that I wanted to return to Abadan.

Mohsen and I wasted no time and went back. Not all the ladies of the radio and television neighborhood had returned, but the female soldiers were there.

Many of the men from Khorramshahr were killed during Operation Beyt al-Moqaddas. Among the martyrs were Gholam Reza, Ali Reza Abkar, Abdol Reza Musavi (Jahan Ara's successor as commander), and Esma'il Khosravi, Rabab Husori's husband. Rabab gave birth to their daughter Vadi'eh several days after her husband's martyrdom.

Habib replaced Mahmud Rabi'i as the person in charge of the Moharrezi district. During the occupation of Khorramshahr, the area was actually the first line of defense for Iranian forces against the Iraqis. Most of the military and officials who visited the sector came to Moharrezi. Ayatollah Khameneh'i and Mr. Mahdavi Kani both came on inspection tours. Because the district was considered a battle zone, entry was strictly forbidden to civilians, especially women. Nevertheless, I insisted Habib take me there. He hated the idea, but when he saw I had my heart set on at least going to the Abadan-Khorramshahr Highway, he took me to the area below Airport Circle.

36

Life Returns to Devastated Khorramshahr

With Khorramshahr liberated, I begged Habib to take me there as soon as he could. I desperately want to see my city, but they had yet to give permission to civilians to inspect the damage and take up residence. When Habib finally said, "Let's go and see Khorramshahr," I couldn't contain myself. After almost two years, I was going home. I thirsted to see it, imagining it was the same old place I had known. Little did I know what had actually happened to the city. The first thing I saw was the bridge over the waterway linking the city to the southern parts (Kut-e Sheikh, Moharrezi, and, finally, the Abadan Road) had been destroyed. We went over a pontoon dubbed "Liberty" to get to the other side.

I couldn't believe my eyes. There was no sign of the city I knew; it had been leveled. I had no idea where I was. As we toured the ruins, Habib had to remind me what had been there before the war. Everything was strange and new to me now. I couldn't tell whether what I was seeing was an avenue, a traffic circle, or a residence—the whole place was reduced to rubble. All that remained of the houses were piles of dirt studded with bits of steel. The only things standing in the broad squares were markers the Iraqis had posted to show where mines were. They were in such a hurry to get out of the city they didn't have time to take them down.

First, we went to the Congregational Mosque, which, though badly damaged, still stood. I went inside and was reminded of the first days of the war. Nothing was left of the Sheybani clinic but a pile of rubble. I rummaged through the debris hoping to find Ali's bag but didn't find anything. Later I learned from Sabah it had been lost.

The city was as unfamiliar on the way back as it was when we entered. Even though the Taleqani district had not been hit as hard as other areas, the homes there had seen so much damage it felt like I was on foreign soil. Seeing what remained of our home brought back memories of father and Ali.

I heard their voices, the sounds they made as they were constructing the house, the house we had all pitched in to make. Saddam's troops not only killed the residents, they destroyed their homes and looted their possessions. They even carted off parts of the metal gate to our yard, which they used to cover their bunkers. The relatively large kitchen and bathroom part of the house was gone. The roof had caved in. But, in spite of it all, the Taleqani district fared better than the other parts of the city.

We went to Jennatabad next. The graves were a mess, and the markers were gone. I went to grieve over father and Ali, but I was too shocked by what I saw to cry.

As we stood over Ali's grave, Habib explained what had happened the day he saw Ali on the battlefield. "Ten days into the battle, we were at Railroad Circle fighting the Iraqis all day and into the night. Then they attacked with a large number of tanks. The boys told me Seyyed Ali had come. 'Which Ali?' I asked them. 'Seyyed Ali Hoseyni.' A few minutes later, I saw Ali crouching before an Iraqi tank with an RPG in his hands. He got up and took aim at the tank, but before he could fire, the tank's canon went off, hitting the wall behind him and demolishing it. The air was so thick with dust and smoke I couldn't see a thing. I was frantic—we were very close friends. It was just his luck, I thought, for him to show up at that moment and be killed. The thought was suddenly interrupted by a figure emerging from the smoke. It was Ali standing there like a man of steel. He had been caught in the blast, but to everyone's relief he had made it. I didn't see him after that. Our fighting with the Iraqis continued. The boys knocked out several of their tanks. Around sunset Jahan Ara ordered us back for a breather. He said we'd been fighting for almost two days straight, and he'd replace us with reinforcements.

We returned to the Darya Bod Rasayi School, which was our base. Taqi Mohsenifar, Ali Vatankhah, boys from the Aqajari unit, a few others, and I stretched out on the floor in the foyer on the first floor and talked. I asked Mohsenifar, who was sitting across from me with an RPG round beside him, where Ali was. He said Ali had gone to see his mother with Hoseyn Ta'i Nezhad. Later we were still talking when Ali Vatankhah and few other boys went over to the door and tried to sleep. I warned them not to, because the spot was directly in the line of fire. They needed to sleep somewhere away from the door closer to our side of the room. They got up, and a few moments later the Iraqis opened fire. Even though the sounds were steadily getting nearer, none of us imagined the Iraqis would bomb the base. Everybody agreed they were firing blind, but just then a shell landed in the yard. The next shell hit in the doorway, and the next landed right in the middle of our group. At that moment the last thing I heard was Ali Vatankhah shouting 'God is great.' I don't know what happened after that. I thought I'd had it. After a while, I opened my eyes, but I couldn't see a thing. I ran my hands over my body. My legs were okay. I still had hands, a head, so I thought I was in heaven. But then I saw I wasn't; my arms and legs were moving but sluggishly. There was something wrong with my eyes and ears. I couldn't get to my feet no matter how hard I tried. The blast made my body feel like lead. I breathed in so much dust I nearly choked to death. Crawling to the doorway was pure hell; it felt like I was treading through flesh and bone. As fresh air entered my lungs, I realized I was outside. Then I called out to Ali Vatankhah. It was pitch dark, and I couldn't see a thing. After a few minutes, Ali emerged from the building, and we stood there not knowing what to do. The Iraqis kept shelling. We went into the alley where we found several soldiers from the Aqajari unit, but, unfamiliar with the neighborhood, the poor guys didn't know where to go. As we were about to leave the alley, I noticed three of them standing behind us. We decided to wait for things to quiet down, but just at that moment a very well dressed man came out of nowhere and asked, 'What happened?' 'They blasted our base and tore the boys to bits,' I told him. 'The shell landed in the base?' he repeated. 'Yeah, a couple of them,' I said. As we spoke it dawned on me that it was odd to find someone dressed so nicely in the middle of a war. But even before I had finished speaking, he was gone, and I never saw him again. Later on I figured out he was one of the Fifth Columnists who were target spotting for the Iraqis. He wanted to make sure the shells had landed were they were supposed to."

When Habib finished, I didn't say anything. I just wanted to go on and see the rest of the city, but the road leading to the slaughterhouse and traffic police headquarters was closed off. The Iraqis were still in Shalamcheh. We turned around, and Habib, sensing I was in a state of shock, continued to explain what had happened while I just listened. We continued touring the city until 2:00 p.m. When we got back to our house, the lump in my throat burst, and I started weeping. It didn't feel like that when I first heard the city had fallen. Perhaps I still had hopes it would be rebuilt. But now I couldn't bear to look at it. I kept thinking about the cruelties inflicted on the city and visualizing all the young people slaughtered and homes destroyed by the enemy.

Some time later, mother along with a few of our relatives on father's side arrived in Khorramshahr for a visit. The next day Habib took us to Jennatabad. Even before we got to the bridge, she was weeping softly and moaning things in Kurdish and Arabic.

Two years had passed since she last saw father and Ali. Their gravestones were covered in soil brought by the rains. It seemed the Iraqis had purposely damaged them to keep people from finding the graves of their loved ones. Mother was frantic. I showed her where father and Ali were buried. She threw herself on the graves and kissed the ground. She spoke mostly to Ali and wept. Modesty apparently kept her from speaking to father in front of others.

As if the agony of losing a husband and a son were still fresh in her mind, she emptied her heart out to them. Her withering howls and cries went on and on. Weeping ourselves, Leila and I tried to comfort her. After a while, I went and sat in a corner, reminiscing about the days I had spent there. After all this time, mother still couldn't believe Ali was gone. At home the slightest thing would revive memories of him, and she would cry. I would often have to escape from her, because she just wouldn't see reason. His was the only voice she'd listen to. She tried to get me to go out with her to find Ali or she would say, "If I could only stand over his corpse and unlock what is in my heart." It reached the point that sometimes I found myself shouting at her. I couldn't help getting angry with her for not accepting her son was dead. I wondered why every so often she had to say things that were torture to me. As I screamed at her and showed how upset I was by beating my head with my fists, she would whimper pathetically. That was when I just had to leave the house and walk aimlessly in the streets until I was calm again. I had no choice but to flee. At times she got so desperate, she'd say, "Why couldn't he have just lost his arms and legs? Why didn't he merely break his back?" No matter how many times I told her that such talk was torment to the souls of father and Ali and that she was ruining any chance of a heavenly reward for herself, she wouldn't listen.

I finally had to take mother to the military sanatorium in Niavaran. I showed her paraplegics, quadriplegics, and soldiers suffering from shock, and said, "Look at the agony they're in. Is that what you want for Ali?" She calmed down and said, "Thank God Ali was martyred."

Some time later I introduced mother to a woman called Afrasiabi, who lost five sons in the war and still kept up her spirits. I reminded her, "We've got to remember there are families who've lost more than two loved ones."

I would say such things to mother even though I myself couldn't stand not having father and Ali around. I missed them so much they would appear in my dreams and guide me. In one dream Ali came to us, upset for some reason. We hugged and kissed. I knew he had been martyred, but because it had been a while since he appeared in my dreams, I complained, "It's been such a long time. What kept you?"

He said, "I've got a house full of guests." Then mother entered the room, and Ali scowled at her and turned away. I said, "Ali, it's been so long since she's seen you. Why are you behaving like that?"

He said, "I can't stand to see her crying so much."

Mother was very moved when I told her my dream. "What should I do?" she asked. "My heart just won't be still."

"By all means have a good cry," I suggested, "but not for us, rather for the sufferings of the blessed Zeynab and Imam Hoseyn."

I was repeating what grandfather would always tell me when the subject of Ashura and Imam Hoseyn came up. "We Seyyeds have come into the world, it seems, to suffer the way our holy forbearers suffered. We are descendants of a prophet who endured great pain. Seyyeds cannot be the same as other folk. God has given us the gifts of pain and suffering so we'll know what our forbearers were forced to go through for Islam, so we'll appreciate our faith."

We stayed a few hours in Jennatabad and around noon took mother to our old municipality-provided home. She peered into every nook and cranny and, with each look, dredged up memories of our life before the war. The Iraqis had looted most of our things and ruined the things that were of no use to them. Clothes, bedding, and foodstuffs father had stored up before the war had been strewn in the yard. The miserable Iraqis even littered the house with rice. They pried open our big cooking oil can, dumped mice in it, and then closed the lid. I looked for my picture album but couldn't find it. The only pictures left were a framed one of father and a group picture on the wall of the room Leila and I shared. Evidently they didn't have time to take them. I found a roll of film among the piles of clothing. Mother salvaged some souvenirs from the debris, but I was so sickened by what I saw that possessions seemed to lose all value. During the war, death could come any moment in the form of shrapnel, a missile, or a mortar shell. I had to be prepared to die, and I wasn't the only one who felt this way. All the folks in the region had this mentality. This was why I had no interest in keepsakes. The only thing of sentimental value was father's old welding motor, which he kept, thinking it might be of use to a soldier.[1]

The day we went to Jennatabad was a bad one for mother. The stress threw her into a depression that went on for several days. She withdrew deeply into herself, and no matter what Leila and I did to

---

[1] In 1991, after the Iraq war with Kuwait, those family members of mine who were in Iraq came to Iran. They told us the Iraqis had used the pictures looted from Iranian homes in large exhibitions marking their conquest of Khorramshahr.

get her out of it and change the subject, we couldn't. Mother insisted on going back to Khorramshahr every day, but because the area hadn't been swept clean, revisiting it was difficult.

At checkpoint after checkpoint on the road, soldiers tried to dissuade people from entering the city. No place was safe, they said. Mines had been placed in various parts. The inhabitants, who had been far from their city for ages, were desperate to go back. Mother insisted on returning and staying for good, but we argued every way we could to convince her it was impossible. The whole time she was in Abadan, we would visit Khorramshahr every few days. We gave the roll of film we found in the rubble to a photographer for developing. Some of the negatives had been burned, but the ones that came out were of Ali and his friends.

As we roamed around the city, a poem performed at the Congregational Mosque after the liberation of Khorramshahr kept running through my mind:

How dispossessed they are
The dear friends have left home.
Our candle is burned,
And so is our moth.
Our wine cups are smashed,
And there is blood in our hearts.
Full of cries and howls
Of the drinkers in the tavern.
Wherever I looked,
Wherever I went,
I saw only blood and ashes,
Ruin after ruin.
Heads lolling to one side,
Hair crimson with blood,
Nowhere is there a hand
To comb the hair.

So long as there is a head on
this body,
These clothes will be a shroud.
The cries of Abu Zarr
Have blocked the enemy's path
Where are the smiles of joy?
Where are the giddy heads and thrills?
The wine jugs are upended,
Spilled is the wine from the goblets.
Torched are the haystacks,
Woe is me! Woe is me!
Woe to my dear friends,
Woe to the blooms of my spring.
The dear friends have left home,
How dispossessed they are! [2]

[2] The poem is by Mr. Parviz Beygi Habibabadi.

Enemy fire intensified after the liberation of Khorramshahr. Our side moved an artillery base near where we lived. The shelling was often so heavy we rarely left home. The houses were shaken to their foundations, while the outsides were being sprayed with or actually penetrated by shrapnel. With the passage of time the destruction grew worse, and the plastic we put over the windows was always being torn away. The Hypocrites continued to harass us as well. One night somebody cut the plastic sheeting at Abbas Parhizkar's house, apparently trying to enter. When they switched on the lights, the intruder ran away. This happened to several people in the area, which is why I slept in the storage closet when Habib wasn't home. The small room had carpeting on the floor and was the safest place I could think of. Even on those sweltering nights in Abadan, I had to be constantly vigilant. I slept with my chador, overcoat, pants, and headscarf at hand. If I was to be martyred, I thought, at least I'd preserve my modesty.

I had become fed up with the scorching heat, but there was no remedy except to grin and bear it. Our cooler didn't work, and it got so bad one day I came down with heat stroke. I said to Habib, "It's impossible to take this heat. You've got to get the cooler to run."

"I won't use things that don't belong to me," he said.

"Fine. When they gave us permission to live here, did it include permission to use the cooler?"

"No."

"I can take it for now, but you've got to think of our child who is about to be born. The baby won't be able to take the heat."

"Any child of mine will have to take hardship," he declared.

Later, having consulted a cleric about the legality of using a cooler that didn't belong to us, Habib was satisfied that it was okay. That same night Hoseyn, Leila's husband, said to Habib, "You're away from home weeks on end. If your wife, given the state she's in, had a problem, there'd be no one to come to her aid."

That night we agreed Hoseyn would bring Leila from Isfahan so she could live with us. I was overjoyed that I would no longer be alone. The bouts of insomnia, the anxiety, and the nights in the storage closet were over.

Leila and I were under the same roof again, talking and recalling the past. My prayers had come true. Some memories brought us to tears, while others made us laugh.

37

Abdollah's Close Call

About to give birth, I naturally went to the Taleqani Hospital on the Abadan-Khorramshahr highway, but the operating rooms there were reserved for wounded soldiers. The doctors advised me that under the circumstances it would be better if I went to a hospital in another city. It was September and I had Zeynab, Sa'id, and Hasan with me, as they had come to Abadan during the school summer vacation. There was no choice but to go back to Tehran. My kidney condition had made it necessary to take painkillers and antibiotics and have x-rays taken, which raised the specter, doctors said, of harm to the fetus. This made me focus all my thoughts and prayers on the health of my baby, but I tried my best to remain optimistic. "God can give me the ugliest baby in the world," I prayed, "so long it's healthy."

A week later Habib joined me in Tehran. I was so sick the last week of my pregnancy I didn't sleep a wink. Not wanting to disturb the others, I would leave the bedroom and pace up and down in the hall. Mother would come out and sit on the steps. On the last night I couldn't even walk to the hallway. I was in torment and that night went to the hospital, which was full of wounded soldiers undergoing operations. My son was born in the late afternoon of the next day. I went into shock and lost consciousness from the intense pain and all the other problems associated with giving birth. I woke up worried about the child's condition. Aware of my fears, doctors assured me the baby was fine. There was an elevated heartbeat, but this was to be expected given the sounds of explosions he was exposed to during my pregnancy. Nevertheless, they kept me and the baby under observation in the hospital for three days.

The baby and I returned to the Kushk Building on October 2, 1982. Aunt Salimeh and Leila, who had a one-month-old herself, were already in Tehran. My mother's room was packed—two babies, our crowd, even guests visiting us.

That night it got dark early, but, still unwell, I couldn't get to sleep and paced in the hall instead. All of a sudden there was a horrific explosion, followed by the sounds of breaking glass. My first thought was that the municipal building across the street had exploded, but people said it was the Telecommunications Building or the Artillery Building on Imam Square. I spent that night in a state of terrible anxiety. The sounds of sirens, ambulances coming and going, and fire engines droned on until morning. On the news the next day they announced many were dead.

Three days later, I realized from the way she reacted that mother wasn't very fond of the names "Hoseyn" or "Ali" for the baby. We called him "Abdollah" instead. After around two and a half weeks, we decided to return to Abadan. Aunt Salimeh suggested we go to Khorramabad first. She wanted show Abdollah to grandfather.

Grandfather was doing his morning prayers when we arrived in Khorramabad. After he finished, he turned to us, and the minute his eyes fell on Abdollah he burst into tears. Mimi asked in her Kurdish accent, "Are you insane, old man? Why are you crying?"

"He's the image of Ali when he was a baby," grandfather explained.

He got up and took baby Abdollah in his arms and kissed him. He whispered the call and the beginning of the prayer into his ear. While we were in Khorramabad, it was mainly grandfather who held Abdollah in his arms. A few days later we left for Abadan.

Mimi came to Khorramshahr for a visit a month after we had returned. Seeing the city after all that time was emotional for her as well. On a visit to Ali's grave, she said, "I never believed I would outlive him."

Mimi had been a great help to our family, especially to Ali and Mohsen. With mother having one baby after another, she was the one who cared for us children more than anyone else. We felt more comfortable speaking to her than mother, who had her own difficulties. Mimi was kinder to us. In Basra she would patiently tell us bedtime stories.

At grandfather's request, we went to their home to find the scroll with the family tree. Everything had been looted. There was no trace of Aunt Salimeh's wedding gifts, which had been stored in boxes, but among the junk the Saddamites left behind we found the family tree. Because it was so dear to him, grandfather had put the scroll in a bamboo flute and hid the flute in a metal pipe. Every time I saw the pipe I was reminded of the bows and arrows of ancient times. Finding the flute made me very happy because I knew this was the best gift we could give grandfather.

It was fall when Mimi went back to grandfather's house, and the weather was getting chilly. With the many holes in the wall our house was drafty, and because there was no heater we froze. Despite the plastic we put around the doors and over the windows, the biting cold found its way inside. Because it was small and heated up quickly, the closet became the baby's room.

Abdollah got bigger and more lovable by the day. He was a trouble-free child and a hit with the neighbors, who were always taking him home.

As there were no children's stores to speak of in Khorramshahr, I had a hard time finding diapers and clothing for Abdollah. It was like we lived on a desert island. I had to ask anyone heading to cities outside the zone to bring back things for the baby. Whenever Ali Shushtari came back from the front to visit his sister, he would ask her to have Abdollah around. Once when I was there and before Ali had even arrived, I heard him tell her to go and get Abdollah. She told him Abdollah was already there.

I knew the Shustari family from childhood. The father was the caretaker at our school. Because of that acquaintance, I felt comfortable saying hello and joking with him, saying, "Brother Shushtari, your name isn't on Abdollah's official visit list, so you'll have to wait your turn."

He said, "You'll have to excuse me this time. I'll be gone soon, and this will probably be the last time I see him again."

"You're forgiven this time, but next time I won't be so lenient!"

"I don't think there'll be a next time. My time is up."

Then he left and, sure enough, he was martyred during the next operation. I was in his sister Fatemeh's home the day they brought the news. She accepted it calmly and went to pray and give thanks for his martyrdom. I appreciated what she was feeling at that moment. As she bowed in prayer, it seemed as if her back was breaking, but she stayed strong, never shedding a tear. When she laughed, though, it was no ordinary laugh.

One night when he was about three months old, Abdollah suddenly became ill. He kept vomiting, but I had no idea why. That night he soiled every stitch of clothing he had. The next morning I got up to feed and clean him. Around 9:00 a.m. I laid him outside on a mattress on the terrace so he could get some sun. I put mosquito netting around him and went to the tanker truck with a basin to wash his things. The water pressure was low, and it took two hours to clean the clothes. Then, with the sound of mortar shells in the distance, I patiently hung them on the line. Used to the explosions, I ignored them and went on with the work.

After all the clothes were on the line, I picked up the basin and was about to step away when I heard a high-pitched whine coming closer and closer. From the sound it seemed like a 230 mm shell. I raced to Abdollah, who was about ten meters away, but it seemed the whole world had gone to pieces. Rocks, shrapnel, and earth went flying through the air. I managed to keep running toward him through the dense cloud of smoke and dust. I yelled out to the Lord of Time at the top of my lungs to give me strength. Pieces of our home came shooting out at me. Terrified by what I might see, I didn't dare open my eyes. I groped for Abdollah's mattress and found the mosquito netting studded with shrapnel. Large chunks of cement studded with stones were strewn around—as if a truck had dumped them there on purpose. I picked up Abdollah and looked him over carefully. To my amazement there was no blood, not even a scratch on his body. It seemed he was still asleep, but then I thought—God forbid he had had a heart attack! I put my ear to his chest and heard his heart beating rapidly. Realizing the baby was fine and had actually slept through the horrid noise, I nuzzled him and wept. This was the first time I had had a good cry since the explosion at the Islamic Republican headquarters.

My screams brought Mrs. Gol Bahar, a neighbor, running from her home. I heard her call out to her husband, "Mohammad, run! Something terrible's happened to Abdollah!" As I said, because there weren't many babies or children in our place, people in the radio and television homes had adopted Abdollah. Before I knew it, I saw the whole neighborhood had gathered in the yard near our house. A few moments later, an ambulance, siren blaring, pulled up. A medic came out and asked, "What happened? Who's hurt?"

"Nobody, thank God!" I said.

Later people would tell the story of how their favorite baby boy caught a 230 mm shell with his hand and hurled it back at the Iraqis.

After that good cry, I got up and went to see what happened to the clothing hanging on the line. It was gone and so was the clothesline. Shredded baby clothes lay here and there among the rocks, and plastic buttons were fused to the scorched cement. At first I wrongly assumed the shell had landed on our house, but it had struck the top of Mrs. Abbaspur's duplex, which was next to ours. The well-built English roof took most of the impact, saving the rest of the house. There was only a big hole in the ceiling. Luckily Mrs. Abbaspur was not home, having gone to the hospital to give birth to her second child. Her husband, Yusof, had been killed by Hypocrites a few months before. He stipulated in his will that the baby, if a boy, should take his name.

Mrs. Abbaspur didn't return to Abadan after the shell hit her home. Relatives came to pack up her things and send them on to her. Watching them emptying the house, I recalled the first time I met the late Mr. Abbaspur. I had been working at the clinic. At that time the uniformed soldiers and paramilitaries, who were sorely needed at the front, had priority. Mr. Abbaspur and Fatemeh, pregnant at the time with their first child, Zohreh, were waiting in line to see the doctor. Mr. Abbaspur complained, "We've been here a long time. How come you're letting the soldiers in ahead of us?" I said, "We take the military first; it makes no difference whether they're regular army or paramilitary, because they have to get back to the front."

Yusof said, "Fine, but I'm paramilitary myself."

"How was I supposed to know that? I'm no mind reader," I said. "You should have said something."

As luck would have it, we became neighbors. Whenever I saw a gecko in our house, I would go out and call out, "Zohreh, Zohreh!" This was a signal to Mr. Abbaspur that another one of those creatures was in our home. Then he would come, slipper in hand, and kill it.

The Abbaspur home remained empty after the shell hit it and I no longer dared put Abdollah out on the terrace. Instead I would pull aside the plastic and blanket and lay him down in front of the open window. Friends joked, "Happy now? What a safe place you've found for the baby! Now if the ceiling falls in, he'll be crushed."

"That's in God's hands," I told them.

38

Hoseyn Eidi Dies

One day in January 1983, Habib came by in a strange mood. "Has something happened?" I asked. He forced a smile and said, "Hoseyn Eidi is dead. He was killed."

The news was a real shock. It was unbelievable. The dark-faced boy with frizzy hair, whom I had known since childhood, was gone. I recalled the first time I saw Hoseyn and Abdollah working at Jennatabad. I didn't think they'd be of any use, but they turned out to be more sympathetic to the grieving and worked harder than all the others. Hoseyn and I were about the same age. He would always call me "sister," and I actually thought of him as a brother. The news of his passing reopened the deep wound made by Ali's death. The grief I felt was so awful I longed for my own death. Habib, as usual, remained his consoling self, telling me, "Martyrdom was the path they chose themselves. There's no cause for grief." That was what he'd usually say, but whenever I asked him to come with me to the cemetery where his martyred comrades were buried, he would make excuses. He was very depressed and withdrawn for a few days. Apparently being around the boys dredged up painful memories. He would say, "I can't understand why I'm still here, when everybody else is gone." Hoseyn served under Habib, and they were very close.

I asked Habib how Hoseyn had died. "We were in the process of clearing areas in Khorramshahr," he said, "and Hoseyn, Mohammad Reza Pur Heydari, and Morteza Kazemi had gathered unexploded mortar shells to load them into a van so they could be defused elsewhere. En route the van hit a pothole, and one of the shells exploded, setting off the rest. This sent Hoseyn and the driver flying from the vehicle, but his entire body was horribly burned. The bodies of Reza Pur Heydari and Morteza Kazemi were mangled beyond recognition. I saw pictures of their corpses. The only thing that remained of Kazemi was a strip of flesh and of Heydari an ankle. They rushed Hoseyn to the hospital, but he was so badly burned he didn't last more than twenty-four hours."

The brothers had made a recording of what Hoseyn said during his last terrible hours. They buried the three of them in Jennatabad, and the army held a memorial service. With the families in attendance, they played the tape of Hoseyn's last words. The sound wasn't clear because even his voice box had been burned, but we could make out him praying to the Lord of Time.

Hoseyn had always been a regular visitor at our home—especially after Abdollah was born. He was very fond of the baby, and the day after the shell hit, he came by to hug and kiss him. "Abdollah," he joked, "you're a regular antiaircraft battery!"

Every time he had to go to Tehran on a mission, Hoseyn would come to our door and ask whether I needed anything for the baby.

Hoseyn's death brought back memories of the first days of the war. I specifically remembered how I felt seeing Abdollah Mo'avi lying neglected in the hospital. At least I had seen Hoseyn whole and healthy before he died. But still, hearing of his death, I wanted to die myself. All the boys I knew were dying one after another, and so were the men in our neighborhood. It was unbelievable for me to be speaking to them one afternoon and to hear they had been killed the next. Here would be a neighbor in the flesh one day, and the next you'd be marching in his funeral procession.

At such times I would turn for comfort to a woman who was like a mother to me, Sima Bandari. She had a knack for getting me through the hard times. "Hoseyn's gone," I said to her, "and I wish I were dead."

Sima said, "When Majid Khayyat Zadeh was killed, Batul Kazeruni said the same thing."

After Hoseyn's death, his mother moved into one of the radio and television homes. They held a memorial service for him in her house, and his forty-day remembrance coincided with Ramadan. Since one of Hoseyn's favorite foods was a fish called *bayah*,[1] his mother prepared a large number of them to break the fast. That night Hoseyn's sister gave birth to a baby girl, but his death had so jarred her mentally she couldn't take the baby. Hoseyn's mother, who was far better off than his sister, cared for the girl instead. I checked in on them regularly to see how they were doing.

---

[1] *Bayah*, a small fish like mullet, are plentiful in the spring and autumn.

39

Family Transitions

With me being in Abadan and my family far away in Tehran, what was happening to my little sister and brothers was a concern. I constantly worried about what were they up to. Who were their friends? I would call regularly to keep tabs on them, asking Hasan to tell me about Mansur and vice versa. I didn't worry about Sa'id, who always had been a quiet, obedient child. Hasan was also a good boy, although he could be very naughty and willful at times. They were still young and I could control them. Mansur, who had gone through a difficult phase and was now on his own, worried me the most. Unfortunately, there was a problem with drugs and even alcohol in the Kushk Building. One of the men ran a drug ring, calling it the "The Association for Mourning Imam Hoseyn." Afraid Mansur might get involved, I overcame my disgust at having to deal with such characters and pulled the boy out of it. I told him, "I don't want you to get mixed up with such people. There's no telling what they'll do in the Imam's name."

All my efforts went into seeing that the kids traveled the right path. Though not perfect myself, I tried to make up for the absence a father or other elders to guide them.

In those years the Komeyl Prayer and Supplication were held either at the Islamic Republican Headquarters or the Motahhari Seminary. Whenever I was in Tehran (both before and after I was married), I would go with the family and, occasionally, others from the building to take part in the ceremonies. I also tried to get the kids in the habit of attending services at the local mosques to keep them from going bad later on. I also taught them the prayers and supplications I had practiced before the war. When summer rolled around, I asked mother to bring the kids to Abadan immediately after their final exams. If she couldn't, I would go to Tehran and fetch them myself. Although they were often a handful, it was better to have them with me than in the city on their own.

Occasionally I went to Tehran in the summer. The Kushk Building Cultural Unit would put on programs for the children. Hasan, Sa'id, and the rest of the children were let loose on the seventh floor, which had a huge hall lined with large windows facing the avenue. They would horse around and participate in the programs. There was a small storage room partitioned off from the rest of the hall, leading to a stairway to the roof. One day Hasan and his playmates, having left their toys in the room, asked the caretaker to open the door for them. He refused. When they insisted, he said, "You'll make a mess if you go in there."

Hasan and one of his friends, a boy named Kurush Lak, decided they would climb out the window and get into the small room from the outside of the building. Holding on to the thin bars and frames of the huge windows, they made their way into the small room and got their toys. Then, retracing their steps, they climbed back into the hall.

I was beside myself when I heard what they had done. I imagined them falling from the seventh floor onto the street, where, even if they survived the fall, a car would run them over.

Even when the kids were in Abadan, I had to watch them like a hawk to see what they were up to. Habib also minded them, especially when they were at our house. Strangely, Habib wouldn't hug or look after Abdollah and, if he had to buy something for the baby, he would always buy gifts for Hasan and Sa'id and give them to the boys first. Things reached such a state that I began to feel jealous for the baby and asked Habib why he didn't kiss his own son. He said, "I can't show my love for him in front of your sister and brothers. It might make them think of their dead father."

One day Habib came home in a red van, which, as usual, was filled with weapons and mortar shells. He ate lunch and went to take a short nap. As soon as Habib entered the house, Hasan and Sa'id left. A short time later they returned and immediately ran up to the second floor. I heard nothing from them, which was odd because they usually made a racket. Habib woke up and went back into the van. A moment later he returned saying, "There were two grenades in there, but now there's only one. Could somebody have taken it?"

"What are you talking about?" I said. "There're so many explosives in this area, who'd bother to steal a grenade?"

"So what happened to it?"

"You probably left it somewhere."

"Impossible. I put it right on the dashboard."

I had a thought and called Hasan and Sa'id to come down. I asked Hasan, "Did you take something from the van?"

"I didn't take anything."

"I think you did. Now bring it here."

Sa'id couldn't keep his mouth shut and admitted, "We took a grenade."

"What did you do with it?"

Hasan said, "Nothing. I gave it to Sa'id and told him to hold it tight while I pulled out the safety."

I felt faint. We had dodged a bullet. Hasan and Sa'id had managed to defuse the grenade. I don't know who taught them how to do that. I looked at Sa'id's palms. They were crosshatched like the outside of the grenade. "You've got to be strict with them," I told Habib. "This time it was a grenade. Next time they might try to defuse a mortar shell."

Habib, who loved the boys very much, said, "There's no way I can be harsh with them. First, they're Seyyeds, and, second, they're the sons of a martyr. What can I say?"

"Saying nothing is worse. You've got to be firm. Slap them in the head, at least."

I finally convinced Habib he had to confront the boys. He slapped Hasan, but, more upset by this than the boys, he quickly climbed into his van and took off. Later I noticed Hasan had disappeared. I searched high and low for him—the yard, the neighbors' houses—but couldn't find him. I even looked on the roof, but there was no place to hide up there. Now beside myself with worry, I went over to Sa'id and asked, "How did you manage to hold on to the grenade in those two little hands of yours?"

"Well, Hasan told me if I let go I'd be blown to bits," he explained. "I got scared and held on with all my might."

Suddenly it hit me: God forbid Hasan is hiding in the small, neighborhood electrical room. I was right. Despite his show of bravery, Hasan was a sensitive child and never expected to be hit. It left a psychological scar. I led him back home. Habib, for his part, returned in a bad mood, complaining, "Why did you make me hit the boy? I couldn't get any work done after that."

Then he went to cuddle Hasan and asked the boy to forgive him several times.

Another of Hasan and Sa'id's favorite pastimes was to play war. They would make dirt piles in the yard and dig two first-class foxholes that faced each other. They also dug trenches with a network of tributaries and filled them with water. It was nice to see them putting so much effort and skill into this, but then again it tore up the garden. Fed up with filling in the holes and ditches they dug, I eventually let them have it. They took my scolding to heart and would repair the damage themselves, only to dig up the place again the next day.

I had no worries as far as Mohsen and Mansur were concerned. Mohsen was employed with the municipality as a fireman, and Mansur spent his time at the front as a paramilitary under Habib's command.

Many times when the area was under constant shelling, the boys in the army would try to send their families to other cities. Habib sent us to his sister's in Ahvaz, which was considered part of the war zone but was still safer than Abadan.

Every day there would be a funeral procession for one of the martyrs. In Ahvaz I visited a graveyard for them called the Rose Garden of Martyrs. I considered it my duty. It also gave me a special feeling. Whenever I was in Tehran, I would go to the office at Behesht-e Zahra where they had voided the IDs of father and Ali. These visits helped keep their memories alive for me.

Once I was in the Rose Garden of Martyrs with Habib's sister and her husband when some uniformed men passed by. Used to seeing his father in uniform, Abdollah started to babble "daddy, daddy" and wiggled his arms and feet. The men walked away, and he started to cry, as though he expected them to cuddle him.

Habib's absences were becoming harder and harder to bear. I was of two minds about them, though. I needed to feel his constant presence, but, at the same time, I wanted to be the wife of a man always at the front. This was one of the conditions of our marriage, a condition many people had a hard time understanding. "Women," they would say, "demand their husbands buy this thing or that for them, but you insist yours should be at the front?"

Habib never came home empty-handed. He'd always arrive with a bouquet of damask roses, which filled the house with their perfume. The ruined houses and alleyways in Moharrezi were teeming with flowers. Even under heavy Iraqi fire, Habib would take pains to pick them. When he handed them to me, I noticed his hands were bleeding from the thorns.

I grew more anxious as time passed about the dangers Habib faced. When he left home, I would stand in the yard with Abdollah in my arms watching him go. I even walked toward the park so I could catch a glimpse of his car as it disappeared in the distance.

Habib's presence at the front being necessary, it was selfish for me to want him all to myself, but he always told me, "If you don't want to live in the zone or if you don't want me to be at the front, just say so and I'll accept it." But I knew he couldn't stand to be away from the war for a moment. And that was how I felt, as well.

When Abdollah was three months old, we moved to another home in the radio and television development. Our first home had taken a mortar hit while we were away in Ahvaz. The door was knocked off its hinges and part of the front of the house was destroyed. Seeing it was no longer habitable, we moved into a smaller but better home in the center of the development. It had a gas stove and a refrigerator. Some of the windows in the home were intact, and it was generally cleaner than the first house. The best thing was that water from the truck outside the house was piped in, which meant there was running water in the kitchen and bathrooms.

The army would occasionally have women gather in one home for safety. Because of the threat posed by Hypocrites, they warned us to be more vigilant when we were alone or out and about. I had heard Hypocrites would monitor the movements of soldiers and took advantage of their absences to decapitate their wives and children. Despite the sweltering heat, on some afternoons there were strange men hanging around the neighborhood and peeking into compounds. For greater safety, all the neighbors would gather in one home.

One night when Abdollah and I were alone, the power went out. In the quiet of the night, I heard a suspicious sound. It was coming from the air conditioning duct and was getting louder and louder. I thought a rat had gotten stuck in the duct. Because the air conditioning didn't work, rats could nest comfortably inside the ducts. In a panic, I didn't know were I could go with Abdollah. The sounds of Saddam's artillery were nothing compared to the noise the rats made. I took Abdollah in my arms and we went to the home of Mrs. Jabbar Beygi, the sister of Jamshid Panahi. I knocked on the door and said, "From the racket in our air conditioner, it seems like rats are about to attack."

Mrs. Jabbar Beygi, who knew I was pregnant, said, "Come on inside."

I said, "No. I don't want to be a bother. Just ask Mr. Jabbar Beygi to do something so the rats will leave us alone tonight."

Ordinarily it was Jabbar Beygi who watched out for us when Habib was not around. He came, inspected the cooler, and made a racket in the duct to drive the rats out of it. But when I got back that night, the sound was still there. Afraid they would hurt Abdollah if I left him alone, I stayed awake all night in that heat, cradling him in my arms. Adding to the misery, the mosquitoes saw the power outage as an opportunity to attack, making my body feel like a pincushion. I was afraid they would sting Abdollah, and he'd come down with one of the diseases they carried.

After a few days, Abdollah and I went to Isfahan, and we traveled with Leila on to Tehran. We had scarcely reached the city when I noticed Abdollah had a fever. This worried me, because I had been repeatedly warned about the water in Abadan, which was known for being a source of cholera and typhus. Even though I feared for the worst, I just told Leila he had caught a cold and was feverish.

"Give him a pill. It's not serious," she said.

I did, but the fever didn't break. For two days I made repeated visits to a pediatrician. He said, "It's a cold," and all I could do was soak his legs. But he got weaker and kept crying. I ultimately had to take him to the hospital, where they gave him a shot. A short time after we got back home, he lost consciousness. He looked like he was dead, and I rushed him back to the hospital. Leila and I were so hysterical the doctors had to usher us out of the examining room and lock the door.

I overheard them saying to each other that whatever they did, the baby showed no response. One doctor injected him with antiseizure medication, and Abdollah began to cry. They opened the door and one of the doctors raced to the dispensary with the baby in his arms. We ran after him. The doctor turned on a faucet and placed Abdollah under it for five minutes. The hospital was cold, but the water was even colder. I couldn't help saying, "He'll freeze to death!"

The doctor said, "Don't worry. It's going to be okay."

After they put Abdollah to bed, his eyes remained open. I waved my hands in front of him, but he didn't blink. "Don't worry," the doctor repeated. "He's unconscious, which is a symptom of the seizure. He'll be better in no time."

Before they admitted Abdollah to the ward, the nurses asked about his father. Uncle Hoseyni told them, "His father's at the front."

They had me sign a release giving them permission to operate, if necessary. At that point mother turned up. When she saw the state the baby was in, she began to scream, "You made him sick, dragging the child from this city to that. How many times did I tell you not to take him to Abadan, where everything's polluted, but you wouldn't listen?"

Uncle Hoseyni stepped in, saying it wasn't time for that kind of talk.

Abdollah remained in the hospital for a week. He had so many drips in him there was no space on his body for another. He swelled up from lack of movement, and he screeched whenever he saw a nurse. I didn't want Habib to worry, so I kept Abdollah's illness a secret. But when I learned from the doctors that the baby had typhoid, I telephoned Habib to say it would be good if he could come to Tehran.

Habib arrived around midnight the next day. There had been no busses, so he had to string together several rides on trucks to get to the city. In the morning we went to the hospital together. When I first brought Abdollah to the hospital, he weighed more than 26 pounds, but he lost almost 10 while he was there. He was very pale. They had shaved his head and, with his sunken, saucer-like eyes, he looked like somebody from Mars.

As soon as he saw Habib, Abdollah seemed to perk up. His condition improved daily until, on the ninth day, he was discharged. A week later, Habib said it was time he went back to the front. I said, "I'm coming with you." Leila, who had been a big help to us during this time, begged me not to go back, but I couldn't stay and returned to Abadan with Habib.

After we got back, it didn't take long for Abdollah's temperature to shoot up again. He showed the same symptoms, but not only did he have a fever, I also developed one. My whole body shook and my voice cracked. Afraid he might go into convulsions, I never left the baby's side. The medicine we had didn't seem to make any difference. At that point I recalled the story about the pomegranate the blessed Zahra lying sick in bed asked her father Ali to get for her. Ali went to get some pomegranates, but on the way back he gave them to a beggar. When he got home he saw a basket of pomegranates, gift from heaven.

Thinking Abdollah would get better if he ate a pomegranate, I had Habib get some from the market, and, after eating one, the baby's fever broke and he was well again.

After Imam Khomeini had removed Banisadr from the post of commander in chief, and after his disgraceful escape from Iran dressed like a woman, our forces were successful in four large-scale military operations. We pushed the enemy artillery back, and the shelling of the city decreased. Fewer planes were able to hit Abadan, as well. The situation at the front stabilized.

But, at the beginning of 1984, the attacks on the city intensified once more. Shalamcheh remained under enemy control, and our boys were getting ready for a new offensive.

The army announced we had to leave our homes for safer areas. Whenever the enemy attacks got worse and there were appeals for us to move, I knew another offensive was in the works. Abdollah had become quite familiar with the sounds of war. As soon as he heard the guns, he would say, "Mommy, sleep."

Almost all the families in our devleopment had gone. Even the caretaker had sent his family away. Mrs. Jabbar Beygi and I were the only ones left. Life under those conditions was very difficult. I began to be afraid in a way that was different from how it was before Abdollah was born. Having a child made the situation much worse. We decided Abdollah and I would go to Tehran, and, to take us there, the army had put a Peykan and a driver at Habib's disposal. The enemy shelled the road heavily between Abadan and Shush, where the driver's nephew lived. Habib accompanied us as far as Khorramabad where grandfather lived and then immediately went back. I was sick all that night from the horrors of the road. The next morning Aunt Salimeh and her children drove on with us to Tehran.

We arrived in the city on February 20, 1984, two months before my second child was due. However, the next day I gave birth to a baby girl we named Hoda.

When I was released from the hospital, we went to live with mother. As she was very frail, I didn't want her to do the housework for me. That winter was very cold, and the Kushk Building had no hot water. Because I insisted on doing the work myself, I landed in the hospital again. I had on my hands eighteen-month-old Abdollah and Hoda, just two months old. I called Leila, who came from Isfahan to take care of the children. Habib also managed to visit me in the hospital, but since he didn't have leave, he had to return to the front. Leila and mother brought Hoda to the hospital three times a day to be breastfed. After a while, the children and I returned to Abadan.

The Iraqis at that time were engaging in the widespread use of chemical weapons in Shalamcheh, Faw, and other cities. I would often smell the chemicals, but I didn't know what they were. The air was full of the smell of bananas, garlic, and cucumbers. On windy days the odor of fruit was everywhere. Habib told me once, "If you smell fruit, try not to inhale it, because the Iraqis are using poison gas in Shalamcheh, and the wind is carrying it here."

That was when I understood what the odors were. At the time Habib had gone to another sector to carry out operations. He said, "I'll probably be out of contact for several months." He urged me to go back to Tehran, which, for the sake of the children's health and Habib's peace of mind, I did—though it wasn't what I wanted. Hoda was eight months old when we arrived in the city. We weren't able to go back to Abadan, where all of our things were.

With all the children around and the constant flood of guests, life in the one room in the Kushk Building was difficult, and I didn't feel comfortable being there. Habib would come for the occasional visit when he had leave, but he told me he felt like an intruder. It was hard on him seeing my family put upon like that.

The home or, in reality, my room was like guest central. If someone had work to do in Tehran or was accepted to university or wanted to see a specialist, we played host to him. Apart from that, the affection mother's brothers and other relatives had for our family was itself the cause of all kinds of congestion. Whenever a single man visited, we had to curtain off part the room to maintain propriety.

When I saw my stay in Tehran would drag on indefinitely, I raised the issue with the Martyrs Foundation. The Foundation wrote to the superintendent of the building, who put two rooms at our disposal. Habib was always annoyed by my constant need for things. He was even opposed to accepting gifts. He would say, "Be thankful for God allowing me to serve at the front."

One time a Kuwaiti merchant, who had heard about the bravery of the Khorramshahri troops, sent the military a number of refrigerators and air conditioners along with boxes of chocolates and baskets with fruit and nuts. At that time most of the old soldiers had families and were living on the bare minimum in the way of appliances and furniture. As a veteran, Habib was entitled to one of the air conditioners, but they were all gone by the time he finally got around to it. We didn't own an air conditioner, and Habib would not hear of using the one belonging to the homeowner because it might constitute theft. One day a truck pulled up in front of our house, and two men delivered a refrigerator, saying it was part of our allowance.

That afternoon when Habib came home and saw the thing in front of the door, he asked, "What's that doing here?"

"I don't know. They brought it and said it was ours."

"Didn't I say I didn't want anything? Why are they doing this?" he asked.

He went to the army and complained. They told him he had been entitled to an air conditioner, but he never picked it up. So he got a refrigerator. Habib told them we already had a refrigerator and stove. We didn't need a thing.

They said, "The appliances you have now belong to the area command, but the refrigerator is yours."

Habib refused to bring the thing into the house. It remained sitting outside in the sun until Leila's husband, Hoseyn Ta'i Nezhad, came and took it to Tehran.

Another time they brought around a machine-made carpet they were selling at cooperative store prices. Each family was entitled to only one length of carpet. Habib, as usual, refused to do anything about it, so Leila's husband once again carted the thing off and stored it in his home in Isfahan. He said to Habib, "It's fine if you won't accept something for free, but this one cost money."

After the first years of marriage, our possessions amounted to a few plates, a kerosene heater/stove, and some blankets the army had given us when we got married. The only thing that was truly ours was a suitcase Habib had. I used it to carry Abdollah's things when we traveled to Isfahan or Tehran.

Now I found myself in the two rooms the building superintendent had found for us on the sixth floor, but without anything to put in them. I covered the floor with two pieces of carpeting I got from mother. Without telling me, mother had bought some things and put them aside for me. When I went to the new apartment, she surprised me by taking them out. A short while later, Hoseyn, learning we had our own place, brought the rug from Isfahan.

When Habib was turning over the radio and television house to the army, he called to ask what he should do with the things in it. I told him to keep them and bring them to Tehran the next time he came.

Habib was pleased to see we had our own apartment when he came to Tehran. Unfortunately, since our home in Abadan had been empty for a time, a number of our things had disappeared—among them books, tapes of mourning ceremonies, and interviews with the martyred brothers in the army.

Some time later, the building superintendent suggested that the two kids and I, mother and my sisters and brothers, including Mohsen (married that fall to my cousin), move to a large space on the seventh floor. He said it was empty and would meet our need for privacy. He also said since many families lacked housing, he could move them into our vacated apartment. Although we knew climbing all the stairs to the seventh floor presented a problem, we all agreed to the move.

The seventh floor was a large open space with floor-to-ceiling windows on either side. Moveable dividers sectioned off the space into two or three rooms. At one end of the hall was another room boxed off with drywall. It had originally been the grillroom for the Bureau of Budget and Planning cafeteria. Since mother's room would always have guests coming and going, I chose a place at the end of the hall, where I could use the grillroom as a kitchen.

In the summer the sun streaming through the large windows was so strong it felt like we were in a hot house without any way of cooling the place. In wintertime, when it rained, water seeped through the cracks in the windows and pooled on the floor at the edge of the carpeting, and it would mold. Putting up carpeting up against the windows to protect us from the drafts was no use, because the room had a false ceiling that allowed the freezing wind to seep in from the roof and stairwell.

When Iraqi planes bombed Tehran or when they fired missiles at us, the windowpanes would rattle, making a terrible noise. I would always have Abdollah and Hoda sleep far from the windows and would position myself between them and the wall to shield them from flying glass.

Abdollah's illness had passed, leaving him with a slight case of asthma. He was put on a strict diet, avoiding all milk products and vegetables. He would often wheeze, and his breathing got so labored at night that he would choke. He tugged on his hair, thinking it would help him breathe. In that childish voice of his, he moaned, "The air is bad, the air is bad."

I placed an inhaler the doctor prescribed in his mouth and squeezed it. Abdollah's difficulty breathing mostly happened when everybody was asleep, and I didn't want to disturb them. At such times, I really missed Habib. I yearned for him to come home, but then, I thought, he was of more use at the front.

Even with a room all to myself, mother was constantly on my mind. While we were on the lower floor, she was always busy cooking with the neighbors in the communal kitchen. She didn't have a chance to sink into one of her depressions. But after we moved to the seventh floor, it was easier for her thoughts to take a downward turn. She put up pictures of the martyrs of Khorramshahr on the wall. She would walk around the house, mumbling to herself in Kurdish and Arabic and weeping. I tried to put up with it or cover my ears so I wouldn't hear her, but no matter what I did, it would make me burst into tears myself. When I realized her tears wouldn't stop until someone came in and comforted her, I went to her room. I saw the children curled up in the corner, and my heart melted. I lay mother's head on my chest and kissed her. I kept speaking to her soothingly until she was calm, but all the while I was in agony on the inside. After mother, it was the children's turn. I took them to the park and bought them something to eat. Then we would stroll along the avenue and go home. During this time there was no one who could understand what I was going through. Some people made pointless expressions of sympathy, while others, knowingly or not, would say hurtful things. Still others would be genuinely kind, but that only made me more heartsick.

In 1985, the army brought Habib to Tehran for a two-year weapons training program. The entire time in the city was a nightmare for him. He would howl when they played martial music on the radio. On the verge of a breakdown, he would pace around, slapping his head, and cursing himself, "Goddamn you, Habib!

How dare you stay here safe and sound in Tehran, while the boys are back there in the thick of it? I wish to God I knew how they were doing."

"Well, what are you waiting for? Go back, instead of eating your heart out here," I said.

"I can't," he said. "The course is important; I've got to finish."

In the end, he didn't even complete one year. This was typical of Habib. As soon as he came to Tehran on leave, he'd be champing at the bit to go back. During those rare times when he did notice how hard life was for me and the kids, he'd say, "If you're not happy with me returning, I won't." But I knew if I had told him not to go back, he'd invent all kinds of excuses to return to the fighting. That was why I pretended it wasn't a problem for me.

Habib often asked me, "What would you do if I were martyred?"

I had seen many women whose husbands had died: the wife of the martyr Abdol Khani, the wife of martyr Abbaspur, and Rabab, the wife of the martyr Khosravi. I had seen a picture of her wiping the blood from her husband's face. She was pregnant at the time and gave birth to their daughter Vadi'eh just days after her husband's martyrdom. I often thought of what I would do if I were in their places. I felt the agony they were feeling, and I grieved for them. I told Habib, "I'm nobody special. I'll just be like the other wives."

But whenever I saw Habib about to write his last will, I begged him not to write that I shouldn't cry for him, that I should stay strong. I said, "I don't have it in me any more to be that strong and do what you want. It would be impossible for me not to cry."

Habib laughed and said, "Fine. Cry as much as you like. How do you know I'm going to die anyway?"

"Whatever happens, I'm ready."

Certain goods were rationed in Tehran in those days because of the war and the economic sanctions. Uncle Hoseyni would leave work at 2:00 p.m., eat lunch quickly, and go out to buy powdered milk for Abdollah and Hoda or get other things needed for the house. Uncles Hoseyni and Nad Ali were a godsend for us at that time. Uncle Hoseyni, always the good manager, saw to it we didn't lack for necessities or funds. But there were times people behaved improperly toward me on the street, and I realized if I had had a man with me, such things wouldn't have happened. Uncle Hoseyni's presence offered some consolation and bucked up my resolve.

Habib's salary when we got married was around 2,000 tumans. It rose gradually to 4,000. At one point early in our marriage I asked him, "Can I give money we don't need to a deserving person or to the front or to earthquake victims?" He said, "The household is in your hands. You want to burn it, go ahead. You want to give it away, fine." Although we were not well off, Habib gave me a free hand with the expenses. Economizing as much as possible, I was able to open a savings account at the Mellat Bank on Ferdowsi Avenue. This meant that if the need arose, Habib wouldn't have to ask others for money.

My brothers Hasan and Sa'id insisted being like Mansur and Mohsen and go to the front, but they were too young to join up. Finally, in 1986, they were able to enlist. Hasan went first and did a six-month tour, while Sa'id did three tours. Each time they enlisted they brought me along in place of mother to sign their applications. Because of my poor track record when it came to telling mother about Ali, I wasted no time telling her about Hasan and Sa'id. I knew if something happened to them, she would never forgive me, but I managed to convince her not to oppose their enlistment. The only thing she said was: "As long as they'll come back safe and sound, let them go."

Hasan had completed two of his final exams for the first year of high school when his call-up notice came. He spent six straight months at the front. Although I didn't like to write letters, we corresponded frequently. I would always leave Habib's letters unanswered, using the telephone instead to answer his. Habib loved to write letters, but, after I didn't respond, he stopped. Nevertheless, he would still send me a letter from time to time.

The circumstances with Hasan were different. I felt obliged to write to him. Habib went to see Hasan several times. They didn't send the boy to the front line; instead, they found a place for him in one of the military police guardhouses in the rear. Although it was in a sensitive area and often under enemy fire, he wasn't thrilled about being a guard.

Hasan's letters bristled with excitement about the war. He wrote once about how one of the boys shot down an Iraqi plane and how they watched it crash. Hasan's enthusiasm was contagious. Before his tour was up, Sa'id started to pester us about joining up. Sa'id was a strange boy, well mannered and studious. His behavior made him the center of attention. The two boys went to the same school, but Hasan was often criticized for acting up, while everyone had nothing but praise for Sa'id. Sa'id's personality and character reminded me of Ali; their features were also very similar, especially with their unibrows.

Whenever the boys had some school activity, they would invite me. I tried to get out of it, saying there were only men at the school, but they insisted.

Sa'id was in a song and theatre troupe, which was part of the High School Student Corps. The leader of the troupe, Seyyed Javad Hashemi, a movie and television actor, wanted to take it on a tour of the front. The boys in the group were all between the ages of thirteen and fifteen. I went to the Cultural Institute on Horr Square and, with mother's approval, saw Mr. Hashemi and signed the papers permitting Sa'id to go to the front. Sa'id wanted to go and fight, but the officials assured families the troupe would only be performing. They entertained troops at bases in Du Kuheh, Hoveyzeh, Bostan, Susangerd, Faw, and elsewhere.

Mansur was wounded in the foot in January 1986 and was laid up at home for eight months. They put a pin in his foot, but as soon as they removed his cast, he went back to the front. One night in September 1987, with military operations taking place in the western part of the country, the martyr Mostafa Chamran appeared to me in a dream. We spoke for a long time, and I asked him what would happen to Hasan, because I was worried about him. He said, "They're going to bring him away." I pressed him on other things, but he would answer with a smile, "Certain events cannot be disclosed." After these and other dreams, I became fed up with everything connected with life. I couldn't get the dreams out of my mind. Dr. Chamran with his unworldly presence and speech consumed my waking moments. I couldn't tell mother about my dreams, but I did share them with Fowziyeh Vatankhah.

A couple of days after the dream, I felt ill and asked Fowziyeh to accompany me to the Amir A'lam Hospital on Kushk Avenue. As we were walking, Fowziyeh began to speak, and I had the feeling she was getting me ready to hear some news. "Come on, out with it. What's on your mind?" I said.

She said, "I saw someone from the Martyr and Wounded Transfer Squad, who was asking about you. We have the interpretation of your dream."

I couldn't control myself and with tears in my eyes, I said, "God, mother can't stand any more pain!"

Fowziyeh quickly tried to reassure me, "I swear to God. Mansur's not dead, but his wounds are very bad, it seems."

"For God's sake, tell me what happened. I'm only worried about mother."

"Don't get me wrong. I'm not trying to console you. The official said he would come to your house himself. He only wanted you to know he'd been wounded. Someone from the squad had come to your house twice but you weren't home. He said nothing to your mother. I only saw him by accident in the hallway."

Although I still felt sick, I changed my mind about going to the hospital. I went to the squad offices in the Health Ministry on Hafez Avenue. They found Mansur's name on a list, which said he had been wounded in the leg and was sent to a hospital in Mashhad.

When I called the hospital, they told me they'd operated on him several times, and that he'd need several more operations. Certain Mansur was in the hospital in Mashhad, I bought a train ticket and went home.

Knowing she would not be able to control herself, I didn't know how to break to the news to mother. She was at her most annoying at such times. Finally I said, "Mother, I'm going to tell you something, but you have to promise you won't have a breakdown."

"What is it? I swear I won't say a word," she promised.

Hardly was Mansur's name out of my mouth, when she started beating herself. "I'm not saying another word," I said.

I got up to leave the room. She said, "Tell me. I'll be quiet—swear to God." She merely sobbed.

"Mansur's been shot in the foot. They brought him to Mashhad and operated. I'm going to visit him in the hospital."

True to her word, mother stayed calm. With Abdollah and Hoda in tow, we went to Mashhad. After finding the address, we went straight to Kamyab Hospital, which was outside of town. They weren't letting people enter, and a crowd had formed by the door. I cut through the crowd and told the guard there was only the four of us in Mashhad to see about my wounded brother.

He glanced at mother and the children and said, "Okay. But you can only go in one at a time."

Not knowing exactly how badly my brother had been injured, I didn't let mother go in first. I left the kids with her and entered the hospital. Although I had been telling her the whole trip not to break down when she was there, because not only would it get on Mansur's already frazzled nerves, it might ruin the morale of the other wounded in the ward, as soon as I got in the room and saw him lying on the bed I couldn't stop from bursting into tears. I hugged and kissed him just the same. He was rail thin, almost half his normal size. Although mother was waiting for me outside, I didn't have the heart to leave him. I sat down beside him, and he asked, "Who's with you?"

"Mother, Hoda, and Abdollah."

Annoyed, he said, "What made you come all this way?"

"We couldn't bear not to come," I said.

At that point one of the nurses came in the room, and Mansur asked her to bring mother and the kids. She left and returned with them. Mother started weeping even before entering the room. I couldn't get her to stop no matter what I did. Her crying caused me to lose control again. She tried so hard to stop the tears that her arms shook and her lips quivered, but they streamed down her cheeks as she sobbed softly. We stayed with Mansur until the evening prayer, when they politely asked us to leave. We went to the holy shrine where Imam Reza is buried and took part in Friday prayers. Later we went to the bazaar to shop and eat, and then returned to the hospital. After the second visit, our thoughts turned to finding a place to stay. We tried every hotel and guesthouse around the shrine with no luck. The air turned chilly around sunset, and the loudspeakers were sounding the call to prayer. I was losing hope and called on Imam Reza to give us shelter in this strange city. We walked toward Fountain Square and roamed around the lanes and alleyways in the old city until we came to a guesthouse called Beyt al-Moqaddas (Jerusalem House).

I went inside and asked the manager if there was a room.

"No," he said.

I turned around to leave and saw that mother and the kids had come in behind me. The manager asked, "Are they with you?" "Yes," I said. "What brings you here?" he asked. I told him we came to see my wounded brother in the hospital.

"This is awkward," he said. "I told you we didn't have a room because they've ordered us not to give rooms to women traveling alone. You have to go to the Holy Precinct Committee and get a letter of introduction, and then I can do whatever you want."

I went to the committee and explained to a brother why we were there. "Why didn't you come to the committee in the first place?" he asked. "The Martyrs Foundation has its own guesthouse for the families." "I didn't know that," I said and went back to the Beyt al-Moqaddas and got a room. It was very small, no more than one and half by two meters, and had a worn carpet on the floor. I had only brought two sheets and a couple of sets of clothes for the kids. I spread one sheet on the floor, and we used mother's cloak to cover the room's rickety wooden window. We washed the grapes we had bought on the way and ate them with some bread for supper. The manager brought some filthy blankets and floor cushions for us, but I couldn't bring myself to use then and sent them back. The kids, who had tired themselves out horsing around, went right to sleep. The room was so cramped mother and I had to sleep curled up next to each other.

We spent the next three days visiting the hospital and the shrine. Abdollah, five at the time, and Hoda, three and a half, were such little devils that they ran me ragged from the time we left the hotel in the morning until late at night when we got back. We said our prayers in the shrine and ate in a restaurant. During visiting hours we went to the hospital. We put Mansur in a wheelchair and rolled him out into the hospital yard.

Mansur's roommates were able to walk with canes and kept the children amused, while we spoke with him. We asked him how he was wounded.

"One night I was riding behind my friend on his motorcycle, racing across the bridge, when we were caught in a hail of shrapnel and mortar fire. A shell landed nearby, and I was thrown from the bike. I had a machine gun strapped to my back, which was loaded in case we had to fight. I fell with my finger on the trigger and accidently sent several rounds into my foot." The combination of the fall, the shrapnel, and the machine gun made a mess of his foot below the ankle. His jaw and teeth were broken, and his right foot and pelvis were in a cast.

Because we couldn't stay in Mashhad long, we asked the hospital authorities to arrange to have Mansur transferred to Tehran. At first they refused, but then they said if we coordinated it with Tehran, they would have no problem with the move.

Three days later we returned to Tehran. One of Fowziyeh Vatankhah's friends was in charge of transferring patients at Imam Khomeini Hospital, and she arranged the transfer. The authorities called asking what hospital we wanted him transferred to.

I said, "It makes no difference. Since we cannot visit him regularly in Mashhad, we want him moved to Tehran. But, if not, he should be treated just like anybody else."

The transfer unit telephoned again to say he was to be moved to Mehrad Hospital on Mir Emad Avenue. They told us to be at the airport at a certain time to meet him.

We went to the airport to find that the plane had arrived early and the patients had been offloaded. It was around midnight. We went to the Mehrad Hospital in a car belonging to one of the martyr families at the Kushk Building. When we got there, they wouldn't let us in, saying everybody was asleep.

I said, "Give me a second to look in on my brother, and I'll be right back."

Mansur was awake, and his friend, Mr. Lashgari, was with him. Relieved, I went home. After a while, they released Mansur from the hospital, and, just like the last time he had been wounded, he remained quite a while convalescing at home. He was annoyed that he had to spend so much time on his back or in a chair and groused constantly about how much his leg itched. The doctors had fitted him with braces and a cast from his ankle to his knee and from the knee to the pelvis. The metal screws in the braces jutted out from the cast. Mansur's body was riddled with shrapnel, and he would dig out the bits that came to the surface of his skin. He poked at his face—especially the area around his eyes—so much the wounds swelled up. I constantly warned him not to fiddle with them because he might sever one of the tiny nerves near his eye, and then he would be in big trouble.

"These are nothing. Don't worry," he'd say.

Mansur told us that when he was at the field hospital in the desert, they wanted to amputate his foot. But he wouldn't let them. After he was transferred to Mashhad, a skilled surgeon, whose name I forget, worked on him for nine hours to fix the foot. Mansur had nothing but praise for this doctor, who told him not expect the foot to be like new, because some parts of it had been so badly crushed they were beyond repair.

Around the time Mansur came home, the weather turned warm. He was at his wits' end, because his leg itched and he couldn't do anything about it. He would bang on the cast in frustration. Mansur's general weakness and instability, and the many times he was under anesthesia during the operations, had a bad effect on him. He would fly into a rage, making me feel helpless. I rubbed the outside of his cast, but it didn't do any good. I pushed a kabob skewer down into it, and this relieved the itch for a time. There was no bath in our building; we had to go to the public bath at the corner of Nejatollahi and Villa Avenues to bathe. After we moved to the seventh floor, we converted the grillroom into a place to wash. We brought Mansur there and, protecting his cast with plastic sheeting, we sponged down the rest of his body with soapy water and rubbed him clean with a damp towel. We poured water over his arms. Knowing that if his wounds got wet it could cause an infection, we were careful to keep them dry. Bathing Mansur wasn't pleasant; it made me think of the times I had hosed down Ali's head when he was doing construction work on our house. After work Ali would have me hold the hose or he would hold it, while I washed his head. The memories brought tears to my eyes, but, not wanting to upset Mansur, I tried to hide my feelings from him.

Mansur's treatments lasted a year. During that time they repeatedly broke open his cast, took x-rays, and refitted him with a new cast. His right leg ended up ten centimeters shorter than his left, which meant he walked with a limp. The leg was so frail and had shriveled up so much, it seemed there was no muscle in it. The doctor said he should go for long walks or do mountain climbing to bring it back. To this day Mansur's right leg is not like the left, but, thank God, he can now stand on his own two feet.

In 1985, the composition of the Kushk Building changed. Instead of the refugee families from Khuzestan, martyr families from Tehran in need of housing moved in. With the passage of time, differences in ethics and background began to emerge and cause problems. Each family was left to its own devices. In the beginning the superintendent of the building was responsible for cleaning and sanitation, but, later on, this was left up to the residents, who were supposed to take turns doing it. Some families took their responsibilities seriously, while others did not. The matter was more than just a case of washing and cleaning up. At the beginning, the Cultural Unit would provide wholesome entertainment, and a clinic was set up to see to the medical needs of the residents. But the Cultural Unit no longer existed. I am not a big believer in the state providing martyr families with every service, but when they put people with different values under the same roof, there has to be proper supervision. Certain irresponsible and inconsiderate families had now taken up residence in the building and were becoming a nuisance to their neighbors.

One family man in particular, an amputee with one leg, engaged in certain immoral acts and medieval practices that disqualified him from receiving benefits. He became a kind of professional beggar and brought a number of others like him into the building. They would pierce their bodies with kabob skewers and use drugs to get into a trance. The man and his wife would lock their children in their room, while they went out for their own amusement. Occasionally they were gone for several days, while the children howled and screamed and banged on the walls. It's not hard to imagine what five bratty boys were capable of when cooped up in a room for a week. Germs and waste literally streamed out of from the room, and, although the neighbors were sickened by the situation, their sympathies lay with the children.

People complained to the Martyr Foundation about what was going on, but it did no good. The man and his family stayed in the building until it was completely vacated, and anyone who had contact with the man became addicts themselves and left their families. Eventually his wife divorced him, his children went astray, and he left Tehran for Mashhad, where he remarried.

There were several cases like this at the Kushk Building. One man was sentenced to a long prison term for smuggling drugs, but after a few years he was pardoned. He reverted to his old ways and enlisted his sons, whom he'd addicted to heroin, in the business.

The son of the previous superintendent of the building formed a gang with several others, who were tough and capable of anything, including armed robbery. A person was killed during one of their robberies, whereupon the police caught some of the members, while others got away. The addicts in the building also stole anything they could get their hands on to support their habits. They even pried off the protective strips of aluminum on the edges of the stairs and sold them. The presence of these elements concerned everyone, especially the girls and women. I didn't have the strength to put up with the situation. In the back of my mind was always the fear that my brothers would become involved with these gangs or Zeynab, now an adolescent, would get into trouble. They were good children, but there was always the possiblity they would be led astray.

Repeated trips to the Martyrs Foundation to complain about the families causing trouble in the building were of no use. The authorities said, "They are also martyr families and have a right to live there."

I said to them, "When you allow drug dealers and other criminals to live in the same place as law-abiding martyr families, it doubles the agony they have had to endure. At least put the criminal elements together somewhere else. Why should the rest of us have to live in fear of our children going astray because of a few bad apples?"

In 1982 Zeynab had started studying at the Shandiz School on Ramsar Avenue.[1] One day the teachers in the school, knowing Zeynab was the daughter of a martyr, brought the fifth-grade class to our home and asked me to tell them about how father and Ali were killed. Hearing I had been in Abadan, they said they would like to see Khorramshahr. I invited them to come. In September 1982, the principal and two teachers were our guests for a few days. Habib arranged for them to tour the areas affected by the war.

After the special schools for the children of martyrs were established, Zeynab enrolled in one called Shahed-e Rowshangar. Because she took part in school activities like Quran recitation, Zeynab became very popular with the teachers. The social studies teacher, Mrs. Ra'is Qasem,[2] and several other teachers were regular visitors to our home. Once, when Mrs. Ra'is Qasem was visiting, I brought up the subject of the bad elements in the building, expressing my concern about Zeynab and the other children. A short time later, Mr. Karroubi, an official with the Martyrs Foundation, came to the school for an inspection tour. Mrs. Ra'is Qasem protested to him that the place where the Foundation housed martyr families was beneath their dignity, a building where drug use and other immoral behavior were common. Mr. Karroubi asked her to give him a full report. Mrs. Ra'is Qasem dictated generally what was going on in the building and specifically what was happening to our family. Zeynab wrote it all down, and the report was given to Mr. Karroubi.

Two years later, in the winter of 1988, mother was issued a dank and dilapidated apartment, which had been confiscated from Zionists.[3] Around the time mother was moving from the Kushk

---

[1] The Shahed Schools had yet to open at that time. Later the name of the school was changed to "Be'sat."

[2] Wife of the former Minister of Foreign Affairs, Mr. Kharrazi.

[3] These were prominent Jews who escaped the country during the Revolution. The apartment was on a lane previously called "Harunian." Later the name was changed to "Seyyed Hoseyn Hoseyni" in honor of my father.

Building, a room on the fourth floor became available. Everyone on the higher floors was ready to give their eyeteeth to get that room. To avoid arguments the superintendent announced he would give the room to anyone with priority. Mother and the kids wanted to leave our building before I was ready, so I didn't know how I would cope all by myself in the humongous room on the seventh floor. It was far from the noise and shouting on the lower floors—especially the part where I was, which, being at the other end of the room, was always plunged in a eerie silence. Ignorant of what happened on the lower floors, we went on about our business as if they didn't exist.

In Khorramshahr, where most families had children, the kids would play in the alley all morning until noon when they got hungry. After lunch, they'd run around the neighborhood until evening. I remember when we were kids, if we did something father didn't like, he only had to give us "the look." The weight of that look was enough to make us bow our heads and remain perfectly still until he said we could go.

That upbringing put us in a world of our own, which prevented us from associated with the ones on the lower floors.

The times I did venture downstairs, it sounded like the neighbors were at each other's throats, and we had been blissfully unaware of it. Because there were no structures near the Kushk Building higher than the fifth floor, people living above that floor had unobstructed views of the surrounding area. With windows on either side of our room, we saw nothing but sky. This gave me the feeling we were living on a ship in the middle of an ocean, a ship that never reached land.

During the times when Tehran was being bombarded, making the building shake and the windows rattle terribly, the feeling of being adrift in the void became stronger.

The effort of going up and down the stairs put pressure on my back. The doctor warned me about moving too much, especially about bending up and down. He said the shrapnel could cut the nerves in my spine and paralyze me. He even advised me to pray in a sitting position.

Although I never liked to be a nuisance to others, Uncle Hoseyni and mother would go out and shop for me. Now with mother leaving, I had to do these things on my own. That was why I turned to Mr. Siyahpush, the superintendent, an energetic and thoughtful man.[4] I told him that I had a slipped disc and, with mother leaving and the two children's father at the front, I couldn't cope in that huge apartment on my own. Mr. Siyahpush sympathized, saying that even though he himself was athletic, he couldn't climb up to the seventh floor without getting winded. He agreed to let us have the apartment on the fourth floor, which caused many of the other residents to complain.

When mother and the kids left the building in 1988, Zeynab was thirteen, Sa'id fifteen, Hasan seventeen, and Mansur twenty-one. Seeing them in a home of their own took a load off my mind. I was left alone with three young children (Fatemeh, my third, was three months old at the time). Having seen some of the misfit young men using drugs in the emergency stairwell, I was concerned that Abdollah and Hoda might come upon them shooting up in the halls as well. This was why I was forced to keep the children inside the apartment and entertain them myself. Although I knew I was no substitute for playing with children their own age, I read to them and told them stories. However, I would let them play with the neighbors' kids as long as I supervised the visits. Occasionally we would go to the park or visit my friends. During these outings, it felt like my spine was breaking. Every time the bones rubbed together I'd let out a short, shrill cry of pain and couldn't move forward or backward for a time. I was forced to sit down where I was, even if it was in the middle of the street, until the pain in my back went away. I didn't want anybody to know why I couldn't move.

There were four other apartments on the fourth floor. In the first was a woman from Tehran living on her own. She was what they called an "oppressed" person, who was given the apartment because of her economic circumstances. In the second was the family of a father martyred in the war who had been married to an Afghan woman. The woman remarried, and the Imam himself officiated at

---

[4] Mr. Siyahpush was a ping-pong coach and a decent individual. He went to the front many times, which helped him understand what we were going through.

her wedding. The woman and her first husband had a boy Abdollah's age. The stepfather was a very respectable man, who stayed away from the building as much as he could. He did look in on the boy and provided him with the best things—including toys and clothing— money could buy. The third apartment contained an Azeri-speaking mother of a martyr, who objected to our getting the apartment instead of her son. "I am the sister of a martyr and my son is the brother of one," she complained. "It wasn't right to give them the apartment." I spoke with the woman, pointing out that her son was quite comfortable living on his own with a job in Tehran, while my husband had to be quite far away and couldn't check in on us. The woman's daughter-in-law also told me that she would never live in a place like our building. But the woman never stopped complaining.

The fourth apartment was occupied by a family in which the father was usually away on a mission or at work from morning until evening. The Azeri-speaking mother, a very neat and tidy woman, lived by herself. Although very admirable for her sanitation, the woman was a real nuisance to the neighbors. There was a communal kitchen on the fourth floor, but any time one of us used it to wash a pot or something, she would show up to complain about how long we were taking. Living on her own without anything better to do, she griped constantly about the children playing in the hall. We had to set up specific times for the kids to play, and, although I told the boys again and again to be considerate of the older people and the sick in the building, they ignored me and played soccer in our hallway. I would regularly hear the racket made by the boys followed by the woman's shouts and curses.

Sometimes I sensed the woman was kind hearted, and it pained her to show an ugly side. I thought that she must have a reason to behave the way she did. One day we had a heart-to-heart chat, and I asked her about her life. She said when she was nine she was married to a much older man who already had a wife. She found being a second wife extremely difficult. No more than a child, all she wanted to do was to play, but her mother-in-law insisted she do the housework and would get furious and beat her when she didn't. It was clear to me that, having been abused as a child, the woman herself had become an abusive adult. After our chat, I tried to be more understanding of her moods.

The Afghan woman was a strange character. As soon as she became friends with a person, she would open up about every detail of her life, from the trivial to the important, droning on and on to the point of driving her listeners crazy. If she fell out with a person, she would do her darnedest to bully the offender into submission. Hating it when people called her Afghan, she protested, "I am the wife of an Iranian, the mother of an Iranian martyr." I would ask her, "Why is it so upsetting to you to be called Afghan? Didn't you yourself say they were a brave people and proud warriors?" But it had no effect on her.

Early one morning the wife of the man always on a mission came to me, saying she needed money. Pleading poverty I said, "I'm sorry. It's the end of the month and Habib hasn't sent his salary yet."

She left my place and then ran into the Afghan lady, and, after apologizing again and again, she borrowed money from her. This led to a loud argument between the Afghan and her husband. She was considerably older than he was and would constantly bring their age difference up to him. All the residents of the fourth floor, especially the woman who borrowed the money, had to endure her vile accusations for months afterward. My room and theirs shared an inner door, which the previous residents had bricked up. Although I had put furniture in front of the door, I could still hear the woman screeching at her husband late into the night. I was pregnant with my fourth child, and the sounds went through my skull like a drill. Unable to sleep, I tried everything I could to drown out the sound of that voice. I played Quran tapes and said prayers, but nothing worked. The next morning, the fights with her husband developed into skirmishes with the neighbors. She would go to the kitchen and was so obsessive about her exclusive right to be there, no one dared disturb her. I tried to keep out of her way, which explains why she was less fierce with me than the other neighbors. But there were times when I would go to the kitchen and find she had gone off somewhere, leaving the water running for no reason.

As I said, most people on the floor took turns policing the common areas: the hallways, stairs, kitchen, and the bathroom. The oppressed Tehrani woman usually was not home, and, when she was, she usually had guests. They would use the common facilities, but she never lifted a finger to clean up after them. It made no difference to her that the mothers of martyrs did the cleaning for her and her guests. It was particularly galling for me to see strange men on the stairs and in the hall, because I would normally hike up my chador and tie it around my waist when I cleaned. If I let it hang down, it got in the way and would get filthy. Because the stairwell was out of the way, not everybody bothered cleaning it. Having strange men about wasn't a problem for the Azeri woman or the Afghan, who, being older, could hike up their chadors without causing a scandal. No one could get the the oppressed woman to work. Therefore, I had no choice but to clean late at night or early in the morning, but it didn't take long for the place to become filthy again. Then people said accusingly, "It's your turn. Why didn't you do some cleaning?"

At the end of our place there was a small room partitioned off by a low wooden wall. The superintendent allowed me to use this room as a kitchen, which was easier on me, because I could use it anytime I wanted without a chador. Mr. Siyahpush also allowed me to extend the walls and create a kind of hallway leading to our door. I also raised the height of the walls so I could work in the kitchen without being seen. The mother of the martyr, who wanted her son to have our place, objected to these alterations. She complained that raising the height of the walls blocked the sunlight, but the only light in the hallway came from small windows at the ends. Because the neighboring buildings came up to the fifth floor on both sides of ours, very little sunlight got through anyway, forcing the manager to keep the fluorescent lights in the hallway on day and night. When there was a power outage, it got pitch dark inside. In spite of all this, I restored the wall to its original height just to mollify the woman.

After various other incidents and things I can't speak about for lack of space, the war finally ended in August 1988. Nevertheless, Habib, because of his specialty, had to stay on in the region. The children were growing up, and their problems were multiplying.

They had reached school age. All responsibilities for raising them fell on my shoulders. In those years people needed coupons to buy kerosene. Without coupons it was so expensive that buying it on the black market didn't pay. The kerosene truck would come to our door and people lined up, making sure to use their coupons before they expired. It was always torture for me to carry the kerosene cans or gas canisters up the stairs. The higher one lived in the building, the more difficult life was. This was what made living on the lower floors so desirable.

While we were at the Kushk Building, grandfather, who had left Khorramabad and was living in Darreh Shahr, visited several times. He was always dressed the same way: the dishdasha with the dark sash around his waist, the cloak on his shoulders, and the turban on his head. The turban came off only when he worked, but he never removed his skullcap. He believed that Seyyeds had to preserve the dignity associated with being related to the Prophet Mohammad. He would always remind us to pay the proper respect to other Seyyeds. The first time he visited us in the building Abdollah was three. He came early in the morning and immediately went to mother's room. Abdollah usually woke early and tried to find his grandfather. As soon as he saw grandfather, he ran back, opened our door and, said in his childish voice, "Mom, come quick! Imam Khomeini's in our house!" Startled, I ran to mother's room and saw grandfather there.

When grandfather came to Tehran, he would spend some time with us and some with Uncle Hoseyni. At that point Uncle Hoseyni's son-in-law, who had never met grandfather, was staying with him. His son-in-law was under the impression from the way the kids called him "Papa" that he was an enlightened man of sorts, educated in Europe, and would appear in a suit, holding a Samsonite briefcase. He asked the children where grandfather came from. When they said "Darreh Shahr," he asked, "Where is that?"

They said, "In Elam Province."

Then the children shouted, "Grandfather's here! He's here!"

"Where?" asked the son-in-law.

After they pointed to him, he said, "Huh? Him? He looks like a cleric. I thought he'd be something else."

They explained to him that "Papa" was not a European word, that it meant "grandfather." Grandfather's briefcase was a saddlebag brought from Iraq holding the scissors he used to trim his beard, a nail clipper, a toothbrush, and his radio. His morning routine was to give the call to prayer, pray, and then listen to the news of the war on the radio.

About two months before he passed away, grandfather came to our house. By that time mother had moved away, and this was the first time I welcomed him in my own home. I tried to be the perfect hostess. I bought a plastic ewer for him so he could do his ablutions without having to trek to the bathroom. Often, when he saw me, grandfather would exclaim, "Lioness!" or something like that, and then say a benediction for me. I had heard he saw Habib from time to time, and would say to him, "I hope you appreciate what a woman you've married."

Grandfather went to mother's place a few days later. I got the kids and joined him there for the few days he would be in town. The kids really love their grandfather. Grandfather was not well during what would be his last visit to the city. Uncle Hoseyni brought him to the doctor for a checkup. His heart, lungs, kidneys, and the rest of his body were fine. It was just that old age had caught up with him, and he needed my help to do certain things like wash his clothes and fetch water for his ablutions. He would always thank me, saying, "I hope I can make it up to you some day." "Grandpa, the little I do you for you doesn't begin to cover the thousands of things you have done for us."

Because there was this feeling we might be seeing grandfather for the last time, those days were very special to us, never to be repeated. He insisted on returning to Darreh Shahr, where Mimi and Uncle Nad Ali and his family had gone after the Iraqis fired missiles at Abadan. Uncle Salim and Aunt Salimeh joined them there later on. Darreh Shahr had been a sleepy little village before the refugees came, but with the influx of people the city grew and a mosque and a hospital were built.[5]

[5] The husband of Aunt Salimeh, whom we called Uncle Abbas, became the caretaker of the mosque.

In the beginning they housed the refugees in half-built homes that had been constructed for foreigners. Some of these structures didn't even have roofs, only brick walls rising from dirt lots. Families from Dehliran, Mehran, Elam, Khorramshahr, and Abadan found refuge there. Prior to my family moving there, I had never heard of the place.[6]

After the refugees settled there, the enemy turned their sights on Darreh Shahr. A popular slogan after the bombardments was: "Darreh Shahr has been lost, but it's still on the map."

Grandfather spent a pleasant month in Tehran. Uncle Hoseyni, who was a kind of adopted child for him, saw to his every need, and grandfather would say in appreciation, "Thank God, there's still honor among families these days." He remained generous and gallant to his dying day. His sons tried to make sure he was well dressed, buying him new coats, pants, and shoes, but he preferred his old clothing and would give away the new things to the needy. Uncle Hoseyni would ask him, "What makes you hand over the clothes we buy you to others? Say the word, and we'll buy things just for them."

"No, they have their pride," he would say, "and don't want to lose face."

As a child in Basra, I saw him do the same thing. He returned home one winter night, having given his clothing away. Mimi got upset and scolded him, "You're going to get sick, old fool! You could have kept wearing a stitch or two until you got home!"

Grandfather passed away in August 1982, two months after his last visit. He was buried according to his wishes in the Imamzadeh Ebrahim cemetery located in the lush hills of Dehliran. He never returned to Khorramabad after the liberation. I think he couldn't bear to visit the graves of father and Ali. He could never accept that

---

[6] Darreh Shahr, known to the ancients as Madakto, was an important city and capital during the Elamite Period (3rd millennium BC). Recent excavations attest to the presence of a highly developed civilization. The present city is 110 kilometers from Andimeshk, near Pol-e Dokhtar. It is situated in a beautiful valley bounded by the Kabir Kuh foothills and the Saymareh River.

they were actually gone. Whenever we invited him, he declined but would recite this poem in Luri instead:

> *A dark cloud has blackened the sky*
> *Who has lived to see a son and father die?*

40

Final Chapter

Habib finally came home for good in 1993.

Until that time he had been in the border areas with soldiers overseeing the United Nations peace. Some of these soldiers were the same ones who had taken us prisoner or had killed our forces. Habib agreed to come to Tehran at a time when the city was secure. Life had been very hard for us the whole time he was away. Things would crop up that needed the presence of a man; I would have to take care of these myself. I never complained, thinking it might weaken his resolve to be at the front. Although I was extremely lonely, I never brought it up to him, because I felt, rather than belonging to us, he belonged to the war effort, to the Lord. I counted his visits to us a gift from God. I felt the same way about Mansur and Mohsen, and, likewise, about Hasan and Sa'id, who joined them later at the front. I braced myself for the news they were gone. Losing father and Ali had steeled my heart, and I was ready to lose everybody, even Habib. Though he was very loving to us, Habib didn't seem to want to be too attached to his children or to me.

Once Habib dreamed he saw Hoseyn Eidi in the lush garden of an imposing building where many of the boys martyred in the war were gathered. Hoseyn said to him, "We've been waiting a long time for you."

Hoseyn said, "If you want, I'll take your ticket so they can sign it."

Habib said, "I'll bring them the ticket myself."

After telling me about the dream, he said angrily, "It's is all your fault I can't go." Habib often ignored Abdollah when he was acting cute and cuddly. He also wouldn't take care of the baby when I had to run an errand, saying, "Do it later." He preferred not to spend all that much time with Abdollah and Hoda.

What puzzled me was how he could be a loving father, and, at the same time, leave his family and appear so unfeeling toward us. While he could be very hard-hearted at times, he could also cry his eyes out when he saw a beggar freezing in the cold. This, I thought, was the Habib I married.

Be that as it may, it is difficult to describe the emotional and physical toll Habib's absences took on me from the time we left Abadan in 1984 until his return. It was devastating at times, and the anguish is still with me. When he visited us at the Kushk Building and saw the state it was in, he'd ask, "Why didn't you say something? You must have infinite patience to put up with this."

"Putting up with it was a duty at the time," I replied.

A while after Habib returned, the six of us (one son: Abdollah, three daughters: Hoda, Fatemeh, and Mina) moved from the Kushk Building to a house Habib found near Ferdowsi Square.

Even after all these years, the pain of losing father and Ali is still fresh for mother. She uses every excuse to visit Khorramshahr. While Abdollah and I were living in the city, she would visit to help with the baby. After we moved to Tehran, she had other excuses:

"I want to spend the months of mourning in Khorramshahr."

"I miss Leila and her children."

"So-and-so has passed away, and I want to go to the funeral."

I knew full well she just wanted to visit the graves of Ali and father—even though the doctor had told her to limit her travel. As a child, mother had lost her mother, which was the reason why everyone, especially grandfather, babied her. Father, for his part, was a believer in hardship. He would say, "Children should learn to put up with difficulties to be successful in the real world." Sure enough, the responsibilities and chores father gave to us when we were kids helped us when we encountered problems later in life.

This was why, when we moved from Sar Bandar, a small town, to Tehran, a huge city, my sister and brothers didn't have any trouble with the change. But the hardships mother experienced living in the camp, with its poor water, food, and sanitation, all the expenses of raising the children—all of it was too much for her. It weighed her down.

She stoops now and has difficulty walking. Her lips quiver and her chin trembles; nevertheless, she is a permanent reminder of what we have endured. She is the tree that still provides shade for her family, never denying them the soothing cool of her being.

My sister and brothers are all busy leading their own lives now. Uncle Salim and Aunt Salimeh remain in Darreh Shahr. Mimi passed away in the last days of winter in 2007. In 2004 I had the opportunity to go back to Basra, and, though my time there was short, I tried to find our old house. I longed to relive the memories of growing up with grandfather and Mimi, to become that child again who played in the yard with Ali or begged to stay up a few more minutes while Mimi told us bedtime stories. That was the time she would sing to me:

O, lovely moon, lovely moon,
Have you seen my grandpa on the path,
With his gun on his shoulder,
Going to the lions' den?

Illustrations

1. Zahra's father, Hoseyn Hoseyni, at the age of 44, just before he was martyred.

2. Zahra's brother, Ali, at age 11

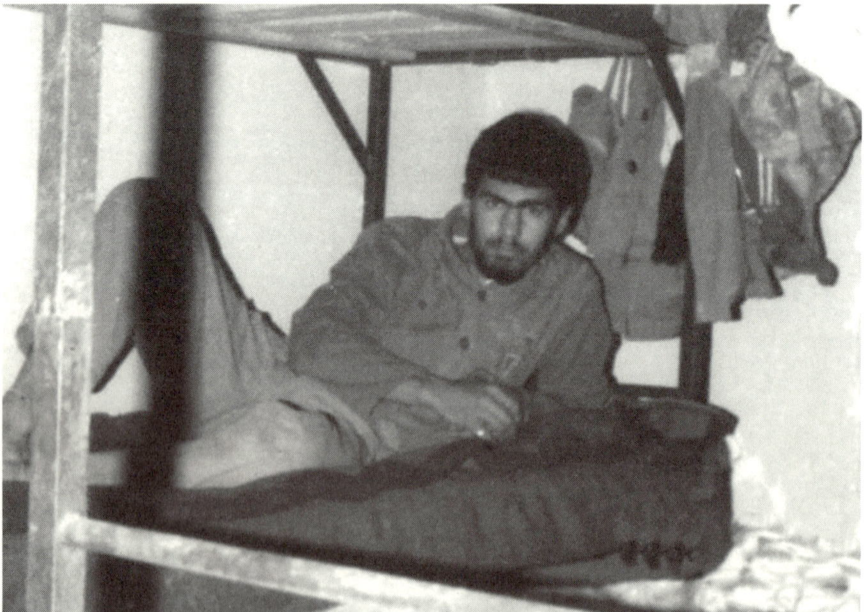

3. Ali in Dezful in 1979 in training

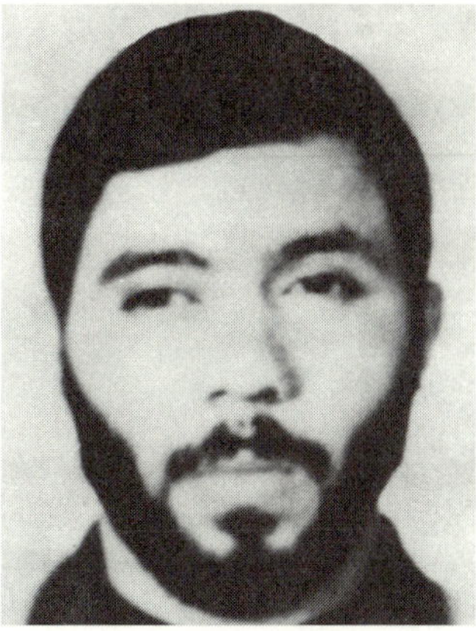

4. Mohammad Farrokhi who was killed in the first days of the war

5. Zahra's sister, Leyla, in winter 1980-81, at the refugee camp

6. A group of girls going to the front

7. Zahra at Refugee Camp B, March 1981

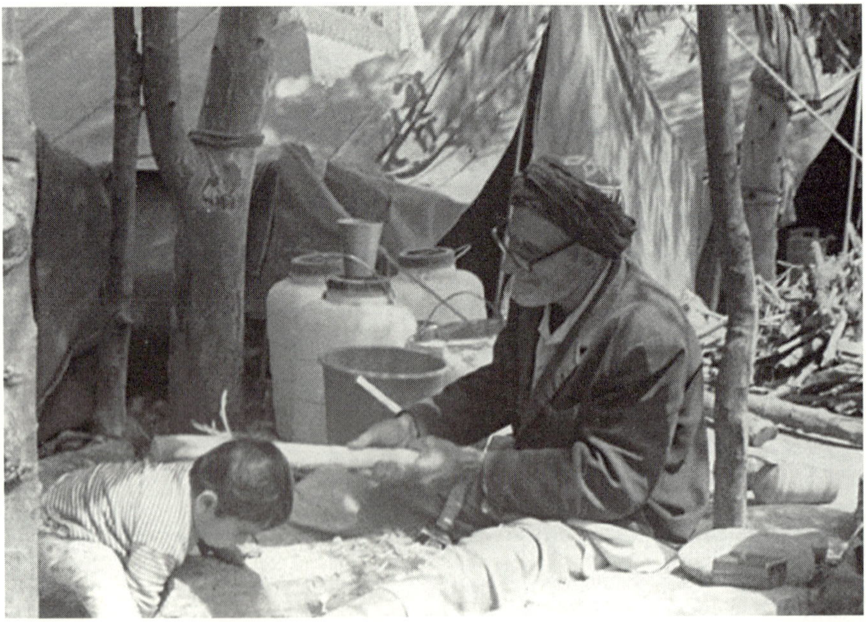

8. Zahra's grandfather at the refugee camp

9. Zahra's mother in the Kushk building after she heard the news of her son's death

10. Ayattolah Khamenei (3rd from left) visiting the troops during the occupation of Khorramshahr. Zahra's husband, Habib, is sitting to his left

11.View of the devastation of Khorramshahr

12. Khorramshahr Bridge, destroyed by Iraqi fire

13. Safa Bazaar, Khorramshahr after being bombed

14. People rejoicing after Khorramshahr was liberated

15. Zahra's daughter, Hoda, celebrating her 6th birthday

16. Zahra, her mother, and daughters Mina and Fatema, visiting the Mausoleum of Ferdowsi in 1999

Names, Places, Terms

Abbas: Abu al-Fazl al-Abbas, also Abolfazl; son of Ali (647-80); half brother of Imam Hoseyn. His forearms were cut off at Karbala when he tried to get water from the Euphrates to help his companions who were dying of thirst; his severed limbs are a prominent feature of Shii iconography. When in the morgue at Jennatabad for the first time, Zahra recalls how her mother often appealed to the two severed arms of the revered Abbas.

Abd al-Baset: Mohammad Abd al-Samad (1927-88), an Egyptian known in the Muslim world for his recitations of the Quran.

Abu Lahab: Literally "Father of the Flame," an early doubter of his nephew, the Prophet Mohammad; condemned in the Quran (111: 3) to "blazing fire."

Alawite(s) or **Alawi:** A minority religious sect founded in the eighth century, very influential in modern Syrian government and politics. The sect is named after Imam Ali, the Prophet Mohammad's cousin and son-in-law.

Ali: Ali ibn Abi Taleb or Talib (600?-661), the first Imam, and son of the Prophet Mohammad's uncle, father of the second Imam Hasan and the third Imam Hoseyn. He was the first male convert to Islam; scribe of the Quran; mortally wounded by on opponent to his Caliphate Abd al-Rahman b. Muljam.

Ali Akbar: Also "Ali the Elder"; son of Imam Hoseyn; valiant fighter; martyred at Karbala.

Ali: A son of Imam Hoseyn (b. around 658); deemed too frail to fight at Karbala; became the fourth Imam; also called Zeyn (Zayn) al-Abedin ("The Ornament of the Believers").

Ali Hoseyni: Zahra Hoseyni's brother.

Ashura: The tenth day of Moharram; day of intense mourning for Hasan and the martyrs of Karbala. Many Shii mark the day with processions, passion plays, and prayer.

Ayatollah: Literally "sign of God." The highest rank attained by Shii clergy. The Ayatollahs in this glossary are listed by last name; thus, Ayatollah Motahhari is under "Motahhari."

Baath(ist): Also Ba'ath; an Arab socialist party formed in 1948 and the most important political force in Iraq under Saddam Hossein.

Bahonar: Hojjat al-Eslam Mohammad Javad (1933-81); anti-monarchist theologian and scholar; Prime Minister of Iran; assassinated in the bombing of Islamic Republican Party meeting in August 1981.

Banisadr: Also Bani Sadr. Abolhassan (Abu al-Hasan) Banisadr (1933-), president of Iran (1980-81) and a close associate of Ayatollah Khomeini, the founder of the Islamic Republic. Having fallen out with leading clerics like Mohammad Beheshti, he went into exile in France, where he still lives. Banisadr formed an alliance with Mas'ud Rajavi, his son-in-law for a time and leader of the Mojahedin-e Khalq.

Basiji: One who is "mobilized"; a member of the volunteer paramilitary force, often composed of adolescents and young men enlisted in the war with Iraq.

Beheshti: Ayatollah Seyyed Mohammad Beheshti (1929-81), close associate of Ayatollah Khomeini, influential cleric in the founding of the Islamic Republic, chief justice; assassinated in an explosion at a meeting of Islamic Republican leaders.

Boupacha, Djamila: Algerian woman (b. 1938); active in the National Liberation Front; arrested by French colonial forces in 1960; tortured and raped in captivity.

Chamran: Dr. Mostafa Chamran (1932-81); PhD in plasma physics from Berkeley; active anti-monarchist in the United States. He served in high positions in post-revolutionary cabinets; commander of the Pasdarans or Guards in the Iran-Iraq War.

Civilian Construction Corps: *Jehad-e Sazandegi* (literally, "Crusade of Reconstruction"); originally set up by order of Ayatollah Khomeini for agricultural and other development projects in deprived areas of Iran; later became a ministry in the government.

Demokrats: Kurdish Democratic Party (KDP); heavily involved in the often hostile relations between Iran under the Pahlavis and Iraq under the Baathist Party.

Dialameh: Dr. Abdol Hamid Dialameh (1954-81); cleric active in reviving Shii religion in the political culture of Iran; representative in parliament after the revolution; killed in bombing of Islamic Republican Party meeting.

Feisal: Feisal b. Hussein (1885-1933); king of the areas known today as Iraq and Syria 1921-33.

Guards: See Pasdar.

Hajj Aqa: Literally "Mr. Hajji"; a way of addressing a respected elderly man.

Hakim: See Tabataba'i.

Hasan Hoseyni; The sixth child in the Hoseyni family.

Hasan al-Bakr: Ahmad Hasan al-Bakr (1914-82), president of Iraq (1968-79) and leading member of the Baath (Ba'th) Party, a socialist, Arab nationalist movement. Saddam Hussein was Hasan al-Bakr's successor as president of Iraq.

Hezb-e Jomhuri: [Islamic] Republican Party Headquarters.

Hojjat al-Eslam: Also Hujjat al-Islam; literally "proof of Islam"; a clerical rank among Shii, one grade below an Ayatollah.

Hoseyn: The son of Imam Ali; third Imam; martyred at Karbala on the tenth day of Moharram (October 10, 680). His son, Ali, Zeyn al-Abedin (Zayn al-'Abedin), became the fourth Imam.

Hoseyn Hoseyni: Zahra al-Hoseyni's father.

Hypocrites: A derogatory term for the Mojahedin-e Khalq, an Islamic-Marxist and anti-monarchist group originally supportive of Ayatollah Khomeini. After breaking with him, they conducted attacks on Revolutionary figures and forces. Because of this break, the group lost their status as "Strivers" (*mojahedin*) on the path of God (Quran 4: 95) and became *monafeqin* (an analogous Arabic form from Quran 4: 61) or "Hypocrites who deliberately turn from the truth." During the Iran-Iraq War, members of the group sided with Saddam Hussein.

Imams: See "Twelve Holy Imams" below.

Jamaran: A neighborhood in north Tehran bounded on the east by the large Bahonar military base and northwest of the royal palace at Niavaran; contains the site of Ayatollah Khomeini's residential compound.

Jennatabad: Literally "Heaven's Abode"; mortuary and cemetery complex in Khorramshahr.

Jomhuri Eslami (Jumhuri Islami): "Islamic Republican"; the Islamic Republic of Iran; name of a political party and its official organ.

Karbala: City in Iraq along the Euphrates; the site of the most consequential ten days in Shii history (October 1-10, 680; October 4-13, according to some). At Karbala forces loyal to the Caliph Yazid killed or took captive members of a small opposition force lead by Imam Hoseyn, the grandson of the Prophet Mohammad. Hoseyn was martyred and beheaded on the tenth day of the month of Moharram (a holy day called "Ashura"). Many Shii view what happens in the present through the prism of what happened at Karbala almost fourteen centuries ago. Every Moharram, believers commemorate the tragedy with mourning processions and passion plays, during which the interval between the events of Karbala and the present collapses. Every place becomes Karbala, every day Ashura, and every person a martyr like Hoseyn. For many Iranians the great slaughter of the Iran-Iraq War was a reliving and renaissance of the killing at Karbala.

Karroubi: Also Karrubi. Mehdi Karroubi (1937-); cleric and politician; leader of parliament 1989-92; head of several political parties and organizations early in the revolution. Under the presidency of Mahmud Ahmadinezhad (2005-2013), declared a dissident and put under house arrest.

Khameneh'i: Ayatollah Seyyed Ali Khameneh'i (1939-); president of Iran 1981-87; successor to Ayatollah Khomeini as supreme leader.

KOMALA: Kurdish for "The Association." The Kurdish Communist Party of Iran.

Komeyl: A supplication among Shii that declares the believer's personal devotion to God; an affirmation of the believers' intent to ignore worldly concerns and devote themselves to the metaphysical.

Leila Hoseyni: The fourth child in author's family; worked with Zahra at Jennatabad.

Lord of Time: (*Imam-e Zaman*) A title of the awaited Twelfth Imam or Mahdi/Mehdi.

Mansur Hoseyni: The author's third oldest brother.

Moharram: The month of morning the martyrs at Karbala. The first ten days of the month are especially important to Shii; they have special prayer sessions, conduct marches during which people beat and, at times, flagellate themselves with whips and chains, and stage passion plays. Moharram, like all Islamic months, is part of the lunar calendar so it can come at any time of the solar year.

Mohsen Hoseyni; The author's second oldest brother; injured in a childhood accident.

Mojahedin-e Khalq: Also Mujahideen and MEK. See Hypocrites.

Montazeri: Hoseyn Ali Montazeri (1922-2009); A prominent theologian; Ayatollah Khomeini's designated successor in 1989; critic of Islamic Republican policies on social questions after falling out with the supreme leader.

Motahhari Ayatollah Morteza (1920-1979): A prominent theorist of a "pure" form of Islam, which excluded unauthentic hybrids like the Islamic Marxism of the Mojahedin-e Khalq.

Now Ruz: Literally "new day," the Persian New Year, a fourteen-day celebration beginning on the first day of spring.

Nodbeh: A prayer-like expression of grief brought on by the absence of the awaited 12th Imam, a messianic figure who, according to Shii belief, is in occultation and will return to establish justice on earth.

Pahlavi: The name of the royal dynasty ruling Iran from 1925 to 1979; consisted of two monarchs: Reza Shah (1878-1949) and his son, Mohammad Reza Shah (1919-80).

Pasdar: A member of the *Sepah-e Pasdaran-e Enqelab* or The Army of the Revolutionary Guards, a military organization, paralleling the regular army and formed after the Islamic Revolution to enforce adherence to Islamic Republican ideology.

Peykan: "The Arrow"; a popular car assembled in Iran, based on the Hillman Hunter.

Rafsanjani: Hojjat al-Eslam Rafsanjani, later Ayatollah (1934-); head of parliament during the Iran-Iraq War; guiding figure in Islamic Republican politics.

Raja'i: Mohammad Ali Raja'i (1933-81), president of Iran in 1981; assassinated in the terror bombing of Islamic Republican headquarters.

Red Crescent: Part of the Red Cross and Red Crescent Movement established in 1929 and recognized in 33 Muslim countries.

Revolutionary Guards: See Pasdar.

Rial: Unit of currency; ten rials = one tuman (also toman); currently about 30,000 rials = $1.00.

Sa'id Hoseyni: The youngest son of the author's family.

SAVAK: *Sazman-e Ettela'at va Amniyat-e Keshvar* or "The Organization of Intelligence and Security of the Country" (*ettela'at*, an Arabic word, begins with the letter *alef* or "a," hence the acronym is SAVAK and not SEVAK); the Iranian secret police founded in the mid-1950s, during the reign of Mohammad Reza Pahlavi with the help and under the direction of the CIA.

Sepah: Literally "army"; the Pasdar are organized into a sepah.

Seyyed(s): Also "al-sayyid," "syed," "sid," "El Cid," etc., descendants of the Prophet Mohammad and therefore often accorded a social status and consideration not given other Muslims.

Persian, ordinarily genderless, occasionally follows the Arabic practice of calling males Seyyed and females Seyyedeh.

Seyyedeh Shah-Pasand Hoseyni: Zahra Hoseyni's mother.

Shahcheragh: A shrine in Shiraz, Iran; tomb of Ahmad and Mohammad, the brothers of Ali Reza, the eighth Imam.

Shahnameh: The Persian national epic written in 50,000 couplets by the poet Abol Qasem Ferdowsi (Abu al-Qasim Firdawsi, 940-1020); source of the creation story and tales about legendary heroes; popular among peoples living in Central Asia and the Middle East.

Shatt or Shatt al-Arab: The waterway separating southeastern Iraq from southwestern Iran; known in Persian as the Arvand River. Many of the most significant battles of the Iran-Iraq War took place along the Shatt.

Sheikh Khaz'al Kaz'al: b. Jabir Merdaw al-Ka'bi (1863-1936); ruler of the semi-autonomous region Mohammerah in Khuzestan under the Qajars. He was protected and paid by the British to protect their oil interests in southwestern Iran; in 1925 he was captured by Reza Khan (later Reza Shah), who put down Arab and other tribes' attempts at setting up autonomous sheikhdoms in Iran.

Shemr: Also Shimr ibn Dhi'l-Jawshan. A hated figure among Shii for delivering the coup de grace to the mortally wounded Imam Hoseyn on the 10th of Moharram (October 10, 680). In the worldview of many Iranians, Saddam Hussein was the "spawn of Shemr" for his attack on Abadan and Khorramshahr.

Tabataba'i: Ayatollah Seyyed Mohsen Hakim Tabataba'i (1889-1970). A prominent Shii cleric born in Iraq; scholar, anti-colonial and anti-Pahlavi activist. He was the principal authority (source of emulation) on religious doctrine and practice from 1961 to 1970.

Taleqani: Azam Talaqani (1954-); active in opposition to the Shah; women's rights activist; member of the first post-revolutionary parliament; daughter of the respected cleric Ayatollah Mahmoud Taleghani (Mahmud Taleqani, 1911-79).

Tavassol: A prayer or "turning to" to God, the Prophet, and the Imams for help during dire circumstances. Personnel at the clinic would perform the prayer communally on Thursday and Friday nights.

Throne Verse: *Ayat al-Kursi* (Quran 2: 255), part of which states: "Nor shall [humanity] understand a bit of His knowledge, except what He wills them to understand. His throne extends over the heavens and the earth"; said when beginning a journey or a very important task.

Tuman also **toman**: unit of currency; at the time of the Iran-Iraq War it was greatly devalued as a result of economic sanctions; currently 3,000 tumans = $1.00.

Twelve Holy Imams: In Shii doctrine, sinless beings preconceived as light in the mind of God; heirs to the Prophets and brought to life through the human agency of Ali and his wife Fatemah al-Zahra ("the radiant"), the daughter of the Prophet Mohammad. Most Shii believe there were/are twelve Imams, the last of whom, Mohammad al-Mahdi or the Hidden Imam, went into occultation in the 10th century and, it is prophesized, shall return as the Redeemer to establish justice on earth.

Zeynab: Also Zaynab and Zainab (ca. 627/28-682) the daughter of Imam Ali and sister of Imam Hoseyn. Zeynab witnessed at Karbala the martyrdom of her brother and two sons, Awn and Mohammad. Because she subsequently stood up to their killers, Zeynab is the archetypal speaker of truth to power for Shii women. Zahra Hoseyni often calls on Zeynab for strength and uses her words to the Caliph Yazid—after Zeynab had witnessed the slaughter of her children and close relatives—"On the plains of Karbala, I saw nothing but beauty" as a way of boosting her morale.

Zeynab: Zahra Hoseyni's younger sister; youngest child and darling of the family.

Zeynab Rudbari: A colleague of Zahra Hoseyni at the Jennatabad mortuary.

Ziyaratnameh: A formulaic set of benedictions in Arabic; contains blessings for the Prophet, his immediate family, and his descendants; text specifically used for visiting the Shahcheragh shrine is at http://www.shahcheragh.

Transliteration

The system used to transliterate non-Roman proper names in this work is similar to those used in academic journals and reference works; however readers will notice a Persian bias in the transliteration of some Arabic names. For example عبدالله is *Abdollah*, not *Abdallah* or *'Abd Allah*. However, certain names for which there are relatively stable forms in English like *Karroubi* (کروبی) or *Saddam Hussein* (صدام حسین) appear as they would in western alphabet publications. Certain romanizations like Shabook are idiosyncratic for comic effect. It should be noted that initial and final ء (*hamzeh*) and ع (*eyn/ayn*) are not shown, while medially they are indicated by ' (apostrophe).

آ	a	ذ	z	ک	k
اَ	a	ر	r	گ	g
اِ	e	ز	z	ل	l
اُ	o	س	s	م	m
ب	b	ش	sh	ن	n
پ	p	ص	s	و	v
ت	t	ض	z	ـُو	u
ث	s	ط	t	ـَو	ow
ج	j	ظ	z	ه	h
چ	ch	ع	'	ی	y
ح	h	غ	gh	ـَی	ey
خ	kh	ف	f	ـِی	i
د	d	ق	q	اضافه	-e/ey

About the Translator

Paul Sprachman teaches Persian at Rutgers University. He has worked and studied in Afghanistan and Iran. He is the translator of a number of works from Persian including *Plagued by the West* by Jalan Al-e Ahmad, *A Man of Many Worlds: The Diaries and Memoirs of Dr. Ghasem Ghani, Journey to Heading 270 Degrees*, by Ahmad Dehqan, and *Chess with the Doomsday Machine* and *A City under Siege: Tales of the Iran-Iraq War* by Habib Ahmadzadeh, and *Revolution Street: A Novel* by Amir Cheheltan. He is also the author of S*uppressed Persian: An Anthology of Forbidden Literaure*, *Language and Culture in Persian,* and *Licensed Fool: The Damnable, Foul-mouthed Obeyd-e Zakani*.

Of Related Interest

Books on or about Iran-Iraq War of 1980-88

Journey to the Heading 270 Degrees

Ahmad Dehqan

Translated from the Persian by Paul Sprachman

2006: ix+250pp. (soft cover)

ISBN:1-56859-196-9

Chess with the Doomsday Machine

Habib Ahmadzadeh

Translated from the Persian by Paul Sprachman

2008: xvii+268pp. (soft cover)

ISBN: 1-56859-215-9

A City Under Siege: Tales of the Iran-Iraq War

Habib Ahmadzadeh

Translated from the Persian by Paul Sprachman

2010: xx+94pp. (soft cover)

ISBN: 1-56859-255-8